NATIONAL CENTER FOR EDUCATION STATISTICS

State Comparisons of Education Statistics: 1969–70 to 1996–97

Thomas D. Snyder
Charlene M. Hoffman

U.S. Department of Education
Office of Educational Research and Improvement   **NCES 98-018**

U.S. Department of Education
Richard W. Riley
Secretary

Office of Educational Research and Improvement
C. Kent McGuire
Assistant Secretary

National Center for Education Statistics
Pascal D. Forgione, Jr.
Commissioner

The National Center for Education Statistics (NCES) is the primary federal entity for collecting, analyzing, and reporting data related to education in the United States and other nations. It fulfills a congressional mandate to collect, collate, analyze, and report full and complete statistics on the condition of education in the United States; conduct and publish reports and specialized analyses of the meaning and significance of such statistics; assist state and local education agencies in improving their statistical systems; and review and report on education activities in foreign countries.

NCES activities are designed to address high priority education data needs; provide consistent, reliable, complete, and accurate indicators of education status and trends; and report timely, useful, and high quality data to the U.S. Department of Education, the Congress, the states, other education policymakers, practitioners, data users, and the general public.

We strive to make our products available in a variety of formats and in language that is appropriate to a variety of audiences. You, as our customer, are the best judge of our success in communicating information effectively. If you have any comments or suggestions about this or any other NCES product or report, we would like to hear from you. Please direct your comments to:

National Center for Education Statistics
Office of Educational Research and Improvement
U.S. Department of Education
555 New Jersey Avenue NW
Washington, DC 20208–5574

November 1998

The NCES World Wide Web Home Page is
http://nces.ed.gov

Suggested Citation
U.S. Department of Education. National Center for Education Statistics. *State Comparisons of Education Statistics: 1969–70 to 1996–97,* NCES 98–018, by Charlene M. Hoffman. Thomas D. Snyder, Project Officer. Washington, DC: 1998.

Contact:
Charlene M. Hoffman
(202) 219–1688

For sale by the U.S. Government Printing Office
Superintendent of Documents, Mail Stop: SSOP, Washington, DC 20402-9328
ISBN 0-16-049807-4

FOREWORD
State Comparisons of Education Statistics: 1969–70 to 1996–97

State Comparisons contains information on elementary and secondary schools and institutions of higher education aggregated at a state level. The report contains a wide array of statistical data ranging from enrollments and enrollment ratios to teacher salaries and institutional finances. The report was designed to meet the needs of state and local education officials and analysts who need convenient access to state level statistics, without consulting numerous volumes and conflicting sources. Many revisions and updates that have occurred over the years have been incorporated in this volume. This up-to-date time series report contains NCES's most frequently requested state level statistics.

State Comparisons reflects an extension of the prior three editions in NCES's historical state education publications. In addition, *State Comparisons* provides detailed analytical tables that highlight more recent data. The *State Comparisons* project also was designed to provide an update of statistical data that may be obtained through the Department's Web site and Encyclopedia of Education Statistics retrieval system.

The analytical tables in *State Comparisons* draw on information available in the *Digest of Education Statistics, 1997* as well as newer data recently released and other material specially arranged for this volume. Examples of special material for this volume include:

- Percentage of students participating in federal special education programs

- Trends in revenues for public elementary and secondary schools, by source

- Size of public school districts

- Distribution of college graduates, by major field of study

- Educational and general expenditures per FTE student, by type and control of institution

These materials supplement the core historical statistics, which provide annual time-series data from 1969–70 to 1994–95, and in some cases 1995–96 or 1996–97. Some historical tables contain somewhat different time periods, because of the limitations of data availability.

ACKNOWLEDGMENTS

Many people have contributed in one way or another to the development of *State Comparisons of Education Statistics: 1969–70 to 1996–97.* Thomas D. Snyder was responsible for the overall development and preparation of this publication. Charlene M. Hoffman provided technical assistance in all phases of its preparation and was responsible for developing tables on degrees conferred. Claire Geddes prepared statistical materials, reviewed the textual materials, and prepared the Guide to Sources. *State Comparisons of Education Statistics* was prepared under the general direction of Martin E. Orland. In the Office of Information Services, Phil Carr designed the cover. Jerry Fairbanks of the U.S. Government Printing Office managed the typesetting.

Producers and users of federal statistics are always indebted to those individuals and institutions who provide the original survey information. In particular, we would like to extend our thanks to the Common Core of Data (CCD) and Integrated Post-secondary Education Data System (IPEDS) state coordinators whose efforts have made this publication possible.

State Comparisons of Education Statistics has been reviewed by individuals within and outside the Department of Education. We wish to thank them for their time and expert advice. In the Office of Educational Research and Improvement (OERI), Marilyn McMillen, Mary Frase, W. Vance Grant, Frank Morgan, and Frank Johnson reviewed the manuscript. Ellen Bradburn (Education Statistics Services Institute), Rolf Blank (Council of Chief State School Officers), Lisa Ross (National Council of Higher Education Loan Programs), and Jewell Gould (American Federation of Teachers) also reviewed the document. Within the Department of Education, reviews were conducted by the Office of Non-Public Education; Office of Bilingual Education, Minority Language Affairs; Office of the Deputy Secretary, Budget Service; and Office of Vocational and Adult Education.

Contents

Figures

Tables

1. Context of Education

2. Elementary and Secondary Education

A. Demographic/enrollment

3. Postsecondary Education

A. Demographic/enrollment

B. Degrees

C. Teachers and staff

D. Institutions and finances

Chapter 1
CONTEXT OF EDUCATION

This chapter presents a selection of tables that are designed to provide essential background information on the education environment in the states. These tables include such frequently required information as educational attainment, population statistics, household income and poverty rates, and limited English proficiency. Numerous studies have found these variables to be related to education achievement.[1] The contextual information also serves as valuable data in its own right. For example, businesses frequently refer to educational attainment data when making marketing and business location decisions.

Educational Attainment

One of the key outcome indicators of education systems is the proportion of the population who complete critical levels of education. For example, completion of a high school education is thought to be a minimum preparation for entry in a modern job market. In reflection of this consensus, reduction of the high school dropout rate has been incorporated into the National Education Goals. The percent of persons 25 and over who obtained a high school credential rose from 75 percent in 1990 to 82 percent in 1996 and the proportion that earned a bachelor's degree rose from 20 to 24 percent (table 1). Figure 1 provides information on the proportion of those who have completed high school or its equivalent for each state. The proportions vary widely among the states ranging from 91 percent in Alaska to 74 percent in South Carolina (figure 1). Many southern states had lower than average rates of high school completion. For example, the ten lowest ranking states on high school completion were southern and southern border states.

However, there was little relationship between state rankings on high school completion and attainment of bachelor's degrees in 1996. While a core of southern states remained at the lower tier of states in terms of college completion, there were many exceptions and some states had dramatic shifts in rankings. For example, the District of Columbia was 38th in terms of high school completion, but was first

in bachelor's degree completion. California, Delaware, Rhode Island, and Maryland also moved up in the rankings by 20 states or more when bachelor's degree completions rather than high school diploma completions were compared. States that declined in ranking by 20 or more in the bachelor's degree comparisons were Maine, Iowa, Indiana, Idaho, and Nevada. About half of the states had differences of 10 states or more between their rankings by high school graduation percent and by bachelor's degree completion percent. Based on 1990 data, there appeared to be more correspondence of rankings of bachelor's and graduate degree percentages. Six of the states had rankings that differed by more than 10 states.

In addition to the dropout information on the population over 25 in table 1, statistics are provided in table 3 that give the dropout percentage among 16- to 19-year-olds, a view of the output of the education system. Five states, Nevada, Arizona, Florida, California, and Georgia, had dropout rates at or exceeding 14 percent in 1990. Six states, Nebraska, North Dakota, Minnesota, Iowa, Wisconsin, and Wyoming, had rates under 7 percent. In general, dropout rates were relatively high among southern and southwestern states and lower among the midwestern and northeastern states.

Poverty

Lower student achievement is associated with coming from a poor family. Students in lower socioeconomic groups consistently score lower on the National Assessment of Educational Progress.[2] Poverty rates among the states ranged widely around the mean of 14 percent in 1995, from a low of 5 percent in New Hampshire to 25 percent in New Mexico (table 2). Among 5- to 17-year-olds, the poverty rate was 19 percent, from a low of 4 percent in New Hampshire to 36 percent in Mississippi. Across states, there was a difference of 32 percentage points in poverty rates for 5- to 17-year-olds compared to a difference of 20 percentage points in poverty rates overall. These data highlight the significant economic hurdles that some state and local govern-

---

[1] For example, see U.S. Department of Education, National Center for Education Statistics, NELS:88, *A Profile of the American Eighth Grader and Two Years Later: Cognitive Gains;* and *School Transitions of NELS:88 Eighth Graders.*

[2] *NAEP 1996 Trends in Academic Progress.*

Figure 1. – Percentage of persons 25 years old and over with a high school diploma or more, by state: 1996

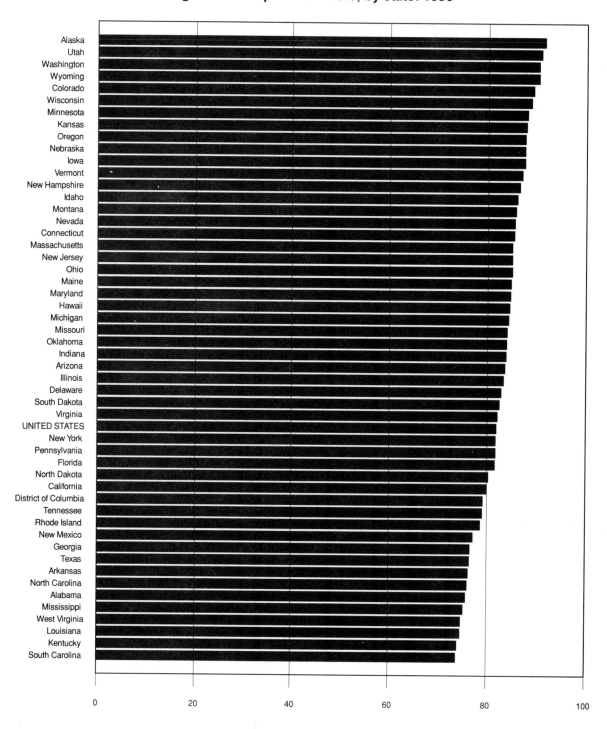

SOURCE: U.S. Department of Commerce, Bureau of the Census, *Current Population Reports, "Educational Attainment in the United States: March 1996."* (This figure was prepared February 1998.)

ments must face in attaining high education achievement levels, relative to peers in more prosperous states.

English Proficiency

Another factor associated with lower levels of education achievement is limited English proficiency (LEP). Large numbers of LEP children can pose significant challenges to local school districts which must provide programs to help children learn English and maintain academic/content subject learning as they learn English. In addition, there may be problems dealing with cultural or linguistic barriers with parents. Local governments may also face demands for adult education programs to address skills for adults, as well as for multilingual versions of administrative forms and other documents.

The proportion of the population 5 years and over with difficulty speaking English varies widely among the states (table 4). Nationally, about 6 percent of the population spoke a non-English language at home and did not speak English "very well" in 1990. However, there are relatively few states with figures around this percent. The distribution of state aver-

ages is skewed because of the very high percentages among the largest states, including California (16.2 percent), Texas (11.3 percent), and New York (10.5 percent). Most of the states have much lower percentages, with 31 states having fewer than 3.0 percent.

In addition to the financial burdens of providing additional language instruction to individuals, other complications are associated with providing social services to linguistically isolated households.[3] Local governments may lack the communication resources needed to interact with large numbers of residents with limited or no English language skills, particularly in areas where a variety of non-English languages exist. These households were most common in California, where nearly 10 percent of the population lived in households where nobody over 13 spoke English "very well." The states with the next highest percentages were Texas (6.3 percent) and New York (6.0 percent). Fourteen states had a rate over 2 percent.

---

[3] Households in which nobody over 13 speaks English at least very well.

Figure 2. – Limited English speaking residents as a percentage of total population, 5 years old and over, by state: April 1990

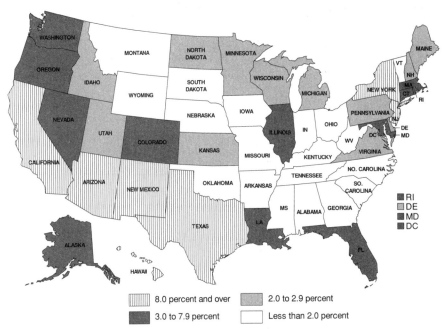

NOTE.—Limited English speaking people are those who speak a language other than English at home and speak English less than very well. English proficiency reported by survey respondents, not based on proficiency assessment.

SOURCE: U.S. Department of Commerce, Bureau of the Census, Decennial Census, unpublished tables. (This figure was prepared December 1994.)

Table 1.—Educational attainment of persons 18 years old and over, by state: 1990 to 1996

State	Percent of population, 25 years old and over, by education level, 1996		Percent of 18- to 24-year-olds who are high school graduates 1993–95 [1]	Distribution of population, 25 years old and over, by education level, 1990				
	Percent with high school diploma or higher	Percent with bachelor's degree or higher		Percent less than high school	Percent high school diploma or higher	Percent with bachelor's degree or higher		
						Total	Bachelor's degree	Graduate or professional degree
1	2	3	4	5	6	7	8	9
United States	**81.8 (0.1)**	**23.6 (0.2)**	**85.3 (0.2)**	**24.8**	**75.2**	**20.3**	**13.1**	**7.2**
Alabama	75.7 (2.3)	18.0 (2.1)	84.0 (1.7)	33.1	66.9	15.7	10.1	5.5
Alaska	91.4 (1.4)	27.2 (2.2)	90.5 (3.9)	13.4	86.6	23.0	15.0	8.0
Arizona	83.5 (2.0)	20.4 (2.1)	84.0 (1.8)	21.3	78.7	20.3	13.3	7.0
Arkansas	76.2 (2.3)	14.6 (1.9)	88.4 (2.0)	33.7	66.3	13.3	8.9	4.5
California	79.8 (0.8)	26.8 (0.9)	78.9 (0.7)	23.8	76.2	23.4	15.3	8.1
Colorado	89.1 (1.7)	30.4 (2.5)	88.4 (1.6)	15.6	84.4	27.0	18.0	9.0
Connecticut	85.3 (2.2)	32.3 (2.9)	94.7 (1.3)	20.8	79.2	27.2	16.2	11.0
Delaware	82.7 (2.2)	27.4 (2.6)	93.3 (2.8)	22.5	77.5	21.4	13.7	7.7
District of Columbia	79.1 (2.7)	34.0 (3.1)	87.7 (4.1)	26.9	73.1	33.3	16.1	17.2
Florida	81.5 (1.0)	20.4 (1.0)	80.7 (1.0)	25.6	74.4	18.3	12.0	6.3
Georgia	76.5 (2.2)	22.4 (2.1)	80.3 (1.4)	29.1	70.9	19.3	12.9	6.4
Hawaii	84.4 (2.1)	23.9 (2.4)	92.0 (2.5)	19.9	80.1	22.9	15.8	7.1
Idaho	85.9 (1.7)	20.3 (2.0)	86.4 (3.0)	20.3	79.7	17.7	12.4	5.3
Illinois	83.2 (1.1)	24.5 (1.3)	86.7 (0.9)	23.8	76.2	21.0	13.6	7.5
Indiana	83.7 (2.1)	16.2 (2.1)	88.5 (1.2)	24.4	75.6	15.6	9.2	6.4
Iowa	87.4 (1.8)	21.3 (2.2)	93.2 (1.3)	19.9	80.1	16.9	11.7	5.2
Kansas	87.7 (1.8)	26.5 (2.4)	90.9 (1.7)	18.7	81.3	21.1	14.1	7.0
Kentucky	74.0 (2.3)	17.5 (2.0)	82.4 (2.0)	35.4	64.6	13.6	8.1	5.5
Louisiana	74.6 (2.5)	19.2 (2.3)	80.5 (1.9)	31.7	68.3	16.1	10.5	5.6
Maine	84.7 (2.0)	19.7 (2.2)	92.9 (2.3)	21.2	78.8	18.8	12.7	6.1
Maryland	84.6 (2.0)	32.5 (2.6)	93.6 (1.1)	21.6	78.4	26.5	15.6	10.9
Massachusetts	84.9 (1.0)	32.4 (1.3)	92.5 (1.1)	20.0	80.0	27.2	16.6	10.6
Michigan	84.2 (1.0)	21.1 (1.2)	88.7 (1.0)	23.2	76.8	17.4	10.9	6.4
Minnesota	87.9 (1.8)	26.3 (2.5)	93.3 (1.1)	17.6	82.4	21.8	15.6	6.3
Mississippi	75.2 (2.3)	16.9 (2.0)	83.9 (2.1)	35.7	64.3	14.7	9.7	5.1
Missouri	83.9 (2.1)	24.3 (2.4)	90.3 (1.3)	26.1	73.9	17.8	11.7	6.1
Montana	85.6 (1.8)	21.9 (2.2)	89.8 (3.5)	19.0	81.0	19.8	14.1	5.7
Nebraska	87.4 (1.8)	24.0 (2.3)	94.5 (1.7)	18.2	81.8	18.9	13.1	5.9
Nevada	85.4 (1.7)	19.0 (1.9)	81.9 (3.4)	21.2	78.8	15.3	10.1	5.2
New Hampshire	86.4 (2.1)	27.6 (2.8)	86.9 (3.2)	17.8	82.2	24.4	16.4	7.9
New Jersey	84.9 (1.0)	28.3 (1.3)	91.8 (1.0)	23.3	76.7	24.9	16.0	8.8
New Mexico	77.1 (2.2)	20.8 (2.1)	82.4 (3.0)	24.9	75.1	20.4	12.1	8.3
New York	81.6 (0.8)	25.6 (0.9)	87.1 (0.8)	25.2	74.8	23.1	13.2	9.9
North Carolina	76.0 (1.1)	21.0 (1.1)	85.5 (1.3)	30.0	70.0	17.4	12.0	5.4
North Dakota	80.2 (2.1)	19.2 (2.1)	96.6 (2.1)	23.3	76.7	18.1	13.5	4.5
Ohio	84.9 (1.0)	22.3 (1.2)	88.4 (0.9)	24.3	75.7	17.0	11.1	5.9
Oklahoma	83.8 (2.0)	20.1 (2.2)	87.0 (1.9)	25.4	74.6	17.8	11.8	6.0
Oregon	87.5 (1.9)	22.8 (2.4)	82.7 (2.1)	18.5	81.5	20.6	13.6	7.0
Pennsylvania	81.6 (1.1)	22.3 (1.2)	89.5 (0.9)	25.3	74.7	17.9	11.3	6.6
Rhode Island	78.6 (2.5)	24.5 (2.6)	89.4 (3.3)	28.0	72.0	21.3	13.5	7.8
South Carolina	73.8 (2.2)	18.1 (1.9)	88.0 (1.6)	31.7	68.3	16.6	11.2	5.4
South Dakota	82.4 (1.9)	20.8 (2.0)	91.5 (3.3)	22.9	77.1	17.2	12.3	4.9
Tennessee	79.0 (2.0)	19.5 (2.0)	84.6 (1.5)	32.9	67.1	16.0	10.5	5.4
Texas	76.4 (1.2)	21.9 (1.1)	79.5 (0.9)	27.9	72.1	20.3	13.9	6.5
Utah	90.7 (1.6)	25.6 (2.4)	93.6 (1.5)	14.9	85.1	22.3	15.4	6.8
Vermont	86.9 (2.0)	27.1 (2.7)	88.1 (4.3)	19.2	80.8	24.3	15.4	8.9
Virginia	82.0 (1.8)	26.3 (2.1)	87.7 (1.2)	24.8	75.2	24.5	15.4	9.1
Washington	90.2 (1.6)	25.6 (2.3)	85.7 (1.4)	16.2	83.8	22.9	15.9	7.0
West Virginia	74.7 (2.3)	14.2 (1.9)	86.8 (2.4)	34.0	66.0	12.3	7.5	4.8
Wisconsin	88.7 (1.6)	24.0 (2.2)	93.7 (1.0)	21.4	78.6	17.7	12.1	5.6
Wyoming	90.2 (1.9)	24.2 (2.7)	90.8 (4.0)	17.0	83.0	18.8	13.1	5.7

[1] Excludes students still enrolled in school. Data reflect 3-year average.

NOTE.—Standard errors appear in parentheses.

SOURCE: U.S. Department of Commerce, Bureau of the Census, Current Population Reports, *Educational Attainment in the United States: March 1996;* and Decennial Census, *Minority Economic Profiles,* unpublished data. U.S. Department of Education, National Center for Education Statistics, *Dropout Rates in the United States, 1995.* (This table was prepared February 1998.)

Table 2.—Household income and poverty rates, by state: 1990, 1994, and 1995

State	Median household income [1]			Percent of persons below the poverty level					
				1990 [2]					
	1989 [2]	1994	1995	Total	Under 5 years	5 years	6 to 11 years	12 to 17 years	18 to 64 years
1	2	3	4	5	6	7	8	9	10
United States	$36,940	$33,178	$34,076	13.1	20.1	19.7	18.3	16.3	11.0
Alabama	29,001	27,967	25,991	18.3	26.1	25.8	24.3	22.3	14.6
Alaska	50,892	46,653	47,954	9.0	13.6	10.6	10.9	9.8	7.9
Arizona	33,848	32,180	30,863	15.7	24.9	24.2	21.8	19.1	14.0
Arkansas	25,990	26,290	25,814	19.1	28.5	26.6	25.2	22.7	15.3
California	43,997	36,332	37,009	12.5	19.0	19.3	18.3	17.1	10.9
Colorado	37,043	38,905	40,706	11.7	17.9	16.5	15.3	12.5	10.3
Connecticut	51,276	42,262	40,243	6.8	11.7	11.9	11.2	8.9	5.3
Delaware	42,863	36,890	34,928	8.7	13.3	12.7	11.8	10.8	7.2
District of Columbia	37,764	30,969	30,748	16.9	27.0	25.5	25.0	24.4	14.3
Florida	33,777	30,124	29,745	12.7	20.3	20.1	18.8	16.8	11.0
Georgia	35,668	32,359	34,099	14.7	22.1	21.3	20.1	18.1	11.4
Hawaii	47,722	43,453	42,851	8.3	12.6	12.6	11.2	10.8	6.9
Idaho	31,042	32,430	32,676	13.3	19.6	18.9	15.9	13.3	12.0
Illinois	39,639	36,075	38,071	11.9	18.9	18.7	17.0	15.0	10.0
Indiana	35,392	28,647	33,385	10.7	16.8	15.8	14.1	11.8	9.1
Iowa	32,236	34,016	35,519	11.5	17.5	15.4	14.1	11.7	10.3
Kansas	33,542	29,125	30,341	11.5	16.8	16.5	14.1	11.6	10.1
Kentucky	27,695	27,349	29,810	19.0	27.9	26.5	24.6	22.4	16.2
Louisiana	26,976	26,404	27,949	23.6	33.4	33.0	31.1	29.7	19.6
Maine	34,233	31,175	33,858	10.8	15.7	15.9	14.0	11.5	8.9
Maryland	48,407	40,309	41,041	8.3	11.9	11.9	11.5	10.2	6.8
Massachusetts	45,415	41,648	38,574	8.9	14.5	14.8	13.8	11.0	7.3
Michigan	38,125	36,284	36,426	13.1	22.1	20.4	18.1	15.7	11.2
Minnesota	37,988	34,597	37,933	10.2	14.8	14.6	12.5	10.6	8.8
Mississippi	24,748	26,120	26,538	25.2	35.8	35.1	33.5	31.9	20.0
Missouri	32,400	31,046	34,825	13.3	20.4	19.2	17.8	15.1	11.1
Montana	28,253	28,414	27,757	16.1	24.3	23.0	20.3	17.1	14.7
Nebraska	31,975	32,695	32,929	11.1	17.3	15.4	13.4	10.8	9.7
Nevada	38,114	36,888	36,084	10.2	15.1	14.4	12.6	11.9	9.1
New Hampshire	44,650	36,244	39,171	6.4	8.5	8.7	7.3	6.2	5.4
New Jersey	50,301	43,478	43,924	7.6	11.7	12.6	11.7	10.4	6.0
New Mexico	29,604	27,667	25,991	20.6	30.3	30.6	27.6	25.2	17.8
New York	40,515	32,803	33,028	13.0	20.6	21.2	19.6	17.0	11.0
North Carolina	32,750	30,967	31,979	13.0	19.2	18.5	17.2	15.3	10.1
North Dakota	28,530	29,079	29,089	14.4	19.6	18.4	17.2	14.7	13.0
Ohio	35,281	32,758	34,941	12.5	21.1	19.9	17.8	14.6	10.7
Oklahoma	28,977	27,756	26,311	16.7	25.3	23.4	21.7	18.5	14.2
Oregon	33,491	32,347	36,374	12.4	19.7	16.1	14.8	13.3	11.5
Pennsylvania	35,727	32,975	34,524	11.1	17.5	17.0	15.7	13.8	9.5
Rhode Island	39,551	32,833	35,359	9.6	16.3	16.1	13.8	11.0	7.6
South Carolina	32,269	30,692	29,071	15.4	22.8	21.8	21.2	19.1	12.0
South Dakota	27,657	30,576	29,578	15.9	23.6	22.2	20.2	17.3	13.6
Tennessee	30,489	29,451	29,015	15.7	23.9	22.5	20.8	18.5	12.5
Texas	33,204	31,627	32,039	18.1	25.6	25.5	24.2	23.0	15.2
Utah	36,220	36,728	36,480	11.4	15.8	14.4	12.0	10.0	11.0
Vermont	36,615	36,817	33,824	9.9	13.5	13.7	12.5	9.8	8.5
Virginia	40,961	38,714	36,222	10.2	14.5	14.5	13.5	11.9	8.4
Washington	38,325	34,483	35,568	10.9	17.0	16.4	14.3	12.2	9.8
West Virginia	25,558	24,232	24,880	19.7	31.7	30.3	25.9	22.4	17.7
Wisconsin	36,185	36,391	40,955	10.7	17.7	16.4	15.0	11.9	9.2
Wyoming	33,302	34,079	31,529	11.9	18.3	16.2	14.1	11.2	10.8

Table 2.—Household income and poverty rates, by state: 1990, 1994, and 1995—Continued

State	Percent of persons below the poverty level				Poverty status of 5- to 17-year-olds, 1995			
	1990 [2]		1995		Number in poverty		Percent in poverty	
	65 to 74 years	75 years and over	Total	Standard error	Number (in thousands)	Standard error	Percent	Standard error
1	11	12	13	14	15	16	17	18
United States	**10.4**	**16.5**	**13.8**	**0.2**	**9,583**	**259**	**19.0**	**0.5**
Alabama	19.2	31.1	20.1	2.0	198	39	22.6	4.0
Alaska	6.4	10.6	7.1	1.3	10	3	6.7	2.2
Arizona	9.3	13.2	16.1	1.8	199	38	24.2	4.2
Arkansas	18.0	29.9	14.9	1.8	108	22	21.7	4.0
California	6.5	9.5	16.7	0.8	1,456	120	23.4	1.7
Colorado	8.5	15.1	8.8	1.4	82	24	10.7	3.0
Connecticut	5.6	9.7	9.7	1.7	120	30	17.8	4.2
Delaware	8.2	13.5	10.3	1.7	23	6	16.6	4.2
District of Columbia	15.5	19.7	22.2	2.3	27	6	31.5	5.6
Florida	9.0	13.5	16.2	1.0	540	63	22.1	2.3
Georgia	16.5	26.7	12.1	1.5	218	49	15.6	3.2
Hawaii	6.7	10.4	10.3	1.7	31	9	14.2	3.9
Idaho	8.7	15.6	14.5	1.7	39	9	16.7	3.6
Illinois	8.9	13.4	12.4	1.0	467	60	20.3	2.4
Indiana	8.7	14.0	9.6	1.5	153	41	14.5	3.6
Iowa	8.1	15.3	12.2	1.7	98	23	15.5	3.4
Kansas	8.5	16.8	10.8	1.6	51	16	10.7	3.2
Kentucky	17.5	25.3	14.7	1.8	139	31	19.3	4.0
Louisiana	20.5	30.1	19.7	1.9	205	39	24.4	4.1
Maine	11.0	18.3	11.2	1.8	31	9	14.3	4.1
Maryland	8.8	13.6	10.1	1.6	119	36	13.3	3.8
Massachusetts	7.3	12.6	11.0	1.2	170	33	16.8	3.0
Michigan	8.7	14.3	12.2	1.0	292	46	14.8	2.2
Minnesota	8.4	17.2	9.2	1.4	101	30	10.4	2.9
Mississippi	24.0	37.1	23.5	2.1	212	32	36.4	4.5
Missouri	11.3	19.7	9.4	1.5	89	31	9.8	3.3
Montana	9.9	16.6	15.3	1.8	31	7	19.0	3.9
Nebraska	8.6	16.8	9.6	1.5	41	12	11.9	3.2
Nevada	8.4	12.3	11.1	1.7	33	11	11.1	3.4
New Hampshire	7.7	13.9	5.3	1.3	8	5	4.3	2.5
New Jersey	6.8	11.3	7.8	0.9	127	29	9.5	2.1
New Mexico	13.7	21.2	25.3	2.1	150	21	34.9	4.1
New York	10.0	14.7	16.5	0.8	805	74	23.6	1.9
North Carolina	15.7	25.9	12.6	1.3	233	41	20.2	3.2
North Dakota	10.8	19.5	12.0	1.7	17	5	13.2	3.4
Ohio	8.7	13.8	11.5	1.0	380	55	17.1	2.3
Oklahoma	13.5	24.1	17.1	1.8	151	29	24.2	4.1
Oregon	8.1	13.1	11.2	1.7	92	25	16.2	4.1
Pennsylvania	8.7	13.5	12.2	0.9	369	52	16.5	2.2
Rhode Island	8.9	15.6	10.6	1.8	27	8	16.4	4.5
South Carolina	17.3	26.5	19.9	2.1	249	43	31.7	4.7
South Dakota	11.1	21.3	14.5	1.8	25	6	17.3	3.7
Tennessee	17.2	26.7	15.5	1.8	204	46	19.6	4.0
Texas	14.9	23.8	17.4	1.0	887	90	23.1	2.1
Utah	6.4	12.5	8.4	1.3	43	12	8.4	2.3
Vermont	9.7	16.3	10.3	1.7	16	5	13.0	3.7
Virginia	11.6	18.5	10.2	1.5	154	42	14.5	3.7
Washington	7.0	12.4	12.5	1.8	156	42	16.6	4.2
West Virginia	14.1	20.8	16.7	1.8	71	15	25.8	4.7
Wisconsin	6.6	12.6	8.5	1.4	123	34	11.2	3.0
Wyoming	8.4	14.3	12.2	1.7	11	3	10.6	3.0

[1] In 1995 dollars adjusted by the Consumer Price Index for all urban consumers.

[2] Based on 1989 incomes collected in the 1990 Census. May differ from data derived from the Current Population Survey.

SOURCE: U.S. Department of Commerce, Bureau of the Census, Decennial Census, *Minority Economic Profiles*, unpublished data; and *Current Population Reports*, Series P-60, "Poverty in the United States," "Money Income of Households, Families, and Persons in the United States," and "Income, Poverty, and Valuation of Noncash Benefits," various years. (This table was prepared June 1998.)

Table 3.—School enrollment rates by age, dropout rates, and housing characteristics, by state: April 1990

State	Percent of age group enrolled in public or private schools							Percent of 16- to 19-year-olds who are dropouts	Percent of housing units built—		Percent of occupied housing units with no telephone
	3 and 4 years old	5 and 6 years old	7 to 15 years old	16 and 17 years old	18 and 19 years old	20 to 24 years old	25 to 34 years old		Between 1980 and March 1990	Before 1940	
1	2	3	4	5	6	7	8	9	10	11	12
United States	28.9	80.1	95.8	90.7	65.5	33.6	11.7	11.2	20.7	18.4	5.2
Alabama	28.3	78.7	95.7	89.3	67.5	33.4	9.6	12.6	23.5	9.3	8.7
Alaska	25.2	77.4	96.2	90.8	51.8	20.5	11.0	9.6	38.0	3.0	8.3
Arizona	23.0	75.1	95.8	87.9	62.1	34.0	14.1	14.3	37.8	3.2	8.5
Arkansas	20.3	75.7	95.7	91.0	61.3	28.1	8.6	10.9	24.2	9.4	10.9
California	29.3	81.1	95.5	89.7	62.0	35.0	15.5	14.3	22.9	10.7	3.0
Colorado	27.7	79.7	96.3	91.8	66.6	36.1	12.9	9.6	24.7	13.0	4.2
Connecticut	40.7	86.5	96.0	92.2	69.3	35.3	10.9	9.2	15.7	25.5	2.6
Delaware	33.3	84.5	96.0	90.3	69.8	35.5	10.7	11.2	24.3	14.3	3.1
District of Columbia	45.9	83.8	93.7	86.8	71.2	40.8	14.5	19.1	5.5	37.7	4.2
Florida	33.3	78.7	95.4	87.9	60.5	30.8	11.6	14.2	35.0	3.7	5.3
Georgia	29.1	76.9	95.5	88.2	60.6	27.8	8.6	14.1	32.1	8.1	8.3
Hawaii	35.7	86.5	96.7	93.2	55.9	28.1	12.0	7.0	20.8	6.7	2.6
Idaho	18.6	77.7	96.8	91.2	65.1	31.8	11.0	9.6	18.0	15.9	5.8
Illinois	31.9	80.8	95.8	90.6	66.0	34.4	11.9	10.4	11.7	27.1	4.6
Indiana	22.2	76.2	95.9	89.8	66.0	33.1	9.7	11.4	14.5	24.2	5.9
Iowa	25.3	82.0	96.2	93.1	74.3	38.6	10.4	6.5	10.0	35.0	3.4
Kansas	24.0	78.0	96.3	92.3	70.0	37.0	11.5	8.4	16.9	24.5	4.4
Kentucky	19.7	77.2	96.3	89.0	58.1	26.8	9.2	13.0	20.0	15.9	10.2
Louisiana	31.3	82.7	95.7	89.5	63.9	31.0	9.7	11.9	22.1	10.6	8.3
Maine	25.1	80.6	96.3	91.8	67.1	27.8	8.8	8.4	20.7	34.9	3.7
Maryland	36.5	85.4	95.3	90.1	63.1	32.4	12.5	11.0	21.6	15.5	3.2
Massachusetts	36.0	83.9	96.1	91.3	72.4	39.1	12.7	9.5	13.8	38.9	2.1
Michigan	31.1	84.8	96.1	92.0	67.9	37.2	12.7	9.9	13.6	20.8	4.1
Minnesota	23.1	76.3	96.3	94.4	74.8	39.0	10.9	6.1	18.5	24.5	2.4
Mississippi	30.2	79.9	95.5	90.5	66.8	31.7	8.7	11.7	24.1	8.6	12.6
Missouri	24.8	75.1	95.9	90.0	64.7	32.6	10.5	11.2	18.3	20.4	5.2
Montana	19.2	75.2	96.7	92.9	69.6	36.0	10.5	7.1	17.5	21.8	6.9
Nebraska	23.0	78.6	96.6	93.5	73.4	38.5	11.9	6.6	12.9	30.7	3.6
Nevada	22.8	73.3	95.8	89.6	50.5	24.1	11.2	14.9	40.1	2.9	5.4
New Hampshire	27.4	76.6	96.3	91.3	68.2	33.2	9.3	9.9	27.7	27.1	3.4
New Jersey	39.8	83.6	95.1	91.6	67.3	32.7	10.4	9.3	14.8	24.6	3.1
New Mexico	21.3	75.6	95.9	90.1	64.1	31.3	13.5	10.8	27.5	8.1	12.4
New York	36.2	85.1	95.6	91.0	71.3	37.6	12.5	10.1	9.4	35.7	5.0
North Carolina	26.7	78.5	95.6	88.5	63.6	29.7	9.8	13.2	28.6	9.9	7.1
North Dakota	15.5	73.8	97.5	95.3	78.3	42.2	10.8	4.3	16.6	24.7	3.5
Ohio	24.4	77.7	95.8	93.3	66.8	33.8	10.4	8.8	12.2	25.8	4.7
Oklahoma	23.1	76.6	96.0	91.7	62.9	33.7	12.0	9.9	22.1	12.4	8.8
Oregon	24.2	76.0	95.5	89.2	63.0	33.0	11.8	11.0	16.6	16.8	4.5
Pennsylvania	29.2	79.7	95.5	91.6	67.6	33.2	9.2	9.4	12.4	35.1	2.6
Rhode Island	28.9	85.2	95.3	88.7	71.0	39.2	12.4	12.9	15.1	34.0	3.1
South Carolina	33.2	83.2	95.9	90.2	62.4	28.8	8.9	11.9	29.0	8.5	9.1
South Dakota	16.5	74.6	96.6	92.2	71.2	34.2	8.5	7.1	14.8	30.4	6.0
Tennessee	23.3	75.4	96.0	89.9	60.0	28.4	8.6	13.6	24.2	10.2	7.1
Texas	26.3	79.9	96.1	90.0	65.3	32.5	12.3	12.5	29.7	7.1	8.6
Utah	24.2	79.6	96.8	93.0	64.3	41.1	15.2	7.9	24.4	13.5	4.0
Vermont	25.9	82.9	96.5	91.0	71.3	35.6	8.3	8.7	22.4	36.5	4.5
Virginia	30.3	82.0	95.8	91.5	63.6	30.8	10.3	10.4	26.3	11.0	5.4
Washington	27.6	77.4	95.7	91.2	64.5	30.9	11.2	10.2	23.1	15.7	3.5
West Virginia	17.4	75.4	96.4	90.9	65.3	29.7	7.9	10.6	17.7	23.7	10.3
Wisconsin	24.4	78.8	96.3	95.2	69.2	36.2	10.7	6.9	14.5	28.5	2.8
Wyoming	22.0	75.2	96.8	94.1	69.9	34.8	12.0	6.3	21.4	15.6	5.6

SOURCE: U.S. Department of Commerce, Bureau of the Census, Decennial Census, unpublished tables; and U.S. Department of Education, National Center for Education Statistics, *Dropout Rates in the United States: 1991.* (This table was prepared February 1995.)

Table 4.—English language proficiency and poverty rates for school-age children, by state: April 1990

State	Persons 5 years old and over									Percent in linguistically isolated households [1]	5- to 17-year-old population		
	Total	Speaks only English at home	Speaks non-English language at home								Total	In poverty [2]	Percent in poverty
			Total	Percent	Ability to speak English			Percent of total population who speaks less than very well					
					Very well	Well	Not well or not at all						
1	2	3	4	5	6	7	8	9	10	11	12	13
United States	230,445,777	198,600,798	31,844,979	13.8	17,862,477	7,310,301	6,672,201	6.1	3.4	45,249,989	7,811,817	17.3
Alabama	3,759,802	3,651,936	107,866	2.9	71,848	22,656	13,362	1.0	0.3	775,493	181,059	23.3
Alaska	495,425	435,260	60,165	12.1	37,685	14,846	7,634	4.5	1.9	117,447	11,952	10.2
Arizona	3,374,806	2,674,519	700,287	20.8	424,380	153,484	122,423	8.2	4.2	688,260	140,990	20.5
Arkansas	2,186,665	2,125,884	60,781	2.8	39,396	11,909	9,476	1.0	0.4	456,464	109,183	23.9
California	27,383,547	18,764,213	8,619,334	31.5	4,196,551	2,010,713	2,412,070	16.2	9.8	5,353,010	938,965	17.5
Colorado	3,042,986	2,722,355	320,631	10.5	210,742	65,502	44,387	3.6	1.8	608,373	85,171	14.0
Connecticut	3,060,000	2,593,825	466,175	15.2	282,157	111,698	72,320	6.0	3.2	521,225	52,757	10.1
Delaware	617,720	575,393	42,327	6.9	27,758	9,130	5,439	2.4	1.0	114,517	12,886	11.3
District of Columbia ...	570,284	498,936	71,348	12.5	42,220	14,572	14,556	5.1	2.9	79,741	19,116	24.0
Florida	12,095,284	9,996,969	2,098,315	17.3	1,137,012	454,892	506,411	7.9	4.5	2,016,641	357,493	17.7
Georgia	5,984,188	5,699,642	284,546	4.8	175,496	60,477	48,573	1.8	0.8	1,231,768	235,392	19.1
Hawaii	1,026,209	771,485	254,724	24.8	130,306	76,827	47,591	12.1	5.5	196,903	21,807	11.1
Idaho	926,703	867,708	58,995	6.4	36,699	10,823	11,473	2.4	1.2	228,212	33,638	14.7
Illinois	10,585,838	9,086,726	1,499,112	14.2	841,129	349,780	308,203	6.2	3.5	2,098,225	337,703	16.1
Indiana	5,146,160	4,900,334	245,826	4.8	158,844	57,770	29,212	1.7	0.7	1,057,308	137,649	13.0
Iowa	2,583,526	2,483,135	100,391	3.9	64,984	21,984	13,423	1.4	0.6	525,677	68,264	13.0
Kansas	2,289,615	2,158,011	131,604	5.7	83,262	28,254	20,088	2.1	1.1	473,224	61,812	13.1
Kentucky	3,434,955	3,348,473	86,482	2.5	57,059	17,742	11,681	0.9	0.2	703,223	165,029	23.5
Louisiana	3,886,353	3,494,359	391,994	10.1	263,689	87,844	40,461	3.3	1.5	892,619	270,834	30.3
Maine	1,142,122	1,036,681	105,441	9.2	77,682	20,614	7,145	2.4	1.1	223,280	28,666	12.8
Maryland	4,425,285	4,030,234	395,051	8.9	246,558	86,309	62,184	3.4	1.6	804,423	86,825	10.8
Massachusetts	5,605,751	4,753,523	852,228	15.2	503,442	190,011	158,775	6.2	3.6	940,602	117,235	12.5
Michigan	8,594,737	8,024,930	569,807	6.6	381,145	118,799	69,863	2.2	1.0	1,756,211	298,022	17.0
Minnesota	4,038,861	3,811,700	227,161	5.6	147,820	48,487	30,854	2.0	1.0	829,983	97,194	11.7
Mississippi	2,378,805	2,312,289	66,516	2.8	42,004	15,434	9,078	1.0	0.3	551,396	179,914	32.6
Missouri	4,748,704	4,570,494	178,210	3.8	115,272	39,521	23,417	1.3	0.5	945,582	155,815	16.5
Montana	740,218	703,198	37,020	5.0	25,563	8,379	3,078	1.5	0.5	162,847	30,726	18.9
Nebraska	1,458,904	1,389,032	69,872	4.8	47,620	13,712	8,540	1.5	0.6	309,406	38,008	12.3
Nevada	1,110,450	964,298	146,152	13.2	83,984	33,477	28,691	5.6	3.3	204,731	24,708	12.1
New Hampshire	1,024,621	935,825	88,796	8.7	63,986	17,258	7,552	2.4	1.1	194,190	13,334	6.9
New Jersey	7,200,696	5,794,548	1,406,148	19.5	797,152	330,728	278,268	8.5	4.6	1,266,825	139,494	11.0
New Mexico	1,390,048	896,049	493,999	35.5	334,379	103,456	56,164	11.5	5.9	320,863	84,834	26.4
New York	16,743,048	12,834,328	3,908,720	23.3	2,143,194	937,207	828,319	10.5	6.0	3,003,785	547,669	18.2
North Carolina	6,172,301	5,931,435	240,866	3.9	154,052	49,332	37,482	1.4	0.5	1,147,194	186,295	16.2
North Dakota	590,839	543,942	46,897	7.9	35,234	8,630	3,033	2.0	0.9	127,540	20,410	16.0
Ohio	10,063,212	9,517,064	546,148	5.4	356,283	124,333	65,532	1.9	0.8	2,014,595	330,029	16.4
Oklahoma	2,921,755	2,775,957	145,798	5.0	93,913	31,449	20,436	1.8	0.8	610,484	123,407	20.2
Oregon	2,640,482	2,448,772	191,710	7.3	113,548	40,234	37,928	3.0	1.5	522,709	72,666	13.9
Pennsylvania	11,085,170	10,278,294	806,876	7.3	513,867	184,976	108,033	2.6	1.3	1,997,752	294,396	14.7
Rhode Island	936,423	776,931	159,492	17.0	93,565	34,376	31,551	7.0	3.9	158,721	20,028	12.6
South Carolina	3,231,539	3,118,376	113,163	3.5	75,406	23,614	14,143	1.2	0.3	663,870	133,363	20.1
South Dakota	641,226	599,232	41,994	6.5	29,491	8,614	3,889	1.9	0.9	143,958	27,130	18.8
Tennessee	4,544,743	4,413,193	131,550	2.9	86,026	27,125	18,399	1.0	0.3	883,189	172,979	19.6
Texas	15,605,822	11,635,518	3,970,304	25.4	2,204,581	953,668	812,055	11.3	6.3	3,445,785	810,533	23.5
Utah	1,553,351	1,432,947	120,404	7.8	79,579	25,043	15,782	2.6	1.2	457,811	51,477	11.2
Vermont	521,521	491,112	30,409	5.8	23,162	4,789	2,458	1.4	0.6	101,822	11,534	11.3
Virginia	5,746,419	5,327,898	418,521	7.3	257,292	92,008	69,221	2.8	1.4	1,061,583	134,522	12.7
Washington	4,501,879	4,098,706	403,173	9.0	237,966	87,786	77,421	3.7	2.0	894,607	118,597	13.3
West Virginia	1,686,932	1,642,729	44,203	2.6	30,609	8,241	5,353	0.8	0.2	336,918	81,665	24.2
Wisconsin	4,531,134	4,267,496	263,638	5.8	170,342	57,149	36,147	2.1	1.0	928,252	125,768	13.5
Wyoming	418,713	394,904	23,809	5.7	16,543	4,639	2,627	1.7	0.7	100,745	12,874	12.8

[1] A linguistically isolated household is one where no person 14 or older speaks English at least very well.

[2] Based on 1989 incomes.

NOTE.—English proficiency reported by survey respondents, not based on proficiency assessment.

SOURCE: U.S. Department of Commerce, Bureau of the Census, Decennial Census, unpublished tables. (This table was prepared November 1994.)

CHAPTER 2
Elementary and Secondary Education

This chapter provides a statistical overview of elementary and secondary education in the United States. It brings together material from preprimary, elementary, and secondary education to present a statistical comparison of state education systems. Tables illustrate the total number of persons enrolled in public schools, the number of teachers and staff, the number of schools, and revenues and expenditures of public schools.

Pupils ordinarily spend from 6 to 8 years in elementary schools, which may be preceded by 1 or 2 years in nursery school and kindergarten. The elementary school program is followed by a 4- to 6-year program in secondary school. Middle schools provide a bridge between elementary and secondary schools and typically serve children in grades 4, 5, or 6 to 6, 7, or 8. Students normally complete the entire program through grade 12 by age 17 or 18. High school graduates who decide to continue their education may enter a technical or vocational institution, a 2-year college, or a 4-year college or university.

The administrative structure of public education in the United States varies widely among local jurisdictions, who share with states the primary responsibility for public education. In general, state education agencies provide coordination of large scale activities and funding to local school districts. Local school districts make significant funding decisions and set many school policies. Local school boards are responsible for making and reviewing school policies. School administrators implement state and local policies and establish school procedures. Normally, school administrators have limited flexibility in school budget authority and must operate within narrow staffing limits. In recent years, significant numbers of "charter schools" have been established. These schools are publicly funded, but their charters grant school administrators wide latitude in funding and staffing decisions.

The number of districts within states ranges from fewer than a dozen to more than a thousand. The enrollment size of school districts ranges from under 5 to over one million. Not only does the size of a school district vary, but the geographical and political boundaries are significantly different. Some districts coincide with county boundaries, others reflect townships, cities, or other types of local jurisdictions. In some areas, school districts cross over political boundaries and are units unto themselves. In some areas of the country, districts provide only elementary or only secondary education and overlap each other. Other districts are combined elementary and secondary districts and serve all children residing within their boundaries. The varied size of districts obviously has an impact on the range of activities undertaken at the school district level. In some areas of the country, smaller districts are served by larger substate organizations that provide administrative, special education, or other services to the member local school districts.

Demographics and Enrollment

Elementary and secondary enrollment in the United States is primarily determined by the size of the school-age population rather than by other demographic or economic characteristics. As a result, the 5- to 17-year-old population is an excellent indicator of the potential enrollment in a particular jurisdiction. In 1996, public elementary and secondary enrollment was about 91 percent of the 5- to 17-year-old population (table 6 and figure 3). Most states were within 4 percent of this figure. The public school enrollment/population ratio is affected by: the relative proportion of students in private schools; dropout rates; and the proportion of students at the elementary age range, where enrollment is nearly universal.

Another demographic influence on the cost of providing education in a state is the proportion of the population that is of school age. This proportion is important since the 5- to 17-year-old population is such an important determinant of the enrollment. A high proportion of 5- to 17-year-olds indicates a relatively large requirement for education expenditures and services. A small population of school-age children can reflect a larger employed population, which suggests a larger tax base on which to draw for school resources. On the other hand, a small proportion of school-age children may indicate a relatively old population with many retired persons. Such a population profile poses a different set of public service requirements, such as a need for more hospitals. State and local governments frequently use demographic data to help develop strategies for providing public services.

Figure 3.– 5- to 17-year-olds as a percentage of total population, by state: 1996

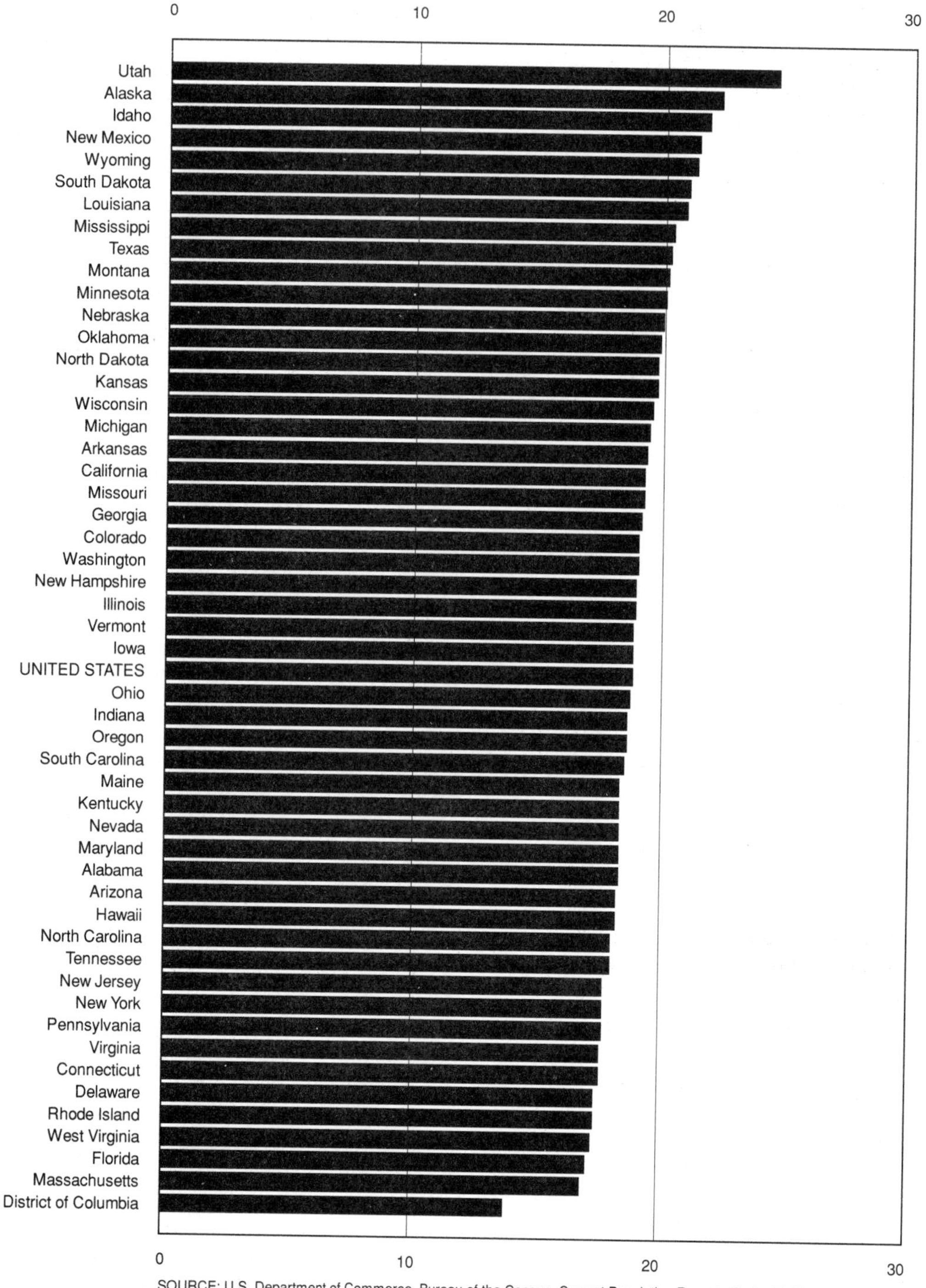

Utah	
Alaska	
Idaho	
New Mexico	
Wyoming	
South Dakota	
Louisiana	
Mississippi	
Texas	
Montana	
Minnesota	
Nebraska	
Oklahoma	
North Dakota	
Kansas	
Wisconsin	
Michigan	
Arkansas	
California	
Missouri	
Georgia	
Colorado	
Washington	
New Hampshire	
Illinois	
Vermont	
Iowa	
UNITED STATES	
Ohio	
Indiana	
Oregon	
South Carolina	
Maine	
Kentucky	
Nevada	
Maryland	
Alabama	
Arizona	
Hawaii	
North Carolina	
Tennessee	
New Jersey	
New York	
Pennsylvania	
Virginia	
Connecticut	
Delaware	
Rhode Island	
West Virginia	
Florida	
Massachusetts	
District of Columbia	

SOURCE: U.S. Department of Commerce, Bureau of the Census, Current Population Reports, Series P-25, and state level reports. (This figure was prepared January 1998.)

The demographic distribution has shifted dramatically since 1970. From 1970 to 1980, the proportion of the population made up of school-age children fell from 26 percent to 21 percent (table 6). The percentage continued to fall during the early 1980s, but has increased slightly since then, reaching nearly 19 percent of the population in 1996. The 5- to 17-year-old proportion of the population in 1996 varied from lows of 14 percent in the District of Columbia (figure 3), and 17 percent in Massachusetts, Florida, West Virginia, Rhode Island, and Delaware, to relatively high percentages in Idaho (22), Alaska (22), and Utah (25).

The ratio of public school students to the 5- to 17-year-old population increased between 1980 and 1990, but has changed little since then. This ratio increased during the 1980s for a variety of reasons, including lower dropout rates, higher public kindergarten and nursery school participation rates, and more older students enrolled in secondary schools. Partly, as a result of the small changes in the proportion of the population that is 5 to 17 years old, public enrollment as a proportion of the population remained stable between 1990 and 1996. This means that the theoretical financial burden of providing a given level of education services to public school children has not shifted significantly between 1990 and 1996.

Tables 5 through 7 contain other statistics that help define the nature of the education enterprise. The proportion of public school enrollment in elementary schools is a useful indicator of the potential for growth in secondary enrollment. Since elementary education is normally less expensive to provide than secondary education, it can also serve as one of the measures of current and future relative demand for more expensive secondary education services. In recent years, the proportion of public school children in secondary schools has fallen due to larger numbers of young children entering elementary school and smaller birth cohorts moving through the secondary schools. Between 1980 and 1990, the proportion of public school children in secondary schools fell from 32 percent to 28 percent. After 1990, the proportion continued to drop slightly to 27 percent in 1991 and 1992, before rising again to 28 percent in 1995. The proportion of public school students at the secondary level in 1995 ranged from 23 percent in the District of Columbia to 32 percent in Iowa. Based on demographic projections, most state secondary school percentages are expected to increase significantly during the middle 1990s through the early 2000s.[1] This suggests an increased demand for relatively more expensive secondary school services.

Enrollment in Private Schools

The proportion of students in private schools has changed little over the past decade. In 1995, approximately 5.0 million or 10 percent of all elementary and secondary students attended private schools (table 8). The proportion varied widely from state to state. The highest proportions of enrollment in private schools were found in Delaware (19 percent), the District of Columbia (18 percent), and Pennsylvania with (16 percent). The private enrollment proportions for Utah (3 percent) and Wyoming (2 percent) were markedly lower.

Enrollment Trends

Enrollment in public elementary and secondary schools grew rapidly during the 1950s and 1960s and peaked in 1971 (table 10).[2] This enrollment rise was caused by what is known as the "baby boom," a dramatic increase in births following World War II. From 1971 to 1984, total elementary and secondary school enrollment decreased every year, reflecting the decline in the school-age population over that period. After these years of decline, enrollment in elementary and secondary schools showed a small increase in the fall of 1985 and has continued to increase through 1995.

A five-year comparison of enrollment trends reveals marked differences from state to state. Public school enrollment rose by 9 percent between 1990 and 1995. However, 2 states and the District of Columbia had enrollment decreases. The decreases were in West Virginia (–5 percent) and in Maine and the District of Columbia (–1 percent). Nevada (32 percent), Florida (17 percent), and Arizona (16 percent) had large increases.

Public school enrollment in the kindergarten through grade eight sector shows a similar pattern over the 1990 to 1995 period (table 11). However, states generally had smaller increases at the elementary level than for the total, and more states had decreases. Five states had decreases over the 1990 to 1995 period. Other states had relatively large increases, including eight states with increases over 10 percent. However, the enrollment increases that occurred during the 1990 to 1995 period were generally smaller than those that occurred over the previous 5-year period. From 1985 to 1990, elementary enrollment rose 11 percent, compared to an increase of 7 percent between 1990 to 1995.

During the early 1990s, public school enrollment from grades 9 to 12 showed a pattern of increases similar to that of the elementary enrollment from the late 1980s (table 12). This pattern of increases in

---

[1] U.S. Department of Education, National Center for Education Statistics, *Projections of Education Statistics to 2008.*

[2] U.S. Department of Education, National Center for Education Statistics, *Digest of Education Statistics, 1997.*

Figure 4. – Percentage change in public elementary and secondary enrollment, by state: Fall 1990 to fall 1995

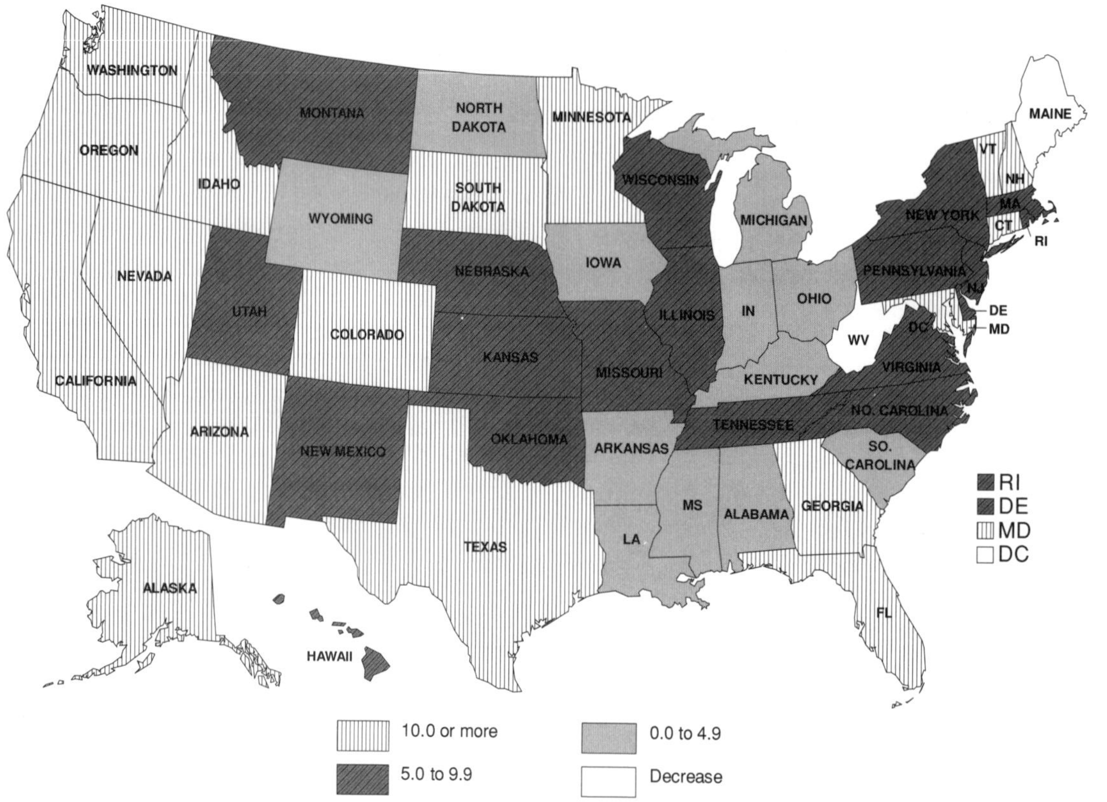

SOURCE: U.S. Department of Education, National Center for Education Statistics, Common Core of Data surveys.
(This figure was prepared February 1998.)

secondary school enrollment represents a large shift from the prior 5-year period. Secondary enrollment fell by 8 percent between 1985 and 1990. In contrast, secondary school enrollment rose 10 percent during the 1990 to 1995 period, but there was a large range among the states. Two states and the District of Columbia had decreases in secondary enrollment, while seven states had increases of 20 percent or more. Nevada had an increase of 34 percent in secondary school enrollment between 1990 and 1995.

Participation in Programs for the Disabled

During the 1970s and early 1980s, increasing numbers and proportions of children were served in programs for the disabled. During the 1976–77 school year, 8 percent of students were served in these programs compared with 13 percent in 1996–97 (tables 8 and 14). However, since 1983–84, the increases have been relatively small. Much of the rise since 1976–77 may be attributed to the increasing proportion of children identified as learning disabled, which rose from 2 percent of enrollment in 1976–77 to 6 percent of enrollment in 1996–97.[3] Also some increase may be due to legislation mandating services (beginning in 1987–88) for 3- to 5-year-olds.

The range in student participation in programs for the disabled varied from state to state by a ratio of about 2 to 1. The highest proportions of children in programs for the disabled were in Rhode Island and Massachusetts (18 percent) and New Jersey (17 percent). The lower participation rates were in Idaho (11 percent) and the District of Columbia (9 percent). More than half of the states had a ratio between 11.0 and 14.0 percent (table 8 and figure 5).

There were some similarities in patterns of changes in participation in federal programs for the disabled and public school enrollment. States with large increases in enrollment often had large increases in disabled program participation. However, some states had increases in program participation in contrast to decreases in total enrollment. Between 1986–87 and 1996–97, 6 states had increases in disabled program enrollment of less than 10 percent compared to 17 states with total enrollment increases of less than 10 percent.[3] Overall, there was a 35 percent increase in disabled program participation between 1986–87 and 1996–97, compared to a 14 percent increase in enrollment. Most of the increases occurred during the latter half of the period, reflecting the pattern of larger overall enrollment increases from 1990 to 1996.

Achievement and Graduates

There was a general improvement in mathematics performance among 8th graders in public schools between 1990 and 1996 (table 15).[4] Among the 29 states participating in the 1990 and the 1996 State Assessment Programs, 26 states showed significant increases and none showed significant decreases. However, there were wide disparities in student performance from state to state. Performance at the basic or above level indicates at least a partial mastery of prerequisite knowledge and skills that are fundamental for proficient 8th grade work. The percentage of 8th graders in public schools who could perform at this level varied from 20 percent in the District of Columbia, 36 percent in Mississippi and 38 percent in Louisiana to 76 percent in Nebraska, 77 percent in North Dakota and Maine, and 78 percent in Iowa. The state differences were reflected in regional differences with 56 percent of students in the Southeast performing at the basic or above level compared to 69 percent of students from the Central region.

Some of the same state patterns were evident at the 4th grade level, with the southeast region trailing the northeast and central regions. Many of the states that had high scoring public school students at the 8th grade level also had high scoring students at the 4th grade level, including Minnesota, North Dakota, and Maine. Overall, about 64 percent of the 4th grade students were able to perform at a basic or above level, which indicates an ability to perform grade appropriate tasks. As among the 8th graders, the range in the percentage of students performing at a given level was relatively wide.

There was little difference in 4th graders' reading proficiency among the regions in 1994 (table 16). The only significant difference was that the Central region scored higher than the Southeast region. However, there was considerable variation in proficiency across the 39 states participating in the assessments. The average reading proficiency level of 4th graders ranged from 228 to 197. This difference is similar to that between the high and low 8th grade mean mathematics performance scores.

High School Graduates

The number of public high school graduates dropped 3 percent between 1986–87 and 1996–97 because of declining numbers of the high-school-age population (table 19). Despite this small general decline, there were increases in 18 states, including an increase of over 25 percent in Utah and a 22 percent increase in Idaho. The trend of the number of high

---

[3] U.S. Department of Education, National Center for Education Statistics, *Digest of Education Statistics, 1998*, forthcoming.

[4] U.S. Department of Education, National Center for Education Statistics, *NAEP 1996 Mathematics Report Card for the Nation and the States,* prepared by Educational Testing Service.

Figure 5. – Students participating in special programs for the disabled as a percentage of public school enrollment, by state: 1996–97

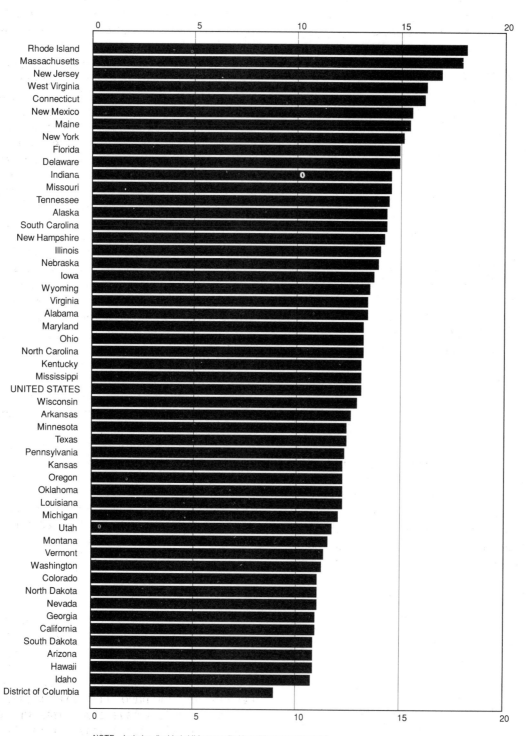

NOTE. - Includes disabled children enrolled in public or private school programs.

SOURCE: U.S. Department of Education, National Center for Education Statistics, Common Core of Data survey; and Office of Special Education and Rehabilitative Services, *Annual Report to Congress on the Implementation of the Individuals with Disabilities Education Act.* (This figure was prepared April 1998.)

school graduates shifted during the period. During the first half of the 10 year period, the number of high school graduates declined by 8 percent, while the number of high school graduates increased by 6 percent between 1991-92 and 1996-97. Most states had increases in the number of high school graduates between 1991-92 and 1996-97, and three states had increases over 20 percent.

Teachers and Staff

Public school systems employed approximately 2.6 million teachers in fall 1995. This represents about 52 percent of the total 5.0 million public school staff (table 20 and figure 8). Large numbers of persons also served in supporting roles, such as instructional aides, school bus drivers, cafeteria workers, janitors, and health personnel. About 3 percent were school district officials or school principals. Calculating the student to staff ratio for various employment categories helps to illustrate typical school staffing patterns. On the average, there were 9 students for every school employee (table 21). There were 909 students for every school district administrator. Also at the district level, there were 310 students for every administrative support staff person and 1,331 for each instruction coordinator. At the school level, there was 1 principal or assistant principal for every 372 students. For each guidance counselor, there were 512 students, and for each librarian, there were 882 students.

States varied widely in the staffing ratios. Utah (13:1) and California (12:1) had the highest ratios of students to staff, with more students per staff member than the national average in most staff categories, including school administrators, teachers, librarians, and guidance counselors. Both states had pupil/teacher ratios that were much higher than the national average of 17 to 1. States with the least number of students per staff member included Missouri, Oklahoma, New Jersey, Maine, and Vermont, all with ratios of less than 7.5:1. These states were characterized by fewer students per staff member in most school level categories and consistently lower than average pupil/teacher ratios. Pupil/teacher ratios ranged among the states from around 14:1 in Virginia, Connecticut, Rhode Island, Maine, New Jersey and Vermont to 24:1 in Utah and California.

Public school teachers are well educated and many have extensive experience. A bachelor's degree is a prerequisite for teaching in most areas, but many teachers have advanced degrees (table 21). A small proportion of teachers, about 1 percent, lack bachelor's degrees. About 4 percent of public school teachers lacked any certification in the field they taught most often.[5] Nearly half of all public school teachers in 1993–94 had advanced degrees, such as the education specialist (5 percent), master's (42 percent), or doctor's (1 percent). The percentage of teachers with advanced degrees ranked from 25 percent or less in Idaho, South Dakota, and North Dakota to highs of 75 percent or more in New York, Kentucky, Indiana, and Connecticut.

In 1993–94 about 10 percent of public school teachers had less than three years of teaching experience; most had considerably more. Nearly two-thirds of the teachers had 10 or more years of experience, and about 30 percent had over 20 years of teaching experience (figure 7). There was a considerable range in average teaching experience from state to state. In four states—Rhode Island, Michigan, Pennsylvania, Massachusetts—and the District of Columbia, 40 percent or more of the teachers had more than 20 years of teaching experience. Alaska, Nevada, Arizona, and Utah had 20 percent or fewer teachers with 20 years or more teaching experience.

An estimated 2.6 million teachers were employed by public schools in the fall of 1995 (table 23). The national total has risen about 18 percent since 1985, but the percent changes for the states ranged widely. Nevada had the largest percentage increase in the number of teachers (79 percent). Other states with increases of 30 percent or more included Hawaii, Georgia, Arizona, Tennessee, Texas, New Mexico, and Virginia. Three states—North Dakota, West Virginia, Wyoming—and the District of Columbia had declines in the number of teachers over the 10-year period. Changes in the numbers of teachers from state to state tended to follow the general pattern of student enrollment trends. Of the 7 states with the largest increases in the number of teachers, five had enrollment increases that exceeded the national average. Of the states with the decreases in the number of teachers, only one had a very small increase in enrollment, the rest had declines.

Changes in enrollment and in numbers of teachers affect the pupil/teacher ratio. The pupil/teacher ratio can serve as a general instructional resource indicator even though it does not reflect average class size (figure 6 and table 22). Average class sizes are larger than what might be inferred from the pupil/teacher ratio, because resource teachers, such as elementary school mathematics or art or physical education teachers, do not have their own classes. Special education teachers have class sizes that generally are much smaller than teachers of regular classes. Average class sizes are consistently higher than pupil/teacher ratios because teacher counts include special education teacher and resource teachers. In

[5] U.S. Department of Education, National Center for Education Statistics, *America's Teachers: Profile of a Profession, 1993–94.*

Figure 6. – Pupil/teacher ratios in public elementary and secondary schools, by state: Fall 1995

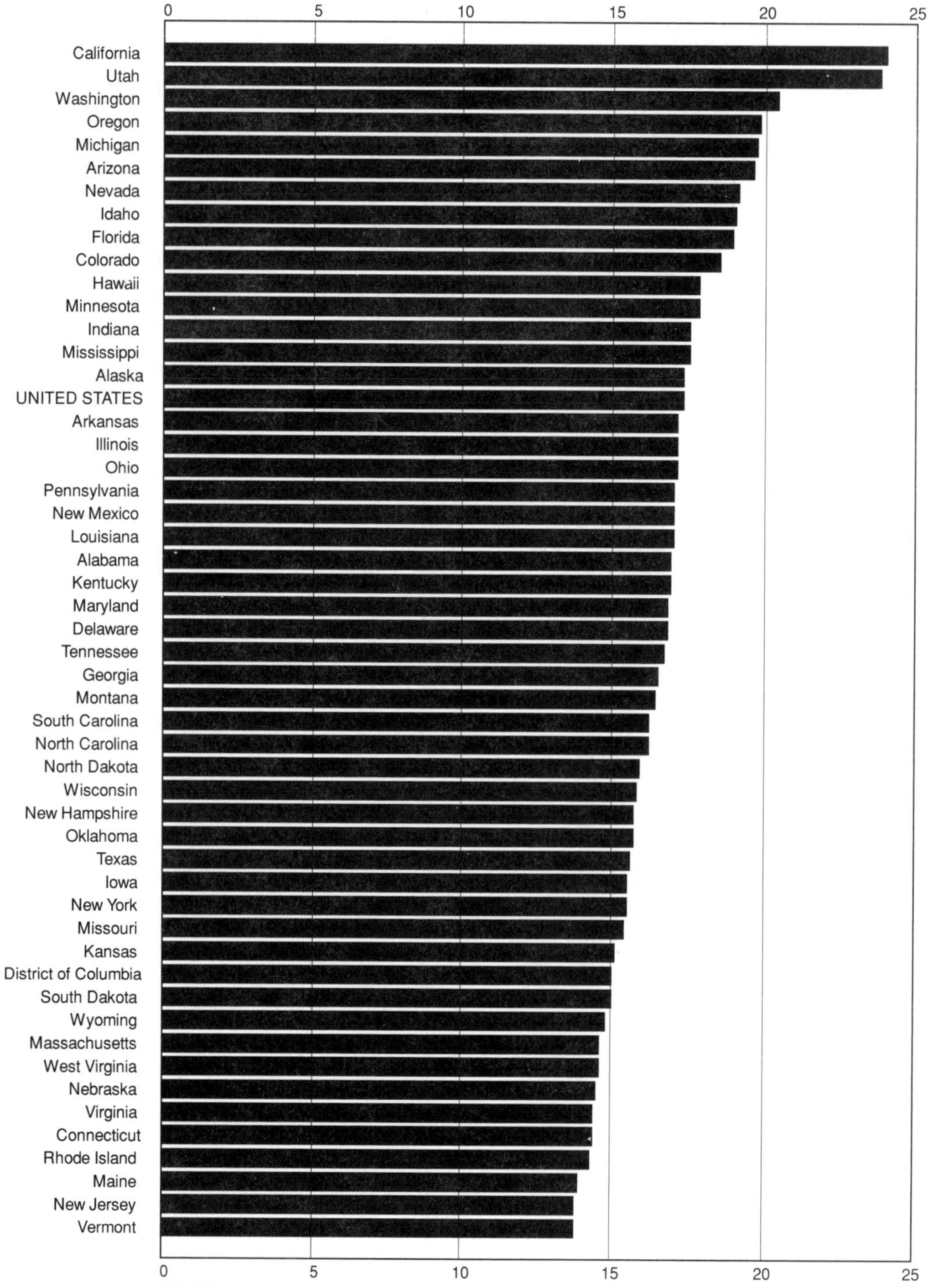

California
Utah
Washington
Oregon
Michigan
Arizona
Nevada
Idaho
Florida
Colorado
Hawaii
Minnesota
Indiana
Mississippi
Alaska
UNITED STATES
Arkansas
Illinois
Ohio
Pennsylvania
New Mexico
Louisiana
Alabama
Kentucky
Maryland
Delaware
Tennessee
Georgia
Montana
South Carolina
North Carolina
North Dakota
Wisconsin
New Hampshire
Oklahoma
Texas
Iowa
New York
Missouri
Kansas
District of Columbia
South Dakota
Wyoming
Massachusetts
West Virginia
Nebraska
Virginia
Connecticut
Rhode Island
Maine
New Jersey
Vermont

SOURCE: U.S. Department of Education, National Center for Education Statistics, Common Core of Data survey. (This figure was prepared February 1998.)

1993–94, California had a pupil/teacher ratio of 24:1 (table 24), but the average class size was 29 for elementary teachers and 30 for secondary teachers (table 21). Similar relationships were typical for other states. New Jersey, the state with the lowest pupil/teacher ratio in 1993–94, had an average elementary class size of 23 and an average secondary class size of 21.

The pupil/teacher ratios declined rapidly during the middle 1970s when enrollments declined and the number of teachers remained stable (table 24). Between 1970 and 1983, the ratio declined from 22.3 to 18.4. The ratio continued to decline more slowly after 1983, reaching 17.2 in 1989. Since 1989, the pupil/teacher ratio has fluctuated within a narrow range indicating that the increase in the number of students and the percentage increase in the number of teachers was about the same. Changes in most states were relatively modest during the 1985 to 1990 and 1990 to 1995 periods. Between 1985 and 1990, 13 states had an increase in the pupil/teacher ratio and only Hawaii had a decrease of more than 2 students per teacher. The balance shifted some between 1990 and 1995, with 23 states and the District of Columbia having increases in the ratio. Two states had declines in the ratio of more than 2 points.

The pattern of overall staffing for public elementary and secondary schools generally mirrored the pattern for the teachers. Between 1985 and 1995, public school enrollment grew by 14 percent, compared to an 18 percent increase for teachers and 20 percent for staff. Staff grew at a fairly consistent pace during these 10 years, about 8 percent in the first five years and 11 percent in the second five (table 25). The general pattern of increases in numbers of staff between 1985 and 1995 was reflected in most of the states. Of the 47 states and the District of Columbia reporting consistent data in 1985 and 1995, only 3 states and the District reported decreases. Thirteen states reported an increase of 30 percent or more.

The drops in public school enrollment and increases in the number of public school staff through the 1970s served to reduce the student/staff ratio from 13.3 in 1970 to 9.8 in 1980 and 9.5 in 1985 (table 26). Increases in enrollment during the following ten years and slightly larger increases in the number of staff yielded further small reductions in the ratio to 9.0 in 1995. Most states had at least a small decline in the pupil/staff ratio between 1985 and 1995. Only Hawaii, California, Minnesota, and Oregon had an increase over 0.5 percent.

Teacher Salaries

The average salary for teachers in 1996–97 was $38,509. The state average salaries ranged very widely from under $28,000 in Mississippi, North Da-

kota, and South Dakota to over $49,000 in New Jersey, New York, Connecticut, and Alaska (table 27). Over the past 25 years, teacher salaries have fluctuated significantly, after adjusting for inflation. Teacher salaries have fallen slightly after reaching all-time highs in 1990–91(table 28). After being adjusted for inflation, teacher salaries rose during the early 1970s, before declining in 1973–74 and 1974–75, because salary increases lagged the rapidly rising inflation rates. After stabilizing in the mid 1970s, teacher salaries dipped again during the late 1970s, as inflation rates took another upward surge. A low point was reached in 1980–81, when average teacher salaries were 14 percent below the 1972–73 high point. Teacher salaries rose during most of the 1980s. During the late 1980s, the changes were very small and average teacher salaries fell 2 percent between 1990-91 and 1996-97.

The national patterns of modest increases in average salaries for teachers during the late 1980s and small decreases during the 1990s were typical for many states. From 1986–87 to 1991–92, average salaries for teachers increased in 30 states. Four states—Connecticut, Vermont, New Hampshire, and Indiana—had relatively large increases of 20 percent or more over the 5-year period, after being adjusted for inflation. Between 1991–92 to 1996–97, the pattern shifted significantly. Nineteen states and the District of Columbia had increases, and none of the increases were over 7 percent. Thirty-one states had decreases, with 12 states having declines of more than 5 percent.

Institutions and Districts

State governments administer elementary and secondary education programs through about 15,000 school districts across the country. Some of these districts have considerable responsibility for raising school funds, typically through property or other local taxes. Others rely on general government units, such as counties, to raise local school funds. School districts make budgets for local schools, subject to requirements set by state school authorities. These requirements may restrict such items as lower or upper spending limits per student or require minimum teacher salaries or establish maximum class sizes. There is a wide range of enrollment sizes among school districts, from a handful of students to 1 million, but most districts are not large (table 29). More than one-third of all school districts have fewer than 500 students. Seven hundred sixty-nine (5 percent) of the districts have 10,000 or more students. Yet these large districts enroll nearly half of all students. About 2 percent of students attend the small districts with fewer than 500 students, yet these districts account for more than one third of all school districts.

Figure 7. – Percentage of public school teachers with more than 20 years of teaching experience, by state: 1993–94

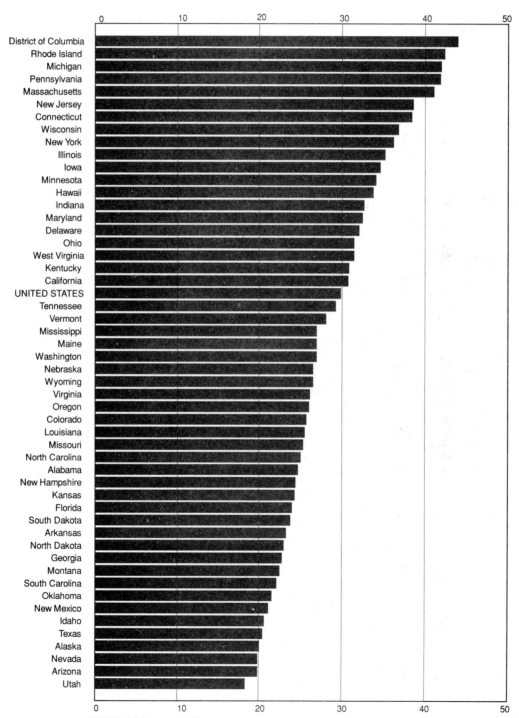

SOURCE: U.S. Department of Education, National Center for Education Statistics, "Schools and Staffing Survey, 1993-94."
(This figure was prepared February 1998.)

Figure 8. – Public school teachers as a percentage of public school system staff, by state: Fall 1995

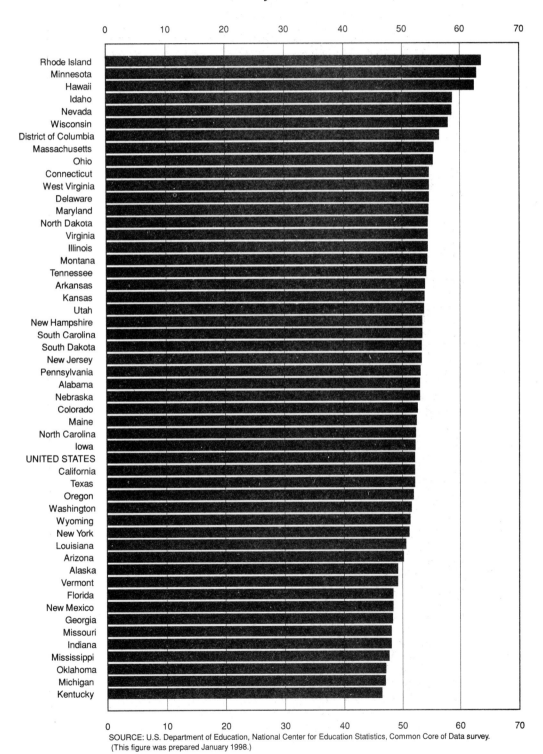

SOURCE: U.S. Department of Education, National Center for Education Statistics, Common Core of Data survey.
(This figure was prepared January 1998.)

States show great diversity in the structure of their school district systems. Some states have relatively large districts, such as states with county-wide systems like Maryland and Florida. Other states, such as Nebraska, have a tradition of very small districts. Nebraska has about the same number of districts as New York, but New York has almost ten times as many students.

In 1995–96, public school systems operated 87,125 schools (table 30). The average school size was 525 students, with the elementary schools (476 students) generally being somewhat smaller than the secondary schools (703 students). There was a considerable range of average enrollment sizes from state to state, but the variation was much narrower than the average size of school districts (figure 9). States with large rural areas such as Alaska, Wyoming, North Dakota, Nebraska, Montana, and South Dakota had the smallest average school sizes. The states with the largest average school sizes—Florida, Hawaii, Georgia, California, and New York—generally had sizeable proportions of their populations in urban areas.

Finances

Public school districts obtain funding for their schools from a variety of federal, state, and local sources. Additional monies come from families and other private sources for school lunches, summer school programs, transportation, books, or other fees (table 31). In 1995–96, 7 percent of public school revenues came from federal sources, 48 percent came from state sources, 43 percent came from local sources and 3 percent came from private sources.

In 1995–96, the average expenditure in ADA per student was $6,146 and about 62 percent of this amount was spent on student instruction (tables 34 and 35 and figures 10 and 11). The proportion of per student expenditures spent on instruction was fairly consistent from state to state. The range was from 49 percent in the District of Columbia and 57 percent in Alaska to 68 percent in New York. But most states (30) were clustered within 2 percentage points of the national average.

The next largest category of school expenditures was operation and maintenance of school facilities. This amounted to 10 percent of expenditures in 1995–96, but the states ranged more widely than did the expenditures for instruction. The ratio of the highest to lowest state for instruction was about 1.8 for operation and maintenance compared to 1.4 for instruction. The highest percentages were in the District of Columbia (15 percent) and Alaska (14 percent). The lowest percentages of 8 percent were tallied in North Carolina, Minnesota, and Vermont.

Another relatively large category was general and school administration, which accounted for 8 percent

of school funds in 1995–96. The range was narrower than for the operation and maintenance expenditures. The highest proportion of funds was 12 percent and the lowest was 7 percent. Most of the states were clustered in a relatively narrow range. Thirty-one states and the District had administration proportions that differed by less than 1 percentage point from the national average.

The remaining amounts of school funds were distributed over a variety of activities. About 5 percent of funds went to health, attendance, and speech services, 4 percent went to curriculum development, staff training, libraries, media, and computer centers, 4 percent went to student transportation, and another 4 percent went to food services. Three percent supported other activities.

The general structure of education spending showed some variations from state to state as described through the percentage breakdowns of school spending, but many of the states were tightly clustered around narrow ranges. This clustering was particularly apparent for some of the larger categories such as operation and maintenance and instruction. However, when the actual spending levels are computed on a per student basis for 1995-96, the high to low range is wider than for measures based on the percentage distribution of expenditures. For example, the percent of expenditures spent on administration ranged from the highest to the lowest state by a ratio of less than 2:1. However, when viewed on an expenditure per student basis, the ratio is more than 4:1, ranging from $1,066 in Alaska to $260 in Utah. Operation and maintenance of plant per student expenditures also ranged by nearly a 4:1 ratio, from $1,383 per student in the District of Columbia to $350 in Utah.

Current expenditures for public elementary and secondary schools totaled $255 billion dollars in 1995–96. This represents an inflation-adjusted increase of 2 percent from the previous year (table 38). Although increases in expenditures have generally been small between 1990–91 and 1995–96, long-term comparisons of inflation-adjusted figures reveal substantial increases. After moderate increases during the mid-1970s and moderate declines during the late 1970s and early 1980s, expenditures began to rise. Expenditures rose 31 percent after inflation between 1985–86 and 1995–96. This increase was reflected in most of the states, with only Alaska and Wyoming showing a decrease. Thirty-seven states showed increases in real expenditures of over 25 percent during these 10 years. About two-thirds of the increase occurred during the 1985–86 to 1990–91 period, rather than during the second half of the ten-year period. During the later 5-year period, 11 states showed increases of more than 15 percent. Three-fifths (30) of the states showed moderate in-

Figure 9. – Average enrollment size of public schools: 1995–96

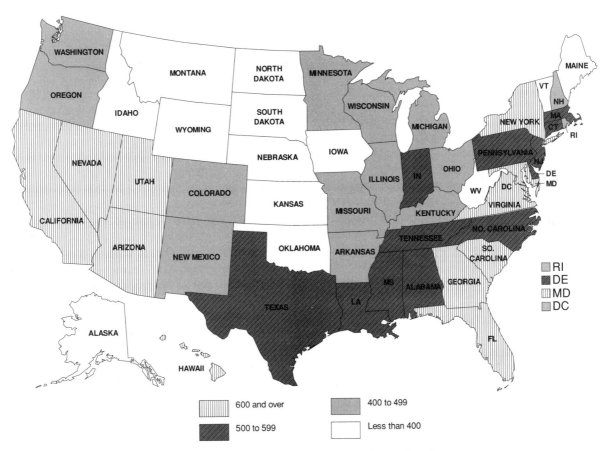

SOURCE: U.S. Department of Education, National Center for Education Statistics, Common Core of Data survey. (This figure was prepared February 1998.)

Figure 10. – Current expenditure per student in average daily attendance in public elementary and secondary schools, by state: 1995–96

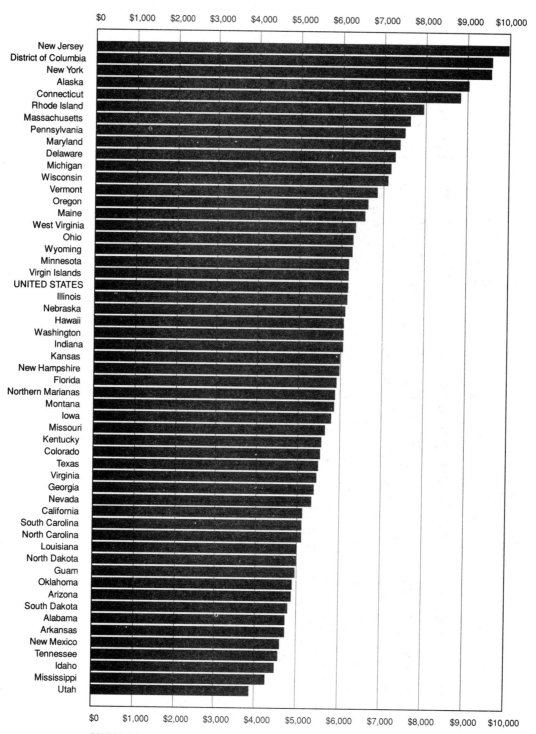

SOURCE: U.S. Department of Education, National Center for Education Statistics, Common Core of Data survey.
(This figure was prepared January 1998.)

Figure 11. – Instruction expenditure per student in average daily attendance in public elementary and secondary schools, by state: 1995–96

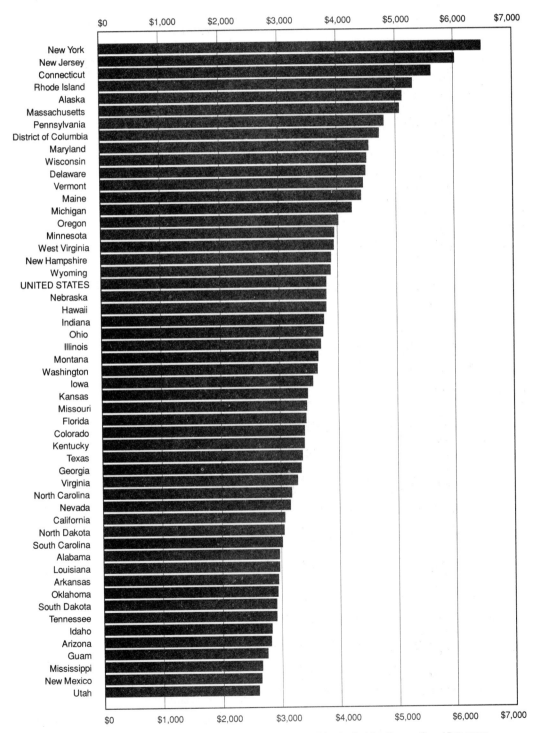

SOURCE: U.S. Department of Education, National Center for Education Statistics, Common Core of Data survey.
(This figure was prepared April 1998.)

creases of 5 to 15 percent; 7 states showed an increase of less than 5 percent, and 2 states and the District of Columbia had a decrease.

When computed on a per pupil in average daily attendance basis, about half of the real spending increases that occurred during the 1985–86 to 1995–96 period disappear. During the first half of the ten-year period expenditures increased at a fast rate, and enrollment rose at a slower rate than during the second half of the ten-year period. This resulted in a much faster growth in expenditures per student during the late 1980s than during the early 1990s (table 40 and figure 15). Between 1985–86 and 1990–91,

expenditure per student rose by 14 percent in constant dollars, compared to the 1 percent increase from 1990–91 to 1995–96.

The substantial increases in per student expenditures of the 1985–86 to 1990–91 period were reflected in many of the states, with 18 states and the District of Columbia having real increases of over 15 percent or more. Seven states had an increase of less than 5 percent, and 5 states had a decrease. Between 1990–91 and 1995–96, the situation shifted significantly. Only Mississippi had an increase of 15 percent or more; 17 states had increases of 5 percent or less and 18 states and the District of Columbia had decreases in expenditure per student.

Table 5.—Estimated total and school-age resident population, by state:[1] 1970 to 1996

[In thousands]

State	1970[2]		1980[2]		1985[3]		1990[2]		1994[3]		1995[3]		1996[3]	
	Total, all ages	5- to 17-year-olds	Total, all ages	5- to 17-year-olds	Total, all ages	5- to 17-year-olds	Total, all ages	5- to 17-year-olds	Total, all ages	5- to 17-year-olds	Total, all ages	5- to 17-year-olds	Total, all ages	5- to 17-year-olds
1	2	3	4	5	6	7	8	9	10	11	12	13	14	15
United States	203,302	52,540	226,546	47,407	237,924	44,782	248,710	45,166	260,372	48,155	262,890	48,974	265,284	49,762
Alabama	3,444	934	3,894	866	3,973	798	4,041	774	4,215	774	4,246	778	4,273	780
Alaska	303	88	402	92	532	112	550	117	601	134	603	135	607	135
Arizona	1,775	486	2,718	578	3,184	601	3,665	686	4,092	781	4,305	795	4,428	807
Arkansas	1,923	498	2,286	496	2,327	461	2,351	455	2,455	469	2,485	478	2,510	484
California	19,971	4,999	23,668	4,681	26,441	4,752	29,760	5,337	31,362	5,831	31,565	5,969	31,878	6,132
Colorado	2,210	589	2,890	592	3,209	599	3,294	607	3,663	692	3,748	709	3,823	728
Connecticut	3,032	768	3,108	638	3,201	549	3,287	520	3,273	555	3,271	565	3,274	575
Delaware	548	148	594	125	618	113	666	114	708	124	717	125	725	126
District of Columbia ..	757	164	638	109	635	88	607	80	568	74	555	76	543	75
Florida	6,791	1,609	9,746	1,789	11,351	1,792	12,938	2,011	13,965	2,319	14,184	2,392	14,400	2,467
Georgia	4,588	1,223	5,463	1,231	5,963	1,195	6,478	1,230	7,063	1,335	7,209	1,370	7,353	1,401
Hawaii	770	204	965	198	1,040	194	1,108	196	1,173	209	1,179	212	1,184	215
Idaho	713	200	944	213	994	223	1,007	228	1,136	252	1,166	255	1,189	258
Illinois	11,110	2,859	11,427	2,401	11,400	2,192	11,431	2,095	11,734	2,168	11,790	2,206	11,847	2,241
Indiana	5,195	1,386	5,490	1,200	5,459	1,087	5,544	1,056	5,750	1,066	5,797	1,079	5,841	1,089
Iowa	2,825	743	2,914	604	2,830	543	2,777	525	2,832	538	2,843	539	2,852	537
Kansas	2,249	573	2,364	468	2,427	452	2,478	472	2,550	503	2,564	505	2,572	507
Kentucky	3,221	844	3,661	800	3,695	745	3,685	703	3,826	708	3,857	710	3,884	710
Louisiana	3,645	1,041	4,206	969	4,408	937	4,220	890	4,315	896	4,338	901	4,351	906
Maine	994	260	1,125	243	1,163	222	1,228	223	1,238	228	1,239	228	1,243	228
Maryland	3,924	1,038	4,217	895	4,413	788	4,781	803	5,000	882	5,039	905	5,072	927
Massachusetts	5,689	1,407	5,737	1,153	5,881	989	6,016	940	6,042	995	6,071	1,015	6,092	1,031
Michigan	8,882	2,450	9,262	2,067	9,076	1,824	9,295	1,754	9,486	1,812	9,538	1,845	9,594	1,865
Minnesota	3,806	1,051	4,076	865	4,184	796	4,375	828	4,572	907	4,615	920	4,658	931
Mississippi	2,217	635	2,521	599	2,588	576	2,573	550	2,668	548	2,696	551	2,716	552
Missouri	4,678	1,183	4,917	1,008	5,000	941	5,117	944	5,275	996	5,319	1,013	5,359	1,027
Montana	694	197	787	167	822	167	799	163	857	176	870	177	879	177
Nebraska	1,485	389	1,570	324	1,585	305	1,578	309	1,626	324	1,639	327	1,652	329
Nevada	489	127	800	160	951	166	1,202	204	1,464	262	1,533	277	1,603	293
New Hampshire	738	189	921	196	997	182	1,109	194	1,135	212	1,148	217	1,162	220
New Jersey	7,171	1,797	7,365	1,528	7,566	1,340	7,730	1,265	7,906	1,354	7,950	1,385	7,988	1,415
New Mexico	1,017	311	1,303	303	1,438	304	1,515	320	1,659	353	1,690	359	1,713	365
New York	18,241	4,358	17,558	3,552	17,792	3,173	17,990	3,000	18,197	3,131	18,191	3,174	18,185	3,220
North Carolina	5,084	1,323	5,882	1,254	6,254	1,175	6,629	1,147	7,079	1,249	7,202	1,285	7,323	1,321
North Dakota	618	175	653	136	677	133	639	127	640	128	642	128	644	127
Ohio	10,657	2,820	10,798	2,307	10,735	2,090	10,847	2,012	11,097	2,064	11,134	2,078	11,173	2,089
Oklahoma	2,559	640	3,025	622	3,271	635	3,146	609	3,254	639	3,275	646	3,301	653
Oregon	2,092	534	2,633	525	2,673	504	2,842	521	3,094	575	3,149	586	3,204	597
Pennsylvania	11,801	2,925	11,864	2,376	11,771	2,079	11,882	1,996	12,058	2,093	12,060	2,114	12,056	2,133
Rhode Island	950	225	947	186	969	163	1,003	159	996	167	992	170	990	172
South Carolina	2,591	720	3,122	703	3,303	663	3,487	663	3,643	674	3,667	680	3,699	684
South Dakota	666	187	691	147	698	139	696	144	724	153	730	153	732	153
Tennessee	3,926	1,002	4,591	972	4,715	903	4,877	882	5,175	928	5,247	944	5,320	958
Texas	11,199	3,002	14,229	3,137	16,273	3,318	16,987	3,437	18,434	3,725	18,801	3,792	19,128	3,870
Utah	1,059	312	1,461	350	1,643	418	1,723	457	1,910	487	1,958	490	2,000	490
Vermont	445	118	511	109	530	100	563	102	581	109	585	110	589	111
Virginia	4,651	1,197	5,347	1,114	5,715	1,039	6,187	1,060	6,550	1,133	6,615	1,156	6,675	1,177
Washington	3,413	881	4,132	826	4,400	816	4,867	893	5,351	1,008	5,448	1,030	5,533	1,051
West Virginia	1,744	442	1,950	414	1,907	383	1,793	337	1,822	320	1,825	318	1,826	315
Wisconsin	4,418	1,203	4,706	1,011	4,748	908	4,892	927	5,084	992	5,122	1,001	5,160	1,006
Wyoming	332	92	470	101	500	108	454	101	476	103	479	103	481	102

[1] Includes Armed Forces residing in each state.
[2] As of April 1.
[3] Estimates as of July 1.

NOTE.—Some data have been revised from previously published figures. Because of rounding, details may not add to totals.

SOURCE: U.S. Department of Commerce, Bureau of the Census, Current Population Reports, Series P-25, No. 1095, CPH-L-74 (1990 data); and forthcoming state level P-25 Reports. (This table was prepared May 1997.)

Table 6.—Estimated school-age population and public school enrollment, by state: 1980 to 1996

[Numbers in thousands]

State	5- to 17-year-old resident population [1]						5- to 17-year-old population as a percent of total population [1]				Public elementary and secondary enrollment as a percent of 5- to 17-year-old population					
	1980 [2]	1985 [3]	1990 [3]	1994 [3]	1995 [3]	1996 [3]	1970 [2]	1980 [2]	1990 [3]	1996 [3]	1980	1985	1990	1994	1995	1996
1	2	3	4	5	6	7	8	9	10	11	12	13	14	15	16	17
United States	47,407	44,782	45,166	48,155	48,974	49,762	25.8	20.9	18.2	18.8	86.2	88.0	91.3	91.6	91.6	90.9
Alabama	866	798	774	774	778	780	27.1	22.2	19.2	18.3	87.6	91.5	93.3	95.2	95.8	95.1
Alaska	92	112	117	134	135	135	29.0	22.9	21.3	22.2	94.0	96.0	97.4	95.1	94.8	93.3
Arizona	578	601	686	781	795	807	27.4	21.3	18.7	18.2	88.9	91.3	93.3	94.4	93.5	92.9
Arkansas	496	461	455	469	478	484	25.9	21.7	19.4	19.3	90.3	93.9	95.9	95.3	94.9	94.4
California	4,681	4,752	5,337	5,831	5,969	6,132	25.0	19.8	17.9	19.2	87.1	89.5	92.8	92.7	92.8	90.3
Colorado	592	599	607	692	709	728	26.7	20.5	18.4	19.0	92.2	92.0	94.6	92.5	92.5	92.5
Connecticut	638	549	520	555	565	575	25.3	20.5	15.8	17.6	83.3	84.2	90.2	91.4	91.7	91.0
Delaware	125	113	114	124	125	126	27.0	21.0	17.1	17.4	79.5	82.4	87.4	86.0	86.6	87.7
District of Columbia	109	88	80	74	76	75	21.7	17.1	13.2	13.8	91.8	98.6	100.9	108.3	105.7	105.5
Florida	1,789	1,792	2,011	2,319	2,392	2,467	23.7	18.4	15.5	17.1	84.4	87.2	92.6	91.1	91.0	90.8
Georgia	1,231	1,195	1,230	1,335	1,370	1,401	26.7	22.5	19.0	19.1	86.8	90.4	93.6	95.2	95.7	94.3
Hawaii	198	194	196	209	212	215	26.5	20.5	17.7	18.2	83.4	84.4	87.6	88.2	88.3	87.7
Idaho	213	223	228	252	255	258	28.1	22.6	22.6	21.7	95.4	93.5	96.9	95.4	95.2	95.1
Illinois	2,401	2,192	2,095	2,168	2,206	2,241	25.7	21.0	18.3	18.9	82.6	83.3	86.9	88.4	88.1	87.5
Indiana	1,200	1,087	1,056	1,066	1,079	1,089	26.7	21.9	19.0	18.6	88.0	88.9	90.4	90.9	90.6	90.4
Iowa	604	543	525	538	539	537	26.3	20.7	18.9	18.8	88.4	89.3	92.1	93.0	93.2	93.9
Kansas	468	452	472	503	505	507	25.5	19.8	19.0	19.7	88.7	90.8	92.6	91.7	91.7	91.7
Kentucky	800	745	703	708	710	710	26.2	21.9	19.1	18.3	83.7	86.4	90.5	92.9	93.0	93.4
Louisiana	969	937	890	896	901	906	28.6	23.0	21.1	20.8	80.2	84.1	88.2	89.1	88.5	85.8
Maine	243	222	223	228	228	228	26.2	21.6	18.2	18.3	91.6	92.7	96.5	93.3	93.5	95.9
Maryland	895	788	803	882	905	927	26.5	21.2	16.8	18.3	83.9	85.2	89.1	89.7	89.0	88.3
Massachusetts	1,153	989	940	995	1,015	1,031	24.7	20.1	15.6	16.9	88.6	85.4	88.8	89.8	90.2	90.9
Michigan	2,067	1,824	1,754	1,812	1,845	1,865	27.6	22.3	18.9	19.4	86.9	87.9	90.3	89.1	89.1	89.1
Minnesota	865	796	828	907	920	931	27.6	21.2	18.9	20.0	87.2	88.5	91.3	90.6	90.8	89.9
Mississippi	599	576	550	548	551	552	28.6	23.8	21.4	20.3	79.6	81.9	91.3	92.3	91.8	91.3
Missouri	1,008	941	944	996	1,013	1,027	25.3	20.5	18.4	19.2	83.8	84.5	86.5	88.2	87.9	86.0
Montana	167	167	163	176	177	177	28.4	21.2	20.4	20.1	92.9	92.0	93.8	93.1	93.6	94.3
Nebraska	324	305	309	324	327	329	26.2	20.6	19.6	19.9	86.6	87.1	88.7	88.6	88.6	88.8
Nevada	160	166	204	262	277	293	26.0	20.0	17.0	18.3	93.4	93.2	98.7	95.9	95.7	96.3
New Hampshire	196	182	194	212	217	220	25.6	21.3	17.5	18.9	85.3	88.4	89.1	89.4	89.6	88.4
New Jersey	1,528	1,340	1,265	1,354	1,385	1,415	25.1	20.7	16.4	17.7	81.5	83.3	86.1	86.7	86.5	86.3
New Mexico	303	304	320	353	359	365	30.6	23.3	21.1	21.3	89.5	91.3	94.3	92.7	91.7	90.6
New York	3,552	3,173	3,000	3,131	3,174	3,220	23.9	20.2	16.7	17.7	80.8	82.6	86.6	88.3	88.6	87.7
North Carolina	1,254	1,175	1,147	1,249	1,285	1,321	26.0	21.3	17.3	18.0	90.1	92.5	94.8	92.6	92.0	90.8
North Dakota	136	133	127	128	128	127	28.3	20.8	19.9	19.7	85.9	89.2	92.8	93.2	93.2	93.2
Ohio	2,307	2,090	2,012	2,064	2,078	2,089	26.5	21.4	18.5	18.7	84.8	85.8	88.0	87.9	88.4	88.1
Oklahoma	622	635	609	639	646	653	25.0	20.6	19.4	19.8	92.9	93.3	95.1	95.5	95.5	95.0
Oregon	525	504	521	575	586	597	25.5	19.9	18.3	18.6	88.5	88.7	90.7	90.8	90.1	90.1
Pennsylvania	2,376	2,079	1,996	2,093	2,114	2,133	24.8	20.0	16.8	17.7	80.4	81.0	83.6	84.3	84.6	84.7
Rhode Island	186	163	159	167	170	172	23.7	19.6	15.9	17.4	80.1	82.4	87.3	88.3	88.1	87.9
South Carolina	703	663	663	674	680	684	27.8	22.5	19.0	18.5	88.1	91.4	93.8	96.2	94.9	94.9
South Dakota	147	139	144	153	153	153	28.1	21.3	20.7	20.9	87.4	89.2	89.7	93.9	94.5	93.4
Tennessee	972	903	882	928	944	958	25.5	21.2	18.1	18.0	87.8	90.2	93.5	95.0	94.7	93.0
Texas	3,137	3,318	3,437	3,725	3,792	3,870	26.8	22.0	20.2	20.2	92.4	94.4	98.4	98.7	98.9	98.4
Utah	350	418	457	487	490	490	29.5	24.0	26.5	24.5	98.2	96.5	97.7	97.4	97.4	97.6
Vermont	109	100	102	109	110	111	26.5	21.3	18.1	18.8	87.9	89.9	93.9	96.3	95.9	96.0
Virginia	1,114	1,039	1,060	1,133	1,156	1,177	25.7	20.8	17.1	17.6	90.7	93.2	94.2	93.6	93.4	93.1
Washington	826	816	893	1,008	1,030	1,051	25.8	20.0	18.3	19.0	91.7	91.8	94.0	93.1	92.9	92.5
West Virginia	414	383	337	320	318	315	25.3	21.2	18.8	17.3	92.6	93.5	95.7	97.2	96.6	96.3
Wisconsin	1,011	908	927	992	1,001	1,006	27.2	21.5	18.9	19.5	82.1	84.6	86.0	86.7	87.0	87.9
Wyoming	101	108	101	103	103	102	27.7	21.5	22.2	21.2	97.3	95.1	97.3	97.1	97.0	96.8

[1] Includes Armed Forces residing in each state.
[2] As of April 1.
[3] Estimates as of July 1.

NOTE.—Because of students outside the normal age range, percents may exceed 100. Because of rounding, details may not add to totals.

SOURCE: U.S. Department of Education, National Center for Education Statistics, Common Core of Data surveys; and U.S. Department of Commerce, Bureau of the Census, *Current Population Reports*, Series P-25, No. 1095, CPH-L-74 (1990 data) and forthcoming state level P-25 Reports. (This table was prepared January 1998.)

Table 7.—Distribution of enrollment in public elementary and secondary schools, by level and state: Fall 1970 to fall 1995

State or other area	Percent of students in kindergarten through grade 8 [1]					Percent of students in grades 9 through grade 12					Change in percentage points at the elementary level		
	Fall 1970	Fall 1980	Fall 1985	Fall 1990	Fall 1995	Fall 1970	Fall 1980	Fall 1985	Fall 1990	Fall 1995	1970 to 1980	1980 to 1990	1990 to 1995
1	2	3	4	5	6	7	8	9	10	11	12	13	14
United States	**70.9**	**67.6**	**68.6**	**72.5**	**72.1**	**29.1**	**32.4**	**31.4**	**27.5**	**27.9**	**–3.3**	**4.9**	**–0.4**
Alabama	70.7	69.6	70.8	73.0	72.3	29.3	30.4	29.2	27.0	27.7	–1.2	3.5	–0.7
Alaska [2]	76.4	69.8	71.9	74.9	73.2	23.6	30.2	28.1	25.1	26.8	–6.6	5.1	–1.7
Arizona	71.4	69.5	70.4	74.9	73.8	28.6	30.5	29.6	25.1	26.2	–1.9	5.4	–1.1
Arkansas	71.2	69.2	70.0	71.9	71.1	28.8	30.8	30.0	28.1	28.9	–1.9	2.6	–0.7
California	69.7	67.0	68.8	73.0	73.0	30.3	33.0	31.2	27.0	27.0	–2.8	6.1	(3)
Colorado	71.0	68.6	68.8	73.1	73.0	29.0	31.4	31.2	26.9	27.0	–2.4	4.6	–0.2
Connecticut	73.6	68.4	69.5	74.1	74.2	26.4	31.6	30.5	25.9	25.8	–5.2	5.6	0.1
Delaware	71.1	62.8	67.9	72.9	71.0	28.9	37.2	32.1	27.1	29.0	–8.2	10.0	–1.8
District of Columbia	77.7	70.9	71.8	75.9	77.5	22.3	29.1	28.2	24.1	22.5	–6.7	5.0	1.6
Florida	71.1	69.0	69.5	73.6	74.1	28.9	31.0	30.5	26.4	25.9	–2.2	4.6	0.6
Georgia	72.8	69.4	70.1	73.7	73.7	27.2	30.6	29.9	26.3	26.3	–3.4	4.3	–0.1
Hawaii	71.5	66.4	69.1	71.5	72.5	28.5	33.6	30.9	28.5	27.5	–5.1	5.1	0.9
Idaho	68.0	70.7	71.6	72.5	69.7	32.0	29.3	28.4	27.5	30.3	2.8	1.8	–2.7
Illinois	71.6	67.3	68.2	71.9	71.5	28.4	32.7	31.8	28.1	28.5	–4.3	4.6	–0.4
Indiana	71.2	67.1	67.7	70.8	70.0	28.8	32.9	32.3	29.2	30.0	–4.1	3.7	–0.8
Iowa	70.4	65.8	66.8	71.3	68.5	29.6	34.2	33.2	28.7	31.5	–4.6	5.5	–2.8
Kansas	69.5	68.1	69.6	73.2	71.0	30.5	31.9	30.4	26.8	29.0	–1.5	5.1	–2.2
Kentucky	71.5	69.2	69.7	72.2	71.0	28.5	30.8	30.3	27.8	29.0	–2.3	2.9	–1.2
Louisiana	73.1	69.9	72.7	74.7	72.8	26.9	30.1	27.3	25.3	27.2	–3.2	4.8	–1.9
Maine	72.3	68.6	69.1	72.1	73.1	27.7	31.4	30.9	27.9	26.9	–3.7	3.5	0.9
Maryland	72.5	65.7	66.5	73.7	73.3	27.5	34.3	33.5	26.3	26.7	–6.8	8.0	–0.4
Massachusetts	71.4	66.2	66.2	72.4	73.7	28.6	33.8	33.8	27.6	26.3	–5.2	6.2	1.3
Michigan	73.3	68.3	67.7	72.3	72.6	26.7	31.7	32.3	27.7	27.4	–4.9	4.0	0.3
Minnesota	68.5	63.9	66.4	72.1	70.2	31.5	36.1	33.6	27.9	29.8	–4.6	8.2	–2.0
Mississippi	72.7	69.1	70.0	74.0	72.3	27.3	30.9	30.0	26.0	27.7	–3.6	4.9	–1.6
Missouri	72.0	67.2	68.4	72.0	71.4	28.0	32.8	31.6	28.0	28.6	–4.8	4.9	–0.6
Montana	68.4	68.1	70.1	72.7	70.3	31.6	31.9	29.9	27.3	29.7	–0.3	4.6	–2.4
Nebraska	69.9	67.4	69.3	72.3	70.1	30.1	32.6	30.7	27.7	29.9	–2.5	4.9	–2.2
Nevada	73.0	67.3	69.1	74.5	73.9	27.0	32.7	30.9	25.5	26.1	–5.7	7.2	–0.5
New Hampshire	71.6	66.9	66.4	73.1	73.0	28.4	33.1	33.6	26.9	27.0	–4.7	6.2	–0.1
New Jersey	71.7	65.8	66.3	71.9	73.5	28.3	34.2	33.7	28.1	26.5	–6.0	6.1	1.6
New Mexico	70.6	68.5	67.5	68.9	69.5	29.4	31.5	32.5	31.1	30.5	–2.0	0.4	0.6
New York	70.4	64.0	65.0	70.4	70.4	29.6	36.0	35.0	29.6	29.6	–6.4	6.3	(3)
North Carolina	70.1	69.6	69.0	72.1	73.6	29.9	30.4	31.0	27.9	26.4	–0.5	2.5	1.6
North Dakota	68.3	65.7	70.6	72.1	69.1	31.7	34.3	29.4	27.9	30.9	–2.6	6.4	–3.0
Ohio	70.0	67.0	67.2	71.0	70.7	30.0	33.0	32.8	29.0	29.3	–3.0	4.0	–0.3
Oklahoma	69.8	69.0	69.9	73.4	72.3	30.2	31.0	30.1	26.6	27.7	–0.7	4.3	–1.1
Oregon	67.8	68.7	68.2	72.0	71.2	32.2	31.3	31.8	28.0	28.8	0.9	3.3	–0.8
Pennsylvania	69.2	64.5	64.9	70.3	70.3	30.8	35.5	35.1	29.7	29.7	–4.7	5.8	(3)
Rhode Island	72.0	65.9	67.2	73.3	73.3	28.0	34.1	32.8	26.7	26.7	–6.1	7.4	(3)
South Carolina	72.0	68.9	69.9	72.7	71.8	28.0	31.1	30.1	27.3	28.2	–3.1	3.8	–0.9
South Dakota	68.5	67.1	70.5	73.7	70.1	31.5	32.9	29.5	26.3	29.9	–1.5	6.6	–3.5
Tennessee	72.1	70.5	70.6	72.5	72.8	27.9	29.5	29.4	27.5	27.2	–1.5	2.0	0.3
Texas	72.0	70.6	72.2	74.2	73.6	28.0	29.4	27.8	25.8	26.4	–1.4	3.6	–0.7
Utah	70.0	72.8	74.1	72.8	68.7	30.0	27.2	25.9	27.2	31.3	2.9	–0.1	–4.1
Vermont	71.6	69.3	69.5	74.0	71.3	28.4	30.7	30.5	26.0	28.7	–2.4	4.7	–2.7
Virginia	71.9	69.6	68.7	72.9	73.0	28.1	30.4	31.3	27.1	27.0	–2.3	3.3	(3)
Washington	70.1	68.0	67.6	73.0	71.1	29.9	32.0	32.4	27.0	28.9	–2.0	4.9	–1.9
West Virginia	70.2	70.5	69.6	69.5	68.7	29.8	29.5	30.4	30.5	31.3	0.3	–1.0	–0.8
Wisconsin	68.3	63.6	65.3	70.9	69.3	31.7	36.4	34.7	29.1	30.7	–4.7	7.3	–1.6
Wyoming	69.5	71.3	72.0	72.2	69.0	30.5	28.7	28.0	27.8	31.0	1.8	0.9	–3.2
Outlying areas	—	—	—	74.5	73.6	—	—	—	25.5	26.4	—	—	–0.9
American Samoa	—	74.4	—	75.3	76.9	—	25.6	—	24.7	23.1	—	1.0	1.5
Guam	77.8	74.2	74.0	73.0	75.5	22.2	25.8	26.0	27.0	24.5	–3.6	–1.2	2.4
Northern Marianas	—	—	—	76.3	77.5	—	—	—	23.7	22.5	—	—	1.2
Puerto Rico	78.9	73.2	74.0	74.5	73.4	21.1	26.8	26.0	25.5	26.6	–5.7	1.3	–1.1
Virgin Islands	—	78.2	73.4	74.7	71.9	—	21.8	26.6	25.3	28.1	—	–3.5	–2.8

[1] Includes prekindergarten students.
[2] Beginning in 1985, data include students enrolled in public schools on federal bases and other special arrangements.
[3] Less than .05 percentage point change.

—Data not available.

SOURCE: U.S. Department of Education, National Center for Education Statistics, Common Core of Data surveys. (This table was prepared January 1998.)

Table 8.—Number of private schools, students, teachers, and high school graduates, and disabled children served under federal programs, by state: 1988–89 to 1996–97

State	Number of private schools [1]				Enrollment in private schools [1,2]	
	Fall 1989	Fall 1991	Fall 1993	Fall 1995	Fall 1989	Fall 1991
1	2	3	4	5	6	7
United States	**26,712 (594)**	**25,998 (224)**	**26,093 (205)**	**27,686 (252)**	**4,824,733 (39,281)**	**4,889,545 (26,741)**
Alabama	254 —	391 (87)	410 (79)	287 —	52,816 —	69,441 (8,390)
Alaska	44 —	87 (25)	66 —	65 —	4,023 —	5,520 (534)
Arizona	189 —	254 —	263 —	296 (39)	31,618 —	39,460 —
Arkansas	162 (50)	154 —	179 (30)	245 (50)	19,388 (1,870)	22,792 —
California	3,091 (43)	3,271 (133)	3,145 (65)	3,470 (51)	560,588 (4,185)	613,068 (16,643)
Colorado	263 (41)	363 (63)	391 (68)	342 (9)	35,781 (1,790)	57,352 (11,374)
Connecticut	323 —	315 —	360 (22)	355 (14)	72,239 —	67,374 —
Delaware	93 (15)	80 —	90 —	112 (17)	21,953 (74)	22,803 —
District of Columbia	117 (46)	88 (9)	80 —	84 —	23,849 (5,450)	17,776 (322)
Florida	1,288 (221)	1,198 (66)	1,262 (83)	1,284 (19)	218,961 (16,499)	205,600 (2,988)
Georgia	484 (70)	503 (32)	580 (81)	525 (20)	84,795 (2,499)	96,683 (4,078)
Hawaii	117 —	123 —	121 —	127 —	35,932 —	36,306 —
Idaho	136 (71)	65 —	78 —	77 —	9,844 (3,602)	6,644 —
Illinois	1,370 (69)	1,375 (26)	1,347 (12)	1,470 (52)	307,973 (5,869)	301,374 (1,158)
Indiana	534 (14)	697 (89)	619 —	661 (30)	89,857 (692)	99,450 (7,004)
Iowa	507 (243)	269 —	290 (30)	274 (26)	60,658 (10,883)	51,431 —
Kansas	211 —	203 —	206 —	265 (52)	34,719 —	35,077 —
Kentucky	323 (67)	318 —	296 —	382 (68)	68,540 (9,031)	65,990 —
Louisiana	451 (27)	438 —	458 (19)	647 (108)	136,465 (1,287)	139,248 —
Maine	119 (8)	122 —	140 —	134 —	16,416 (1,475)	14,854 —
Maryland	521 (62)	516 —	522 —	606 (11)	119,464 (9,963)	113,774 —
Massachusetts	612 (82)	655 (46)	648 (29)	655 (38)	124,603 (5,285)	125,006 (3,419)
Michigan	1,054 (98)	1,027 (14)	1,075 —	1,034 —	189,629 (2,283)	187,095 (710)
Minnesota	630 (96)	604 (38)	542 —	570 (36)	96,593 (8,179)	93,404 (2,401)
Mississippi	394 (137)	275 (6)	221 (30)	182 —	55,037 (6,293)	58,757 (1,377)
Missouri	1,046 (314)	616 (46)	719 (69)	775 (104)	124,085 (5,558)	116,440 (1,884)
Montana	148 (35)	108 —	82 —	88 —	13,969 (1,876)	9,644 —
Nebraska	213 —	236 —	223 —	279 (62)	36,458 —	39,673 —
Nevada	83 (46)	51 —	58 —	63 —	9,713 (1,926)	8,482 —
New Hampshire	143 (35)	181 (50)	130 —	210 (72)	21,742 (827)	18,712 (1,330)
New Jersey	891 (95)	956 (65)	878 —	914 —	218,440 (21,195)	209,913 (8,195)
New Mexico	371 (182)	186 —	166 —	194 (23)	33,036 (11,897)	23,236 —
New York	1,993 (157)	2,058 (29)	1,985 (59)	1,997 (35)	497,426 (29,501)	498,668 (7,158)
North Carolina	279 —	476 (28)	463 (18)	542 (37)	48,350 —	63,255 (5,224)
North Dakota	55 —	63 —	59 —	55 —	7,045 —	7,518 —
Ohio	1,248 (198)	1,096 (67)	1,016 (58)	1,071 (124)	263,379 (12,247)	269,064 (13,362)
Oklahoma	102 —	244 (105)	190 (62)	135 —	19,934 —	34,025 (9,317)
Oregon	389 (142)	282 (52)	250 —	410 (106)	32,991 (4,559)	30,918 (1,003)
Pennsylvania	1,896 (261)	1,879 (53)	1,846 (54)	1,894 (27)	361,183 (14,868)	359,440 (6,920)
Rhode Island	96 —	111 —	112 —	128 —	22,599 —	21,242 —
South Carolina	374 (109)	307 (42)	297 (21)	282 —	57,024 (12,631)	46,086 (2,013)
South Dakota	278 (189)	106 —	96 —	93 —	16,854 (7,198)	10,539 —
Tennessee	411 (95)	474 (50)	496 (54)	504 (47)	73,015 (5,591)	82,969 (2,953)
Texas	1,409 (259)	951 (13)	1,353 (98)	1,593 (120)	199,524 (19,202)	170,670 (472)
Utah	33 —	56 —	66 —	97 (28)	6,254 —	9,836 —
Vermont	63 —	81 —	85 —	84 —	7,552 —	8,351 —
Virginia	412 (32)	525 (51)	515 (55)	493 (24)	66,847 (1,302)	80,887 (1,872)
Washington	464 (65)	429 (15)	486 (53)	504 (44)	64,491 (5,798)	66,556 (2,798)
West Virginia	97 —	148 —	145 —	135 —	11,233 —	12,908 —
Wisconsin	901 (44)	955 (13)	954 —	961 —	137,901 (2,906)	142,399 (220)
Wyoming	29 —	27 —	35 —	37 —	1,952 —	1,840 —

Table 8.—Number of private schools, students, teachers, and high school graduates, and disabled children served under federal programs, by state: 1988–89 to 1996–97—Continued

State	Enrollment in private schools [1,2]				Teachers in private schools [1]	
	Fall 1993	Fall 1995	Percent change in enrollment, 1989 to 1995	As a percent of total enrollment, 1995	Fall 1989	Fall 1991
1	8	9	10	11	12	13
United States	4,836,442 (12,875)	5,032,200 (20,482)	4.3	10.1	331,533 (3,214)	339,267 (1,829)
Alabama	72,630 (4,724)	66,958 —	26.8	8.2	3,894 —	5,022 (540)
Alaska	5,884 —	6,113 —	52.0	4.6	369 —	516 (118)
Arizona	41,957 —	44,134 (3,181)	39.6	5.6	2,038 —	2,771 —
Arkansas	29,011 (3,995)	27,454 (547)	41.6	5.7	1,422 (179)	1,566 —
California	569,062 (1,987)	629,344 (12,386)	12.3	10.2	35,418 (284)	37,861 (1,165)
Colorado	53,732 (7,798)	48,977 (147)	36.9	6.9	2,766 (116)	4,242 (893)
Connecticut	70,198 (1,875)	70,605 (1,022)	−2.3	12.0	6,339 —	5,987 —
Delaware	22,308 —	25,528 (1,850)	16.3	19.1	1,601 (54)	1,547 —
District of Columbia	15,854 —	17,468 —	−26.8	18.0	2,588 (713)	1,834 (61)
Florida	233,743 (3,789)	253,831 (2,811)	15.9	10.4	15,779 (1,617)	15,302 (358)
Georgia	97,726 (3,586)	97,807 (983)	15.3	6.9	6,612 (239)	7,838 (307)
Hawaii	30,537 —	34,541 —	−3.9	15.6	2,268 —	2,486 —
Idaho	8,019 —	9,210 —	−6.4	3.7	779 (318)	467 —
Illinois	293,038 (794)	300,981 (1,597)	−2.3	13.4	18,001 (597)	17,880 (211)
Indiana	91,986 —	99,258 (1,269)	10.5	9.2	5,879 (119)	6,762 (680)
Iowa	50,602 (211)	49,461 (1,041)	−18.5	9.0	4,137 (878)	3,408 —
Kansas	37,045 —	39,306 (775)	13.2	7.8	2,257 —	2,347 —
Kentucky	58,058 —	67,181 (1,995)	−2.0	9.2	4,632 (898)	4,705 —
Louisiana	145,512 (4,036)	147,147 (4,944)	7.8	15.6	8,537 (107)	8,746 —
Maine	16,999 —	16,896 —	2.9	7.3	1,526 (111)	1,311 —
Maryland	112,481 —	125,092 (427)	4.7	13.4	9,126 (945)	8,846 —
Massachusetts	126,744 (1,362)	125,696 (2,936)	0.9	12.1	10,688 (627)	10,891 (342)
Michigan	187,741 —	189,065 —	−0.3	10.3	11,039 (155)	11,176 (100)
Minnesota	86,051 —	86,477 (430)	−10.5	9.4	6,319 (558)	6,307 (284)
Mississippi	58,655 (1,564)	50,166 —	−8.9	9.0	3,914 (557)	4,149 (53)
Missouri	117,466 (616)	126,985 (7,179)	2.3	12.5	8,806 (855)	7,950 (252)
Montana	9,111 —	8,458 —	−39.5	4.9	1,064 (110)	766 —
Nebraska	39,564 —	41,320 (2,034)	13.3	12.5	2,276 —	2,634 —
Nevada	10,723 —	12,251 —	26.1	4.4	587 (193)	486 —
New Hampshire	18,386 —	22,633 (2,311)	4.1	10.4	1,937 (115)	1,929 (181)
New Jersey	195,921 —	207,275 —	−5.1	14.8	15,742 (2,054)	15,178 (582)
New Mexico	20,007 —	22,893 (2,149)	−30.7	6.5	3,208 (1,345)	1,813 —
New York	473,119 (4,776)	466,239 (936)	−6.3	14.2	34,160 (1,412)	35,615 (755)
North Carolina	69,000 (1,803)	81,437 (5,583)	68.4	6.4	4,124 —	5,466 (418)
North Dakota	7,577 —	7,321 —	3.9	5.8	478 —	535 —
Ohio	246,805 (3,480)	255,277 (3,674)	−3.1	12.2	15,736 (878)	15,591 (640)
Oklahoma	25,837 (3,584)	24,653 —	23.7	3.8	1,469 —	2,521 (612)
Oregon	34,092 —	43,501 (3,843)	31.9	7.6	2,487 (496)	2,213 (210)
Pennsylvania	342,298 (4,260)	346,800 (5,848)	−4.0	16.2	22,480 (898)	23,127 (529)
Rhode Island	23,153 —	23,543 —	4.2	13.6	1,761 —	1,861 —
South Carolina	51,600 (1,819)	50,162 —	−12.0	7.2	4,842 (1,290)	3,609 (252)
South Dakota	9,575 —	10,056 —	−40.3	6.5	1,184 (509)	827 —
Tennessee	84,538 (2,909)	80,701 (2,337)	10.5	8.3	5,628 (533)	6,404 (244)
Texas	211,337 (7,591)	229,353 (6,768)	15.0	5.8	14,891 (1,377)	13,320 (67)
Utah	9,793 —	12,840 (2,439)	105.3	2.6	446 —	817 —
Vermont	9,107 —	9,669 —	28.0	8.4	822 —	913 —
Virginia	84,438 (4,584)	86,507 (782)	29.4	7.4	5,655 (139)	7,115 (173)
Washington	70,205 (1,858)	74,890 (2,546)	16.1	7.3	4,199 (354)	4,463 (190)
West Virginia	13,539 —	13,241 —	17.9	4.1	892 —	1,074 —
Wisconsin	141,762 —	143,231 —	3.9	14.1	8,586 (316)	8,920 (50)
Wyoming	1,919 —	2,272 —	16.4	2.2	149 —	148 —

Table 8.—Number of private schools, students, teachers, and high school graduates, and disabled children served under federal programs, by state: 1988–89 to 1996–97—Continued

State	Teachers in private schools [1]			Pupil/teacher ratio in private schools [1]			
	Fall 1993	Fall 1995	Percent change in teachers, 1989 to 1995	Fall 1989	Fall 1991	Fall 1993	Fall 1995
1	14	15	16	17	18	19	20
United States	**338,162 (1,319)**	**361,909 (1,618)**	**9.2**	**14.6**	**14.4**	**14.3**	**13.9**
Alabama	5,424 (456)	4,814 —	23.6	13.6	13.8	13.4	13.9
Alaska	476 —	530 —	43.6	10.9	10.7	12.4	11.5
Arizona	2,796 —	3,070 (205)	50.6	15.5	14.2	15.0	14.4
Arkansas	2,023 (335)	2,081 (108)	46.3	13.6	14.6	14.3	13.2
California	35,170 (248)	41,073 (695)	16.0	15.8	16.2	16.2	15.3
Colorado	4,115 (632)	3,843 (44)	38.9	12.9	13.5	13.1	12.7
Connecticut	6,345 (125)	6,381 (107)	0.7	11.4	11.3	11.1	11.1
Delaware	1,780 —	1,878 (147)	17.3	13.7	14.7	12.5	13.6
District of Columbia	1,544 —	1,852 —	−28.4	9.2	9.7	10.3	9.4
Florida	16,842 (424)	19,093 (337)	21.0	13.9	13.4	13.9	13.3
Georgia	8,283 (300)	8,282 (117)	25.3	12.8	12.3	11.8	11.8
Hawaii	2,144 —	2,532 —	11.6	15.8	14.6	14.2	13.6
Idaho	552 —	607 —	−22.1	12.6	14.2	14.5	15.2
Illinois	17,550 (70)	18,617 (194)	3.4	17.1	16.9	16.7	16.2
Indiana	6,139 —	6,653 (147)	13.2	15.3	14.7	15.0	14.9
Iowa	3,291 (34)	3,309 (78)	−20.0	14.7	15.1	15.4	14.9
Kansas	2,382 —	2,623 (105)	16.2	15.4	14.9	15.5	15.0
Kentucky	3,815 —	4,581 (362)	−1.1	14.8	14.0	15.2	14.7
Louisiana	9,286 (301)	9,849 (517)	15.4	16.0	15.9	15.7	14.9
Maine	1,535 —	1,531 —	0.3	10.8	11.3	11.1	11.0
Maryland	8,646 —	10,142 (64)	11.1	13.1	12.9	13.0	12.3
Massachusetts	11,329 (168)	11,068 (268)	3.6	11.7	11.5	11.2	11.4
Michigan	11,322 —	11,550 —	4.6	17.2	16.7	16.6	16.4
Minnesota	5,595 —	5,835 (72)	−7.7	15.3	14.8	15.4	14.8
Mississippi	3,995 (150)	3,447 —	−11.9	14.1	14.2	14.7	14.6
Missouri	7,973 (85)	9,162 (816)	4.0	14.1	14.6	14.7	13.9
Montana	684 —	673 —	−36.7	13.1	12.6	13.3	12.6
Nebraska	2,575 —	2,695 (160)	18.4	16.0	15.1	15.4	15.3
Nevada	654 —	711 —	21.1	16.5	17.4	16.4	17.2
New Hampshire	1,742 —	2,101 (217)	8.5	11.2	9.7	10.6	10.8
New Jersey	14,281 —	15,585 —	−1.0	13.9	13.8	13.7	13.3
New Mexico	1,569 —	1,756 (114)	−45.3	10.3	12.8	12.8	13.0
New York	34,771 (482)	35,328 (234)	3.4	14.6	14.0	13.6	13.2
North Carolina	5,746 (147)	6,990 (442)	69.5	11.7	11.6	12.0	11.7
North Dakota	529 —	523 —	9.4	14.7	14.0	14.3	14.0
Ohio	14,872 (306)	15,085 (228)	−4.1	16.7	17.3	16.6	16.9
Oklahoma	2,250 (450)	2,014 —	37.1	13.6	13.5	11.5	12.2
Oregon	2,254 —	3,431 (513)	38.0	13.3	14.0	15.1	12.7
Pennsylvania	21,880 (235)	23,085 (356)	2.7	16.1	15.5	15.6	15.0
Rhode Island	1,835 —	1,941 —	10.2	12.8	11.4	12.6	12.1
South Carolina	3,989 (155)	3,943 —	−18.6	11.8	12.8	12.9	12.7
South Dakota	707 —	724 —	−38.9	14.2	12.7	13.5	13.9
Tennessee	6,684 (162)	6,388 (184)	13.5	13.0	13.0	12.6	12.6
Texas	16,726 (708)	19,042 (717)	27.9	13.4	12.8	12.6	12.0
Utah	749 —	1,013 (134)	127.1	14.0	12.0	13.1	12.7
Vermont	945 —	977 —	18.9	9.2	9.1	9.6	9.9
Virginia	7,391 (621)	7,723 (142)	36.6	11.8	11.4	11.4	11.2
Washington	4,798 (348)	5,132 (231)	22.2	15.4	14.9	14.6	14.6
West Virginia	1,085 —	1,113 —	24.8	12.6	12.0	12.5	11.9
Wisconsin	8,927 —	9,312 —	8.5	16.1	16.0	15.9	15.4
Wyoming	167 —	221 —	48.3	13.1	12.4	11.5	10.3

Table 8.—Number of private schools, students, teachers, and high school graduates, and disabled children served under federal programs, by state: 1988–89 to 1996–97—Continued

State	High school graduates from private schools [1]					Disabled children, birth to 21 years old, 1996–97 [3]	
	1988–89	1990–91	1992–93	1994–95	Percent change in graduates, 1988–89 to 1994–95	Total	As a percent of public school enrollment [4]
1	21	22	23	24	25	26	27
United States	285,105 (4,117)	258,095 (1,979)	247,278 (697)	245,543 (1,009)	–13.9	5,919,767	13.0
Alabama	3,496 —	3,853 (311)	4,174 (348)	3,581 —	2.4	99,302	13.3
Alaska	102 —	178 (51)	213 —	178 —	74.5	18,061	13.9
Arizona	1,565 —	2,039 —	2,415 —	2,221 (208)	41.9	81,099	10.1
Arkansas	920 (46)	944 —	1,023 —	1,081 —	17.5	57,475	12.6
California	29,628 (754)	27,702 (573)	24,436 (65)	26,353 (103)	–11.1	604,075	10.6
Colorado	2,142 (57)	2,384 (664)	1,826 (283)	1,928 —	–10.0	73,992	11.0
Connecticut	7,687 —	6,361 —	6,291 (46)	5,166 —	–32.8	84,412	16.0
Delaware	1,805 (80)	1,347 —	1,446 —	1,436 —	–20.4	16,421	14.9
District of Columbia	2,035 (558)	1,241 —	1,054 —	1,242 —	–39.0	7,059	9.0
Florida	11,550 (785)	9,892 (125)	9,820 (54)	10,151 (88)	–12.1	334,707	14.9
Georgia	6,699 —	6,070 (9)	5,630 (127)	5,075 —	–24.2	144,512	10.7
Hawaii	2,578 —	2,771 —	1,886 —	2,603 —	1.0	20,350	10.8
Idaho	472 (194)	317 —	341 —	380 —	–19.5	26,128	10.7
Illinois	16,288 (69)	15,538 (26)	14,724 (98)	14,681 (115)	–9.9	275,198	13.9
Indiana	4,316 —	4,303 (366)	4,061 —	4,055 (181)	–6.0	142,667	14.5
Iowa	4,551 (1,621)	2,386 —	2,495 —	2,601 —	–42.8	69,060	13.7
Kansas	1,550 —	1,468 —	1,668 —	1,621 —	4.6	56,845	12.2
Kentucky	3,444 —	3,368 —	2,949 —	3,242 (8)	–5.9	87,137	13.3
Louisiana	8,432 (73)	7,552 —	7,844 —	7,457 (96)	–11.6	94,727	11.9
Maine	2,025 (32)	1,684 —	1,914 —	1,759 —	–13.1	33,678	15.8
Maryland	6,832 (116)	6,569 —	5,648 —	6,235 —	–8.7	108,453	13.2
Massachusetts	10,035 (182)	10,269 (20)	10,281 —	8,561 (15)	–14.7	168,082	18.0
Michigan	12,071 —	9,674 —	8,925 —	8,805 —	–27.1	198,772	11.8
Minnesota	4,687 (115)	3,815 (163)	3,453 —	3,373 —	–28.0	103,929	12.3
Mississippi	3,349 —	3,729 (313)	3,901 (180)	3,174 —	–5.2	66,161	13.1
Missouri	7,173 (325)	5,857 —	5,839 (212)	5,894 (152)	–17.8	127,864	14.2
Montana	509 (114)	431 —	355 —	356 —	–30.1	19,119	11.6
Nebraska	1,912 —	1,995 —	1,904 —	1,783 (50)	–6.7	40,578	13.9
Nevada	388 —	308 —	646 —	381 —	–1.8	30,913	11.0
New Hampshire	2,178 (32)	1,881 (20)	1,730 —	1,730 (36)	–20.6	27,592	13.9
New Jersey	16,703 (3,069)	13,385 (766)	11,025 —	12,030 —	–28.0	206,252	17.1
New Mexico	1,307 (477)	1,045 —	1,029 —	947 —	–27.5	51,280	15.4
New York	26,975 (262)	28,359 (1,552)	26,625 (125)	25,489 —	–5.5	427,907	15.1
North Carolina	2,600 —	3,191 (407)	2,983 —	3,144 —	20.9	158,272	13.1
North Dakota	471 —	391 —	332 —	381 —	–19.1	12,991	10.8
Ohio	16,012 (935)	12,314 (48)	12,398 (172)	12,639 —	–21.1	243,312	13.2
Oklahoma	1,105 —	1,480 (102)	1,536 (288)	1,296 —	17.3	75,601	12.2
Oregon	1,545 (91)	1,511 (97)	1,700 —	2,042 (76)	32.2	65,543	12.2
Pennsylvania	20,751 (57)	19,634 (65)	18,532 (304)	18,138 (927)	–12.6	222,494	12.3
Rhode Island	1,827 —	1,485 —	1,408 —	1,354 —	–25.9	27,354	18.1
South Carolina	4,770 (2,099)	2,312 (89)	2,383 —	2,378 —	–50.1	92,787	14.2
South Dakota	470 —	390 —	254 —	436 —	–7.2	15,485	10.8
Tennessee	5,949 (269)	4,901 —	4,970 —	4,427 (27)	–25.6	128,672	14.2
Texas	9,552 (1,376)	7,334 (13)	8,447 (469)	8,767 (209)	–8.2	472,661	12.3
Utah	398 —	537 —	590 —	590 —	48.2	55,848	11.6
Vermont	652 —	965 —	1,120 —	1,081 —	65.8	12,076	11.4
Virginia	4,214 —	4,536 —	4,580 —	4,463 —	5.9	146,840	13.4
Washington	3,031 (311)	2,734 (54)	2,644 —	2,998 —	–1.1	109,227	11.2
West Virginia	679 —	646 —	672 —	698 —	2.8	49,092	16.1
Wisconsin	5,649 (109)	5,010 —	5,129 —	5,119 —	–9.4	114,407	13.0
Wyoming	24 —	11 —	31 —	24 —	(5)	13,298	13.4

[1] NCES employed an area frame sample to account for noninclusion of schools at the national level. However, caution should be exercised in interpreting state by state characteristics since the samples were not designed to produce such numbers.

[2] Includes special, vocational/technical, and alternative schools. Excludes prekindergarten enrollment and kindergarten enrollment in schools that do not offer a first grade or higher.

[3] Children served under Individuals with Disabilities Education Act and Chapter 1 of the Education Consolidation and Improvement Act, State Operated Program. Individuals with Disabilities Education Act (IDEA), formerly known as the Education of the Handicapped Act, now extends the right to a free and appropriate education to 3- to 5-year-old disabled children.

[4] Based on the enrollment in public schools, kindergarten through grade 12, including a number of prekindergarten students.

[5] Change of less than .05 percent.

—Data not available.

NOTE.—Standard errors appear in parentheses.

SOURCE: U.S. Department of Education, Office of Special Education and Rehabilitative Services, *Annual Report to Congress on the Implementation of The Individuals with Disabilities Education Act;* and National Center for Education Statistics, Private School Survey, various years; and Common Core of Data survey. (This table was prepared August 1998.)

Table 9.—Enrollment in public elementary and secondary schools, by race or ethnicity and state: Fall 1986 and fall 1995

State or other area	Percent distribution, fall 1986						Percent distribution, fall 1995					
	Total	White [1]	Black [1]	Hispanic	Asian or Pacific Islander	American Indian/ Alaskan Native	Total	White [1]	Black [1]	Hispanic	Asian or Pacific Islander	American Indian/ Alaskan Native
1	2	3	4	5	6	7	8	9	10	11	12	13
United States	100.0	70.4	16.1	9.9	2.8	0.9	100.0	64.8	16.8	13.5	3.7	1.1
Alabama	100.0	62.0	37.0	0.1	0.4	0.5	100.0	62.1	36.0	0.5	0.6	0.7
Alaska	100.0	65.7	4.3	1.7	3.3	25.1	100.0	63.7	4.6	2.7	4.4	24.5
Arizona	100.0	62.2	4.0	26.4	1.3	6.1	100.0	56.9	4.3	30.0	1.7	7.2
Arkansas	100.0	74.7	24.2	0.4	0.6	0.2	100.0	73.9	23.6	1.5	0.7	0.4
California	100.0	53.7	9.0	27.5	9.1	0.7	100.0	40.4	8.8	38.7	11.2	0.9
Colorado	100.0	78.7	4.5	13.7	2.0	1.0	100.0	72.5	5.5	18.4	2.5	1.1
Connecticut	100.0	77.2	12.1	8.9	1.5	0.2	100.0	72.0	13.5	11.8	2.4	0.3
Delaware	100.0	68.3	27.7	2.5	1.4	0.2	100.0	64.7	29.4	4.0	1.7	0.2
District of Columbia	100.0	4.0	91.1	3.9	0.9	0.1	100.0	4.0	87.6	7.0	1.4	(2)
Florida	100.0	65.4	23.7	9.5	1.2	0.2	100.0	57.5	25.3	15.3	1.8	0.2
Georgia	100.0	60.7	37.9	0.6	0.8	(2)	100.0	58.2	37.8	2.2	1.6	0.1
Hawaii	100.0	23.5	2.3	2.2	71.7	0.3	100.0	22.9	2.6	4.9	69.3	0.4
Idaho	100.0	92.6	0.3	4.9	0.8	1.3	100.0	88.4	0.6	8.4	1.2	1.3
Illinois	100.0	69.8	18.7	9.2	2.3	0.1	100.0	63.6	21.1	12.2	3.0	0.1
Indiana	100.0	88.7	9.0	1.7	0.5	0.1	100.0	85.6	11.1	2.3	0.8	0.2
Iowa	100.0	94.6	3.0	0.9	1.2	0.3	100.0	92.7	3.3	2.1	1.5	0.4
Kansas	100.0	85.6	7.6	4.4	1.9	0.6	100.0	82.6	8.5	6.0	1.8	1.1
Kentucky	100.0	89.2	10.2	0.1	0.5	(2)	100.0	89.1	9.8	0.4	0.6	0.1
Louisiana	100.0	56.5	41.3	0.8	1.1	0.3	100.0	51.0	46.0	1.1	1.3	0.5
Maine	100.0	98.3	0.5	0.2	0.8	0.2	100.0	97.3	0.8	0.4	0.9	0.6
Maryland	100.0	59.7	35.3	1.7	3.1	0.2	100.0	57.5	35.0	3.3	3.8	0.3
Massachusetts	100.0	83.7	7.4	6.0	2.8	0.1	100.0	78.5	8.2	9.3	3.8	0.2
Michigan	100.0	76.4	19.8	1.8	1.2	0.8	100.0	76.4	18.4	2.7	1.5	1.0
Minnesota	100.0	93.9	2.1	0.9	1.7	1.5	100.0	87.4	4.8	2.0	3.9	1.9
Mississippi	100.0	43.9	55.5	0.1	0.4	0.1	100.0	47.7	51.0	0.3	0.6	0.4
Missouri	100.0	83.4	14.9	0.7	0.8	0.2	100.0	81.7	16.1	1.0	1.0	0.2
Montana	100.0	92.7	0.3	0.9	0.5	5.5	100.0	87.5	0.5	1.4	0.8	9.8
Nebraska	100.0	91.4	4.4	2.4	0.8	1.0	100.0	87.2	5.9	4.4	1.3	1.4
Nevada	100.0	77.4	9.6	7.5	3.2	2.3	100.0	66.5	9.8	17.2	4.5	1.9
New Hampshire	100.0	98.0	0.7	0.5	0.8	0.1	100.0	96.7	0.9	1.2	1.1	0.2
New Jersey	100.0	69.1	17.4	10.7	2.7	0.1	100.0	62.5	18.5	13.5	5.4	0.2
New Mexico	100.0	43.1	2.3	45.1	0.8	8.7	100.0	39.5	2.4	46.8	1.0	10.4
New York	100.0	68.4	16.5	12.3	2.7	0.2	100.0	56.9	20.2	17.4	5.0	0.4
North Carolina	100.0	68.4	28.9	0.4	0.6	1.7	100.0	64.6	30.7	1.9	1.3	1.5
North Dakota	100.0	92.4	0.6	1.1	0.8	5.0	100.0	90.8	0.8	1.1	0.8	6.6
Ohio	100.0	83.1	15.0	1.0	0.7	0.1	100.0	82.2	15.3	1.4	1.0	0.1
Oklahoma	100.0	79.0	7.8	1.6	1.0	10.6	100.0	69.4	10.5	3.9	1.3	15.0
Oregon	100.0	89.8	2.2	3.9	2.4	1.7	100.0	85.3	2.6	6.8	3.4	2.0
Pennsylvania	100.0	84.4	12.6	1.8	1.2	0.1	100.0	80.6	14.0	3.5	1.8	0.1
Rhode Island	100.0	87.9	5.6	3.7	2.4	0.3	100.0	78.9	7.0	10.3	3.3	0.5
South Carolina	100.0	54.6	44.5	0.2	0.6	0.1	100.0	56.3	42.1	0.7	0.8	0.2
South Dakota	100.0	90.6	0.5	0.6	0.7	7.6	100.0	83.7	0.9	0.7	0.7	13.9
Tennessee	100.0	76.5	22.6	0.2	0.6	(2)	100.0	75.3	23.1	0.7	0.8	0.1
Texas	100.0	51.0	14.4	32.5	2.0	0.2	100.0	46.4	14.3	36.7	2.3	0.3
Utah	100.0	93.7	0.4	3.0	1.5	1.5	100.0	90.4	0.7	5.3	2.2	1.4
Vermont	100.0	98.4	0.3	0.2	0.6	0.6	100.0	97.3	0.7	0.4	1.0	0.6
Virginia	100.0	72.6	23.7	1.0	2.6	0.1	100.0	66.6	26.5	3.2	3.5	0.2
Washington	100.0	84.5	4.2	3.8	5.1	2.3	100.0	78.3	4.7	7.8	6.5	2.6
West Virginia	100.0	95.9	3.7	0.1	0.3	(2)	100.0	95.2	4.0	0.3	0.4	0.1
Wisconsin	100.0	86.6	8.9	1.9	1.7	1.0	100.0	83.2	9.4	3.3	2.8	1.3
Wyoming	100.0	90.7	0.9	5.9	0.6	1.9	100.0	89.3	1.0	6.1	0.8	2.7
Outlying areas												
American Samoa	—	—	—	—	—	—	100.0	—	—	—	100.0	—
Guam	—	—	—	—	—	—	100.0	6.7	1.3	0.5	91.5	—
Northern Marianas	—	—	—	—	—	—	100.0	0.7	—	—	99.3	—
Puerto Rico	—	—	—	—	—	—	100.0	—	—	100.0	—	—
Virgin Islands	—	—	—	—	—	—	100.0	0.9	84.5	14.3	0.4	—

[1] Excludes persons of Hispanic origin.
[2] Less than 0.05 percent.
—Data not available.

NOTE.—The 1986–87 data were derived from the 1986 Elementary and Secondary School Civil Rights sample survey of public school districts. Because of rounding, details may not add to totals.

SOURCE: U.S. Department of Education, Office for Civil Rights, *1986 State Summaries of Elementary and Secondary School Civil Rights Survey;* and National Center for Education Statistics, Common Core of Data survey. (This table was prepared April 1997.)

Table 10.—Enrollment [1] in public elementary and secondary schools, by state: Fall 1970 to fall 1995

State or other area	Fall 1970	Fall 1971	Fall 1972	Fall 1973	Fall 1974	Fall 1975	Fall 1976	Fall 1977	Fall 1978	Fall 1979
1	2	3	4	5	6	7	8	9	10	11
United States	**45,893,960**	**46,071,327**	**45,726,408**	**45,444,787**	**45,073,441**	**44,819,327**	**44,310,966**	**43,577,373**	**42,550,893**	**41,650,712**
Alabama	805,205	806,315	783,383	770,739	764,341	759,346	752,507	761,880	761,666	754,181
Alaska [2]	79,845	84,381	85,332	82,505	86,576	89,295	91,190	90,344	90,728	88,573
Arizona	439,524	464,478	485,088	521,240	487,040	492,995	502,817	513,817	509,830	509,252
Arkansas	463,320	461,260	461,431	450,114	454,406	456,703	460,593	458,778	456,698	453,125
California	4,633,198	4,601,550	4,500,978	4,459,328	4,427,443	4,419,571	4,380,400	4,303,665	4,187,967	4,119,511
Colorado	550,060	564,502	574,248	573,154	568,060	568,851	564,087	561,807	558,285	550,527
Connecticut	662,205	666,867	664,761	667,088	660,067	652,449	635,000	616,389	593,757	566,634
Delaware	132,745	135,013	134,317	132,940	130,616	127,476	122,273	118,000	111,034	104,035
District of Columbia	145,704	142,512	139,918	136,036	131,691	129,969	125,848	119,875	113,858	106,156
Florida	1,427,896	1,478,504	1,514,359	1,537,952	1,557,054	1,551,373	1,537,336	1,535,570	1,513,819	1,508,337
Georgia	1,098,901	1,093,407	1,090,280	1,085,881	1,081,485	1,090,292	1,095,142	1,089,625	1,093,256	1,078,462
Hawaii	180,641	183,654	181,979	178,511	177,030	176,430	174,943	172,356	170,761	168,660
Idaho	182,333	185,114	184,663	189,133	187,552	196,616	200,005	201,433	203,022	202,758
Illinois	2,356,636	2,379,646	2,354,562	2,320,672	2,296,241	2,269,892	2,238,129	2,173,352	2,039,430	2,043,239
Indiana	1,231,458	1,230,796	1,220,543	1,207,420	1,186,800	1,173,863	1,163,179	1,143,722	1,113,331	1,083,826
Iowa	660,104	652,958	646,408	631,132	617,485	612,111	605,127	588,760	568,540	548,317
Kansas	513,394	505,267	491,765	479,344	471,460	465,355	458,330	446,592	433,538	422,924
Kentucky	717,205	720,309	714,632	709,764	701,373	691,612	694,000	697,000	692,999	677,123
Louisiana	842,365	851,074	845,841	842,152	840,742	847,202	839,499	839,000	816,669	800,435
Maine	244,670	246,406	250,448	245,467	250,643	250,931	248,822	245,768	240,016	227,823
Maryland	916,244	922,051	920,896	911,097	894,209	880,927	860,929	836,912	809,933	777,725
Massachusetts	1,167,713	1,191,179	1,202,597	1,205,142	1,210,100	1,198,410	1,169,000	1,116,810	1,081,464	1,035,724
Michigan	2,152,256	2,182,885	2,164,949	2,123,611	2,137,612	2,073,288	2,035,703	1,968,975	1,911,345	1,860,498
Minnesota	920,839	913,955	909,653	900,377	889,535	879,944	862,591	836,420	807,716	778,056
Mississippi	534,395	529,366	526,366	519,786	513,476	512,407	510,209	502,025	493,710	482,039
Missouri	1,039,477	1,023,374	1,030,008	1,019,803	1,001,705	965,360	950,142	931,232	900,002	872,933
Montana	176,712	178,367	179,877	173,559	172,158	171,788	170,552	168,732	164,326	158,208
Nebraska	329,110	332,375	329,192	323,211	318,792	315,669	312,024	306,207	297,796	287,288
Nevada	127,550	130,186	131,660	135,406	137,051	139,745	141,791	143,444	146,281	147,734
New Hampshire	158,756	164,102	168,094	171,482	172,117	174,597	175,496	174,618	172,389	170,546
New Jersey	1,482,000	1,497,841	1,510,519	1,481,605	1,466,956	1,458,000	1,427,000	1,381,528	1,337,327	1,287,809
New Mexico	281,372	284,948	285,094	283,550	282,382	274,612	284,719	281,896	279,249	275,572
New York	3,489,245	3,538,474	3,508,004	3,465,450	3,434,116	3,417,453	3,338,809	3,222,612	3,093,885	2,969,216
North Carolina	1,192,187	1,176,308	1,161,326	1,173,415	1,177,860	1,184,996	1,191,316	1,181,831	1,162,810	1,150,053
North Dakota	147,013	144,419	141,535	138,302	133,241	131,331	129,106	125,085	122,021	117,688
Ohio	2,425,643	2,438,743	2,422,654	2,378,349	2,330,150	2,292,647	2,249,440	2,181,979	2,102,440	2,025,256
Oklahoma	626,956	625,740	607,084	600,948	596,380	594,816	597,665	594,468	588,870	583,458
Oregon	479,527	478,502	471,395	476,518	476,583	477,559	474,707	473,279	471,374	467,128
Pennsylvania	2,363,817	2,370,665	2,361,285	2,321,437	2,277,451	2,246,147	2,193,673	2,128,873	2,046,746	1,968,801
Rhode Island	188,090	190,696	189,693	184,624	178,662	176,317	172,373	166,629	161,285	154,699
South Carolina	637,800	648,643	623,778	626,914	627,205	629,729	620,711	620,723	624,931	624,795
South Dakota	166,305	165,267	162,398	157,522	153,592	151,217	148,080	143,630	138,228	133,840
Tennessee	899,893	897,598	891,775	902,704	872,819	876,926	841,974	878,424	873,036	866,117
Texas	2,839,900	2,811,700	2,738,131	2,782,151	2,785,296	2,812,888	2,822,754	2,842,842	2,867,254	2,872,719
Utah	304,002	305,740	305,916	305,800	306,388	309,708	314,471	317,332	325,026	333,049
Vermont	103,130	105,340	106,517	106,236	105,376	104,874	104,356	102,934	101,292	98,338
Virginia	1,078,754	1,074,073	1,069,345	1,085,295	1,093,309	1,103,669	1,100,723	1,082,184	1,055,238	1,031,403
Washington	817,712	805,049	790,502	788,324	785,457	785,449	780,730	776,463	769,246	764,879
West Virginia	399,531	403,377	409,989	409,184	404,441	404,119	404,771	401,369	395,722	387,966
Wisconsin	993,736	999,921	995,223	987,022	974,333	964,219	945,337	917,863	886,419	857,855
Wyoming	86,886	86,430	86,017	85,391	86,584	88,184	90,587	92,321	94,328	95,422
Outlying areas	—	—	—	—	—	—	—	—	—	—
American Samoa	—	8,018	8,165	10,296	10,186	10,119	9,950	9,291	—	—
Guam	24,757	26,000	26,922	27,329	28,184	28,591	28,570	—	—	27,582
Northern Marianas	—	—	—	—	—	—	—	—	4,513	4,407
Puerto Rico	686,777	697,410	711,238	712,588	—	697,159	688,592	—	721,419	—
Trust Territories	29,723	—	—	—	—	—	—	—	—	—
Virgin Islands	—	18,860	20,826	22,022	23,343	24,512	25,026	25,571	25,138	25,553

Table 10.—Enrollment [1] in public elementary and secondary schools, by state: Fall 1970 to fall 1995—Continued

State or other area	Fall 1980	Fall 1981	Fall 1982	Fall 1983	Fall 1984	Fall 1985	Fall 1986	Fall 1987	Fall 1988	Fall 1989
1	12	13	14	15	16	17	18	19	20	21
United States	40,877,481	40,044,093	39,565,610	39,252,308	39,208,252	39,421,961	39,753,172	40,008,213	40,188,690	40,542,707
Alabama	758,721	743,448	724,037	721,901	712,586	730,460	733,735	729,234	724,751	723,743
Alaska [2]	86,514	90,858	89,413	98,206	104,599	107,345	107,848	106,869	106,481	109,280
Arizona	513,790	507,199	510,296	506,682	530,062	548,252	534,538	572,421	574,890	607,615
Arkansas	447,700	437,121	432,565	432,120	432,668	433,410	437,438	437,036	436,387	434,960
California	4,076,421	4,046,156	4,065,486	4,089,017	4,151,110	4,255,554	4,377,989	4,488,398	4,618,120	4,771,978
Colorado	546,033	544,174	545,209	542,196	545,427	550,642	558,415	560,236	560,081	562,755
Connecticut	531,459	505,386	486,470	477,585	468,145	462,026	468,847	465,465	460,637	461,560
Delaware	99,403	95,072	92,646	91,406	91,767	92,901	94,410	95,659	96,678	97,808
District of Columbia	100,049	94,975	91,105	88,843	87,397	87,092	85,612	86,435	84,792	81,301
Florida	1,510,225	1,487,721	1,484,734	1,495,543	1,524,107	1,562,283	1,607,320	1,664,774	1,720,930	1,789,925
Georgia	1,068,737	1,056,117	1,053,689	1,050,859	1,062,315	1,079,594	1,096,425	1,110,947	1,107,994	1,126,535
Hawaii	165,068	162,805	162,024	162,241	163,860	164,169	164,640	166,160	167,488	169,493
Idaho	203,247	204,524	202,973	206,352	208,080	208,669	208,391	212,444	214,615	214,932
Illinois	1,983,463	1,924,084	1,880,289	1,853,316	1,834,355	1,826,478	1,825,185	1,811,446	1,794,916	1,797,355
Indiana	1,055,589	1,025,172	999,542	984,384	972,659	966,106	966,780	964,129	960,994	954,165
Iowa	533,857	516,216	504,983	497,287	491,011	485,332	481,286	480,826	478,200	478,486
Kansas	415,291	409,909	407,074	405,222	405,347	410,229	416,091	421,112	426,596	430,864
Kentucky	669,798	658,350	651,084	647,414	644,421	643,833	642,778	642,696	637,627	630,688
Louisiana	777,560	782,053	784,027	800,193	800,941	788,349	795,188	793,093	786,683	783,025
Maine	222,497	216,293	211,986	209,753	207,537	206,101	211,752	211,817	212,902	213,775
Maryland	750,665	721,841	699,201	683,491	673,840	671,560	675,747	683,797	688,947	698,806
Massachusetts	1,021,885	947,037	908,984	878,844	859,391	844,330	833,918	825,320	823,428	825,588
Michigan	1,797,052	1,724,787	1,674,697	1,635,963	1,609,448	1,602,747	1,597,154	1,589,287	1,582,785	1,576,785
Minnesota	754,318	733,741	715,190	705,236	701,697	705,140	711,134	721,481	726,950	739,553
Mississippi	477,059	471,615	468,294	467,744	466,058	471,195	498,639	505,550	503,326	502,020
Missouri	844,648	818,705	802,535	795,453	793,793	795,107	800,606	802,060	806,639	807,934
Montana	155,193	153,435	152,335	153,646	154,412	153,869	153,327	152,207	152,191	151,265
Nebraska	280,430	273,340	269,009	266,998	265,599	265,819	267,139	268,100	269,434	270,920
Nevada	149,481	151,339	151,104	150,442	151,633	154,948	161,239	168,353	176,474	186,834
New Hampshire	167,232	163,827	160,197	159,030	158,614	160,974	163,717	166,045	169,413	171,696
New Jersey	1,246,008	1,199,643	1,172,520	1,147,841	1,129,223	1,116,194	1,107,467	1,092,982	1,080,871	1,076,005
New Mexico	271,198	268,091	268,632	269,711	272,478	277,551	281,943	287,229	292,425	296,057
New York	2,871,724	2,783,017	2,718,678	2,674,818	2,645,811	2,621,378	2,607,719	2,594,070	2,573,715	2,565,841
North Carolina	1,129,376	1,108,960	1,096,815	1,089,606	1,088,724	1,086,165	1,085,248	1,085,976	1,083,156	1,080,744
North Dakota	116,885	117,708	117,078	117,213	118,711	118,570	118,703	119,004	118,809	117,816
Ohio	1,957,381	1,898,501	1,860,245	1,827,300	1,805,440	1,793,965	1,793,508	1,793,431	1,778,544	1,764,410
Oklahoma	577,807	582,572	593,825	591,389	589,690	592,327	593,183	584,212	580,426	578,580
Oregon	464,599	457,165	448,184	447,109	446,884	447,527	449,307	455,895	461,752	472,394
Pennsylvania	1,909,292	1,839,015	1,783,969	1,737,952	1,701,880	1,683,221	1,674,161	1,668,542	1,659,714	1,655,279
Rhode Island	148,956	143,414	139,959	136,412	134,610	133,949	134,690	134,800	133,585	135,729
South Carolina	619,223	609,158	608,518	604,553	602,718	606,643	611,629	614,921	615,774	616,177
South Dakota	128,507	125,657	123,897	123,060	123,314	124,291	125,458	126,817	126,910	127,329
Tennessee	853,569	838,297	828,264	822,057	817,212	813,753	818,073	823,783	821,580	819,660
Texas	2,900,073	2,935,547	2,985,659	2,989,796	3,040,305	3,131,705	3,209,515	3,236,787	3,283,707	3,328,514
Utah	343,618	355,554	370,183	378,208	390,141	403,305	415,994	423,386	431,119	438,554
Vermont	95.815	93,183	91,454	90,416	90,089	90,157	92,112	92,755	93,381	94,779
Virginia	1,010,371	989,548	975,727	966,110	965,222	968,104	975,135	979,417	982,393	985,346
Washington	757,639	750,188	739,215	736,239	741,177	749,706	761,428	775,755	790,918	810,232
West Virginia	383,503	377,772	375,115	371,251	362,941	357,923	351,837	344,236	335,912	327,540
Wisconsin	830,247	804,262	784,830	774,646	767,542	768,234	767,819	772,363	774,857	782,905
Wyoming	98,305	99,541	101,665	99,254	101,261	102,779	100,955	98,455	97,793	97,172
Outlying areas	—	787,224	—	808,546	—	—	—	739,860	729,069	717,270
American Samoa	9,647	9,896	—	10,124	—	—	11,055	11,248	11,764	12,258
Guam	26,420	25,084	25,676	26,249	—	26,043	25,676	25,936	26,041	26,493
Northern Marianas	—	5,300	—	4,499	4,841	—	—	5,819	6,079	6,101
Puerto Rico	712,880	721,419	708,794	701,925	692,923	686,914	679,489	672,837	661,693	651,225
Trust Territories	—	—	—	39,623	—	—	—	—	—	—
Virgin Islands	25,201	25,525	25,699	26,126	26,122	25,448	24,435	24,020	23,492	21,193

Table 10.—Enrollment [1] in public elementary and secondary schools, by state: Fall 1970 to fall 1995—Continued

State or other area	Fall 1990	Fall 1991	Fall 1992	Fall 1993	Fall 1994	Fall 1995	Percentage change			
							Fall 1970 to fall 1995	Fall 1985 to fall 1990	Fall 1990 to fall 1995	Fall 1985 to fall 1995
1	22	23	24	25	26	27	28	29	30	31
United States	**41,216,683**	**42,046,878**	**42,823,312**	**43,464,916**	**44,111,482**	**44,840,481**	**−2.3**	**4.6**	**8.8**	**13.7**
Alabama	721,806	722,004	731,634	734,288	736,531	746,149	−7.3	−1.2	3.4	2.1
Alaska [2]	113,903	118,680	122,487	125,948	127,057	127,618	59.8	6.1	12.0	18.9
Arizona	639,853	656,980	673,477	709,453	737,424	743,566	69.2	16.7	16.2	35.6
Arkansas	436,286	438,518	441,490	444,271	447,565	453,257	−2.2	0.7	3.9	4.6
California	4,950,474	5,107,145	5,254,844	5,327,231	5,407,475	5,536,406	19.5	16.3	11.8	30.1
Colorado	574,213	593,030	612,635	625,062	640,521	656,279	19.3	4.3	14.3	19.2
Connecticut	469,123	481,050	488,476	496,298	506,824	517,935	−21.8	1.5	10.4	12.1
Delaware	99,658	102,196	104,321	105,547	106,813	108,461	−18.3	7.3	8.8	16.7
District of Columbia	80,694	80,618	80,937	80,678	80,450	79,802	−45.2	−7.3	−1.1	−8.4
Florida	1,861,592	1,932,131	1,981,407	2,040,763	2,111,188	2,176,222	52.4	19.2	16.9	39.3
Georgia	1,151,687	1,177,569	1,207,186	1,235,304	1,270,948	1,311,126	19.3	6.7	13.8	21.4
Hawaii	171,708	174,747	177,448	180,410	183,795	187,180	3.6	4.6	9.0	14.0
Idaho	220,840	225,680	231,668	236,774	240,448	243,097	33.3	5.8	10.1	16.5
Illinois	1,821,407	1,848,166	1,873,567	1,893,078	1,916,172	1,943,623	−17.5	−0.3	6.7	6.4
Indiana	954,525	956,988	960,630	965,633	969,022	977,263	−20.6	−1.2	2.4	1.2
Iowa	483,652	491,363	494,839	498,519	500,440	502,343	−23.9	−0.3	3.9	3.5
Kansas	437,034	445,390	451,536	457,614	460,838	463,008	−9.8	6.5	5.9	12.9
Kentucky	636,401	646,024	655,041	655,265	657,642	659,821	−8.0	−1.2	3.7	2.5
Louisiana	784,757	794,128	797,985	800,560	797,933	797,366	−5.3	−0.5	1.6	1.1
Maine	215,149	216,400	216,453	216,995	212,601	213,569	−12.7	4.4	−0.7	3.6
Maryland	715,176	736,238	751,850	772,638	790,938	805,544	−12.1	6.5	12.6	20.0
Massachusetts	834,314	846,155	859,948	877,726	893,727	915,007	−21.6	−1.2	9.7	8.4
Michigan	1,584,431	1,593,561	1,603,610	1,599,377	1,614,784	1,641,456	−23.7	−1.1	3.6	2.4
Minnesota	756,374	773,571	793,724	810,233	821,693	835,166	−9.3	7.3	10.4	18.4
Mississippi	502,417	504,127	506,668	505,907	505,962	506,272	−5.3	6.6	0.8	7.4
Missouri	816,558	842,965	859,357	866,378	878,541	889,881	−14.4	2.7	9.0	11.9
Montana	152,974	155,779	160,011	163,009	164,341	165,547	−6.3	−0.6	8.2	7.6
Nebraska	274,081	279,552	282,414	285,097	287,100	289,744	−12.0	3.1	5.7	9.0
Nevada	201,316	211,810	222,974	235,800	250,747	265,041	107.8	29.9	31.7	71.1
New Hampshire	172,785	177,138	181,247	185,360	189,319	194,171	22.3	7.3	12.4	20.6
New Jersey	1,089,646	1,109,796	1,130,560	1,151,307	1,174,206	1,197,381	−19.2	−2.4	9.9	7.3
New Mexico	301,881	308,667	315,668	322,292	327,248	329,640	17.2	8.8	9.2	18.8
New York	2,598,337	2,643,993	2,689,686	2,733,813	2,766,208	2,813,230	−19.4	−0.9	8.3	7.3
North Carolina	1,086,871	1,097,598	1,114,083	1,133,231	1,156,767	1,183,090	−0.8	0.1	8.9	8.9
North Dakota	117,825	118,376	118,734	119,127	119,288	119,100	−19.0	−0.6	1.1	0.4
Ohio	1,771,089	1,783,767	1,795,199	1,807,319	1,814,290	1,836,015	−24.3	−1.3	3.7	2.3
Oklahoma	579,087	588,263	597,096	604,076	609,718	616,393	−1.7	−2.2	6.4	4.1
Oregon	472,394	498,614	510,122	516,611	521,945	527,914	10.1	5.6	11.8	18.0
Pennsylvania	1,667,834	1,692,797	1,717,613	1,744,082	1,764,946	1,787,533	−24.4	−0.9	7.2	6.2
Rhode Island	138,813	142,144	143,798	145,676	147,487	149,799	−20.4	3.6	7.9	11.8
South Carolina	622,112	627,470	640,464	643,696	648,725	645,586	1.2	2.5	3.8	6.4
South Dakota	129,164	131,576	134,573	142,825	143,482	144,685	−13.0	3.9	12.0	16.4
Tennessee	824,595	833,651	855,231	866,557	881,425	893,770	−0.7	1.3	8.4	9.8
Texas	3,382,887	3,464,371	3,541,769	3,608,262	3,677,171	3,748,167	32.0	8.0	10.8	19.7
Utah	446,652	456,430	463,870	471,365	474,675	477,121	56.9	10.7	6.8	18.3
Vermont	95,762	97,137	98,558	102,755	104,533	105,565	2.4	6.2	10.2	17.1
Virginia	998,601	1,016,204	1,031,925	1,045,471	1,060,809	1,079,854	0.1	3.2	8.1	11.5
Washington	839,709	869,327	896,475	915,952	938,314	956,572	17.0	12.0	13.9	27.6
West Virginia	322,389	320,249	318,296	314,383	310,511	307,112	−23.1	−9.9	−4.7	−14.2
Wisconsin	797,621	814,671	829,415	844,001	860,581	870,175	−12.4	3.8	9.1	13.3
Wyoming	98,226	102,074	100,313	100,899	100,314	99,859	14.9	−4.4	1.7	−2.8
Outlying areas	711,787	713,533	712,078	707,804	699,306	706,702	—	—	−0.7	—
American Samoa	12,463	13,365	13,994	14,484	14,445	14,576	—	—	17.0	—
Guam	26,391	28,334	30,077	30,920	32,185	32,960	33.1	1.3	24.9	26.6
Northern Marianas	6,449	7,096	8,086	8,188	8,429	8,809	—	—	36.6	—
Puerto Rico	644,734	642,392	637,034	631,460	621,121	627,620	−8.6	−6.1	−2.7	−8.6
Trust Territories	—	—	—	—	—	—				
Virgin Islands	21,750	22,346	22,887	22,752	23,126	22,737	—	−14.5	4.5	−10.7

[1] Includes a number of prekindergarten students.
[2] Beginning in 1983, data include students enrolled in public schools on federal bases and other special arrangements.
—Data not available or not applicable.

SOURCE: U.S. Department of Education, National Center for Education Statistics, "Statistics of Public Elementary and Secondary Day Schools," various years; and Common Core of Data surveys. (This table was prepared April 1997.)

Table 11.—Elementary enrollment [1] in public schools, by state:
Fall 1970 to fall 1995

State or other area	Fall 1970	Fall 1971	Fall 1972	Fall 1973	Fall 1974	Fall 1975	Fall 1976	Fall 1977	Fall 1978	Fall 1979
1	2	3	4	5	6	7	8	9	10	11
United States	32,558,308	32,318,229	31,878,600	31,400,809	30,970,723	30,515,131	29,996,835	29,374,503	28,463,348	28,034,345
Alabama	569,547	568,396	546,545	534,814	528,318	520,405	513,140	524,957	509616	519,077
Alaska [2]	61,030	61,675	63,568	60,562	61,338	64,574	65,059	63,292	62802	61,065
Arizona	313,697	331,105	346,981	367,997	346,599	349,831	354,281	358,889	349695	353,408
Arkansas	329,750	325,969	324,524	316,665	317,303	317,458	319,166	316,401	313738	312,011
California	3,230,905	3,166,351	3,114,208	3,060,277	3,019,441	2,992,901	2,940,300	2,919,607	2728637	2,786,484
Colorado	390,593	395,644	399,955	395,218	387,959	383,694	377,685	375,105	374158	369,928
Connecticut	487,416	483,836	476,604	440,965	459,965	449,787	434,403	416,769	396975	377,762
Delaware	94,328	94,691	92,728	90,325	87,713	84,389	80,001	76,231	69811	65,134
District of Columbia	113,194	109,874	106,322	101,825	98,114	94,105	89,925	85,581	79963	75,180
Florida	1,015,811	1,032,505	1,052,596	1,065,459	1,077,734	1,061,282	1,042,342	1,036,314	1027152	1,031,452
Georgia	799,522	769,493	784,681	777,831	768,560	750,505	768,603	760,208	763196	745,910
Hawaii	129,146	130,289	127,868	124,035	122,394	120,621	118,420	115,344	113341	111,693
Idaho	123,933	125,223	124,549	126,671	124,985	133,335	135,816	137,107	139481	141,193
Illinois	1,687,909	1,699,218	1,650,506	1,609,242	1,572,145	1,538,579	1,506,052	1,451,242	1365164	1,367,133
Indiana	876,558	866,813	852,836	834,093	813,073	795,838	784,235	766,821	720671	723,064
Iowa	464,543	453,678	446,828	431,222	417,417	408,460	399,473	385,452	369307	357,588
Kansas	357,029	346,276	333,980	322,309	314,240	310,964	305,360	298,019	290299	284,761
Kentucky	513,148	508,932	500,774	494,467	485,582	475,098	476,329	480,247	477570	466,201
Louisiana	615,562	619,045	605,075	598,256	590,432	592,479	581,588	577,452	565844	555,095
Maine	176,804	177,552	178,782	174,566	174,439	172,350	170,531	166,704	161797	155,882
Maryland	664,024	661,928	653,642	640,228	621,561	606,512	587,384	562,498	535565	510,259
Massachusetts	833,171	838,069	841,553	846,540	836,500	813,410	786,700	755,921	721266	684,910
Michigan	1,576,554	1,542,904	1,512,777	1,472,500	1,482,208	1,418,905	1,386,286	1,336,464	1294499	1,268,210
Minnesota	630,930	627,456	618,161	601,738	586,588	572,827	554,497	533,211	512834	496,170
Mississippi	388,647	382,949	377,964	369,467	361,214	356,234	353,173	346,632	340084	325,650
Missouri	748,299	724,917	719,061	700,674	680,224	645,886	630,956	614,938	593923	579,470
Montana	120,825	122,041	123,209	119,416	115,142	114,646	112,930	111,843	109463	105,735
Nebraska	229,920	230,659	226,829	220,281	214,830	210,445	206,422	201,769	194376	189,646
Nevada	93,108	94,042	93,530	95,401	95,667	95,763	95,909	95,448	96682	97,819
New Hampshire	113,700	116,626	118,466	120,351	119,983	120,395	120,399	119,413	117241	114,526
New Jersey	1,063,276	1,058,768	1,069,560	1,029,202	1,010,969	998,000	961,080	932,320	884390	847,766
New Mexico	198,595	200,315	198,813	190,895	188,073	183,144	192,085	188,864	187102	186,215
New York	2,457,791	2,468,560	2,419,467	2,365,215	2,320,664	2,290,285	2,213,230	2,109,573	2000069	1,905,387
North Carolina	835,739	820,497	812,207	814,431	818,594	817,537	825,381	816,645	800807	796,033
North Dakota	100,441	97,557	94,319	90,351	85,746	83,747	82,000	79,220	77544	75,542
Ohio	1,698,298	1,697,512	1,665,936	1,617,374	1,584,740	1,535,447	1,504,071	1,455,646	1396760	1,351,413
Oklahoma	437,332	437,612	421,676	414,717	411,516	408,378	406,149	403,438	398510	398,695
Oregon	325,065	322,252	318,256	321,619	321,201	321,449	316,521	316,712	317533	317,045
Pennsylvania	1,634,940	1,621,816	1,596,209	1,551,631	1,509,909	1,480,733	1,441,357	1,390,197	1326561	1,270,676
Rhode Island	135,389	136,343	134,924	130,419	124,327	121,297	117,202	112,370	107292	102,189
South Carolina	459,145	460,481	436,245	444,616	446,310	443,431	425,184	421,990	428682	428,924
South Dakota	113,976	113,150	110,361	106,179	102,559	99,844	97,296	93,987	90437	88,400
Tennessee	648,633	639,287	634,375	643,309	617,603	626,230	603,714	608,498	616060	610,435
Texas	2,045,900	2,006,400	1,955,050	1,991,736	1,987,794	1,991,629	1,998,615	1,983,801	1999905	2,004,224
Utah	212,669	212,644	212,522	211,110	210,961	212,452	216,106	219,746	228391	237,872
Vermont	73,891	76,411	76,017	75,441	74,637	73,452	72,655	71,071	69618	67,755
Virginia	775,497	764,866	752,046	753,005	756,245	759,305	752,495	734,350	730918	714,954
Washington	572,881	556,913	542,250	537,865	533,540	530,116	523,501	518,282	513000	515,258
West Virginia	280,426	283,862	287,307	286,084	283,337	283,044	284,994	282,510	269979	272,847
Wisconsin	678,430	675,159	666,965	654,945	640,873	625,149	603,642	582,510	559786	543,581
Wyoming	60,391	59,668	58,993	57,270	59,457	58,784	62,192	62,894	64854	66,718
Outlying areas	—	—	—	—	—	—	—	—	—	—
American Samoa	—	6,013	5,981	8,204	8,013	8,022	7,746	7,022	—	—
Guam	19,259	20,242	20,710	20,843	21,178	21,311	21,245	—	—	20,193
Northern Marianas	—	—	—	—	—	—	—	—	3353	3,267
Puerto Rico	541,621	547,186	555,515	553,149	—	523,245	530,054	—	534421	—
Trust Territories	25,709	—	—	—	—	—	—	—	—	—
Virgin Islands	—	15,365	15,367	16,811	18,898	19,697	19,530	20,373	19163	19,330

Table 11.—Elementary enrollment [1] in public schools, by state: Fall 1970 to fall 1995—Continued

State or other area	Fall 1980	Fall 1981	Fall 1982	Fall 1983	Fall 1984	Fall 1985	Fall 1986	Fall 1987	Fall 1988	Fall 1989
1	12	13	14	15	16	17	18	19	20	21
United States	**27,646,536**	**27,280,220**	**27,160,518**	**26,980,962**	**26,904,517**	**27,034,244**	**27,420,063**	**27,932,682**	**28,501,413**	**29,152,224**
Alabama	527,753	518,534	509,952	510,814	514,355	517,361	518,982	521,004	521,650	525,730
Alaska [2]	60,417	63,756	63,211	70,284	75,206	77,211	77,906	77,885	78,518	81,698
Arizona	357,112	355,275	359,229	354,415	373,235	386,057	371,419	412,501	417,579	451,311
Arkansas	309,909	305,030	304,443	304,975	304,518	303,536	306,851	307,248	309,268	311,060
California	2,729,725	2,769,788	2,801,818	2,813,524	2,845,962	2,926,705	3,045,684	3,171,170	3,316,797	3,470,198
Colorado	374,366	376,043	379,599	376,775	376,216	378,735	386,304	391,986	399,853	407,525
Connecticut	363,590	347,490	335,997	328,574	323,391	321,203	321,823	326,250	331,697	338,378
Delaware	62,464	60,287	61,367	61,181	61,961	63,082	64,807	66,714	68,886	70,699
District of Columbia	70,978	67,547	64,696	63,297	62,808	62,494	62,456	62,857	62,334	60,662
Florida	1,041,859	1,035,323	1,038,998	1,044,107	1,061,736	1,086,250	1,120,938	1,171,809	1,232,007	1,303,439
Georgia	741,675	736,565	739,178	738,258	745,837	756,752	777,991	795,032	807,864	828,426
Hawaii	109,597	111,383	112,410	112,698	113,716	113,496	115,076	117,514	120,385	123,496
Idaho	143,759	145,547	145,416	148,363	148,937	149,380	149,613	153,356	155,505	156,602
Illinois	1,334,909	1,304,192	1,286,858	1,271,525	1,254,477	1,246,496	1,249,340	1,251,790	1,259,124	1,280,021
Indiana	708,419	690,810	679,033	670,440	661,779	654,061	653,613	658,656	667,647	671,036
Iowa	351,155	341,218	337,728	333,198	328,835	324,332	323,536	328,436	333,988	338,422
Kansas	282,725	282,014	282,879	282,389	282,182	285,671	291,564	298,516	306,751	313,588
Kentucky	463,804	458,781	457,505	454,931	451,111	448,768	446,901	449,033	451,805	451,858
Louisiana	543,598	543,275	561,411	577,234	578,911	573,068	580,771	582,742	581,095	581,702
Maine	152,642	148,769	146,848	145,814	143,986	142,443	143,671	145,499	148,904	152,267
Maryland	492,842	472,288	461,794	451,716	446,244	446,321	456,045	472,909	489,115	507,007
Massachusetts	676,314	620,543	596,990	578,306	566,028	559,057	559,418	565,042	577,795	590,238
Michigan	1,227,437	1,182,083	1,140,534	1,113,691	1,090,362	1,085,582	1,089,757	1,097,004	1,113,595	1,127,921
Minnesota	482,025	480,008	471,670	466,578	464,107	467,957	479,130	496,553	511,279	528,507
Mississippi	329,760	328,016	326,998	327,509	325,454	329,981	356,052	364,129	367,593	369,513
Missouri	567,198	553,012	546,751	546,155	545,062	544,197	549,348	557,073	567,860	576,243
Montana	105,680	106,235	106,869	108,268	108,796	107,918	107,572	108,017	109,526	109,791
Nebraska	189,029	186,755	186,265	185,941	184,618	184,296	185,282	188,166	191,302	194,227
Nevada	100,597	102,635	102,639	102,358	104,963	107,070	112,164	119,077	127,414	137,455
New Hampshire	111,902	109,959	107,349	106,303	105,525	106,912	109,948	114,098	119,785	124,410
New Jersey	819,567	788,163	776,608	761,464	747,182	740,497	742,324	747,402	755,073	765,810
New Mexico	185,874	187,192	189,968	191,824	194,928	187,479	191,037	195,413	200,129	203,157
New York	1,838,492	1,786,679	1,761,336	1,735,517	1,712,219	1,703,430	1,713,465	1,735,527	1,760,596	1,790,143
North Carolina	785,881	772,876	768,755	761,053	755,313	749,451	748,451	753,595	761,069	769,825
North Dakota	76,787	79,579	81,171	82,321	83,635	83,702	83,930	84,379	85,182	84,920
Ohio	1,312,353	1,277,103	1,258,642	1,240,344	1,220,019	1,206,174	1,208,110	1,219,978	1,229,384	1,238,917
Oklahoma	398,895	408,579	423,140	420,913	416,664	414,279	417,287	410,995	413,656	420,940
Oregon	319,129	315,388	308,964	307,121	305,628	305,418	308,527	317,920	328,226	340,264
Pennsylvania	1,231,428	1,186,821	1,157,356	1,130,767	1,102,776	1,092,558	1,097,671	1,111,648	1,131,662	1,147,986
Rhode Island	98,190	94,365	92,451	90,705	89,710	89,971	91,964	93,623	95,285	98,412
South Carolina	426,384	420,664	424,362	423,016	422,417	424,125	427,751	431,585	437,826	443,712
South Dakota	86,178	85,887	85,990	86,324	86,724	87,644	89,373	91,362	92,556	93,596
Tennessee	602,044	593,556	590,839	587,014	581,452	574,517	577,045	582,432	585,972	590,121
Texas	2,048,684	2,098,126	2,149,813	2,155,012	2,188,511	2,260,679	2,317,454	2,350,856	2,392,079	2,443,245
Utah	250,242	261,722	275,145	280,792	289,340	298,760	308,389	313,953	319,423	324,004
Vermont	66,359	64,988	64,181	63,452	62,738	62,703	63,392	65,012	66,761	69,103
Virginia	703,322	690,736	682,630	674,016	667,215	665,151	673,237	685,172	699,064	712,297
Washington	515,430	513,018	507,515	503,551	502,392	506,890	521,333	540,936	563,100	585,818
West Virginia	270,309	266,944	266,950	263,254	255,112	249,034	243,538	236,926	231,819	227,251
Wisconsin	527,655	512,831	503,871	500,778	497,175	501,402	509,584	521,533	535,215	549,143
Wyoming	70,093	71,842	74,396	72,103	73,049	73,988	72,239	70,369	70,415	70,130
Outlying areas	—	—	—	603,235	—	—	—	547,434	541,207	535,242
American Samoa	7,174	7,350	—	7,535	—	—	8,133	8,313	8,911	9,309
Guam	19,603	18,932	19,168	19,331	—	19,266	18,522	18,713	18,659	19,291
Northern Marianas	—	3,964	—	3,215	3,531	—	—	4,424	4,699	4,626
Puerto Rico	521,865	—	522,366	519,143	512,205	507,973	503,012	498,853	491,836	486,247
Trust Territories	—	—	—	34,105	—	—	—	—	—	—
Virgin Islands	19,716	19,588	19,294	19,906	19,131	18,690	17,778	17,131	17,102	15,769

Table 11.—Elementary enrollment [1] in public schools, by state: Fall 1970 to fall 1995—Continued

State or other area	Fall 1990	Fall 1991	Fall 1992	Fall 1993	Fall 1994	Fall 1995	Percentage change			
							Fall 1970 to fall 1995	Fall 1985 to fall 1990	Fall 1990 to fall 1995	Fall 1985 to fall 1995
1	22	23	24	25	26	27	28	29	30	31
United States	29,878,245	30,505,625	31,088,304	31,088,304	31,504,032	31,898,249	−2.0	10.5	6.8	18.0
Alabama	527,097	526,473	535,248	535,248	535,637	535,246	−6.0	1.9	1.5	3.5
Alaska [2]	85,297	89,124	91,640	91,640	93,601	93,719	53.6	10.5	9.9	21.4
Arizona	479,050	490,242	497,917	497,917	526,412	542,904	73.1	24.1	13.3	40.6
Arkansas	313,512	315,147	317,598	317,598	317,713	319,282	−3.2	3.3	1.8	5.2
California	3,614,798	3,720,302	3,850,790	3,850,790	3,903,137	3,955,868	22.4	23.5	9.4	35.2
Colorado	419,929	435,621	451,321	451,321	459,930	469,755	20.3	10.9	11.9	24.0
Connecticut	347,396	355,463	361,548	361,548	368,632	375,638	−22.9	8.2	8.1	16.9
Delaware	72,606	74,555	75,983	75,983	76,617	76,819	−18.6	15.1	5.8	21.8
District of Columbia	61,274	61,019	61,133	61,133	61,434	62,126	−45.1	−2.0	1.4	−0.6
Florida	1,369,934	1,427,613	1,469,850	1,469,850	1,515,194	1,569,666	54.5	26.1	14.6	44.5
Georgia	849,082	868,130	891,647	891,647	910,425	934,650	16.9	12.2	10.1	23.5
Hawaii	122,840	126,855	128,610	128,610	131,638	133,675	3.5	8.2	8.8	17.8
Idaho	160,097	161,458	164,634	164,634	166,999	168,887	36.3	7.2	5.5	13.1
Illinois	1,309,640	1,327,834	1,344,549	1,344,549	1,356,329	1,368,041	−19.0	5.1	4.5	9.8
Indiana	675,851	676,481	677,249	677,249	679,066	678,970	−22.5	3.3	0.5	3.8
Iowa	344,874	348,231	348,648	348,648	348,006	345,865	−25.5	6.3	0.3	6.6
Kansas	319,697	325,126	328,244	328,244	329,708	329,211	−7.8	11.9	3.0	15.2
Kentucky	459,216	466,170	469,897	469,897	467,315	467,005	−9.0	2.3	1.7	4.1
Louisiana	586,183	590,660	590,824	590,824	587,490	583,892	−5.1	2.3	−0.4	1.9
Maine	155,218	156,764	156,368	156,368	156,528	155,903	−11.8	9.0	0.4	9.4
Maryland	526,859	543,492	555,565	555,565	569,497	580,903	−12.5	18.0	10.3	30.2
Massachusetts	604,234	615,990	629,649	629,649	645,518	658,507	−21.0	8.1	9.0	17.8
Michigan	1,144,878	1,158,568	1,164,879	1,164,879	1,159,968	1,170,251	−25.8	5.5	2.2	7.8
Minnesota	545,556	556,735	569,298	569,298	576,980	581,426	−7.8	16.6	6.6	24.2
Mississippi	371,674	369,936	370,006	370,006	368,688	366,846	−5.6	12.6	−1.3	11.2
Missouri	588,104	611,603	621,712	621,712	622,171	628,286	−16.0	8.1	6.8	15.5
Montana	111,172	112,780	115,315	115,315	116,668	116,748	−3.4	3.0	5.0	8.2
Nebraska	198,080	201,367	202,439	202,439	203,426	203,055	−11.7	7.5	2.5	10.2
Nevada	149,882	157,713	165,348	165,348	175,054	185,336	99.1	40.0	23.7	73.1
New Hampshire	126,309	129,698	133,182	133,182	136,211	138,851	22.1	18.1	9.9	29.9
New Jersey	783,558	800,696	817,661	817,661	843,526	862,331	−18.9	5.8	10.1	16.5
New Mexico	208,087	212,836	217,418	217,418	226,287	229,168	15.4	11.0	10.1	22.2
New York	1,827,936	1,862,215	1,893,303	1,893,303	1,920,609	1,949,245	−20.7	7.3	6.6	14.4
North Carolina	783,132	794,773	810,576	810,576	828,171	847,463	1.4	4.5	8.2	13.1
North Dakota	84,943	84,941	84,569	84,569	84,127	83,419	−16.9	1.5	−1.8	−0.3
Ohio	1,257,580	1,277,403	1,283,869	1,283,869	1,290,197	1,295,289	−23.7	4.3	3.0	7.4
Oklahoma	424,901	432,334	438,796	438,796	441,094	442,607	1.2	2.6	4.2	6.8
Oregon	340,264	359,348	365,416	365,416	368,141	371,967	14.4	11.4	9.3	21.8
Pennsylvania	1,172,164	1,195,012	1,215,974	1,215,974	1,233,113	1,243,983	−23.9	7.3	6.1	13.9
Rhode Island	101,797	104,146	105,677	105,677	107,047	107,913	−20.3	13.1	6.0	19.9
South Carolina	452,033	456,039	467,305	467,305	466,951	468,850	2.1	6.6	3.7	10.5
South Dakota	95,169	96,423	97,882	97,882	102,281	101,805	−10.7	8.6	7.0	16.2
Tennessee	598,111	604,571	621,801	621,801	630,015	640,604	−1.2	4.1	7.1	11.5
Texas	2,510,955	2,574,983	2,634,346	2,634,346	2,681,053	2,720,623	33.0	11.1	8.4	20.3
Utah	325,019	326,969	329,883	329,883	329,926	328,482	54.5	8.8	1.1	9.9
Vermont	70,860	72,702	73,865	73,865	74,828	75,590	2.3	13.0	6.7	20.6
Virginia	728,282	741,005	757,847	757,847	767,347	774,319	−0.2	9.5	6.3	16.4
Washington	612,597	632,781	651,743	651,743	660,424	673,107	17.5	20.9	9.9	32.8
West Virginia	224,057	221,545	219,037	219,037	215,784	212,808	−24.1	−10.0	−5.0	−14.5
Wisconsin	565,520	579,863	588,447	588,447	595,717	601,215	−11.4	12.8	6.3	19.9
Wyoming	70,941	73,890	71,798	71,798	71,402	70,130	16.1	−4.1	−1.1	−5.2
Outlying areas	530,151	528,129	525,711	505,283	500,177	514,114	—	—	3.0	—
American Samoa	9,390	10,050	10,582	10,582	10,974	11,054	—	—	17.7	—
Guam	19,276	20,800	22,428	2,000	2,000	24,189	25.6	0.1	25.5	25.6
Northern Marianas	4,918	5,628	6,133	6,133	6,380	6,559	—	—	33.4	—
Puerto Rico	480,319	474,976	469,764	469,764	464,117	455,653	−15.9	−5.4	−5.1	−10.3
Trust Territories	—	—	—	—	—	—	—	—	—	—
Virgin Islands	16,248	16,675	16,804	16,804	16,706	16,659	—	−13.1	2.5	−10.9

[1] Includes kindergarten through grade 8 enrollment and a number of prekindergarten students.

[2] Beginning in 1983, data includes students enrolled in public schools on federal bases and other special arrangements.

—Data not available or not applicable.

SOURCE: U.S. Department of Education, National Center for Education Statistics, "Statistics of Public Elementary and Secondary Day Schools," various years; and Common Core of Data surveys. (This table was prepared April 1997.)

Table 12.—Secondary enrollment [1] in public schools, by state: Fall 1970 to fall 1995

State or other area	Fall 1970	Fall 1971	Fall 1972	Fall 1973	Fall 1974	Fall 1975	Fall 1976	Fall 1977	Fall 1978	Fall 1979
1	2	3	4	5	6	7	8	9	10	11
United States	**13,335,652**	**13,753,098**	**13,847,808**	**14,043,978**	**14,102,718**	**14,304,196**	**14,314,131**	**14,202,870**	**14,087,545**	**13,616,367**
Alabama	235,658	237,919	236,838	235,925	236,023	238,941	239,367	236,923	252,050	235,104
Alaska [2]	18,815	22,706	21,764	21,943	25,238	24,721	26,131	27,052	27,926	27,508
Arizona	125,827	133,373	138,107	153,243	140,441	143,164	148,536	154,928	160,135	155,844
Arkansas	133,570	135,291	136,907	133,449	137,103	139,245	141,427	142,377	142,960	141,114
California	1,402,293	1,435,199	1,386,770	1,399,051	1,408,002	1,426,670	1,440,100	1,384,058	1,459,330	1,333,027
Colorado	159,467	168,858	174,293	177,936	180,101	185,157	186,402	186,702	184,127	180,599
Connecticut	174,789	183,031	188,157	226,123	200,102	202,662	200,597	199,620	196,782	188,872
Delaware	38,417	40,322	41,589	42,615	42,903	43,087	42,272	41,769	41,223	38,901
District of Columbia	32,510	32,638	33,596	34,211	33,577	35,864	35,923	34,294	33,895	30,976
Florida	412,085	445,999	461,763	472,493	479,320	490,091	494,994	499,256	486,667	476,885
Georgia	299,379	323,914	305,599	308,050	312,925	339,787	326,539	329,417	330,060	332,552
Hawaii	51,495	53,365	54,111	54,476	54,636	55,809	56,523	57,012	57,420	56,967
Idaho	58,400	59,891	60,114	62,462	62,567	63,281	64,189	64,326	63,541	61,565
Illinois	668,727	680,428	704,056	711,430	724,096	731,313	732,077	722,110	674,266	676,106
Indiana	354,900	363,983	367,707	373,327	373,727	378,025	378,944	376,901	392,660	360,762
Iowa	195,561	199,280	199,580	199,910	200,068	203,651	205,654	203,308	199,233	190,729
Kansas	156,365	158,991	157,785	157,035	157,220	154,391	152,970	148,573	143,239	138,163
Kentucky	204,057	211,377	213,858	215,297	215,791	216,514	217,671	216,753	215,429	210,922
Louisiana	226,803	232,029	240,766	243,896	250,310	254,723	257,911	261,548	250,825	245,340
Maine	67,866	68,854	71,666	70,901	76,204	78,581	78,291	79,064	78,219	71,941
Maryland	252,220	260,123	267,254	270,869	272,648	274,415	273,545	274,414	274,368	267,466
Massachusetts	334,542	353,110	361,044	358,602	373,600	385,000	382,300	360,889	360,198	350,814
Michigan	575,702	639,981	652,172	651,111	655,404	654,383	649,417	632,511	616,846	592,288
Minnesota	289,909	286,499	291,492	298,639	302,947	307,117	308,094	303,209	294,882	281,886
Mississippi	145,748	146,417	148,402	150,319	152,262	156,173	157,036	155,393	153,626	156,389
Missouri	291,178	298,457	310,947	319,129	321,481	319,474	319,186	316,294	306,079	293,463
Montana	55,887	56,326	56,668	54,143	57,016	57,142	57,622	56,889	54,863	52,473
Nebraska	99,190	101,716	102,363	102,930	103,962	105,224	105,602	104,438	103,420	97,642
Nevada	34,442	36,144	38,130	40,005	41,384	43,982	45,882	47,996	49,599	49,915
New Hampshire	45,056	47,476	49,628	51,131	52,134	54,202	55,097	55,205	55,148	56,020
New Jersey	418,724	439,073	440,959	452,403	455,987	460,000	465,920	449,208	452,937	440,043
New Mexico	82,777	84,633	86,281	92,655	94,309	91,468	92,634	93,032	92,147	89,357
New York	1,031,454	1,069,914	1,088,537	1,100,235	1,113,452	1,127,168	1,125,579	1,113,039	1,093,816	1,063,829
North Carolina	356,448	355,811	349,119	358,984	359,266	367,459	365,935	365,186	362,003	354,020
North Dakota	46,572	46,862	47,216	47,951	47,495	47,584	47,106	45,865	44,477	42,146
Ohio	727,345	741,231	756,718	760,975	745,410	757,200	745,369	726,333	705,680	673,843
Oklahoma	189,624	188,128	185,408	186,231	184,864	186,438	191,516	191,030	190,360	184,763
Oregon	154,462	156,250	153,139	154,899	155,382	156,110	158,186	156,567	153,841	150,083
Pennsylvania	728,877	748,849	765,076	769,806	767,542	765,414	752,316	738,676	720,185	698,125
Rhode Island	52,701	54,353	54,769	54,205	54,335	55,020	55,171	54,259	53,993	52,510
South Carolina	178,655	188,162	187,533	182,298	180,895	186,298	195,527	198,733	196,249	195,871
South Dakota	52,329	52,117	52,037	51,343	51,033	51,373	50,784	49,643	47,791	45,440
Tennessee	251,260	258,311	257,400	259,395	255,216	250,696	238,260	269,926	256,976	255,682
Texas	794,000	805,300	783,081	790,415	797,502	821,259	824,139	859,041	867,349	868,495
Utah	91,333	93,096	93,394	94,690	95,427	97,256	98,365	97,586	96,635	95,177
Vermont	29,239	28,929	30,500	30,795	30,739	31,422	31,701	31,863	31,674	30,583
Virginia	303,257	309,207	317,299	332,290	337,064	344,364	348,228	347,834	324,320	316,449
Washington	244,831	248,136	248,252	250,459	251,917	255,333	257,229	258,181	256,246	249,621
West Virginia	119,105	119,515	122,682	123,100	121,104	121,075	119,777	118,859	125,743	115,119
Wisconsin	315,306	324,762	328,258	332,077	333,460	339,070	341,695	335,353	326,633	314,274
Wyoming	26,495	26,762	27,024	28,121	27,127	29,400	28,395	29,427	29,474	28,704
Outlying areas	—	—	—	—	—	—	—	—	—	—
American Samoa		2,005	2,184	2,092	2,173	2,097	2,204	2,269	—	—
Guam	5,498	5,758	6,212	6,486	7,006	7,280	7,325	—	—	7,389
Northern Marianas	—	—	—	—	—	—	—	—	1,160	1,140
Puerto Rico	145,156	150,224	155,723	159,439	—	173,914	158,538	—	186,998	—
Trust Territories	4,014	—	—	—	—	—	—	—	—	—
Virgin Islands	—	3,495	5,459	5,211	4,445	4,815	5,496	5,198	5,975	6,223

Table 12.—Secondary enrollment [1] in public schools, by state: Fall 1970 to fall 1995—Continued

State or other area	Fall 1980	Fall 1981	Fall 1982	Fall 1983	Fall 1984	Fall 1985	Fall 1986	Fall 1987	Fall 1988	Fall 1989
1	12	13	14	15	16	17	18	19	20	21
United States	**13,230,945**	**12,763,873**	**12,405,092**	**12,271,346**	**12,303,735**	**12,387,717**	**12,333,109**	**12,075,531**	**11,687,277**	**11,390,483**
Alabama	230,968	224,914	214,085	211,087	198,231	213,099	214,753	208,230	203,101	198,013
Alaska [2]	26,097	27,102	26,202	27,922	29,393	30,134	29,942	28,984	27,963	27,582
Arizona	156,678	151,924	151,067	152,267	156,827	162,195	163,119	159,920	157,311	156,304
Arkansas	137,791	132,091	128,122	127,145	128,150	129,874	130,587	129,788	127,119	123,900
California	1,346,696	1,276,368	1,263,668	1,275,493	1,305,148	1,328,849	1,332,305	1,317,228	1,301,323	1,301,780
Colorado	171,667	168,131	165,610	165,421	169,211	171,907	172,111	168,250	160,228	155,230
Connecticut	167,869	157,896	150,473	149,011	144,754	140,823	147,024	139,215	128,940	123,182
Delaware	36,939	34,785	31,279	30,225	29,806	29,819	29,603	28,945	27,792	27,109
District of Columbia	29,071	27,428	26,409	25,546	24,589	24,598	23,156	23,578	22,458	20,639
Florida	468,366	452,398	445,736	451,436	462,371	476,033	486,382	492,965	488,923	486,486
Georgia	327,062	319,552	314,511	312,601	316,478	322,842	318,434	315,915	300,130	298,109
Hawaii	55,471	51,422	49,614	49,543	50,144	50,673	49,564	48,646	47,103	45,997
Idaho	59,488	58,977	57,557	57,989	59,143	59,289	58,778	59,088	59,110	58,330
Illinois	648,554	619,892	593,431	581,791	579,878	579,982	575,845	559,656	535,792	517,334
Indiana	347,170	334,362	320,509	313,944	310,880	312,045	313,167	305,473	293,347	283,129
Iowa	182,702	174,998	167,255	164,089	162,176	161,000	157,750	152,390	144,212	140,064
Kansas	132,566	127,895	124,195	122,833	123,165	124,558	124,527	122,596	119,845	117,276
Kentucky	205,994	199,569	193,579	192,483	193,310	195,065	195,877	193,663	185,822	178,830
Louisiana	233,962	238,778	222,616	222,959	222,030	215,281	214,417	210,351	205,588	201,323
Maine	69,855	67,524	65,138	63,939	63,551	63,658	68,081	66,318	63,998	61,508
Maryland	257,823	249,553	237,407	231,775	227,596	225,239	219,702	210,888	199,832	191,799
Massachusetts	345,571	326,494	311,994	300,538	293,363	285,273	274,500	260,278	245,633	235,350
Michigan	569,615	542,704	534,163	522,272	519,086	517,165	507,397	492,283	469,190	448,864
Minnesota	272,293	253,733	243,520	238,658	237,590	237,183	232,004	224,928	215,671	211,046
Mississippi	147,299	143,599	141,296	140,235	140,604	141,214	142,587	141,421	135,733	132,507
Missouri	277,450	265,693	255,784	249,298	248,731	250,910	251,258	244,987	238,779	231,691
Montana	49,513	47,200	45,466	45,378	45,616	45,951	45,755	44,190	42,665	41,474
Nebraska	91,401	86,585	82,744	81,057	80,981	81,523	81,857	79,934	78,132	76,693
Nevada	48,884	48,704	48,465	48,084	46,670	47,878	49,075	49,276	49,060	49,379
New Hampshire	55,330	53,868	52,848	52,727	53,089	54,062	53,769	51,947	49,628	47,286
New Jersey	426,441	411,480	395,912	386,377	382,041	375,697	365,143	345,580	325,798	310,195
New Mexico	85,324	80,899	78,664	77,887	77,550	90,072	90,906	91,816	92,296	92,900
New York	1,033,232	996,338	957,342	939,301	933,592	917,948	894,254	858,543	813,119	775,698
North Carolina	343,495	336,084	328,060	328,553	333,411	336,714	336,797	332,381	322,087	310,919
North Dakota	40,098	38,129	35,907	34,892	35,076	34,868	34,773	34,625	33,627	32,896
Ohio	645,028	621,398	601,603	586,956	585,421	587,791	585,398	573,453	549,160	525,493
Oklahoma	178,912	173,993	170,685	170,476	173,026	178,048	175,896	173,217	166,770	157,640
Oregon	145,470	141,777	139,220	139,988	141,256	142,109	140,780	137,975	133,526	132,130
Pennsylvania	677,864	652,194	626,613	607,185	599,104	590,663	576,490	556,894	528,052	507,293
Rhode Island	50,766	49,049	47,508	45,707	44,900	43,978	42,726	41,177	38,300	37,317
South Carolina	192,839	188,494	184,156	181,537	180,301	182,518	183,878	183,336	177,948	172,465
South Dakota	42,329	39,770	37,907	36,736	36,590	36,647	36,085	35,455	34,354	33,733
Tennessee	251,525	244,741	237,425	235,043	235,760	239,236	241,028	241,351	235,608	229,539
Texas	851,389	837,421	835,846	834,784	851,794	871,026	892,061	885,931	891,628	885,269
Utah	93,376	93,832	95,038	97,416	100,801	104,545	107,605	109,433	111,696	114,550
Vermont	29,456	28,195	27,273	26,964	27,351	27,454	28,720	27,743	26,620	25,676
Virginia	307,049	298,812	293,097	292,094	298,007	302,953	301,898	294,245	283,329	273,049
Washington	242,209	237,170	231,700	232,688	238,785	242,816	240,095	234,819	227,818	224,414
West Virginia	113,194	110,828	108,165	107,997	107,829	108,889	108,299	107,310	104,093	100,289
Wisconsin	302,592	291,431	280,959	273,868	270,367	266,832	258,235	250,830	239,642	233,762
Wyoming	28,212	27,699	27,269	27,151	28,212	28,791	28,716	28,086	27,378	27,042
Outlying areas	—	—	—	205,311	—	—	—	192,426	187,862	182,028
American Samoa	2,473	2,546	—	2,589	—	—	2,922	2,935	2,853	2,949
Guam	6,817	6,152	6,508	6,918	—	6,777	7,154	7,223	7,382	7,202
Northern Marianas	—	1,336		1,284	1,310			1,395	1,380	1,475
Puerto Rico	191,015	—	186,428	182,782	180,718	178,941	176,477	173,984	169,857	164,978
Trust Territories				5,518						
Virgin Islands	5,485	5,937	6,405	6,220	6,991	6,758	6,657	6,889	6,390	5,424

Table 12.—Secondary enrollment [1] in public schools, by state:
Fall 1970 to fall 1995—Continued

| State or other area | Fall 1990 | Fall 1991 | Fall 1992 | Fall 1993 | Fall 1994 | Fall 1995 | Percentage change | | | |
							Fall 1970 to fall 1995	Fall 1985 to fall 1990	Fall 1990 to fall 1995	Fall 1985 to fall 1995
1	22	23	24	25	26	27	28	29	30	31
United States	**11,338,438**	**11,541,253**	**11,735,008**	**11,960,884**	**12,213,233**	**12,499,980**	**-6.3**	**-8.5**	**10.2**	**0.9**
Alabama	194,709	195,531	196,386	198,651	201,285	206,840	-12.2	-8.6	6.2	-2.9
Alaska [2]	28,606	29,556	30,847	32,347	33,338	34,184	81.7	-5.1	19.5	13.4
Arizona	160,803	166,738	175,560	183,041	194,520	195,040	55.0	-0.9	21.3	20.3
Arkansas	122,774	123,371	123,892	126,558	128,283	130,817	-2.1	-5.5	6.6	0.7
California	1,335,676	1,386,843	1,404,054	1,424,094	1,451,607	1,495,182	6.6	0.5	11.9	12.5
Colorado	154,284	157,409	161,314	165,132	170,766	177,398	11.2	-10.3	15.0	3.2
Connecticut	121,727	125,587	126,928	127,666	131,186	133,661	-23.5	-13.6	9.8	-5.1
Delaware	27,052	27,641	28,338	28,930	29,994	31,433	-18.2	-9.3	16.2	5.4
District of Columbia	19,420	19,599	19,804	19,244	18,324	17,966	-44.7	-21.1	-7.5	-27.0
Florida	491,658	504,518	511,557	525,569	541,522	562,712	36.6	3.3	14.5	18.2
Georgia	302,605	309,439	315,539	324,879	336,298	345,419	15.4	-6.3	14.1	7.0
Hawaii	48,868	47,892	48,838	48,772	50,120	51,509	(3)	-3.6	5.4	1.6
Idaho	60,743	64,222	67,034	69,775	71,561	73,541	25.9	2.5	21.1	24.0
Illinois	511,767	520,332	529,018	536,749	548,131	553,148	-17.3	-11.8	8.1	-4.6
Indiana	278,674	280,507	283,381	286,567	290,052	292,915	-17.5	-10.7	5.1	-6.1
Iowa	138,778	143,132	146,191	150,513	154,575	158,346	-19.0	-13.8	14.1	-1.6
Kansas	117,337	120,264	123,292	127,906	131,627	134,307	-14.1	-5.8	14.5	7.8
Kentucky	177,185	179,854	185,144	187,950	190,637	191,579	-6.1	-9.2	8.1	-1.8
Louisiana	198,574	203,468	207,161	213,070	214,041	217,018	-4.3	-7.8	9.3	0.8
Maine	59,931	59,636	60,085	60,467	56,698	57,553	-15.2	-5.9	-4.0	-9.6
Maryland	188,317	192,746	196,285	203,141	210,035	215,389	-14.6	-16.4	14.4	-4.4
Massachusetts	230,080	230,165	230,299	232,208	235,220	240,419	-28.1	-19.3	4.5	-15.7
Michigan	439,553	434,993	438,731	439,409	444,533	449,785	-21.9	-15.0	2.3	-13.0
Minnesota	210,818	216,836	224,426	233,253	240,267	249,086	-14.1	-11.1	18.2	5.0
Mississippi	130,743	134,191	136,662	137,219	139,116	140,086	-3.9	-7.4	7.1	-0.8
Missouri	228,454	231,362	237,645	244,207	250,255	254,110	-12.7	-8.9	11.2	1.3
Montana	41,802	42,999	44,696	46,341	47,593	49,144	-12.1	-9.0	17.6	6.9
Nebraska	76,001	78,185	79,975	81,671	84,045	86,722	-12.6	-6.8	14.1	6.4
Nevada	51,434	54,097	57,626	60,746	65,411	69,149	100.8	7.4	34.4	44.4
New Hampshire	46,476	47,440	48,065	49,149	50,468	52,450	16.4	-14.0	12.9	-3.0
New Jersey	306,088	309,100	312,899	307,781	311,875	317,031	-24.3	-18.5	3.6	-15.6
New Mexico	93,794	95,831	98,250	96,005	98,080	100,401	21.3	4.1	7.0	11.5
New York	770,401	781,778	796,383	813,204	816,963	833,022	-19.2	-16.1	8.1	-9.3
North Carolina	303,739	302,825	303,507	305,060	309,304	311,770	-12.5	-9.8	2.6	-7.4
North Dakota	32,882	33,435	34,165	35,000	35,869	36,767	-21.1	-5.7	11.8	5.4
Ohio	513,509	506,364	511,330	517,122	519,001	538,702	-25.9	-12.6	4.9	-8.4
Oklahoma	154,186	155,929	158,300	162,982	167,111	170,613	-10.0	-13.4	10.7	-4.2
Oregon	132,130	139,266	144,706	148,470	149,978	151,948	-1.6	-7.0	15.0	6.9
Pennsylvania	495,670	497,785	501,639	510,969	520,963	530,912	-27.2	-16.1	7.1	-10.1
RhodeIsland	37,016	37,998	38,121	38,629	39,574	39,984	-24.1	-15.8	8.0	-9.1
South Carolina	170,079	171,431	173,159	176,745	179,875	182,281	2.0	-6.8	7.2	-0.1
South Dakota	33,995	35,153	36,691	40,544	41,677	43,194	-17.5	-7.2	27.1	17.9
Tennessee	226,484	229,080	233,430	236,542	240,821	243,169	-3.2	-5.3	7.4	1.6
Texas	871,932	889,388	907,423	927,209	956,548	990,894	24.8	0.1	13.6	13.8
Utah	121,633	129,461	133,987	141,439	146,193	149,331	63.5	16.3	22.8	42.8
Vermont	24,902	24,435	24,693	27,927	28,943	30,338	3.8	-9.3	21.8	10.5
Virginia	270,319	275,199	274,078	278,124	286,490	291,909	-3.7	-10.8	8.0	-3.6
Washington	227,112	236,546	244,732	255,528	265,207	276,563	13.0	-6.5	21.8	13.9
West Virginia	98,332	98,704	99,259	98,599	97,703	96,104	-19.3	-9.7	-2.3	-11.7
Wisconsin	232,101	234,808	240,968	248,284	259,366	267,211	-15.3	-13.0	15.1	0.1
Wyoming	27,285	28,184	28,515	29,497	30,184	30,928	16.7	-5.2	13.4	7.4
Outlying areas	181,636	185,404	186,367	186,474	185,192	186,866	—	—	2.9	—
American Samoa	3,073	3,315	3,412	3,510	3,391	3,369	—	—	9.6	—
Guam	7,115	7,534	7,649	7,767	7,996	8,083	47.0	5.0	13.6	19.3
Northern Marianas	1,531	1,468	1,953	1,808	1,870	1,984	—	—	29.6	—
Puerto Rico	164,415	167,416	167,270	167,343	165,468	167,035	15.1	-8.1	1.6	-6.7
Trust Territories	—	—	—	—	—	—	—	—	—	—
Virgin Islands	5,502	5,671	6,083	6,046	6,467	6,395	—	-18.6	16.2	-5.4

[1] Includes grades 9 through 12.
[2] Beginning in 1983, data include students enrolled in public schools on federal bases and other special arrangements.
[3] Less than 0.05 percent.

—Data not available or not applicable.

SOURCE: U.S. Department of Education, National Center for Education Statistics, "Statistics of Public Elementary and Secondary Day Schools," various years; and Common Core of Data surveys. (This table was prepared April 1997.)

Table 13.—Average daily attendance in public elementary and secondary schools, by state: 1969–70 to 1995–96

State or other area	1969–70	1970–71	1971–72	1972–73	1973–74	1974–75	1975–76	1976–77	1977–78	1978–79
1	2	3	4	5	6	7	8	9	10	11
United States	41,934,376	42,427,909	42,204,272	42,179,200	41,438,054	41,523,866	41,269,720	40,831,630	40,079,590	39,075,837
Alabama	777,123	754,014	745,818	736,000	723,399	720,643	716,371	707,332	702,880	716,744
Alaska	72,489	76,630	77,924	78,100	77,866	79,388	81,564	83,198	82,377	81,620
Arizona	391,526	403,326	428,043	441,800	451,078	470,494	455,692	468,384	470,279	475,265
Arkansas	414,158	415,267	412,405	410,900	418,602	423,648	428,720	427,385	433,282	427,961
California [1]	4,418,423	4,609,740	4,453,800	4,538,800	4,364,168	4,531,540	4,366,617	4,501,948	4,425,876	4,110,778
Colorado	500,388	512,449	525,128	533,900	532,248	529,539	527,434	526,905	523,536	510,372
Connecticut	618,881	625,439	621,461	620,100	615,443	608,638	596,175	584,805	555,449	541,079
Delaware	120,819	122,324	124,061	123,300	121,106	120,354	116,553	111,269	107,049	99,730
District of Columbia	138,600	132,419	130,040	117,200	125,953	122,685	119,255	105,203	99,863	106,292
Florida	1,312,693	1,333,414	1,353,547	1,370,600	1,401,774	1,432,716	1,435,570	1,446,745	1,444,646	1,407,914
Georgia	1,019,427	1,006,879	1,000,444	990,100	987,767	989,686	998,898	1,000,732	997,603	990,860
Hawaii	168,140	167,329	168,912	166,500	161,458	163,246	162,903	159,936	157,312	154,263
Idaho	170,920	173,444	175,746	174,400	173,795	173,416	182,215	186,886	187,769	189,634
Illinois	2,084,844	2,121,330	2,106,306	2,107,600	2,027,959	2,057,396	1,990,158	1,992,575	1,935,346	1,829,714
Indiana	1,111,043	1,130,514	1,112,047	1,113,500	1,078,995	1,076,162	1,049,889	1,055,230	1,033,180	1,010,338
Iowa	624,403	625,756	619,602	610,500	589,892	585,153	574,773	568,342	551,136	532,867
Kansas	470,296	466,026	457,153	450,400	428,388	424,985	419,022	414,580	405,469	392,500
Kentucky	647,970	662,116	666,989	660,600	652,364	645,420	622,484	636,910	637,644	632,615
Louisiana	776,555	774,312	771,940	774,300	761,593	761,532	768,097	782,535	751,221	743,364
Maine	225,146	228,270	230,976	230,900	228,360	228,172	227,841	226,411	222,550	216,965
Maryland	785,989	799,780	837,000	807,400	803,569	777,780	793,848	755,579	736,403	715,155
Massachusetts	1,056,207	1,186,783	1,076,273	1,136,400	1,066,005	1,153,485	1,070,996	1,046,854	1,001,857	970,302
Michigan	1,991,235	2,003,894	2,008,147	2,017,800	1,985,245	1,922,914	1,971,774	1,864,145	1,811,457	1,759,868
Minnesota	864,595	843,929	836,106	839,200	815,996	810,460	827,239	809,613	784,314	771,312
Mississippi	524,623	497,846	494,060	491,400	483,585	481,314	479,076	476,225	470,006	461,434
Missouri	906,132	915,385	919,749	912,500	891,564	881,147	864,958	849,443	823,733	797,512
Montana	162,664	164,185	161,494	158,900	160,870	159,399	156,473	155,453	152,187	149,306
Nebraska	314,516	316,960	314,858	310,700	303,198	301,170	296,915	293,808	286,095	278,806
Nevada	113,421	117,534	120,450	121,300	123,261	124,373	128,106	129,947	131,471	133,754
New Hampshire	140,203	145,614	153,788	157,900	156,518	158,096	159,836	160,499	158,980	157,668
New Jersey	1,322,124	1,341,155	1,337,129	1,350,800	1,328,399	1,328,551	1,310,042	1,279,498	1,236,759	1,200,781
New Mexico	259,997	258,394	260,106	257,200	254,986	254,358	256,764	260,226	259,354	256,909
New York	3,099,192	3,073,573	3,106,191	3,090,700	2,978,886	2,939,023	3,012,893	2,833,758	2,743,544	2,665,405
North Carolina	1,104,295	1,101,860	1,082,650	1,070,400	1,108,630	1,084,862	1,120,207	1,101,891	1,095,128	1,081,803
North Dakota	141,961	141,411	138,799	136,700	133,231	128,644	126,277	124,465	121,136	117,626
Ohio	2,246,282	2,238,641	2,245,779	2,217,300	2,162,033	2,134,485	2,103,243	2,058,284	1,985,160	1,914,227
Oklahoma	560,993	565,028	577,804	567,600	559,132	557,684	558,528	558,354	554,274	549,516
Oregon	436,736	438,776	435,328	430,900	429,480	428,108	425,126	426,586	425,042	422,372
Pennsylvania	2,169,225	2,192,316	2,179,947	2,163,900	2,125,465	2,090,865	2,064,312	1,999,727	1,940,316	1,877,427
Rhode Island	163,205	163,914	173,017	166,400	164,812	156,216	158,752	156,503	150,161	144,895
South Carolina	600,292	586,998	582,104	577,200	568,491	566,719	591,900	563,433	579,442	574,238
South Dakota	158,543	157,291	156,675	153,500	149,097	146,739	141,120	140,573	134,004	130,204
Tennessee	836,010	849,882	846,190	832,300	817,902	823,394	826,335	821,698	819,028	865,509
Texas	2,432,420	2,489,263	2,499,248	2,497,600	2,512,739	2,529,015	2,549,517	2,566,545	2,587,556	2,592,022
Utah	287,405	276,860	277,578	278,700	276,787	278,838	289,171	284,172	305,976	294,721
Vermont	97,772	104,576	103,324	102,800	99,375	97,575	98,015	96,851	96,234	97,213
Virginia	995,580	1,006,230	994,317	985,900	995,524	1,008,811	1,018,034	1,014,801	994,248	975,899
Washington	764,735	762,006	746,269	730,100	730,605	728,047	723,083	723,418	713,713	713,967
West Virginia	372,278	370,951	376,849	382,800	374,226	366,785	366,395	368,588	360,828	352,890
Wisconsin	880,609	894,178	899,861	903,500	876,167	879,526	858,407	839,356	810,773	794,783
Wyoming	81,293	81,698	80,840	79,900	80,104	80,670	82,147	84,026	85,944	87,438
Outlying areas	—	—	—	—	—	—	—	734,648	—	—
American Samoa	—	—	7,517	7,700	—	8,164	7,461	8,921	—	—
Guam	20,315	22,926	24,201	24,900	24,081	26,426	26,318	25,677	24,956	23,614
Northern Marianas	—	—	—	—	—	—	—	—	4,107	—
Puerto Rico	—	637,068	650,992	660,000	—	617,724	669,400	646,150	676,777	673,015
Trust Territories	—	—	—	—	—	—	—	30,122	—	—
Virgin Islands	—	—	17,680	19,400	20,572	22,128	21,793	23,778	24,136	23,289

Table 13.—Average daily attendance in public elementary and secondary schools, by state: 1969–70 to 1995–96—Continued

State or other area	1979–80	1980–81	1981–82	1982–83	1983–84	1984–85	1985–86	1986–87	1987–88	1988–89
1	12	13	14	15	16	17	18	19	20	21
United States	**38,288,911**	**37,703,744**	**37,094,652**	**36,635,868**	**36,362,978**	**36,404,261**	**36,523,103**	**36,863,867**	**37,050,707**	**37,268,072**
Alabama	711,432	701,925	690,084	682,814	679,742	684,211	686,716	690,256	689,340	684,453
Alaska	79,945	83,745	87,253	85,435	80,264	96,257	98,535	96,004	94,917	95,776
Arizona	481,905	476,149	468,081	478,664	482,185	477,520	494,504	518,277	534,812	549,219
Arkansas	423,610	417,080	410,426	406,588	404,282	405,077	408,601	409,388	405,196	403,106
California [1]	4,044,736	4,014,917	4,016,214	4,042,996	4,098,300	4,139,461	4,245,090	4,429,792	4,531,459	4,695,920
Colorado	513,475	508,750	514,808	506,425	503,162	505,321	507,876	513,587	514,838	514,232
Connecticut	507,362	501,085	484,161	470,572	452,061	446,981	452,058	444,285	441,150	435,227
Delaware	94,058	89,609	86,052	85,144	84,118	84,407	84,936	86,655	87,821	88,397
District of Columbia	91,576	85,773	82,521	79,827	77,859	76,023	76,241	76,822	79,801	74,398
Florida	1,464,461	1,389,487	1,454,118	1,368,520	1,388,717	1,416,104	1,442,921	1,489,146	1,536,866	1,587,882
Georgia	989,433	988,612	979,047	978,853	978,530	989,713	1,004,799	1,023,127	1,033,459	1,039,977
Hawaii	151,563	151,713	148,636	149,696	150,137	150,572	151,174	152,287	155,220	156,114
Idaho	189,199	190,144	190,872	192,707	194,533	197,902	198,141	198,449	199,563	201,219
Illinois	1,770,435	1,765,357	1,678,944	1,647,984	1,616,711	1,600,380	1,604,265	1,574,128	1,584,745	1,560,461
Indiana	983,444	944,424	925,411	902,672	893,464	883,592	870,463	873,733	877,942	882,175
Iowa	510,081	501,403	487,405	476,406	467,965	461,392	454,341	453,150	450,858	449,418
Kansas	382,019	374,451	371,061	370,064	368,354	369,524	371,655	378,073	384,660	385,364
Kentucky	619,868	614,676	607,376	587,615	585,861	579,441	577,190	579,226	578,550	573,221
Louisiana	727,601	715,844	716,995	709,170	724,153	732,864	732,230	736,474	729,492	744,142
Maine	211,400	207,554	201,427	197,239	200,159	198,125	198,358	197,539	197,225	194,350
Maryland	686,336	664,866	637,792	615,097	602,077	596,478	592,383	595,618	601,415	608,699
Massachusetts	935,960	950,675	852,031	826,758	806,193	779,869	745,991	727,680	749,030	756,285
Michigan	1,758,427	1,711,139	1,662,798	1,618,445	1,514,671	1,490,452	1,481,068	1,476,471	1,473,542	1,454,871
Minnesota	748,606	710,836	700,897	672,804	663,780	669,930	669,385	674,245	679,729	690,266
Mississippi	454,401	446,515	441,880	439,405	437,790	435,587	448,117	473,424	479,402	477,439
Missouri	777,269	756,536	732,526	717,994	715,182	712,197	714,230	724,710	725,661	726,451
Montana	144,608	141,641	139,434	138,801	139,387	139,905	138,829	139,199	139,018	138,016
Nebraska	270,524	263,797	258,654	254,452	252,484	250,647	250,975	252,457	252,399	253,426
Nevada	134,995	138,481	139,543	139,600	139,115	140,402	143,941	149,136	153,252	162,415
New Hampshire	154,187	150,316	148,251	146,309	144,733	144,655	147,561	149,963	152,000	152,536
New Jersey	1,140,111	1,121,272	1,110,685	1,083,217	1,037,865	1,043,047	1,029,797	1,024,611	1,008,749	968,176
New Mexico	253,453	240,496	239,710	245,919	246,451	248,758	252,892	243,340	248,231	280,921
New York	2,530,289	2,475,055	2,396,594	2,344,091	2,321,800	2,309,169	2,276,842	2,266,283	2,247,588	2,234,976
North Carolina	1,072,150	1,055,651	1,039,849	1,032,030	1,022,138	1,018,795	1,014,795	1,020,702	1,016,742	1,004,837
North Dakota	118,986	111,759	112,836	111,782	111,630	109,427	108,947	109,074	109,512	109,271
Ohio	1,849,283	1,801,914	1,748,908	1,718,878	1,693,851	1,675,530	1,660,718	1,664,709	1,612,592	1,597,117
Oklahoma	548,065	542,800	546,689	556,115	553,236	552,835	553,370	550,949	547,149	542,693
Oregon	418,593	417,009	410,107	404,458	401,398	401,154	401,476	402,855	406,054	409,717
Pennsylvania	1,808,630	1,754,782	1,691,235	1,641,763	1,601,944	1,571,831	1,560,746	1,554,642	1,539,310	1,532,806
Rhode Island	139,195	135,096	129,780	127,206	123,501	122,653	122,109	122,024	124,559	123,321
South Carolina	569,612	580,132	575,248	574,293	602,183	559,340	558,716	564,508	567,091	567,133
South Dakota	124,934	121,663	119,023	117,495	117,192	117,137	118,269	118,902	119,868	119,400
Tennessee	806,696	797,237	785,336	778,321	774,346	769,862	762,225	766,521	766,651	764,354
Texas	2,608,817	2,647,288	2,664,282	2,724,989	2,745,339	2,879,823	2,923,741	2,977,783	2,991,242	3,033,684
Utah	312,813	323,048	334,577	348,717	356,072	366,574	379,249	386,306	397,214	403,294
Vermont	95,045	90,884	88,448	87,403	86,404	85,734	85,875	85,985	87,760	88,532
Virginia	955,105	938,794	919,481	908,989	900,378	901,994	904,347	911,261	914,354	914,445
Washington	710,929	704,655	695,771	687,094	685,068	688,759	696,372	708,584	721,952	736,345
West Virginia	353,264	351,823	348,632	346,368	343,320	336,196	330,145	324,791	319,330	309,691
Wisconsin	770,554	743,505	729,889	713,196	699,089	696,071	694,351	682,560	698,963	700,389
Wyoming	89,471	91,381	92,874	94,488	93,804	94,583	95,547	94,176	92,434	91,515
Outlying areas	—	—	—	—	—	—	699,036	691,775	683,436	671,206
American Samoa	—	—	—	—	—	10,580	10,816	10,559	10,579	11,222
Guam	—	22,343	—	—	—	23,632	23,220	23,409	23,172	23,203
Northern Marianas	—	—	—	—	—	5,548	4,921	5,071	5,851	6,677
Puerto Rico	656,709	671,661	—	—	—	649,651	636,268	629,922	621,731	608,945
Trust Territories	—	—	—	—	—	—	—	—	—	—
Virgin Islands	—	23,312	—	—	—	—	23,811	22,814	22,103	21,159

Table 13.—Average daily attendance in public elementary and secondary schools, by state: 1969–70 to 1995–96—Continued

State or other area	1989–90	1990–91	1991–92	1992–93	1993–94	1994–95	1995–96	Percentage change			
								1970–71 to 1995–96	1985–86 to 1990–91	1990–91 to 1995–96	1985–86 to 1995–96
1	22	23	24	25	26	27	28	29	30	31	32
United States	37,799,296	38,426,543	38,960,783	39,570,462	40,146,393	40,720,763	41,501,596	–2.2	5.2	8.0	13.6
Alabama	683,833	682,524	681,840	694,078	696,071	687,047	687,076	–8.9	–0.6	0.7	0.1
Alaska	98,213	102,585	110,277	110,797	112,869	113,874	115,958	51.3	4.1	13.0	17.7
Arizona	557,252	573,140	593,413	610,558	631,450	658,084	684,740	69.8	15.9	19.5	38.5
Arkansas	403,025	408,145	410,902	413,076	416,479	420,229	423,520	2.0	–0.1	3.8	3.7
California [1]	4,893,341	5,065,647	4,993,009	5,066,708	5,108,907	5,198,308	5,351,475	16.1	19.3	5.6	26.1
Colorado	519,419	521,899	532,525	568,158	579,682	594,019	608,633	18.8	2.8	16.6	19.8
Connecticut	439,524	450,808	457,476	468,992	465,487	481,742	495,188	–20.8	–0.3	9.8	9.5
Delaware	89,838	91,052	93,909	95,660	97,247	98,793	99,941	–18.3	7.2	9.8	17.7
District of Columbia	71,468	69,092	70,939	71,201	70,079	71,446	71,001	–46.4	–9.4	2.8	–6.9
Florida	1,646,583	1,714,394	1,776,539	1,818,011	1,873,199	1,927,172	1,947,777	46.1	18.8	13.6	35.0
Georgia	1,054,097	1,075,728	1,098,966	1,125,385	1,148,319	1,181,724	1,232,852	22.4	7.1	14.6	22.7
Hawaii	157,360	160,193	163,212	165,851	169,779	169,254	171,977	2.8	6.0	7.4	13.8
Idaho	203,987	209,085	213,843	217,933	223,489	225,986	228,371	31.7	5.5	9.2	15.3
Illinois	1,587,733	1,618,101	1,630,534	1,685,678	1,709,915	1,734,175	1,750,417	–17.5	0.9	8.2	9.1
Indiana	884,568	888,177	895,794	897,799	899,585	900,017	909,553	–19.5	2.0	2.4	4.5
Iowa	450,224	456,614	462,360	467,788	477,916	478,285	477,053	–23.8	0.5	4.5	5.0
Kansas	388,986	397,609	405,083	408,689	410,862	413,699	416,674	–10.6	7.0	4.8	12.1
Kentucky	569,795	569,713	574,226	579,446	578,020	572,952	571,934	–13.6	–1.3	0.4	–0.9
Louisiana	727,125	720,551	732,485	722,626	732,202	730,148	710,925	–8.2	–1.6	–1.3	–2.9
Maine	195,089	196,229	198,413	200,462	199,125	199,387	200,700	–12.1	–1.1	2.3	1.2
Maryland	620,617	637,370	653,203	668,778	687,455	701,594	719,433	–10.0	7.6	12.9	21.4
Massachusetts	763,231	770,802	785,840	796,897	810,028	831,918	845,270	–28.8	3.3	9.7	13.3
Michigan	1,446,996	1,452,700	1,460,795	1,467,900	1,474,413	1,492,653	1,554,358	–22.4	–1.9	7.0	4.9
Minnesota	699,001	714,072	727,838	744,567	756,725	770,549	786,241	–6.8	6.7	10.1	17.5
Mississippi	476,048	474,029	473,398	473,262	471,367	470,974	470,657	–5.5	5.8	–0.7	5.0
Missouri	729,693	733,680	747,760	759,529	778,605	794,177	805,404	–12.0	2.7	9.8	12.8
Montana	135,406	138,341	141,316	144,718	146,849	148,325	148,616	–9.5	–0.4	7.4	7.0
Nebraska	254,754	257,587	262,429	267,975	267,931	268,732	270,938	–14.5	2.6	5.2	8.0
Nevada	173,149	185,755	195,463	204,440	217,681	229,862	243,718	107.4	29.0	31.2	69.3
New Hampshire	154,915	156,579	160,203	172,376	175,968	179,892	187,067	28.5	6.1	19.5	26.8
New Jersey	997,561	1,016,159	1,036,885	1,053,135	1,079,653	1,102,565	1,125,877	–16.1	–1.3	10.8	9.3
New Mexico	290,245	291,215	321,955	304,661	310,610	314,822	330,851	28.0	15.2	13.6	30.8
New York	2,244,110	2,278,531	2,319,738	2,347,468	2,404,426	2,388,973	2,463,349	–19.9	0.1	8.1	8.2
North Carolina	1,012,274	1,012,613	1,023,186	1,035,258	1,051,295	1,071,640	1,096,812	–0.5	–0.2	8.3	8.1
North Dakota	109,659	109,691	110,635	111,174	111,770	111,502	111,870	–20.9	0.7	2.0	2.7
Ohio	1,584,735	1,603,025	1,602,418	1,594,191	1,609,855	1,627,984	1,661,014	–25.8	–3.5	3.6	(2)
Oklahoma	543,170	548,387	556,609	560,744	566,155	570,381	574,538	1.7	–0.9	4.8	3.8
Oregon	419,771	431,806	444,272	452,509	455,492	458,107	462,108	5.3	7.6	7.0	15.1
Pennsylvania	1,524,839	1,542,077	1,568,279	1,588,514	1,609,125	1,629,877	1,651,741	–24.7	–1.2	7.1	5.8
Rhode Island	125,934	129,856	132,278	134,736	135,016	136,229	137,870	–15.9	6.3	6.2	12.9
South Carolina	569,029	573,138	578,236	581,775	586,178	608,699	605,526	3.2	2.6	5.7	8.4
South Dakota	119,823	121,403	124,171	126,916	127,550	128,335	127,754	–18.8	2.6	5.2	8.0
Tennessee	761,766	767,738	774,596	786,146	796,744	806,895	819,831	–3.5	0.7	6.8	7.6
Texas	3,075,333	3,085,648	3,175,400	3,237,958	3,306,297	3,364,830	3,435,010	38.0	5.5	11.3	17.5
Utah	408,917	417,609	426,507	432,781	439,484	442,617	444,679	60.6	10.1	6.5	17.3
Vermont	87,832	88,901	90,908	96,121	97,550	98,608	100,166	–4.2	3.5	12.7	16.6
Virginia	989,197	1,011,513	1,023,683	1,049,901	1,065,071	1,079,496	1,098,862	9.2	11.9	8.6	21.5
Washington	755,141	781,371	808,090	833,641	850,813	870,163	888,142	16.6	12.2	13.7	27.5
West Virginia	301,947	300,067	296,191	294,202	291,238	287,937	285,548	–23.0	–9.1	–4.8	–13.5
Wisconsin	711,466	731,088	748,830	765,184	769,717	782,395	799,391	–10.6	5.3	9.3	15.1
Wyoming	91,277	92,506	93,926	94,109	94,650	93,691	93,190	14.1	–3.2	0.7	–2.5
Outlying areas	658,500	661,066	623,472	620,592	661,948	621,030	622,238	—	–5.4	–5.9	–11.0
American Samoa	11,448	12,272	12,935	14,150	14,094	14,000	14,074	—	13.5	14.7	30.1
Guam	23,883	25,330	25,330	30,417	31,711	31,779	31,998	39.6	9.1	26.3	37.8
Northern Marianas	6,809	6,062	6,194	7,334	7,278	7,351	7,511	—	23.2	23.9	52.6
Puerto Rico	597,436	597,418	558,515	548,067	588,484	547,561	548,788	–13.9	–6.1	–8.1	–13.7
Trust Territories	—	—	—	—	—	—	—	—	—	—	—
Virgin Islands	18,924	19,984	20,498	20,624	20,381	20,339	19,867	—	–16.1	–0.6	–16.6

[1] Data for California are not strictly comparable with those for other states because California's attendance figures include excused absences.

[2] Less than .05 percent.

—Data not available or not applicable.

SOURCE: U.S. Department of Education, National Center for Education Statistics, "Revenues and Expenditures for Public Elementary and Secondary Education," various years; Statistics of State School Systems, various years; and Common Core of Data surveys. (This table was prepared February 1998.)

Table 14.—Number of children with disabilities served under IDEA-B and Chapter 1 of ESEA (state operated programs), by state: 1976–77 to 1996–97

State or other area	1976–77	1977–78	1978–79	1979–80	1980–81	1981–82	1982–83	1983–84	1984–85	1985–86	1986–87	1987–88
1	2	3	4	5	6	7	8	9	10	11	12	13
United States	3,691,833	3,755,354	3,893,611	4,010,109	4,146,424	4,202,831	4,259,642	4,303,630	4,320,458	4,322,080	4,379,004	4,452,206
Alabama	53,987	60,265	69,749	72,378	76,296	76,397	81,609	84,428	88,976	91,107	91,231	95,130
Alaska	9,597	9,739	9,341	10,242	10,352	11,007	12,017	11,110	11,360	11,895	12,211	12,845
Arizona	43,045	41,624	45,814	48,303	51,202	52,137	51,862	51,679	52,198	51,805	53,219	54,018
Arkansas	28,487	34,741	40,345	45,027	49,096	49,863	49,004	48,723	48,043	47,322	48,222	47,031
California	332,291	324,976	334,887	355,533	362,503	359,888	364,318	363,613	369,142	378,888	391,217	410,175
Colorado	47,943	44,770	46,676	47,228	48,677	46,147	45,126	45,634	46,805	47,953	49,515	52,042
Connecticut	62,085	60,697	61,539	62,551	67,072	66,311	66,010	65,426	65,478	65,426	64,758	64,441
Delaware	14,307	14,054	13,679	14,434	14,416	14,440	14,405	15,018	15,018	15,322	15,275	14,623
District of Columbia	9,261	5,722	7,312	5,217	6,308	6,129	5,809	7,009	7,394	7,069	7,114	7,161
Florida	117,257	125,427	128,463	136,963	144,532	149,838	155,609	158,653	165,302	172,821	181,651	194,200
Georgia	85,209	86,491	97,786	101,847	111,981	115,779	112,555	109,038	102,448	93,295	93,229	92,957
Hawaii	10,544	11,005	11,002	11,382	12,018	12,678	12,876	12,738	12,394	11,947	11,658	11,835
Idaho	14,573	17,396	17,544	18,066	16,833	17,154	17,673	17,953	18,144	19,159	18,640	19,136
Illinois	229,797	239,522	241,981	250,463	246,954	255,775	261,769	257,426	245,647	242,333	248,169	250,704
Indiana	87,644	85,360	96,836	98,818	98,916	97,647	100,228	102,996	104,183	104,417	105,978	107,682
Iowa	51,055	52,406	56,683	58,969	61,015	56,894	56,109	56,534	57,500	56,476	56,205	56,415
Kansas	37,623	35,363	37,088	38,733	40,637	42,544	44,159	42,907	41,419	41,176	42,373	42,930
Kentucky	57,057	59,350	62,975	67,087	70,628	72,057	73,170	74,492	74,901	73,560	73,711	76,573
Louisiana	86,989	87,995	93,369	85,640	82,723	81,879	86,009	85,732	81,379	76,628	73,852	68,782
Maine	23,701	21,410	24,283	24,307	25,638	25,947	26,485	27,069	27,452	27,845	26,841	28,193
Maryland	84,184	87,636	88,571	93,763	98,682	93,296	90,879	90,668	90,462	89,041	90,294	89,892
Massachusetts	131,992	136,873	140,576	141,869	141,580	139,747	138,480	139,338	140,890	141,448	143,636	145,681
Michigan	153,113	154,448	155,363	155,385	155,988	154,061	155,771	158,293	162,317	161,862	161,446	161,128
Minnesota	72,136	74,087	79,329	82,346	80,744	77,916	77,658	78,916	80,640	81,488	82,407	82,967
Mississippi	29,219	32,374	39,240	42,430	46,495	49,456	50,883	51,688	52,068	53,084	55,683	58,589
Missouri	94,387	90,580	99,542	98,134	101,076	100,931	99,984	99,141	98,570	99,378	99,692	99,721
Montana	8,610	10,444	12,549	12,781	13,424	14,279	15,215	15,480	15,930	15,376	15,369	15,343
Nebraska	25,270	27,443	31,252	30,386	30,740	31,812	30,448	30,375	30,273	30,453	30,171	30,450
Nevada	11,133	10,619	11,405	11,207	11,786	12,456	13,326	13,557	14,087	14,178	14,743	15,122
New Hampshire	9,916	10,302	10,850	12,627	12,525	14,179	14,143	15,233	15,561	16,071	16,323	16,755
New Jersey	145,077	150,046	151,992	149,578	158,469	163,686	161,481	165,622	166,982	170,512	172,018	172,829
New Mexico	15,149	16,727	19,239	20,479	24,030	24,454	26,334	27,125	28,188	29,556	29,816	31,265
New York	240,250	233,264	208,906	218,587	230,093	250,404	264,835	280,857	289,320	289,583	292,981	288,363
North Carolina	98,035	97,807	108,197	114,894	119,018	120,041	120,586	121,755	119,688	112,934	109,214	109,276
North Dakota	8,976	9,124	9,660	9,776	9,426	10,212	10,802	11,569	11,941	11,850	12,279	12,483
Ohio	168,314	176,453	190,989	201,352	207,875	210,445	202,234	201,150	201,169	198,956	199,211	198,240
Oklahoma	44,181	50,004	57,809	60,997	63,547	65,479	65,819	65,401	65,093	65,081	65,285	63,735
Oregon	37,258	36,316	41,260	44,145	44,809	45,278	46,201	46,872	48,153	46,575	47,487	48,382
Pennsylvania	206,792	182,840	186,522	190,244	198,108	190,919	196,277	196,442	196,779	202,357	203,258	208,518
Rhode Island	15,971	14,092	14,328	16,071	17,577	18,435	18,589	18,354	19,045	19,152	19,527	19,855
South Carolina	72,357	71,144	70,336	71,466	69,973	69,476	71,705	72,452	72,610	72,157	73,299	74,968
South Dakota	9,936	9,098	9,479	9,850	10,138	11,522	11,841	11,870	13,008	13,629	14,034	14,420
Tennessee	99,251	96,378	93,054	93,004	95,168	102,459	106,091	103,867	98,954	95,380	96,433	98,289
Texas	233,552	281,468	273,499	267,612	275,921	281,873	289,343	295,637	294,830	293,418	301,222	311,459
Utah	37,204	36,169	35,265	36,127	35,898	37,584	38,968	41,144	41,809	41,791	42,811	44,824
Vermont	6,382	7,632	12,130	12,424	12,059	11,563	9,309	9,880	10,256	10,665	11,405	11,930
Virginia	77,616	81,329	87,173	91,051	97,972	99,571	100,713	102,556	103,374	102,814	103,727	105,641
Washington	57,705	51,088	51,876	54,049	63,509	63,916	64,295	66,855	67,859	68,451	70,282	73,613
West Virginia	30,135	29,874	31,293	33,964	36,573	39,554	42,418	42,796	44,153	46,409	47,556	46,422
Wisconsin	58,019	59,316	60,483	65,611	69,957	71,593	72,219	73,823	74,861	75,945	76,067	77,968
Wyoming	7,261	8,068	9,542	9,873	10,837	10,844	11,144	11,511	11,041	10,654	10,893	10,894
Bureau of Indian Affairs	—	3,998	4,550	4,839	4,630	4,859	4,849	5,225	5,364	5,388	5,366	6,311
Outlying areas	16,768	21,946	25,462	26,110	31,265	—	—	—	—	—	—	—
American Samoa	139	208	240	167	220	204	244	428	116	201	178	248
Guam	2,597	4,016	2,619	1,790	2,085	2,123	2,031	2,065	1,995	1,929	1,852	1,883
Northern Marianas	—	17	65	58	154	—	—	—	—	—	585	804
Palau	—	—	—	—	—	—	—	—	—	—	—	—
Puerto Rico	11,200	15,330	19,968	21,035	25,333	27,852	35,173	35,153	40,327	44,620	39,858	37,694
Trust Territories	1,120	1,243	1,480	1,742	1,917	—	—	—	—	—	—	—
Virgin Islands	1,712	1,132	1,090	1,318	1,556	272	1,237	123	135	1,414	124	1,445

Table 14.—Number of children with disabilities served under IDEA-B and Chapter 1 of ESEA (state operated programs), by state: 1976–77 to 1996–97—Continued

| State or other area | 1988–89 | 1989–90 | 1990–91 | 1991–92 | 1992–93 | 1993–94 | 1994–95 | 1995–96 | 1996–97 | Percentage change | | | |
										1976–77 to 1996–97	1986–87 to 1991–92	1991–92 to 1996–97	1986–87 to 1996–97
1	14	15	16	17	18	19	20	21	22	23	24	25	26
United States	**4,526,963**	**4,647,566**	**4,768,739**	**4,954,966**	**5,182,651**	**5,370,501**	**5,546,432**	**5,753,007**	**5,927,959**	**60.6**	**13.2**	**19.6**	**35.4**
Alabama	103,211	100,195	94,945	96,975	97,685	100,174	100,473	99,594	99,302	83.9	6.3	2.4	8.8
Alaska	13,392	14,135	14,745	16,106	17,400	18,006	17,942	18,036	18,061	88.2	31.9	12.1	47.9
Arizona	55,156	56,603	57,235	61,076	66,410	70,167	73,914	77,688	81,099	88.4	14.8	32.8	52.4
Arkansas	47,659	47,376	47,835	49,018	52,407	53,985	54,279	56,055	57,475	101.8	1.7	17.3	19.2
California	430,522	448,747	469,282	494,058	524,700	548,336	563,489	583,789	604,075	81.8	26.3	22.3	54.4
Colorado	53,017	55,022	57,102	60,357	65,730	68,720	71,496	73,633	73,992	54.3	21.9	22.6	49.4
Connecticut	63,503	63,474	64,562	66,192	69,546	71,863	75,695	78,549	84,412	36.0	2.2	27.5	30.3
Delaware	13,908	13,726	14,294	14,435	15,104	16,139	16,701	17,012	16,421	14.8	–5.5	13.8	7.5
District of Columbia	7,213	6,153	6,290	7,104	7,563	7,740	6,831	7,398	7,059	–23.8	–0.1	–0.6	–0.8
Florida	207,939	221,350	236,013	253,606	266,430	286,772	301,723	320,955	334,707	185.4	39.6	32.0	84.3
Georgia	94,065	98,479	101,997	107,660	118,144	125,846	132,451	138,514	144,512	69.6	15.5	34.2	55.0
Hawaii	12,255	12,825	13,169	14,163	17,123	18,101	19,020	19,903	20,350	93.0	21.5	43.7	74.6
Idaho	19,436	21,846	22,017	22,755	23,302	23,571	23,737	24,671	26,128	79.3	22.1	14.8	40.2
Illinois	235,654	249,158	239,185	245,931	249,719	253,412	258,461	265,456	275,198	19.8	–0.9	11.9	10.9
Indiana	109,838	112,118	114,643	118,924	124,695	129,440	132,714	138,150	142,667	62.8	12.2	20.0	34.6
Iowa	57,563	58,580	60,695	61,510	62,531	63,373	65,034	66,914	69,060	35.3	9.4	12.3	22.9
Kansas	43,416	43,708	45,212	47,063	49,013	50,567	52,861	55,031	56,845	51.1	11.1	20.8	34.2
Kentucky	76,500	78,618	79,421	81,681	81,524	80,539	82,021	84,524	87,137	52.7	10.8	6.7	18.2
Louisiana	69,365	71,082	73,663	78,760	82,388	87,236	91,344	93,304	94,727	8.9	6.6	20.3	28.3
Maine	27,908	28,190	27,987	27,891	29,761	30,106	31,037	32,719	33,678	42.1	3.9	20.7	25.5
Maryland	87,019	87,905	91,940	92,520	94,922	97,998	100,565	104,558	108,453	28.8	2.5	17.2	20.1
Massachusetts	149,770	152,325	154,616	156,633	164,197	160,275	164,784	165,680	168,082	27.3	9.0	7.3	17.0
Michigan	160,917	163,204	166,927	172,238	177,053	181,709	186,431	193,152	198,772	29.8	6.7	15.4	23.1
Minnesota	81,565	79,980	80,896	83,028	86,323	90,850	96,539	100,888	103,929	44.1	0.8	25.2	26.1
Mississippi	59,180	59,900	60,934	61,197	63,280	64,287	65,912	67,520	66,161	126.4	9.9	8.1	18.8
Missouri	100,665	100,667	101,955	105,521	110,603	114,008	119,148	123,811	127,864	35.5	5.8	21.2	28.3
Montana	15,830	16,491	17,204	18,038	18,725	18,401	18,161	18,876	19,119	122.1	17.4	6.0	24.4
Nebraska	31,458	31,384	32,761	35,975	35,704	37,203	38,763	39,926	40,578	60.6	19.2	12.8	34.5
Nevada	16,070	17,047	18,440	20,530	23,074	25,242	27,091	29,043	30,913	177.7	39.3	50.6	109.7
New Hampshire	17,685	19,242	19,658	21,047	22,992	23,373	24,546	26,163	27,592	178.3	28.9	31.1	69.0
New Jersey	174,982	177,158	181,319	184,621	188,511	190,407	194,940	200,469	206,252	42.2	7.3	11.7	19.9
New Mexico	31,605	33,216	36,037	38,207	41,961	44,424	46,844	49,325	51,280	238.5	28.1	34.2	72.0
New York	294,675	295,692	307,458	324,677	339,686	365,697	383,822	407,421	427,907	78.1	10.8	31.8	46.1
North Carolina	113,922	119,573	123,126	127,867	139,153	142,735	145,510	151,414	158,272	61.4	17.1	23.8	44.9
North Dakota	12,729	12,905	12,504	12,679	12,714	12,440	12,386	12,581	12,991	44.7	3.3	2.5	5.8
Ohio	200,527	200,623	205,440	210,268	228,139	233,820	239,696	242,734	243,312	44.6	5.6	15.7	22.1
Oklahoma	64,247	65,417	65,653	68,576	71,603	73,130	72,496	73,495	75,601	71.1	5.0	10.2	15.8
Oregon	49,079	55,919	55,149	56,702	58,016	63,212	60,619	66,156	65,543	75.9	19.4	15.6	38.0
Pennsylvania	213,606	217,868	219,428	214,035	209,578	211,422	213,785	218,556	222,494	7.6	5.3	4.0	9.5
Rhode Island	20,172	20,468	21,076	21,588	22,942	23,582	24,494	26,048	27,354	71.3	10.6	26.7	40.1
South Carolina	76,148	76,965	77,765	79,872	81,103	81,930	84,217	88,419	92,787	28.2	9.0	16.2	26.6
South Dakota	14,414	14,625	14,987	15,284	15,557	15,923	16,114	15,888	15,485	55.8	8.9	1.3	10.3
Tennessee	100,171	101,194	104,898	111,315	116,577	120,524	126,909	129,617	128,672	29.6	15.4	15.6	33.4
Texas	324,056	335,481	350,636	367,860	390,073	412,039	430,010	451,590	472,661	102.4	22.1	28.5	56.9
Utah	43,763	44,777	47,747	50,009	52,045	52,338	52,778	54,527	55,848	50.1	16.8	11.7	30.5
Vermont	12,685	13,748	12,263	11,101	10,584	10,526	11,034	11,587	12,076	89.2	–2.7	8.8	5.9
Virginia	105,766	106,221	113,971	122,647	127,484	131,879	138,252	143,985	146,840	89.2	18.2	19.7	41.6
Washington	77,041	82,189	85,395	91,286	96,650	101,534	106,725	108,851	109,227	89.3	29.9	19.7	55.4
West Virginia	45,034	43,840	43,135	44,338	45,469	44,730	46,853	48,151	49,092	62.9	–6.8	10.7	3.2
Wisconsin	79,743	82,695	86,930	91,742	97,952	102,412	105,536	110,029	114,407	97.2	20.6	24.7	50.4
Wyoming	10,919	10,865	11,202	11,935	12,228	12,480	12,573	12,983	13,298	83.1	9.6	11.4	22.1
Bureau of Indian Affairs	—	6,597	6,997	6,365	6,578	5,878	7,676	7,669	8,192	—	18.6	28.7	52.7
Outlying areas	41,155	—	39,445	39,203	43,580	52,830	49,139	51,823	55,243	229.5	—	40.9	—
American Samoa	334	397	363	322	433	418	479	400	415	198.6	80.9	28.9	133.1
Guam	1,847	1,793	1,750	1,619	1,710	1,918	1,909	1,980	2,099	–19.2	–12.6	29.6	13.3
Northern Marianas	890	212	411	426	401	496	256	331	379	—	–27.2	–11.0	–35.2
Palau	—	—	459	456	390	447	152	120	116	—	—	–74.6	—
Puerto Rico	36,243	36,197	35,129	34,981	39,118	48,105	44,693	47,230	50,726	352.9	–12.2	45.0	27.3
Trust Territories	421	—	—	—	—	—	—	—	—	—	—	—	—
Virgin Islands	1,420	1,438	1,333	1,399	1,528	1,446	1,650	1,762	1,508	–11.9	1,028.2	7.8	1,116.1

—Data not available or not applicable.

NOTE.—IDEA-B is the Individuals with Disabilities Education Act (formerly known as EHA-B). IDEA-B child count includes children ages 3–21 from 1976–77 to 1984–85 and ages 3–22+ from 1985–86 to 1991–92. Chapter 1 of Elementary and Secondary Education Act (state operated programs) child count includes children ages 0–20 from 1976–77 to 1987–88 and ages 0–21 from 1988–89 to 1994–95. Includes children enrolled in public or private school programs.

SOURCE: U.S. Department of Education, Office of Special Education and Rehabilitative Services, "Annual Report to Congress on the Implementation of The Education of the Handicapped Act," various years. (This table was prepared May 1998.)

Table 15.—Mathematics achievement of 8th graders and 4th graders in public schools, by region and state: 1990, 1992, and 1996

Region and state	Average proficiency, all content areas			Percent attaining mathematics achievement levels:[1] 1996			
	1990	1992	1996	Below basic	Basic or above [2]	Proficient or above [3]	Advanced [4]
1	2	3	4	5	6	7	8
United States	262 (1.4)	266 (1.0)	271 (1.1)	38 (1.1)	62 (1.1)	24 (1.1)	4 (0.5)
Region							
Northeast	270 (3.3)	267 (3.0)	277 (3.1)	33 (3.1)	67 (3.1)	27 (3.7)	5 (1.9)
Southeast	254 (2.6)	258 (1.2)	266 (2.6)	44 (3.2)	56 (3.2)	18 (1.8)	3 (0.6)
Central	265 (2.3)	273 (2.2)	277 (3.1)	31 (3.4)	69 (3.4)	29 (2.5)	5 (1.0)
West	261 (2.6)	267 (2.1)	269 (2.2)	41 (2.2)	59 (2.2)	22 (1.9)	3 (0.6)
State							
Alabama	253 (1.1)	251 (1.7)	257 (2.1)	55 (2.6)	45 (2.6)	12 (1.8)	1 (0.4)
Alaska	— —	— —	278 (1.8)	32 (2.3)	68 (2.3)	30 (1.6)	7 (1.1)
Arizona	260 (1.3)	5 265 (1.3)	268 (1.6)	43 (1.9)	57 (1.9)	18 (1.2)	2 (0.3)
Arkansas	256 (0.9)	255 (1.2)	262 (1.5)	48 (1.8)	52 (1.8)	13 (1.0)	2 (0.4)
California	256 (1.3)	260 (1.7)	263 (1.9)	49 (2.1)	51 (2.1)	17 (1.5)	3 (0.5)
Colorado	267 (0.9)	5 272 (1.1)	276 (1.1)	33 (1.3)	67 (1.3)	25 (1.3)	3 (0.5)
Connecticut	270 (1.0)	5 273 (1.1)	280 (1.1)	30 (1.4)	70 (1.4)	31 (1.5)	5 (0.6)
Delaware	261 (0.9)	262 (1.0)	267 (0.9)	45 (1.3)	55 (1.3)	19 (1.0)	3 (0.6)
District of Columbia	231 (0.9)	5 234 (0.9)	233 (1.3)	80 (1.2)	20 (1.2)	5 (0.8)	1 (0.3)
Florida	255 (1.3)	259 (1.5)	264 (1.8)	46 (2.1)	54 (2.1)	17 (1.3)	2 (0.4)
Georgia	259 (1.3)	259 (1.2)	262 (1.6)	49 (2.0)	51 (2.0)	16 (1.8)	2 (0.5)
Hawaii	251 (0.8)	5 257 (0.9)	262 (1.0)	49 (1.5)	51 (1.5)	16 (0.9)	2 (0.4)
Idaho	271 (0.8)	5 274 (0.8)	— —	— —	— —	— —	— —
Indiana	267 (1.1)	269 (1.2)	276 (1.4)	32 (2.0)	68 (2.0)	24 (1.7)	3 (0.5)
Iowa	278 (1.1)	5 283 (1.0)	284 (1.3)	22 (1.4)	78 (1.4)	31 (1.8)	4 (0.6)
Kentucky	257 (1.2)	5 261 (1.1)	267 (1.1)	44 (1.6)	56 (1.6)	16 (1.2)	1 (0.3)
Louisiana	246 (1.2)	249 (1.7)	252 (1.6)	62 (2.0)	38 (2.0)	7 (1.1)	0 (0.2)
Maine	— —	278 (1.0)	284 (1.3)	23 (1.5)	77 (1.5)	31 (1.7)	6 (0.7)
Maryland	261 (1.4)	264 (1.3)	270 (2.1)	43 (2.2)	57 (2.2)	24 (2.3)	5 (1.0)
Massachusetts	— —	272 (1.0)	278 (1.7)	32 (2.3)	68 (2.3)	28 (1.8)	5 (0.8)
Michigan	264 (1.2)	267 (1.4)	277 (1.8)	33 (2.1)	67 (2.1)	28 (1.8)	4 (0.8)
Minnesota	275 (0.9)	5 282 (1.0)	284 (1.3)	25 (1.5)	75 (1.5)	34 (1.8)	6 (0.8)
Mississippi	— —	246 (1.2)	250 (1.2)	64 (1.3)	36 (1.3)	7 (0.8)	0 (0.2)
Missouri	— —	270 (1.2)	273 (1.4)	36 (2.0)	64 (2.0)	22 (1.4)	2 (0.5)
Montana	— —	— —	283 (1.3)	25 (1.7)	75 (1.7)	32 (1.5)	5 (0.5)
Nebraska	276 (1.0)	277 (1.1)	283 (1.0)	24 (1.1)	76 (1.1)	31 (1.5)	5 (0.7)
Nevada	— —	— —	— —	— —	— —	— —	— —
New Hampshire	273 (0.9)	5 278 (1.0)	— —	— —	— —	— —	— —
New Jersey	270 (1.1)	271 (1.6)	— —	— —	— —	— —	— —
New Mexico	256 (0.7)	5 259 (0.9)	262 (1.2)	49 (1.6)	51 (1.6)	14 (1.1)	2 (0.3)
New York	261 (1.4)	266 (2.1)	270 (1.7)	39 (2.0)	61 (2.0)	22 (1.5)	3 (0.5)
North Carolina	250 (1.1)	5 258 (1.2)	268 (1.4)	44 (1.8)	56 (1.8)	20 (1.3)	3 (0.6)
North Dakota	281 (1.2)	283 (1.2)	284 (0.9)	23 (1.2)	77 (1.2)	33 (1.5)	4 (0.7)
Ohio	264 (1.0)	267 (1.5)	— —	— —	— —	— —	— —
Oregon	— —	— —	276 (1.5)	33 (1.7)	67 (1.7)	26 (1.6)	4 (0.7)
Oklahoma	263 (1.3)	5 267 (1.2)	— —	— —	— —	— —	— —
Pennsylvania	266 (1.6)	271 (1.5)	— —	— —	— —	— —	— —
Rhode Island	260 (0.6)	5 265 (0.7)	269 (0.9)	40 (1.6)	60 (1.6)	20 (1.3)	3 (0.4)
South Carolina	— —	260 (1.0)	261 (1.5)	52 (1.7)	48 (1.7)	14 (1.2)	2 (0.4)
Tennessee	— —	258 (1.4)	263 (1.4)	47 (1.8)	53 (1.8)	15 (1.3)	2 (0.3)
Texas	258 (1.4)	5 264 (1.3)	270 (1.4)	41 (1.8)	59 (1.8)	21 (1.5)	3 (0.4)
Utah	— —	274 (0.7)	277 (1.0)	30 (1.5)	70 (1.5)	24 (1.3)	3 (0.4)
Vermont	— —	— —	279 (1.0)	28 (1.7)	72 (1.7)	27 (1.4)	4 (0.6)
Virginia	264 (1.5)	267 (1.2)	270 (1.6)	42 (2.0)	58 (2.0)	21 (1.2)	3 (0.4)
Washington	— —	— —	276 (1.3)	33 (1.6)	67 (1.6)	26 (1.2)	4 (0.7)
West Virginia	256 (1.0)	258 (1.0)	265 (1.0)	46 (1.6)	54 (1.6)	14 (0.9)	1 (0.4)
Wisconsin	274 (1.3)	277 (1.5)	283 (1.5)	25 (2.0)	75 (2.0)	32 (2.0)	5 (0.8)
Wyoming	272 (0.7)	5 274 (0.9)	275 (0.9)	32 (1.2)	68 (1.2)	22 (1.0)	2 (0.6)
Department of Defense Domestic Dependent Elementary and Secondary Schools	— —	— —	269 (2.3)	43 (3.1)	57 (3.1)	21 (2.4)	5 (1.1)
Department of Defense Overseas Schools	— —	— —	275 (0.9)	35 (1.4)	65 (1.4)	23 (0.2)	3 (0.6)
Guam	233 (0.7)	235 (1.0)	239 (1.7)	71 (1.6)	29 (1.6)	6 (0.8)	— —
Virgin Islands	219 (0.9)	222 (1.1)	— —	— —	— —	— —	— —

Table 15.—Mathematics achievement of 8th graders and 4th graders in public schools, by region and state: 1990, 1992, and 1996—Continued

Region and state	4th grade					
	Average proficiency, all content areas		Percent attaining mathematics achievement levels,[1] 1996			
	1992	1996	Below basic	Basic or above[2]	Proficient or above[3]	Advanced[4]
1	9	10	11	12	13	14
United States	**217 (0.8)**	**224 (1.0)**	**36 (1.4)**	**64 (1.4)**	**21 (1.0)**	**2 (0.3)**
Region						
Northeast	223 (2.1)	228 (2.0)	30 (2.9)	70 (2.9)	26 (1.6)	3 (0.9)
Southeast	209 (1.9)	218 (1.9)	45 (2.9)	55 (2.9)	16 (2.4)	2 (0.8)
Central	222 (2.2)	231 (2.9)	25 (2.6)	75 (2.6)	27 (2.1)	2 (0.6)
West	217 (1.6)	220 (1.7)	42 (2.8)	58 (2.8)	18 (1.7)	2 (0.5)
State						
Alabama	207 (1.6)	212 (1.2)	52 (2.0)	48 (2.0)	11 (1.1)	1 (0.2)
Alaska	— —	224 (1.3)	35 (2.0)	65 (2.0)	21 (1.2)	2 (0.5)
Arizona	214 (1.1)	218 (1.7)	43 (2.4)	57 (2.4)	15 (1.6)	1 (0.4)
Arkansas	209 (0.9)	216 (1.5)	46 (2.2)	54 (2.2)	13 (1.4)	1 (0.3)
California	207 (1.6)	209 (1.8)	54 (2.4)	46 (2.4)	11 (1.5)	1 (0.4)
Colorado	220 (1.0)	226 (1.0)	33 (1.6)	67 (1.6)	22 (1.3)	2 (0.3)
Connecticut	226 (1.2)	232 (1.1)	25 (1.5)	75 (1.5)	31 (1.7)	3 (0.5)
Delaware	217 (0.8)	215 (0.6)	46 (1.1)	54 (1.1)	16 (1.2)	1 (0.4)
District of Columbia	191 (0.5)	187 (1.1)	80 (0.8)	20 (0.8)	5 (0.5)	1 (0.4)
Florida	212 (1.5)	216 (1.2)	45 (1.7)	55 (1.7)	15 (1.1)	1 (0.2)
Georgia	214 (1.3)	215 (1.5)	47 (2.1)	53 (2.1)	13 (1.3)	1 (0.3)
Hawaii	213 (1.3)	215 (1.5)	47 (1.6)	53 (1.6)	16 (1.1)	2 (0.4)
Idaho	220 (1.0)	— —	— —	— —	— —	— —
Indiana	220 (1.1)	229 (1.0)	28 (1.7)	72 (1.7)	24 (1.6)	2 (0.5)
Iowa	229 (1.1)	229 (1.1)	26 (1.4)	74 (1.4)	22 (1.4)	1 (0.4)
Kentucky	214 (1.0)	220 (1.1)	40 (1.8)	60 (1.8)	16 (1.1)	1 (0.3)
Louisiana	203 (1.4)	209 (1.1)	56 (1.8)	44 (1.8)	8 (0.9)	0 (0.2)
Maine	231 (1.0)	232 (1.0)	25 (1.4)	75 (1.4)	27 (1.4)	3 (0.6)
Maryland	216 (1.3)	221 (1.6)	41 (1.8)	59 (1.8)	22 (1.7)	3 (0.7)
Massachusetts	226 (1.2)	229 (1.4)	29 (1.8)	71 (1.8)	24 (1.9)	2 (0.5)
Michigan	219 (1.8)	226 (1.3)	32 (1.8)	68 (1.8)	23 (1.5)	2 (0.5)
Minnesota	227 (0.9)	232 (1.1)	24 (1.5)	76 (1.5)	29 (1.5)	3 (0.5)
Mississippi	200 (1.1)	208 (1.2)	58 (1.9)	42 (1.9)	8 (0.9)	0 (0.2)
Missouri	221 (1.2)	225 (1.1)	34 (1.7)	66 (1.7)	20 (1.3)	1 (0.3)
Montana	— —	228 (1.2)	29 (1.9)	71 (1.9)	22 (1.6)	1 (0.4)
Nebraska	224 (1.3)	228 (1.2)	30 (1.6)	70 (1.6)	24 (1.4)	2 (0.3)
Nevada	— —	218 (1.3)	43 (1.8)	57 (1.8)	14 (1.2)	1 (0.3)
New Hampshire	229 (1.2)	— —	— —	— —	— —	— —
New Jersey	226 (1.5)	227 (1.5)	32 (2.1)	68 (2.1)	25 (1.7)	3 (0.7)
New Mexico	212 (1.5)	214 (1.8)	49 (2.4)	51 (2.4)	13 (1.2)	1 (0.3)
New York	217 (1.3)	223 (1.2)	36 (1.8)	64 (1.8)	20 (1.2)	2 (0.4)
North Carolina	211 (1.1)	224 (1.2)	36 (1.6)	64 (1.6)	21 (1.3)	2 (0.4)
North Dakota	228 (0.8)	231 (1.2)	25 (1.9)	75 (1.9)	24 (1.3)	2 (0.5)
Ohio	217 (1.2)	— —	— —	— —	— —	— —
Oregon	— —	223 (1.4)	35 (2.2)	65 (2.2)	21 (1.3)	2 (0.5)
Oklahoma	219 (1.0)	— —	— —	— —	— —	— —
Pennsylvania	223 (1.4)	226 (1.2)	32 (1.8)	68 (1.8)	20 (1.5)	1 (0.3)
Rhode Island	214 (1.6)	220 (1.4)	39 (2.0)	61 (2.0)	17 (1.3)	1 (0.3)
South Carolina	211 (1.1)	213 (1.3)	52 (2.0)	48 (2.0)	12 (1.3)	1 (0.3)
Tennessee	209 (1.4)	219 (1.4)	42 (2.0)	58 (2.0)	17 (1.5)	1 (0.3)
Texas	217 (1.3)	229 (1.4)	31 (1.9)	69 (1.9)	25 (1.5)	3 (0.5)
Utah	223 (1.0)	227 (1.2)	31 (1.6)	69 (1.6)	23 (1.3)	2 (0.4)
Vermont	— —	225 (1.2)	33 (2.1)	67 (2.1)	23 (1.1)	3 (0.5)
Virginia	220 (1.3)	223 (1.4)	38 (2.2)	62 (2.2)	19 (1.5)	2 (0.5)
Washington	— —	225 (1.2)	33 (1.8)	67 (1.8)	21 (1.2)	1 (0.2)
West Virginia	214 (1.1)	223 (1.0)	37 (1.6)	63 (1.6)	19 (1.2)	2 (0.5)
Wisconsin	228 (1.1)	231 (1.0)	26 (1.2)	74 (1.2)	27 (1.3)	3 (0.6)
Wyoming	224 (1.0)	223 (1.4)	36 (1.7)	64 (1.7)	19 (1.2)	1 (0.3)
Department of Defense Domestic Dependent Elementary and Secondary Schools	— —	224 (1.0)	2 (0.6)	20 (1.5)	64 (1.7)	36 (1.7)
Department of Defense Overseas Schools	— —	223 (0.7)	36 (1.4)	64 (1.4)	19 (0.5)	1 (0.0)
Guam	193 (0.8)	188 (1.3)	77 (1.4)	23 (1.4)	3 (0.5)	0 (0.2)
Virgin Islands	— —	— —	— —	— —	— —	— —

[1] Achievement levels are in developmental status.

[2] This level denotes partial mastery of prerequisite knowledge and skills that are fundamental for proficient work at this grade level.

[3] This level represents solid academic mastery for this grade level. Students reaching this level have demonstrated competency over challenging subject matter, including subject-matter knowledge, application of such knowledge to real-world situations, and analytical skills appropriate to the subject matter.

[4] This level signifies superior performance.

[5] Statistically significant increases from 1990 to 1992.

—Data not available.

NOTE.—These test scores are from the National Assessment of Educational Progress (NAEP). In 1990, 37 states, territories, and jurisdictions participated in the State Trial Assessment of 8th graders. In 1992, 44 states, territories, or jurisdictions participated in the 8th grade assessment, and 43 participated in the 4th grade assessment. In 1996, there were 44 participants for 8th grade, and 47 for 4th grade. Standard errors are in parentheses.

SOURCE: U.S. Department of Education, National Center for Education Statistics, National Assessment of Educational Progress, *NAEP 1992 Mathematics Report Card for the Nation and the States,* and *1996 Report Card for the Nation and the States,* prepared by Educational Testing Service. (This table was prepared February 1998.)

Table 16.—Average proficiency in reading for 4th graders in public schools,[1] by selected characteristics, region, and state: 1994

Region and state	Average	Race/ethnicity[2]			Sex	
		White	Black	Hispanic	Male	Female
1	2	3	4	5	6	7
United States	**212 (1.1)**	**223 (1.3)**	**186 (1.7)**	**188 (2.7)**	**207 (1.3)**	**218 (1.2)**
Region						
Northeast	212 (2.2)	224 (2.5)	184 (2.1)	191 (4.2)	207 (3.0)	216 (2.2)
Southeast	208 (2.0)	219 (2.4)	188 (2.5)	184 (4.1)	202 (2.5)	215 (2.2)
Central	218 (2.7)	225 (2.8)	182 (6.4)	199 (6.7)	212 (2.6)	225 (3.0)
West	212 (2.2)	222 (2.0)	186 (4.8)	186 (4.4)	5207 (2.5)	217 (2.5)
State						
Alabama	208 (1.5)	220 (1.5)	188 (1.9)	178 (4.3)	203 (1.9)	213 (1.6)
Arizona	206 (1.9)	220 (1.6)	183 (5.7)	188 (2.6)	201 (2.2)	211 (2.1)
Arkansas	209 (1.7)	218 (1.7)	183 (2.3)	192 (4.2)	204 (1.9)	213 (1.8)
California	197 (1.8)	211 (2.0)	182 (4.9)	174 (2.4)	194 (1.9)	200 (2.2)
Colorado	213 (1.3)	222 (1.3)	191 (4.7)	193 (2.1)	209 (1.8)	218 (1.5)
Connecticut	222 (1.6)	234 (1.3)	190 (4.8)	190 (3.9)	218 (1.8)	226 (2.0)
Delaware	206 (1.1)	215 (1.3)	188 (2.4)	190 (3.1)	200 (2.1)	212 (1.5)
Florida	205 (1.7)	218 (1.6)	183 (2.4)	189 (3.1)	199 (2.1)	210 (1.8)
Georgia	207 (2.4)	222 (1.9)	185 (3.2)	184 (5.7)	201 (3.0)	212 (2.2)
Hawaii	201 (1.7)	219 (2.1)	189 (4.5)	185 (4.0)	194 (2.1)	208 (1.7)
Indiana	220 (1.3)	225 (1.4)	193 (2.5)	201 (3.5)	216 (1.5)	223 (1.5)
Iowa	223 (1.3)	225 (1.2)	5 186 (7.0)	204 (4.1)	219 (1.6)	227 (1.5)
Kentucky	212 (1.6)	215 (1.6)	190 (3.4)	196 (4.1)	206 (1.8)	217 (2.0)
Louisiana	197 (1.3)	213 (1.4)	180 (1.6)	175 (5.0)	193 (1.6)	200 (1.7)
Maine	228 (1.3)	229 (1.3)	(4) (4)	218 (4.6)	225 (1.6)	231 (1.6)
Maryland	210 (1.5)	223 (1.5)	185 (2.3)	197 (3.5)	205 (1.8)	214 (1.8)
Massachusetts	223 (1.3)	231 (1.2)	199 (3.1)	194 (2.8)	5 221 (1.5)	226 (1.5)
Minnesota	218 (1.4)	222 (1.1)	173 (8.0)	202 (4.4)	214 (1.5)	223 (1.9)
Mississippi	202 (1.6)	220 (2.0)	187 (2.1)	181 (3.9)	196 (1.6)	207 (1.9)
Missouri	217 (1.5)	223 (1.3)	192 (4.1)	200 (3.9)	213 (1.9)	221 (1.8)
Montana[6]	222 (1.4)	226 (1.3)	(4) (4)	208 (3.2)	218 (1.6)	227 (1.7)
Nebraska[6]	220 (1.5)	224 (1.4)	5 190 (5.5)	205 (3.9)	216 (1.5)	224 (1.9)
New Hampshire[6]	223 (1.5)	224 (1.5)	(4) (4)	213 (4.8)	218 (1.6)	229 (1.8)
New Jersey	219 (1.2)	231 (1.2)	193 (3.4)	200 (2.5)	216 (1.5)	222 (1.3)
New Mexico	205 (1.7)	219 (1.7)	196 (7.0)	196 (2.2)	201 (2.1)	208 (1.8)
New York	212 (1.4)	226 (1.7)	191 (1.9)	193 (2.6)	207 (1.8)	216 (1.6)
North Carolina	214 (1.5)	225 (1.6)	193 (1.9)	189 (4.4)	209 (1.7)	220 (1.8)
North Dakota	225 (1.2)	228 (1.2)	(4) (4)	212 (2.9)	221 (1.5)	230 (1.5)
Pennsylvania[6]	215 (1.6)	224 (1.3)	180 (3.8)	187 (3.9)	211 (1.8)	220 (1.9)
Rhode Island[6]	220 (1.3)	226 (1.4)	197 (2.4)	195 (2.8)	215 (1.5)	225 (1.5)
South Carolina	203 (1.4)	219 (1.4)	184 (1.7)	182 (3.3)	199 (1.7)	208 (1.6)
Tennessee[6]	213 (1.7)	220 (1.8)	188 (3.0)	196 (6.7)	208 (2.1)	217 (1.9)
Texas	212 (1.9)	227 (1.7)	191 (4.4)	198 (1.9)	210 (2.0)	214 (2.1)
Utah	217 (1.3)	221 (1.3)	(4) (4)	199 (2.5)	213 (1.7)	222 (1.3)
Virginia	213 (1.5)	224 (1.6)	192 (1.9)	206 (3.4)	208 (1.8)	219 (1.5)
Washington	213 (1.5)	217 (1.5)	198 (3.1)	190 (3.6)	209 (1.8)	217 (1.7)
West Virginia	213 (1.1)	215 (1.0)	202 (4.2)	192 (4.8)	208 (1.4)	218 (1.4)
Wisconsin[6]	224 (1.1)	228 (1.1)	197 (3.5)	203 (4.3)	221 (1.2)	227 (1.5)
Wyoming	221 (1.2)	224 (1.2)	(4) (4)	209 (3.1)	218 (1.3)	224 (1.6)
Department of Defense Overseas Schools	218 (0.9)	224 (1.2)	205 (1.9)	211 (1.7)	213 (1.3)	223 (1.0)
Guam	181 (1.2)	192 (4.2)	171 (8.0)	171 (2.3)	172 (1.4)	190 (1.7)

Table 16.—Average proficiency in reading for 4th graders in public schools,[1] by selected characteristics, region, and state: 1994—Continued

Region and state	Percent of students reading for fun on their own time almost every day	Percent of students watching television 6 or more hours per day	Parental education [3]			
			Did not finish high school	Graduated high school	Some education after high school	Graduated college
1	8	9	10	11	12	13
United States	**45 (0.7)**	**22 (0.7)**	**188 (3.5)**	**206 (1.9)**	**222 (2.2)**	**222 (1.4)**
Region						
Northeast	45 (1.2)	25 (2.0)	(4) (4)	202 (3.3)	222 (4.4)	221 (3.1)
Southeast	40 (1.3)	25 (1.7)	186 (4.8)	207 (3.9)	222 (3.0)	216 (3.0)
Central	46 (1.4)	19 (1.6)	(4) (4)	215 (4.0)	221 (5.1)	226 (3.0)
West	46 (1.5)	17 (1.2)	188 (6.6)	201 (3.9)	221 (5.1)	223 (2.4)
State						
Alabama	41 (1.2)	21 (1.1)	197 (3.0)	201 (2.6)	217 (3.2)	217 (1.9)
Arizona	44 (1.2)	16 (1.1)	189 (3.5)	200 (3.3)	219 (3.5)	218 (2.3)
Arkansas	41 (1.1)	25 (1.6)	196 (3.8)	203 (2.2)	221 (3.1)	215 (2.0)
California	45 (1.3)	21 (1.3)	166 (4.3)	191 (4.2)	207 (3.4)	207 (2.1)
Colorado	47 (1.1)	31 (1.0)	192 (5.9)	213 (3.0)	220 (2.7)	222 (1.4)
Connecticut	48 (1.3)	20 (1.2)	204 (6.9)	209 (3.6)	234 (2.9)	231 (1.7)
Delaware	42 (1.1)	26 (1.3)	185 (4.6)	202 (3.2)	217 (3.3)	214 (1.4)
Florida	41 (0.9)	24 (1.1)	187 (4.8)	195 (3.2)	219 (3.3)	212 (2.3)
Georgia	45 (1.3)	22 (1.5)	185 (5.4)	199 (3.4)	219 (3.2)	217 (2.9)
Hawaii	42 (1.1)	20 (1.1)	192 (5.3)	194 (2.7)	215 (5.0)	208 (1.9)
Indiana	41 (1.1)	18 (1.1)	198 (4.6)	216 (2.6)	230 (2.8)	229 (1.5)
Iowa	50 (1.3)	13 (1.1)	211 (4.5)	219 (2.1)	232 (2.9)	229 (1.6)
Kentucky	40 (1.1)	25 (1.1)	195 (3.2)	212 (2.0)	222 (2.9)	218 (2.1)
Louisiana	38 (1.3)	28 (1.4)	188 (2.4)	196 (2.1)	209 (2.6)	200 (2.2)
Maine	46 (1.3)	12 (0.8)	214 (3.3)	225 (2.5)	237 (2.4)	236 (1.5)
Maryland	45 (1.3)	23 (1.5)	195 (5.1)	202 (4.1)	215 (3.3)	217 (2.2)
Massachusetts	46 (1.2)	14 (1.2)	206 (3.4)	212 (3.1)	230 (2.3)	232 (1.6)
Minnesota	48 (1.3)	12 (0.9)	(4) (4)	212 (3.2)	220 (2.8)	229 (1.6)
Mississippi	39 (0.9)	28 (1.1)	192 (3.2)	199 (2.8)	213 (3.8)	207 (2.1)
Missouri	44 (1.2)	21 (1.1)	199 (3.7)	216 (2.4)	227 (3.3)	225 (2.0)
Montana [6]	49 (1.2)	12 (1.1)	211 (4.2)	219 (2.2)	227 (2.8)	230 (1.8)
Nebraska [6]	46 (1.2)	14 (1.3)	(4) (4)	215 (2.5)	232 (2.9)	231 (1.5)
New Hampshire [6]	47 (1.5)	14 (1.4)	207 (5.6)	220 (2.6)	236 (2.7)	231 (2.0)
New Jersey	43 (1.1)	23 (1.3)	193 (5.9)	209 (3.1)	225 (2.8)	230 (1.4)
New Mexico	44 (1.0)	13 (1.0)	188 (4.8)	200 (3.2)	220 (2.9)	215 (1.9)
New York	49 (1.1)	22 (1.5)	196 (4.2)	208 (2.7)	224 (3.3)	220 (2.0)
North Carolina	46 (1.1)	19 (1.0)	195 (2.9)	204 (2.2)	226 (2.6)	223 (2.0)
North Dakota	47 (1.3)	11 (1.0)	(4) (4)	217 (2.5)	232 (2.9)	233 (1.3)
Pennsylvania [6]	43 (1.1)	19 (1.4)	187 (5.7)	210 (2.2)	221 (2.9)	224 (2.3)
Rhode Island [6]	48 (0.9)	16 (1.1)	203 (4.9)	217 (2.5)	230 (2.6)	228 (1.6)
South Carolina	44 (1.1)	24 (1.2)	189 (3.0)	193 (2.5)	216 (4.1)	213 (2.0)
Tennessee [6]	39 (1.5)	20 (1.5)	200 (3.7)	213 (3.3)	225 (3.9)	219 (2.7)
Texas	42 (1.4)	20 (1.3)	195 (3.2)	207 (3.1)	224 (2.7)	222 (3.0)
Utah	47 (1.2)	9 (0.9)	(4) (4)	211 (2.6)	225 (2.5)	226 (1.5)
Virginia	47 (1.4)	24 (1.3)	196 (4.3)	207 (2.6)	220 (3.1)	221 (1.9)
Washington	48 (1.2)	13 (0.9)	197 (4.6)	209 (2.7)	216 (2.4)	223 (1.7)
West Virginia	39 (1.1)	19 (1.1)	196 (3.1)	213 (2.2)	226 (2.9)	221 (1.5)
Wisconsin [6]	49 (1.3)	14 (1.0)	212 (4.1)	223 (2.5)	228 (2.5)	233 (1.6)
Wyoming	51 (1.0)	12 (0.7)	203 (4.1)	215 (2.1)	230 (2.1)	228 (1.5)
Department of Defense Overseas Schools	48 (0.9)	19 (0.9)	(4) (4)	209 (2.3)	226 (2.3)	223 (1.4)
Guam	44 (1.3)	23 (0.8)	164 (4.8)	176 (2.6)	189 (4.3)	185 (1.8)

[1] As measured by the National Assessment of Educational Progress (NAEP). Some states did not participate in the test.

[2] Children from other racial/ethnic groups are included in totals, but not shown separately.

[3] Parents' highest level of education. Data not shown for students who did not know parents' level of education.

[4] Sample size is insufficient to permit a reliable estimate.

[5] The nature of the sample does not allow accurate determination of the variability of this value.

[6] Did not satisfy one or more of the guidelines for school sample participation rates. Data are subject to appreciable nonresponse bias.

NOTE.—These test scores are from the National Assessment of Educational Progress (NAEP). The NAEP scores have been evaluated at certain performance levels.

A score of 300 implies an ability to find, understand, summarize, and explain relatively complicated literary and informational material. A score of 250 implies an ability to search for specific information, interrelate ideas, and make generalizations about literature, science, and social studies materials. A score of 200 implies an ability to understand, combine ideas, and make inferences based on short uncomplicated passages about specific or sequentially related information. A score of 150 implies an ability to follow brief written directions and carry out simple, discrete reading tasks. Scale ranges from 0 to 500. Excludes states not participating in the survey. Some data have been revised from previously published figures. Standard errors are in parentheses.

SOURCE: U.S. Department of Education, National Center for Education Statistics, National Assessment of Educational Progress, *NAEP 1994 Reading Report Card for the Nation and the States,* prepared by Educational Testing Service. (This table was prepared February 1998.)

Table 17.—Graduation requirements in mathematics, NCTM standards, length of school year, student homework, attitudes towards mathematics, television watching habits, and household composition of 8th grade students in public schools, by region and state: 1992[1]

Region and state	Math units required for graduation	Year of revision of state guides with NCTM standards[2]	Length of school year, 1992	Passing test in math required for graduation in 1993	Percent of students with 4 or more hours of math instruction each week	Percent of students reporting					
						Spending 30 minutes or more on math homework each day	Spending 1 or 2 hours on all homework each day	Spending more than 2 hours on all homework each day	Positive attitudes towards math[3]	Both parents living at home	Watching 6 or more hours of television each day
1	2	3	4	5	6	7	8	9	10	11	12
Total	—	—	—	—	32	64	59	8	59	75	13
Region											
Northeast	—	—	—	—	35	59	62	8	56	75	14
Southeast	—	—	—	—	37	65	56	7	59	71	17
Central	—	—	—	—	24	63	65	6	63	79	11
West	—	—	—	—	30	68	56	10	56	75	12
State											
Alabama	2	1989	175	Yes	60	65	59	7	62	72	20
Alaska	2	1994	180	No	—	—	—	—	—	—	—
Arizona	2	1992	175	No	34	65	56	5	54	76	9
Arkansas	3	1993	178	No	42	61	56	7	60	75	20
California	2	1991	180	No	43	67	63	10	56	74	10
Colorado	(4)	1994	(5)	No	27	65	61	7	58	77	7
Connecticut	3	Devel.,1995	180	No	21	61	70	9	59	79	11
Delaware	2	Devel.,1994	180	No	30	57	62	5	63	73	17
District of Columbia	3	1993	180	No	52	63	63	10	73	45	31
Florida	3	Devel.,1994	180	Yes	40	62	57	7	61	71	15
Georgia	3	1992	180	Yes	56	65	59	7	66	71	18
Hawaii	3	Devel.,1994	180	Yes	34	68	55	11	54	75	22
Idaho	2	1994	180	No	28	63	57	5	56	83	7
Illinois	2	Devel.,1994	180	No	—	—	—	—	—	—	—
Indiana	2	1991	180	No	32	62	60	6	61	78	9
Iowa	(4)	1987	180	No	20	61	63	4	63	83	7
Kansas	2	1991	180	No	—	—	—	—	—	—	—
Kentucky	3	1993	175	No	47	61	54	6	57	78	13
Louisiana	3	Devel.,1994	180	Yes	54	62	61	10	63	71	20
Maine	2	Devel.,1994	175	No	12	66	70	8	61	81	8
Maryland	3	1985	180	Yes	45	60	65	7	61	73	17
Massachusetts	(4)	1994	180	No	28	67	70	9	57	77	8
Michigan	3	Devel.,1994	180	Yes	39	67	61	7	60	75	13
Minnesota	1	Devel.,1994	175	No	41	64	59	5	57	85	5
Mississippi	2	1993	180	Yes	60	68	60	8	67	70	21
Missouri	2	1990	174	No	44	66	60	6	60	77	12
Montana	2	Devel.,1995	180	No	—	—	—	—	—	—	—
Nebraska	(4)	Devel.,1994	(5)	No	25	69	61	5	60	81	8
Nevada	2	1993	180	Yes	—	—	—	—	—	—	—
New Hampshire	2	1993	180	No	38	62	68	9	58	81	7
New Jersey	3	1993	180	Yes	28	62	68	10	62	78	13
New Mexico	3	1992	180	Yes	26	65	56	7	56	75	11
New York	2	Devel.,1994	180	Yes	20	54	66	9	62	75	15
North Carolina	2	1992	180	Yes	52	64	64	7	65	73	16
North Dakota	2	1993	180	No	44	70	63	6	55	85	5
Ohio	2	1990	182	Yes	26	62	62	6	62	74	12
Oklahoma	2	1993	175	No	37	69	59	7	58	78	11
Oregon	2	Devel.,1994	(5)	No	—	—	—	—	—	—	—
Pennsylvania	3	none	180	No	24	58	63	4	59	79	9
Rhode Island	2	Devel.,1994	180	No	43	62	67	7	56	78	9
South Carolina	3	1993	180	Yes	59	61	61	7	70	73	17
South Dakota	2	Devel.,1995	175	No	—	—	—	—	—	—	—
Tennessee	2	1991	180	Yes	60	67	62	6	58	73	14
Texas	3	1991	175	Yes	38	67	57	8	61	75	12
Utah	2	1993	180	No	28	62	56	5	55	85	5
Vermont	(6)	Devel.,1994	175	No	—	—	—	—	—	—	—
Virginia	2	1988	180	Yes	38	65	63	7	63	77	15
Washington	2	Devel.,1994	180	No	—	—	—	—	—	—	—
West Virginia	2	1992	180	Yes	40	57	55	5	58	78	13
Wisconsin	2	Devel.,1995	180	No	32	59	61	5	59	80	8
Wyoming	(4)	1990	175	No	24	60	55	5	58	81	8
Outlying areas											
Guam	—	—	—	—	28	68	47	12	50	79	20
Virgin Islands	—	—	180	—	31	61	47	11	75	56	32

[1] Data are for 1992 unless otherwise specified.

[2] Standards recommended by the National Council of Teachers of Mathematics.

[3] Percent of students agreeing or strongly agreeing with positive statements about mathematics.

[4] Local board determines.

[5] No statewide policy.

[6] 5 units of math and science combined.

—Data not available or not applicable.

SOURCE: U.S. Department of Education, National Center for Education Statistics, National Assessment of Educational Progress, *The State of Mathematics Achievement*, by Educational Testing Service; and Council of Chief State School Officers, *State Education Indicators*. (This table was prepared June 1994.)

Table 18.—High school graduates and 12th grade enrollment in public secondary schools, by state: 1985–86, 1990–91, and 1995–96

State or other area	1985–86			1990–91			1995–96		
	High school graduates, 1985–86	12th grade enrollment, 1985	Graduates as a percent of 12th grade enrollment	High school graduates, 1990–91	12th grade enrollment, 1990	Graduates as a percent of 12th grade enrollment	High school graduates, 1995–96 [1]	12th grade enrollment, 1995	Graduates as a percent of 12th grade enrollment
1	2	3	4	5	6	7	8	9	10
United States	**2,382,616**	**2,549,614**	**93.5**	**2,234,893**	**2,381,083**	**93.9**	**2,281,317**	**2,487,135**	**91.7**
Alabama	39,620	43,626	90.8	39,042	42,031	92.9	35,043	40,981	85.5
Alaska	5,464	6,481	84.3	5,458	6,486	84.2	5,945	7,111	83.6
Arizona	27,533	34,297	80.3	31,282	34,645	90.3	30,008	39,197	76.6
Arkansas	26,227	28,201	93.0	25,668	27,734	92.6	25,094	27,083	92.7
California	229,026	243,398	94.1	234,164	244,142	95.9	259,071	287,428	90.1
Colorado	32,621	35,538	91.8	31,293	33,582	93.2	32,608	35,480	91.9
Connecticut	33,571	32,006	104.9	27,290	27,859	98.0	26,319	28,282	93.1
Delaware	5,791	6,580	88.0	5,223	5,897	88.6	5,609	6,211	90.3
District of Columbia	3,875	4,193	92.4	3,369	3,481	96.8	2,696	2,972	90.7
Florida	83,029	90,510	91.7	87,419	94,776	92.2	89,242	99,519	89.7
Georgia	59,082	63,157	93.5	60,088	62,379	96.3	56,271	63,736	88.3
Hawaii	9,958	9,911	100.5	8,974	9,234	97.2	9,387	10,478	89.6
Idaho	12,059	13,035	92.5	11,961	13,095	91.3	14,667	16,093	91.1
Illinois	114,319	117,626	97.2	103,329	105,541	97.9	110,486	107,244	103.0
Indiana	59,817	66,223	90.3	57,892	62,740	92.3	56,368	62,659	90.0
Iowa	34,279	35,906	95.5	28,593	30,928	92.5	31,689	34,565	91.7
Kansas	25,587	27,215	94.0	24,414	26,089	93.6	25,786	28,491	90.5
Kentucky	37,288	39,284	94.9	35,835	37,577	95.4	36,641	38,797	94.4
Louisiana	39,965	42,753	93.5	33,489	37,983	88.2	36,467	40,663	89.7
Maine	13,006	13,705	94.9	13,151	13,817	95.2	11,795	12,670	93.1
Maryland	46,700	48,250	96.8	39,014	40,529	96.3	41,785	42,974	97.2
Massachusetts	60,360	64,529	93.5	50,216	53,484	93.9	47,993	51,911	92.5
Michigan	101,042	105,600	95.7	88,234	91,769	96.1	85,530	87,840	97.4
Minnesota	51,988	56,735	91.6	46,474	51,324	90.6	50,481	57,793	87.3
Mississippi	25,134	27,301	92.1	23,665	26,411	89.6	23,032	25,741	89.5
Missouri	49,204	52,904	93.0	46,928	49,925	94.0	48,870	52,939	92.3
Montana	9,761	10,294	94.8	9,013	9,609	93.8	10,139	10,897	93.0
Nebraska	17,845	18,834	94.7	16,500	17,680	93.3	18,014	19,275	93.5
Nevada	8,784	10,127	86.7	9,370	11,197	83.7	10,374	14,143	73.4
New Hampshire	10,648	11,558	92.1	10,059	10,408	96.6	10,094	10,996	91.8
New Jersey	78,781	81,505	96.7	67,003	67,716	98.9	[2]67,516	65,647	102.8
New Mexico	15,468	16,934	91.3	15,157	15,454	98.1	15,402	17,078	90.2
New York	162,165	170,394	95.2	133,562	142,514	93.7	135,569	142,841	94.9
North Carolina	65,865	69,127	95.3	62,792	65,720	95.5	57,014	59,653	95.6
North Dakota	7,610	7,984	95.3	7,573	7,960	95.1	8,027	8,513	94.3
Ohio	119,561	130,558	91.6	107,484	118,605	90.6	103,435	114,879	90.0
Oklahoma	34,452	37,308	92.3	33,007	35,671	92.5	33,060	35,733	92.5
Oregon	26,286	30,847	85.2	24,597	30,018	81.9	26,570	33,202	80.0
Pennsylvania	122,871	127,390	96.5	104,770	108,592	96.5	105,981	111,050	95.4
Rhode Island	8,908	9,590	92.9	7,744	8,167	94.8	7,689	8,263	93.1
South Carolina	34,500	37,012	93.2	32,999	35,393	93.2	30,313	34,800	87.1
South Dakota	7,870	8,378	93.9	7,127	7,758	91.9	8,532	9,116	93.6
Tennessee	43,263	49,581	87.3	44,847	49,050	91.4	43,792	49,319	88.8
Texas	161,150	172,742	93.3	174,306	178,390	97.7	171,844	186,229	92.3
Utah	19,774	22,453	88.1	22,219	26,263	84.6	26,293	32,006	82.2
Vermont	5,794	6,116	94.7	5,212	5,424	96.1	5,870	6,507	90.2
Virginia	63,113	65,792	95.9	58,441	61,328	95.3	58,166	62,204	93.5
Washington	45,805	54,850	83.5	42,514	51,856	82.0	49,862	59,612	83.6
West Virginia	21,870	22,564	96.9	21,064	22,045	95.6	20,335	21,844	93.1
Wisconsin	58,340	62,661	93.1	49,340	54,562	90.4	52,651	57,791	91.1
Wyoming	5,587	6,051	92.3	5,728	6,245	91.7	5,892	6,679	88.2
Outlying areas	34,089	37,697	90.4	32,194	34,669	92.9	—	36,293	—
American Samoa	608	—	—	597	599	99.7	719	756	95.1
Guam	840	1,295	64.9	1,014	1,120	90.5	—	1,433	—
Northern Marianas	—	—	—	273	326	83.7	325	467	69.6
Puerto Rico	31,597	35,514	89.0	29,329	31,496	93.1	29,499	32,535	90.7
Virgin Islands	1,044	888	117.6	981	1,128	87.0	937	1,102	64.7

[1] Preliminary data.

[2] Data imputed by NCES based on previous year's data.

—Data not available or not applicable.

NOTE.—Percentages may exceed 100.0 because of inconsistent reporting of enrollment and graduates and transfers into the public schools.

SOURCE: U.S. Department of Education, National Center for Education Statistics, "Statistics of Public Elementary and Secondary Day Schools," various years; and Common Core of Data surveys. (This table was prepared February 1998.)

Table 19.—Public high school graduates, by state: 1970–71 to 1996–97

State or other area	1970–71	1971–72	1972–73	1973–74	1974–75	1975–76	1976–77	1977–78	1978–79	1979–80
1	2	3	4	5	6	7	8	9	10	11
United States	**2,637,642**	**2,699,553**	**2,728,822**	**2,763,317**	**2,822,502**	**2,837,129**	**2,837,340**	**2,824,636**	**2,801,152**	**2,747,678**
Alabama	44,722	44,806	44,441	45,502	46,633	46,695	46,763	46,509	47,137	45,190
Alaska	3,534	3,760	3,970	4,248	4,220	4,223	4,526	4,832	5,038	5,223
Arizona	23,407	23,953	24,012	24,924	25,665	26,019	29,855	30,814	30,059	28,633
Arkansas	25,965	25,892	25,705	24,384	26,836	27,029	27,628	28,064	28,302	29,052
California	262,661	270,518	268,021	268,493	273,411	272,500	266,143	261,698	250,708	249,217
Colorado	31,910	33,454	33,358	34,353	34,963	35,555	36,647	37,373	37,234	36,804
Connecticut	35,155	37,804	37,871	39,171	[2] 42,792	40,612	39,485	38,860	38,369	37,683
Delaware	7,342	7,666	7,733	8,165	8,235	8,212	8,164	8,166	8,090	7,582
District of Columbia [4]	4,760	4,965	5,213	5,540	5,367	5,106	5,335	5,186	5,812	4,959
Florida	73,150	78,574	81,773	74,830	86,481	[2] 89,444	88,137	91,613	87,633	87,324
Georgia	57,082	58,358	57,755	58,026	59,803	61,059	62,234	61,095	62,179	61,621
Hawaii	10,471	11,185	11,147	11,426	11,283	11,284	11,637	11,190	11,637	11,493
Idaho	12,360	12,829	12,714	12,776	12,631	11,940	13,029	13,301	13,432	13,187
Illinois	128,843	128,843	135,735	139,104	[2] 141,316	146,612	142,040	140,690	139,230	135,579
Indiana	70,596	72,501	73,155	73,377	74,104	77,712	76,406	74,336	75,182	73,143
Iowa	43,546	44,426	44,521	43,508	43,005	[2] 42,318	43,720	44,168	44,488	43,445
Kansas	33,442	34,163	33,941	33,374	32,458	[2] 32,212	33,216	32,763	32,132	30,890
Kentucky	38,486	40,707	40,607	41,351	42,368	[2] 41,761	41,755	41,611	41,402	41,203
Louisiana	44,446	45,563	45,704	46,808	47,691	47,446	[2] 48,219	47,183	46,861	46,297
Maine	13,857	14,356	14,377	14,491	14,830	15,200	15,205	15,364	15,402	15,445
Maryland	48,219	50,370	52,813	54,128	55,408	56,063	55,503	55,455	55,114	54,270
Massachusetts	62,153	67,487	72,696	[2] 78,000	[2] 79,000	81,207	[2] 75,386	78,348	76,097	73,802
Michigan	131,598	126,409	130,286	134,336	135,509	130,872	135,337	132,759	130,586	124,316
Minnesota	60,966	63,135	63,394	63,981	66,535	66,424	68,166	67,475	66,096	64,908
Mississippi	26,729	26,529	26,128	25,664	27,243	27,617	27,639	28,186	28,168	27,586
Missouri	57,422	58,876	60,068	62,183	62,375	63,942	64,471	64,564	64,163	62,265
Montana	11,500	10,652	10,504	12,135	12,293	12,136	12,328	12,184	12,068	12,135
Nebraska	21,410	21,720	22,459	22,276	22,249	22,237	[2] 23,067	23,322	23,147	22,410
Nevada	5,899	6,206	6,414	6,960	7,232	7,566	7,992	8,233	8,319	8,473
New Hampshire	9,119	9,290	9,849	9,932	11,050	10,663	11,477	11,360	11,853	11,722
New Jersey	87,718	88,106	91,629	93,918	[2] 96,000	[2] 97,985	97,494	97,079	97,643	94,564
New Mexico	16,261	16,999	17,248	17,364	18,438	17,843	17,988	18,444	18,762	18,424
New York	192,807	199,771	204,037	207,413	210,780	214,234	212,907	210,720	208,335	204,064
North Carolina	68,821	70,242	69,322	69,062	70,094	70,498	71,146	70,953	72,464	70,862
North Dakota	11,003	10,515	10,563	10,824	10,690	10,771	10,839	10,526	10,385	9,928
Ohio	145,076	149,472	152,428	153,874	158,179	157,583	156,220	152,002	150,651	144,169
Oklahoma	38,062	38,409	37,349	36,770	37,809	37,663	38,577	39,005	39,225	39,305
Oregon	32,757	31,882	31,221	30,806	30,668	30,561	30,258	29,998	30,228	29,939
Pennsylvania	153,568	157,415	154,045	159,934	163,124	163,812	160,665	156,918	155,442	146,458
Rhode Island	10,435	10,909	10,802	11,117	11,042	10,831	10,796	10,884	11,243	10,864
South Carolina	35,992	37,071	36,150	38,837	38,312	38,073	37,780	38,735	38,079	38,697
South Dakota	11,875	11,945	12,164	11,894	11,725	11,340	11,293	11,349	11,092	10,689
Tennessee	50,500	51,622	52,115	49,641	49,363	50,118	49,290	47,515	47,403	49,845
Texas	148,105	153,653	153,529	156,984	159,487	159,855	163,574	167,983	168,518	171,449
Utah	19,097	18,971	18,993	18,901	19,532	19,673	19,743	20,324	20,045	20,035
Vermont	5,939	5,885	6,303	6,316	6,455	6,559	6,699	6,773	6,721	6,733
Virginia	59,672	62,372	62,589	63,846	65,570	66,061	66,738	66,270	67,027	66,621
Washington	50,902	51,563	50,988	51,868	50,990	51,012	50,876	51,101	51,108	50,402
West Virginia	25,485	22,159	24,541	25,401	24,631	24,879	24,719	23,986	23,570	23,369
Wisconsin	67,182	69,817	70,789	69,341	70,979	70,355	72,367	71,295	71,291	69,332
Wyoming	5,635	5,778	5,653	5,760	5,648	5,757	5,861	6,074	5,982	6,072
Outlying Areas	24,847	26,868	26,152	26,145	29,277	28,058	—	—	—	—
American Samoa	367	406	446	448	448	394	—	—	—	—
Guam	1,022	1,031	1,056	1,002	1,117	1,206	—	—	—	—
Northern Marianas	—	—	—	—	—	—	—	—	—	—
Puerto Rico	23,026	24,901	24,081	24,081	27,071	25,788	—	—	—	—
Virgin Islands	432	530	569	614	641	670	—	—	—	—

Table 19.—Public high school graduates, by state: 1970–71 to 1996–97—Continued

State or other area	1980–81	1981–82	1982–83	1983–84	1984–85	1985–86	1986–87	1987–88	1988–89	1989–90
1	12	13	14	15	16	17	18	19	20	21
United States	**2,725,254**	**2,704,758**	**2,597,604**	**[1]2,494,797**	**2,413,917**	**2,382,616**	**[1]2,428,803**	**2,500,191**	**2,458,800**	**[1]2,320,337**
Alabama	44,894	45,409	44,352	42,021	40,002	39,620	42,463	43,799	43,437	40,485
Alaska	5,343	5,477	5,622	5,457	5,184	5,464	5,692	5,907	5,631	5,386
Arizona	28,416	28,049	26,530	28,332	27,877	27,533	29,549	29,777	31,919	32,103
Arkansas	29,577	29,710	28,447	27,049	26,342	26,227	27,101	27,776	27,920	26,475
California	242,172	241,343	236,897	232,199	225,448	229,026	237,414	249,617	244,629	236,291
Colorado	35,993	35,494	34,875	32,954	32,255	32,621	34,200	35,977	35,520	32,967
Connecticut	38,369	37,706	36,204	33,679	32,126	33,571	31,141	32,383	30,862	27,878
Delaware	7,349	7,144	6,924	6,410	5,893	5,791	5,895	5,963	6,104	5,550
District of Columbia[4]	4,848	4,871	4,909	4,073	3,940	3,875	3,842	3,882	3,565	3,626
Florida	88,755	90,736	86,871	85,908	81,140	83,029	82,184	89,206	90,759	88,934
Georgia	62,963	64,489	63,293	60,718	58,654	59,082	60,018	61,765	61,937	56,605
Hawaii	11,472	11,563	10,757	10,454	10,092	9,958	10,371	10,575	10,404	10,325
Idaho	12,679	12,560	12,126	11,732	12,148	12,059	12,243	12,425	12,520	11,971
Illinois	136,795	136,534	128,814	122,561	117,027	114,319	116,075	119,090	116,660	108,119
Indiana	73,381	73,984	70,549	65,710	63,308	59,817	60,364	64,037	63,571	60,012
Iowa	42,635	41,509	39,569	37,248	36,087	34,279	34,580	35,218	34,294	31,796
Kansas	29,397	28,298	28,316	26,730	25,983	25,587	26,933	27,036	26,848	25,367
Kentucky	41,714	42,531	40,478	39,645	37,999	37,288	36,948	39,484	38,883	38,005
Louisiana	46,199	39,895	39,539	39,400	39,742	39,965	39,084	39,058	37,198	36,053
Maine	15,554	14,764	14,600	13,935	13,924	13,006	13,692	13,808	13,857	13,839
Maryland	54,050	54,621	52,446	50,684	48,299	46,700	46,107	47,175	45,791	41,566
Massachusetts	74,831	73,414	71,219	65,885	63,411	60,360	61,010	59,515	57,328	[5]55,941
Michigan	124,372	121,030	112,950	[3]108,926	105,908	101,042	102,725	106,151	101,784	93,807
Minnesota	64,166	62,145	59,015	55,376	53,352	51,988	53,533	54,645	53,122	49,087
Mississippi	28,083	28,023	27,271	26,324	25,315	25,134	26,201	27,896	24,241	25,182
Missouri	60,359	59,872	56,420	53,388	51,290	49,204	50,840	51,316	51,968	48,957
Montana	11,634	11,162	10,689	10,224	10,016	9,761	10,073	10,311	10,490	9,370
Nebraska	21,411	21,027	19,986	18,674	18,036	17,845	18,129	18,300	18,690	17,664
Nevada	9,069	9,240	8,979	8,726	8,572	8,784	[3]9,506	9,404	9,464	9,477
New Hampshire	11,552	11,669	11,470	11,478	11,052	10,648	10,796	11,685	11,340	10,766
New Jersey	93,168	93,750	90,048	85,569	81,547	78,781	79,376	80,863	76,263	69,824
New Mexico	17,915	17,635	16,530	15,914	15,622	15,468	15,701	15,868	15,481	14,884
New York	198,465	194,605	184,022	174,762	166,752	162,165	163,765	165,379	154,580	143,318
North Carolina	69,395	71,210	68,783	66,803	67,245	65,865	65,421	67,836	69,970	64,782
North Dakota	9,924	9,504	8,886	8,569	8,146	7,610	7,821	8,432	8,077	7,690
Ohio	143,503	139,899	133,524	127,837	122,281	119,561	121,121	124,503	125,036	114,513
Oklahoma	38,875	38,347	36,799	35,254	34,626	34,452	35,514	36,145	36,773	35,606
Oregon	28,729	28,780	28,099	27,214	26,870	26,286	27,165	28,058	26,903	25,473
Pennsylvania	144,518	143,356	137,494	132,412	127,226	122,871	121,219	124,376	118,921	110,527
Rhode Island	10,719	10,545	10,533	9,820	9,382	8,908	8,771	8,855	8,554	7,825
South Carolina	38,347	38,647	37,570	36,800	34,500	34,500	36,000	36,113	37,020	32,483
South Dakota	10,385	9,864	9,206	8,638	8,206	7,870	8,074	8,415	8,181	7,650
Tennessee	50,648	51,447	46,704	44,711	43,293	43,263	44,731	47,904	48,553	46,094
Texas	171,665	172,085	168,897	161,580	159,234	161,150	168,430	171,436	176,951	172,480
Utah	19,886	19,400	19,210	19,350	19,606	19,774	20,930	22,226	22,934	21,196
Vermont	6,424	6,513	6,011	6,002	5,769	5,794	5,968	6,177	5,963	6,127
Virginia	67,126	67,809	65,571	62,177	60,959	63,113	65,008	65,688	65,004	60,605
Washington	50,046	50,148	45,809	44,919	45,431	45,805	49,873	51,754	48,941	45,941
West Virginia	23,580	23,589	23,561	22,613	22,262	21,870	22,401	22,406	22,886	21,854
Wisconsin	67,743	67,357	64,321	62,189	58,851	58,340	56,872	58,428	54,994	52,038
Wyoming	6,161	5,999	5,909	5,764	5,687	5,587	5,933	6,148	6,079	5,823
Outlying Areas	—	—	—	34,429	33,626	34,089	33,141	34,674	34,347	32,272
American Samoa	—	—	—	—	—	608	647	633	569	703
Guam	—	—	—	—	1,099	840	898	898	936	1,033
Northern Marianas	—	—	—	265	—	289	285	200	227	
Puerto Rico	—	—	—	33,166	31,519	31,597	30,137	31,832	31,617	29,049
Virgin Islands	—	—	—	998	1,008	1,044	1,170	1,026	1,025	1,260

Table 19.—Public high school graduates, by state: 1970–71 to 1996–97—Continued

State or other area	1990–91	1991–92	1992–93	1993–94	1994–95	1995–96	Estimated 1996–97	Percentage change			
								1970–71 to 1996–97	1986–87 to 1991–92	1991–92 to 1996–97	1986–87 to 1996–97
1	22	23	24	25	26	27	28	29	30	31	32
United States	**2,234,893**	**2,226,016**	**2,233,241**	**2,220,849**	**2,273,541**	**¹2,281,317**	**¹2,359,572**	**–10.5**	**–8.3**	**6.0**	**–2.9**
Alabama	39,042	38,680	36,007	34,447	36,268	35,043	²34,726	–22.4	–8.9	–10.2	–18.2
Alaska	5,458	5,535	5,535	5,747	5,765	5,945	5,984	69.3	–2.8	8.1	5.1
Arizona	31,282	31,264	31,747	31,799	30,989	30,008	³32,886	40.5	5.8	5.2	11.3
Arkansas	25,668	25,845	25,655	24,990	24,636	25,094	25,069	–3.5	–4.6	–3.0	–7.5
California	234,164	244,594	249,320	253,083	255,200	259,071	269,294	2.5	3.0	10.1	13.4
Colorado	31,293	31,059	31,839	31,867	32,409	32,608	²34,221	7.2	–9.2	10.2	0.1
Connecticut	27,290	27,079	26,799	26,330	26,445	26,319	26,850	–23.6	–13.0	–0.8	–13.8
Delaware	5,223	5,325	5,492	5,230	5,234	5,609	²5,623	–23.4	–9.7	5.6	–4.6
District of Columbia⁴	3,369	3,385	3,136	3,207	2,974	2,696	³2,709	–43.1	–11.9	–20.0	–29.5
Florida	87,419	93,674	89,428	88,032	89,827	89,242	²92,267	26.1	14.0	–1.5	12.3
Georgia	60,088	57,742	57,602	56,356	56,660	56,271	61,004	6.9	–3.8	5.6	1.6
Hawaii	8,974	9,160	8,854	9,369	9,407	9,387	³9,595	–8.4	–11.7	4.7	–7.5
Idaho	11,961	12,734	12,974	13,281	14,198	14,667	14,900	20.6	4.0	17.0	21.7
Illinois	103,329	102,742	103,628	102,126	105,164	110,486	²110,186	–14.5	–11.5	7.2	–5.1
Indiana	57,892	56,630	57,559	54,650	56,058	56,368	56,569	–19.9	–6.2	–0.1	–6.3
Iowa	28,593	29,224	30,677	30,247	31,268	31,689	32,735	–24.8	–15.5	12.0	–5.3
Kansas	24,414	24,129	24,720	25,319	26,125	25,786	26,726	–20.1	–10.4	10.8	–0.8
Kentucky	35,835	33,896	36,361	38,454	37,626	36,641	³37,146	–3.5	–8.3	9.6	0.5
Louisiana	33,489	32,247	33,682	34,822	36,480	36,467	²36,727	–17.4	–17.5	13.9	–6.0
Maine	13,151	13,177	12,103	11,384	11,501	11,795	²12,405	–10.5	–3.8	–5.9	–9.4
Maryland	39,014	39,720	39,523	39,091	41,387	41,785	²43,365	–10.1	–13.9	9.2	–5.9
Massachusetts	50,216	50,317	48,321	47,453	47,679	47,993	48,933	–21.3	–17.5	–2.8	–19.8
Michigan	88,234	87,756	85,302	83,385	84,628	85,530	88,000	–33.1	–14.6	0.3	–14.3
Minnesota	46,474	46,228	48,002	47,514	49,354	50,481	52,340	–14.1	–13.6	13.2	–2.2
Mississippi	23,665	22,912	23,597	23,379	23,837	23,032	23,255	–13.0	–12.6	1.5	–11.2
Missouri	46,928	46,556	46,864	46,566	48,862	48,870	²50,223	–12.5	–8.4	7.9	–1.2
Montana	9,013	9,046	9,389	9,601	10,134	10,139	10,320	–10.3	–10.2	14.1	2.5
Nebraska	16,500	17,057	17,569	17,072	17,969	18,014	19,183	–10.4	–5.9	12.5	5.8
Nevada	9,370	8,811	9,042	9,485	10,038	10,374	²11,299	91.5	–7.3	28.2	18.9
New Hampshire	10,059	10,329	10,065	9,933	10,145	10,094	9,398	3.1	–4.3	–9.0	–12.9
New Jersey	67,003	66,669	67,134	66,125	67,403	³67,516	³69,715	–20.5	–16.0	4.6	–12.2
New Mexico	15,157	14,824	15,172	14,892	14,928	15,402	15,700	–3.4	–5.6	5.9	(6)
New York	133,562	134,573	132,963	132,708	132,401	135,569	137,600	–28.6	–17.8	2.2	–16.0
North Carolina	62,792	61,157	60,460	57,738	59,540	57,014	²57,886	–15.9	–6.5	–5.3	–11.5
North Dakota	7,573	7,438	7,310	7,522	7,817	8,027	²7,990	–27.4	–4.9	7.4	2.2
Ohio	107,484	104,522	109,200	107,700	109,418	103,435	106,924	–26.3	–13.7	2.3	–11.7
Oklahoma	33,007	32,670	30,542	31,872	33,319	33,060	33,224	–12.7	–8.0	1.7	–6.4
Oregon	24,597	25,305	26,301	26,338	26,713	26,570	²27,799	–15.1	–6.8	9.9	2.3
Pennsylvania	104,770	103,881	103,715	101,958	104,146	105,981	109,160	–28.9	–14.3	5.1	–9.9
Rhode Island	7,744	7,859	7,640	7,450	7,826	7,689	7,734	–25.9	–10.4	–1.6	–11.8
South Carolina	32,999	30,698	31,297	30,603	30,680	30,313	32,800	–8.9	–14.7	6.8	–8.9
South Dakota	7,127	7,261	7,952	8,442	8,355	8,532	9,108	–23.3	–10.1	25.4	12.8
Tennessee	44,847	45,138	44,166	40,643	43,556	43,792	²45,962	–9.0	0.9	1.8	2.8
Texas	174,306	162,270	160,546	163,191	170,322	171,844	180,369	21.8	–3.7	11.2	7.1
Utah	22,219	23,513	24,197	26,407	27,670	26,293	²31,032	62.5	12.3	32.0	48.3
Vermont	5,212	5,231	5,215	5,414	5,871	5,870	²6,102	2.7	–12.3	16.7	2.2
Virginia	58,441	57,338	56,948	56,140	58,260	58,166	²62,258	4.3	–11.8	8.6	–4.2
Washington	42,514	44,381	45,262	47,235	49,294	49,862	52,900	3.9	–11.0	19.2	6.1
West Virginia	21,064	20,054	20,228	19,884	20,131	20,335	²19,547	–23.3	–10.5	–2.5	–12.7
Wisconsin	49,340	48,563	50,027	48,371	51,735	52,651	55,500	–17.4	–14.6	14.3	–2.4
Wyoming	5,728	5,818	6,174	5,997	5,889	5,892	²6,324	12.2	–1.9	8.7	6.6
Outlying Areas	32,194	32,274	31,860	30,655	32,743	—	31,743	27.8	–2.6	–1.6	–4.2
American Samoa	597	680	712	738	695	719	²705	92.1	5.1	3.7	9.0
Guam	1,014	1,018	912	985	987	—	²1,076	5.3	13.4	5.7	19.8
Northern Marianas	273	264	245	328	319	325	²310	—	–8.7	17.4	7.3
Puerto Rico	29,329	29,396	29,064	27,718	29,747	29,499	28,740	24.8	–2.5	–2.2	–4.6
Virgin Islands	981	916	927	886	995	937	²912	111.1	–21.7	–0.4	–22.1

¹ National total includes estimates for nonreporting states.
² Data estimated by reporting state.
³ Data imputed by the National Center for Education Statistics based on previous year's data.
⁴ Beginning in 1983–84, graduates from adult programs are excluded.
⁵ Data from *Projections of Education Statistics to 2002* published by the National Center for Education Statistics.

⁶ Less than 0.05 percent.
—Data not available or not applicable.

SOURCE: U.S. Department of Education, National Center for Education Statistics, "Statistics of Public Elementary and Secondary Day Schools," various years; and Common Core of Data and "Early Estimates" surveys. (This table was prepared February 1998.)

Table 20.—Staff employed in public school systems, by type of assignment and state: Fall 1995

[In full-time equivalents]

State or other area	Total	School district staff			School staff						Student support staff	Other support services staff
		Officials and adminis- trators	Adminis- trative support staff	Instruction coordina- tors	Principals and assistant principals	School and library support staff	Teachers	Instruc- tional aides	Guidance counselors	Librarians		
1	2	3	4	5	6	7	8	9	10	11	12	13
United States [1]	4,994,358	49,315	144,842	33,683	120,629	237,389	2,598,220	494,289	87,528	50,862	142,655	1,034,946
Alabama	83,256	428	1,039	980	2,221	2,768	44,056	6,657	1,684	1,259	468	21,696
Alaska [2]	15,022	294	549	112	436	886	7,379	1,751	225	147	819	2,424
Arizona	75,931	428	641	182	1,611	6,123	38,017	9,613	1,050	737	7,312	10,217
Arkansas	49,178	554	583	179	1,460	1,646	26,449	3,523	1,223	952	387	12,222
California [3]	444,014	2,155	19,920	4,685	10,335	28,571	230,849	56,822	5,115	896	9,989	74,677
Colorado	67,447	846	2,211	775	1,749	4,749	35,388	5,919	1,080	700	1,608	12,422
Connecticut	66,133	955	1,611	453	1,823	3,246	36,070	7,520	1,116	672	3,239	9,428
Delaware	11,869	87	388	58	399	472	6,463	861	215	122	498	2,306
District of Columbia	9,410	402	290	144	305	442	5,305	327	217	143	53	1,782
Florida	237,721	1,739	12,267	812	5,964	12,110	114,938	24,111	4,794	2,560	7,147	51,279
Georgia [4]	165,058	2,127	3,488	691	3,754	6,423	79,480	21,709	2,476	1,987	2,699	40,224
Hawaii	16,841	141	263	438	483	704	10,500	937	540	287	512	2,036
Idaho	21,814	114	443	210	661	876	12,784	1,914	520	185	381	3,726
Illinois	209,036	3,292	5,114	1,656	5,132	9,984	113,538	21,137	2,823	1,941	6,503	37,916
Indiana	116,363	928	496	1,368	2,818	7,872	55,821	14,421	1,720	1,021	1,650	28,248
Iowa	62,075	519	756	382	1,762	4,465	32,318	6,083	1,331	662	2,192	11,605
Kansas	57,265	1,253	961	74	1,671	2,487	30,729	4,760	1,087	972	2,298	10,973
Kentucky	84,425	1,170	2,188	434	1,906	3,147	39,120	10,916	1,282	1,173	2,093	20,996
Louisiana	93,070	265	689	1,026	2,379	2,907	46,980	10,026	2,610	1,172	2,248	22,768
Maine	29,413	448	660	113	853	1,393	15,392	3,776	600	238	1,049	4,891
Maryland	87,868	720	719	701	2,647	3,765	47,819	7,318	1,830	1,043	1,443	19,863
Massachusetts	113,154	991	5,788	1,065	2,166	3,073	62,710	12,867	2,090	611	1,860	19,933
Michigan	177,495	2,250	3,264	497	5,079	7,890	83,179	14,318	2,871	1,450	6,704	49,993
Minnesota	74,891	1,288	1,735	487	1,589	3,316	46,971	6,088	902	986	2,863	8,666
Mississippi	60,855	906	1,433	418	1,493	2,110	28,997	8,758	824	750	2,221	12,945
Missouri	120,621	638	4,578	1,244	2,579	8,189	57,951	7,228	2,593	1,368	1,758	32,495
Montana [4,5]	18,586	156	469	155	489	907	10,076	1,938	403	348	68	3,577
Nebraska	37,894	612	684	236	953	1,479	20,028	3,578	755	575	996	7,998
Nevada	23,742	184	489	101	680	1,340	13,878	1,489	498	241	605	4,237
New Hampshire	23,143	360	455	144	479	812	12,346	3,519	620	281	447	3,680
New Jersey	163,069	1,680	6,826	1,305	4,383	8,393	86,706	13,936	3,150	1,781	8,767	26,142
New Mexico	40,124	435	1,887	553	859	2,694	19,398	4,574	645	259	1,039	7,781
New York	355,723	2,737	23,774	1,263	6,878	7,110	181,559	28,001	5,456	2,998	8,720	87,227
North Carolina [4]	140,204	1,285	2,977	720	3,993	5,794	73,201	22,287	2,976	2,176	2,720	22,075
North Dakota	13,804	435	164	54	394	475	7,501	1,471	248	183	364	2,515
Ohio	194,579	5,242	9,467	353	971	12,597	107,347	10,092	3,219	1,628	1,252	42,411
Oklahoma [4]	83,802	533	94	590	1,456	5,754	39,364	7,186	1,390	902	12,589	13,944
Oregon	51,458	874	1,315	341	1,622	3,410	26,680	6,381	1,229	612	997	7,997
Pennsylvania	198,087	1,344	7,175	1,594	4,087	9,840	104,921	14,831	3,676	2,202	9,904	38,513
Rhode Island	16,517	148	426	78	361	804	10,482	1,458	309	75	378	1,998
South Carolina [4,5]	74,859	264	1,830	467	2,224	3,537	39,922	7,558	1,517	1,097	2,494	13,949
South Dakota [4]	18,126	268	400	148	473	878	9,641	2,302	354	202	269	3,191
Tennessee	98,948	918	2,297	761	4,654	4,572	53,403	9,992	1,456	1,386	2,927	16,582
Texas	462,661	2,580	2,451	1,100	11,251	18,644	240,371	43,046	8,219	4,252	3,679	127,068
Utah	37,385	109	715	465	926	2,098	20,039	5,037	596	291	369	6,740
Vermont	15,640	152	278	294	411	719	7,676	2,931	332	216	1,668	963
Virginia [3]	137,546	1,760	1,739	1,483	3,535	5,627	74,731	12,072	3,111	1,950	3,147	28,391
Washington [2,4]	91,322	1,015	2,540	841	2,501	4,760	46,907	8,582	1,758	1,263	3,695	17,460
West Virginia	38,645	279	1,896	322	1,095	366	21,073	2,957	611	357	886	8,803
Wisconsin	95,105	842	2,276	1,090	2,353	4,463	55,033	8,361	1,925	1,416	4,005	13,341
Wyoming	13,164	165	144	41	326	702	6,734	1,350	257	137	676	2,632
Outlying areas												
American Samoa	1,417	30	38	26	60	81	728	15	19	6	48	366
Guam	3,728	15	288	18	62	40	1,802	476	80	30	146	771
Northern Marianas	1,054	9	88	17	30	54	422	216	28	4	75	111
Puerto Rico	69,731	314	111	618	1,382	4,738	39,328	—	886	865	1,995	19,494
Virgin Islands	3,421	36	322	21	86	106	1,622	298	86	46	431	367

[1] Includes imputations for undercounts in designated states.
[2] Includes imputation for instruction coordinators.
[3] Includes imputation for prekindergarten teachers.
[4] Includes imputation for support staff.
[5] Includes imputation for instruction aides.

—Data not available or not applicable.

SOURCE: U.S. Department of Education, National Center for Education Statistics, Common Core of Data survey; and unpublished estimates. (This table was prepared April 1997.)

Table 21.—Students per staff employed in public school systems, by type of assignment and state: Fall 1995

State or other area	Total	School district staff			School staff						Student services staff	Other support staff
		Officials and administrators	Administrative support staff	Instruction coordinators	Principals and assistant principals	School and library support staff	Teachers	Instructional aides	Guidance counselors	Librarians		
1	2	3	4	5	6	7	8	9	10	11	12	13
United States [1]	9.0	909.3	309.6	1,331.2	371.7	188.9	17.3	90.7	512.3	881.6	314.3	43.3
Alabama	9.0	1,743.3	718.1	761.4	336.0	269.6	16.9	112.1	443.1	592.7	1,594.3	34.4
Alaska [2]	8.5	434.1	232.5	1,139.4	292.7	144.0	17.3	72.9	567.2	868.1	155.8	52.6
Arizona	9.8	1,737.3	1,160.0	4,085.5	461.6	121.4	19.6	77.4	708.2	1,008.9	101.7	72.8
Arkansas	9.2	818.2	777.5	2,532.2	310.5	275.4	17.1	128.7	370.6	476.1	1,171.2	37.1
California [3]	12.5	2,569.1	277.9	1,181.7	535.7	193.8	24.0	97.4	1,082.4	6,179.0	554.3	74.1
Colorado	9.7	775.7	296.8	846.8	375.2	138.2	18.5	110.9	607.7	937.5	408.1	52.8
Connecticut	7.8	542.3	321.5	1,143.3	284.1	159.6	14.4	68.9	464.1	770.7	159.9	54.9
Delaware	9.1	1,246.7	279.5	1,870.0	271.8	229.8	16.8	126.0	504.5	889.0	217.8	47.0
District of Columbia	8.5	198.5	275.2	554.2	261.6	180.5	15.0	244.0	367.8	558.1	1,505.7	44.8
Florida	9.2	1,251.4	177.4	2,680.1	364.9	179.7	18.9	90.3	453.9	850.1	304.5	42.4
Georgia [4]	7.9	616.4	375.9	1,897.4	349.3	204.1	16.5	60.4	529.5	659.9	485.8	32.6
Hawaii	11.1	1,327.5	711.7	427.4	387.5	265.9	17.8	199.8	346.6	652.2	365.6	91.9
Idaho	11.1	2,132.4	548.8	1,157.6	367.8	277.5	19.0	127.0	467.5	1,314.0	638.0	65.2
Illinois	9.3	590.4	380.1	1,173.7	378.7	194.7	17.1	92.0	688.5	1,001.4	298.9	51.3
Indiana	8.4	1,053.1	1,970.3	714.4	346.8	124.1	17.5	67.8	568.2	957.2	592.3	34.6
Iowa	8.1	967.9	664.5	1,315.0	285.1	112.5	15.5	82.6	377.4	758.8	229.2	43.3
Kansas	8.1	369.5	481.8	6,256.9	277.1	186.2	15.1	97.3	426.0	476.3	201.5	42.2
Kentucky	7.8	563.9	301.6	1,520.3	346.2	209.7	16.9	60.4	514.7	562.5	315.3	31.4
Louisiana	8.6	3,008.9	1,157.3	777.2	335.2	274.3	17.0	79.5	305.5	680.3	354.7	35.0
Maine	7.3	476.7	323.6	1,890.0	250.4	153.3	13.9	56.6	355.9	897.3	203.6	43.7
Maryland	9.2	1,118.8	1,120.4	1,149.1	304.3	214.0	16.8	110.1	440.2	772.3	558.2	40.6
Massachusetts	8.1	923.3	158.1	859.2	422.4	297.8	14.6	71.1	437.8	1,497.6	491.9	45.9
Michigan	9.2	729.5	502.9	3,302.7	323.2	208.0	19.7	114.6	571.7	1,132.0	244.8	32.8
Minnesota	11.2	648.4	481.4	1,714.9	525.6	251.9	17.8	137.2	925.9	847.0	291.7	96.4
Mississippi	8.3	558.8	353.3	1,211.2	339.1	239.9	17.5	57.8	614.4	675.0	227.9	39.1
Missouri	7.4	1,394.8	194.4	715.3	345.0	108.7	15.4	123.1	343.2	650.5	506.2	27.4
Montana [4,5]	8.9	1,061.2	353.0	1,068.0	338.5	182.5	16.4	85.4	410.8	475.7	2,434.5	46.3
Nebraska	7.6	473.4	423.6	1,227.7	304.0	195.9	14.5	81.0	383.8	503.9	290.9	36.2
Nevada	11.2	1,440.4	542.0	2,624.2	389.8	197.8	19.1	178.0	532.2	1,099.8	438.1	62.6
New Hampshire	8.4	539.4	426.7	1,348.4	405.4	239.1	15.7	55.2	313.2	691.0	434.4	52.8
New Jersey	7.3	712.7	175.4	917.5	273.2	142.7	13.8	85.9	380.1	672.3	136.6	45.8
New Mexico	8.2	757.8	174.7	596.1	383.7	122.4	17.0	72.1	511.1	1,272.7	317.3	42.4
New York	7.9	1,027.9	118.3	2,227.4	409.0	395.7	15.5	100.5	515.6	938.4	322.6	32.3
North Carolina [4]	8.4	920.7	397.4	1,643.2	296.3	204.2	16.2	53.1	397.5	543.7	435.0	53.6
North Dakota	8.6	273.8	726.2	2,205.6	302.3	250.7	15.9	81.0	480.2	650.8	327.2	47.4
Ohio	9.4	350.3	193.9	5,201.2	1,890.8	145.8	17.1	181.9	570.4	1,127.8	1,466.5	43.3
Oklahoma [4]	7.4	1,156.5	6,557.4	1,044.7	423.3	107.1	15.7	85.8	443.4	683.4	49.0	44.2
Oregon	10.3	604.0	401.5	1,548.1	325.5	154.8	19.8	82.7	429.5	862.6	529.5	66.0
Pennsylvania	9.0	1,330.0	249.1	1,121.4	437.4	181.7	17.0	120.5	486.3	811.8	180.5	46.4
Rhode Island	9.1	1,012.2	351.6	1,920.5	415.0	186.3	14.3	102.7	484.8	1,997.3	396.3	75.0
South Carolina [4,5]	8.6	2,445.4	352.8	1,382.4	290.3	182.5	16.2	85.4	425.6	588.5	258.9	46.3
South Dakota [4]	8.0	539.9	361.7	977.6	305.9	164.8	15.0	62.9	408.7	716.3	537.9	45.3
Tennessee	9.0	973.6	389.1	1,174.5	192.0	195.5	16.7	89.4	613.9	644.9	305.4	53.9
Texas	8.1	1,452.8	1,529.2	3,407.4	333.1	201.0	15.6	87.1	456.0	881.5	1,018.8	29.5
Utah	12.8	4,377.3	667.3	1,026.1	515.2	227.4	23.8	94.7	800.5	1,639.6	1,293.0	70.8
Vermont	6.7	694.5	379.7	359.1	256.8	146.8	13.8	36.0	318.0	488.7	63.3	109.6
Virginia [3]	7.9	613.6	621.0	728.2	305.5	191.9	14.4	89.5	347.1	553.8	343.1	38.0
Washington [2,4]	10.5	942.4	376.6	1,137.4	382.5	201.0	20.4	111.5	544.1	757.4	258.9	54.8
West Virginia	7.9	1,100.8	162.0	953.8	280.5	839.1	14.6	103.9	502.6	860.3	346.6	34.9
Wisconsin	9.1	1,033.5	382.3	798.3	369.8	195.0	15.8	104.1	452.0	614.5	217.3	65.2
Wyoming	7.6	605.2	693.5	2,435.6	306.3	142.2	14.8	74.0	388.6	728.9	147.7	37.9
Outlying areas												
American Samoa	10.3	485.9	383.6	560.6	242.9	180.0	20.0	971.7	767.2	2,429.3	303.7	39.8
Guam	8.8	2,197.3	114.4	1,831.1	531.6	824.0	18.3	69.2	412.0	1,098.7	225.8	42.7
Northern Marianas	8.4	978.8	100.1	518.2	293.6	163.1	20.9	40.8	314.6	2,202.3	117.5	79.4
Puerto Rico	9.0	1,998.8	5,654.2	1,015.6	454.1	132.5	16.0	—	708.4	725.6	314.6	32.2
Virgin Islands	6.6	631.6	70.6	1,082.7	264.4	214.5	14.0	76.3	264.4	494.3	52.8	62.0

[1] U.S. totals include underreporting and nonreporting states.
[2] Includes imputations for instruction coordinators.
[3] Includes imputations for prekindergarten teachers.
[4] Includes imputations for support staff.
[5] Includes imputations for instruction aides.

—Data not available or not applicable.

SOURCE: U.S. Department of Education, National Center for Education Statistics, Common Core of Data survey. (This table was prepared January 1998.)

Table 22.—Highest degree earned, number of years teaching experience, and average class size for teachers in public elementary and secondary schools, by state: 1993–94

State	Total [1]	Percent of teachers, by highest degree [2]				Percent of teachers, by years of full-time teaching experience				Average class size [3]	
		Bachelor's	Master's	Education specialist	Doctor's	Less than 3	3 to 9	10 to 20	Over 20	Elementary	Secondary
1	2	3	4	5	6	7	8	9	10	11	12
United States	2,561,294	52.0 (0.3)	42.0 (0.3)	4.6 (0.1)	0.7 (0.1)	9.7 (0.2)	25.5 (0.3)	35.0 (0.3)	29.8 (0.3)	24.1 (0.1)	23.6 (0.1)
Alabama	44,791	38.5 (1.9)	52.6 (1.7)	7.8 (0.8)	0.7 (0.3)	11.1 (0.8)	22.0 (1.5)	42.2 (1.9)	24.7 (1.5)	21.7 (0.4)	24.2 (0.2)
Alaska	8,152	59.0 (1.1)	35.3 (1.0)	4.2 (0.5)	0.2 (0.1)	8.0 (0.6)	29.3 (1.4)	42.7 (1.4)	20.0 (1.1)	22.6 (0.5)	22.0 (0.5)
Arizona	37,600	51.4 (1.8)	43.3 (1.7)	4.0 (0.6)	0.7 (0.2)	13.1 (1.0)	29.1 (1.6)	38.1 (1.7)	19.8 (1.4)	25.8 (0.4)	25.5 (0.3)
Arkansas	30,621	64.9 (2.1)	32.5 (1.7)	1.8 (0.6)	0.5 (0.1)	9.2 (0.8)	27.3 (1.7)	40.2 (1.8)	23.3 (1.6)	21.0 (0.4)	21.3 (0.3)
California	209,032	58.6 (1.8)	32.6 (1.8)	6.8 (0.7)	1.0 (0.2)	9.8 (0.8)	27.8 (1.9)	31.8 (1.7)	30.7 (1.7)	29.3 (0.3)	29.7 (0.4)
Colorado	35,723	46.5 (1.7)	49.4 (1.7)	2.5 (0.6)	0.5 (0.1)	9.4 (0.8)	26.1 (1.6)	38.7 (1.6)	25.7 (1.4)	24.7 (0.3)	24.5 (0.4)
Connecticut	35,465	19.6 (1.1)	62.4 (1.5)	15.7 (0.7)	1.4 (0.4)	6.4 (0.6)	19.8 (1.1)	35.5 (1.7)	38.3 (1.6)	21.4 (0.2)	19.7 (0.2)
Delaware	7,027	46.0 (1.6)	48.3 (1.8)	5.1 (0.9)	0.2 (0.1)	7.7 (1.0)	24.1 (1.9)	36.2 (2.3)	32.0 (2.1)	24.8 (0.4)	24.1 (0.4)
District of Columbia	5,185	41.2 (1.8)	54.4 (1.7)	2.4 (0.8)	2.0 (0.7)	10.8 (1.4)	14.7 (2.1)	30.6 (2.2)	43.9 (3.4)	21.8 (0.3)	20.7 (0.6)
Florida	106,535	57.2 (1.2)	37.0 (1.2)	3.3 (0.6)	1.4 (0.4)	8.7 (0.9)	29.4 (1.6)	37.8 (1.7)	24.0 (1.4)	26.0 (0.3)	26.6 (0.4)
Georgia	74,907	48.9 (1.5)	42.5 (1.6)	7.7 (0.8)	0.2 (0.1)	13.3 (1.1)	28.3 (1.4)	35.6 (1.4)	22.8 (1.3)	22.2 (0.2)	24.2 (0.3)
Hawaii	11,137	47.8 (2.1)	21.7 (1.5)	27.5 (2.2)	1.1 (0.4)	16.2 (1.4)	28.1 (1.6)	22.0 (1.4)	33.7 (2.2)	23.6 (0.3)	23.6 (0.8)
Idaho	12,166	74.4 (1.6)	21.7 (1.5)	2.6 (0.5)	0.6 (0.2)	12.4 (1.2)	33.3 (1.5)	33.7 (1.3)	20.6 (1.2)	24.0 (0.5)	23.7 (0.4)
Illinois	111,511	49.7 (1.3)	46.1 (1.4)	3.4 (0.5)	0.5 (0.2)	9.0 (0.6)	25.1 (1.0)	30.8 (1.3)	35.1 (1.3)	24.5 (0.3)	24.0 (0.3)
Indiana	57,732	21.4 (1.7)	72.9 (1.7)	4.9 (0.6)	0.1 (0.1)	5.6 (0.8)	24.7 (2.0)	37.1 (2.2)	32.6 (2.0)	21.9 (0.4)	23.0 (0.3)
Iowa	35,861	67.3 (1.8)	31.3 (1.9)	1.2 (0.5)	0.2 (0.1)	10.1 (1.0)	23.3 (1.7)	32.1 (2.1)	34.5 (2.3)	22.5 (0.6)	21.4 (0.5)
Kansas	31,164	53.5 (1.4)	42.8 (1.2)	2.3 (0.5)	1.1 (0.3)	12.3 (0.8)	28.2 (1.3)	35.2 (1.3)	24.3 (1.1)	20.6 (0.3)	20.7 (0.4)
Kentucky	41,571	23.4 (2.2)	56.8 (2.4)	18.7 (1.5)	0.8 (0.4)	9.5 (1.6)	26.8 (2.3)	32.9 (2.2)	30.8 (2.2)	24.4 (0.9)	23.5 (0.4)
Louisiana	48,948	60.5 (1.6)	31.2 (1.5)	6.9 (0.7)	0.5 (0.1)	9.7 (0.8)	29.8 (1.3)	35.1 (1.4)	25.5 (1.3)	22.9 (0.3)	23.7 (0.3)
Maine	15,658	68.4 (1.9)	28.4 (1.9)	1.6 (0.4)	0.2 (0.1)	7.0 (0.7)	28.7 (1.9)	37.4 (1.8)	26.9 (1.8)	21.5 (1.1)	18.5 (0.4)
Maryland	43,862	43.3 (1.9)	49.7 (2.3)	6.2 (1.1)	0.6 (0.2)	11.7 (0.9)	23.6 (1.6)	32.4 (1.4)	32.4 (1.5)	26.3 (0.7)	25.0 (0.3)
Massachusetts	58,416	38.8 (1.2)	54.8 (1.4)	3.9 (0.5)	0.9 (0.1)	8.4 (0.7)	17.1 (1.0)	33.6 (1.3)	41.0 (1.1)	23.1 (0.4)	20.9 (0.3)
Michigan	83,288	46.6 (1.9)	48.1 (1.8)	4.7 (0.8)	0.6 (0.3)	7.4 (1.0)	21.5 (1.8)	29.4 (2.1)	41.9 (2.2)	27.3 (1.9)	25.5 (0.3)
Minnesota	44,150	63.4 (2.1)	33.6 (2.0)	2.6 (0.6)	0.4 (0.2)	13.0 (1.1)	20.0 (1.5)	33.0 (1.7)	34.0 (1.8)	24.5 (1.0)	25.9 (0.4)
Mississippi	29,851	56.3 (1.5)	37.5 (1.7)	4.3 (0.9)	0.4 (0.1)	10.5 (0.8)	22.8 (1.4)	39.8 (1.8)	26.9 (1.2)	23.6 (0.4)	22.5 (0.4)
Missouri	62,454	54.3 (2.0)	42.4 (1.9)	2.2 (0.5)	0.6 (0.2)	10.6 (1.1)	26.9 (2.0)	37.2 (2.2)	25.3 (1.9)	23.7 (0.5)	22.5 (0.4)
Montana	12,851	71.3 (1.3)	26.0 (1.1)	1.8 (0.4)	0.5 (0.2)	11.1 (0.7)	27.5 (1.3)	39.0 (1.3)	22.5 (1.1)	21.2 (0.8)	19.3 (0.4)
Nebraska	20,411	61.5 (1.7)	36.0 (1.6)	1.9 (0.4)	0.4 (0.2)	10.1 (1.0)	24.4 (1.4)	39.0 (1.1)	26.5 (1.6)	20.0 (0.8)	18.7 (0.4)
Nevada	12,822	50.5 (2.2)	42.8 (2.3)	5.7 (0.9)	0.6 (0.3)	12.0 (1.1)	33.2 (2.4)	35.0 (1.8)	19.8 (1.8)	24.4 (0.7)	26.6 (0.6)
New Hampshire	12,299	60.2 (2.0)	35.9 (1.9)	2.6 (0.6)	0.7 (0.3)	10.6 (1.2)	26.8 (1.7)	38.2 (1.6)	24.4 (1.6)	21.8 (0.4)	20.5 (0.4)
New Jersey	83,935	56.2 (2.9)	37.4 (2.7)	4.8 (1.0)	1.0 (0.3)	5.8 (0.8)	21.1 (2.0)	34.6 (2.4)	38.5 (1.9)	23.2 (0.8)	20.5 (0.4)
New Mexico	19,265	53.2 (1.6)	43.6 (1.6)	2.2 (0.5)	0.4 (0.2)	12.5 (1.0)	32.5 (1.4)	33.9 (1.6)	21.1 (1.5)	21.9 (0.3)	24.5 (0.4)
New York	178,701	25.0 (1.9)	68.1 (1.9)	5.3 (0.8)	1.5 (0.6)	10.3 (1.2)	23.9 (1.7)	29.7 (1.6)	36.1 (2.0)	23.9 (0.4)	23.2 (0.4)
North Carolina	72,305	61.8 (1.5)	35.0 (1.6)	1.2 (0.4)	0.5 (0.3)	9.7 (0.7)	26.6 (1.4)	38.8 (1.3)	25.0 (1.3)	24.8 (0.2)	22.4 (0.3)
North Dakota	8,404	79.3 (1.1)	18.0 (0.9)	1.6 (0.3)	0.2 (0.1)	12.1 (1.0)	27.2 (1.0)	37.7 (1.5)	23.0 (1.4)	20.7 (0.7)	19.7 (0.5)
Ohio	111,518	53.2 (2.2)	41.8 (2.3)	3.1 (0.7)	0.4 (0.2)	6.8 (0.8)	23.2 (1.8)	38.6 (2.1)	31.4 (2.1)	25.0 (1.2)	22.3 (0.4)
Oklahoma	42,220	56.9 (1.8)	39.5 (1.9)	3.2 (0.5)	0.4 (0.2)	10.4 (0.8)	27.0 (1.7)	41.2 (1.8)	21.5 (1.1)	20.5 (0.4)	20.5 (0.3)
Oregon	25,706	51.5 (1.9)	43.1 (1.9)	4.0 (0.9)	0.8 (0.5)	7.4 (0.8)	27.0 (1.6)	39.6 (1.7)	26.0 (1.7)	24.4 (0.3)	23.9 (0.4)
Pennsylvania	114,571	46.7 (2.3)	45.6 (1.9)	6.9 (1.7)	0.3 (0.2)	6.9 (1.0)	18.3 (2.0)	33.0 (2.2)	41.8 (2.2)	25.2 (0.6)	24.1 (0.3)
Rhode Island	9,217	40.1 (2.5)	53.3 (2.4)	5.7 (0.9)	1.0 (0.5)	7.2 (1.1)	21.9 (1.8)	28.6 (1.7)	42.3 (2.0)	23.2 (0.6)	20.8 (0.5)
South Carolina	39,623	48.8 (2.5)	43.4 (2.6)	5.6 (0.9)	0.7 (0.3)	10.5 (1.4)	25.1 (1.9)	42.3 (1.9)	22.1 (1.7)	23.3 (0.7)	22.5 (0.4)
South Dakota	10,579	75.1 (1.2)	23.2 (1.1)	1.5 (0.3)	0.1 (0.1)	10.4 (0.7)	28.6 (1.2)	37.3 (1.1)	23.8 (1.2)	19.2 (0.3)	20.9 (0.4)
Tennessee	47,662	51.2 (2.0)	42.0 (2.0)	4.8 (0.8)	1.2 (0.4)	12.4 (1.1)	22.9 (1.9)	35.5 (2.0)	29.2 (2.2)	24.4 (1.2)	25.2 (0.4)
Texas	223,800	69.7 (1.3)	26.8 (1.5)	1.8 (0.4)	0.9 (0.5)	12.1 (0.9)	30.1 (1.5)	37.5 (1.4)	20.4 (1.4)	20.1 (0.2)	22.5 (0.4)
Utah	19,884	70.6 (1.4)	23.5 (1.3)	4.2 (0.7)	0.4 (0.1)	12.7 (0.8)	32.8 (1.4)	36.1 (1.4)	18.3 (1.0)	27.5 (0.4)	28.8 (0.2)
Vermont	7,327	49.4 (1.8)	47.5 (1.8)	2.1 (0.8)	0.5 (0.4)	12.3 (1.5)	25.3 (1.9)	34.4 (1.9)	28.0 (1.8)	19.7 (0.8)	19.2 (0.4)
Virginia	64,937	64.4 (2.1)	31.3 (2.0)	2.4 (0.6)	0.5 (0.2)	10.5 (1.2)	26.0 (2.2)	37.5 (2.0)	26.1 (1.9)	22.6 (0.3)	21.6 (0.3)
Washington	48,452	56.3 (1.9)	37.5 (2.2)	3.6 (0.9)	1.0 (0.3)	10.8 (0.9)	30.1 (2.0)	32.2 (1.9)	26.9 (1.6)	25.9 (1.3)	25.5 (0.2)
West Virginia	21,473	41.7 (1.7)	53.1 (1.7)	4.3 (0.6)	(4) —	4.4 (0.8)	21.6 (1.6)	42.7 (1.5)	31.4 (1.7)	20.9 (0.6)	22.5 (0.3)
Wisconsin	62,958	59.3 (1.7)	38.1 (1.6)	1.7 (0.4)	0.6 (0.3)	9.1 (0.8)	24.7 (1.8)	29.5 (2.2)	36.7 (2.2)	23.1 (0.4)	23.1 (0.4)
Wyoming	7,567	71.3 (1.0)	26.5 (0.9)	1.4 (0.3)	0.4 (0.1)	9.4 (0.8)	22.6 (1.2)	41.6 (1.3)	26.5 (1.3)	21.0 (0.3)	19.3 (0.3)

[1] Data are based on a head count of all teachers rather than on the number of full-time equivalent teachers appearing in other tables.

[2] Teachers with less than a bachelor's degree are not shown.

[3] Elementary teachers are those who taught self-contained classes at the elementary level and secondary teachers are those who taught departmentalized classes (e.g., science, art, social science, or other course subjects) at the secondary level. Excludes special education teachers. Teachers were classified as elementary or secondary on the basis of the grades they taught, rather than on the level of the school in which they taught.

[4] Less than 0.05 percent.

—Data not applicable.

NOTE.—Excludes prekindergarten teachers. Details may not add to totals due to rounding. Standard errors appear in parentheses.

SOURCE: U.S. Department of Education, National Center for Education Statistics, "Schools and Staffing Survey, 1993–94"; and Condition of Education, 1997, Supplemental tables. (This table was prepared February 1998.)

Table 23.—Teachers in public elementary and secondary schools, by state: Fall 1970 to fall 1995

State or other area	Fall 1970	Fall 1971	Fall 1972	Fall 1973	Fall 1974	Fall 1975	Fall 1976	Fall 1977	Fall 1978	Fall 1979
1	2	3	4	5	6	7	8	9	10	11
United States	**2,058,744**	**[1] 2,062,933**	**[1] 2,105,716**	**2,135,879**	**2,164,548**	**2,197,670**	**[1] 2,189,197**	**[1] 2,208,672**	**[1] 2,206,803**	**2,184,877**
Alabama	33,026	33,172	33,730	34,234	35,380	36,675	[2] 37,259	[3] 37,980	40,771	31,967
Alaska	3,821	4,087	4,142	4,046	4,090	4,577	4,475	4,915	5,057	5,130
Arizona	18,772	19,010	20,368	21,352	21,206	22,978	23,482	24,189	25,654	26,205
Arkansas	21,122	20,305	20,611	20,053	20,678	21,256	21,821	22,463	23,112	23,851
California	193,000	199,178	198,483	200,475	202,929	205,000	206,563	207,000	207,000	194,237
Colorado	24,450	24,593	25,476	26,392	26,279	28,451	29,259	29,158	29,461	29,675
Connecticut	31,323	33,909	34,077	34,750	35,474	35,673	36,299	36,425	35,739	35,225
Delaware	6,034	6,220	6,220	6,280	6,349	6,335	6,235	6,029	6,014	6,021
District of Columbia	7,486	6,529	6,561	6,580	6,928	6,642	6,057	6,022	5,964	5,946
Florida	62,419	63,245	66,563	67,532	70,842	72,836	73,505	70,598	71,856	71,853
Georgia	44,007	44,732	44,536	45,375	46,446	47,382	46,451	52,920	53,000	52,292
Hawaii	7,985	8,235	8,310	7,877	7,806	7,860	7,914	7,891	7,940	7,207
Idaho	8,047	8,024	7,664	8,263	8,563	9,009	9,277	9,561	9,830	9,697
Illinois	111,827	[3] 110,000	109,824	110,831	112,749	113,589	[2] 110,500	[3] 107,000	112,904	107,211
Indiana	50,421	52,297	[3] 52,400	52,046	49,302	53,088	53,089	52,649	53,657	53,426
Iowa	32,659	32,494	32,749	32,708	32,715	33,100	33,334	33,331	33,511	32,911
Kansas	25,884	24,743	[3] 25,360	25,529	25,573	25,668	25,633	25,613	26,812	26,184
Kentucky	30,180	31,020	31,465	31,412	31,755	31,962	[2] 32,300	[3] 32,860	32,835	32,959
Louisiana	36,469	37,203	41,837	41,884	42,132	41,054	40,428	[3] 40,794	41,756	44,688
Maine	11,170	11,400	12,213	11,612	12,017	12,304	13,230	13,425	13,878	10,748
Maryland	40,810	41,998	41,681	42,793	42,802	42,378	42,891	42,637	42,543	41,738
Massachusetts	55,300	54,763	60,233	66,249	67,220	64,100	62,982	[3] 66,224	66,962	69,313
Michigan	93,000	89,236	89,969	91,429	90,481	89,847	87,999	87,452	87,622	86,650
Minnesota	43,809	44,535	43,944	43,621	43,817	44,779	45,024	44,631	44,488	44,149
Mississippi	22,533	22,849	23,329	23,472	23,580	23,881	24,130	24,831	25,685	25,805
Missouri	48,286	43,872	45,414	46,680	47,391	49,283	48,563	49,618	48,800	48,755
Montana	8,406	8,480	8,875	8,903	9,015	9,052	9,580	9,650	9,682	9,521
Nebraska	17,230	16,642	[3] 16,999	17,289	17,367	17,707	17,852	17,943	17,731	18,325
Nevada	4,967	5,329	5,411	5,571	5,616	5,750	5,995	6,391	6,294	6,986
New Hampshire	7,441	[3] 7,450	8,564	8,675	9,360	8,775	9,624	9,600	8,874	9,425
New Jersey	72,140	76,260	79,347	79,156	80,448	80,410	[2] 80,010	78,701	[3] 78,000	77,429
New Mexico	11,620	12,272	12,320	12,520	12,651	12,883	12,887	13,832	13,909	14,144
New York	177,066	180,071	185,368	186,386	188,961	180,880	172,102	174,991	158,146	158,621
North Carolina	49,565	49,402	49,571	51,277	51,221	52,379	52,906	53,836	55,309	56,369
North Dakota	7,659	7,490	7,454	7,569	7,577	7,594	7,551	7,389	7,381	7,560
Ohio	104,680	100,776	103,487	105,127	104,512	105,875	105,588	105,286	102,645	101,482
Oklahoma	28,184	27,515	27,401	27,611	28,986	29,762	30,405	31,177	32,136	33,210
Oregon	21,641	22,831	22,216	22,250	22,300	23,808	23,942	24,312	24,579	24,780
Pennsylvania	108,772	109,035	111,682	113,089	115,668	116,255	114,425	112,956	110,833	111,615
Rhode Island	8,988	9,226	9,484	9,426	9,329	9,196	9,162	9,112	9,314	9,255
South Carolina	28,578	25,729	26,957	26,960	27,804	28,695	30,917	29,666	30,022	31,658
South Dakota	8,698	8,269	8,253	8,127	8,118	8,083	8,163	8,072	8,179	8,122
Tennessee	35,450	36,089	36,200	37,150	39,278	39,855	40,135	40,029	41,220	40,978
Texas	129,440	125,050	127,237	130,517	133,759	143,390	[2] 142,400	147,544	154,913	153,727
Utah	11,736	12,127	12,248	12,320	12,468	12,521	12,779	12,871	13,425	13,974
Vermont	5,750	6,169	6,192	6,262	6,224	6,421	[2] 6,314	[3] 6,170	6,480	[3] 6,628
Virginia	47,903	48,774	49,743	51,761	53,280	58,330	59,538	60,082	56,739	56,868
Washington	33,380	[3] 33,480	32,733	32,689	33,584	33,698	[2] 33,690	[3] 33,691	34,893	35,498
West Virginia	16,582	17,248	17,958	18,474	18,992	19,590	20,175	20,674	19,765	21,387
Wisconsin	44,460	44,898	48,122	48,432	48,541	51,847	49,366	52,940	47,677	48,264
Wyoming	4,568	4,672	4,735	4,863	4,985	5,207	4,991	5,541	5,806	5,208
Outlying Areas	—	—	—	—	—	—	—	—	—	—
American Samoa	400	400	400	623	666	342	378	488	—	—
Guam	1,048	1,142	1,183	1,247	1,326	1,229	1,294	1,294	—	1,248
Northern Marianas	—	—	—	—	—	—	—	—	—	236
Puerto Rico	23,142	23,820	24,552	25,439	25,000	25,796	24,761	24,761	32,048	—
Trust Territories	—	—	—	—	—	—	—	—	—	—
Virgin Islands	—	980	1,023	1,135	1,341	1,408	1,361	1,421	1,660	1,479

Table 23.—Teachers in public elementary and secondary schools, by state: Fall 1970 to fall 1995—Continued

State or other area	Fall 1980	Fall 1981	Fall 1982	Fall 1983	Fall 1984	Fall 1985	Fall 1986	Fall 1987	Fall 1988	Fall 1989
1	12	13	14	15	16	17	18	19	20	21
United States	**2,184,216**	**[1] 2,127,402**	**2,132,792**	**2,138,821**	**2,167,950**	**2,205,987**	**[1] 2,243,579**	**2,279,241**	**2,323,213**	**2,356,702**
Alabama	36,172	[2] 36,000	35,619	35,875	36,647	36,138	36,971	37,716	38,845	39,928
Alaska	5,225	5,665	5,710	6,259	6,127	6,814	6,448	6,113	6,272	6,492
Arizona	25,713	25,601	26,190	26,268	26,900	27,935	29,104	30,707	31,617	32,134
Arkansas	24,078	23,497	23,713	23,696	23,985	24,767	24,944	25,572	27,730	25,585
California	193,846	175,000	174,674	174,290	178,310	184,151	190,484	195,864	203,342	212,687
Colorado	29,840	29,462	29,375	28,417	28,824	29,894	30,704	31,168	31,398	31,954
Connecticut	34,584	33,723	32,760	32,317	32,618	32,903	34,252	35,050	35,502	34,618
Delaware	5,626	5,331	5,409	5,429	5,577	5,745	5,883	5,951	5,898	5,982
District of Columbia	5,238	5,132	5,355	5,569	5,889	6,137	5,984	6,232	5,936	6,055
Florida	73,983	74,872	83,301	85,028	86,264	88,973	91,969	95,857	100,370	104,127
Georgia	56,514	56,217	56,510	56,555	56,294	57,374	57,881	62,280	59,916	61,487
Hawaii	7,185	7,165	7,077	7,007	7,078	7,276	7,291	7,684	8,737	8,866
Idaho	9,938	9,798	9,790	9,847	10,147	10,255	10,234	10,258	10,425	10,715
Illinois	108,064	103,793	104,619	102,130	102,013	102,657	104,609	105,217	105,097	106,183
Indiana	53,099	51,303	50,528	50,509	51,308	51,976	52,896	53,749	54,029	54,370
Iowa	32,745	31,244	32,110	31,779	31,882	31,770	30,958	30,873	30,327	30,423
Kansas	26,366	26,179	26,056	26,096	26,331	26,686	27,064	27,317	28,122	28,727
Kentucky	32,892	31,666	32,237	32,458	32,850	33,506	34,507	35,239	35,788	35,731
Louisiana	43,930	39,967	42,697	42,200	42,180	42,609	42,929	42,920	43,203	44,608
Maine	11,775	[2] 12,000	12,910	13,492	13,261	14,226	13,685	14,204	14,593	15,206
Maryland	40,863	39,120	37,760	37,275	38,030	38,433	39,491	40,093	40,899	41,646
Massachusetts	64,987	62,227	56,498	56,873	56,504	56,845	58,066	59,517	60,068	59,040
Michigan	84,377	78,768	80,364	79,982	81,185	82,193	83,130	79,972	79,847	80,150
Minnesota	44,142	42,836	39,775	39,392	40,108	41,314	40,957	42,132	42,750	43,101
Mississippi	25,933	24,430	25,176	24,955	25,388	26,102	26,219	26,930	27,283	27,591
Missouri	48,878	48,135	46,047	46,761	47,366	48,170	48,902	49,632	50,693	51,362
Montana	9,370	9,310	9,517	9,479	9,597	9,705	9,818	9,659	9,626	9,627
Nebraska	16,796	17,410	17,381	17,548	17,656	17,687	17,748	17,713	18,003	18,464
Nevada	7,129	7,180	7,222	7,366	7,496	7,751	7,908	8,348	8,699	9,175
New Hampshire	8,448	9,729	9,758	9,821	10,065	10,104	10,300	10,363	10,442	10,572
New Jersey	76,550	75,231	74,303	73,593	73,774	74,236	75,558	78,335	79,698	79,597
New Mexico	14,089	14,296	14,323	14,532	14,538	14,781	14,876	15,175	15,770	16,150
New York	155,320	157,201	157,250	158,440	163,044	165,573	168,940	170,236	172,807	174,610
North Carolina	56,222	55,833	55,261	55,126	56,084	57,638	58,103	59,771	61,933	63,160
North Dakota	7,375	6,995	7,071	7,067	7,794	7,796	7,779	7,632	7,731	7,809
Ohio	100,527	96,449	94,126	96,927	98,061	98,264	98,894	99,708	101,021	101,417
Oklahoma	33,901	33,904	34,960	34,999	34,894	35,752	35,041	34,515	35,116	35,631
Oregon	22,596	22,480	24,074	24,409	24,444	24,605	24,615	24,911	25,147	25,630
Pennsylvania	109,928	107,103	103,855	102,207	101,484	101,665	102,993	103,307	104,379	105,415
Rhode Island	9,192	8,895	8,854	8,848	8,752	8,844	8,916	8,934	9,216	9,369
South Carolina	32,214	32,007	32,244	32,323	33,764	34,645	35,349	35,701	35,877	36,337
South Dakota	7,964	7,964	7,974	8,355	8,579	8,340	8,031	8,172	8,260	8,191
Tennessee	41,162	40,875	39,660	39,409	39,636	40,023	41,103	42,082	42,657	42,824
Texas	159,531	159,640	167,835	170,439	172,865	181,051	186,385	187,159	196,616	199,397
Utah	14,372	14,463	14,616	15,245	15,821	16,229	16,886	17,124	17,602	17,611
Vermont	6,476	6,103	6,189	6,242	6,327	6,397	[2] 6,397	6,656	6,852	6,852
Virginia	57,027	55,471	56,038	56,388	57,498	57,339	58,141	59,928	60,883	62,138
Washington	35,514	34,576	34,056	34,757	35,706	36,202	37,065	38,344	38,780	40,279
West Virginia	21,668	21,870	22,159	22,503	22,732	22,733	22,931	22,702	22,177	21,653
Wisconsin	48,491	46,652	45,047	45,311	47,082	46,482	47,039	47,721	48,541	49,329
Wyoming	6,361	6,634	6,759	7,028	7,191	7,296	7,201	6,798	6,693	6,697
Outlying Areas	—	—	—	—	—	—	—	37,027	37,365	37,661
American Samoa	559	—	—	—	—	—	623	656	674	659
Guam	1,466	—	1,330	1,334	—	1,329	1,430	1,407	1,403	1,622
Northern Marianas	—	—	—	258	310	—	—	305	334	358
Puerto Rico	31,964	—	32,845	32,247	32,520	32,683	32,361	33,069	33,357	33,427
Trust Territories	—	—	—	—	—	—	—	—	—	—
Virgin Islands	1,567	—	1,647	2,281	1,665	1,631	1,606	1,590	1,597	1,595

Table 23.—Teachers in public elementary and secondary schools, by state:
Fall 1970 to fall 1995—Continued

State or other area	Fall 1990	Fall 1991	Fall 1992	Fall 1993	Fall 1994	Fall 1995	Percentage change			
							Fall 1970 to fall 1995	Fall 1985 to fall 1990	Fall 1990 to fall 1995	Fall 1985 to fall 1995
1	22	23	24	25	26	27	28	29	30	31
United States	**2,398,169**	**2,432,243**	**2,458,956**	**2,503,901**	**2,551,875**	**2,598,220**	**26.2**	**8.7**	**8.3**	**17.8**
Alabama	36,266	40,480	41,961	43,003	42,791	44,056	33.4	0.4	21.5	21.9
Alaska	6,710	7,118	7,282	7,193	7,205	7,379	93.1	-1.5	10.0	8.3
Arizona	32,987	33,978	36,076	37,493	38,132	38,017	102.5	18.1	15.2	36.1
Arkansas	25,984	25,785	26,017	26,014	26,181	26,449	25.2	4.9	1.8	6.8
California	217,228	224,000	218,566	221,787	225,016	230,849	19.6	18.0	6.3	25.4
Colorado	32,342	33,093	33,419	33,661	34,894	35,388	44.7	8.2	9.4	18.4
Connecticut	34,785	34,383	34,193	34,526	35,316	36,070	15.2	5.7	3.7	9.6
Delaware	5,961	6,095	6,252	6,380	6,416	6,463	7.1	3.8	8.4	12.5
District of Columbia	5,950	6,346	6,064	6,056	6,110	5,305	-29.1	-3.0	-10.8	-13.6
Florida	108,088	109,939	107,590	110,653	110,674	114,938	84.1	21.5	6.3	29.2
Georgia	63,058	63,816	66,942	74,172	77,914	79,480	80.6	9.9	26.0	38.5
Hawaii	9,083	9,451	10,083	10,111	10,240	10,500	31.5	24.8	15.6	44.3
Idaho	11,254	11,626	11,827	12,007	12,582	12,784	58.9	9.7	13.6	24.7
Illinois	108,775	110,153	111,461	110,874	110,830	113,538	1.5	6.0	4.4	10.6
Indiana	54,806	54,509	54,552	55,107	55,496	55,821	10.7	5.4	1.9	7.4
Iowa	31,045	31,395	31,403	31,616	31,726	32,318	-1.0	-2.3	4.1	1.7
Kansas	29,140	29,324	29,753	30,283	30,579	30,729	18.7	9.2	5.5	15.2
Kentucky	36,777	37,571	37,868	37,324	38,784	39,120	29.6	9.8	6.4	16.8
Louisiana	45,401	46,170	46,904	46,913	47,599	46,980	28.8	6.6	3.5	10.3
Maine	15,513	15,416	15,375	15,344	15,404	15,392	37.8	9.0	-0.8	8.2
Maryland	42,562	43,616	44,495	44,171	46,565	47,819	17.2	10.7	12.4	24.4
Massachusetts	54,003	55,963	57,225	58,766	60,489	62,710	13.4	-5.0	16.1	10.3
Michigan	80,008	82,967	82,301	80,267	80,522	83,179	-10.6	-2.7	4.0	1.2
Minnesota	43,574	44,903	45,050	46,956	46,958	46,971	7.2	5.5	7.8	13.7
Mississippi	28,062	28,111	27,829	28,376	28,866	28,997	28.7	7.5	3.3	11.1
Missouri	52,359	52,643	52,984	54,860	56,606	57,951	20.0	8.7	10.7	20.3
Montana	9,613	9,883	10,135	9,949	10,079	10,076	19.9	-0.9	4.8	3.8
Nebraska	18,764	19,069	19,323	19,616	19,774	20,028	16.2	6.1	6.7	13.2
Nevada	10,373	11,409	11,953	12,579	13,414	13,878	179.4	33.8	33.8	79.0
New Hampshire	10,637	11,464	11,654	11,972	12,109	12,346	65.9	5.3	16.1	22.2
New Jersey	79,886	80,515	83,057	84,564	85,258	86,706	20.2	7.6	8.5	16.8
New Mexico	16,703	17,498	17,912	18,404	19,025	19,398	66.9	13.0	16.1	31.2
New York	176,390	171,914	176,375	179,413	182,273	181,559	2.5	6.5	2.9	9.7
North Carolina	64,283	65,326	66,630	69,421	71,592	73,201	47.7	11.5	13.9	27.0
North Dakota	7,591	7,733	7,794	7,755	7,796	7,501	-2.1	-2.6	-1.2	-3.8
Ohio	103,088	103,372	106,233	107,444	109,085	107,347	2.5	4.9	4.1	9.2
Oklahoma	37,221	37,650	38,433	39,031	39,406	39,364	39.7	4.1	5.8	10.1
Oregon	26,174	26,745	26,634	26,488	26,208	26,680	23.3	6.4	1.9	8.4
Pennsylvania	100,275	100,475	100,912	101,302	102,988	104,921	-3.5	-1.4	4.6	3.2
Rhode Island	9,522	9,709	10,069	9,823	10,066	10,482	16.6	7.7	10.1	18.5
South Carolina	36,963	37,115	37,295	38,620	39,437	39,922	39.7	6.7	8.0	15.2
South Dakota	8,511	8,868	8,767	9,557	9,985	9,641	10.8	2.1	13.3	15.6
Tennessee	43,051	43,062	43,566	46,066	47,406	53,403	50.6	7.6	24.0	33.4
Texas	219,298	219,192	219,385	224,830	234,213	240,371	85.7	21.1	9.6	32.8
Utah	17,884	18,305	19,191	19,053	19,524	20,039	70.7	10.2	12.0	23.5
Vermont	7,257	7,031	7,521	7,330	7,566	7,676	33.5	13.4	5.8	20.0
Virginia	63,638	64,537	68,181	70,859	72,505	74,731	56.0	11.0	17.4	30.3
Washington	41,764	42,931	44,295	45,524	46,439	46,907	40.5	15.4	12.3	29.6
West Virginia	21,476	20,997	20,961	21,029	21,024	21,073	27.1	-5.5	-1.9	-7.3
Wisconsin	49,302	52,028	53,387	52,822	54,054	55,033	23.8	6.1	11.6	18.4
Wyoming	6,784	6,564	5,821	6,537	6,754	6,734	47.4	-7.0	-0.7	-7.7
Outlying Areas	38,456	41,472	42,754	44,117	44,391	43,902	—	—	14.2	—
American Samoa	662	671	725	656	698	728	82.0	—	10.0	—
Guam	1,543	1,499	1,628	1,644	1,826	1,802	71.9	16.1	16.8	35.6
Northern Marianas	416	430	425	431	406	422	—	—	1.4	—
Puerto Rico	34,260	37,291	38,381	39,816	39,933	39,328	69.9	4.8	14.8	20.3
Trust Territories	—	—	—	—	—	—				
Virgin Islands	1,575	1,581	1,595	1,570	1,528	1,622	—	-3.4	3.0	-0.6

[1] National total includes estimates for nonreporting states.
[2] Data estimated by NCES.
[3] Data estimated by reporting state.
—Data not available or not applicable.

SOURCE: U.S. Department of Education, National Center for Education Statistics, *Statistics of Public Elementary and Secondary Day Schools,* various years; and Common Core of Data surveys. (This table was prepared February 1998.)

Table 24.—Pupil/teacher ratios in public elementary and secondary schools, by state: Fall 1970 to fall 1995

State or other area	Fall 1970	Fall 1971	Fall 1972	Fall 1973	Fall 1974	Fall 1975	Fall 1976	Fall 1977	Fall 1978	Fall 1979
1	2	3	4	5	6	7	8	9	10	11
United States	**22.3**	**[1] 22.3**	**[1] 21.7**	**21.3**	**20.8**	**20.4**	**[1] 20.2**	**[1] 19.7**	**[1] 19.3**	**[1] 19.1**
Alabama	24.4	24.3	23.2	22.5	21.6	20.7	[2] 20.2	[3] 20.1	18.7	23.6
Alaska [4]	20.9	20.6	20.6	20.4	21.2	19.5	20.4	18.4	17.9	17.3
Arizona	23.4	24.4	23.8	24.4	23.0	21.5	21.4	21.2	19.9	19.4
Arkansas	21.9	22.7	22.4	22.4	22.0	21.5	21.1	20.4	19.8	19.0
California	24.0	23.1	22.7	22.2	21.8	21.6	21.2	20.8	20.2	21.2
Colorado	22.5	23.0	22.5	21.7	21.6	20.0	19.3	19.3	18.9	18.6
Connecticut	21.1	19.7	19.5	19.2	18.6	18.3	17.5	16.9	16.6	16.1
Delaware	22.0	21.7	21.6	21.2	20.6	20.1	19.6	19.6	18.5	17.3
District of Columbia	19.5	21.8	21.3	20.7	19.0	19.6	20.8	19.9	19.1	17.9
Florida	22.9	23.4	22.8	22.8	22.0	21.3	20.9	21.8	21.1	21.0
Georgia	25.0	24.4	24.5	23.9	23.3	23.0	23.6	20.6	20.6	20.6
Hawaii	22.6	22.3	21.9	22.7	22.7	22.4	22.1	21.8	21.5	23.4
Idaho	22.7	23.1	24.1	22.9	21.9	21.8	21.6	21.1	20.7	20.9
Illinois	21.1	[3] 21.6	21.4	20.9	20.4	20.0	[2] 20.3	[3] 20.3	18.1	19.1
Indiana	24.4	23.5	[3] 23.3	23.2	24.1	22.1	21.9	21.7	20.7	20.3
Iowa	20.2	20.1	19.7	19.3	18.9	18.5	18.2	17.7	17.0	16.7
Kansas	19.8	20.4	[3] 19.4	18.8	18.4	18.1	17.9	17.4	16.2	16.2
Kentucky	23.8	23.2	22.7	22.6	22.1	21.6	[2] 21.5	[3] 21.2	21.1	20.5
Louisiana	23.1	22.9	20.2	20.1	20.0	20.6	20.8	[3] 20.6	19.6	17.9
Maine	21.9	21.6	20.5	21.1	20.9	20.4	18.8	18.3	17.3	21.2
Maryland	22.5	22.0	22.1	21.3	20.9	20.8	20.1	19.6	19.0	18.6
Massachusetts	21.1	21.8	20.0	18.2	18.0	18.7	18.6	[3] 16.9	16.2	14.9
Michigan	23.1	24.5	24.1	23.2	23.6	23.1	23.1	22.5	21.8	21.5
Minnesota	21.0	20.5	20.7	20.6	20.3	19.7	19.2	18.7	18.2	17.6
Mississippi	23.7	23.2	22.6	22.1	21.8	21.5	21.1	20.2	19.2	18.7
Missouri	21.5	23.3	22.7	21.8	21.1	19.6	19.6	18.8	18.4	17.9
Montana	21.0	21.0	20.3	19.5	19.1	19.0	17.8	17.5	17.0	16.6
Nebraska	19.1	20.0	[3] 19.4	18.7	18.4	17.8	17.5	17.1	16.8	15.7
Nevada	25.7	24.4	24.3	24.3	24.4	24.3	23.7	22.4	23.2	21.1
New Hampshire	21.3	[3] 22.0	19.6	19.8	18.4	19.9	18.2	18.2	19.4	18.1
New Jersey	20.5	19.6	19.0	18.7	18.2	18.1	[2] 17.8	17.6	[3] 17.1	16.6
New Mexico	24.2	23.2	23.1	22.6	22.3	21.3	22.1	20.4	20.1	19.5
New York	19.7	19.7	18.9	18.6	18.2	18.9	19.4	18.4	19.6	18.7
North Carolina	24.1	23.8	23.4	22.9	23.0	22.6	22.5	22.0	21.0	20.4
North Dakota	19.2	19.3	19.0	18.3	17.6	17.3	17.1	16.9	16.5	15.6
Ohio	23.2	24.2	23.4	22.6	22.3	21.7	21.3	20.7	20.5	20.0
Oklahoma	22.2	22.7	22.2	21.8	20.6	20.0	19.7	19.1	18.3	17.6
Oregon	22.2	21.0	21.2	21.4	21.4	20.1	19.8	19.5	19.2	18.9
Pennsylvania	21.7	21.7	21.1	20.5	19.7	19.3	19.2	18.8	18.5	17.6
Rhode Island	20.9	20.7	20.0	19.6	19.2	19.2	18.8	18.3	17.3	16.7
South Carolina	22.3	25.2	23.1	23.3	22.6	21.9	20.1	20.9	20.8	19.7
South Dakota	19.1	20.0	19.7	19.4	18.9	18.7	18.1	17.8	16.9	16.5
Tennessee	25.4	24.9	24.6	24.3	22.2	22.0	21.0	21.9	21.2	21.1
Texas	21.9	22.5	21.5	21.3	20.8	19.6	[2] 19.8	19.3	18.5	18.7
Utah	25.9	25.2	25.0	24.8	24.6	24.7	24.6	24.7	24.2	23.8
Vermont	17.9	17.1	17.2	17.0	16.9	16.3	[2] 16.5	[3] 16.7	15.6	[3] 14.8
Virginia	22.5	22.0	21.5	21.0	20.5	18.9	18.5	18.0	18.6	18.1
Washington	24.5	[3] 24.0	24.2	24.1	23.4	23.3	[2] 23.2	[3] 23.0	22.0	21.5
West Virginia	24.1	23.4	22.8	22.1	21.3	20.6	20.1	19.4	20.0	18.1
Wisconsin	22.4	22.3	20.7	20.4	20.1	18.6	19.1	17.3	18.6	17.8
Wyoming	19.0	18.5	18.2	17.6	17.4	16.9	18.2	16.7	16.2	18.3
Outlying areas	—	—	—	—	—	—	—	—	—	—
American Samoa	—	20.0	20.4	16.5	15.3	29.6	26.3	19.0	—	—
Guam	23.6	22.8	22.8	21.9	21.3	23.3	22.1	—	—	22.1
Northern Marianas	—	—	—	—	—	—	—	—	—	18.7
Puerto Rico	29.7	29.3	29.0	28.0	—	27.0	27.8	—	22.5	—
Trust Territories	—	—	—	—	—	—	—	—	—	—
Virgin Islands	—	19.2	20.4	19.4	17.4	17.4	18.4	18.0	15.1	17.3

Table 24.—Pupil/teacher ratios in public elementary and secondary schools, by state: Fall 1970 to fall 1995—Continued

State or other area	Fall 1980	Fall 1981	Fall 1982	Fall 1983	Fall 1984	Fall 1985	Fall 1986	Fall 1987	Fall 1988	Fall 1989
1	12	13	14	15	16	17	18	19	20	21
United States	**18.7**	**[1]18.8**	**18.6**	**18.4**	**18.1**	**17.9**	**[1]17.7**	**17.6**	**17.3**	**17.2**
Alabama	21.0	[2]20.7	20.3	20.1	19.4	20.2	19.8	19.3	18.7	18.1
Alaska[4]	16.6	16.0	15.7	15.7	17.1	15.8	16.7	17.5	17.0	16.8
Arizona	20.0	19.8	19.5	19.3	19.7	19.6	18.4	18.6	18.2	18.9
Arkansas	18.6	18.6	18.2	18.2	18.0	17.5	17.5	17.1	15.7	17.0
California	21.0	23.1	23.3	23.5	23.3	23.1	23.0	22.9	22.7	22.4
Colorado	18.3	18.5	18.6	19.1	18.9	18.4	18.2	18.0	17.8	17.6
Connecticut	15.4	15.0	14.8	14.8	14.4	14.0	13.7	13.3	13.0	13.3
Delaware	17.7	17.8	17.1	16.8	16.5	16.2	16.0	16.1	16.4	16.4
District of Columbia	19.1	18.5	17.0	16.0	14.8	14.2	14.3	13.9	14.3	13.4
Florida	20.4	19.9	17.8	17.6	17.7	17.6	17.5	17.4	17.1	17.2
Georgia	18.9	18.8	18.6	18.6	18.9	18.8	18.9	17.8	18.5	18.3
Hawaii	23.0	22.7	22.9	23.2	23.2	22.6	22.6	21.6	19.2	19.1
Idaho	20.5	20.9	20.7	21.0	20.5	20.3	20.4	20.7	20.6	20.1
Illinois	18.4	18.5	18.0	18.1	18.0	17.8	17.4	17.2	17.1	16.9
Indiana	19.9	20.0	19.8	19.5	19.0	18.6	18.3	17.9	17.8	17.5
Iowa	16.3	16.5	15.7	15.6	15.4	15.3	15.5	15.6	15.8	15.7
Kansas	15.8	15.7	15.6	15.5	15.4	15.4	15.4	15.4	15.2	15.0
Kentucky	20.4	20.8	20.2	19.9	19.6	19.2	18.6	18.2	17.8	17.7
Louisiana	17.7	19.6	18.4	19.0	19.0	18.5	18.5	18.5	18.2	17.6
Maine	18.9	[2]18.0	16.4	15.5	15.7	14.5	15.5	14.9	14.6	14.1
Maryland	18.4	18.5	18.5	18.3	17.7	17.5	17.1	17.1	16.8	16.8
Massachusetts	15.7	15.2	16.1	15.5	15.2	14.9	14.4	13.9	13.7	14.0
Michigan	21.3	21.9	20.8	20.5	19.8	19.5	19.2	19.9	19.8	19.7
Minnesota	17.1	17.1	18.0	17.9	17.5	17.1	17.4	17.1	17.0	17.2
Mississippi	18.4	19.3	18.6	18.7	18.4	18.1	19.0	18.8	18.4	18.2
Missouri	17.3	17.0	17.4	17.0	16.8	16.5	16.4	16.2	15.9	15.7
Montana	16.6	16.5	16.0	16.2	16.1	15.9	15.6	15.8	15.8	15.7
Nebraska	16.7	15.7	15.5	15.2	15.0	15.0	15.1	15.1	15.0	14.7
Nevada	21.0	21.1	20.9	20.4	20.2	20.0	20.4	20.2	20.3	20.4
New Hampshire	19.8	16.8	16.4	16.2	15.8	15.9	15.9	16.0	16.2	16.2
New Jersey	16.3	15.9	15.8	15.6	15.3	15.0	14.7	14.0	13.6	13.5
New Mexico	19.2	18.8	18.8	18.6	18.7	18.7	19.0	18.9	18.5	18.3
New York	18.5	17.7	17.3	16.9	16.2	15.8	15.4	15.2	14.9	14.7
North Carolina	20.1	19.9	19.8	19.8	19.4	18.8	18.7	18.2	17.5	17.1
North Dakota	15.8	16.8	16.8	16.6	16.6	15.2	15.2	15.3	15.6	15.1
Ohio	19.5	19.7	19.8	18.9	18.4	18.3	18.1	18.0	17.6	17.4
Oklahoma	17.0	17.2	17.0	16.9	16.9	16.6	16.9	16.9	16.5	16.2
Oregon	20.6	20.3	18.6	18.3	18.3	18.2	18.3	18.3	18.4	18.4
Pennsylvania	17.4	17.2	17.2	17.0	16.8	16.6	16.3	16.2	15.9	15.7
Rhode Island	16.2	16.1	15.8	15.4	15.4	15.1	15.1	15.1	14.5	14.5
South Carolina	19.2	19.0	18.9	18.7	17.9	17.5	17.3	17.2	17.2	17.0
South Dakota	16.1	15.8	15.5	14.7	14.4	14.9	15.6	15.5	15.4	15.5
Tennessee	20.7	20.5	20.9	20.9	20.6	20.3	19.9	19.6	19.3	19.1
Texas	18.2	18.4	17.8	17.5	17.6	17.3	17.2	17.3	16.7	16.7
Utah	23.9	24.6	25.3	24.8	24.7	24.9	24.6	24.7	24.5	24.9
Vermont	14.8	15.3	14.8	14.5	14.2	14.1	[2]14.4	13.9	13.6	13.8
Virginia	17.7	17.8	17.4	17.1	16.8	16.9	16.8	16.3	16.1	15.9
Washington	21.3	21.7	21.7	21.2	20.8	20.7	20.5	20.2	20.4	20.1
West Virginia	17.7	17.3	16.9	16.5	16.0	15.7	15.3	15.2	15.1	15.1
Wisconsin	17.1	17.2	17.4	17.1	16.3	16.5	16.3	16.2	16.0	15.9
Wyoming	15.5	15.0	15.0	14.1	14.1	14.1	14.0	14.5	14.6	14.5
Outlying areas	—	—	—	—	—	—	—	20.0	19.5	19.0
American Samoa	17.3	—	—	—	—	—	17.7	17.1	17.5	16.3
Guam	18.0	—	19.3	19.7	—	19.6	18.0	18.4	18.6	17.0
Northern Marianas	—	—	—	17.4	15.6	—	—	19.1	18.2	19.5
Puerto Rico	22.3	—	21.6	21.8	21.3	21.0	21.0	20.3	19.8	13.3
Trust Territories	—	—	—	—	—	—	—	—	—	—
Virgin Islands	16.1	—	15.6	11.5	15.7	15.6	15.2	15.1	14.7	13.3

Table 24.—Pupil/teacher ratios in public elementary and secondary schools, by state: Fall 1970 to fall 1995—Continued

State or other area	Fall 1990	Fall 1991	Fall 1992	Fall 1993	Fall 1994	Fall 1995	Difference in ratio			
							Fall 1970 to Fall 1995	Fall 1985 to Fall 1990	Fall 1990 to Fall 1995	Fall 1985 to Fall 1995
1	22	23	24	25	26	27	28	29	30	31
United States	**17.2**	**17.3**	**17.4**	**17.4**	**17.3**	**17.3**	−5.0	−0.7	0.1	−0.6
Alabama	19.9	17.8	17.4	17.1	17.2	16.9	−7.4	−0.3	−3.0	−3.3
Alaska [4]	17.0	16.7	16.8	17.5	17.6	17.3	−3.6	1.2	0.3	1.5
Arizona	19.4	19.3	18.7	18.9	19.3	19.6	−3.9	−0.2	0.2	−0.1
Arkansas	16.8	17.0	17.0	17.1	17.1	17.1	−4.8	−0.7	0.3	−0.4
California	22.8	22.8	24.0	24.0	24.0	24.0	−0.0	−0.3	1.2	0.9
Colorado	17.8	17.9	18.3	18.6	18.4	18.5	−4.0	−0.7	0.8	0.1
Connecticut	13.5	14.0	14.3	14.4	14.4	14.4	−6.8	−0.6	0.9	0.3
Delaware	16.7	16.8	16.7	16.5	16.6	16.8	−5.2	0.5	0.1	0.6
District of Columbia	13.6	12.7	13.3	13.3	13.2	15.0	−4.4	−0.6	1.5	0.9
Florida	17.2	17.6	18.4	18.4	19.1	18.9	−3.9	−0.3	1.7	1.4
Georgia	18.3	18.5	18.0	16.7	16.3	16.5	−8.5	−0.6	−1.8	−2.3
Hawaii	18.9	18.5	17.6	17.8	17.9	17.8	−4.8	−3.7	−1.1	−4.7
Idaho	19.6	19.4	19.6	19.7	19.1	19.0	−3.6	−0.7	−0.6	−1.3
Illinois	16.7	16.8	16.8	17.1	17.3	17.1	−4.0	−1.0	0.4	−0.7
Indiana	17.4	17.6	17.6	17.5	17.5	17.5	−6.9	−1.2	0.1	−1.1
Iowa	15.6	15.7	15.8	15.8	15.8	15.5	−4.7	0.3	−0.0	0.3
Kansas	15.0	15.2	15.2	15.1	15.1	15.1	−4.8	−0.4	0.1	−0.3
Kentucky	17.3	17.2	17.3	17.6	17.0	16.9	−6.9	−1.9	−0.4	−2.3
Louisiana	17.3	17.2	17.0	17.1	16.8	17.0	−6.1	−1.2	−0.3	−1.5
Maine	13.9	14.0	14.1	14.1	13.8	13.9	−8.0	−0.6	0.0	−0.6
Maryland	16.8	16.9	16.9	17.5	17.0	16.8	−5.6	−0.7	0.0	−0.6
Massachusetts	15.4	15.1	15.0	14.9	14.8	14.6	−6.5	0.6	−0.9	−0.3
Michigan	19.8	19.2	19.5	19.9	20.1	19.7	−3.4	0.3	−0.1	0.2
Minnesota	17.4	17.2	17.6	17.3	17.5	17.8	−3.2	0.3	0.4	0.7
Mississippi	17.9	17.9	18.2	17.8	17.5	17.5	−6.3	−0.1	−0.4	−0.6
Missouri	15.6	16.0	16.2	15.8	15.5	15.4	−6.2	−0.9	−0.2	−1.2
Montana	15.9	15.8	15.8	16.4	16.3	16.4	−4.6	0.1	0.5	0.6
Nebraska	14.6	14.7	14.6	14.5	14.5	14.5	−4.6	−0.4	−0.1	−0.6
Nevada	19.4	18.6	18.7	18.7	18.7	19.1	−6.6	−0.6	−0.3	−0.9
New Hampshire	16.2	15.5	15.6	15.5	15.6	15.7	−5.6	0.3	−0.5	−0.2
New Jersey	13.6	13.8	13.6	13.6	13.8	13.8	−6.7	−1.4	0.2	−1.2
New Mexico	18.1	17.6	17.6	17.5	17.2	17.0	−7.2	−0.7	−1.1	−1.8
New York	14.7	15.4	15.2	15.2	15.2	15.5	−4.2	−1.1	0.8	−0.3
North Carolina	16.9	16.8	16.7	16.3	16.2	16.2	−7.9	−1.9	−0.7	−2.7
North Dakota	15.5	15.3	15.2	15.4	15.3	15.9	−3.3	0.3	0.4	0.7
Ohio	17.2	17.3	16.9	16.8	16.6	17.1	−6.1	−1.1	−0.1	−1.2
Oklahoma	15.6	15.6	15.5	15.5	15.5	15.7	−6.6	−1.0	0.1	−0.9
Oregon	18.0	18.6	19.2	19.5	19.9	19.8	−2.4	−0.1	1.7	1.6
Pennsylvania	16.6	16.8	17.0	17.0	17.1	17.0	−4.7	0.1	0.4	0.5
Rhode Island	14.6	14.6	14.3	14.8	14.7	14.3	−6.6	−0.6	−0.3	−0.9
South Carolina	16.8	16.9	17.2	16.7	16.4	16.2	−6.1	−0.7	−0.7	−1.3
South Dakota	15.2	14.8	15.3	14.9	14.4	15.0	−4.1	0.3	−0.2	0.1
Tennessee	19.2	19.4	19.6	18.8	18.6	16.7	−8.6	−1.2	−2.4	−3.6
Texas	15.4	15.8	16.1	16.0	15.7	15.6	−6.3	−1.9	0.2	−1.7
Utah	25.0	24.9	24.2	24.7	24.3	23.8	−2.1	0.1	−1.2	−1.0
Vermont	13.2	13.8	13.1	14.0	13.8	13.8	−4.2	−0.9	0.6	−0.3
Virginia	15.7	15.7	15.1	14.8	14.6	14.4	−8.1	−1.2	−1.2	−2.4
Washington	20.1	20.2	20.2	20.1	20.2	20.4	−4.1	−0.6	0.3	−0.3
West Virginia	15.0	15.3	15.2	14.9	14.8	14.6	−9.5	−0.7	−0.4	−1.2
Wisconsin	16.2	15.7	15.5	16.0	15.9	15.8	−6.5	−0.3	−0.4	−0.7
Wyoming	14.5	15.6	17.2	15.4	14.9	14.8	−4.2	0.4	0.4	0.7
Outlying areas	18.5	17.2	16.7	16.0	15.8	16.1	16.1	18.5	−2.4	16.1
American Samoa	17.1	18.9	18.5	18.8	17.6	18.3	18.3	17.1	1.2	18.3
Guam	15.5	16.5	19.0	19.0	20.8	20.9	−2.7	−4.1	5.4	1.3
Northern Marianas	18.8	17.2	16.6	15.9	15.6	16.0	16.0	18.8	−2.9	16.0
Puerto Rico	13.8	14.1	14.3	14.5	15.1	14.0	−15.7	−7.2	0.2	−7.0
Trust Territories	—	—	—	—	—	—	—	—	—	—
Virgin Islands	13.8	14.1	14.3	14.5	15.1	14.0	14.0	−1.8	0.2	−1.6

[1] National total includes estimates for indicated states.
[2] Data estimated by NCES.
[3] Data estimated by reporting state.
[4] Beginning in 1983, data include students enrolled in public schools on federal bases and other special arrangements.

—Data not available or not applicable.

SOURCE: U.S. Department of Education, National Center for Education Statistics, *Statistics of Public Elementary and Secondary Day Schools*, various years; and Common Core of Data surveys. (This table was prepared April 1997.)

Table 25.—Staff employed in public elementary and secondary schools, by state:
Fall 1970 to fall 1995

State or other area	Estimated fall 1970	Fall 1971	Fall 1972	Fall 1973	Fall 1974	Fall 1975	Fall 1976	Fall 1977	Fall 1978	Fall 1979
1	2	3	4	5	6	7	8	9	10	11
United States	3,448,357	3,547,502	3,562,968	3,656,551	3,745,000	3,997,347	3,884,000	3,912,449	3,895,706	4,062,800
Alabama	56,485	57,372	55,295	55,922	59,049	64,523	[3]61,554	[3]64,223	63,917	55,229
Alaska	[4]5,288	[4]5,597	[4]5,471	[4]6,765	[4]7,224	[4]8,176	[4]8,401	8,449	9,216	9,556
Arizona	[4]33,807	39,876	33,699	38,017	39,861	40,874	43,306	44,347	40,968	51,526
Arkansas	32,801	33,059	32,745	30,752	34,657	38,886	39,623	41,353	42,996	44,703
California	322,923	322,994	338,659	347,916	359,335	[5]373,680	[3]371,950	[3]381,820	[3]381,820	[6]412,463
Colorado	42,560	45,548	48,222	48,626	53,534	55,488	[3]56,000	52,502	54,918	[4]34,885
Connecticut	[4]42,694	[4]40,072	[4]39,973	[4]40,145	40,889	[7]56,171	[7]40,786	[4]41,181	[4]40,334	[4]39,894
Delaware	9,287	9,682	10,400	10,380	10,542	11,811	11,516	11,121	11,414	11,521
District of Columbia	13,216	12,262	12,116	12,230	12,885	12,632	12,689	10,896	12,100	12,281
Florida	119,703	130,205	132,295	136,628	140,938	169,023	142,511	142,993	147,946	151,530
Georgia	82,034	85,502	86,565	88,450	85,246	[6]86,447	91,831	97,730	97,910	98,090
Hawaii	11,610	12,547	13,631	12,710	12,875	[4]12,231	13,251	13,490	14,321	14,250
Idaho	13,742	14,188	14,463	13,798	13,917	14,428	15,182	15,693	16,576	16,466
Illinois	159,449	161,024	190,892	191,556	196,337	241,543	[3]194,440	[3]190,138	[4]152,584	195,634
Indiana	86,620	94,052	[3]96,285	[3]96,221	[5]86,433	[5]98,954	92,460	[8]94,233	97,401	96,682
Iowa	55,552	53,867	52,876	51,398	52,395	65,192	61,264	[5]62,021	64,841	63,299
Kansas	43,802	43,828	[3]43,558	44,707	45,361	44,799	45,092	45,593	47,572	47,648
Kentucky	54,674	56,982	57,621	58,202	59,484	59,752	[3]60,752	[3]61,272	62,532	62,750
Louisiana	68,012	71,487	75,588	76,819	76,378	79,757	79,600	[3]81,619	[3]80,713	85,710
Maine	18,121	17,581	[4]13,676	15,057	15,926	19,976	[4]17,173	17,496	20,192	19,297
Maryland	70,566	75,174	75,560	77,340	77,978	78,704	80,197	79,122	79,354	79,059
Massachusetts	89,234	92,915	98,438	[3]112,454	112,112	[6]104,539	[3]113,193	[3]114,728	[3]104,605	119,668
Michigan	156,290	158,123	166,279	170,340	173,637	180,533	175,770	174,823	179,838	178,440
Minnesota	72,200	73,033	73,457	76,441	78,217	79,145	79,181	77,427	77,575	77,032
Mississippi	42,784	45,484	46,737	45,982	45,947	46,803	47,482	48,302	49,869	51,833
Missouri	80,204	82,766	82,814	85,055	87,202	88,535	85,803	86,170	89,446	90,532
Montana	[4]10,040	[4]10,157	[6]10,039	[4]9,921	[3]10,317	[3,5]14,524	[4]10,971	[4]10,982	[4]11,158	[4]11,024
Nebraska	27,456	28,147	[3]31,380	29,152	29,715	30,698	30,820	31,429	31,760	32,676
Nevada	8,746	9,159	8,568	9,266	9,731	10,232	10,247	[5]11,142	[4]7,250	[4]7,994
New Hampshire	11,371	11,879	12,915	10,462	12,555	13,951	13,945	[5]13,997	15,054	16,209
New Jersey	116,600	119,123	[6]124,851	130,578	[6]130,702	137,444	[3]135,217	[5]134,061	[4]92,230	139,479
New Mexico	20,669	20,546	22,867	22,365	21,403	24,457	25,143	25,809	27,058	25,970
New York	304,740	319,244	[3]306,138	[3]311,996	299,080	313,238	[3]304,750	[3]287,610	289,370	296,978
North Carolina	86,806	86,338	91,845	97,218	101,151	101,468	97,729	102,736	107,513	111,031
North Dakota	11,859	11,544	12,067	12,595	12,788	12,592	12,726	12,784	12,932	12,650
Ohio	160,669	163,428	177,264	182,500	183,374	177,775	186,205	186,165	190,101	191,586
Oklahoma	51,338	52,184	[4]42,298	44,418	48,594	55,096	52,229	53,655	56,542	58,293
Oregon	41,890	42,678	43,089	43,414	43,490	54,391	46,414	46,202	46,997	48,195
Pennsylvania	182,518	187,122	193,329	197,163	[3]196,000	207,695	204,250	[3]200,949	200,639	202,733
Rhode Island	14,452	14,714	15,106	15,016	14,985	15,120	15,246	15,024	14,840	15,093
South Carolina	46,411	46,313	47,828	48,092	[4]32,974	[3,4]43,236	[4]34,491	[4]35,386	[4]42,393	[7]42,342
South Dakota	14,246	14,238	13,816	14,113	14,427	17,515	14,424	14,219	14,504	14,288
Tennessee	65,765	69,387	67,099	68,281	68,195	74,591	76,234	76,274	77,515	79,347
Texas	206,090	211,907	[4]152,603	162,548	221,931	230,037	[3]250,575	[5]270,424	[3]284,060	300,460
Utah	20,412	21,090	20,900	20,720	21,365	20,437	22,638	[3]22,353	23,465	25,093
Vermont	9,681	9,694	10,166	10,459	10,432	11,685	11,350	[3]11,558	12,051	12,752
Virginia	83,482	87,833	87,407	91,350	95,120	105,522	99,757	100,945	102,941	104,462
Washington	54,329	55,480	55,543	58,570	60,250	60,176	[3]59,483	[3]59,490	61,799	63,399
West Virginia	30,697	32,857	34,461	35,262	35,552	36,756	35,156	35,811	36,939	37,902
Wisconsin	76,938	79,555	76,260	78,909	83,548	86,829	83,785	85,180	84,939	82,496
Wyoming	7,493	7,665	7,814	8,272	8,962	9,280	9,208	9,522	10,698	10,370
Outlying areas	—	46,857	—	—	—	—	—	—	—	—
American Samoa	—	1,110	—	1,014	1,081	504	750	824	—	—
Guam	2,090	2,280	2,382	2,706	2,743	2,299	2,556	—	—	2,516
Northern Marianas	—	—	—	—	—	—	—	—	441	399
Puerto Rico	—	39,211	41,370	42,267	—	29,429	28,777	—	46,098	—
Trust Territories	—	2,267	—	—	—	—	—	—	—	—
Virgin Islands	—	1,989	1,878	1,996	2,422	2,678	2,709	2,785	3,055	3,011

Table 25.—Staff employed in public elementary and secondary schools, by state: Fall 1970 to fall 1995—Continued

State or other area	Fall 1980	Fall 1981	Fall 1982	Fall 1983	Fall 1984	Fall 1985	Fall 1986	Fall 1987	Fall 1988	Fall 1989
1	12	13	14	15	16	17	18	19	20	21
United States	**4,168,286**	**4,015,297**	**[1] 4,051,879**	**[1] 4,036,306**	**[1] 4,062,271**	**[1] 4,159,624**	**[1] 4,232,805**	**[1] 4,311,941**	**[1] 4,319,356**	**[1] 4,431,033**
Alabama	64,356	70,052	65,554	64,413	68,421	68,992	70,907	70,655	72,955	79,786
Alaska	10,380	11,170	[4] 8,384	11,113	13,187	13,370	[4] 9,810	[4] 7,285	13,500	13,438
Arizona	51,171	50,334	50,270	50,371	51,524	53,675	56,207	59,095	60,014	60,965
Arkansas	44,892	44,006	44,088	44,260	44,859	46,411	46,372	47,741	50,734	49,401
California	420,211	[6] 380,188	392,341	380,604	354,654	378,883	385,244	392,299	404,769	419,673
Colorado	56,410	55,244	55,720	53,977	55,079	58,199	58,537	59,263	59,814	60,603
Connecticut	59,300	[6] 54,875	[4] 37,463	[4] 36,989	[4] 37,267	[4] 37,720	[4] 39,284	[4] 40,214	[4] 40,870	62,367
Delaware	10,644	9,974	9,980	9,916	10,083	10,370	10,597	10,790	10,766	10,914
District of Columbia	11,072	10,529	10,081	10,038	10,510	10,471	11,945	11,130	10,157	10,619
Florida	156,705	155,992	160,524	161,371	165,754	172,552	177,639	184,608	197,403	206,351
Georgia	102,508	102,226	110,422	110,482	105,637	108,735	111,317	119,320	120,669	125,939
Hawaii	14,255	15,099	15,318	14,987	15,410	17,100	15,892	18,036	20,730	14,723
Idaho	16,801	15,429	15,310	15,449	15,878	16,036	16,039	16,205	16,558	17,160
Illinois	192,408	167,424	181,481	177,601	175,892	181,515	185,572	186,595	186,235	187,682
Indiana	105,076	100,816	98,586	99,140	100,465	102,274	104,482	105,326	105,430	106,870
Iowa	63,232	57,359	58,427	58,288	58,997	58,779	56,825	56,670	56,220	56,925
Kansas	48,578	48,011	44,757	45,223	45,856	46,549	47,227	47,569	48,828	50,175
Kentucky	64,693	61,061	62,676	62,465	63,683	65,557	67,721	69,192	71,685	71,377
Louisiana	86,204	83,961	85,457	86,380	86,363	88,403	88,591	88,794	88,361	[6] 89,468
Maine	20,291	20,282	21,308	23,652	21,985	23,253	22,966	24,410	25,450	26,317
Maryland	78,148	74,354	71,285	70,993	71,293	71,264	72,931	73,717	75,229	76,623
Massachusetts	114,455	103,174	96,177	97,224	97,231	98,560	101,905	103,471	106,327	104,058
Michigan	175,271	159,922	166,950	162,735	166,728	168,603	171,931	170,162	169,610	170,889
Minnesota	73,122	[6] 74,296	72,378	70,758	72,101	70,721	69,836	74,027	75,885	76,268
Mississippi	52,464	48,749	49,134	51,115	53,188	55,580	[4] 40,687	[4] 42,540	[4] 43,227	56,361
Missouri	91,038	92,406	87,895	88,344	88,201	90,339	91,609	96,736	97,946	101,595
Montana	[4] 10,878	[6] 15,446	[4] 12,226	[4] 12,313	[4] 12,576	[4] 12,752	[4] 12,613	[4] 12,477	[4] 12,414	[4] 12,543
Nebraska	31,622	31,022	30,383	30,578	30,878	30,896	31,576	31,809	32,292	33,325
Nevada	[4] 8,147	[6] 11,611	12,975	12,703	13,301	[4] 8,865	[4] 9,212	[4] 9,736	[4] 10,136	[4] 10,311
New Hampshire	15,278	15,726	15,789	16,003	16,428	16,958	18,387	18,635	19,185	20,556
New Jersey	139,423	136,730	135,765	134,670	135,416	137,638	139,541	141,257	144,051	146,617
New Mexico	26,790	27,387	27,118	27,320	27,728	27,786	28,548	29,347	30,159	32,165
New York	310,100	290,251	308,728	309,574	320,080	311,704	317,782	327,428	312,426	345,072
North Carolina	112,414	107,118	106,685	106,239	107,902	109,934	110,628	114,243	[4] 119,161	122,470
North Dakota	12,393	12,156	12,308	12,359	13,511	13,671	13,693	13,533	13,789	14,132
Ohio	192,577	183,015	178,549	177,623	180,399	182,105	182,796	184,130	186,631	187,944
Oklahoma	59,465	59,636	61,590	60,772	64,812	66,858	65,253	63,822	64,076	65,741
Oregon	49,204	47,701	45,934	45,742	45,842	46,425	46,598	47,211	47,317	48,225
Pennsylvania	201,010	196,694	188,903	185,466	183,958	182,910	184,868	185,629	188,279	190,175
Rhode Island	15,131	14,375	14,118	14,080	13,916	13,962	14,317	14,569	14,795	15,184
South Carolina	61,986	58,710	58,304	58,106	58,956	61,132	61,847	62,557	61,908	63,333
South Dakota	14,068	14,012	14,065	15,376	15,719	14,559	13,903	14,202	13,898	14,129
Tennessee	81,020	80,465	77,867	76,134	76,277	78,321	80,968	83,256	84,500	86,049
Texas	299,201	313,905	[4] 240,477	[4] 241,678	[4] 223,330	357,365	374,986	377,240	327,296	332,948
Utah	26,973	26,493	25,845	26,428	27,443	28,589	29,635	29,976	30,774	31,351
Vermont	12,485	11,408	11,532	11,688	11,888	12,238	—	12,321	11,959	11,959
Virginia	105,399	100,838	102,664	102,820	106,219	105,659	108,455	114,439	117,291	120,203
Washington	63,494	60,822	59,622	61,012	63,107	64,159	65,955	68,405	69,610	72,517
West Virginia	40,055	39,977	40,128	40,299	41,252	41,347	41,653	41,415	40,433	39,407
Wisconsin	83,440	80,360	76,858	77,072	78,535	77,805	79,386	80,340	82,307	83,561
Wyoming	12,048	12,504	12,903	13,552	14,063	14,374	14,326	13,373	13,275	13,421
Outlying areas	—	—	—	—	—	—	48,384	50,170	70,320	70,678
American Samoa	1,004	—	—	—	—	—	1,162	1,206	1,255	1,240
Guam	2,838	—	2,600	—	—	2,395	2,985	2,884	2,778	2,985
Northern Marianas	—	—	—	—	513	—	—	512	643	688
Puerto Rico	54,635	—	37,583	—	42,123	41,242	40,979	42,314	62,322	62,441
Trust Territories	—	—	—	—	—	—	—	—	—	—
Virgin Islands	3,267	—	3,919	—	3,406	3,329	3,258	3,254	3,322	3,324

Table 25.—Staff employed in public elementary and secondary schools, by state: Fall 1970 to fall 1995—Continued

State or other area	Fall 1990	Fall 1991	Fall 1992	Fall 1993	Fall 1994	Fall 1995	Percentage change			
							Fall 1970 to Fall 1995	Fall 1985 to Fall 1990	Fall 1990 to Fall 1995	Fall 1985 to Fall 1995
1	22	23	24	25	26	27	28	29	30	31
United States	[1] 4,494,076	[1] 4,559,359	[1] 4,708,286	[1] 4,808,080	[1] 4,904,757	4,994,358	44.8	8.0	11.1	20.1
Alabama	74,462	81,950	[2] 78,882	[2] 80,923	[2] 81,544	83,256	47.4	7.9	11.8	20.7
Alaska	13,327	13,992	14,792	15,689	[2] 15,150	15,022	—	−0.3	12.7	12.4
Arizona	63,485	65,505	71,591	74,679	74,540	75,931	—	18.3	19.6	41.5
Arkansas	49,746	51,652	48,880	50,502	50,201	49,178	49.9	7.2	−1.1	6.0
California	419,776	429,387	[2] 427,610	[2] 431,093	[2] 436,140	444,014	37.5	10.8	5.8	17.2
Colorado	61,444	62,592	62,785	62,927	64,985	67,447	58.5	5.6	9.8	15.9
Connecticut	61,800	60,500	63,648	62,014	64,742	66,133	—	—	7.0	—
Delaware	10,794	10,987	11,390	11,640	11,759	11,869	27.8	4.1	10.0	14.5
District of Columbia	10,200	11,143	10,567	10,591	10,507	9,410	−28.8	−2.6	−7.7	−10.1
Florida	216,854	219,733	217,356	226,911	226,975	237,721	98.6	25.7	9.6	37.8
Georgia	128,950	132,921	[2] 142,840	[2] 156,005	[2] 161,390	165,058	101.2	18.6	28.0	51.8
Hawaii	15,174	15,559	17,731	18,292	16,567	16,841	45.1	−11.3	11.0	−1.5
Idaho	18,059	18,621	19,571	19,983	21,194	21,814	58.7	12.6	20.8	36.0
Illinois	192,005	196,930	199,380	198,862	204,413	209,036	31.1	5.8	8.9	15.2
Indiana	108,097	108,746	111,919	113,892	115,441	116,363	34.3	5.7	7.6	13.8
Iowa	58,524	60,305	60,208	60,267	60,469	62,075	11.7	−0.4	6.1	5.6
Kansas	51,280	51,637	54,185	55,783	56,790	57,265	30.7	10.2	11.7	23.0
Kentucky	74,244	77,165	79,191	81,279	81,720	84,425	54.4	13.3	13.7	28.8
Louisiana	91,119	[4] 66,339	92,180	93,197	96,124	93,070	36.8	3.1	2.1	5.3
Maine	27,060	27,082	28,937	28,865	29,264	29,413	62.3	16.4	8.7	26.5
Maryland	78,945	79,925	80,861	82,753	84,699	87,868	24.5	10.8	11.3	23.3
Massachusetts	94,403	98,974	101,278	104,196	108,281	113,154	26.8	−4.2	19.9	14.8
Michigan	172,378	178,111	173,863	169,283	164,766	177,495	13.6	2.2	3.0	5.3
Minnesota	77,518	78,273	79,215	74,859	74,914	74,891	3.7	9.6	−3.4	5.9
Mississippi	58,116	59,200	57,876	59,853	60,708	60,855	42.2	4.6	4.7	9.5
Missouri	103,482	100,735	[2] 109,417	[2] 112,810	116,974	120,621	50.4	14.5	16.6	33.5
Montana	[4] 12,580	[4] 13,078	[2] 18,760	[2] 18,717	[2] 18,452	18,586	—	—	—	—
Nebraska	35,149	34,676	[2] 35,648	[2] 36,832	37,144	37,894	38.0	13.8	7.8	22.7
Nevada	[4] 11,608	[4] 13,145	[2] 21,452	[2] 22,418	23,098	23,742	171.5	—	—	—
New Hampshire	20,535	20,480	21,262	21,913	22,336	23,143	103.5	21.1	12.7	36.5
New Jersey	147,375	148,491	151,460	160,202	161,586	163,069	39.9	7.1	10.6	18.5
New Mexico	33,191	34,509	34,803	36,694	39,016	40,124	94.1	19.5	20.9	44.4
New York	346,656	338,335	343,900	353,603	356,386	355,723	16.7	11.2	2.6	14.1
North Carolina	125,599	126,332	[2] 129,445	[2] 133,059	[2] 137,791	140,204	61.5	14.2	11.6	27.5
North Dakota	13,941	13,594	13,797	13,780	13,919	13,804	16.4	2.0	−1.0	1.0
Ohio	190,848	194,727	200,793	201,828	200,141	194,579	21.1	4.8	2.0	6.8
Oklahoma	68,720	69,725	72,166	73,067	[2] 78,270	83,802	63.2	2.8	21.9	25.3
Oregon	49,212	50,479	51,681	50,392	50,377	51,458	22.8	6.0	4.6	10.8
Pennsylvania	191,171	190,607	191,370	190,885	193,696	198,087	8.5	4.5	3.6	8.3
Rhode Island	15,829	15,452	15,833	15,442	15,438	16,517	14.3	13.4	4.3	18.3
South Carolina	65,991	66,597	67,106	71,433	[2] 74,196	74,859	61.3	7.9	13.4	22.5
South Dakota	15,108	14,753	15,671	17,201	[2] 17,989	18,126	27.2	3.8	20.0	24.5
Tennessee	87,232	84,518	86,790	92,349	96,281	98,948	50.5	11.4	13.4	26.3
Texas	332,220	337,473	420,243	433,102	450,462	462,661	124.5	−7.0	39.3	29.5
Utah	32,383	33,297	34,838	35,301	36,186	37,385	83.2	13.3	15.4	30.8
Vermont	13,543	13,923	14,970	14,928	[5] 15,337	15,640	61.5	10.7	15.5	27.8
Virginia	129,816	[6] 130,621	[4] 126,619	[3] 130,033	[2] 133,485	137,546	64.8	22.9	6.0	30.2
Washington	75,730	78,039	81,398	87,734	[2] 90,438	91,322	68.1	18.0	20.6	42.3
West Virginia	39,092	38,550	38,487	38,486	38,481	38,645	25.9	−5.5	−1.1	−6.5
Wisconsin	84,861	88,249	92,139	88,640	100,996	95,105	23.6	9.1	12.1	22.2
Wyoming	12,787	13,134	11,502	12,893	12,999	13,164	75.7	−11.0	2.9	−8.4
Outlying areas	70,176	76,386	76,959	77,608	79,182	79,351	—	—	13.1	—
American Samoa	1,258	1,277	1,350	1,339	1,340	1,417	—	—	12.6	—
Guam	2,936	2,965	3,517	3,839	4,730	3,728	78.4	22.6	27.0	55.7
Northern Marianas	814	906	1,096	1,101	1,051	1,054	—	—	29.5	—
Puerto Rico	61,888	67,948	67,643	68,005	68,868	69,731	—	50.1	12.7	69.1
Trust Territories	—	—	—	—	—	—	—	—	—	—
Virgin Islands	3,280	3,290	3,353	3,324	3,193	3,421	—	−1.5	4.3	2.8

[1] U.S. totals include imputations for underreporting and nonreporting states.
[2] Some data have been imputed.
[3] Data estimated by reporting state.
[4] Support staff not reported or underreported.
[5] Data partially estimated.
[6] Estimated by NCES.
[7] Estimated by state and does not include any nonprofessional staff.
[8] Data are for school year 1976–77.

—Data not available or not applicable.

NOTE—Inconsistent reporting practices may affect percent changes over time. Percent change calculations were not made in cases where data were known to be incomplete.

SOURCE: U.S. Department of Education, National Center for Education Statistics, *Statistics of State School Systems*, various years; and Common Core of Data surveys. (This table was prepared April 1997.)

**Table 26.—Pupil/staff ratios in public elementary and secondary schools, by state:
Fall 1970 to fall 1995**

State or other area	Estimated fall 1970	Fall 1971	Fall 1972	Fall 1973	Fall 1974	Fall 1975	Fall 1976	Fall 1977	Fall 1978	Fall 1979
1	2	3	4	5	6	7	8	9	10	11
United States	**13.3**	**13.0**	**12.8**	**12.4**	**12.0**	**11.2**	**11.4**	**11.1**	**10.9**	**10.3**
Alabama	14.3	14.1	14.2	13.8	12.9	11.8	[2]12.2	[2]11.9	11.9	13.7
Alaska	[3]15.1	[3]15.1	[3]15.6	[3]12.2	[3]12.0	[3]10.9	[3]10.9	10.7	9.8	9.3
Arizona	[3]13.0	11.6	14.4	13.7	12.2	12.1	11.6	11.6	12.4	9.9
Arkansas	14.1	14.0	14.1	14.6	13.1	11.7	11.6	11.1	10.6	10.1
California	14.3	14.2	13.3	12.8	12.3	[4]11.8	[2]11.8	[2]11.3	[2]11.0	[5]10.0
Colorado	12.9	12.4	11.9	11.8	10.6	10.3	[2]10.1	10.7	10.2	[3]15.8
Connecticut	[3]15.5	[3]16.6	[3]16.6	[3]16.6	16.1	[6]11.6	[6]15.6	[3]15.0	[3]14.7	[3]14.2
Delaware	14.3	13.9	12.9	12.8	12.4	10.8	10.6	10.6	9.7	9.0
District of Columbia	11.0	11.6	11.5	11.1	10.2	10.3	9.9	11.0	9.4	8.6
Florida	11.9	11.4	11.4	11.3	11.0	9.2	10.8	10.7	10.2	10.0
Georgia	13.4	12.8	12.6	12.3	12.7	[5]12.6	11.9	11.1	11.2	11.0
Hawaii	15.6	14.6	13.4	14.0	13.7	[3]14.4	13.2	12.8	11.9	11.8
Idaho	13.3	13.0	12.8	13.7	13.5	13.6	13.2	12.8	12.2	12.3
Illinois	14.8	14.8	12.3	12.1	11.7	9.4	[2]11.5	[2]11.4	[3]13.4	10.4
Indiana	14.2	13.1	[2]12.7	[2]12.5	[4]13.7	[4]11.9	12.6	[7]12.1	11.4	11.2
Iowa	11.9	12.1	12.2	12.3	11.8	9.4	9.9	[4]9.5	8.8	8.7
Kansas	11.7	11.5	[2]11.3	10.7	10.4	10.4	10.2	9.8	9.1	8.9
Kentucky	13.1	12.6	12.4	12.2	11.8	11.6	[2]11.4	[2]11.4	11.1	10.8
Louisiana	12.4	11.9	11.2	11.0	11.0	10.6	10.5	[2]10.3	[2]10.1	9.3
Maine	13.5	14.0	[3]18.3	16.3	15.7	12.6	[3]14.5	14.0	11.9	11.8
Maryland	13.0	12.3	12.2	11.8	11.5	11.2	10.7	10.6	10.2	9.8
Massachusetts	13.1	12.8	12.2	[2]10.7	10.8	[5]11.5	[2]10.3	[2]9.7	[2]10.3	8.7
Michigan	13.8	13.8	13.0	12.5	12.3	11.5	11.6	11.3	10.6	10.4
Minnesota	12.8	12.5	12.4	11.8	11.4	11.1	10.9	10.8	10.4	10.1
Mississippi	12.5	11.6	11.3	11.3	11.2	10.9	10.7	10.4	9.9	9.3
Missouri	13.0	12.4	12.4	12.0	11.5	10.9	11.1	10.8	10.1	9.6
Montana	[3]17.6	[3]17.6	[5]17.9	[3]17.5	[2]16.7	[4,6]11.8	[3]15.5	[3]15.4	[3]14.7	[3]14.4
Nebraska	12.0	11.8	[2]10.5	11.1	10.7	10.3	10.1	9.7	9.4	8.8
Nevada	14.6	14.2	15.4	14.6	14.1	13.7	13.8	[4]12.9	[3]20.2	[3]18.5
New Hampshire	14.0	13.8	13.0	16.4	13.7	12.5	12.6	[4]12.5	11.5	10.5
New Jersey	12.7	12.6	[5]12.1	11.3	[5]11.2	10.6	[2]10.6	[4]10.3	[3]14.5	9.2
New Mexico	13.6	13.9	12.5	12.7	13.2	11.2	11.3	10.9	10.3	10.6
New York	11.4	11.1	[2]11.5	[2]11.1	11.5	10.9	[2]11.0	[2]11.2	10.7	10.0
North Carolina	13.7	13.6	12.6	12.1	11.6	11.7	12.2	11.5	10.8	10.4
North Dakota	12.4	12.5	11.7	11.0	10.4	10.4	10.1	9.8	9.4	9.3
Ohio	15.1	14.9	13.7	13.0	12.7	12.9	12.1	11.7	11.1	10.6
Oklahoma	12.2	12.0	[3]14.4	13.5	12.3	10.8	11.4	11.1	10.4	10.0
Oregon	11.4	11.2	10.9	11.0	11.0	8.8	10.2	10.2	10.0	9.7
Pennsylvania	13.0	12.7	12.2	11.8	[2]11.6	10.8	10.7	[2]10.6	10.2	9.7
Rhode Island	13.0	13.0	12.6	12.3	11.9	11.7	11.3	11.1	10.9	10.2
South Carolina	13.7	14.0	13.0	13.0	[3]19.0	[4,5]14.6	[3]18.0	[3]17.5	[3]14.7	[6]14.8
South Dakota	11.7	11.6	11.8	11.2	10.6	8.6	10.3	10.1	9.5	9.4
Tennessee	13.7	12.9	13.3	13.2	12.8	11.8	11.0	11.5	11.3	10.9
Texas	13.8	13.3	[3]17.9	17.1	12.6	12.2	[2]11.3	[4]10.5	[2]10.1	9.6
Utah	14.9	14.5	14.6	14.8	14.3	15.2	13.9	[2]14.2	13.9	13.3
Vermont	10.7	10.9	10.5	10.2	10.1	9.0	9.2	[2]8.9	8.4	7.7
Virginia	12.9	12.2	12.2	11.9	11.5	10.5	11.0	10.7	10.3	9.9
Washington	15.1	14.5	14.2	13.5	13.0	13.1	[2]13.1	[2]13.1	12.4	12.1
West Virginia	13.0	12.3	11.9	11.6	11.4	11.0	11.5	11.2	10.7	10.2
Wisconsin	12.9	12.6	13.1	12.5	11.7	11.1	11.3	10.8	10.4	10.4
Wyoming	11.6	11.3	11.0	10.3	9.7	9.5	9.8	9.7	8.8	9.2
Outlying areas	354.7	16.0	16.8	16.1	9.9	21.8	21.6	9.7	15.1	9.7
American Samoa	—	7.2	—	10.2	9.4	20.1	13.3	11.3	—	—
Guam	11.8	11.4	11.3	10.1	10.3	12.4	11.2	—	—	11.0
Northern Marianas	—	—	—	—	—	—	—	—	10.2	11.0
Puerto Rico	—	17.8	17.2	16.9	—	23.7	23.9	—	15.6	—
Trust Territories	—	—	—	—	—	—	—	—	—	—
Virgin Islands	—	9.5	11.1	11.0	9.6	9.2	9.2	9.2	8.2	8.5

Table 26.—Pupil/staff ratios in public elementary and secondary schools, by state: Fall 1970 to fall 1995—Continued

State or other area	Fall 1980	Fall 1981	Fall 1982	Fall 1983	Fall 1984	Fall 1985	Fall 1986	Fall 1987	Fall 1988	Fall 1989
1	12	13	14	15	16	17	18	19	20	21
United States	**9.8**	**10.0**	**¹9.8**	**¹9.7**	**¹9.7**	**¹9.5**	**¹9.4**	**¹9.3**	**¹9.3**	**¹9.1**
Alabama	11.8	10.6	11.0	11.2	10.4	10.6	10.3	10.3	9.9	9.1
Alaska	8.3	8.1	³10.7	8.8	7.9	8.0	³11.0	³14.7	7.9	8.1
Arizona	10.0	10.1	10.2	10.1	10.3	10.2	9.5	9.7	9.6	10.0
Arkansas	10.0	9.9	9.8	9.8	9.6	9.3	9.4	9.2	8.6	8.8
California	9.7	⁵10.6	10.4	10.7	11.7	11.2	11.4	11.4	11.4	11.4
Colorado	9.7	9.9	9.8	10.0	9.9	9.5	9.5	9.5	9.4	9.3
Connecticut	9.0	⁵9.2	³13.0	³12.9	³12.6	³12.2	³11.9	³11.6	³11.3	7.4
Delaware	9.3	9.5	9.3	9.2	9.1	9.0	8.9	8.9	9.0	9.0
District of Columbia	9.0	9.0	9.0	8.9	8.3	8.3	7.2	7.8	8.3	7.7
Florida	9.6	9.5	9.2	9.3	9.2	9.1	9.0	9.0	8.7	8.7
Georgia	10.4	10.3	9.5	9.5	10.1	9.9	9.8	9.3	9.2	8.9
Hawaii	11.6	10.8	10.6	10.8	10.6	9.6	10.4	9.2	8.1	11.5
Idaho	12.1	13.3	13.3	13.4	13.1	13.0	13.0	13.1	13.0	12.5
Illinois	10.3	11.5	10.4	10.4	10.4	10.1	9.8	9.7	9.6	9.6
Indiana	10.0	10.2	10.1	9.9	9.7	9.4	9.3	9.2	9.1	8.9
Iowa	8.4	9.0	8.6	8.5	8.3	8.3	8.5	8.5	8.5	8.4
Kansas	8.5	8.5	9.1	9.0	8.8	8.8	8.8	8.9	8.7	8.6
Kentucky	10.4	10.8	10.4	10.4	10.1	9.8	9.5	9.3	8.9	8.8
Louisiana	9.0	9.3	9.2	9.3	9.3	8.9	9.0	8.9	8.9	⁵8.8
Maine	11.0	10.7	9.9	8.9	9.4	8.9	9.2	8.7	8.4	8.1
Maryland	9.6	9.7	9.8	9.6	9.5	9.4	9.3	9.3	9.2	9.1
Massachusetts	8.9	9.2	9.5	9.0	8.8	8.6	8.2	8.0	7.7	7.9
Michigan	10.3	10.8	10.0	10.1	9.7	9.5	9.3	9.3	9.3	9.2
Minnesota	10.3	⁵9.9	9.9	10.0	9.7	10.0	10.2	9.7	9.6	9.7
Mississippi	9.1	9.7	9.5	9.2	8.8	8.5	³12.3	³11.9	³11.6	8.9
Missouri	9.3	8.9	9.1	9.0	9.0	8.8	8.7	8.3	8.2	8.0
Montana	³14.3	⁵9.9	³12.5	³12.5	³12.3	³12.1	³12.2	³12.2	³12.3	³12.1
Nebraska	8.9	8.8	8.9	8.7	8.6	8.6	8.5	8.4	8.3	8.1
Nevada	³18.3	⁵13.0	11.6	11.8	11.4	³17.5	³17.5	³17.3	³17.4	³18.1
New Hampshire	10.9	10.4	10.1	9.9	9.7	9.5	8.9	8.9	8.8	8.4
New Jersey	8.9	8.8	8.6	8.5	8.3	8.1	7.9	7.7	7.5	7.3
New Mexico	10.1	9.8	9.9	9.9	9.8	10.0	9.9	9.8	9.7	9.2
New York	9.3	9.6	8.8	8.6	8.3	8.4	8.2	7.9	8.2	7.4
North Carolina	10.0	10.4	10.3	10.3	10.1	9.9	9.8	9.5	³9.1	8.8
North Dakota	9.4	9.7	9.5	9.5	8.8	8.7	8.7	8.8	8.6	8.3
Ohio	10.2	10.4	10.4	10.3	10.0	9.9	9.8	9.7	9.5	9.4
Oklahoma	9.7	9.8	9.6	9.7	9.1	8.9	9.1	9.2	9.1	8.8
Oregon	9.4	9.6	9.8	9.8	9.7	9.6	9.6	9.7	9.8	9.8
Pennsylvania	9.5	9.3	9.4	9.4	9.3	9.2	9.1	9.0	8.8	8.7
Rhode Island	9.8	10.0	9.9	9.7	9.7	9.6	9.4	9.3	9.0	8.9
South Carolina	10.0	10.4	10.4	10.4	10.2	9.9	9.9	9.8	9.9	9.7
South Dakota	9.1	9.0	8.8	8.0	7.8	8.5	9.0	8.9	9.1	9.0
Tennessee	10.5	10.4	10.6	10.8	10.7	10.4	10.1	9.9	9.7	9.5
Texas	9.7	9.4	³12.4	³12.4	³13.6	8.8	8.6	8.6	10.0	10.0
Utah	12.7	13.4	14.3	14.3	14.2	14.1	14.0	14.1	14.0	14.0
Vermont	7.7	8.2	7.9	7.7	7.6	7.4	—	7.5	7.8	7.9
Virginia	9.6	9.8	9.5	9.4	9.1	9.2	9.0	8.6	8.4	8.2
Washington	11.9	12.3	12.4	12.1	11.7	11.7	11.5	11.3	11.4	11.2
West Virginia	9.6	9.4	9.3	9.2	8.8	8.7	8.4	8.3	8.3	8.3
Wisconsin	10.0	10.0	10.2	10.1	9.8	9.9	9.7	9.6	9.4	9.4
Wyoming	8.2	8.0	7.9	7.3	7.2	7.2	7.0	7.4	7.4	7.2
Outlying areas	12.5	—	17.2	—	15.7	15.7	15.3	14.7	10.4	10.1
American Samoa	9.6	—	—	—	—	—	9.5	9.3	9.4	9.9
Guam	9.3	—	9.9	—	—	10.9	8.6	9.0	9.4	8.9
Northern Marianas	—	—	—	—	9.4	—	—	11.4	9.5	8.9
Puerto Rico	13.0	—	18.9	—	16.4	16.7	16.6	15.9	10.6	10.4
Trust Territories	—	—	—	—	—	—	—	—	—	—
Virgin Islands	7.7	—	6.6	—	7.7	7.6	7.5	7.4	7.1	6.4

Table 26.—Pupil/staff ratios in public elementary and secondary schools, by state: Fall 1970 to fall 1995—Continued

State or other area	Fall 1990	Fall 1991	Fall 1992	Fall 1993	Fall 1994	Fall 1995	Difference in ratio			
							Fall 1970 to Fall 1995	Fall 1985 to Fall 1990	Fall 1990 to Fall 1995	Fall 1985 to Fall 1995
1	22	23	24	25	26	27	28	29	30	31
United States	[1]9.2	[1]9.2	[1]9.1	[1]9.0	[1]9.0	[1]9.0	-4.3	-0.3	-0.2	-0.5
Alabama	9.7	8.8	9.3	9.1	9.0	9.0	-5.3	-0.9	-0.7	-1.6
Alaska	8.5	8.5	8.3	8.0	8.4	8.5	—	0.5	-0.1	0.5
Arizona	10.1	10.0	9.4	9.5	9.9	9.8	—	-0.1	-0.3	-0.4
Arkansas	8.8	8.5	9.0	8.8	8.9	9.2	-4.9	-0.6	0.4	-0.1
California	11.8	11.9	12.3	12.4	12.4	12.5	-1.9	0.6	0.7	1.2
Colorado	9.3	9.5	9.8	9.9	9.9	9.7	-3.2	-0.1	0.4	0.3
Connecticut	7.6	8.0	7.7	8.0	7.8	7.8	—	—	0.2	—
Delaware	9.2	9.3	9.2	9.1	9.1	9.1	-5.2	0.3	-0.1	0.2
District of Columbia	7.9	7.2	7.7	7.6	7.7	8.5	-2.5	-0.4	0.6	0.2
Florida	8.6	8.8	9.1	9.0	9.3	9.2	-2.8	-0.5	0.6	0.1
Georgia	8.9	8.9	8.5	7.9	7.9	7.9	-5.5	-1.0	-1.0	-2.0
Hawaii	11.3	11.2	10.0	9.9	11.1	11.1	-4.4	1.7	-0.2	1.5
Idaho	12.2	12.1	11.8	11.8	11.3	11.1	-2.1	-0.8	-1.1	-1.9
Illinois	9.5	9.4	9.4	9.5	9.4	9.3	-5.5	-0.6	-0.2	-0.8
Indiana	8.8	8.8	8.6	8.5	8.4	8.4	-5.8	8.0	-0.4	-1.0
Iowa	8.3	8.1	8.2	8.3	8.3	8.1	-3.8	0.0	-0.2	-0.2
Kansas	8.5	8.6	8.3	8.2	8.1	8.1	-3.6	-0.3	-0.4	-0.7
Kentucky	8.6	8.4	8.3	8.1	8.0	7.8	-5.3	-1.2	-0.8	-2.0
Louisiana	8.6	[3]12.0	[3]8.7	8.6	8.3	8.6	-3.8	-0.3	(8)	-0.4
Maine	8.0	8.0	7.5	7.5	7.3	7.3	-6.2	-0.9	-0.7	-1.6
Maryland	9.1	9.2	9.3	9.3	9.3	9.2	-3.8	-0.4	0.1	-0.3
Massachusetts	8.8	8.5	8.5	8.4	8.3	8.1	-5.0	0.3	-0.8	-0.5
Michigan	9.2	8.9	9.2	9.4	9.8	9.2	-4.5	-0.3	0.1	-0.3
Minnesota	9.8	9.9	10.0	10.8	11.0	11.2	-1.6	-0.2	1.4	1.2
Mississippi	8.6	8.5	8.8	8.5	8.3	8.3	-4.2	0.2	-0.3	-0.2
Missouri	7.9	8.4	7.9	7.7	7.5	7.4	-5.6	-0.9	-0.5	-1.4
Montana	[3]12.2	[3]11.9	[3]8.5	8.7	8.9	8.9	—	—	—	—
Nebraska	7.8	8.1	7.9	7.7	7.7	7.6	-4.3	-0.8	-0.2	-1.0
Nevada	[3]17.3	[3]16.1	10.4	10.5	10.9	11.2	-3.4	—	—	—
New Hampshire	8.4	8.6	8.5	8.5	8.5	8.4	-5.6	-1.1	(8)	-1.1
New Jersey	7.4	7.5	7.5	7.2	7.3	7.3	-5.4	-0.7	-0.1	-0.8
New Mexico	9.1	8.9	9.1	8.8	8.4	8.2	-5.4	-0.9	-0.9	-1.8
New York	7.5	7.8	7.8	7.7	7.8	7.9	-3.5	-0.9	0.4	-0.5
North Carolina	8.7	8.7	8.6	8.5	8.4	8.4	-5.3	-1.2	-0.2	-1.4
North Dakota	8.5	8.7	8.6	8.6	8.6	8.6	-3.8	-0.2	0.2	(8)
Ohio	9.3	9.2	8.9	9.0	9.1	9.4	-5.7	-0.6	0.2	-0.4
Oklahoma	8.4	8.4	8.3	8.3	7.8	7.4	-4.9	-0.4	-1.1	-1.5
Oregon	9.6	9.9	9.9	10.3	10.4	10.3	-1.2	-0.0	0.7	0.6
Pennsylvania	8.7	8.9	9.0	9.1	9.1	9.0	-3.9	-0.5	0.3	-0.2
Rhode Island	8.8	9.2	9.1	9.4	9.6	9.1	-3.9	-0.8	0.3	-0.5
South Carolina	9.4	9.4	9.5	9.0	8.7	8.6	-5.1	-0.5	-0.8	-1.3
South Dakota	8.5	8.9	8.6	8.3	8.0	8.0	-3.7	0.0	-0.6	-0.6
Tennessee	9.5	9.9	9.9	9.4	9.2	9.0	-4.7	-0.9	-0.4	-1.4
Texas	10.2	10.3	8.4	8.3	8.2	8.1	-5.7	1.4	-2.1	-0.7
Utah	13.8	13.7	13.3	13.4	13.1	12.8	-2.1	-0.3	-1.0	-1.3
Vermont	7.1	7.0	6.6	6.9	6.8	6.7	-3.9	-0.3	-0.3	-0.6
Virginia	7.7	[5]7.8	[3]8.1	8.0	7.9	7.9	-5.1	-1.5	0.2	-1.3
Washington	11.1	11.1	11.0	10.4	10.4	10.5	-4.6	-0.6	-0.6	-1.2
West Virginia	8.2	8.3	8.3	8.2	8.1	7.9	-5.1	-0.4	-0.3	-0.7
Wisconsin	9.4	9.2	9.0	9.5	8.5	9.1	-3.8	-0.5	-0.2	-0.7
Wyoming	7.7	7.8	8.7	7.8	7.7	7.6	-4.0	0.5	-0.1	0.4
Outlying areas	10.1	9.3	9.3	9.1	8.8	8.9	-345.8	-5.6	-1.2	-6.8
American Samoa	9.9	10.5	10.4	10.8	10.8	10.3	10.3	9.9	0.4	10.3
Guam	9.0	9.6	8.6	8.1	6.8	8.8	-3.0	-1.9	-0.1	-2.0
Northern Marianas	7.9	7.8	7.4	7.4	8.0	8.4	8.4	7.9	0.4	8.4
Puerto Rico	10.4	9.5	9.4	9.3	9.0	9.0	9.0	-6.2	-1.4	-7.7
Trust Territories	—	—	—	—	—	—	—	—	—	—
Virgin Islands	6.6	6.8	6.8	6.8	7.2	6.6	6.6	-1.0	(8)	-1.0

[1] U.S. totals include imputations for underreporting and nonreporting states.

[2] Data estimated by reporting state.

[3] Support staff not reported or underreported.

[4] Data partially estimated.

[5] Estimated by NCES.

[6] Estimated by state and does not include any nonprofessional staff.

[7] Data are for school year 1976–77.

[8] Less than 0.05 percent change.

—Data not available or not applicable.

NOTE—Inconsistent reporting practices may affect ratio differences over time. Ratio difference calculations were not made in cases where data were known to be incomplete.

SOURCE: U.S. Department of Education, National Center for Education Statistics, *Statistics of State School Systems*, various years; and Common Core of Data surveys. (This table was prepared April 1997.)

Table 27.—Estimated average annual teacher salaries (in current dollars) in public elementary and secondary schools, by state: 1970–71 to 1996–97

State	1970–71	1971–72	1972–73	1973–74	1974–75	1975–76	1976–77	1977–78	1978–79	1979–80
1	2	3	4	5	6	7	8	9	10	11
United States	**$9,268**	**$9,705**	**$10,174**	**$10,770**	**$11,641**	**$12,600**	**$13,354**	**$14,198**	**$15,032**	**$15,970**
Alabama	7,377	7,737	8,105	9,227	9,304	10,501	10,499	11,666	12,948	13,060
Alaska	13,570	14,129	14,663	15,667	16,381	19,308	20,880	22,541	24,150	27,210
Arizona	9,281	9,915	10,063	10,428	10,807	11,776	12,911	13,614	14,430	15,054
Arkansas	6,525	6,842	7,333	7,820	8,651	9,595	9,733	10,398	11,121	12,299
California	11,025	11,418	12,072	13,106	14,315	15,285	16,316	17,149	17,579	18,020
Colorado	8,615	9,264	9,666	10,131	10,929	12,031	13,202	14,018	14,990	16,205
Connecticut	10,079	10,295	10,604	11,038	11,805	12,818	13,659	14,299	15,482	16,229
Delaware	9,725	10,420	10,593	11,303	12,009	12,539	13,152	13,741	15,117	16,148
District of Columbia	10,607	11,020	12,127	12,733	14,355	15,681	17,065	18,235	19,486	22,190
Florida	8,797	8,938	9,250	9,989	10,287	10,502	12,146	12,780	13,186	14,149
Georgia	7,494	7,917	8,685	9,365	10,135	10,834	11,170	12,111	13,274	13,853
Hawaii	10,285	10,321	10,531	11,114	13,684	15,209	16,770	17,722	18,357	19,920
Idaho	7,068	7,367	7,657	8,260	9,242	10,212	10,972	11,726	12,607	13,611
Illinois	10,249	10,624	11,341	11,984	13,165	14,092	14,657	15,926	16,517	17,601
Indiana	9,421	9,772	10,047	10,492	11,186	11,962	12,776	13,408	14,285	15,599
Iowa	9,085	9,187	9,597	9,854	10,655	12,132	12,533	13,340	14,186	15,203
Kansas	8,027	8,251	8,505	8,895	9,332	10,864	11,280	12,033	12,746	13,690
Kentucky	7,198	7,362	7,796	8,301	8,941	9,784	10,925	11,723	13,170	14,520
Louisiana	8,306	8,766	8,837	9,166	9,800	10,657	10,878	11,116	12,478	13,760
Maine	8,127	8,546	8,977	9,238	9,806	10,620	11,116	11,739	12,275	13,071
Maryland	10,091	10,463	11,159	˙11,741	12,626	13,702	14,696	15,810	16,587	17,558
Massachusetts	9,611	10,178	10,519	11,128	12,734	13,519	14,311	15,200	17,007	17,253
Michigan	10,962	11,620	11,877	12,473	13,862	14,602	15,525	16,440	18,004	19,663
Minnesota	9,778	10,218	10,553	11,076	11,790	12,726	13,963	14,167	15,509	15,912
Mississippi	6,004	6,530	6,908	7,606	8,033	9,276	9,399	10,432	11,100	11,850
Missouri	8,183	8,682	9,059	9,526	9,990	10,802	11,449	12,154	12,711	13,682
Montana	8,130	8,529	8,949	9,428	9,994	11,044	11,740	12,668	13,651	14,537
Nebraska	8,125	8,465	8,704	9,168	9,264	10,409	11,172	11,853	12,635	13,516
Nevada	9,517	10,192	10,864	11,576	12,227	12,768	13,472	14,288	15,336	16,295
New Hampshire	8,311	8,457	9,157	9,611	9,998	10,250	10,495	11,100	11,838	13,017
New Jersey	10,025	10,726	11,739	11,897	12,594	13,606	14,518	15,369	16,186	17,161
New Mexico	8,114	8,227	8,715	9,181	10,005	10,806	11,854	12,840	14,087	14,887
New York	11,034	11,828	12,359	13,362	14,700	16,315	17,149	17,831	18,512	19,812
North Carolina	7,772	8,587	9,080	10,229	10,990	11,260	11,892	12,770	13,674	14,117
North Dakota	7,253	7,586	8,052	8,472	9,239	10,315	10,683	11,298	12,012	13,263
Ohio	8,677	8,780	9,628	10,101	10,730	11,557	12,511	13,306	14,279	15,269
Oklahoma	7,657	7,700	7,794	8,230	8,942	9,702	10,527	11,519	12,233	13,107
Oregon	9,048	9,478	9,550	9,927	10,809	12,283	13,044	13,838	14,924	16,266
Pennsylvania	9,186	9,901	10,389	10,921	11,618	12,614	13,431	14,459	15,511	16,515
Rhode Island	9,301	9,910	10,606	11,407	12,371	13,001	14,109	15,985	16,778	18,002
South Carolina	6,950	7,354	8,004	8,550	9,465	9,916	10,500	11,420	12,121	13,063
South Dakota	7,392	7,628	7,860	8,109	8,708	9,408	10,183	10,850	11,419	12,348
Tennessee	7,550	7,995	8,298	8,841	9,916	10,327	11,159	11,919	12,921	13,972
Texas	8,147	8,472	8,681	8,922	9,788	11,318	11,564	12,538	13,038	14,132
Utah	8,049	8,454	8,499	9,141	10,052	11,180	12,168	13,890	13,890	14,909
Vermont	8,256	8,494	8,867	8,937	9,679	10,101	10,804	11,305	11,786	12,484
Virginia	8,581	9,084	9,513	9,919	10,671	11,302	12,047	12,544	13,272	14,060
Washington	9,900	10,176	10,591	11,295	12,415	13,687	14,921	16,114	17,357	18,820
West Virginia	7,626	8,110	8,099	8,313	9,106	10,436	11,428	12,061	12,752	13,710
Wisconsin	9,634	10,012	10,414	10,830	11,433	12,351	13,242	14,045	14,906	16,006
Wyoming	8,694	9,234	9,294	9,689	10,317	12,055	13,082	14,115	14,469	16,012

Table 27.—Estimated average annual teacher salaries (in current dollars) in public elementary and secondary schools, by state: 1970–71 to 1996–97—Continued

State	1980–81	1981–82	1982–83	1983–84	1984–85	1985–86	1986–87	1987–88	1988–89	1989–90
1	12	13	14	15	16	17	18	19	20	21
United States	$17,644	$19,274	$20,695	$21,935	$23,600	$25,199	$26,569	$28,034	$29,564	$31,367
Alabama	15,496	15,612	17,619	17,682	20,295	23,090	23,200	23,320	24,815	24,828
Alaska	29,030	31,924	33,983	37,807	38,461	39,115	39,769	40,424	41,754	43,153
Arizona	17,158	19,211	21,119	21,642	23,380	24,680	25,972	27,388	28,499	29,402
Arkansas	13,273	14,506	15,029	16,929	18,696	19,519	19,904	20,340	21,395	22,352
California	20,893	22,755	23,614	24,843	27,410	29,130	31,219	33,159	34,684	37,998
Colorado	17,734	19,577	21,470	23,276	24,454	25,892	27,387	28,651	29,558	30,758
Connecticut	17,404	18,858	20,731	22,627	24,468	26,610	28,902	33,487	37,343	40,461
Delaware	18,025	19,290	20,625	20,934	22,924	24,624	27,467	29,573	31,585	33,377
District of Columbia	22,882	24,265	26,633	28,667	31,709	33,211	33,797	34,705	37,231	38,402
Florida	15,406	16,780	18,275	19,497	20,836	22,250	23,833	25,198	26,974	28,803
Georgia	15,445	16,363	17,412	18,630	20,610	23,046	24,200	26,190	26,920	28,006
Hawaii	21,147	22,542	24,796	24,357	24,628	25,845	26,815	28,785	30,778	32,047
Idaho	15,109	16,401	17,585	17,985	20,033	20,969	21,480	22,242	22,734	23,861
Illinois	19,426	21,020	22,315	24,191	25,477	26,897	28,238	29,663	31,145	32,794
Indiana	17,211	18,636	20,150	21,538	22,853	24,325	22,581	27,029	29,161	30,902
Iowa	16,961	18,270	19,257	20,149	20,934	21,663	22,581	24,842	25,778	26,747
Kansas	15,250	16,712	18,231	19,411	21,121	22,644	23,459	24,647	27,360	28,744
Kentucky	15,750	17,290	18,385	19,660	20,230	20,948	22,476	24,253	24,930	26,292
Louisiana	16,010	17,930	18,420	18,400	19,490	20,303	21,196	21,209	22,470	24,300
Maine	13,994	15,105	16,248	17,328	18,330	19,583	21,257	23,425	24,938	26,881
Maryland	18,998	21,120	22,922	23,870	25,861	26,800	28,893	30,933	33,895	36,319
Massachusetts	18,798	20,249	21,841	22,958	24,618	26,496	28,922	30,379	32,221	34,712
Michigan	21,779	24,304	25,712	27,104	28,440	30,067	31,412	33,151	34,670	37,072
Minnesota	17,777	19,907	22,876	24,350	25,450	27,360	28,340	29,900	30,660	32,190
Mississippi	13,017	14,135	14,320	15,812	15,923	18,472	19,447	20,563	22,578	24,292
Missouri	15,421	16,413	17,521	19,269	20,452	21,945	23,435	24,709	26,006	27,094
Montana	15,967	17,770	19,702	20,690	21,705	22,482	23,206	23,798	24,421	25,081
Nebraska	14,882	16,570	17,412	18,785	19,848	20,939	21,834	22,683	23,845	25,522
Nevada	17,700	19,940	22,070	22,360	22,520	25,610	26,960	27,600	28,840	30,590
New Hampshire	13,702	14,894	16,549	17,376	18,577	20,263	21,869	24,019	26,702	28,986
New Jersey	18,245	19,910	21,536	23,264	24,830	27,170	28,718	30,720	33,037	35,676
New Mexico	16,812	18,690	20,380	20,571	21,811	21,982	23,976	24,523	24,297	24,756
New York	21,326	23,437	25,000	27,319	28,213	30,490	32,000	34,500	36,654	38,925
North Carolina	15,861	16,947	17,585	18,311	20,812	22,340	23,879	24,900	25,738	27,883
North Dakota	14,881	17,426	18,770	19,260	20,090	20,816	21,284	21,660	22,249	23,016
Ohio	16,904	18,550	20,004	21,290	22,878	24,518	26,288	27,606	29,671	31,218
Oklahoma	15,182	16,210	18,270	18,630	19,019	21,419	21,468	21,630	22,370	23,070
Oregon	18,047	20,305	21,746	23,155	24,378	25,660	26,690	28,060	29,390	30,840
Pennsylvania	17,890	19,482	21,178	22,703	24,192	25,853	27,422	29,177	31,248	33,338
Rhode Island	20,088	21,659	23,175	25,337	27,693	29,470	31,079	32,858	34,233	36,057
South Carolina	14,353	15,615	16,523	17,384	20,143	21,595	23,201	24,728	25,623	27,217
South Dakota	13,668	14,717	15,595	16,480	17,380	18,095	18,781	19,758	20,530	21,300
Tennessee	15,118	16,285	17,380	17,910	20,474	21,384	22,627	23,785	25,619	27,052
Texas	15,728	17,582	19,550	20,170	23,264	24,463	24,903	25,558	26,527	27,496
Utah	16,900	18,106	19,859	20,007	21,170	22,553	22,956	22,555	22,852	23,686
Vermont	13,540	14,715	16,271	17,606	18,999	20,796	21,835	24,507	27,106	29,012
Virginia	15,535	17,008	18,535	19,676	21,272	23,095	25,039	27,189	28,967	30,938
Washington	21,268	22,954	23,488	24,365	25,505	26,209	27,285	28,217	29,199	30,457
West Virginia	14,948	17,129	17,322	17,489	19,563	20,627	21,446	21,736	21,904	22,842
Wisconsin	17,606	19,387	21,496	22,811	24,577	26,347	27,815	29,122	30,779	31,921
Wyoming	18,718	21,249	23,690	25,197	26,398	27,224	28,103	27,134	27,634	28,141

Table 27.—Estimated average annual teacher salaries (in current dollars) in public elementary and secondary schools, by state: 1970–71 to 1996–97—Continued

State	1990–91	1991–92	1992–93	1993–94	1994–95	1995–96	1996–97	Percentage change			
								1970–71 to 1996–97	1986–87 to 1991–92	1991–92 to 1996–97	1986–87 to 1996–97
1	22	23	24	25	26	27	28	29	30	31	32
United States	**$33,084**	**$34,063**	**$35,030**	**$35,733**	**$36,609**	**$37,560**	**$38,509**	315.5	28.2	13.1	44.9
Alabama	26,874	26,971	26,953	28,705	31,144	31,313	32,549	341.2	16.3	20.7	40.3
Alaska	43,427	44,661	46,701	47,512	47,951	49,620	50,647	273.2	12.3	13.4	27.4
Arizona	30,773	31,176	31,352	31,800	32,175	32,484	33,350	259.3	20.0	7.0	28.4
Arkansas	23,611	27,070	27,433	28,098	28,934	29,322	29,975	359.4	36.0	10.7	50.6
California	39,598	39,922	40,035	40,264	41,078	42,259	43,474	294.3	27.9	8.9	39.3
Colorado	31,819	33,072	33,541	33,826	34,571	35,364	36,175	319.9	20.8	9.4	32.1
Connecticut	43,808	46,971	48,343	49,769	50,045	50,254	50,426	400.3	62.5	7.4	74.5
Delaware	35,246	34,548	36,217	37,469	39,076	40,533	41,436	326.1	25.8	19.9	50.9
District of Columbia	39,497	38,798	38,702	42,543	43,700	43,700	45,012	324.4	14.8	16.0	33.2
Florida	30,555	31,070	31,172	31,944	32,588	33,330	33,881	285.1	30.4	9.0	42.2
Georgia	28,976	29,372	30,223	30,712	32,291	34,002	36,042	380.9	21.4	22.7	48.9
Hawaii	32,541	34,528	36,470	36,564	38,518	35,807	35,842	248.5	28.8	3.8	33.7
Idaho	25,485	26,334	27,011	27,756	29,783	30,891	31,818	350.2	22.6	20.8	48.1
Illinois	34,605	36,461	38,632	39,387	39,431	40,919	42,679	316.4	29.1	17.1	51.1
Indiana	32,757	34,006	35,066	35,712	36,785	37,675	38,575	309.5	50.6	13.4	70.8
Iowa	27,977	29,202	30,130	30,760	31,511	32,372	33,275	266.3	29.3	13.9	47.4
Kansas	29,767	30,731	32,863	33,914	34,652	35,134	35,837	346.5	31.0	16.6	52.8
Kentucky	29,115	30,870	31,115	31,625	32,257	33,080	33,950	371.7	37.3	10.0	51.1
Louisiana	26,240	25,963	26,102	26,095	26,461	26,800	28,347	241.3	22.5	9.2	33.7
Maine	28,531	30,097	30,250	30,996	31,972	32,869	33,800	315.9	41.6	12.3	59.0
Maryland	38,382	38,728	38,753	39,453	40,661	41,160	41,148	307.8	34.0	6.2	42.4
Massachusetts	36,460	37,845	38,774	39,023	40,795	42,264	43,806	355.8	30.9	15.8	51.5
Michigan	39,449	41,490	43,901	44,856	41,895	44,796	44,251	303.7	32.1	6.7	40.9
Minnesota	33,126	34,451	35,093	35,440	35,948	36,937	37,975	288.4	21.6	10.2	34.0
Mississippi	24,366	24,367	24,367	25,153	26,818	27,692	27,720	361.7	25.3	13.8	42.5
Missouri	28,286	28,895	29,375	30,319	31,189	33,341	34,342	319.7	23.3	18.9	46.5
Montana	26,774	27,590	27,617	28,200	28,785	29,364	29,950	268.4	18.9	8.6	29.1
Nebraska	26,592	27,231	28,754	29,564	30,922	31,496	31,768	291.0	24.7	16.7	45.5
Nevada	32,209	33,857	34,119	33,955	34,836	36,167	37,340	292.4	25.6	10.3	38.5
New Hampshire	31,200	33,170	33,931	34,121	34,720	35,792	36,867	343.6	51.7	11.1	68.6
New Jersey	38,411	41,027	42,680	44,693	46,087	47,910	49,349	392.3	42.9	20.3	71.8
New Mexico	25,735	26,239	26,532	27,202	28,493	29,074	29,715	266.2	9.4	13.2	23.9
New York	42,080	43,335	44,999	45,772	47,612	48,115	49,560	349.2	35.4	14.4	54.9
North Carolina	29,276	28,791	29,315	29,728	30,793	30,411	31,225	301.8	20.6	8.5	30.8
North Dakota	23,574	24,495	25,211	25,506	26,327	26,969	27,711	282.1	15.1	13.1	30.2
Ohio	32,615	32,932	34,519	35,673	36,802	37,835	38,831	347.5	25.3	17.9	47.7
Oklahoma	24,457	25,339	25,918	27,009	28,172	28,404	29,270	282.3	18.0	15.5	36.3
Oregon	32,300	34,100	35,880	37,713	38,555	39,706	40,900	352.0	27.8	19.9	53.2
Pennsylvania	36,057	38,715	41,215	42,411	44,510	46,087	47,429	416.3	41.2	22.5	73.0
Rhode Island	34,997	36,417	37,933	39,261	40,729	42,160	43,019	362.5	17.2	18.1	38.4
South Carolina	28,301	28,068	29,224	29,566	30,279	31,622	32,659	369.9	21.0	16.4	40.8
South Dakota	22,376	23,291	24,289	25,259	25,994	26,346	26,764	262.1	24.0	14.9	42.5
Tennessee	28,248	28,621	28,960	30,514	32,477	33,126	33,789	347.5	26.5	18.1	49.3
Texas	28,321	29,041	29,935	30,529	31,223	32,000	32,644	300.7	16.6	12.4	31.1
Utah	25,578	26,339	27,239	27,706	29,082	30,588	31,750	294.5	14.7	20.5	38.3
Vermont	31,236	33,646	32,824	34,517	35,406	36,295	37,200	350.6	54.1	10.6	70.4
Virginia	32,153	31,764	32,257	33,009	33,987	34,792	35,837	317.6	26.9	12.8	43.1
Washington	33,079	34,823	35,759	35,863	36,151	37,853	37,860	282.4	27.6	8.7	38.8
West Virginia	25,967	27,366	30,301	30,549	31,944	32,155	33,159	334.8	27.6	21.2	54.6
Wisconsin	33,209	35,227	35,926	35,990	37,746	38,182	38,950	304.3	26.6	10.6	40.0
Wyoming	28,948	30,425	30,080	30,952	31,285	31,571	31,721	264.9	8.3	4.3	12.9

SOURCE: National Education Association, *Estimates of School Statistics;* and unpublished data.

Table 28.—Estimated average annual teacher salaries (in constant 1996–97 dollars [1]) in public elementary and secondary schools, by state: 1970–71 to 1996–97

State	1970–71	1971–72	1972–73	1973–74	1974–75	1975–76	1976–77	1977–78	1978–79	1979–80
1	2	3	4	5	6	7	8	9	10	11
United States	$37,074	$37,478	$37,767	$36,706	$35,717	$36,104	$36,156	$36,022	$34,872	$32,689
Alabama	29,509	29,878	30,087	31,448	28,546	30,089	28,426	29,598	30,037	26,733
Alaska	54,283	54,562	54,431	53,396	50,260	55,325	56,532	57,189	56,024	55,697
Arizona	37,126	38,289	37,355	35,541	33,158	33,743	34,956	34,540	33,475	30,814
Arkansas	26,101	26,422	27,221	26,652	26,543	27,493	26,352	26,381	25,799	25,175
California	44,102	44,093	44,813	44,668	43,921	43,797	44,175	43,509	40,780	36,885
Colorado	34,462	35,775	35,881	34,529	33,532	34,473	35,744	35,565	34,774	33,170
Connecticut	40,318	39,756	39,363	37,620	36,220	36,728	36,982	36,278	35,916	33,219
Delaware	38,902	40,239	39,322	38,523	36,846	35,929	35,609	34,863	35,069	33,054
District of Columbia	42,430	42,556	45,017	43,397	44,044	44,932	46,203	46,265	45,204	45,421
Florida	35,190	34,516	34,337	34,045	31,563	30,092	32,885	32,425	30,589	28,962
Georgia	29,978	30,573	32,240	31,918	31,096	31,043	30,243	30,727	30,793	28,356
Hawaii	41,142	39,856	39,092	37,879	41,985	43,579	45,405	44,963	42,585	40,775
Idaho	28,273	28,449	28,424	28,152	28,356	29,261	29,707	29,750	29,246	27,861
Illinois	40,998	41,026	42,099	40,844	40,393	40,379	39,684	40,406	38,317	36,028
Indiana	37,686	37,736	37,296	35,759	34,321	34,276	34,591	34,018	33,139	31,930
Iowa	36,342	35,477	35,625	33,585	32,692	34,763	33,933	33,845	32,909	31,119
Kansas	32,110	31,863	31,571	30,316	28,632	31,129	30,540	30,529	29,568	28,022
Kentucky	28,793	28,430	28,940	28,292	27,433	28,035	29,579	29,743	30,552	29,721
Louisiana	33,226	33,851	32,804	31,240	30,068	30,536	29,452	31,658	30,167	28,166
Maine	32,510	33,002	33,324	31,485	30,087	30,430	30,096	29,783	28,476	26,755
Maryland	40,366	40,405	41,423	40,016	38,739	39,261	39,789	40,112	38,479	35,940
Massachusetts	38,446	39,304	39,048	37,927	39,070	38,737	38,747	38,564	39,453	35,315
Michigan	43,850	44,873	44,089	42,511	42,531	41,840	42,034	41,710	41,766	40,248
Minnesota	39,114	39,459	39,174	37,749	36,174	36,465	37,805	35,944	35,978	32,570
Mississippi	24,017	25,217	25,643	25,923	24,647	26,579	25,448	26,467	25,750	24,256
Missouri	32,734	33,527	33,628	32,467	30,651	30,952	30,998	30,836	29,487	28,006
Montana	32,522	32,936	33,220	32,133	30,664	31,645	31,786	32,140	31,668	29,756
Nebraska	32,502	32,689	32,310	31,247	28,424	29,826	30,248	30,073	29,311	27,666
Nevada	38,070	39,358	40,328	39,453	37,515	36,585	36,475	36,250	35,577	33,354
New Hampshire	33,246	32,658	33,992	32,756	30,676	29,370	28,415	28,162	27,462	26,645
New Jersey	40,102	41,420	43,576	40,548	38,641	38,986	39,307	38,993	37,549	35,127
New Mexico	32,458	31,770	32,351	31,291	30,697	30,963	32,095	32,577	32,679	30,472
New York	44,138	45,676	45,878	45,541	45,102	46,749	46,431	45,240	42,945	40,553
North Carolina	31,090	33,160	33,706	34,863	33,719	32,264	32,197	32,399	31,721	28,896
North Dakota	29,013	29,295	29,890	28,874	28,347	29,556	28,924	28,664	27,866	27,148
Ohio	34,710	33,906	35,740	34,426	32,922	33,115	33,873	33,759	33,125	31,254
Oklahoma	30,630	29,735	28,932	28,050	27,436	27,800	28,502	29,225	28,378	26,829
Oregon	36,194	36,601	35,451	33,833	33,164	35,195	35,316	35,109	34,621	33,295
Pennsylvania	36,746	38,234	38,565	37,221	35,646	36,144	36,364	36,684	35,983	33,805
Rhode Island	37,206	38,269	39,371	38,878	37,957	37,253	38,200	40,556	38,922	36,849
South Carolina	27,801	28,399	29,712	29,140	29,040	28,413	28,429	28,974	28,119	26,739
South Dakota	29,569	29,457	29,177	27,637	26,718	26,957	27,570	27,528	26,490	25,275
Tennessee	30,202	30,874	30,803	30,132	30,424	29,591	30,213	30,240	29,974	28,599
Texas	32,590	32,716	32,225	30,408	30,032	32,430	31,309	31,811	30,246	28,927
Utah	32,198	32,647	31,549	31,154	30,842	32,035	32,945	35,241	32,222	30,517
Vermont	33,026	32,801	32,915	30,459	29,697	28,943	29,252	28,682	27,341	25,554
Virginia	34,326	35,079	35,313	33,806	32,741	32,384	32,617	31,826	30,789	28,780
Washington	39,602	39,296	39,315	38,496	38,092	39,218	40,398	40,883	40,265	38,523
West Virginia	30,506	31,318	30,064	28,332	27,939	29,903	30,941	30,600	29,582	28,063
Wisconsin	38,538	38,663	38,658	36,911	35,079	35,390	35,853	35,634	34,579	32,763
Wyoming	34,778	35,659	34,500	33,022	31,655	34,542	35,419	35,812	33,566	32,775

Table 28.—Estimated average annual teacher salaries (in constant 1996–97 dollars[1]) in public elementary and secondary schools, by state: 1970–71 to 1996–97—Continued

State	1980–81	1981–82	1982–83	1983–84	1984–85	1985–86	1986–87	1987–88	1988–89	1989–90
1	12	13	14	15	16	17	18	19	20	21
United States	$32,367	$32,546	$33,506	$34,246	$35,457	$36,799	$37,957	$38,456	$38,765	$39,256
Alabama	28,426	26,362	28,526	27,606	30,492	33,719	33,144	31,990	32,538	31,072
Alaska	53,254	53,906	55,020	59,026	57,785	57,121	56,814	55,452	54,748	54,006
Arizona	31,475	32,439	34,192	33,788	35,127	36,041	37,104	37,570	37,368	36,796
Arkansas	24,348	24,494	24,332	26,430	28,090	28,504	28,435	27,902	28,053	27,973
California	38,327	38,423	38,232	38,786	41,182	42,539	44,600	45,486	45,478	47,554
Colorado	32,532	33,057	34,761	36,339	36,741	37,811	39,125	39,302	38,757	38,493
Connecticut	31,927	31,843	33,564	35,326	36,762	38,859	41,290	45,936	48,964	50,637
Delaware	33,066	32,573	33,393	32,683	34,442	35,959	39,239	40,567	41,415	41,771
District of Columbia	41,976	40,973	43,120	44,756	47,641	48,499	48,283	47,607	48,818	48,060
Florida	28,261	28,334	29,588	30,440	31,305	32,492	34,048	34,566	35,369	36,047
Georgia	28,333	27,630	28,191	29,086	30,965	33,655	34,572	35,927	35,298	35,049
Hawaii	38,793	38,064	40,146	38,027	37,002	37,742	38,308	39,486	40,356	40,107
Idaho	27,716	27,694	28,471	28,079	30,098	30,622	30,686	30,511	29,809	29,862
Illinois	35,636	35,494	36,129	37,768	38,278	39,278	40,341	40,691	40,838	41,041
Indiana	31,572	31,468	32,623	33,626	34,335	35,522	32,259	37,077	38,236	38,674
Iowa	31,114	30,850	31,178	31,457	31,452	31,635	32,259	34,077	33,800	33,474
Kansas	27,975	28,219	29,517	30,305	31,733	33,068	33,514	33,810	35,875	35,973
Kentucky	28,892	29,195	29,766	30,694	30,394	30,591	32,109	33,269	32,688	32,904
Louisiana	29,369	30,276	29,823	28,727	29,282	29,649	30,281	29,094	29,463	30,411
Maine	25,671	25,506	26,306	27,053	27,540	28,598	30,368	32,134	32,699	33,641
Maryland	34,851	35,663	37,111	37,267	38,854	39,137	41,277	42,433	44,443	45,453
Massachusetts	34,484	34,192	35,361	35,843	36,987	38,693	41,318	41,673	42,248	43,442
Michigan	39,952	41,039	41,629	42,316	42,729	43,908	44,875	45,475	45,460	46,395
Minnesota	32,611	33,614	37,037	38,016	38,237	39,954	40,487	41,016	40,202	40,285
Mississippi	23,879	23,868	23,185	24,686	23,923	26,975	27,782	28,208	29,604	30,401
Missouri	28,289	27,715	28,367	30,084	30,728	32,047	33,479	33,895	34,099	33,908
Montana	29,290	30,006	31,898	32,302	32,610	32,831	33,152	32,645	32,021	31,389
Nebraska	27,300	27,980	28,191	29,328	29,820	30,578	31,192	31,116	31,266	31,941
Nevada	32,470	33,670	35,732	34,909	33,835	37,399	38,515	37,861	37,815	38,283
New Hampshire	25,135	25,150	26,793	27,128	27,911	29,591	31,242	32,948	35,012	36,276
New Jersey	33,469	33,619	34,867	36,321	37,305	39,677	41,027	42,141	43,318	44,648
New Mexico	30,841	31,559	32,996	32,116	32,770	32,101	34,252	33,640	31,858	30,982
New York	39,121	39,575	40,476	42,652	42,388	44,525	45,715	47,326	48,061	48,714
North Carolina	29,096	28,616	28,471	28,588	31,269	32,624	34,114	34,157	33,748	34,895
North Dakota	27,298	29,425	30,389	30,070	30,184	30,398	30,406	29,712	29,173	28,804
Ohio	31,009	31,323	32,387	33,239	34,373	35,804	37,555	37,869	38,905	39,069
Oklahoma	27,850	27,372	29,580	29,086	28,575	31,279	30,669	29,671	29,332	28,872
Oregon	33,106	34,286	35,207	36,151	36,626	37,472	38,129	38,492	38,536	38,596
Pennsylvania	32,818	32,897	34,288	35,445	36,347	37,754	39,175	40,024	40,973	41,722
Rhode Island	36,850	36,573	37,521	39,557	41,607	43,036	44,400	45,073	44,887	45,125
South Carolina	26,330	26,367	26,751	27,141	30,264	31,536	33,145	33,921	33,597	34,062
South Dakota	25,073	24,851	25,249	25,729	26,112	26,425	26,831	27,103	26,919	26,657
Tennessee	27,733	27,498	28,139	27,962	30,761	31,228	32,325	32,627	33,592	33,855
Texas	28,852	29,688	31,652	31,490	34,953	35,724	35,577	35,060	34,782	34,411
Utah	31,002	30,573	32,152	31,236	31,807	32,935	32,795	30,940	29,964	29,643
Vermont	24,838	24,847	26,343	27,487	28,545	30,369	31,194	33,618	35,542	36,308
Virginia	28,498	28,719	30,009	30,719	31,960	33,726	35,771	37,297	37,982	38,719
Washington	39,015	38,759	38,028	38,040	38,320	38,274	38,979	38,707	38,286	38,117
West Virginia	27,421	28,924	28,045	27,305	29,392	30,122	30,638	29,817	28,721	28,587
Wisconsin	32,297	32,736	34,803	35,614	36,925	38,475	39,737	39,949	40,358	39,949
Wyoming	34,337	35,880	38,355	39,339	39,661	39,756	40,148	37,221	36,234	35,218

Table 28.—Estimated average annual teacher salaries (in constant 1996–97 dollars [1]) in public elementary and secondary schools, by state: 1970–71 to 1996–97—Continued

State	1990–91	1991–92	1992–93	1993–94	1994–95	1995–96	1996–97	Percentage change			
								1970–71 to 1996–97	1986–87 to 1991–92	1991–92 to 1996–97	1986–87 to 1996–97
1	22	23	24	25	26	27	28	29	30	31	32
United States	$39,258	$39,165	$39,057	$38,834	$38,678	$38,632	$38,509	3.9	3.2	–1.7	1.5
Alabama	31,889	31,011	30,051	31,196	32,904	32,206	32,549	10.3	–6.4	5.0	–1.8
Alaska	51,531	51,350	52,069	51,636	50,661	51,036	50,647	–6.7	–9.6	–1.4	–10.9
Arizona	36,516	35,845	34,956	34,560	33,993	33,411	33,350	–10.2	–3.4	–7.0	–10.1
Arkansas	28,017	31,124	30,586	30,537	30,569	30,159	29,975	14.8	9.5	–3.7	5.4
California	46,988	45,901	44,637	43,759	43,399	43,465	43,474	–1.4	2.9	–5.3	–2.5
Colorado	37,757	38,025	37,396	36,762	36,525	36,373	36,175	5.0	–2.8	–4.9	–7.5
Connecticut	51,983	54,006	53,900	54,089	52,873	51,688	50,426	25.1	30.8	–6.6	22.1
Delaware	41,823	39,722	40,380	40,721	41,284	41,689	41,436	6.5	1.2	4.3	5.6
District of Columbia	46,868	44,609	43,151	46,236	46,170	44,947	45,012	6.1	–7.6	0.9	–6.8
Florida	36,257	35,723	34,755	34,717	34,430	34,281	33,881	–3.7	4.9	–5.2	–0.5
Georgia	34,383	33,771	33,697	33,378	34,116	34,972	36,042	20.2	–2.3	6.7	4.3
Hawaii	38,614	39,699	40,662	39,738	40,695	36,829	35,842	–12.9	3.6	–9.7	–6.4
Idaho	30,241	30,278	30,116	30,165	31,466	31,772	31,818	12.5	–1.3	5.1	3.7
Illinois	41,063	41,922	43,073	42,806	41,659	42,086	42,679	4.1	3.9	1.8	5.8
Indiana	38,870	39,099	39,097	38,812	38,864	38,750	38,575	2.4	21.2	–1.3	19.6
Iowa	33,198	33,576	33,593	33,430	33,292	33,296	33,275	–8.4	4.1	–0.9	3.1
Kansas	35,322	35,334	36,641	36,858	36,610	36,136	35,837	11.6	5.4	1.4	6.9
Kentucky	34,548	35,494	34,692	34,370	34,080	34,024	33,950	17.9	10.5	–4.3	5.7
Louisiana	31,137	29,852	29,102	28,360	27,956	27,565	28,347	–14.7	–1.4	–5.0	–6.4
Maine	33,855	34,605	33,727	33,686	33,779	33,807	33,800	4.0	14.0	–2.3	11.3
Maryland	45,545	44,528	43,208	42,877	42,959	42,334	41,148	1.9	7.9	–7.6	–0.3
Massachusetts	43,264	43,513	43,231	42,410	43,100	43,470	43,806	13.9	5.3	0.7	6.0
Michigan	46,811	47,704	48,947	48,749	44,263	46,074	44,251	0.9	6.3	–7.2	–1.4
Minnesota	39,308	39,611	39,127	38,516	37,980	37,991	37,975	–2.9	–2.2	–4.1	–6.2
Mississippi	28,913	28,017	27,168	27,336	28,334	28,482	27,720	15.4	0.8	–1.1	–0.2
Missouri	33,565	33,223	32,752	32,951	32,952	34,292	34,342	4.9	–0.8	3.4	2.6
Montana	31,770	31,722	30,792	30,648	30,412	30,202	29,950	–7.9	–4.3	–5.6	–9.7
Nebraska	31,554	31,310	32,059	32,130	32,669	32,395	31,768	–2.3	0.4	1.5	1.8
Nevada	38,220	38,928	38,041	36,902	36,805	37,199	37,340	–1.9	1.1	–4.1	–3.1
New Hampshire	37,022	38,138	37,831	37,083	36,682	36,813	36,867	10.9	22.1	–3.3	18.0
New Jersey	45,579	47,172	47,586	48,572	48,692	49,277	49,349	23.1	15.0	4.6	20.3
New Mexico	30,538	30,169	29,582	29,563	30,103	29,904	29,715	–8.4	–11.9	–1.5	–13.2
New York	49,933	49,825	50,172	49,745	50,303	49,488	49,560	12.3	9.0	–0.5	8.4
North Carolina	34,739	33,103	32,685	32,308	32,533	31,279	31,225	0.4	–3.0	–5.7	–8.5
North Dakota	27,973	28,164	28,109	27,720	27,815	27,738	27,711	–4.5	–7.4	–1.6	–8.9
Ohio	38,701	37,864	38,487	38,769	38,882	38,914	38,831	11.9	0.8	2.6	3.4
Oklahoma	29,021	29,134	28,897	29,353	29,764	29,214	29,270	–4.4	–5.0	0.5	–4.6
Oregon	38,328	39,207	40,004	40,986	40,734	40,839	40,900	13.0	2.8	4.3	7.3
Pennsylvania	42,786	44,514	45,953	46,092	47,025	47,402	47,429	29.1	13.6	6.5	21.1
Rhode Island	41,528	41,871	42,293	42,669	43,031	43,363	43,019	15.6	–5.7	2.7	–3.1
South Carolina	33,582	32,272	32,583	32,132	31,990	32,524	32,659	17.5	–2.6	1.2	–1.5
South Dakota	26,552	26,779	27,081	27,451	27,463	27,098	26,764	–9.5	–0.2	–0.1	–0.2
Tennessee	33,520	32,908	32,289	33,162	34,312	34,071	33,789	11.9	1.8	2.7	4.5
Texas	33,606	33,391	33,376	33,179	32,988	32,913	32,644	0.2	–6.1	–2.2	–8.2
Utah	30,351	30,284	30,370	30,111	30,726	31,461	31,750	–1.4	–7.7	4.8	–3.2
Vermont	37,065	38,685	38,827	37,513	37,407	37,331	37,200	12.6	24.0	–3.8	19.3
Virginia	38,153	36,521	35,965	35,874	35,908	35,785	35,837	4.4	2.1	–1.9	0.2
Washington	39,252	40,039	39,869	38,976	38,194	38,933	37,860	–4.4	2.7	–5.4	–2.9
West Virginia	30,813	31,465	33,784	33,201	33,749	33,072	33,159	8.7	2.7	5.4	8.2
Wisconsin	39,406	40,503	40,056	39,114	39,879	39,271	38,950	1.1	1.9	–3.8	–2.0
Wyoming	34,350	34,982	33,538	33,638	33,053	32,472	31,721	–8.8	–12.9	–9.3	–21.0

[1] Based on the Consumer Price Index prepared by the Bureau of Labor Statistics, U.S. Department of Labor. Price index does not account for different rates of change in the cost of living among states.

SOURCE: National Education Association, *Estimates of School Statistics;* and unpublished data. (This table was prepared March 1998.)

Table 29.—Number and percentage distribution of enrollment of regular public elementary and secondary school districts, by enrollment size and state: 1995–96

State or other area	Number of regular school districts and supervisory union components, by enrollment size								Distribution of enrollment, by size of regular school districts and supervisory union components							
	Total	Less than 500[1]	500 to 999	1,000 to 2,499	2,500 to 4,999	5,000 to 9,999	10,000 to 24,999	25,000 or more	Total[2]	Less than 500	500 to 999	1,000 to 2,499	2,500 to 4,999	5,000 to 9,999	10,000 to 24,999	25,000 or more
1	2	3	4	5	6	7	8	9	10	11	12	13	14	15	16	17
United States	14,883	5,134	2,386	3,554	2,027	1,013	553	216	44,380,367	2.3	3.9	13.1	16.0	15.7	18.6	30.5
Alabama	127	0	1	37	52	26	7	4	735,912	0.0	0.1	9.4	24.2	25.5	15.9	24.9
Alaska	56	31	11	6	3	1	3	1	127,185	6.2	5.8	8.7	7.3	4.3	30.4	37.2
Arizona	227	95	21	52	23	15	17	4	745,008	1.9	2.0	11.9	10.4	13.1	35.0	25.7
Arkansas	314	93	108	71	26	13	3	0	452,907	6.4	17.1	24.3	19.7	19.8	12.8	0.0
California	1,006	314	129	170	133	123	103	34	5,409,887	1.2	1.7	5.6	8.8	16.2	29.6	36.9
Colorado	176	75	29	30	20	4	12	6	655,679	2.8	3.1	7.1	11.4	3.8	30.5	41.4
Connecticut	166	27	24	47	41	21	6	0	499,815	1.6	3.5	16.2	28.7	29.4	20.6	0.0
Delaware	19	0	1	4	7	3	4	0	108,461	0.0	0.6	5.5	23.3	18.4	52.2	0.0
District of Columbia	1	0	0	0	0	0	0	1	79,802	0.0	0.0	0.0	0.0	0.0	0.0	100.0
Florida	67	0	0	10	9	13	11	24	2,175,352	0.0	0.0	0.9	1.6	4.2	8.3	85.0
Georgia	181	9	4	55	54	30	19	10	1,311,126	0.2	0.3	7.4	14.6	15.9	20.2	41.4
Hawaii	1	0	0	0	0	0	0	1	187,104	0.0	0.0	0.0	0.0	0.0	0.0	100.0
Idaho	112	36	21	30	13	8	3	1	243,097	3.7	6.1	19.7	19.3	22.2	18.0	11.0
Illinois	916	269	230	263	95	41	15	3	1,924,970	3.8	8.6	21.4	17.0	14.2	10.5	24.5
Indiana	295	9	30	149	58	32	15	2	975,455	0.2	2.5	25.2	20.0	22.6	21.7	7.9
Iowa	390	122	151	83	21	6	6	1	502,343	7.5	21.2	25.2	15.5	7.8	16.2	6.5
Kansas	304	125	82	66	16	9	4	2	463,008	8.4	12.5	22.4	12.5	13.0	14.5	16.7
Kentucky	176	11	25	58	54	19	7	2	639,531	0.6	3.2	15.9	28.5	19.7	12.4	19.7
Louisiana	66	0	0	8	19	18	14	7	796,087	0.0	0.0	2.0	8.9	16.2	28.9	44.0
Maine	285	174	34	55	21	1	0	0	213,601	10.5	11.2	41.3	33.2	3.9	0.0	0.0
Maryland	24	0	0	0	3	5	7	9	805,544	0.0	0.0	0.0	3.6	13.4	81.7	
Massachusetts	353	149	25	73	68	28	9	1	784,297	1.5	2.3	16.6	30.4	23.3	17.8	8.1
Michigan	633	151	87	210	117	44	21	3	1,631,459	1.2	4.0	21.1	24.2	17.6	17.8	13.9
Minnesota	419	155	81	111	38	20	10	4	830,777	3.9	7.1	20.3	16.7	17.1	16.3	18.5
Mississippi	153	5	9	63	52	20	3	1	503,602	0.4	1.4	21.8	35.2	26.5	8.3	6.5
Missouri	536	233	127	97	47	15	15	2	873,661	6.4	10.3	18.0	18.8	11.6	26.0	9.0
Montana	481	408	37	25	6	4	1	0	165,390	28.9	15.0	21.2	12.5	15.7	6.6	0.0
Nebraska	680	592	47	25	10	3	1	2	288,692	22.1	10.7	13.3	13.6	8.0	6.3	26.0
Nevada	17	3	1	4	3	4	0	2	265,041	0.3	0.4	2.2	4.8	11.3	0.0	80.9
New Hampshire	178	90	29	39	17	1	2	0	194,171	8.9	10.4	32.2	30.8	2.8	14.8	0.0
New Jersey	608	186	122	167	80	40	11	2	1,190,724	3.8	7.4	22.5	23.8	22.7	13.3	6.5
New Mexico	89	26	22	12	13	9	6	1	329,661	2.0	4.7	6.5	14.6	19.9	25.3	27.0
New York	719	107	105	287	138	68	11	3	2,788,343	0.9	2.7	16.5	17.4	16.3	5.5	40.7
North Carolina	119	0	2	18	33	33	26	7	1,181,600	0.0	0.1	2.8	10.2	20.2	34.7	32.0
North Dakota	243	204	24	6	5	2	2	0	119,102	30.2	13.3	8.0	14.8	15.0	18.7	0.0
Ohio	661	61	103	285	140	53	13	6	1,837,628	0.2	4.5	25.8	25.7	19.5	8.6	15.7
Oklahoma	551	324	102	87	18	10	8	2	616,106	13.5	11.6	21.1	10.0	10.3	20.5	13.1
Oregon	248	114	31	49	31	13	7	3	527,502	3.4	4.3	15.0	21.4	17.3	16.7	21.9
Pennsylvania	501	7	41	211	174	53	13	2	1,764,117	0.1	1.9	20.6	33.6	20.7	8.9	14.2
Rhode Island	36	3	2	7	17	4	3	0	148,977	0.6	1.0	8.8	39.4	19.1	31.1	0.0
South Carolina	95	4	7	24	22	20	13	5	637,517	0.2	0.9	6.4	12.2	24.0	28.6	27.7
South Dakota	177	119	30	17	9	0	2	0	136,394	21.7	14.7	17.9	21.6	0.0	24.1	0.0
Tennessee	140	6	10	40	42	26	12	4	881,749	0.2	0.9	7.4	17.6	20.1	22.3	31.6
Texas	1,044	364	203	218	115	67	44	33	3,740,260	2.5	4.0	9.4	10.9	11.7	18.6	42.9
Utah	40	3	2	9	8	6	6	6	474,907	0.2	0.2	3.0	6.2	8.1	18.3	64.0
Vermont	284	218	46	18	2	0	0	0	104,150	34.0	32.1	27.6	6.2	0.0	0.0	0.0
Virginia	141	11	7	36	37	26	15	9	1,079,854	0.1	0.5	5.7	11.8	17.3	19.8	44.7
Washington	296	100	46	59	38	25	25	3	956,572	2.1	3.7	10.1	14.0	18.1	40.4	11.6
West Virginia	55	0	0	17	15	15	7	1	306,451	0.0	0.0	9.5	18.9	32.8	28.3	10.5
Wisconsin	428	89	125	132	57	14	9	2	869,930	3.3	10.7	23.3	21.9	11.6	15.0	14.2
Wyoming	49	12	12	14	7	2	2	0	99,859	3.3	9.5	22.8	23.8	13.8	26.9	0.0
Outlying areas																
American Samoa	1	0	0	0	0	0	1	0	14,576	0.0	0.0	0.0	0.0	0.0	100.0	0.0
Guam	1	0	0	0	0	0	0	1	32,014	0.0	0.0	0.0	0.0	0.0	0.0	100.0
Northern Marianas	1	0	0	0	0	1	0	0	8,444	0.0	0.0	0.0	0.0	100.0	0.0	0.0
Puerto Rico	1	0	0	0	0	0	0	1	621,121	0.0	0.0	0.0	0.0	0.0	0.0	100.0
Virgin Islands	1	0	0	0	0	0	1	0	22,221	0.0	0.0	0.0	0.0	0.0	100.0	0.0

[1] Includes districts not reporting an enrollment figure.

[2] Enrollment totals may differ slightly from data reported in other tables. This table reflects data reported by school districts rather than state education agencies. Excludes data for districts not reporting enrollment.

SOURCE: U.S. Department of Education, National Center for Education Statistics, Common Core of Data survey. (This table was prepared January 1998.)

Table 30.—Number and size of public elementary and secondary schools, by type and state: 1990–91 and 1995–96

State or other area	Total,[1] all schools, 1990–91	Number of schools, 1995–96							Average size of schools, 1995–96[2]				
		Total[1]	Elementary schools[3]	Secondary schools[4]	Combined elementary/secondary schools[5]	Other[6]	Alternative schools[7]	Special education schools[7]	All schools	All elementary schools[3]	Regular elementary schools[8]	All secondary schools[4]	Regular secondary schools[9]
1	2	3	4	5	6	7	8	9	10	11	12	13	14
United States	84,538	87,125	61,165	20,997	2,796	2,167	3,243	1,992	525	476	481	703	771
Alabama	1,297	1,319	864	298	154	3	18	17	559	490	496	708	736
Alaska	498	495	186	87	208	14	36	3	265	371	374	453	520
Arizona	1,049	1,133	817	240	15	61	43	16	671	587	593	1,008	1,067
Arkansas	1,098	1,098	674	414	7	3	0	0	416	394	391	447	447
California	7,913	7,876	5,750	1,866	182	78	756	127	694	620	623	960	1,352
Colorado	1,344	1,486	1,034	356	22	74	102	9	463	431	431	588	657
Connecticut	985	1,045	763	188	26	68	54	18	520	469	469	778	819
Delaware	173	181	120	42	19	0	2	28	599	560	593	930	989
District of Columbia ...	181	186	126	41	2	17	7	11	431	419	420	569	580
Florida	2,516	2,760	1,914	443	346	57	262	104	809	782	798	1,159	1,561
Georgia	1,734	1,763	1,383	307	73	0	19	8	744	657	658	1,146	1,204
Hawaii	235	246	186	44	16	0	1	4	761	627	630	1,367	1,462
Idaho	582	618	384	209	18	7	45	14	398	370	371	470	583
Illinois	4,239	4,142	3,061	898	32	151	44	240	474	423	433	701	730
Indiana	1,915	1,924	1,406	448	34	36	33	44	524	442	445	809	833
Iowa	1,588	1,556	1,075	443	28	10	26	18	323	288	290	408	425
Kansas	1,477	1,487	1,048	426	9	4	18	1	312	287	288	377	381
Kentucky	1,400	1,402	1,002	360	3	37	49	8	467	418	422	625	689
Louisiana	1,533	1,470	1,006	319	119	26	56	39	542	498	501	764	821
Maine	747	726	550	158	14	4	0	2	307	261	261	506	506
Maryland	1,220	1,276	1,038	213	20	5	27	47	631	547	562	1,080	1,176
Massachusetts	1,842	1,850	1,465	336	27	22	29	7	500	430	431	789	842
Michigan	3,313	3,748	2,514	811	92	331	135	159	478	434	436	671	724
Minnesota	1,590	2,157	1,190	686	92	189	513	108	426	426	474	457	670
Mississippi	972	1,011	571	314	75	51	35	0	570	518	518	672	672
Missouri	2,199	2,256	1,447	627	30	152	61	67	422	388	389	527	535
Montana	900	894	532	361	0	1	3	2	185	188	189	181	183
Nebraska	1,506	1,411	1,010	354	26	21	0	63	208	168	174	334	335
Nevada	354	423	313	96	9	5	23	12	633	586	597	845	1,023
New Hampshire	439	460	357	98	5	0	0	0	422	373	373	581	581
New Jersey	2,272	2,279	1,770	427	7	75	0	79	526	456	457	887	936
New Mexico	681	721	536	178	3	4	25	14	456	404	409	624	695
New York	4,010	4,149	2,972	940	145	92	65	83	678	611	611	946	968
North Carolina	1,955	1,985	1,538	393	44	10	48	27	599	537	542	882	941
North Dakota	663	613	352	224	4	33	0	31	211	192	192	242	242
Ohio	3,731	3,865	2,694	948	130	93	10	34	496	428	429	724	739
Oklahoma	1,880	1,830	1,216	604	0	10	0	15	336	338	339	333	335
Oregon	1,199	1,216	913	252	46	5	35	15	432	377	383	684	718
Pennsylvania	3,260	3,182	2,350	788	30	14	10	11	574	483	483	855	860
Rhode Island	309	310	249	57	2	2	3	4	485	406	406	850	907
South Carolina	1,097	1,095	795	289	11	0	18	11	606	540	542	836	892
South Dakota	802	824	506	301	2	15	11	15	177	183	184	173	174
Tennessee	1,543	1,563	1,133	338	53	39	14	17	586	511	511	876	918
Texas	5,991	6,638	4,515	1,721	402	0	345	221	563	551	559	679	821
Utah	714	735	476	227	10	22	40	24	647	547	548	917	1,073
Vermont	397	384	271	55	17	41	1	60	292	240	254	611	621
Virginia	1,811	1,889	1,384	394	20	91	60	48	606	528	529	981	1,041
Washington	1,936	2,124	1,315	534	105	170	122	81	491	451	461	640	786
West Virginia	1,015	877	624	209	29	15	12	12	365	294	295	622	650
Wisconsin	2,018	2,037	1,486	518	33	0	18	9	427	373	374	580	592
Wyoming	415	410	284	117	0	9	9	5	249	209	209	347	360
Department of Defense dependents schools ...	—	171	116	41	14	0	0	0	478	488	488	475	475
Outlying areas													
American Samoa	30	31	24	6	0	1	0	1	470	467	467	551	600
Guam	35	35	30	5	0	0	0	1	957	843	849	1,617	1,617
Northern Marianas	26	24	20	4	0	0	0	0	362	274	274	803	803
Puerto Rico	1,619	1,561	972	359	191	39	10	22	406	304	305	643	656
Virgin Islands	33	34	23	10	1	0	0	0	673	505	505	1,136	1,136

[1] Includes "other" schools.
[2] Average for schools reporting enrollment data.
[3] Includes schools beginning with grade 6 or below and with no grade higher than 8.
[4] Includes schools with no grade lower than 7.
[5] Includes schools beginning with grade 6 or below and ending with grade 9 or above.
[6] Includes special education, alternative, and other schools not classified by grade span.

[7] Also tabulated under the elementary, secondary, combined, or other school classification as appropriate.
[8] Excludes elementary special education and alternative schools.
[9] Excludes secondary special education, alternative, and vocational schools.
—Data not available or not applicable.

SOURCE: U.S. Department of Education, National Center for Education Statistics, Common Core of Data survey. (This table was prepared January 1998.)

Table 31.—Revenues for public elementary and secondary schools, by source and state: 1995–96

[Amounts in thousands of dollars]

State or other area	Total	Federal		State		Local and intermediate		Private [1]	
		Amount	Percent of total	Amount	Percent of total	Amount	Percent of total	Amount	Percent of total
1	2	3	4	5	6	7	8	9	10
United States	[2]$287,702,844	$19,104,019	6.6	$136,670,754	47.5	$124,308,202	43.2	[2]$7,619,869	2.6
Alabama	3,771,940	348,717	9.2	2,310,952	61.3	790,919	21.0	321,353	8.5
Alaska	1,183,127	130,903	11.1	782,559	66.1	239,553	20.2	30,112	2.5
Arizona	4,151,421	375,299	9.0	1,829,488	44.1	1,850,818	44.6	95,817	2.3
Arkansas	2,204,845	188,064	8.5	1,322,273	60.0	580,387	26.3	114,121	5.2
California	30,858,564	2,742,893	8.9	17,207,011	55.8	10,546,059	34.2	362,602	1.2
Colorado	3,804,992	200,537	5.3	1,665,138	43.8	1,811,053	47.6	128,263	3.4
Connecticut	[2]4,786,247	177,394	3.7	1,819,099	38.0	2,656,280	55.5	[2]133,474	2.8
Delaware	822,226	54,837	6.7	547,837	66.6	207,183	25.2	12,369	1.5
District of Columbia	675,409	54,405	8.1	—	—	617,760	91.5	3,244	0.5
Florida	13,214,948	972,473	7.4	6,422,329	48.6	5,317,562	40.2	502,583	3.8
Georgia	7,627,823	520,690	6.8	3,956,281	51.9	3,005,940	39.4	144,911	1.9
Hawaii	1,201,888	94,261	7.8	1,079,096	89.8	5,294	0.4	23,238	1.9
Idaho	1,179,927	83,787	7.1	758,538	64.3	316,851	26.9	20,750	1.8
Illinois	12,290,140	745,113	6.1	3,359,525	27.3	7,898,466	64.3	287,036	2.3
Indiana	6,191,534	319,237	5.2	3,362,035	54.3	2,312,251	37.3	198,012	3.2
Iowa	3,033,687	154,638	5.1	1,486,472	49.0	1,231,268	40.6	161,308	5.3
Kansas	2,948,036	160,308	5.4	1,690,101	57.3	1,022,587	34.7	75,040	2.5
Kentucky	3,492,890	290,625	8.3	2,280,140	65.3	895,219	25.6	26,906	0.8
Louisiana	[2]3,934,998	477,761	12.1	1,978,050	50.3	1,374,937	34.9	[2]104,250	2.6
Maine	1,451,987	80,876	5.6	681,853	47.0	673,602	46.4	15,656	1.1
Maryland	5,695,850	281,709	4.9	2,175,948	38.2	3,058,142	53.7	180,051	3.2
Massachusetts	6,772,855	318,591	4.7	2,593,935	38.3	3,749,747	55.4	110,582	1.6
Michigan	12,698,697	777,325	6.1	8,483,312	66.8	3,184,072	25.1	253,987	2.0
Minnesota	5,939,765	253,845	4.3	3,458,503	58.2	2,000,762	33.7	226,655	3.8
Mississippi	2,225,798	304,024	13.7	1,285,426	57.8	560,821	25.2	75,527	3.4
Missouri	5,263,003	317,991	6.0	2,113,958	40.2	2,618,966	49.8	212,088	4.0
Montana	941,538	92,802	9.9	457,958	48.6	350,452	37.2	40,326	4.3
Nebraska	1,876,494	104,388	5.6	593,662	31.6	1,067,218	56.9	111,226	5.9
Nevada	1,554,888	69,857	4.5	497,744	32.0	930,476	59.8	56,810	3.7
New Hampshire	1,217,104	40,623	3.3	84,764	7.0	1,060,083	87.1	31,633	2.6
New Jersey	11,882,657	402,135	3.4	4,582,794	38.6	6,615,530	55.7	282,198	2.4
New Mexico	1,783,804	216,810	12.2	1,318,739	73.9	209,699	11.8	38,556	2.2
New York	25,849,431	1,507,150	5.8	10,261,383	39.7	13,840,857	53.5	240,040	0.9
North Carolina	6,154,971	443,121	7.2	3,971,825	64.5	1,565,289	25.4	174,735	2.8
North Dakota	618,322	71,300	11.5	260,260	42.1	253,276	41.0	33,486	5.4
Ohio	11,794,089	738,880	6.3	4,797,764	40.7	5,775,786	49.0	481,659	4.1
Oklahoma	2,856,688	266,970	9.3	1,694,433	59.3	738,270	25.8	157,016	5.5
Oregon	3,366,831	218,785	6.5	1,821,888	54.1	1,203,913	35.8	122,245	3.6
Pennsylvania	14,047,905	776,499	5.5	5,589,707	39.8	7,425,427	52.9	256,273	1.8
Rhode Island	1,138,171	57,906	5.1	472,134	41.5	593,824	52.2	14,308	1.3
South Carolina	3,697,232	308,082	8.3	1,955,378	52.9	1,271,210	34.4	162,561	4.4
South Dakota	717,005	70,519	9.8	213,290	29.7	410,705	57.3	22,491	3.1
Tennessee	4,142,148	358,035	8.6	1,985,414	47.9	1,530,085	36.9	268,614	6.5
Texas	21,689,792	1,557,597	7.2	9,312,159	42.9	10,246,162	47.2	573,876	2.6
Utah	2,066,218	137,707	6.7	1,209,925	58.6	612,311	29.6	106,275	5.1
Vermont	773,448	36,481	4.7	215,275	27.8	501,925	64.9	19,767	2.6
Virginia	[2]6,826,448	361,752	5.3	2,123,203	31.1	4,106,568	60.2	[2]234,925	3.4
Washington	6,327,993	365,988	5.8	4,302,300	68.0	1,464,556	23.1	195,150	3.1
West Virginia	1,990,094	160,084	8.0	1,253,995	63.0	544,803	27.4	31,213	1.6
Wisconsin	6,304,318	273,225	4.3	2,705,278	42.9	3,192,597	50.6	133,219	2.1
Wyoming	662,660	41,022	6.2	339,624	51.3	270,684	40.8	11,331	1.7
Outlying areas									
American Samoa	45,087	34,218	75.9	10,801	24.0	0	0.0	68	0.2
Guam	171,464	19,524	11.4	0	—	150,544	87.8	1,397	0.8
Northern Marianas	44,418	11,785	26.5	32,504	73.2	70	0.2	58	0.1
Puerto Rico	1,821,858	536,899	29.5	1,284,218	70.5	256	(3)	484	(3)
Virgin Islands	142,016	24,495	17.2	0	—	117,434	82.7	87	0.1

[1] Includes revenues from gifts, and tuition and fees from patrons. U.S. total includes imputations for nonreporting states.
[2] Data have been adjusted to reflect gross revenues for student activities.
[3] Less than .05 percent.
—Data not available or not applicable.

NOTE.—Excludes revenues for state education agencies. Because of rounding, details may not add to totals.

SOURCE: U.S. Department of Education, National Center for Education Statistics, Common Core of Data survey. (This table was prepared February 1998.)

Table 32.—Revenues (in current dollars) for public elementary and secondary schools, by source and state: 1969–70 to 1995–96

[Amounts in thousands]

State or other area	Federal							
	1969–70	1974–75	1979–80	1984–85	1989–90	1993–94	1994–95	1995–96
1	2	3	4	5	6	7.	8	9
United States	$3,219,557	$5,811,595	$9,503,537	$9,105,569	$12,700,784	$18,341,483	$18,581,511	$19,104,019
Alabama	86,485	134,492	147,145	221,569	286,598	346,246	343,927	348,717
Alaska	22,082	48,843	38,939	60,329	127,584	138,061	129,911	130,903
Arizona	42,142	73,646	148,434	140,596	216,488	332,091	354,242	375,299
Arkansas	47,801	71,412	114,914	121,745	153,637	176,931	199,163	188,064
California	281,729	609,440	1,099,332	1,118,191	1,605,281	2,572,258	2,751,519	2,742,893
Colorado	46,450	59,173	96,668	104,270	132,246	185,835	193,865	200,537
Connecticut	26,691	55,851	85,822	80,735	97,828	163,091	177,446	177,394
Delaware	10,547	18,310	37,055	29,099	39,616	53,531	53,885	54,837
District of Columbia	45,192	93,992	68,242	39,700	54,591	79,433	66,716	54,405
Florida	122,884	225,480	367,634	406,173	595,711	921,140	971,277	972,473
Georgia	102,995	172,370	272,377	269,008	329,253	518,047	512,456	520,690
Hawaii	20,461	28,518	55,918	57,901	76,099	84,217	86,882	94,261
Idaho	14,127	20,422	34,482	41,830	56,891	80,589	84,012	83,787
Illinois	123,792	236,355	384,575	243,757	531,923	743,760	780,212	745,113
Indiana	52,353	95,495	161,019	146,135	211,441	299,738	306,971	319,237
Iowa	34,454	51,218	83,422	78,344	105,270	147,123	151,225	154,638
Kansas	34,255	49,763	71,781	75,124	103,598	148,303	152,757	160,308
Kentucky	79,270	124,471	174,707	182,881	220,813	329,830	301,243	290,625
Louisiana	70,967	131,225	223,104	263,337	309,117	439,492	458,344	477,761
Maine	14,144	23,303	40,527	39,338	62,805	78,641	79,403	80,876
Maryland	70,073	110,038	168,882	148,478	196,285	268,305	279,464	281,709
Massachusetts	56,909	100,421	210,451	185,553	240,192	334,600	352,760	318,591
Michigan	91,048	215,728	349,179	298,280	482,031	714,960	734,290	777,325
Minnesota	56,434	81,190	123,907	122,648	165,059	236,773	247,964	253,845
Mississippi	67,038	106,931	182,672	155,767	243,774	307,241	310,249	304,024
Missouri	61,543	108,972	188,333	163,099	205,179	297,101	317,002	317,991
Montana	9,066	26,817	37,537	52,916	63,726	84,632	91,912	92,802
Nebraska	18,389	33,624	49,455	61,032	79,742	106,686	104,608	104,388
Nevada	10,653	13,651	20,100	22,046	36,018	58,827	67,369	69,857
New Hampshire	8,492	12,180	21,683	23,365	24,944	35,284	35,169	40,623
New Jersey	82,435	174,037	271,261	250,514	336,351	406,261	383,016	402,135
New Mexico	39,223	63,207	102,762	117,847	150,229	193,924	199,231	216,810
New York	234,621	501,436	776,950	665,613	1,014,296	1,472,573	1,196,994	1,507,150
North Carolina	126,942	195,830	278,427	258,002	300,405	454,606	443,701	443,121
North Dakota	16,882	19,765	30,257	35,963	47,517	67,042	73,400	71,300
Ohio	108,589	198,266	334,147	343,556	463,554	668,428	714,840	738,880
Oklahoma	48,741	81,551	175,230	97,793	121,530	263,440	260,760	266,970
Oregon	24,664	58,952	118,379	108,871	155,250	212,437	224,139	218,785
Pennsylvania	138,553	266,894	511,119	334,543	534,118	724,185	746,601	776,499
Rhode Island	11,095	20,423	37,560	24,449	41,524	60,415	59,458	57,906
South Carolina	67,067	107,480	175,992	176,497	217,395	294,566	299,232	308,082
South Dakota	16,890	34,862	42,384	50,468	57,774	69,536	69,162	70,519
Tennessee	79,577	108,380	196,082	200,983	261,676	347,887	348,729	358,035
Texas	209,923	411,915	680,365	785,737	1,012,383	1,516,708	1,511,000	1,557,597
Utah	21,156	33,470	55,247	61,801	86,986	126,294	133,543	137,707
Vermont	6,071	11,043	19,147	18,570	24,464	35,655	34,424	36,481
Virginia	117,380	168,080	233,071	224,206	268,730	370,560	368,102	361,752
Washington	55,380	98,658	191,930	156,121	243,402	334,306	357,615	365,988
West Virginia	37,943	53,534	81,570	85,953	106,072	151,207	156,555	160,084
Wisconsin	41,567	59,984	118,496	134,184	174,249	249,844	262,315	273,225
Wyoming	6,392	10,496	14,861	20,653	29,140	38,846	42,453	41,022
Outlying areas								
American Samoa	—	2,712	—	—	18,345	34,722	37,858	34,218
Guam	6,134	7,572	—	—	18,069	16,765	17,132	19,524
Northern Marianas	—	—	—	—	6,959	11,042	11,663	11,785
Puerto Rico	—	113,731	—	—	338,346	473,394	474,419	536,899
Virgin Islands	—	5,161	—	—	65,021	25,169	25,435	24,495

Table 32.—Revenues (in current dollars) for public elementary and secondary schools, by source and state: 1969–70 to 1995–96—Continued

[Amounts in thousands]

State or other area	State							
	1969–70	1974–75	1979–80	1984–85	1989–90	1993–94	1994–95	1995–96
1	10	11	12	13	14	15	16	17
United States	**$16,062,776**	**$27,060,563**	**$45,348,814**	**$67,168,684**	**$98,238,633**	**$117,474,209**	**$127,719,673**	**$136,670,754**
Alabama	283,934	448,738	771,521	1,177,874	1,534,021	1,850,898	2,161,685	2,310,952
Alaska	57,604	116,645	300,275	529,071	622,798	777,478	815,286	782,559
Arizona	170,347	321,411	467,528	927,626	1,194,354	1,474,316	1,664,966	1,829,488
Arkansas	110,438	207,249	337,994	565,647	905,487	1,164,432	1,266,778	1,322,273
California	1,535,872	2,752,652	6,839,343	9,538,739	16,260,203	16,324,953	15,670,329	17,207,011
Colorado	119,252	333,443	608,987	881,851	1,055,366	1,466,584	1,578,428	1,665,138
Connecticut	285,281	273,433	326,847	877,947	1,575,131	1,653,755	1,748,802	1,819,099
Delaware	112,650	145,000	190,911	258,729	362,161	441,043	479,319	547,837
District of Columbia	—	—	—	—	—	—	—	—
Florida	631,337	1,150,956	1,836,027	2,901,656	4,914,474	5,945,110	6,286,323	6,422,329
Georgia	382,296	529,937	1,043,025	1,591,324	2,759,335	3,360,515	3,530,615	3,956,281
Hawaii	159,705	212,117	309,244	474,224	714,986	1,025,813	1,062,296	1,079,096
Idaho	47,673	80,070	208,385	273,583	427,757	576,967	666,387	758,538
Illinois	768,305	1,326,162	1,755,999	1,982,143	2,952,592	3,196,325	3,361,268	3,359,525
Indiana	342,330	678,367	1,025,118	1,900,364	2,510,251	3,097,205	3,391,558	3,362,035
Iowa	158,414	307,735	508,810	727,422	1,056,130	1,339,923	1,381,238	1,486,472
Kansas	136,311	232,570	444,501	675,419	920,867	1,558,260	1,655,905	1,690,101
Kentucky	235,153	369,687	700,888	908,402	1,540,138	2,105,658	2,132,169	2,280,140
Louisiana	332,099	545,254	834,888	1,347,787	1,696,645	1,912,880	1,999,368	1,978,050
Maine	70,156	123,338	183,167	313,055	613,447	641,322	670,517	681,853
Maryland	294,525	685,687	770,253	1,039,913	1,609,649	2,002,376	2,059,241	2,175,948
Massachusetts	257,361	648,357	1,093,958	1,458,838	1,765,255	2,125,314	2,376,538	2,593,935
Michigan	856,213	1,255,055	1,930,132	2,135,482	2,251,071	3,200,682	8,023,133	8,483,312
Minnesota	443,505	748,726	1,210,736	1,507,245	2,088,236	2,840,930	2,939,545	3,458,503
Mississippi	169,456	242,432	408,378	559,926	884,024	1,024,792	1,185,185	1,285,426
Missouri	260,541	414,652	643,923	868,820	1,480,193	1,733,542	1,892,112	2,113,958
Montana	38,752	76,537	192,655	306,779	324,888	451,223	453,778	457,958
Nebraska	46,983	84,547	108,020	225,735	314,371	547,921	582,430	593,662
Nevada	37,771	60,380	155,271	163,723	326,773	416,469	412,904	497,744
New Hampshire	14,410	15,759	26,887	24,015	75,684	89,552	83,611	84,764
New Jersey	411,062	810,676	1,490,648	2,247,339	3,486,521	4,564,512	4,361,977	4,582,794
New Mexico	128,305	204,256	394,600	693,888	893,539	1,153,974	1,261,807	1,318,739
New York	2,098,377	2,963,620	3,605,453	5,484,459	8,044,917	9,090,191	10,127,462	10,261,383
North Carolina	464,526	812,576	1,217,699	1,820,625	3,127,946	3,559,792	3,867,413	3,971,825
North Dakota	31,157	67,933	119,304	217,762	218,041	240,860	249,273	260,260
Ohio	515,496	1,093,265	1,990,318	2,701,654	3,774,795	4,280,781	4,410,699	4,797,764
Oklahoma	148,693	315,416	693,736	915,282	1,237,503	1,811,319	1,644,176	1,694,433
Oregon	98,278	188,202	412,249	489,088	637,971	1,215,454	1,521,760	1,821,888
Pennsylvania	1,052,230	1,739,929	2,115,837	3,362,755	4,511,630	5,075,591	5,325,072	5,589,707
Rhode Island	64,055	99,978	119,319	212,034	363,539	399,395	437,494	472,134
South Carolina	262,886	386,035	444,383	1,021,999	1,347,999	1,478,065	1,598,971	1,955,378
South Dakota	16,544	23,179	63,191	96,094	130,552	168,964	183,552	213,290
Tennessee	251,804	438,839	537,402	736,509	1,330,928	1,707,740	1,855,784	1,985,414
Texas	839,946	1,496,356	2,878,079	5,191,850	5,847,048	7,542,112	7,908,524	9,312,159
Utah	113,123	187,113	340,425	541,149	751,040	981,014	1,054,222	1,209,925
Vermont	41,391	44,438	62,766	103,624	181,330	220,614	224,941	215,275
Virginia	292,457	470,705	837,529	1,037,411	1,687,176	1,895,429	2,052,415	2,123,203
Washington	424,927	575,610	1,480,974	2,100,938	3,000,965	3,988,235	4,103,287	4,302,300
West Virginia	148,151	207,497	433,141	716,579	928,128	1,214,154	1,234,701	1,253,995
Wisconsin	272,979	508,347	787,595	1,098,385	1,703,555	2,188,298	2,460,520	2,705,278
Wyoming	27,715	39,697	90,494	235,923	297,225	351,479	303,908	339,624
Outlying areas								
American Samoa	—	5,835	—	—	8,511	6,699	6,987	10,801
Guam	24,689	—	—	—	—	—	—	—
Northern Marianas	—	—	—	—	19,935	30,215	32,321	32,504
Puerto Rico	—	329,609	—	—	820,287	1,036,657	1,166,632	1,284,218
Virgin Islands	—	28,785	—	—	—	—	—	—

Table 32.—Revenues (in current dollars) for public elementary and secondary schools, by source and state: 1969–70 to 1995–96—Continued

[Amounts in thousands]

State or other area	Local (including intermediate and private)							
	1969–70	1974–75	1979–80	1984–85	1989–90	1993–94	1994–95	1995–96
1	18	19	20	21	22	23	24	25
United States	$20,984,589	$31,573,079	$42,028,813	$61,020,419	$97,608,157	$124,343,776	$126,836,715	$131,928,071
Alabama	100,717	161,356	291,275	389,430	737,217	924,176	1,036,264	1,112,271
Alaska	19,542	29,096	77,411	150,331	209,740	243,720	261,803	269,664
Arizona	138,732	316,290	596,936	511,211	1,331,784	1,743,769	1,764,078	1,946,634
Arkansas	94,025	142,648	239,824	329,591	535,304	673,537	709,168	694,508
California	2,996,349	3,520,110	2,375,482	3,465,257	6,454,798	10,153,198	10,469,453	10,908,661
Colorado	289,400	421,543	792,686	1,243,427	1,579,494	1,716,177	1,906,870	1,939,316
Connecticut	286,001	682,743	804,728	1,148,247	1,973,894	[1] 2,286,368	[1] 2,505,354	[1] 2,789,754
Delaware	29,053	49,266	67,893	86,790	150,087	[1] 189,837	211,832	219,552
District of Columbia	129,829	150,551	242,489	351,655	601,325	656,289	634,584	621,004
Florida	393,958	752,330	1,061,458	2,031,772	4,079,776	5,060,862	5,548,253	5,820,145
Georgia	235,572	448,762	614,932	1,018,767	2,197,874	2,752,132	2,922,401	3,150,851
Hawaii	6,063	—	—	555	19,546	30,143	28,736	28,531
Idaho	59,832	116,674	117,561	155,761	226,193	297,525	338,198	337,601
Illinois	1,581,295	2,015,683	2,473,023	3,224,487	5,489,255	7,382,634	7,874,839	8,185,502
Indiana	473,109	755,005	748,257	1,187,538	1,678,756	2,521,658	2,663,999	2,510,262
Iowa	445,162	537,554	712,041	837,998	988,310	1,295,575	1,348,713	1,392,576
Kansas	266,224	331,861	526,986	796,353	1,060,850	988,471	1,074,683	1,097,627
Kentucky	136,422	211,748	216,712	335,593	526,207	758,915	807,514	922,126
Louisiana	187,799	273,701	466,537	854,813	1,088,021	[1] 1,256,061	[1] 1,380,151	[1] 1,479,187
Maine	103,070	132,836	184,552	278,389	478,416	607,983	650,519	689,258
Maryland	494,627	752,843	1,052,161	1,450,528	2,511,029	2,874,555	3,220,899	3,238,193
Massachusetts	808,097	1,296,427	1,941,853	1,848,239	3,112,058	3,767,277	3,820,170	3,860,329
Michigan	954,803	1,793,435	2,600,569	3,906,153	5,661,857	7,218,441	3,167,888	3,438,060
Minnesota	436,042	524,273	777,953	1,075,246	1,735,023	2,082,557	2,419,058	2,227,417
Mississippi	84,914	117,898	137,895	229,239	445,666	547,345	604,361	636,348
Missouri	509,837	605,456	939,159	1,227,416	2,014,567	2,496,185	2,682,270	2,831,054
Montana	112,630	142,224	170,687	255,824	318,980	341,953	369,702	390,778
Nebraska	177,640	266,102	489,691	601,105	965,600	1,020,228	1,110,747	1,178,445
Nevada	57,297	97,531	126,402	220,612	497,673	793,834	890,257	987,286
New Hampshire	98,252	181,227	277,900	432,593	800,215	972,323	1,030,893	1,091,716
New Jersey	1,035,303	1,668,212	2,356,662	3,020,834	5,112,618	6,331,135	6,740,389	6,897,728
New Mexico	41,866	62,857	123,501	113,627	181,661	219,925	234,320	248,255
New York	2,224,430	4,023,289	5,096,839	7,145,570	10,685,333	13,212,423	13,565,448	14,080,897
North Carolina	189,989	320,535	516,784	738,316	1,309,694	[1] 1,545,913	1,629,405	1,740,025
North Dakota	73,759	79,260	120,834	156,909	221,490	255,449	269,807	286,762
Ohio	1,276,935	1,649,562	2,020,049	2,973,281	4,471,160	5,550,027	5,899,001	6,257,445
Oklahoma	187,149	246,653	376,964	500,625	813,514	1,003,152	862,774	895,286
Oregon	325,404	494,000	696,338	1,161,980	1,746,513	1,646,788	1,548,114	1,326,158
Pennsylvania	1,080,116	1,613,715	2,526,384	3,616,633	5,290,312	6,801,585	7,199,491	7,681,700
Rhode Island	89,611	154,134	207,642	289,704	453,885	563,051	583,307	608,131
South Carolina	110,744	177,996	366,254	551,415	1,130,826	1,427,782	1,551,999	1,433,772
South Dakota	88,128	125,758	168,790	226,933	315,623	408,526	438,972	433,196
Tennessee	214,938	333,858	540,048	800,219	1,315,110	1,594,003	1,703,793	1,798,699
Texas	770,940	1,333,040	2,303,900	4,612,876	7,088,686	9,685,482	10,259,359	10,820,037
Utah	84,433	122,596	257,355	442,652	496,690	678,450	752,482	718,585
Vermont	55,297	97,953	136,802	204,640	356,749	447,670	494,541	521,692
Virginia	421,718	757,867	1,045,656	1,940,437	3,204,574	[1] 3,896,841	[1] 4,035,863	[1] 4,341,493
Washington	281,153	445,368	459,236	575,976	947,925	1,401,075	1,515,538	1,659,705
West Virginia	93,899	138,816	220,868	282,814	378,965	514,091	549,170	576,016
Wisconsin	591,421	829,277	1,203,358	1,653,431	2,362,628	3,223,098	3,262,927	3,325,816
Wyoming	41,063	71,160	159,495	366,629	254,684	283,581	286,359	282,014
Outlying areas								
American Samoa	—	—	—	—	81	263	306	68
Guam	—	—	—	—	95,689	151,696	154,734	151,940
Northern Marianas	—	—	—	—	12	150	139	128
Puerto Rico	—	—	—	—	887	796	529	740
Virgin Islands	—	—	—	—	109,437	107,542	117,526	117,521

[1] Includes some imputations.

—Data not available or not applicable.

NOTE.—Excludes revenues for state education agencies. Beginning in 1989–90, survey was expanded and coverage of state funds on behalf of public school districts was improved. Because of rounding, details may not add to totals.

SOURCE: U.S. Department of Education, National Center for Education Statistics, *Statistics of State School Systems;* and Common Core of Data survey. (This table was prepared February 1998.)

Table 33.—Percentage distribution of revenues for public elementary and secondary schools, by source and state: 1969–70 to 1995–96

State or other area	Federal								State			
	1969–70	1974–75	1979–80	1984–85	1989–90	1993–94	1994–95	1995–96	1969–70	1974–75	1979–80	1984–85
1	2	3	4	5	6	7	8	9	10	11	12	13
United States	8.00	9.02	9.81	6.63	6.09	7.05	6.80	6.64	39.89	41.99	46.81	48.92
Alabama	18.36	18.06	12.16	12.39	11.20	11.09	9.71	9.25	60.27	60.27	63.77	65.84
Alaska	22.25	25.10	9.35	8.16	13.29	11.91	10.76	11.06	58.05	59.95	72.07	71.52
Arizona	12.00	10.35	12.24	8.90	7.89	9.35	9.36	9.04	48.50	45.18	38.55	58.73
Arkansas	18.95	16.95	16.59	11.97	9.64	8.78	9.16	8.53	43.78	49.19	48.79	55.62
California	5.85	8.86	10.66	7.92	6.60	8.85	9.52	8.89	31.90	40.00	66.31	67.54
Colorado	10.21	7.27	6.45	4.68	4.78	5.52	5.27	5.27	26.20	40.96	40.64	39.55
Connecticut	4.46	5.52	7.05	3.83	2.68	3.97	4.00	3.71	47.71	27.02	26.85	41.67
Delaware	6.93	8.61	12.52	7.77	7.18	7.82	7.23	6.67	73.99	68.21	64.53	69.06
District of Columbia	25.82	38.44	21.96	10.14	8.32	10.80	9.51	8.06	0.00	0.00	0.00	0.00
Florida	10.70	10.59	11.26	7.61	6.21	7.72	7.58	7.36	54.99	54.07	56.23	54.34
Georgia	14.29	14.97	14.11	9.34	6.23	7.81	7.36	6.83	53.03	46.04	54.03	55.27
Hawaii	10.99	11.85	15.31	10.87	9.39	7.39	7.38	7.84	85.76	88.15	84.69	89.03
Idaho	11.61	9.40	9.57	8.88	8.00	8.44	7.72	7.10	39.19	36.87	57.82	58.06
Illinois	5.00	6.61	8.34	4.47	5.93	6.57	6.49	6.06	31.06	37.06	38.06	36.37
Indiana	6.03	6.25	8.32	4.52	4.80	5.06	4.82	5.16	39.45	44.37	52.99	58.76
Iowa	5.40	5.71	6.40	4.77	4.90	5.29	5.25	5.10	24.83	34.33	39.01	44.25
Kansas	7.84	8.10	6.88	4.86	4.97	5.50	5.30	5.44	31.21	37.87	42.61	43.66
Kentucky	17.58	17.63	15.99	12.82	9.65	10.33	9.29	8.32	52.16	52.37	64.17	63.66
Louisiana	12.01	13.81	14.63	10.68	9.99	12.18	11.94	12.14	56.21	57.38	54.76	54.66
Maine	7.55	8.34	9.93	6.24	5.44	5.92	5.67	5.57	37.44	44.13	44.87	49.63
Maryland	8.16	7.11	8.48	5.63	4.55	5.21	5.03	4.95	34.28	44.28	38.68	39.41
Massachusetts	5.07	4.91	6.48	5.31	4.69	5.37	5.39	4.70	22.93	31.70	33.70	41.77
Michigan	4.79	6.61	7.16	4.70	5.74	6.42	6.16	6.12	45.01	38.45	39.55	33.68
Minnesota	6.03	6.00	5.87	4.53	4.14	4.59	4.42	4.27	47.38	55.29	57.31	55.72
Mississippi	20.86	22.88	25.06	16.48	15.49	16.35	14.78	13.66	52.72	51.88	56.02	59.26
Missouri	7.40	9.65	10.63	7.22	5.55	6.56	6.48	6.04	31.32	36.72	36.35	38.45
Montana	5.65	10.92	9.36	8.60	9.01	9.64	10.04	9.86	24.15	31.17	48.06	49.84
Nebraska	7.57	8.75	7.64	6.87	5.86	6.37	5.82	5.56	19.33	22.00	16.69	25.42
Nevada	10.08	7.96	6.66	5.42	4.19	4.64	4.92	4.49	35.73	35.19	51.45	40.29
New Hampshire	7.01	5.82	6.64	4.87	2.77	3.22	3.06	3.34	11.89	7.53	8.24	5.00
New Jersey	5.39	6.56	6.59	4.54	3.76	3.59	3.33	3.38	26.89	30.56	36.19	40.72
New Mexico	18.73	19.14	16.55	12.74	12.26	12.37	11.75	12.15	61.27	61.84	63.56	74.99
New York	5.15	6.70	8.20	5.01	5.14	6.19	4.81	5.83	46.04	39.58	38.04	41.25
North Carolina	16.24	14.74	13.83	9.16	6.34	8.18	7.47	7.20	59.44	61.14	60.49	64.63
North Dakota	13.86	11.84	11.19	8.76	9.76	11.90	12.39	11.53	25.58	40.69	44.12	53.03
Ohio	5.71	6.74	7.69	5.71	5.32	6.37	6.48	6.26	27.12	37.17	45.81	44.89
Oklahoma	12.67	12.67	14.06	6.46	5.59	8.56	9.42	9.35	38.66	49.01	55.68	60.47
Oregon	5.50	7.95	9.65	6.19	6.11	6.91	6.80	6.50	21.92	25.39	33.60	27.79
Pennsylvania	6.10	7.37	9.92	4.57	5.17	5.75	5.63	5.53	46.34	48.06	41.06	45.98
Rhode Island	6.73	7.44	10.30	4.65	4.83	5.91	5.50	5.09	38.88	36.42	32.73	40.30
South Carolina	15.22	16.01	17.84	10.09	8.06	9.20	8.67	8.33	59.65	57.49	45.04	58.40
South Dakota	13.89	18.97	15.45	13.51	11.46	10.75	10.00	9.84	13.61	12.61	23.03	25.73
Tennessee	14.57	12.30	15.40	11.57	9.00	9.53	8.92	8.64	46.09	49.81	42.20	42.38
Texas	11.53	12.71	11.61	7.42	7.26	8.09	7.68	7.18	46.13	46.17	49.09	49.02
Utah	9.67	9.75	8.46	5.91	6.52	7.07	6.88	6.66	51.72	54.52	52.13	51.75
Vermont	5.91	7.20	8.75	5.68	4.35	5.07	4.57	4.72	40.28	28.96	28.70	31.71
Virginia	14.12	12.03	11.01	7.00	5.21	6.01	5.70	5.30	35.17	33.70	39.58	32.40
Washington	7.27	8.81	9.00	5.51	5.81	5.84	5.98	5.78	55.80	51.41	69.46	74.16
West Virginia	13.55	13.39	11.09	7.92	7.51	8.05	8.07	8.04	52.91	51.89	58.88	66.02
Wisconsin	4.59	4.29	5.62	4.65	4.11	4.41	4.38	4.33	30.13	36.37	37.34	38.06
Wyoming	8.50	8.65	5.61	3.31	5.02	5.76	6.71	6.19	36.87	32.71	34.17	37.86
Outlying areas												
American Samoa	—	31.73	—	—	68.10	83.30	83.85	75.89	—	68.27	—	—
Guam	19.90	100.00	—	—	15.88	9.95	9.97	11.39	80.10	—	—	—
Northern Marianas	—	—	—	—	25.87	26.67	26.43	26.53	—	—	—	—
Puerto Rico	—	25.65	—	—	29.18	31.33	28.90	29.47	—	74.35	—	—
Virgin Islands	—	15.20	—	—	37.27	18.97	17.79	17.25	—	84.80	—	—

Table 33.—Percentage distribution of revenues for public elementary and secondary schools, by source and state: 1969–70 to 1995–96—Continued

State or other area	State				Local (including intermediate and private)							
	1989–90	1993–94	1994–95	1995–96	1969–70	1974–75	1979–80	1984–85	1989–90	1993–94	1994–95	1995–96
1	14	15	16	17	18	19	20	21	22	23	24	25
United States	**47.11**	**45.15**	**46.76**	**47.50**	**52.11**	**48.99**	**43.38**	**44.44**	**46.80**	**47.80**	**46.44**	**45.86**
Alabama	59.97	59.30	61.03	61.27	21.38	21.67	24.07	21.77	28.82	29.61	29.26	29.49
Alaska	64.87	67.07	67.55	66.14	19.69	14.95	18.58	20.32	21.85	21.02	21.69	22.79
Arizona	43.55	41.53	44.01	44.07	39.50	44.46	49.22	32.37	48.56	49.12	46.63	46.89
Arkansas	56.79	57.79	58.24	59.97	37.27	33.86	34.62	32.41	33.57	33.43	32.60	31.50
California	66.86	56.20	54.24	55.76	62.24	51.15	23.03	24.54	26.54	34.95	36.24	35.35
Colorado	38.14	43.54	42.90	43.76	63.59	51.78	52.90	55.77	57.08	50.95	51.83	50.97
Connecticut	43.19	40.30	39.46	38.01	47.83	67.46	66.10	54.50	54.13	[1] 55.72	[1] 56.53	[1] 58.29
Delaware	65.63	64.44	64.34	66.63	19.08	23.18	22.95	23.17	27.20	[1] 27.74	28.43	26.70
District of Columbia	0.00	0.00	0.00	0.00	74.18	61.56	78.04	89.86	91.68	89.20	90.49	91.94
Florida	51.25	49.85	49.09	48.60	34.31	35.34	32.51	38.05	42.54	42.43	43.33	44.04
Georgia	52.20	50.68	50.69	51.87	32.68	38.99	31.86	35.38	41.58	41.51	41.96	41.31
Hawaii	88.20	89.97	90.18	89.78	3.26	0.00	0.00	0.10	2.41	2.64	2.44	2.37
Idaho	60.18	60.41	61.22	64.29	49.19	53.73	32.62	33.06	31.82	31.15	31.07	28.61
Illinois	32.90	28.23	27.97	27.34	63.93	56.33	53.60	59.16	61.17	65.20	65.53	66.60
Indiana	57.05	52.33	53.31	54.30	54.52	49.38	38.68	36.72	38.15	42.61	41.87	40.54
Iowa	49.13	48.15	47.94	49.00	69.77	59.96	54.59	50.98	45.97	46.56	46.81	45.90
Kansas	44.16	57.82	57.43	57.33	60.95	54.03	50.51	51.48	50.87	36.68	37.27	37.23
Kentucky	67.34	65.92	65.79	65.28	30.26	30.00	19.84	23.52	23.01	23.76	24.92	26.40
Louisiana	54.84	53.01	52.10	50.27	31.78	28.81	30.60	34.66	35.17	[1] 34.81	[1] 35.96	[1] 37.59
Maine	53.13	48.29	47.88	46.96	55.01	47.53	45.21	44.13	41.43	45.78	46.45	47.47
Maryland	37.29	38.92	37.04	38.20	57.57	48.62	52.84	54.97	58.17	55.87	57.93	56.85
Massachusetts	34.49	34.13	36.29	38.30	72.00	63.39	59.82	52.92	60.81	60.50	58.33	57.00
Michigan	26.81	28.75	67.28	66.80	50.20	54.94	53.29	61.61	67.44	64.83	26.56	27.07
Minnesota	52.36	55.05	52.43	58.23	46.59	38.71	36.82	39.75	43.50	40.36	43.15	37.50
Mississippi	56.18	54.53	56.44	57.75	26.42	25.23	18.92	24.26	28.32	29.12	28.78	28.59
Missouri	40.01	38.29	38.68	40.17	61.28	53.62	53.02	54.33	54.45	55.14	54.84	53.79
Montana	45.91	51.40	49.57	48.64	70.20	57.91	42.58	41.56	45.08	38.96	40.39	41.50
Nebraska	23.12	32.71	32.40	31.64	73.10	69.25	75.67	67.70	71.02	60.92	61.78	62.80
Nevada	37.98	32.82	30.13	32.01	54.20	56.85	41.89	54.29	57.84	62.55	64.96	63.50
New Hampshire	8.40	8.16	7.27	6.96	81.10	86.64	85.12	90.13	88.83	88.62	89.67	89.70
New Jersey	39.02	40.39	37.98	38.57	67.72	62.88	57.22	54.74	57.22	56.02	58.69	58.05
New Mexico	72.92	73.60	74.43	73.93	19.99	19.03	19.89	12.28	14.82	14.03	13.82	13.92
New York	40.75	38.23	40.69	39.70	48.81	53.73	53.77	53.74	54.12	55.57	54.50	54.47
North Carolina	66.02	64.02	65.10	64.53	24.31	24.12	25.67	26.21	27.64	[1] 27.80	27.43	28.27
North Dakota	44.77	42.75	42.07	42.09	60.56	47.47	44.69	38.21	45.48	45.34	45.54	46.38
Ohio	43.34	40.77	40.01	40.68	67.17	56.09	46.50	49.40	51.34	52.86	53.51	53.06
Oklahoma	56.96	58.85	59.41	59.31	48.66	38.32	30.26	33.07	37.45	32.59	31.17	31.34
Oregon	25.12	39.53	46.20	54.11	72.58	66.65	56.75	66.02	68.77	53.56	47.00	39.39
Pennsylvania	43.65	40.28	40.13	39.79	47.56	44.57	49.02	49.45	51.18	53.98	54.25	54.68
Rhode Island	42.32	39.05	40.50	41.48	54.39	56.14	56.96	55.06	52.84	55.05	54.00	53.43
South Carolina	50.00	46.18	46.34	52.89	25.13	26.51	37.12	31.51	41.94	44.61	44.98	38.78
South Dakota	25.91	26.11	26.54	29.75	72.50	68.42	61.52	60.76	62.63	63.14	63.46	60.42
Tennessee	45.77	46.79	47.48	47.93	39.34	37.89	42.41	46.05	45.23	43.68	43.59	43.42
Texas	41.92	40.24	40.19	42.93	42.34	41.13	39.30	43.56	50.82	51.67	52.13	49.89
Utah	56.27	54.94	54.33	58.56	38.60	35.72	39.41	42.33	37.21	37.99	38.78	34.78
Vermont	32.23	31.34	29.84	27.83	53.81	63.84	62.55	62.61	63.42	63.59	65.60	67.45
Virginia	32.69	30.76	31.79	31.10	50.71	54.26	49.41	60.60	62.10	[1] 63.23	[1] 62.51	[1] 63.60
Washington	71.58	69.68	68.66	67.99	36.92	39.78	21.54	20.33	22.61	24.48	25.36	26.23
West Virginia	65.68	64.60	63.63	63.01	33.54	34.72	30.03	26.06	26.82	27.35	28.30	28.94
Wisconsin	40.17	38.65	41.11	42.91	65.28	59.34	57.05	57.29	55.72	56.93	54.51	52.75
Wyoming	51.15	52.16	48.03	51.25	54.63	58.64	60.22	58.83	43.83	42.08	45.26	42.56
Outlying areas												
American Samoa	31.60	16.07	15.47	23.96	—	—	—	—	0.30	0.63	0.68	0.15
Guam	—	—	—	—	—	—	—	—	84.12	90.05	90.03	88.61
Northern Marianas	74.09	72.97	73.25	73.18	—	—	—	—	0.04	0.36	0.31	0.29
Puerto Rico	70.74	68.61	71.07	70.49	—	—	—	—	0.08	0.05	0.03	0.04
Virgin Islands	—	—	—	—	—	—	—	—	62.73	81.03	82.21	82.75

[1] Includes some imputations.

—Data not available or not applicable.

NOTE.—Excludes revenues for state education agencies. Beginning in 1988–89, survey was expanded and coverage of state funds on behalf of public school districts was improved. Because of rounding, details may not add to totals.

SOURCE: U.S. Department of Education, National Center for Education Statistics, *Statistics of State School Systems;* and Common Core of Data survey. (This table was prepared February 1998.)

Table 34.—Percentage distribution of current expenditures for public elementary and secondary education, by function and state: 1995–96

State or other area	Total	Instruction	Student services								Food services	Enterprise operations[3]
			Total	Students[1]	Instruc-tional[2]	General administra-tion	School administra-tion	Operation and mainte-nance	Student transpor-tation	Other support services		
1	2	3	4	5	6	7	8	9	10	11	12	13
United States	[4]100.0	61.7	33.8	4.8	3.9	2.3	5.8	10.1	4.1	2.8	4.2	[4]0.3
Alabama	100.0	62.7	29.9	3.4	3.3	2.2	5.9	8.9	4.1	2.1	7.3	0.0
Alaska	100.0	56.6	40.2	5.0	5.6	5.8	6.1	14.1	3.4	0.2	2.8	0.4
Arizona	100.0	57.7	35.8	4.4	3.2	4.0	5.5	11.4	4.0	3.4	5.2	1.3
Arkansas	100.0	62.4	30.7	4.1	3.8	3.4	5.6	8.6	3.8	1.5	6.0	0.9
California	100.0	59.8	36.0	5.3	4.6	0.6	7.6	10.5	2.8	4.5	4.3	0.0
Colorado	100.0	61.6	34.4	4.3	3.7	2.8	6.7	8.9	2.9	5.1	3.6	0.4
Connecticut	[4]100.0	63.7	31.2	5.2	2.9	2.0	5.5	9.4	4.4	1.9	2.7	[5]2.3
Delaware	100.0	61.6	33.6	4.8	1.4	1.1	5.6	9.9	5.8	4.9	4.8	0.3
District of Columbia	100.0	49.3	46.1	12.6	5.1	2.9	5.5	14.5	2.2	3.3	4.3	0.3
Florida	100.0	58.1	36.9	4.5	5.6	1.1	6.7	11.6	4.3	3.1	4.9	0.0
Georgia	100.0	62.1	31.8	4.0	4.9	1.4	6.3	8.7	3.8	2.7	6.0	0.1
Hawaii	100.0	62.6	31.0	6.2	3.8	0.7	6.3	10.1	1.9	2.0	6.4	0.0
Idaho	100.0	63.1	32.4	5.3	3.1	2.5	6.1	9.3	4.6	1.5	4.5	0.0
Illinois	100.0	60.2	36.3	5.0	3.7	3.0	5.5	11.1	4.7	3.2	3.5	0.0
Indiana	100.0	62.1	33.4	4.2	2.8	1.8	5.6	11.0	5.7	2.3	4.4	0.0
Iowa	100.0	61.4	33.6	6.2	4.5	3.0	5.2	8.8	3.1	2.8	4.5	0.4
Kansas	100.0	57.9	37.1	4.9	4.1	3.9	6.7	11.3	4.1	2.0	4.9	0.0
Kentucky	100.0	61.2	34.1	3.9	2.7	4.0	6.1	10.1	5.8	1.5	4.6	0.0
Louisiana	[4]100.0	59.2	31.9	3.8	4.0	2.3	5.5	9.0	5.6	1.7	7.5	[5]1.4
Maine	100.0	67.2	29.2	2.9	2.8	1.9	5.7	9.5	4.7	1.7	3.6	0.0
Maryland	100.0	61.4	33.8	4.1	4.1	0.5	8.2	9.9	5.0	1.9	3.1	1.6
Massachusetts	100.0	66.4	30.3	4.6	3.2	2.2	4.7	9.3	4.4	1.8	3.3	0.0
Michigan	100.0	59.1	38.0	6.3	4.3	2.0	6.1	10.8	4.3	4.1	2.9	0.0
Minnesota	100.0	63.9	32.1	3.2	5.5	2.4	4.3	8.5	5.3	3.0	4.0	0.0
Mississippi	100.0	62.3	30.2	3.6	3.8	3.0	5.5	8.7	4.1	1.5	7.5	0.0
Missouri	100.0	61.1	34.5	4.3	3.9	3.2	5.9	9.7	5.6	1.9	4.3	0.0
Montana	100.0	62.3	33.5	4.5	3.4	3.2	5.3	10.5	4.4	2.2	4.1	0.1
Nebraska	100.0	62.4	29.6	4.0	3.5	3.7	5.1	8.8	2.9	1.7	3.8	4.2
Nevada	100.0	59.3	37.3	3.8	2.8	2.0	7.3	10.1	4.4	7.0	3.4	0.0
New Hampshire	100.0	65.1	31.4	5.5	2.7	3.5	5.7	8.8	4.4	0.8	3.5	0.0
New Jersey	100.0	60.5	36.2	6.7	3.1	2.9	5.6	11.0	5.0	2.0	3.0	0.4
New Mexico	100.0	57.5	36.8	7.9	4.6	2.7	4.9	10.3	4.9	1.4	5.1	0.6
New York	100.0	67.8	29.5	4.0	2.3	2.4	4.2	9.3	5.0	2.4	2.7	0.0
North Carolina	100.0	62.3	31.2	5.0	3.6	1.9	6.6	8.5	3.7	1.9	6.5	0.0
North Dakota	100.0	61.0	30.2	3.0	2.2	5.1	4.7	9.0	4.4	1.8	5.1	3.7
Ohio	100.0	59.6	36.7	5.0	4.9	2.5	6.0	9.7	2.6	6.0	3.7	0.0
Oklahoma	100.0	59.9	33.9	5.4	2.9	4.2	5.5	10.4	3.3	2.2	5.3	0.9
Oregon	100.0	60.6	35.8	4.8	4.6	2.2	6.7	9.2	4.1	4.3	3.4	0.1
Pennsylvania	100.0	64.0	32.4	4.6	3.1	2.9	4.5	10.2	4.4	2.6	3.5	0.1
Rhode Island	100.0	66.6	30.7	6.2	3.2	2.2	4.9	9.0	4.1	1.1	2.7	0.0
South Carolina	100.0	59.0	34.5	6.6	5.7	1.4	6.3	9.3	3.0	2.2	5.9	0.6
South Dakota	100.0	60.7	33.6	4.1	3.5	2.9	5.8	10.0	4.0	3.2	5.3	0.4
Tennessee	100.0	63.8	30.9	3.2	5.2	2.3	5.5	9.6	3.6	1.4	5.3	0.0
Texas	100.0	61.4	32.9	4.6	4.3	3.7	5.5	11.1	2.8	0.9	5.5	0.3
Utah	100.0	67.0	27.1	3.0	3.7	1.0	5.7	9.0	2.8	1.8	5.5	0.4
Vermont	100.0	64.9	32.1	5.9	3.0	3.0	6.6	8.2	3.3	2.0	3.0	0.1
Virginia	[4]100.0	60.3	34.3	4.8	5.4	1.1	6.0	10.5	4.5	2.0	3.9	[5]1.5
Washington	100.0	60.1	35.2	5.9	4.8	2.7	5.1	10.4	4.0	2.4	3.2	1.5
West Virginia	100.0	62.1	32.0	3.2	2.6	2.6	5.8	10.0	6.4	1.4	5.8	0.0
Wisconsin	100.0	63.3	33.6	4.2	4.7	2.7	5.3	9.2	4.2	3.3	3.1	0.0
Wyoming	100.0	62.0	34.4	5.6	3.1	2.2	6.0	11.0	3.9	2.5	3.6	0.0
Outlying areas												
American Samoa	100.0	41.0	35.8	11.8	5.1	1.6	5.4	6.0	1.9	4.0	23.2	0.0
Guam	100.0	55.4	38.7	10.8	2.2	0.9	4.9	9.6	6.7	3.6	5.9	0.0
Northern Marianas	100.0	80.3	12.9	0.3	0.4	10.5	0.0	0.4	0.9	0.3	6.8	0.0
Puerto Rico	100.0	71.8	15.0	3.1	0.0	5.9	1.1	2.6	2.2	0.1	13.1	0.0
Virgin Islands	100.0	56.8	37.6	5.1	6.3	7.6	5.6	5.7	2.6	4.7	5.5	0.1

[1] Includes expenditures for health, attendance, and speech pathology services.

[2] Includes expenditures for curriculum development, staff training, libraries, and media and computer centers.

[3] Includes expenditures for operations funded by sales of products or services (e.g., school bookstore or computer time).

[4] Includes imputations for enterprise operations.

[5] Estimated by NCES.

NOTE.—Excludes expenditures for state education agencies. "0.0" indicates none or less than .05 percent. Because of rounding, details may not add to totals.

SOURCE: U.S. Department of Education, National Center for Education Statistics, Common Core of Data survey. (This table was prepared February 1998.)

Table 35.—Current expenditures per pupil in average daily attendance in public elementary and secondary education, by function and state: 1995–96

State or other area	Total	Instruction	Student services								Food services	Enterprise operations [3]
			Total	Students [1]	Instructional [2]	General administration	School administration	Operation and maintenance	Student transportation	Other support services		
1	2	3	4	5	6	7	8	9	10	11	12	13
United States	[4]$6,146	$3,795	$2,076	$295	$243	$141	$357	$620	$250	$170	$257	[4]$19
Alabama	4,716	2,958	1,412	158	156	105	278	422	192	101	346	0
Alaska	9,012	5,100	3,623	453	506	519	547	1,269	309	20	250	0
Arizona	4,860	2,806	1,741	212	154	197	266	553	196	164	252	39
Arkansas	4,710	2,938	1,448	192	178	162	264	404	178	69	283	61
California	5,108	3,052	1,837	271	234	31	390	535	144	231	218	1
Colorado	5,521	3,400	1,900	235	204	156	370	492	161	283	200	22
Connecticut	[4]8,817	5,616	2,754	460	256	176	489	825	384	166	242	[5]205
Delaware	7,267	4,478	2,442	351	104	80	409	719	421	359	346	0
District of Columbia	9,565	4,717	4,408	1,207	486	280	528	1,383	208	315	411	0
Florida	5,894	3,427	2,176	266	330	65	396	686	252	181	291	0
Georgia	5,377	3,339	1,711	217	263	76	338	466	207	144	323	5
Hawaii	6,051	3,790	1,874	376	227	45	381	611	112	121	387	0
Idaho	4,465	2,817	1,448	234	137	113	273	416	207	68	200	0
Illinois	6,128	3,691	2,224	309	229	184	337	681	289	194	213	0
Indiana	6,040	3,752	2,020	256	170	110	339	662	343	140	268	0
Iowa	5,772	3,547	1,942	357	261	172	301	508	181	162	258	25
Kansas	5,971	3,460	2,217	295	245	233	403	675	247	119	295	0
Kentucky	5,545	3,396	1,891	218	149	220	340	560	323	81	258	0
Louisiana	[4]4,988	2,954	1,590	189	199	114	276	449	279	83	372	[5]72
Maine	6,546	4,396	1,911	193	184	126	371	622	305	110	238	0
Maryland	7,382	4,536	2,497	305	302	40	609	734	370	138	232	118
Massachusetts	7,613	5,059	2,304	353	241	170	358	709	339	134	251	0
Michigan	7,166	4,235	2,721	452	308	146	438	775	306	296	209	0
Minnesota	6,162	3,938	1,976	195	336	147	266	521	330	183	248	0
Mississippi	4,250	2,649	1,282	155	163	128	234	368	173	62	318	1
Missouri	5,626	3,440	1,944	240	221	178	334	548	317	106	243	0
Montana	5,847	3,643	1,959	262	199	187	311	611	258	131	241	3
Nebraska	6,083	3,793	1,801	242	210	223	313	533	175	105	232	257
Nevada	5,320	3,153	1,986	202	147	104	388	538	235	373	182	0
New Hampshire	5,958	3,879	1,869	326	162	208	337	524	264	48	210	0
New Jersey	9,955	6,018	3,608	664	306	293	558	1,093	496	197	294	36
New Mexico	4,587	2,636	1,687	362	209	124	227	475	226	65	235	28
New York	9,549	6,474	2,819	382	215	226	400	886	476	233	256	0
North Carolina	5,090	3,173	1,587	253	184	98	335	432	191	94	330	0
North Dakota	4,979	3,039	1,503	148	111	254	232	446	221	91	253	184
Ohio	6,266	3,733	2,300	311	308	159	373	605	165	378	231	2
Oklahoma	4,881	2,925	1,652	265	140	203	269	509	159	106	260	43
Oregon	6,615	4,008	2,371	319	307	144	440	607	269	285	227	9
Pennsylvania	7,492	4,797	2,424	347	234	218	339	762	329	196	263	7
Rhode Island	7,936	5,283	2,439	493	256	178	387	717	322	86	214	0
South Carolina	5,096	3,008	1,758	335	290	72	323	473	154	111	299	31
South Dakota	4,780	2,901	1,605	197	165	140	278	478	193	155	255	19
Tennessee	4,548	2,901	1,405	146	238	103	250	437	165	66	242	0
Texas	5,473	3,360	1,799	251	238	202	301	607	152	49	300	15
Utah	3,867	2,591	1,048	115	144	39	221	350	109	69	212	16
Vermont	6,837	4,434	2,194	407	207	204	454	561	228	134	202	7
Virginia	[4]5,433	3,277	1,861	261	294	58	327	572	242	107	210	[5]84
Washington	6,044	3,631	2,129	356	293	164	306	626	240	144	196	88
West Virginia	6,325	3,930	2,026	201	165	166	367	634	407	86	368	1
Wisconsin	7,094	4,493	2,384	295	333	194	375	656	299	232	217	1
Wyoming	6,243	3,871	2,149	352	193	137	377	689	243	158	223	0
Outlying areas												
American Samoa	2,159	885	773	254	110	36	116	130	42	86	501	0
Guam	4,947	2,743	1,912	534	110	44	243	475	331	176	292	0
Northern Marianas	5,863	4,707	759	20	24	618	0	26	54	16	397	0
Puerto Rico	3,039	2,183	457	94	0	179	35	79	66	4	399	0
Virgin Islands	6,155	3,497	2,316	311	388	468	342	353	162	291	339	3

[1] Includes expenditures for health, attendance, and speech pathology services.

[2] Includes expenditures for curriculum development, staff training, libraries, and media and computer centers.

[3] Includes expenditures for operations funded by sales of products or services (e.g., school bookstore or computer time).

[4] Includes imputations for enterprise operations.

[5] Estimated by NCES.

NOTE.—Excludes expenditures for state education agencies. "0" indicates none or less than $0.50. Because of rounding, details may not add to totals.

SOURCE: U.S. Department of Education, National Center for Education Statistics, Common Core of Data survey. (This table was prepared February 1998.)

Table 36.—Current expenditures per pupil in fall enrollment in public elementary and secondary education, by function and state: 1995–96

State or other area	Total	Instruction	Student services								Food services	Enterprise operations [3]
			Total	Students [1]	Instructional [2]	General administration	School administration	Operation and maintenance	Student transportation	Other support services		
1	2	3	4	5	6	7	8	9	10	11	12	13
United States	[4]$5,689	$3,512	$1,922	$273	$225	$131	$331	$574	$232	$157	$237	[4]$17
Alabama	4,343	2,724	1,300	146	143	96	256	388	177	93	318	0
Alaska	8,189	4,634	3,292	412	460	472	497	1,153	281	18	227	35
Arizona	4,476	2,584	1,603	195	142	181	245	510	180	151	232	56
Arkansas	4,401	2,745	1,353	180	167	151	247	378	167	65	264	39
California	4,937	2,950	1,775	262	226	30	377	517	139	223	211	1
Colorado	5,121	3,153	1,762	218	189	144	343	456	150	262	185	20
Connecticut	[4]8,430	5,369	2,633	439	244	168	468	789	367	158	231	[5]196
Delaware	6,696	4,126	2,251	323	96	73	377	662	388	331	319	0
District of Columbia	8,510	4,197	3,922	1,074	433	249	470	1,230	185	281	366	26
Florida	5,275	3,067	1,948	238	295	58	355	614	226	162	260	0
Georgia	5,056	3,139	1,609	204	248	72	318	438	194	135	304	4
Hawaii	5,560	3,482	1,722	346	209	41	350	561	103	112	356	0
Idaho	4,194	2,646	1,360	220	128	106	256	391	194	64	188	0
Illinois	5,519	3,324	2,003	278	206	166	304	613	260	175	192	0
Indiana	5,621	3,492	1,880	239	158	103	315	616	319	130	250	0
Iowa	5,481	3,368	1,844	339	248	163	286	483	172	154	245	24
Kansas	5,374	3,113	1,995	266	221	209	362	608	223	107	265	0
Kentucky	4,807	2,944	1,639	189	129	191	295	485	280	70	223	0
Louisiana	[4]4,447	2,634	1,418	169	178	102	246	400	249	74	331	[5]64
Maine	6,151	4,131	1,796	181	173	119	349	585	286	104	224	0
Maryland	6,593	4,051	2,230	272	269	36	544	655	330	123	207	106
Massachusetts	7,033	4,673	2,128	326	223	157	331	655	313	124	232	0
Michigan	6,785	4,011	2,577	428	291	138	415	734	290	280	233	0
Minnesota	5,801	3,707	1,861	183	316	138	250	490	310	172	296	1
Mississippi	3,951	2,462	1,192	144	152	119	217	342	160	57	296	0
Missouri	5,092	3,113	1,759	217	200	162	302	496	287	96	220	0
Montana	5,249	3,271	1,759	235	179	168	279	549	231	118	216	3
Nebraska	5,688	3,547	1,684	226	197	209	293	499	163	98	217	241
Nevada	4,892	2,899	1,826	186	135	96	357	494	216	343	167	0
New Hampshire	5,740	3,737	1,801	314	156	200	325	505	255	46	202	0
New Jersey	9,361	5,659	3,392	624	287	276	525	1,028	467	186	276	34
New Mexico	4,604	2,646	1,694	363	210	124	227	476	227	65	236	29
New York	8,361	5,669	2,468	335	188	198	350	776	417	204	224	0
North Carolina	4,719	2,941	1,471	235	170	91	310	401	177	88	306	0
North Dakota	4,677	2,854	1,412	139	104	239	218	419	208	85	238	173
Ohio	5,669	3,377	2,081	282	279	144	338	547	149	342	209	2
Oklahoma	4,549	2,726	1,540	247	131	189	251	475	149	99	242	40
Oregon	5,790	3,509	2,076	280	268	126	385	531	236	249	198	7
Pennsylvania	6,922	4,432	2,240	320	216	201	313	704	304	181	243	7
Rhode Island	7,304	4,863	2,245	454	236	164	356	660	296	79	197	0
South Carolina	4,779	2,821	1,649	314	272	67	303	443	145	104	281	29
South Dakota	4,220	2,561	1,417	174	146	124	246	422	170	137	225	17
Tennessee	4,172	2,661	1,289	134	218	94	230	400	151	60	222	0
Texas	5,016	3,079	1,649	230	218	185	276	556	139	45	275	14
Utah	3,604	2,415	977	108	134	36	206	326	102	65	198	15
Vermont	6,488	4,207	2,082	386	196	193	431	532	217	127	192	7
Virginia	[4]5,528	3,335	1,894	265	300	59	333	582	246	109	213	[5]86
Washington	5,611	3,372	1,976	330	272	152	284	581	223	134	182	82
West Virginia	5,881	3,654	1,884	187	154	154	342	589	379	80	342	1
Wisconsin	6,517	4,127	2,190	271	306	178	344	603	275	213	199	0
Wyoming	5,826	3,613	2,005	328	180	128	352	643	227	147	208	0
Outlying areas												
American Samoa	2,084	855	746	245	106	34	112	126	40	83	484	0
Guam	4,803	2,663	1,856	518	107	43	236	461	321	171	283	0
Northern Marianas	4,999	4,014	647	17	21	527	0	22	46	14	339	0
Puerto Rico	2,657	1,909	399	82	0	156	30	69	58	3	349	0
Virgin Islands	5,378	3,056	2,024	272	339	409	299	309	142	254	296	3

[1] Includes expenditures for health, attendance, and speech pathology services.

[2] Includes expenditures for curriculum development, staff training, libraries, and media and computer centers.

[3] Includes expenditures for operations funded by sales of products or services (e.g., school bookstore or computer time).

[4] Includes imputations for enterprise operations.

[5] Estimated by NCES.

NOTE.—Excludes expenditures for state education agencies. "0" indicates none or less than $0.50. Because of rounding, details may not add to totals.

SOURCE: U.S. Department of Education, National Center for Education Statistics, Common Core of Data survey. (This table was prepared July 1998.)

Table 37.—Current expenditures (in current dollars) for public elementary and secondary schools, by state: 1969–70 to 1995–96
[Amounts in thousands]

State or other area	1969–70	1970–71	1971–72	1972–73	1973–74	1974–75	1975–76	1976–77	1977–78	1978–79
1	2	3	4	5	6	7	8	9	10	11
United States	**$34,217,773**	**$38,656,967**	**$41,817,782**	**$45,422,500**	**$50,024,638**	**$56,660,671**	**$62,054,108**	**$66,864,475**	**$73,058,027**	**$78,951,243**
Alabama	422,730	456,283	500,513	526,525	618,002	670,764	796,263	869,748	984,764	1,119,944
Alaska	81,374	115,461	129,519	137,148	159,826	193,594	245,390	281,317	298,601	335,620
Arizona	281,941	315,804	371,615	400,455	457,201	571,906	658,546	735,562	769,488	817,496
Arkansas	235,083	249,195	273,130	292,542	330,191	378,620	429,390	465,638	521,803	577,026
California	3,831,595	4,177,175	4,445,041	4,863,143	5,392,182	6,194,757	6,968,424	7,509,475	8,249,419	8,451,747
Colorado	369,218	431,224	480,878	524,238	592,019	681,555	768,193	871,358	992,166	1,125,403
Connecticut	588,710	660,672	717,551	775,817	842,578	947,159	937,596	1,017,451	1,089,532	1,155,991
Delaware	108,747	128,104	135,582	155,158	167,912	182,185	198,959	213,513	222,141	236,170
District of Columbia	141,138	155,983	163,553	178,018	202,437	218,251	238,162	259,064	270,218	272,385
Florida	961,273	1,105,590	1,175,382	1,267,872	1,468,562	1,868,914	1,953,356	2,011,723	2,195,240	2,333,226
Georgia	599,371	719,065	709,404	864,369	882,484	1,044,071	1,160,339	1,300,517	1,334,758	1,471,196
Hawaii	141,324	171,145	175,897	176,353	213,945	224,907	263,292	293,654	317,286	329,041
Idaho	103,107	112,742	122,699	134,438	150,322	176,248	205,975	220,694	259,159	287,584
Illinois	1,896,067	2,197,975	2,296,916	2,597,749	2,721,821	3,119,258	3,331,841	3,504,967	3,763,471	4,029,182
Indiana	809,105	914,233	982,085	1,020,774	1,099,760	1,198,698	1,318,290	1,427,296	1,527,942	1,707,906
Iowa	527,086	564,100	620,170	639,324	669,570	736,592	871,239	952,610	1,011,370	1,122,858
Kansas	362,593	383,508	402,905	445,890	481,105	539,050	508,747	639,317	676,412	776,231
Kentucky	353,265	443,373	454,576	475,864	513,899	583,650	654,992	719,821	818,002	950,203
Louisiana	503,217	612,817	675,062	705,782	754,600	860,901	959,455	1,006,323	1,134,847	1,192,077
Maine	155,907	171,437	192,253	199,429	225,348	252,798	256,056	294,991	321,766	349,073
Maryland	721,794	830,978	907,061	975,346	1,058,258	1,217,565	1,337,431	1,436,175	1,542,756	1,680,166
Massachusetts	907,341	1,100,118	1,131,709	1,292,082	1,544,264	1,707,970	2,022,429	2,168,539	2,326,283	2,476,847
Michigan	1,799,945	2,017,644	2,234,112	2,398,367	2,675,285	2,931,214	3,207,045	3,380,877	3,815,974	4,304,689
Minnesota	781,243	885,060	960,946	1,033,395	1,094,191	1,251,186	1,359,329	1,461,873	1,554,749	1,655,666
Mississippi	262,760	299,931	324,378	348,116	377,228	421,815	464,766	536,849	612,758	695,343
Missouri	642,030	698,781	778,390	843,148	915,094	1,012,373	1,082,500	1,167,463	1,263,662	1,376,073
Montana	127,176	137,930	145,328	162,515	186,861	215,368	248,144	276,564	301,276	325,216
Nebraska	231,612	274,023	286,804	310,398	338,309	382,700	416,435	474,638	495,336	548,289
Nevada	87,273	96,370	110,819	118,749	132,789	147,805	173,544	188,334	216,216	242,250
New Hampshire	101,370	116,625	130,191	147,491	159,165	186,567	200,780	226,560	233,253	263,519
New Jersey	1,343,564	1,578,338	1,740,442	1,919,464	2,122,253	2,368,495	2,485,608	2,753,830	3,000,341	3,276,083
New Mexico	183,736	192,672	214,798	228,141	245,605	283,266	316,060	368,023	411,134	461,432
New York	4,111,839	4,815,666	5,140,817	5,457,178	6,193,669	6,783,934	7,049,414	7,074,875	7,735,405	8,062,894
North Carolina	676,193	756,140	802,012	879,885	1,017,522	1,184,564	1,247,383	1,373,365	1,524,885	1,721,015
North Dakota	97,895	104,966	115,351	123,443	133,444	142,938	167,451	180,193	194,871	212,362
Ohio	1,639,805	1,786,912	1,921,109	2,119,540	2,271,288	2,492,310	2,737,250	2,952,327	3,153,739	3,424,464
Oklahoma	339,105	381,812	422,567	443,616	500,496	572,680	642,800	737,118	818,005	950,297
Oregon	403,844	443,829	489,904	526,080	576,492	668,900	759,338	819,785	895,676	1,021,449
Pennsylvania	1,912,644	2,087,296	2,360,334	2,694,594	2,833,269	3,165,615	3,461,881	3,704,461	3,963,849	4,224,662
Rhode Island	145,443	164,222	181,673	200,522	217,597	249,363	215,574	281,839	312,857	345,900
South Carolina	367,689	386,902	424,243	466,907	508,076	585,047	631,687	682,387	779,087	865,965
South Dakota	109,375	121,997	129,029	136,886	145,114	157,111	185,149	188,066	198,580	218,334
Tennessee	473,226	529,662	568,971	606,086	689,558	815,751	810,097	986,698	1,090,099	1,196,717
Texas	1,518,181	1,749,696	1,963,886	2,104,828	2,288,893	2,689,288	3,208,656	3,512,137	4,054,608	4,382,123
Utah	179,981	194,017	213,274	227,008	249,765	285,406	326,219	365,270	410,289	473,410
Vermont	78,921	89,291	102,788	107,321	118,227	133,298	135,165	149,003	161,801	176,918
Virginia	704,677	797,357	874,423	942,565	1,056,604	1,210,575	1,334,580	1,467,142	1,495,069	1,630,612
Washington	699,984	707,410	765,420	806,442	900,888	1,015,312	1,124,835	1,213,890	1,422,661	1,551,198
West Virginia	249,404	269,175	308,867	315,491	339,433	384,058	448,865	501,084	544,792	589,751
Wisconsin	777,288	880,189	957,606	1,013,082	1,091,953	1,239,249	1,391,164	1,490,191	1,601,583	1,766,708
Wyoming	69,584	76,072	85,799	92,926	99,284	115,070	138,024	149,880	168,048	190,532
Outlying areas										
American Samoa	—	—	5,412	6,128	—	7,190	7,676	6,961	—	—
Guam	16,652	17,173	24,373	25,352	32,789	47,487	32,471	41,066	43,881	46,317
Northern Marianas	—	—	—	—	—	—	—	—	—	—
Puerto Rico	—	267,464	329,134	353,734	—	444,505	422,850	443,940	549,469	599,594
Trust Territories	—	—	9,063	—	—	—	17,644	—	4,111	—
Virgin Islands	—	—	23,832	21,735	—	32,560	32,983	35,010	37,641	46,500

Table 37.—Current expenditures (in current dollars) for public elementary and secondary schools, by state: 1969–70 to 1995–96—Continued

[Amounts in thousands]

State or other area	1979–80	1980–81	1981–82	1982–83	1983–84	1984–85	1985–86	1986–87	1987–88	1988–89
1	12	13	14	15	16	17	18	19	20	21
United States	$86,984,142	$94,321,093	$101,108,524	$108,267,717	$115,392,342	$126,337,491	$137,164,965	$146,364,922	$157,097,951	$173,098,906
Alabama	1,146,713	1,393,137	1,423,748	1,486,521	1,396,804	1,590,856	1,761,154	1,775,997	1,873,390	2,188,020
Alaska	377,947	476,368	550,784	625,818	692,418	754,967	818,219	769,015	756,577	739,020
Arizona	949,753	1,075,362	1,152,564	1,242,928	1,326,552	1,436,844	1,649,832	1,836,908	2,002,395	2,143,148
Arkansas	666,949	709,394	755,680	801,194	903,510	1,005,347	1,085,943	1,118,904	1,211,156	1,319,370
California	9,172,158	9,936,642	10,727,266	11,050,354	12,143,642	13,477,768	15,040,898	16,512,668	17,402,063	19,417,178
Colorado	1,243,049	1,369,883	1,500,214	1,605,885	1,697,085	1,868,058	2,018,579	2,129,964	2,172,563	2,324,625
Connecticut	1,227,892	1,440,881	1,543,483	1,711,013	1,818,683	2,117,798	2,144,094	2,414,708	2,748,567	2,984,542
Delaware	269,108	270,439	275,210	294,222	323,760	353,191	391,558	418,116	440,631	479,327
District of Columbia	298,448	295,155	312,940	340,027	371,113	387,918	406,910	441,135	489,357	584,035
Florida	2,766,468	3,336,657	3,552,127	3,747,760	4,071,134	4,589,068	5,092,668	5,650,083	6,288,977	7,245,515
Georgia	1,608,028	1,688,714	1,976,268	2,123,586	2,301,496	2,629,681	2,979,980	3,254,786	3,549,038	4,006,069
Hawaii	351,889	395,038	425,342	484,858	500,554	521,692	575,456	576,749	608,264	643,319
Idaho	313,927	352,912	371,290	398,996	417,426	467,532	492,092	513,011	532,274	570,013
Illinois	4,579,355	4,773,179	4,928,668	5,108,290	5,332,566	5,662,354	6,066,390	6,463,564	6,923,298	7,655,153
Indiana	1,851,292	1,898,194	2,133,789	2,239,069	2,434,738	2,696,072	2,851,080	3,106,616	3,330,525	3,779,468
Iowa	1,186,659	1,337,504	1,400,580	1,474,443	1,532,171	1,599,674	1,644,359	1,708,440	1,859,173	1,925,623
Kansas	830,133	958,281	1,044,483	1,131,758	1,209,537	1,315,469	1,423,225	1,486,814	1,568,041	1,712,260
Kentucky	1,054,459	1,096,472	1,157,496	1,233,797	1,354,120	1,384,722	1,434,962	1,583,158	1,741,799	1,918,741
Louisiana	1,303,902	1,767,692	1,857,207	1,908,595	1,950,869	2,191,478	2,333,748	2,260,393	2,289,241	2,468,307
Maine	385,492	401,355	447,360	484,744	540,351	599,189	688,673	760,446	839,860	921,931
Maryland	1,783,056	1,937,159	2,062,775	2,118,972	2,322,690	2,446,771	2,634,209	2,845,404	3,128,165	3,505,018
Massachusetts	2,638,734	2,794,762	2,673,115	2,792,653	2,898,355	3,139,486	3,403,505	3,744,131	4,098,062	4,516,604
Michigan	4,642,847	5,196,249	5,221,346	5,351,620	5,386,329	5,735,303	6,184,767	6,427,556	6,913,261	7,492,267
Minnesota	1,786,768	1,900,322	2,035,842	2,075,572	2,253,402	2,461,571	2,637,722	2,818,390	2,981,209	3,282,296
Mississippi	756,018	716,878	753,648	869,764	982,605	1,023,720	1,058,301	1,112,535	1,221,560	1,365,846
Missouri	1,504,988	1,643,258	1,715,761	1,772,111	1,965,436	2,106,539	2,277,576	2,515,846	2,747,234	3,096,666
Montana	358,118	380,092	418,027	456,519	502,290	538,245	567,901	583,861	590,226	592,454
Nebraska	581,615	629,017	699,487	759,197	813,214	870,019	911,983	948,149	995,235	1,105,009
Nevada	281,901	287,752	338,208	364,766	374,201	397,254	495,147	513,014	555,272	628,657
New Hampshire	295,400	340,518	372,027	402,307	431,288	473,151	522,604	589,850	677,507	733,240
New Jersey	3,638,533	3,648,914	4,080,209	4,340,960	4,666,185	4,697,534	5,735,895	6,099,473	6,621,860	7,309,147
New Mexico	515,451	560,213	647,867	713,599	721,641	784,442	808,036	865,789	916,305	975,552
New York	8,760,500	9,259,948	10,258,454	10,985,481	11,879,638	12,681,301	13,686,039	14,724,687	16,073,392	17,127,596
North Carolina	1,880,862	2,112,417	2,191,269	2,206,325	2,353,506	2,674,774	2,991,747	3,193,337	3,424,194	3,892,971
North Dakota	228,483	254,197	307,659	318,784	337,961	365,341	379,470	374,941	385,427	431,814
Ohio	3,836,576	4,149,858	4,357,731	4,600,475	5,051,057	5,504,161	5,856,999	6,114,426	6,446,903	7,484,434
Oklahoma	1,055,844	1,193,373	1,461,497	1,560,103	1,581,443	1,575,467	1,740,981	1,707,396	1,692,283	1,833,743
Oregon	1,126,812	1,292,624	1,352,825	1,417,393	1,475,990	1,560,242	1,662,372	1,747,125	1,944,657	2,123,241
Pennsylvania	4,584,320	4,955,115	5,158,103	5,506,931	5,843,492	6,660,369	6,750,520	7,176,886	7,679,986	8,579,546
Rhode Island	362,046	395,389	394,485	454,062	486,328	525,824	569,935	608,318	663,800	747,852
South Carolina	997,984	1,006,088	1,096,871	1,158,595	1,314,792	1,556,552	1,708,603	1,814,160	1,932,502	2,118,732
South Dakota	238,332	242,215	273,794	292,102	314,627	338,800	360,832	368,266	389,436	428,014
Tennessee	1,319,303	1,429,938	1,488,430	1,577,915	1,627,147	1,836,012	1,990,889	2,167,026	2,352,183	2,668,341
Texas	4,997,689	5,310,181	5,939,849	7,442,159	7,642,784	8,996,476	9,642,812	10,152,521	10,791,854	11,761,447
Utah	518,251	587,648	626,218	702,162	730,904	813,817	906,484	932,740	974,666	1,043,759
Vermont	189,811	224,901	247,035	267,530	290,206	313,026	346,164	378,264	456,992	485,226
Virginia	1,881,519	2,045,412	2,191,853	2,414,130	2,584,005	2,845,540	3,183,707	3,444,952	3,793,475	4,151,050
Washington	1,825,782	1,791,477	1,844,060	2,206,231	2,373,841	2,565,957	2,702,652	2,808,636	3,005,980	3,209,992
West Virginia	678,386	754,889	904,080	957,707	988,532	1,090,514	1,164,882	1,229,069	1,231,966	1,202,486
Wisconsin	1,908,523	2,035,879	2,142,172	2,305,552	2,455,671	2,655,729	2,893,797	3,086,878	3,318,247	3,688,311
Wyoming	226,067	271,153	317,328	382,182	424,251	453,874	488,616	489,825	466,921	491,930
Outlying areas										
American Samoa	—	—	—	—	—	13,348	14,997	19,497	20,186	22,314
Guam	—	—	50,000	51,173	54,251	58,815	78,545	78,278	76,359	94,368
Northern Marianas	—	—	—	7,714	5,534	9,394	12,556	15,714	19,694	16,118
Puerto Rico	—	713,000	670,000	745,360	822,589	856,743	842,827	872,050	935,392	1,030,387
Trust Territories	—	—	—	—	—	34,002	—	—	—	—
Virgin Islands	—	—	62,000	70,975	70,411	—	76,751	97,585	89,217	111,750

Table 37.—Current expenditures (in current dollars) for public elementary and secondary schools, by state: 1969–70 to 1995–96—Continued

[Amounts in thousands]

State or other area	1989–90	1990–91	1991–92	1992–93	1993–94	1994–95	1995–96	Percentage change			
								1969–70 to 1995–96	1985–86 to 1990–91	1990–91 to 1995–96	1985–86 to 1995–96
1	22	23	24	25	26	27	28	29	30	31	32
United States	$188,229,359	$202,037,752	$211,210,190	$220,948,052	$231,542,764	$243,877,582	$255,079,736	645.5	47.3	26.3	86.0
Alabama	2,275,233	2,475,216	2,465,523	2,610,514	2,809,713	3,026,287	3,240,364	666.5	40.5	30.9	84.0
Alaska	828,051	854,499	931,869	967,765	1,002,515	1,020,675	1,045,022	1,184.2	4.4	22.3	27.7
Arizona	2,258,660	2,469,543	2,599,586	2,753,504	2,911,304	3,144,540	3,327,969	1,080.4	49.7	34.8	101.7
Arkansas	1,404,545	1,510,092	1,656,201	1,703,621	1,782,645	1,873,595	1,994,748	748.5	39.1	32.1	83.7
California	21,485,782	22,748,218	23,696,863	24,219,792	25,140,639	25,949,033	27,334,639	613.4	51.2	20.2	81.7
Colorado	2,451,833	2,642,850	2,754,087	2,919,916	2,954,793	3,232,976	3,360,529	810.2	30.9	27.2	66.5
Connecticut	3,444,520	3,540,411	3,665,505	3,739,497	3,943,891	4,247,328	4,366,123	641.6	65.1	23.3	103.6
Delaware	520,953	543,933	572,152	600,161	643,915	694,473	726,241	567.8	38.9	33.5	85.5
District of Columbia	639,983	647,901	677,422	670,677	713,427	666,938	679,106	381.2	59.2	4.8	66.9
Florida	8,228,531	9,045,710	9,314,079	9,661,012	10,331,896	11,019,735	11,480,359	1,094.3	77.6	26.9	125.4
Georgia	4,505,962	4,804,225	4,856,583	5,273,143	5,643,843	6,136,689	6,629,646	1,006.1	61.2	38.0	122.5
Hawaii	700,012	827,579	884,591	946,074	998,143	1,028,729	1,040,682	636.4	43.8	25.8	80.8
Idaho	627,794	708,045	760,440	804,231	859,088	951,350	1,019,594	888.9	43.9	44.0	107.2
Illinois	8,125,493	8,932,538	9,244,655	9,942,737	10,076,889	10,640,279	10,727,091	465.8	47.2	20.1	76.8
Indiana	4,074,578	4,379,142	4,544,829	4,797,946	5,064,685	5,243,761	5,493,653	579.0	53.6	25.5	92.7
Iowa	2,004,742	2,136,561	2,356,196	2,459,141	2,527,434	2,622,510	2,753,425	422.4	29.9	28.9	67.4
Kansas	1,848,302	1,938,012	2,028,440	2,224,080	2,325,247	2,406,580	2,488,077	586.2	36.2	28.4	74.8
Kentucky	2,134,011	2,480,363	2,709,623	2,823,134	2,952,119	2,988,892	3,171,495	797.8	72.9	27.9	121.0
Louisiana	2,838,283	3,023,690	3,188,024	3,199,919	3,309,018	3,475,926	3,545,832	604.6	29.6	17.3	51.9
Maine	1,048,195	1,070,965	1,121,360	1,217,418	1,208,411	1,281,706	1,313,759	742.7	55.5	22.7	90.8
Maryland	3,894,644	4,240,862	4,362,679	4,556,266	4,783,023	5,083,380	5,311,207	635.8	61.0	25.2	101.6
Massachusetts	4,760,390	4,906,828	5,035,973	5,281,067	5,637,337	6,062,303	6,435,458	609.3	44.2	31.2	89.1
Michigan	8,025,621	8,545,805	9,156,501	9,532,994	9,816,830	10,440,206	11,137,877	518.8	38.2	30.3	80.1
Minnesota	3,474,398	3,740,820	3,936,695	4,135,284	4,328,093	4,622,930	4,844,879	520.2	41.8	29.5	83.7
Mississippi	1,472,710	1,510,552	1,536,295	1,600,752	1,725,386	1,921,480	2,000,321	661.3	42.7	32.4	89.0
Missouri	3,288,738	3,487,786	3,611,613	3,710,426	3,981,614	4,275,217	4,531,192	605.8	53.1	29.9	98.9
Montana	641,345	719,963	751,710	785,159	822,015	844,257	868,892	583.2	26.8	20.7	53.0
Nebraska	1,233,431	1,297,643	1,381,290	1,430,039	1,513,971	1,594,928	1,648,104	611.6	42.3	27.0	80.7
Nevada	712,898	864,379	962,800	1,035,623	1,099,685	1,186,132	1,296,629	1,385.7	74.6	50.0	161.9
New Hampshire	821,671	890,116	927,625	972,963	1,007,129	1,053,966	1,114,540	999.5	70.3	25.2	113.3
New Jersey	8,119,336	8,897,612	9,660,899	9,915,482	10,448,096	10,776,982	11,208,558	734.2	55.1	26.0	95.4
New Mexico	1,020,148	1,134,156	1,212,189	1,240,310	1,323,459	1,441,078	1,517,517	725.9	40.4	33.8	87.8
New York	18,090,978	19,514,583	19,781,384	20,898,267	22,059,949	22,989,629	23,522,461	472.1	42.6	20.5	71.9
North Carolina	4,342,826	4,605,384	4,660,027	4,930,823	5,145,416	5,440,426	5,582,994	725.7	53.9	21.2	86.6
North Dakota	459,391	460,581	491,293	511,095	522,377	534,632	557,043	469.0	21.4	20.9	46.8
Ohio	7,994,379	8,407,428	9,124,731	9,173,393	9,612,678	10,030,956	10,408,022	534.7	43.5	23.8	77.7
Oklahoma	1,905,332	2,107,513	2,268,958	2,442,320	2,680,113	2,763,721	2,804,088	726.9	21.1	33.1	61.1
Oregon	2,297,944	2,453,934	2,626,803	2,849,009	2,852,723	2,948,539	3,056,801	656.9	47.6	24.6	83.9
Pennsylvania	9,496,788	10,087,322	10,371,796	10,944,392	11,236,417	11,587,027	12,374,073	547.0	49.4	22.7	83.3
Rhode Island	801,908	823,655	865,898	934,815	990,094	1,050,969	1,094,185	652.3	44.5	32.8	92.0
South Carolina	2,322,618	2,494,254	2,564,949	2,690,009	2,790,878	2,920,230	3,085,495	739.2	46.0	23.7	80.6
South Dakota	447,074	481,304	518,156	553,005	584,894	612,825	610,640	458.3	33.4	26.9	69.2
Tennessee	2,790,808	2,903,209	2,859,755	3,139,223	3,305,579	3,540,682	3,728,486	687.9	45.8	28.4	87.3
Texas	12,763,954	13,695,327	14,709,628	15,121,655	16,193,722	17,572,269	18,801,462	1,138.4	42.0	37.3	95.0
Utah	1,130,135	1,235,916	1,296,723	1,376,319	1,511,205	1,618,047	1,719,782	855.5	36.3	39.2	89.7
Vermont	546,901	599,018	606,410	616,212	643,828	665,559	684,864	767.8	73.0	14.3	97.8
Virginia	4,621,071	4,958,213	4,993,480	5,228,326	5,441,384	5,750,318	5,969,608	747.1	55.7	20.4	87.5
Washington	3,550,819	3,906,471	4,259,048	4,679,698	4,892,690	5,138,928	5,367,559	666.8	44.5	37.4	98.6
West Virginia	1,316,637	1,473,640	1,503,980	1,626,005	1,663,868	1,758,557	1,806,004	624.1	26.5	22.6	55.0
Wisconsin	3,929,920	4,292,434	4,597,004	4,954,900	5,170,343	5,422,264	5,670,826	629.6	48.3	32.1	96.0
Wyoming	509,084	521,549	545,870	547,938	558,353	577,144	581,817	736.1	6.7	11.6	19.1
Outlying areas											
American Samoa	21,838	24,946	26,972	23,636	25,161	28,643	30,382	—	66.3	21.8	102.6
Guam	101,130	116,406	132,494	161,477	160,797	161,434	158,303	850.7	48.2	36.0	101.5
Northern Marianas	20,476	26,822	32,498	38,784	32,824	45,008	44,037	—	113.6	64.2	250.7
Puerto Rico	1,045,407	1,142,863	1,207,235	1,295,452	1,360,762	1,501,485	1,667,640	—	35.6	45.9	97.9
Trust Territories	—	—	—	—	—	—	—	—			
Virgin Islands	128,065	119,950	121,660	120,510	120,556	122,094	122,286	—	56.3	1.9	59.3

NOTE—Beginning in 1980–81, expenditures for state administration are excluded. Beginning in 1988–89, survey was expanded and coverage of state expenditures for public school districts was improved. Because of rounding, details may not add to totals.

SOURCE: U.S. Department of Education, National Center for Education Statistics, *Revenues and Expenditures for Public Elementary and Secondary Schools,* various years; *Statistics of State School Systems,* various years; and Common Core of Data surveys. (This table was prepared February 1998.)

Table 38.—Current expenditures (in constant 1995–96 dollars[1]) for public elementary and secondary schools, by state: 1969–70 to 1995–96

[Amounts in thousands]

State or other area	1969–70	1970–71	1971–72	1972–73	1973–74	1974–75	1975–76	1976–77	1977–78	1978–79
1	2	3	4	5	6	7	8	9	10	11
United States	$139,950,918	$150,346,165	$157,007,225	$163,936,093	$165,765,288	$169,023,665	$172,876,045	$176,013,109	$180,215,943	$178,072,512
Alabama	1,728,968	1,774,593	1,879,204	1,900,302	2,047,856	2,000,947	2,218,303	2,289,512	2,429,167	2,526,005
Alaska	332,820	449,055	486,286	494,986	529,611	577,508	683,630	740,535	736,574	756,982
Arizona	1,153,141	1,228,237	1,395,250	1,445,298	1,515,015	1,706,045	1,834,638	1,936,283	1,898,135	1,843,841
Arkansas	961,491	969,179	1,025,482	1,055,825	1,094,145	1,129,456	1,196,234	1,225,739	1,287,158	1,301,467
California	15,671,249	16,246,030	16,689,158	17,551,757	17,867,927	18,479,494	19,413,277	19,767,837	20,349,261	19,062,699
Colorado	1,510,104	1,677,133	1,805,484	1,892,048	1,961,757	2,033,137	2,140,103	2,293,751	2,447,426	2,538,318
Connecticut	2,407,828	2,569,511	2,694,086	2,800,031	2,792,028	2,825,457	2,612,041	2,678,324	2,687,604	2,607,308
Delaware	444,776	498,227	509,050	559,987	556,405	543,474	554,278	562,049	547,966	532,675
District of Columbia	577,255	606,655	614,069	642,492	670,810	651,062	663,494	681,956	666,560	614,357
Florida	3,931,613	4,299,903	4,413,038	4,575,926	4,866,334	5,575,132	5,441,839	5,295,631	5,415,110	5,262,532
Georgia	2,451,431	2,796,615	2,663,497	3,119,627	2,924,263	3,114,554	3,232,579	3,423,463	3,292,515	3,318,245
Hawaii	578,016	665,624	660,415	636,482	708,944	670,917	733,503	773,011	782,665	742,144
Idaho	421,708	438,481	460,680	485,205	498,118	525,763	573,824	580,952	639,281	648,638
Illinois	7,754,927	8,548,449	8,623,901	9,375,636	9,019,225	9,305,015	9,282,149	9,226,426	9,283,545	9,087,717
Indiana	3,309,245	3,555,670	3,687,294	3,684,115	3,644,245	3,575,819	3,672,614	3,757,194	3,769,052	3,852,138
Iowa	2,155,785	2,193,919	2,328,463	2,307,409	2,218,736	2,197,317	2,427,178	2,507,637	2,494,798	2,532,578
Kansas	1,483,008	1,491,554	1,512,730	1,609,279	1,594,225	1,608,033	1,417,314	1,682,929	1,668,540	1,750,769
Kentucky	1,444,856	1,724,383	1,706,731	1,717,459	1,702,893	1,741,078	1,824,737	1,894,847	2,017,807	2,143,159
Louisiana	2,058,161	2,383,391	2,534,558	2,547,265	2,500,498	2,568,142	2,672,938	2,649,031	2,799,385	2,688,699
Maine	637,661	666,759	721,825	719,767	746,730	754,118	713,344	776,530	793,717	787,325
Maryland	2,952,142	3,231,872	3,405,612	3,520,159	3,506,721	3,632,101	3,725,938	3,780,567	3,805,595	3,789,571
Massachusetts	3,711,031	4,278,621	4,249,065	4,663,303	5,117,186	5,095,022	5,634,269	5,708,432	5,738,360	5,586,465
Michigan	7,361,787	7,847,099	8,388,100	8,656,039	8,865,019	8,744,064	8,934,481	8,899,773	9,413,057	9,709,116
Minnesota	3,195,289	3,442,209	3,607,926	3,729,666	3,625,791	3,732,396	3,786,944	3,848,214	3,835,178	3,734,312
Mississippi	1,074,690	1,166,503	1,217,896	1,256,399	1,250,010	1,258,311	1,294,788	1,413,194	1,511,521	1,568,328
Missouri	2,625,907	2,717,726	2,922,509	3,043,038	3,032,322	3,019,996	3,015,728	3,073,213	3,117,139	3,103,697
Montana	520,151	536,443	545,642	586,539	619,196	642,461	691,302	728,023	743,173	733,516
Nebraska	947,295	1,065,741	1,076,822	1,120,269	1,121,045	1,141,627	1,160,143	1,249,430	1,221,870	1,236,652
Nevada	356,947	374,806	416,076	428,582	440,019	440,915	483,475	495,768	533,351	546,389
New Hampshire	414,604	453,582	488,809	532,315	527,421	556,545	559,351	596,393	575,377	594,360
New Jersey	5,495,186	6,138,533	6,534,588	6,927,611	7,032,452	7,065,425	6,924,636	7,249,144	7,401,093	7,389,122
New Mexico	751,481	749,347	806,471	823,392	813,855	845,007	880,509	968,779	1,014,165	1,040,748
New York	16,817,449	18,729,274	19,301,488	19,695,711	20,523,793	20,237,060	19,638,906	18,623,802	19,081,316	18,185,651
North Carolina	2,765,634	2,940,809	3,011,199	3,175,627	3,371,735	3,533,657	3,475,074	3,615,227	3,761,511	3,881,705
North Dakota	400,391	408,238	433,092	445,523	442,190	426,396	466,500	474,338	480,698	478,977
Ohio	6,706,813	6,949,727	7,212,912	7,649,713	7,526,306	7,434,776	7,625,683	7,771,664	7,779,488	7,723,791
Oklahoma	1,386,942	1,484,958	1,586,552	1,601,072	1,658,480	1,708,354	1,790,771	1,940,379	2,017,814	2,143,371
Oregon	1,651,725	1,726,157	1,839,372	1,898,696	1,910,306	1,995,386	2,115,434	2,157,991	2,209,409	2,303,852
Pennsylvania	7,822,727	8,117,992	8,862,007	9,725,163	9,388,527	9,443,302	9,644,427	9,751,571	9,777,828	9,528,617
Rhode Island	594,863	638,699	682,102	723,712	721,045	743,871	600,566	741,909	771,740	780,169
South Carolina	1,503,850	1,504,754	1,592,844	1,685,132	1,683,598	1,745,246	1,759,812	1,796,306	1,921,813	1,953,162
South Dakota	447,344	474,475	484,447	494,041	480,860	468,676	515,805	495,062	489,847	492,447
Tennessee	1,935,497	2,059,982	2,136,234	2,187,448	2,284,970	2,433,456	2,256,843	2,597,370	2,689,003	2,699,165
Texas	6,209,370	6,804,985	7,373,521	7,596,616	7,584,643	8,022,378	8,938,969	9,245,300	10,001,707	9,883,766
Utah	736,123	754,578	800,749	819,303	827,640	851,391	908,811	961,532	1,012,081	1,067,764
Vermont	322,787	347,274	385,923	387,336	391,766	397,639	376,555	392,233	399,123	399,034
Virginia	2,882,134	3,101,112	3,283,071	3,401,848	3,501,240	3,611,250	3,717,996	3,862,084	3,687,963	3,677,804
Washington	2,862,939	2,751,286	2,873,813	2,910,561	2,985,248	3,028,763	3,133,669	3,195,427	3,509,350	3,498,687
West Virginia	1,020,064	1,046,886	1,159,659	1,138,651	1,124,770	1,145,678	1,250,489	1,319,047	1,343,866	1,330,168
Wisconsin	3,179,113	3,423,265	3,595,386	3,656,353	3,618,375	3,696,787	3,875,633	3,922,758	3,950,706	3,984,765
Wyoming	284,599	295,862	322,137	335,383	328,995	343,264	384,520	394,542	414,533	429,740
Outlying areas										
American Samoa	—	—	20,320	22,117	—	21,448	21,385	18,324	—	—
Guam	68,107	66,790	91,510	91,499	108,652	141,658	90,461	108,102	108,243	104,467
Northern Marianas	—	—	—	—	—	—	—	—	—	—
Puerto Rico	—	1,040,231	1,235,752	1,276,675	—	1,325,997	1,178,014	1,168,621	1,355,403	1,352,369
Trust Territories	—	—	34,028	—	—	—	49,154	—	10,141	—
Virgin Islands	—	—	89,479	78,445	—	97,129	91,887	92,160	92,851	104,880

Table 38.—Current expenditures (in constant 1995–96 dollars[1]) for public elementary and secondary schools, by state: 1969–70 to 1995–96—Continued

[Amounts in thousands]

State or other area	1979–80	1980–81	1981–82	1982–83	1983–84	1984–85	1985–86	1986–87	1987–88	1988–89
1	12	13	14	15	16	17	18	19	20	21
United States	$173,110,017	$168,226,365	$165,992,976	$170,426,513	$175,158,099	$184,548,511	$194,748,864	$203,297,407	$209,523,604	$220,672,825
Alabama	2,282,111	2,484,729	2,337,411	2,339,964	2,120,258	2,323,856	2,500,513	2,466,818	2,498,565	2,789,368
Alaska	752,165	849,626	904,239	985,113	1,051,046	1,102,824	1,161,720	1,068,143	1,009,057	942,129
Arizona	1,890,135	1,917,962	1,892,200	1,956,519	2,013,620	2,098,881	2,342,456	2,551,421	2,670,620	2,732,164
Arkansas	1,327,317	1,265,240	1,240,623	1,261,176	1,371,470	1,468,569	1,541,838	1,554,131	1,615,335	1,681,982
California	18,253,815	17,722,496	17,611,283	17,394,597	18,433,262	19,687,759	21,355,291	22,935,704	23,209,361	24,753,730
Colorado	2,473,833	2,443,255	2,462,947	2,527,858	2,576,065	2,728,781	2,866,008	2,958,469	2,897,576	2,963,517
Connecticut	2,443,668	2,569,883	2,533,984	2,693,342	2,760,643	3,093,591	3,044,216	3,353,972	3,665,800	3,804,804
Delaware	535,561	482,341	451,821	463,141	491,447	515,927	555,939	580,753	587,675	611,064
District of Columbia	593,951	526,424	513,763	535,244	563,325	566,654	577,737	612,726	652,662	744,549
Florida	5,505,639	5,951,094	5,831,636	5,899,429	6,179,718	6,703,518	7,230,645	7,847,831	8,387,692	9,236,848
Georgia	3,200,190	3,011,905	3,244,500	3,342,782	3,493,522	3,841,328	4,231,020	4,520,821	4,733,399	5,107,084
Hawaii	700,306	704,570	698,297	763,225	759,809	762,066	817,041	801,090	811,250	820,127
Idaho	624,757	629,436	609,558	628,068	633,626	682,951	698,679	712,560	709,901	726,673
Illinois	9,113,526	8,513,202	8,091,546	8,041,068	8,094,490	8,271,329	8,613,151	8,977,737	9,233,694	9,759,070
Indiana	3,684,317	3,385,523	3,503,107	3,524,566	3,695,775	3,938,309	4,048,006	4,315,016	4,441,964	4,818,204
Iowa	2,361,609	2,385,505	2,299,375	2,320,952	2,325,736	2,336,737	2,334,685	2,372,983	2,479,604	2,454,854
Kansas	1,652,075	1,709,142	1,714,760	1,781,524	1,835,999	1,921,582	2,020,716	2,065,150	2,091,317	2,182,852
Kentucky	2,098,514	1,955,612	1,900,297	1,942,146	2,055,466	2,022,744	2,037,380	2,198,969	2,323,060	2,446,082
Louisiana	2,594,938	3,152,767	3,049,034	3,004,360	2,961,293	3,201,219	3,313,490	3,139,632	3,053,191	3,146,688
Maine	767,180	715,837	734,445	763,046	820,218	875,270	977,789	1,056,241	1,120,132	1,175,311
Maryland	3,548,519	3,455,020	3,386,521	3,335,519	3,525,693	3,574,141	3,740,089	3,952,199	4,172,075	4,468,326
Massachusetts	5,251,432	4,984,597	4,388,535	4,395,974	4,399,515	4,586,030	4,832,347	5,200,509	5,465,639	5,757,932
Michigan	9,239,883	9,267,769	8,572,044	8,424,099	8,176,098	8,377,890	8,781,224	8,927,723	9,220,308	9,551,417
Minnesota	3,555,906	3,389,319	3,342,304	3,267,202	3,420,518	3,595,760	3,745,078	3,914,677	3,976,077	4,184,391
Mississippi	1,504,576	1,278,588	1,237,287	1,369,114	1,491,531	1,495,407	1,502,592	1,545,285	1,629,211	1,741,230
Missouri	2,995,126	2,930,832	2,816,818	2,789,518	2,983,405	3,077,144	3,233,737	3,494,450	3,664,023	3,947,743
Montana	712,702	677,913	686,288	718,616	762,444	786,246	806,314	810,970	787,192	755,282
Nebraska	1,157,491	1,121,883	1,148,369	1,195,068	1,234,406	1,270,887	1,294,846	1,316,957	1,327,358	1,408,705
Nevada	561,021	513,220	555,246	574,186	568,013	580,292	703,017	712,564	740,574	801,435
New Hampshire	587,885	607,331	610,768	633,280	654,667	691,159	742,002	819,288	903,600	934,761
New Jersey	7,241,165	6,508,020	6,698,605	6,833,197	7,082,967	6,861,961	8,143,909	8,472,023	8,831,661	9,317,969
New Mexico	1,025,816	999,168	1,063,623	1,123,291	1,095,404	1,145,880	1,147,262	1,202,560	1,222,088	1,243,670
New York	17,434,561	16,515,578	16,841,620	17,292,479	18,032,521	18,524,313	19,431,643	20,452,241	21,437,294	21,834,887
North Carolina	3,743,166	3,767,601	3,597,474	3,473,023	3,572,470	3,907,198	4,247,726	4,435,469	4,566,893	4,962,902
North Dakota	454,712	453,373	505,093	501,805	513,003	533,675	538,778	520,784	514,049	550,492
Ohio	7,635,297	7,401,478	7,154,221	7,241,705	7,667,177	8,040,248	8,315,854	8,492,793	8,598,320	9,541,431
Oklahoma	2,101,270	2,128,440	2,399,385	2,455,791	2,400,528	2,301,376	2,471,871	2,371,532	2,257,020	2,337,723
Oregon	2,242,506	2,305,459	2,220,974	2,231,148	2,240,457	2,279,136	2,360,261	2,426,715	2,593,614	2,706,786
Pennsylvania	9,123,407	8,837,694	8,468,216	8,668,577	8,870,042	9,729,188	9,584,489	9,968,525	10,242,899	10,937,520
Rhode Island	720,520	705,196	647,638	714,749	738,214	768,102	809,203	844,939	885,319	953,389
South Carolina	1,986,121	1,794,408	1,800,767	1,823,769	1,995,769	2,273,746	2,425,900	2,519,825	2,577,403	2,701,037
South Dakota	474,312	432,003	449,496	459,804	477,583	494,905	512,314	511,512	519,396	545,647
Tennessee	2,625,589	2,550,366	2,443,601	2,483,830	2,469,904	2,681,969	2,826,694	3,009,948	3,137,137	3,401,699
Texas	9,946,066	9,470,972	9,751,633	11,714,861	11,601,251	13,141,675	13,691,008	14,101,610	14,393,238	14,993,923
Utah	1,031,388	1,048,099	1,028,081	1,105,288	1,109,465	1,188,790	1,287,040	1,295,554	1,299,925	1,330,622
Vermont	377,749	401,122	405,565	421,125	440,514	457,255	491,489	525,400	609,496	618,584
Virginia	3,744,473	3,648,094	3,598,433	3,800,133	3,922,352	4,156,646	4,520,274	4,784,957	5,059,408	5,291,910
Washington	3,633,549	3,195,188	3,027,450	3,472,875	3,603,337	3,748,242	3,837,265	3,901,129	4,009,115	4,092,215
West Virginia	1,350,078	1,346,382	1,484,256	1,507,547	1,500,528	1,592,977	1,653,917	1,707,148	1,643,089	1,532,973
Wisconsin	3,798,215	3,631,092	3,516,870	3,629,218	3,727,549	3,879,378	4,108,657	4,287,600	4,425,589	4,701,993
Wyoming	449,903	483,615	520,967	601,601	643,986	663,000	693,745	680,355	622,738	627,131
Outlying areas										
American Samoa	—	—	—	—	—	19,498	21,293	27,081	26,923	28,446
Guam	—	—	82,087	80,553	82,350	85,914	111,519	108,727	101,841	120,304
Northern Marianas	—	—	—	12,143	8,400	13,722	17,828	21,827	26,266	20,548
Puerto Rico	—	1,271,671	1,099,960	1,173,287	1,248,637	1,251,494	1,196,658	1,211,257	1,247,545	1,313,576
Trust Territories	—	—	—	—	—	49,669	—	—	—	—
Virgin Islands	—	—	101,787	111,723	106,879	—	108,972	135,543	118,990	142,463

Table 38.—Current expenditures (in constant 1995–96 dollars[1]) for public elementary and secondary schools, by state: 1969–70 to 1995–96—Continued

[Amounts in thousands]

State or other area	1989–90	1990–91	1991–92	1992–93	1993–94	1994–95	1995–96	Percentage change			
								1969–70 to 1995–96	1985–86 to 1990–91	1990–91 to 1995–96	1985–86 to 1995–96
1	22	23	24	25	26	27	28	29	30	31	32
United States	$229,032,770	$233,090,890	$236,107,710	$239,512,184	$244,659,356	$250,512,515	$255,079,736	82.3	19.7	9.4	31.0
Alabama	2,768,446	2,855,656	2,756,159	2,829,851	2,968,879	3,108,620	3,240,364	87.4	14.2	13.5	29.6
Alaska	1,007,551	985,835	1,041,718	1,049,077	1,059,306	1,048,444	1,045,022	214.0	–15.1	6.0	–10.0
Arizona	2,748,281	2,849,111	2,906,026	2,984,855	3,076,226	3,230,090	3,327,969	188.6	21.6	16.8	42.1
Arkansas	1,709,016	1,742,193	1,851,435	1,846,760	1,883,630	1,924,568	1,994,748	107.5	13.0	14.5	29.4
California	26,143,362	26,244,612	26,490,256	26,254,747	26,564,823	26,655,002	27,334,639	74.4	22.9	4.2	28.0
Colorado	2,983,329	3,049,055	3,078,739	3,165,249	3,122,178	3,320,933	3,360,529	122.5	6.4	10.2	17.3
Connecticut	4,191,205	4,084,571	4,097,596	4,053,691	4,167,307	4,362,880	4,366,123	81.3	34.2	6.9	43.4
Delaware	633,883	627,535	639,598	650,586	680,392	713,367	726,241	63.3	12.9	15.7	30.6
District of Columbia	778,715	747,483	757,277	727,028	753,842	685,083	679,106	17.6	29.4	–9.1	17.5
Florida	10,012,270	10,436,033	10,412,026	10,472,734	10,917,184	11,319,538	11,480,359	192.0	44.3	10.0	58.8
Georgia	5,482,741	5,542,633	5,429,078	5,716,195	5,963,559	6,303,643	6,629,646	170.4	31.0	19.6	56.7
Hawaii	851,758	954,778	988,866	1,025,563	1,054,687	1,056,717	1,040,682	80.0	16.9	9.0	27.4
Idaho	763,884	816,871	850,081	871,802	907,754	977,233	1,019,594	141.8	16.9	24.8	45.9
Illinois	9,886,896	10,305,467	10,334,417	10,778,130	10,647,731	10,929,758	10,727,091	38.3	19.6	4.1	24.5
Indiana	4,957,844	5,052,215	5,080,575	5,201,071	5,351,592	5,386,422	5,493,653	66.0	24.8	8.7	35.7
Iowa	2,439,320	2,464,950	2,633,945	2,665,759	2,670,610	2,693,858	2,753,425	27.7	5.6	11.7	17.9
Kansas	2,248,968	2,235,883	2,267,553	2,410,948	2,456,969	2,472,054	2,488,077	67.8	10.6	11.3	23.1
Kentucky	2,596,611	2,861,594	3,029,034	3,060,334	3,119,353	3,070,208	3,171,495	119.5	40.5	10.8	55.7
Louisiana	3,453,552	3,488,431	3,563,830	3,468,777	3,496,469	3,570,492	3,545,832	72.3	5.3	1.6	7.0
Maine	1,275,417	1,235,572	1,253,546	1,319,706	1,276,866	1,316,576	1,313,759	106.0	26.4	6.3	34.4
Maryland	4,738,906	4,892,681	4,876,952	4,939,085	5,053,975	5,221,679	5,311,207	79.9	30.8	8.6	42.0
Massachusetts	5,792,324	5,661,006	5,629,614	5,724,784	5,956,685	6,227,234	6,435,458	73.4	17.1	13.7	33.2
Michigan	9,765,374	9,859,292	10,235,872	10,333,959	10,372,941	10,724,242	11,137,877	51.3	12.3	13.0	26.8
Minnesota	4,227,561	4,315,783	4,400,754	4,482,732	4,573,274	4,748,702	4,844,879	51.6	15.2	12.3	29.4
Mississippi	1,791,956	1,742,724	1,717,394	1,735,247	1,823,127	1,973,755	2,000,321	86.1	16.0	14.8	33.1
Missouri	4,001,653	4,023,858	4,037,351	4,022,177	4,207,168	4,391,529	4,531,192	72.6	24.4	12.6	40.1
Montana	780,373	830,621	840,322	851,129	868,581	867,226	868,892	67.0	3.0	4.6	7.8
Nebraska	1,500,808	1,497,090	1,544,117	1,550,192	1,599,735	1,638,320	1,648,104	74.0	15.6	10.1	27.3
Nevada	867,437	997,233	1,076,295	1,122,636	1,161,980	1,218,402	1,296,629	263.3	41.9	30.0	84.4
New Hampshire	999,788	1,026,926	1,036,973	1,054,712	1,064,182	1,082,640	1,114,540	168.8	38.4	8.5	50.2
New Jersey	9,879,405	10,265,172	10,799,729	10,748,585	11,039,967	11,070,180	11,208,558	104.0	26.0	9.2	37.6
New Mexico	1,241,291	1,308,475	1,355,083	1,344,521	1,398,431	1,480,283	1,517,517	101.9	14.1	16.0	32.3
New York	22,012,649	22,513,968	22,113,219	22,654,147	23,309,616	23,615,085	23,522,461	39.9	15.9	4.5	21.1
North Carolina	5,284,242	5,313,230	5,209,353	5,345,112	5,436,898	5,588,438	5,582,994	101.9	25.1	5.1	31.4
North Dakota	558,975	531,372	549,206	554,037	551,969	549,177	557,043	39.1	–1.4	4.8	3.4
Ohio	9,727,360	9,699,647	10,200,358	9,944,145	10,157,224	10,303,859	10,408,022	55.2	16.6	7.3	25.2
Oklahoma	2,318,360	2,431,437	2,536,424	2,647,525	2,831,938	2,838,910	2,804,088	102.2	–1.6	15.3	13.4
Oregon	2,796,080	2,831,102	2,936,452	3,088,384	3,014,326	3,028,757	3,056,801	85.1	19.9	8.0	29.5
Pennsylvania	11,555,453	11,637,740	11,594,426	11,863,943	11,872,945	11,902,264	12,374,073	58.2	21.4	6.3	29.1
Rhode Island	975,741	950,251	967,970	1,013,358	1,046,182	1,079,562	1,094,185	83.9	17.4	15.1	35.2
South Carolina	2,826,104	2,877,620	2,867,305	2,916,024	2,948,977	2,999,677	3,085,495	105.2	18.6	7.2	27.2
South Dakota	543,988	555,281	579,236	599,469	618,027	629,497	610,640	36.5	8.4	10.0	19.2
Tennessee	3,395,785	3,349,431	3,196,863	3,402,981	3,492,835	3,637,010	3,728,486	92.6	18.5	11.3	31.9
Texas	15,530,860	15,800,294	16,443,604	16,392,182	17,111,075	18,050,340	18,801,642	202.8	15.4	19.0	37.3
Utah	1,375,120	1,425,876	1,449,582	1,491,958	1,596,813	1,662,067	1,719,782	133.6	10.8	20.6	33.6
Vermont	665,456	691,087	677,894	667,987	680,300	683,666	684,864	112.2	40.6	–0.9	39.3
Virginia	5,622,804	5,720,288	5,582,113	5,667,612	5,749,631	5,906,762	5,969,608	107.1	26.5	4.4	32.1
Washington	4,320,548	4,506,895	4,761,106	5,072,888	5,169,855	5,278,737	5,367,559	87.5	17.5	19.1	39.9
West Virginia	1,602,051	1,700,138	1,681,270	1,762,623	1,758,124	1,806,400	1,806,004	77.0	2.8	6.2	9.2
Wisconsin	4,781,828	4,952,180	5,138,901	5,371,213	5,463,236	5,569,782	5,670,826	78.4	20.5	14.5	38.0
Wyoming	619,441	601,711	610,218	593,976	589,983	592,846	581,817	104.4	–13.3	–3.3	–16.1
Outlying areas											
American Samoa	26,571	28,780	30,151	25,622	26,586	29,423	30,382	—	35.2	5.6	42.7
Guam	123,053	134,297	148,113	175,045	169,905	165,826	158,303	132.4	20.4	17.9	42.0
Northern Marianas	24,915	30,944	36,328	42,043	34,684	46,233	44,037	—	73.6	42.3	147.0
Puerto Rico	1,272,025	1,318,520	1,349,545	1,404,296	1,437,847	1,542,335	1,667,640	—	10.2	26.5	39.4
Trust Territories	—	—	—	—	—	—	—	—	—	—	—
Virgin Islands	155,827	138,386	136,001	130,635	127,385	125,416	122,286	—	27.0	–11.6	12.2

[1] Based on the Consumer Price Index, by the Bureau of Labor Statistics, U.S. Department of Labor, adjusted to a school year basis. These data do not reflect differences in inflation rates from state to state.
—Data not available or not applicable.

NOTE—Beginning in 1980–81, expenditures for state administration are excluded. Beginning in 1988–89, survey was expanded and coverage of state expenditures for public school districts was improved. Because of rounding, details may not add to totals.

SOURCE: U.S. Department of Education, National Center for Education Statistics, *Revenues and Expenditures for Public Elementary and Secondary Schools*, various years; *Statistics of State School Systems*, various years; and Common Core of Data surveys. (This table was prepared February 1998.)

Table 39.—Current expenditures (in current dollars) per pupil in average daily attendance in public elementary and secondary schools, by state: 1969–70 to 1995–96

State or other area	1969–70	1970–71	1971–72	1972–73	1973–74	1974–75	1975–76	1976–77	1977–78	1978–79
1	2	3	4	5	6	7	8	9	10	11
United States	**$816**	**$911**	**$990**	**$1,077**	**$1,207**	**$1,365**	**$1,504**	**$1,638**	**$1,823**	**$2,020**
Alabama	544	605	671	715	854	931	1,112	1,230	1,401	1,563
Alaska	1,123	1,507	1,662	1,756	2,053	2,439	3,009	3,381	3,625	4,112
Arizona	720	783	868	906	1,014	1,216	1,445	1,570	1,636	1,720
Arkansas	568	600	662	712	789	894	1,002	1,090	1,204	1,348
California	867	906	998	1,071	1,236	1,367	1,596	1,668	1,864	2,056
Colorado	738	841	916	982	1,112	1,287	1,456	1,654	1,895	2,205
Connecticut	951	1,056	1,155	1,251	1,369	1,556	1,573	1,740	1,962	2,136
Delaware	900	1,047	1,093	1,258	1,386	1,514	1,707	1,919	2,075	2,368
District of Columbia	1,018	1,178	1,258	1,519	1,607	1,779	1,997	2,463	2,706	2,563
Florida	732	829	868	925	1,048	1,304	1,361	1,391	1,520	1,657
Georgia	588	714	709	873	893	1,055	1,162	1,300	1,338	1,485
Hawaii	841	1,023	1,041	1,059	1,325	1,378	1,616	1,836	2,017	2,133
Idaho	603	650	698	771	865	1,016	1,130	1,181	1,380	1,517
Illinois	909	1,036	1,090	1,233	1,342	1,516	1,674	1,759	1,945	2,202
Indiana	728	809	883	917	1,019	1,114	1,256	1,353	1,479	1,690
Iowa	844	901	1,001	1,047	1,135	1,259	1,516	1,676	1,835	2,107
Kansas	771	823	881	990	1,123	1,268	1,214	1,542	1,668	1,978
Kentucky	545	670	682	720	788	904	1,052	1,130	1,283	1,502
Louisiana	648	791	875	912	991	1,130	1,249	1,286	1,511	1,604
Maine	692	751	832	864	987	1,108	1,124	1,303	1,446	1,609
Maryland	918	1,039	1,084	1,208	1,317	1,565	1,685	1,901	2,095	2,349
Massachusetts	859	927	1,052	1,137	1,449	1,481	1,888	2,071	2,322	2,553
Michigan	904	1,007	1,113	1,189	1,348	1,524	1,626	1,814	2,107	2,446
Minnesota	904	1,049	1,149	1,231	1,341	1,544	1,643	1,806	1,982	2,147
Mississippi	501	602	657	708	780	876	970	1,127	1,304	1,507
Missouri	709	763	846	924	1,026	1,149	1,252	1,374	1,534	1,725
Montana	782	840	900	1,023	1,162	1,351	1,586	1,779	1,980	2,178
Nebraska	736	865	911	999	1,116	1,271	1,403	1,615	1,731	1,967
Nevada	769	820	920	979	1,077	1,188	1,355	1,449	1,645	1,811
New Hampshire	723	801	847	934	1,017	1,180	1,256	1,412	1,467	1,671
New Jersey	1,016	1,177	1,302	1,421	1,598	1,783	1,897	2,152	2,426	2,728
New Mexico	707	746	826	887	963	1,114	1,231	1,414	1,585	1,796
New York	1,327	1,567	1,655	1,766	2,079	2,308	2,340	2,497	2,819	3,025
North Carolina	612	686	741	822	918	1,092	1,114	1,246	1,392	1,591
North Dakota	690	742	831	903	1,002	1,111	1,326	1,448	1,609	1,805
Ohio	730	798	855	956	1,051	1,168	1,301	1,434	1,589	1,789
Oklahoma	604	676	731	782	895	1,027	1,151	1,320	1,476	1,729
Oregon	925	1,012	1,125	1,221	1,342	1,562	1,786	1,922	2,107	2,418
Pennsylvania	882	952	1,083	1,245	1,333	1,514	1,677	1,852	2,043	2,250
Rhode Island	891	1,002	1,050	1,205	1,320	1,596	1,358	1,801	2,083	2,387
South Carolina	613	659	729	809	894	1,032	1,067	1,211	1,345	1,508
South Dakota	690	776	824	892	973	1,071	1,312	1,338	1,482	1,677
Tennessee	566	623	672	728	843	991	980	1,201	1,331	1,383
Texas	624	703	786	843	911	1,063	1,259	1,368	1,567	1,691
Utah	626	701	768	815	902	1,024	1,128	1,285	1,341	1,606
Vermont	807	854	995	1,044	1,190	1,366	1,379	1,538	1,681	1,820
Virginia	708	792	879	956	1,061	1,200	1,311	1,446	1,504	1,671
Washington	915	928	1,026	1,105	1,233	1,395	1,556	1,678	1,993	2,173
West Virginia	670	726	820	824	907	1,047	1,225	1,359	1,510	1,671
Wisconsin	883	984	1,064	1,121	1,246	1,409	1,621	1,775	1,975	2,223
Wyoming	856	931	1,061	1,163	1,239	1,426	1,680	1,784	1,955	2,179
Outlying areas										
American Samoa	—	—	720	796	—	881	1,029	780	—	—
Guam	820	749	1,007	1,018	1,362	1,797	1,234	1,599	1,758	1,961
Northern Marianas	—	—	—	—	—	—	—	—	—	—
Puerto Rico	—	420	506	536	—	720	632	687	812	891
Trust Territories	—	—	—	—	—	—	—	—	—	—
Virgin Islands	—	—	1,348	1,120	—	1,471	1,513	1,472	1,560	1,997

Table 39.—Current expenditures (in current dollars) per pupil in average daily attendance in public elementary and secondary schools, by state: 1969–70 to 1995–96—Continued

State or other area	1979–80	1980–81	1981–82	1982–83	1983–84	1984–85	1985–86	1986–87	1987–88	1988–89
1	12	13	14	15	16	17	18	19	20	21
United States	$2,272	$2,502	$2,726	$2,955	$3,173	$3,470	$3,756	$3,970	$4,240	$4,645
Alabama	1,612	1,985	2,063	2,177	2,055	2,325	2,565	2,573	2,718	3,197
Alaska	4,728	5,688	6,312	7,325	8,627	7,843	8,304	8,010	7,971	7,716
Arizona	1,971	2,258	2,462	2,597	2,751	3,009	3,336	3,544	3,744	3,902
Arkansas	1,574	1,701	1,841	1,971	2,235	2,482	2,658	2,733	2,989	3,273
California	2,268	2,475	2,671	2,733	2,963	3,256	3,543	3,728	3,840	4,135
Colorado	2,421	2,693	2,914	3,171	3,373	3,697	3,975	4,147	4,220	4,521
Connecticut	2,420	2,876	3,188	3,636	4,023	4,738	4,743	5,435	6,230	6,857
Delaware	2,861	3,018	3,198	3,456	3,849	4,184	4,610	4,825	5,017	5,422
District of Columbia	3,259	3,441	3,792	4,260	4,766	5,103	5,337	5,742	6,132	7,850
Florida	1,889	2,401	2,443	2,739	2,932	3,241	3,529	3,794	4,092	4,563
Georgia	1,625	1,708	2,019	2,169	2,352	2,657	2,966	3,181	3,434	3,852
Hawaii	2,322	2,604	2,862	3,239	3,334	3,465	3,807	3,787	3,919	4,121
Idaho	1,659	1,856	1,945	2,070	2,146	2,362	2,484	2,585	2,667	2,833
Illinois	2,587	2,704	2,936	3,100	3,298	3,538	3,781	4,106	4,369	4,906
Indiana	1,882	2,010	2,306	2,480	2,725	3,051	3,275	3,556	3,794	4,284
Iowa	2,326	2,668	2,874	3,095	3,274	3,467	3,619	3,770	4,124	4,285
Kansas	2,173	2,559	2,815	3,058	3,284	3,560	3,829	3,933	4,076	4,443
Kentucky	1,701	1,784	1,906	2,100	2,311	2,390	2,486	2,733	3,011	3,347
Louisiana	1,792	2,469	2,590	2,691	2,694	2,990	3,187	3,069	3,138	3,317
Maine	1,824	1,934	2,221	2,458	2,700	3,024	3,472	3,850	4,258	4,744
Maryland	2,598	2,914	3,234	3,445	3,858	4,102	4,447	4,777	5,201	5,758
Massachusetts	2,819	2,940	3,137	3,378	3,595	4,026	4,562	5,145	5,471	5,972
Michigan	2,640	3,037	3,140	3,307	3,556	3,848	4,176	4,353	4,692	5,150
Minnesota	2,387	2,673	2,905	3,085	3,395	3,674	3,941	4,180	4,386	4,755
Mississippi	1,664	1,605	1,706	1,979	2,244	2,350	2,362	2,350	2,548	2,861
Missouri	1,936	2,172	2,342	2,468	2,748	2,958	3,189	3,472	3,786	4,263
Montana	2,476	2,683	2,998	3,289	3,604	3,847	4,091	4,194	4,246	4,293
Nebraska	2,150	2,384	2,704	2,984	3,221	3,471	3,634	3,756	3,943	4,360
Nevada	2,088	2,078	2,424	2,613	2,690	2,829	3,440	3,440	3,623	3,871
New Hampshire	1,916	2,265	2,509	2,750	2,980	3,271	3,542	3,933	4,457	4,807
New Jersey	3,191	3,254	3,674	4,007	4,496	4,504	5,570	5,953	6,564	7,549
New Mexico	2,034	2,329	2,703	2,902	2,928	3,153	3,195	3,558	3,691	3,473
New York	3,462	3,741	4,280	4,686	5,117	5,492	6,011	6,497	7,151	7,663
North Carolina	1,754	2,001	2,107	2,138	2,303	2,625	2,948	3,129	3,368	3,874
North Dakota	1,920	2,275	2,727	2,852	3,028	3,339	3,483	3,437	3,519	3,952
Ohio	2,075	2,303	2,492	2,676	2,982	3,285	3,527	3,673	3,998	4,686
Oklahoma	1,926	2,199	2,673	2,805	2,859	2,850	3,146	3,099	3,093	3,379
Oregon	2,692	3,100	3,299	3,504	3,677	3,889	4,141	4,337	4,789	5,182
Pennsylvania	2,535	2,824	3,050	3,354	3,648	4,237	4,325	4,616	4,989	5,597
Rhode Island	2,601	2,927	3,040	3,570	3,938	4,287	4,667	4,985	5,329	6,064
South Carolina	1,752	1,734	1,907	2,017	2,183	2,783	3,058	3,214	3,408	3,736
South Dakota	1,908	1,991	2,300	2,486	2,685	2,892	3,051	3,097	3,249	3,585
Tennessee	1,635	1,794	1,895	2,027	2,101	2,385	2,612	2,827	3,068	3,491
Texas	1,916	2,006	2,229	2,731	2,784	3,124	3,298	3,409	3,608	3,877
Utah	1,657	1,819	1,872	2,014	2,053	2,220	2,390	2,415	2,454	2,588
Vermont	1,997	2,475	2,793	3,061	3,359	3,651	4,031	4,399	5,207	5,481
Virginia	1,970	2,179	2,384	2,656	2,870	3,155	3,520	3,780	4,149	4,539
Washington	2,568	2,542	2,650	3,211	3,465	3,725	3,881	3,964	4,164	4,359
West Virginia	1,920	2,146	2,593	2,765	2,879	3,244	3,528	3,784	3,858	3,883
Wisconsin	2,477	2,738	2,935	3,233	3,513	3,815	4,168	4,523	4,747	5,266
Wyoming	2,527	2,967	3,417	4,045	4,523	4,799	5,114	5,201	5,051	5,375
Outlying areas										
American Samoa	—	—	—	—	—	1,262	1,387	1,846	1,908	1,988
Guam	—	—	2,133	—	2,301	2,489	3,383	3,344	3,295	4,067
Northern Marianas	—	—	—	—	1,142	1,693	2,552	3,099	3,366	2,414
Puerto Rico	—	1,062	961	—	1,247	1,319	1,325	1,384	1,504	1,692
Trust Territories	—	—	—	—	—	—	—	—	—	—
Virgin Islands	—	—	2,646	—	2,710	—	3,223	4,277	4,036	5,281

Table 39.—Current expenditures (in current dollars) per pupil in average daily attendance in public elementary and secondary schools, by state: 1969–70 to 1995–96—Continued

State or other area	1989–90	1990–91	1991–92	1992–93	1993–94	1994–95	1995–96	Percentage change			
								1969–70 to 1995–96	1985–86 to 1990–91	1990–91 to 1995–96	1985–86 to 1995–96
1	22	23	24	25	26	27	28	29	30	31	32
United States	**$4,980**	**$5,258**	**$5,421**	**$5,584**	**$5,767**	**$5,989**	**$6,146**	**653.2**	**40.0**	**16.9**	**63.7**
Alabama	3,327	3,627	3,616	3,761	4,037	4,405	4,716	767.0	41.4	30.0	83.9
Alaska	8,431	8,330	8,450	8,735	8,882	8,963	9,012	702.8	0.3	8.2	8.5
Arizona	4,053	4,309	4,381	4,510	4,611	4,778	4,860	574.9	29.1	12.8	45.7
Arkansas	3,485	3,700	4,031	4,124	4,280	4,459	4,710	729.8	39.2	27.3	77.2
California	4,391	4,491	4,746	4,780	4,921	4,992	5,108	489.0	26.7	13.7	44.2
Colorado	4,720	5,064	5,172	5,139	5,097	5,443	5,521	648.3	27.4	9.0	38.9
Connecticut	7,837	7,853	8,012	7,973	8,473	8,817	8,817	826.9	65.6	12.3	85.9
Delaware	5,799	5,974	6,093	6,274	6,621	7,030	7,267	707.3	29.6	21.6	57.6
District of Columbia ...	8,955	9,377	9,549	9,419	10,180	9,335	9,565	839.3	75.7	2.0	79.2
Florida	4,997	5,276	5,243	5,314	5,516	5,718	5,894	704.9	49.5	11.7	67.0
Georgia	4,275	4,466	4,419	4,686	4,915	5,193	5,377	814.6	50.6	20.4	81.3
Hawaii	4,448	5,166	5,420	5,704	5,879	6,078	6,051	620.0	35.7	17.1	59.0
Idaho	3,078	3,386	3,556	3,690	3,844	4,210	4,465	640.1	36.4	31.8	79.8
Illinois	5,118	5,520	5,670	5,898	5,893	6,136	6,128	573.8	46.0	11.0	62.1
Indiana	4,606	4,930	5,074	5,344	5,630	5,826	6,040	729.4	50.5	22.5	84.4
Iowa	4,453	4,679	5,096	5,257	5,288	5,483	5,772	583.7	29.3	23.4	59.5
Kansas	4,752	4,874	5,007	5,442	5,659	5,817	5,971	674.5	27.3	22.5	55.9
Kentucky	3,745	4,354	4,719	4,872	5,107	5,217	5,545	917.1	75.1	27.4	123.0
Louisiana	3,903	4,196	4,352	4,428	4,519	4,761	4,988	669.7	31.7	18.9	56.5
Maine	5,373	5,458	5,652	6,073	6,069	6,428	6,546	845.3	57.2	19.9	88.5
Maryland	6,275	6,654	6,679	6,813	6,958	7,245	7,382	703.9	49.6	11.0	66.0
Massachusetts	6,237	6,366	6,408	6,627	6,959	7,287	7,613	786.3	39.5	19.6	66.9
Michigan	5,546	5,883	6,268	6,494	6,658	6,994	7,166	692.7	40.9	21.8	71.6
Minnesota	4,971	5,239	5,409	5,554	5,720	6,000	6,162	582.0	32.9	17.6	56.4
Mississippi	3,094	3,187	3,245	3,382	3,660	4,080	4,250	748.6	34.9	33.4	80.0
Missouri	4,507	4,754	4,830	4,885	5,114	5,383	5,626	694.0	49.1	18.3	76.4
Montana	4,736	5,204	5,319	5,425	5,598	5,692	5,847	647.8	27.2	12.3	42.9
Nebraska	4,842	5,038	5,263	5,336	5,651	5,935	6,083	726.0	38.6	20.7	67.4
Nevada	4,117	4,653	4,926	5,066	5,052	5,160	5,320	591.4	35.3	14.3	54.7
New Hampshire	5,304	5,685	5,790	5,644	5,723	5,859	5,958	724.0	60.5	4.8	68.2
New Jersey	8,139	8,756	9,317	9,415	9,677	9,774	9,955	879.7	57.2	13.7	78.7
New Mexico	3,515	3,895	3,765	4,071	4,261	4,577	4,587	549.0	21.9	17.8	43.6
New York	8,062	8,565	8,527	8,902	9,175	9,623	9,549	619.7	42.5	11.5	58.9
North Carolina	4,290	4,548	4,554	4,763	4,894	5,077	5,090	731.3	54.3	11.9	72.7
North Dakota	4,189	4,199	4,441	4,597	4,674	4,795	4,979	622.1	20.6	18.6	43.0
Ohio	5,045	5,245	5,694	5,754	5,971	6,162	6,266	758.4	48.7	19.5	77.7
Oklahoma	3,508	3,843	4,076	4,355	4,734	4,845	4,881	707.4	22.2	27.0	55.1
Oregon	5,474	5,683	5,913	6,296	6,263	6,436	6,615	615.4	37.2	16.4	59.8
Pennsylvania	6,228	6,541	6,613	6,890	6,983	7,109	7,492	749.7	51.2	14.5	73.2
Rhode Island	6,368	6,343	6,546	6,938	7,333	7,715	7,936	790.6	35.9	25.1	70.0
South Carolina	4,082	4,352	4,436	4,624	4,761	4,797	5,096	731.9	42.3	17.1	66.6
South Dakota	3,731	3,965	4,173	4,357	4,586	4,775	4,780	592.9	29.9	20.6	56.7
Tennessee	3,664	3,782	3,692	3,993	4,149	4,388	4,548	703.4	44.8	20.3	74.1
Texas	4,150	4,438	4,632	4,670	4,898	5,222	5,473	777.0	34.6	23.3	66.0
Utah	2,764	2,960	3,040	3,180	3,439	3,656	3,867	517.6	23.8	30.7	61.8
Vermont	6,227	6,738	6,671	6,411	6,600	6,750	6,837	747.0	67.2	1.5	69.6
Virginia	4,672	4,902	4,878	4,980	5,109	5,327	5,433	667.5	39.2	10.8	54.3
Washington	4,702	5,000	5,271	5,614	5,751	5,906	6,044	560.3	28.8	20.9	55.7
West Virginia	4,360	4,911	5,078	5,527	5,713	6,107	6,325	844.1	39.2	28.8	79.3
Wisconsin	5,524	5,871	6,139	6,475	6,717	6,930	7,094	703.7	40.9	20.8	70.2
Wyoming	5,577	5,638	5,812	5,822	5,899	6,160	6,243	629.4	10.2	10.7	22.1
Outlying areas											
American Samoa	1,908	2,033	2,085	1,670	1,785	2,046	2,159	—	46.6	6.2	55.7
Guam	4,234	4,596	5,231	5,309	5,071	5,080	4,947	503.6	35.9	7.7	46.3
Northern Marianas	3,007	4,425	5,247	5,288	4,510	6,123	5,863	—	73.4	32.5	129.8
Puerto Rico	1,750	1,913	2,162	2,364	2,312	2,742	3,039	—	44.4	58.8	129.4
Trust Territories	—	—	—	—	—	—	—	—	—	—	—
Virgin Islands	6,767	6,002	5,935	5,843	5,915	6,003	6,155	—	86.2	2.5	91.0

—Data not available or not applicable.

NOTE—Beginning in 1980–81, expenditures for state administration are excluded. Beginning in 1988–89, survey was expanded and coverage of state expenditures for public school districts was improved. Because of rounding, details may not add to totals.

SOURCE: U.S. Department of Education, National Center for Education Statistics, *Revenues and Expenditures for Public Elementary and Secondary Schools,* various years; *Statistics of State School Systems,* various years; and Common Core of Data surveys. (This table was prepared February 1998.)

Table 40.—Current expenditures (in constant 1995–96 dollars [1]) per pupil in average daily attendance in public elementary and secondary schools, by state: 1969–70 to 1995–96

State or other area	1969–70	1970–71	1971–72	1972–73	1973–74	1974–75	1975–76	1976–77	1977–78	1978–79
1	2	3	4	5	6	7	8	9	10	11
United States	**$3,337**	**$3,544**	**$3,720**	**$3,887**	**$4,000**	**$4,071**	**$4,189**	**$4,311**	**$4,496**	**$4,557**
Alabama	2,225	2,354	2,520	2,582	2,831	2,777	3,097	3,237	3,456	3,524
Alaska	4,591	5,860	6,241	6,338	6,802	7,274	8,382	8,901	8,942	9,274
Arizona	2,945	3,045	3,260	3,271	3,359	3,626	4,026	4,134	4,036	3,880
Arkansas	2,322	2,334	2,487	2,570	2,614	2,666	2,790	2,868	2,971	3,041
California	3,547	3,524	3,747	3,867	4,094	4,078	4,446	4,391	4,598	4,637
Colorado	3,018	3,273	3,438	3,544	3,686	3,839	4,058	4,353	4,675	4,973
Connecticut	3,891	4,108	4,335	4,515	4,537	4,642	4,381	4,580	4,839	4,819
Delaware	3,681	4,073	4,103	4,542	4,594	4,516	4,756	5,051	5,119	5,341
District of Columbia	4,165	4,581	4,722	5,482	5,326	5,307	5,564	6,482	6,675	5,780
Florida	2,995	3,225	3,260	3,339	3,472	3,891	3,791	3,660	3,748	3,738
Georgia	2,405	2,778	2,662	3,151	2,960	3,147	3,236	3,421	3,300	3,349
Hawaii	3,438	3,978	3,910	3,823	4,391	4,110	4,503	4,833	4,975	4,811
Idaho	2,467	2,528	2,621	2,782	2,866	3,032	3,149	3,109	3,405	3,420
Illinois	3,720	4,030	4,094	4,448	4,447	4,523	4,664	4,630	4,797	4,967
Indiana	2,979	3,145	3,316	3,309	3,378	3,323	3,498	3,561	3,648	3,813
Iowa	3,453	3,506	3,758	3,780	3,761	3,755	4,223	4,412	4,527	4,753
Kansas	3,153	3,201	3,309	3,573	3,721	3,784	3,382	4,059	4,115	4,461
Kentucky	2,230	2,604	2,559	2,600	2,610	2,698	2,931	2,975	3,164	3,388
Louisiana	2,650	3,078	3,283	3,290	3,283	3,372	3,480	3,385	3,726	3,617
Maine	2,832	2,921	3,125	3,117	3,270	3,305	3,131	3,430	3,566	3,629
Maryland	3,756	4,041	4,069	4,360	4,364	4,670	4,694	5,004	5,168	5,299
Massachusetts	3,514	3,605	3,948	4,104	4,800	4,417	5,261	5,453	5,728	5,757
Michigan	3,697	3,916	4,177	4,290	4,465	4,547	4,531	4,774	5,196	5,517
Minnesota	3,696	4,079	4,315	4,444	4,443	4,605	4,578	4,753	4,890	4,842
Mississippi	2,048	2,343	2,465	2,557	2,585	2,614	2,703	2,967	3,216	3,399
Missouri	2,898	2,969	3,178	3,335	3,401	3,427	3,487	3,618	3,784	3,892
Montana	3,198	3,267	3,379	3,691	3,849	4,031	4,418	4,683	4,883	4,913
Nebraska	3,012	3,362	3,420	3,606	3,697	3,791	3,907	4,253	4,271	4,436
Nevada	3,147	3,189	3,454	3,533	3,570	3,545	3,774	3,815	4,057	4,085
New Hampshire	2,957	3,115	3,178	3,371	3,370	3,520	3,500	3,716	3,619	3,770
New Jersey	4,156	4,577	4,887	5,129	5,294	5,318	5,286	5,666	5,984	6,154
New Mexico	2,890	2,900	3,101	3,201	3,192	3,322	3,429	3,723	3,910	4,051
New York	5,426	6,094	6,214	6,373	6,890	6,886	6,518	6,572	6,955	6,823
North Carolina	2,504	2,669	2,781	2,967	3,041	3,257	3,102	3,281	3,435	3,588
North Dakota	2,820	2,887	3,120	3,259	3,319	3,315	3,694	3,811	3,968	4,072
Ohio	2,986	3,104	3,212	3,450	3,481	3,483	3,626	3,776	3,919	4,035
Oklahoma	2,472	2,628	2,746	2,821	2,966	3,063	3,206	3,475	3,640	3,900
Oregon	3,782	3,934	4,225	4,406	4,448	4,661	4,976	5,059	5,198	5,455
Pennsylvania	3,606	3,703	4,065	4,494	4,417	4,516	4,672	4,876	5,039	5,075
Rhode Island	3,645	3,897	3,942	4,349	4,375	4,762	3,783	4,741	5,139	5,384
South Carolina	2,505	2,563	2,736	2,919	2,962	3,080	2,973	3,188	3,317	3,401
South Dakota	2,822	3,017	3,092	3,219	3,225	3,194	3,655	3,522	3,655	3,782
Tennessee	2,315	2,424	2,525	2,628	2,794	2,955	2,731	3,161	3,283	3,119
Texas	2,553	2,734	2,950	3,042	3,018	3,172	3,506	3,602	3,865	3,813
Utah	2,561	2,725	2,885	2,940	2,990	3,053	3,143	3,384	3,308	3,623
Vermont	3,301	3,321	3,735	3,768	3,942	4,075	3,842	4,050	4,147	4,105
Virginia	2,895	3,082	3,302	3,450	3,517	3,580	3,652	3,806	3,709	3,769
Washington	3,744	3,611	3,851	3,987	4,086	4,160	4,334	4,417	4,917	4,900
West Virginia	2,740	2,822	3,077	2,975	3,006	3,124	3,413	3,579	3,724	3,769
Wisconsin	3,610	3,828	3,995	4,047	4,130	4,203	4,515	4,674	4,873	5,014
Wyoming	3,501	3,621	3,985	4,198	4,107	4,255	4,681	4,695	4,823	4,915
Outlying areas										
American Samoa	—	—	2,703	2,872	—	2,627	2,866	2,054	—	—
Guam	3,353	2,913	3,781	3,675	4,512	5,361	3,437	4,210	4,337	4,424
Northern Marianas	—	—	—	—	—	—	—	—	—	—
Puerto Rico	—	1,633	1,898	1,934	—	2,147	1,760	1,809	2,003	2,009
Trust Territories	—	—	—	—	—	—	—	—	—	—
Virgin Islands	—	—	5,061	4,044	—	4,389	4,216	3,876	3,847	4,503

Table 40.—Current expenditures (in constant 1995–96 dollars [1]) per pupil in average daily attendance in public elementary and secondary schools, by state: 1969–70 to 1995–96—Continued

State or other area	1979–80	1980–81	1981–82	1982–83	1983–84	1984–85	1985–86	1986–87	1987–88	1988–89
1	12	13	14	15	16	17	18	19	20	21
United States	$4,521	$4,462	$4,475	$4,652	$4,817	$5,069	$5,332	$5,515	$5,655	$5,921
Alabama	3,208	3,540	3,387	3,427	3,119	3,396	3,641	3,574	3,625	4,075
Alaska	9,409	10,145	10,363	11,531	13,095	11,457	11,790	11,126	10,631	9,837
Arizona	3,922	4,028	4,042	4,087	4,176	4,395	4,737	4,923	4,994	4,975
Arkansas	3,133	3,034	3,023	3,102	3,392	3,625	3,773	3,796	3,987	4,173
California	4,513	4,414	4,385	4,302	4,498	4,756	5,031	5,178	5,122	5,271
Colorado	4,818	4,802	4,784	4,992	5,120	5,400	5,643	5,760	5,628	5,763
Connecticut	4,816	5,129	5,234	5,724	6,107	6,921	6,734	7,549	8,310	8,742
Delaware	5,694	5,383	5,251	5,440	5,842	6,112	6,545	6,702	6,692	6,913
District of Columbia	6,486	6,137	6,226	6,705	7,235	7,454	7,578	7,976	8,179	10,008
Florida	3,759	4,283	4,010	4,311	4,450	4,734	5,011	5,270	5,458	5,817
Georgia	3,234	3,047	3,314	3,415	3,570	3,881	4,211	4,419	4,580	4,911
Hawaii	4,621	4,644	4,698	5,099	5,061	5,061	5,405	5,260	5,226	5,253
Idaho	3,302	3,310	3,194	3,259	3,257	3,451	3,526	3,591	3,557	3,611
Illinois	5,148	4,822	4,819	4,879	5,007	5,168	5,369	5,703	5,827	6,254
Indiana	3,746	3,585	3,785	3,905	4,136	4,457	4,650	4,939	5,060	5,462
Iowa	4,630	4,758	4,718	4,872	4,970	5,065	5,139	5,237	5,500	5,462
Kansas	4,325	4,564	4,621	4,814	4,984	5,200	5,437	5,462	5,437	5,664
Kentucky	3,385	3,182	3,129	3,305	3,508	3,491	3,530	3,796	4,015	4,267
Louisiana	3,566	4,404	4,253	4,236	4,089	4,368	4,525	4,263	4,185	4,229
Maine	3,629	3,449	3,646	3,869	4,098	4,418	4,929	5,347	5,679	6,047
Maryland	5,170	5,197	5,310	5,423	5,856	5,992	6,314	6,635	6,937	7,341
Massachusetts	5,611	5,243	5,151	5,317	5,457	5,881	6,478	7,147	7,297	7,613
Michigan	5,255	5,416	5,155	5,205	5,398	5,621	5,929	6,047	6,257	6,565
Minnesota	4,750	4,768	4,769	4,856	5,153	5,367	5,595	5,806	5,850	6,062
Mississippi	3,311	2,863	2,800	3,116	3,407	3,433	3,353	3,264	3,398	3,647
Missouri	3,853	3,874	3,845	3,885	4,172	4,321	4,528	4,822	5,049	5,434
Montana	4,929	4,786	4,922	5,177	5,470	5,620	5,808	5,826	5,663	5,472
Nebraska	4,279	4,253	4,440	4,697	4,889	5,070	5,159	5,217	5,259	5,559
Nevada	4,156	3,706	3,979	4,113	4,083	4,133	4,884	4,778	4,832	4,934
New Hampshire	3,813	4,040	4,120	4,328	4,523	4,778	5,028	5,463	5,945	6,128
New Jersey	6,351	5,804	6,031	6,308	6,825	6,579	7,908	8,269	8,755	9,624
New Mexico	4,047	4,155	4,437	4,568	4,445	4,606	4,537	4,942	4,923	4,427
New York	6,890	6,673	7,027	7,377	7,767	8,022	8,534	9,025	9,538	9,770
North Carolina	3,491	3,569	3,460	3,365	3,495	3,835	4,186	4,346	4,492	4,939
North Dakota	3,822	4,057	4,476	4,489	4,596	4,877	4,945	4,775	4,694	5,038
Ohio	4,129	4,108	4,091	4,213	4,526	4,799	5,007	5,102	5,332	5,974
Oklahoma	3,834	3,921	4,389	4,416	4,339	4,163	4,467	4,304	4,125	4,308
Oregon	5,357	5,529	5,416	5,516	5,582	5,681	5,879	6,024	6,387	6,606
Pennsylvania	5,044	5,036	5,007	5,280	5,537	6,190	6,141	6,412	6,654	7,136
Rhode Island	5,176	5,220	4,990	5,619	5,977	6,262	6,627	6,924	7,108	7,731
South Carolina	3,487	3,093	3,130	3,176	3,314	4,065	4,342	4,464	4,545	4,763
South Dakota	3,797	3,551	3,777	3,913	4,075	4,225	4,332	4,302	4,333	4,570
Tennessee	3,255	3,199	3,112	3,191	3,190	3,484	3,708	3,927	4,092	4,450
Texas	3,812	3,578	3,660	4,299	4,226	4,563	4,683	4,736	4,812	4,942
Utah	3,297	3,244	3,073	3,170	3,116	3,243	3,394	3,354	3,273	3,299
Vermont	3,974	4,414	4,585	4,818	5,098	5,333	5,723	6,110	6,945	6,987
Virginia	3,920	3,886	3,914	4,181	4,356	4,608	4,998	5,251	5,533	5,787
Washington	5,111	4,534	4,351	5,054	5,260	5,442	5,510	5,506	5,553	5,557
West Virginia	3,822	3,827	4,257	4,352	4,371	4,738	5,010	5,256	5,145	4,950
Wisconsin	4,929	4,884	4,818	5,089	5,332	5,573	5,917	6,282	6,332	6,713
Wyoming	5,028	5,292	5,609	6,367	6,865	7,010	7,261	7,224	6,737	6,853
Outlying areas										
American Samoa	—	—	—	—	—	1,843	1,969	2,565	2,545	2,535
Guam	—	—	3,502	—	3,493	3,636	4,803	4,645	4,395	5,185
Northern Marianas	—	—	—	—	1,733	2,473	3,623	4,304	4,489	3,077
Puerto Rico	—	1,893	1,578	—	1,893	1,926	1,881	1,923	2,007	2,157
Trust Territories	—	—	—	—	—	—	—	—	—	—
Virgin Islands	—	—	4,344	—	4,114	—	4,577	5,941	5,383	6,733

Table 40.—Current expenditures (in constant 1995–96 dollars¹) per pupil in average daily attendance in public elementary and secondary schools, by state: 1969–70 to 1995–96—Continued

State or other area	1989–90	1990–91	1991–92	1992–93	1993–94	1994–95	1995–96	Percentage change			
								1969–70 to 1995–96	1985–86 to 1990–91	1990–91 to 1995–96	1985–86 to 1995–96
1	22	23	24	25	26	27	28	29	30	31	32
United States	$6,059	$6,066	$6,060	$6,053	$6,094	$6,152	$6,146	84.2	13.8	1.3	15.3
Alabama	4,048	4,184	4,042	4,077	4,265	4,525	4,716	112.0	14.9	12.7	29.5
Alaska	10,259	9,610	9,446	9,468	9,385	9,207	9,012	96.3	−18.5	−6.2	−23.6
Arizona	4,932	4,971	4,897	4,889	4,872	4,908	4,860	65.0	4.9	−2.2	2.6
Arkansas	4,240	4,269	4,506	4,471	4,523	4,580	4,710	102.9	13.1	10.3	24.8
California	5,343	5,181	5,305	5,182	5,200	5,128	5,108	44.0	3.0	−1.4	1.5
Colorado	5,744	5,842	5,781	5,571	5,386	5,591	5,521	83.0	3.5	−5.5	−2.2
Connecticut	9,536	9,061	8,957	8,643	8,953	9,056	8,817	126.6	34.5	−2.7	30.9
Delaware	7,056	6,892	6,811	6,801	6,997	7,221	7,267	97.4	5.3	5.4	11.0
District of Columbia ...	10,896	10,819	10,675	10,211	10,757	9,589	9,565	129.7	42.8	−11.6	26.2
Florida	6,081	6,087	5,861	5,761	5,828	5,874	5,894	96.8	21.5	−3.2	17.6
Georgia	5,201	5,152	4,940	5,079	5,193	5,334	5,377	123.6	22.4	4.4	27.7
Hawaii	5,413	5,960	6,059	6,184	6,212	6,243	6,051	76.0	10.3	1.5	12.0
Idaho	3,745	3,907	3,975	4,000	4,062	4,324	4,465	81.0	10.8	14.3	26.6
Illinois	6,227	6,369	6,338	6,394	6,227	6,303	6,128	64.8	18.6	−3.8	14.1
Indiana	5,605	5,688	5,672	5,793	5,949	5,985	6,040	102.8	22.3	6.2	29.9
Iowa	5,418	5,398	5,697	5,699	5,588	5,632	5,772	67.2	5.1	6.9	12.3
Kansas	5,782	5,623	5,598	5,899	5,980	5,975	5,971	89.4	3.4	6.2	9.8
Kentucky	4,557	5,023	5,275	5,281	5,397	5,359	5,545	148.7	42.3	10.4	57.1
Louisiana	4,750	4,841	4,865	4,800	4,775	4,890	4,988	88.2	7.0	3.0	10.2
Maine	6,538	6,297	6,318	6,583	6,412	6,603	6,546	131.1	27.7	4.0	32.8
Maryland	7,636	7,676	7,466	7,385	7,352	7,443	7,382	96.6	21.6	−3.8	16.9
Massachusetts	7,589	7,344	7,164	7,184	7,354	7,485	7,613	116.7	13.4	3.7	17.5
Michigan	6,749	6,787	7,007	7,040	7,035	7,185	7,166	93.8	14.5	5.6	20.9
Minnesota	6,048	6,044	6,046	6,021	6,044	6,163	6,162	66.7	8.0	2.0	10.1
Mississippi	3,764	3,676	3,628	3,667	3,868	4,191	4,250	107.5	9.6	15.6	26.7
Missouri	5,484	5,484	5,399	5,296	5,403	5,530	5,626	94.1	21.1	2.6	24.3
Montana	5,763	6,004	5,946	5,881	5,915	5,847	5,847	82.8	3.4	−2.6	0.7
Nebraska	5,891	5,812	5,884	5,785	5,971	6,096	6,083	102.0	12.7	4.7	17.9
Nevada	5,010	5,369	5,506	5,491	5,338	5,301	5,320	69.1	9.9	−0.9	8.9
New Hampshire	6,454	6,559	6,473	6,119	6,048	6,018	5,958	101.5	30.4	−9.2	18.5
New Jersey	9,904	10,102	10,416	10,206	10,225	10,040	9,955	139.5	27.7	−1.5	25.9
New Mexico	4,277	4,493	4,209	4,413	4,502	4,702	4,587	58.7	−1.0	2.1	1.1
New York	9,809	9,881	9,533	9,650	9,694	9,885	9,549	76.0	15.8	−3.4	11.9
North Carolina	5,220	5,247	5,091	5,163	5,172	5,215	5,090	103.2	25.4	−3.0	21.6
North Dakota	5,097	4,844	4,964	4,984	4,938	4,925	4,979	76.5	−2.0	2.8	0.7
Ohio	6,138	6,051	6,366	6,238	6,309	6,329	6,266	109.9	20.8	3.6	25.1
Oklahoma	4,268	4,434	4,557	4,721	5,002	4,977	4,881	97.4	−0.7	10.1	9.3
Oregon	6,661	6,556	6,610	6,825	6,618	6,611	6,615	74.9	11.5	0.9	12.5
Pennsylvania	7,578	7,547	7,393	7,469	7,379	7,303	7,492	107.7	22.9	−0.7	22.0
Rhode Island	7,748	7,318	7,318	7,521	7,521	7,925	7,936	117.7	10.4	8.5	19.8
South Carolina	4,967	5,021	4,959	5,012	5,031	4,928	5,096	103.4	15.6	1.5	17.4
South Dakota	4,540	4,574	4,665	4,723	4,845	4,905	4,780	69.4	5.6	4.5	10.3
Tennessee	4,458	4,363	4,127	4,329	4,384	4,507	4,548	96.4	17.6	4.2	22.6
Texas	5,050	5,121	5,178	5,063	5,175	5,364	5,473	114.4	9.4	6.9	16.9
Utah	3,363	3,414	3,399	3,447	3,633	3,755	3,867	51.0	0.6	13.3	14.0
Vermont	7,576	7,774	7,457	6,949	6,974	6,933	6,837	107.1	35.8	−12.0	19.5
Virginia	5,684	5,655	5,453	5,398	5,398	5,472	5,433	87.7	13.1	−3.9	8.7
Washington	5,722	5,768	5,892	6,085	6,076	6,066	6,044	61.4	4.7	4.8	9.7
West Virginia	5,306	5,666	5,676	5,991	6,037	6,274	6,325	130.8	13.1	11.6	26.2
Wisconsin	6,721	6,774	6,863	7,020	7,098	7,119	7,094	96.5	14.5	4.7	19.9
Wyoming	6,786	6,505	6,497	6,312	6,233	6,328	6,243	78.3	−10.4	−4.0	−14.0
Outlying areas											
American Samoa	2,321	2,345	2,331	1,811	1,886	2,102	2,159	—	19.1	−8.0	9.7
Guam	5,152	5,302	5,847	5,755	5,358	5,218	4,947	47.6	10.4	−6.7	3.0
Northern Marianas	3,659	5,105	5,865	5,733	4,766	6,289	5,863	—	40.9	14.9	61.8
Puerto Rico	2,129	2,207	2,416	2,562	2,443	2,817	3,039	—	17.3	37.7	61.6
Trust Territories	—	—	—	—	—	—	—	—	—	—	—
Virgin Islands	8,234	6,925	6,635	6,334	6,250	6,166	6,155	—	51.3	−11.1	34.5

¹ Based on the Consumer Price Index, prepared by the Bureau of Labor Statistics, U.S. Department of Labor, adjusted to a school-year basis. These data do not reflect differences in inflation rates from state to state.

—Data not available or not applicable.

NOTE—Beginning in 1980–81, expenditures for state administration are excluded. Beginning in 1988–89, survey was expanded and coverage of state expenditures for public school districts was improved. Because of rounding, details may not add to totals.

SOURCE: U.S. Department of Education, National Center for Education Statistics, *Revenues and Expenditures for Public Elementary and Secondary Schools*, various years; *Statistics of State School Systems*, various years; and Common Core of Data surveys. (This table was prepared July 1998.)

Table 41.—Current expenditures (in current dollars) per pupil in fall enrollment in public elementary and secondary schools, by state: 1969–70 to 1995–96

State or other area	1969–70	1970–71	1971–72	1972–73	1973–74	1974–75	1975–76	1976–77	1977–78	1978–79
1	2	3	4	5	6	7	8	9	10	11
United States	$751	$842	$908	$993	$1,101	$1,257	$1,385	$1,509	$1,677	$1,855
Alabama	512	567	621	672	802	878	1,049	1,156	1,293	1,470
Alaska	1,059	1,446	1,535	1,607	1,937	2,236	2,748	3,085	3,305	3,699
Arizona	674	719	800	826	877	1,174	1,336	1,463	1,498	1,603
Arkansas	511	538	592	634	734	833	940	1,011	1,137	1,263
California	833	902	966	1,080	1,209	1,399	1,577	1,714	1,917	2,018
Colorado	686	784	852	913	1,033	1,200	1,350	1,545	1,766	2,016
Connecticut	911	998	1,076	1,167	1,263	1,435	1,437	1,602	1,768	1,947
Delaware	833	965	1,004	1,155	1,263	1,395	1,561	1,746	1,883	2,127
District of Columbia	947	1,071	1,148	1,272	1,488	1,657	1,832	2,059	2,254	2,392
Florida	683	774	795	837	955	1,200	1,259	1,309	1,430	1,541
Georgia	539	654	649	793	813	965	1,064	1,188	1,225	1,346
Hawaii	792	947	958	969	1,198	1,270	1,492	1,679	1,841	1,927
Idaho	573	618	663	728	795	940	1,048	1,103	1,287	1,417
Illinois	816	933	965	1,103	1,173	1,358	1,468	1,566	1,732	1,976
Indiana	661	742	798	836	911	1,010	1,123	1,227	1,336	1,534
Iowa	798	855	950	989	1,061	1,193	1,423	1,574	1,718	1,975
Kansas	699	747	797	907	1,004	1,143	1,093	1,395	1,515	1,790
Kentucky	502	618	631	666	724	832	947	1,037	1,174	1,371
Louisiana	589	727	793	834	896	1,024	1,132	1,199	1,353	1,460
Maine	649	701	780	796	918	1,009	1,020	1,186	1,309	1,454
Maryland	809	907	984	1,059	1,162	1,362	1,518	1,668	1,843	2,074
Massachusetts	791	942	950	1,074	1,281	1,411	1,688	1,855	2,083	2,290
Michigan	841	937	1,023	1,108	1,260	1,371	1,547	1,661	1,938	2,252
Minnesota	855	961	1,051	1,136	1,215	1,407	1,545	1,695	1,859	2,050
Mississippi	457	561	613	661	726	821	907	1,052	1,221	1,408
Missouri	596	672	761	819	897	1,011	1,121	1,229	1,357	1,529
Montana	728	781	815	903	1,077	1,251	1,444	1,622	1,786	1,979
Nebraska	700	833	863	943	1,047	1,200	1,319	1,521	1,618	1,841
Nevada	706	756	851	902	981	1,078	1,242	1,328	1,507	1,656
New Hampshire	666	735	793	877	928	1,084	1,150	1,291	1,336	1,529
New Jersey	924	1,065	1,162	1,271	1,432	1,615	1,705	1,930	2,172	2,450
New Mexico	665	685	754	800	866	1,003	1,151	1,293	1,458	1,652
New York	1,194	1,380	1,453	1,556	1,787	1,975	2,063	2,119	2,400	2,606
North Carolina	570	634	682	758	867	1,006	1,053	1,153	1,290	1,480
North Dakota	662	714	799	872	965	1,073	1,275	1,396	1,558	1,740
Ohio	677	737	788	875	955	1,070	1,194	1,312	1,445	1,629
Oklahoma	554	609	675	731	833	960	1,081	1,233	1,376	1,614
Oregon	843	926	1,024	1,116	1,210	1,404	1,590	1,727	1,892	2,167
Pennsylvania	815	883	996	1,141	1,220	1,390	1,541	1,689	1,862	2,064
Rhode Island	807	873	953	1,057	1,179	1,396	1,223	1,635	1,878	2,145
South Carolina	567	607	654	749	810	933	1,003	1,099	1,255	1,386
South Dakota	656	734	781	843	921	1,023	1,224	1,270	1,383	1,580
Tennessee	531	589	634	680	764	935	924	1,172	1,241	1,371
Texas	551	616	698	698	769	966	1,141	1,244	1,426	1,528
Utah	595	638	698	742	817	932	1,053	1,162	1,293	1,457
Vermont	790	866	976	1,008	1,113	1,265	1,289	1,428	1,572	1,747
Virginia	654	739	814	881	974	1,107	1,209	1,333	1,382	1,545
Washington	853	865	951	1,020	1,143	1,293	1,432	1,555	1,832	2,017
West Virginia	621	674	766	770	830	950	1,111	1,238	1,357	1,490
Wisconsin	793	886	958	1,018	1,106	1,272	1,443	1,576	1,745	1,993
Wyoming	805	876	993	1,080	1,163	1,329	1,565	1,655	1,820	2,020
Outlying areas										
American Samoa	—	—	675	751	—	706	759	700	—	—
Guam	766	694	937	942	1,200	1,685	1,136	1,437	—	—
Northern Marianas	—	—	—	—	—	—	—	—	—	—
Puerto Rico	—	389	472	497	—	—	607	645	—	831
Trust Territories	—	—	—	—	—	—	—	—	—	—
Virgin Islands	—	—	1,264	1,044	—	1,395	1,346	1,399	1,472	1,850

Table 41.—Current expenditures (in current dollars) per pupil in fall enrollment in public elementary and secondary schools, by state: 1969–70 to 1995–96—Continued

State or other area	1979–80	1980–81	1981–82	1982–83	1983–84	1984–85	1985–86	1986–87	1987–88	1988–89
1	12	13	14	15	16	17	18	19	20	21
United States	**$2,088**	**$2,307**	**$2,525**	**$2,736**	**$2,940**	**$3,222**	**$3,479**	**$3,682**	**$3,927**	**$4,307**
Alabama	1,520	1,836	1,915	2,053	1,935	2,233	2,411	2,420	2,569	3,019
Alaska	4,267	5,506	6,062	6,999	7,051	7,218	7,622	7,131	7,079	6,940
Arizona	1,865	2,093	2,272	2,436	2,618	2,711	3,009	3,436	3,498	3,728
Arkansas	1,472	1,585	1,729	1,852	2,091	2,324	2,506	2,558	2,771	3,023
California	2,227	2,438	2,651	2,718	2,970	3,247	3,534	3,772	3,877	4,205
Colorado	2,258	2,509	2,757	2,945	3,130	3,425	3,666	3,814	3,878	4,151
Connecticut	2,167	2,711	3,054	3,517	3,808	4,524	4,641	5,150	5,905	6,479
Delaware	2,587	2,721	2,895	3,176	3,542	3,849	4,215	4,429	4,606	4,958
District of Columbia ...	2,811	2,950	3,295	3,732	4,177	4,439	4,672	5,153	5,662	6,888
Florida	1,834	2,209	2,388	2,524	2,722	3,011	3,260	3,515	3,778	4,210
Georgia	1,491	1,580	1,871	2,015	2,190	2,475	2,760	2,969	3,195	3,616
Hawaii	2,086	2,393	2,613	2,993	3,085	3,184	3,505	3,503	3,661	3,841
Idaho	1,548	1,736	1,815	1,966	2,023	2,247	2,358	2,462	2,505	2,656
Illinois	2,241	2,406	2,562	2,717	2,877	3,087	3,321	3,541	3,822	4,265
Indiana	1,708	1,798	2,081	2,240	2,473	2,772	2,951	3,213	3,454	3,933
Iowa	2,164	2,505	2,713	2,920	3,081	3,258	3,388	3,550	3,867	4,027
Kansas	1,963	2,307	2,548	2,780	2,985	3,245	3,469	3,573	3,724	4,014
Kentucky	1,557	1,637	1,758	1,895	2,092	2,149	2,229	2,463	2,710	3,009
Louisiana	1,629	2,273	2,375	2,434	2,438	2,736	2,960	2,843	2,886	3,138
Maine	1,692	1,804	2,068	2,287	2,576	2,887	3,341	3,591	3,965	4,330
Maryland	2,293	2,581	2,858	3,031	3,398	3,631	3,923	4,211	4,575	5,088
Massachusetts	2,548	2,735	2,823	3,072	3,298	3,653	4,031	4,490	4,965	5,485
Michigan	2,495	2,892	3,027	3,196	3,292	3,564	3,859	4,024	4,350	4,734
Minnesota	2,296	2,519	2,775	2,902	3,195	3,508	3,741	3,963	4,132	4,515
Mississippi	1,568	1,503	1,598	1,857	2,101	2,197	2,246	2,231	2,416	2,714
Missouri	1,724	1,945	2,096	2,208	2,471	2,654	2,864	3,142	3,425	3,839
Montana	2,264	2,449	2,724	2,997	3,269	3,486	3,691	3,808	3,878	3,893
Nebraska	2,025	2,243	2,559	2,822	3,046	3,276	3,431	3,549	3,712	4,101
Nevada	1,908	1,925	2,235	2,414	2,487	2,620	3,196	3,182	3,298	3,562
New Hampshire	1,732	2,036	2,271	2,511	2,712	2,983	3,247	3,603	4,080	4,328
New Jersey	2,825	2,928	3,401	3,702	4,065	4,160	5,139	5,508	6,059	6,762
New Mexico	1,870	2,066	2,417	2,656	2,676	2,879	2,911	3,071	3,190	3,336
New York	2,950	3,225	3,686	4,041	4,441	4,793	5,221	5,647	6,196	6,655
North Carolina	1,635	1,870	1,976	2,012	2,160	2,457	2,754	2,942	3,153	3,594
North Dakota	1,941	2,175	2,614	2,723	2,883	3,078	3,200	3,159	3,239	3,635
Ohio	1,894	2,120	2,295	2,473	2,764	3,049	3,265	3,409	3,595	4,208
Oklahoma	1,810	2,065	2,509	2,627	2,674	2,672	2,939	2,878	2,897	3,159
Oregon	2,412	2,782	2,959	3,163	3,301	3,491	3,715	3,888	4,266	4,598
Pennsylvania	2,328	2,595	2,805	3,087	3,362	3,914	4,010	4,287	4,603	5,169
Rhode Island	2,340	2,654	2,751	3,244	3,565	3,906	4,255	4,516	4,924	5,598
South Carolina	1,597	1,625	1,801	1,904	2,175	2,583	2,816	2,966	3,143	3,441
South Dakota	1,781	1,885	2,179	2,358	2,557	2,747	2,903	2,935	3,071	3,373
Tennessee	1,523	1,675	1,776	1,905	1,979	2,247	2,447	2,649	2,855	3,248
Texas	1,740	1,831	2,023	2,493	2,556	2,959	3,079	3,163	3,334	3,582
Utah	1,556	1,710	1,761	1,897	1,933	2,086	2,248	2,242	2,302	2,421
Vermont	1,930	2,347	2,651	2,925	3,210	3,475	3,840	4,107	4,927	5,196
Virginia	1,824	2,024	2,215	2,474	2,675	2,948	3,289	3,533	3,873	4,225
Washington	2,387	2,365	2,458	2,985	3,224	3,462	3,605	3,689	3,875	4,059
West Virginia	1,749	1,968	2,393	2,553	2,663	3,005	3,255	3,493	3,579	3,580
Wisconsin	2,225	2,452	2,664	2,938	3,170	3,460	3,767	4,020	4,296	4,760
Wyoming	2,369	2,758	3,188	3,759	4,274	4,482	4,754	4,852	4,742	5,030
Outlying areas										
American Samoa	—	—	—	—	—	—	—	1,764	1,795	1,897
Guam	—	—	1,993	1,993	2,067	—	3,016	3,049	2,944	3,624
Northern Marianas	—	—	—	—	1,230	1,941	—	—	3,384	2,651
Puerto Rico	—	1,000	929	1,052	1,172	1,236	1,227	1,283	1,390	1,557
Trust Territories	—	—	—	—	—	—	—	—	—	—
Virgin Islands	—	—	2,429	2,762	2,695	—	3,016	3,994	3,714	4,757

Table 41.—Current expenditures (in current dollars) per pupil in fall enrollment in public elementary and secondary schools, by state: 1969–70 to 1995–96—Continued

State or other area	1989–90	1990–91	1991–92	1992–93	1993–94	1994–95	1995–96	Percentage change			
								1969–70 to 1995–96	1985–86 to 1990–91	1990–91 to 1995–96	1985–86 to 1995–96
1	22	23	24	25	26	27	28	29	30	31	32
United States	$4,643	$4,902	$5,023	$5,160	$5,327	$5,529	$5,689	657.3	40.9	16.1	63.5
Alabama	3,144	3,429	3,415	3,568	3,826	4,109	4,343	748.8	42.2	26.6	80.1
Alaska	7,577	7,502	7,852	7,901	7,960	8,033	8,189	673.1	–1.6	9.2	7.4
Arizona	3,717	3,860	3,957	4,088	4,104	4,264	4,476	563.7	28.3	16.0	48.7
Arkansas	3,229	3,461	3,777	3,859	4,013	4,186	4,401	761.4	38.1	27.1	75.6
California	4,502	4,595	4,640	4,609	4,719	4,799	4,937	492.4	30.0	7.4	39.7
Colorado	4,357	4,603	4,644	4,766	4,727	5,047	5,121	646.4	25.6	11.3	39.7
Connecticut	7,463	7,547	7,620	7,655	7,947	8,380	8,430	825.6	62.6	11.7	81.7
Delaware	5,326	5,458	5,599	5,753	6,101	6,502	6,696	703.3	29.5	22.7	58.9
District of Columbia ...	7,872	8,029	8,403	8,286	8,843	8,290	8,510	798.7	71.8	6.0	82.1
Florida	4,597	4,859	4,821	4,876	5,063	5,220	5,275	672.7	49.1	8.6	61.8
Georgia	4,000	4,171	4,124	4,368	4,569	4,828	5,056	838.5	51.1	21.2	83.2
Hawaii	4,130	4,820	5,062	5,332	5,533	5,597	5,560	602.0	37.5	15.4	58.6
Idaho	2,921	3,206	3,370	3,471	3,628	3,957	4,194	631.7	36.0	30.8	77.9
Illinois	4,521	4,904	5,002	5,307	5,323	5,553	5,519	576.6	47.7	12.5	66.2
Indiana	4,270	4,588	4,749	4,995	5,245	5,411	5,621	750.2	55.5	22.5	90.5
Iowa	4,190	4,418	4,795	4,970	5,070	5,240	5,481	586.7	30.4	24.1	61.8
Kansas	4,290	4,434	4,554	4,926	5,081	5,222	5,374	669.0	27.8	21.2	54.9
Kentucky	3,384	3,897	4,194	4,310	4,505	4,545	4,807	857.5	74.9	23.3	115.7
Louisiana	3,625	3,853	4,014	4,010	4,133	4,356	4,447	654.5	30.2	15.4	50.2
Maine	4,903	4,978	5,182	5,624	5,569	6,029	6,151	847.6	49.0	23.6	84.1
Maryland	5,573	5,930	5,926	6,060	6,191	6,427	6,593	714.8	51.2	11.2	68.1
Massachusetts	5,766	5,881	5,952	6,141	6,423	6,783	7,033	789.5	45.9	19.6	74.5
Michigan	5,090	5,394	5,746	5,945	6,138	6,465	6,785	706.3	39.8	25.8	75.8
Minnesota	4,698	4,946	5,089	5,210	5,342	5,626	5,801	578.6	32.2	17.3	55.1
Mississippi	2,934	3,007	3,047	3,159	3,410	3,798	3,951	765.0	33.9	31.4	75.9
Missouri	4,071	4,271	4,284	4,318	4,596	4,866	5,092	754.4	49.1	19.2	77.8
Montana	4,240	4,706	4,825	4,907	5,043	5,137	5,249	621.3	27.5	11.5	42.2
Nebraska	4,553	4,735	4,941	5,064	5,310	5,555	5,688	712.9	38.0	20.1	65.8
Nevada	3,816	4,294	4,546	4,645	4,664	4,730	4,892	593.2	34.4	13.9	53.1
New Hampshire	4,786	5,152	5,237	5,368	5,433	5,567	5,740	761.8	58.7	11.4	76.8
New Jersey	7,546	8,166	8,705	8,770	9,075	9,178	9,361	913.3	58.9	14.6	82.2
New Mexico	3,446	3,757	3,927	3,929	4,106	4,404	4,604	592.2	29.0	22.5	58.1
New York	7,051	7,510	7,482	7,770	8,069	8,311	8,361	600.1	43.9	11.3	60.2
North Carolina	4,018	4,237	4,246	4,426	4,540	4,703	4,719	727.4	53.8	11.4	71.3
North Dakota	3,899	3,909	4,150	4,305	4,385	4,482	4,677	606.1	22.1	19.6	46.1
Ohio	4,531	4,747	5,115	5,110	5,319	5,529	5,669	737.9	45.4	19.4	73.6
Oklahoma	3,293	3,639	3,857	4,090	4,437	4,533	4,549	721.5	23.8	25.0	54.8
Oregon	4,864	5,195	5,268	5,585	5,522	5,649	5,790	586.7	39.8	11.5	55.9
Pennsylvania	5,737	6,048	6,127	6,372	6,443	6,565	6,922	749.1	50.8	14.5	72.6
Rhode Island	5,908	5,934	6,092	6,501	6,797	7,126	7,304	805.4	39.5	23.1	71.7
South Carolina	3,769	4,009	4,088	4,200	4,336	4,501	4,779	742.5	42.4	19.2	69.7
South Dakota	3,511	3,726	3,938	4,109	4,095	4,271	4,220	543.2	28.4	13.3	45.4
Tennessee	3,405	3,521	3,430	3,671	3,815	4,017	4,172	685.8	43.9	18.5	70.5
Texas	3,835	4,048	4,246	4,270	4,488	4,779	5,016	810.1	31.5	23.9	62.9
Utah	2,577	2,767	2,841	2,967	3,206	3,409	3,604	505.6	23.1	30.3	60.4
Vermont	5,770	6,255	6,243	6,252	6,266	6,367	6,488	721.7	62.9	3.7	69.0
Virginia	4,690	4,965	4,914	5,067	5,205	5,421	5,528	744.7	51.0	11.3	68.1
Washington	4,382	4,652	4,899	5,220	5,342	5,477	5,611	557.7	29.0	20.6	55.7
West Virginia	4,020	4,571	4,696	5,108	5,292	5,663	5,881	846.4	40.4	28.7	80.7
Wisconsin	5,020	5,382	5,643	5,974	6,126	6,301	6,517	721.7	42.9	21.1	73.0
Wyoming	5,239	5,310	5,348	5,462	5,534	5,753	5,826	623.8	11.7	9.7	22.6
Outlying areas											
American Samoa	1,781	2,002	2,018	1,689	1,737	1,983	2,084	—	—	4.1	—
Guam	3,817	4,411	4,676	5,369	5,200	5,016	4,803	526.6	46.2	8.9	59.2
Northern Marianas	3,356	4,159	4,580	4,796	4,009	5,340	4,999	—	—	20.2	—
Puerto Rico	1,605	1,773	1,879	2,034	2,155	2,417	2,657	—	44.5	49.9	116.6
Trust Territories	—	—	—	—	—	—	—	—	—	—	—
Virgin Islands	6,043	5,515	5,444	5,265	5,299	5,280	5,378	—	82.9	–2.5	78.3

—Data not available or not applicable.

NOTE—Beginning in 1980–81, expenditures for state administration are excluded. Beginning in 1988–89, survey was expanded and coverage of state expenditures for public school districts was improved. Because of rounding, details may not add to totals.

SOURCE: U.S. Department of Education, National Center for Education Statistics, *Revenues and Expenditures for Public Elementary and Secondary Schools*, various years; *Statistics of State School Systems*, various years; and Common Core of Data surveys. (This table was prepared July 1998.)

Table 42.—Current expenditures (in constant 1995–96 dollars[1]) per pupil in fall enrollment in public elementary and secondary schools, by state: 1969–70 to 1995–96

State or other area	1969–70	1970–71	1971–72	1972–73	1973–74	1974–75	1975–76	1976–77	1977–78	1978–79
1	2	3	4	5	6	7	8	9	10	11
United States	**$3,072**	**$3,276**	**$3,408**	**$3,585**	**$3,648**	**$3,750**	**$3,857**	**$3,972**	**$4,136**	**$4,185**
Alabama	2,093	2,204	2,331	2,426	2,657	2,618	2,921	3,043	3,188	3,316
Alaska	4,332	5,624	5,763	5,801	6,419	6,671	7,656	8,121	8,153	8,343
Arizona	2,758	2,794	3,004	2,979	2,907	3,503	3,721	3,851	3,694	3,617
Arkansas	2,090	2,092	2,223	2,288	2,431	2,486	2,619	2,661	2,806	2,850
California	3,408	3,506	3,627	3,900	4,007	4,174	4,393	4,513	4,728	4,552
Colorado	2,806	3,049	3,198	3,295	3,423	3,579	3,762	4,066	4,356	4,547
Connecticut	3,725	3,880	4,040	4,212	4,185	4,281	4,003	4,218	4,360	4,391
Delaware	3,409	3,753	3,770	4,169	4,185	4,161	4,348	4,597	4,644	4,797
District of Columbia ...	3,873	4,164	4,309	4,592	4,931	4,944	5,105	5,419	5,560	5,396
Florida	2,792	3,011	2,985	3,022	3,164	3,581	3,508	3,445	3,526	3,476
Georgia	2,204	2,545	2,436	2,861	2,693	2,880	2,965	3,126	3,022	3,035
Hawaii	3,239	3,685	3,596	3,498	3,971	3,790	4,157	4,419	4,541	4,346
Idaho	2,344	2,405	2,489	2,628	2,634	2,803	2,919	2,905	3,174	3,195
Illinois	3,336	3,627	3,624	3,982	3,886	4,052	4,089	4,122	4,272	4,456
Indiana	2,704	2,887	2,996	3,018	3,018	3,013	3,129	3,230	3,295	3,460
Iowa	3,264	3,324	3,566	3,570	3,515	3,558	3,965	4,144	4,237	4,455
Kansas	2,858	2,905	2,994	3,272	3,326	3,411	3,046	3,672	3,736	4,038
Kentucky	2,053	2,404	2,369	2,403	2,399	2,482	2,638	2,730	2,895	3,093
Louisiana	2,411	2,829	2,978	3,012	2,969	3,055	3,155	3,155	3,337	3,292
Maine	2,655	2,725	2,929	2,874	3,042	3,009	2,843	3,121	3,230	3,280
Maryland	3,310	3,527	3,694	3,823	3,849	4,062	4,230	4,391	4,547	4,679
Massachusetts	3,234	3,664	3,567	3,878	4,246	4,210	4,701	4,883	5,138	5,166
Michigan	3,442	3,646	3,843	3,998	4,175	4,091	4,309	4,372	4,781	5,080
Minnesota	3,496	3,738	3,948	4,100	4,027	4,196	4,304	4,461	4,585	4,623
Mississippi	1,868	2,183	2,301	2,387	2,405	2,451	2,527	2,770	3,011	3,177
Missouri	2,438	2,615	2,856	2,954	2,973	3,015	3,124	3,234	3,347	3,449
Montana	2,976	3,036	3,059	3,261	3,568	3,732	4,024	4,269	4,404	4,464
Nebraska	2,862	3,238	3,240	3,403	3,468	3,581	3,675	4,004	3,990	4,153
Nevada	2,886	2,939	3,196	3,255	3,250	3,217	3,460	3,496	3,718	3,735
New Hampshire	2,724	2,857	2,979	3,167	3,076	3,234	3,204	3,398	3,295	3,448
New Jersey	3,778	4,142	4,363	4,586	4,747	4,816	4,749	5,080	5,357	5,525
New Mexico	2,720	2,663	2,830	2,888	2,870	2,992	3,206	3,403	3,598	3,727
New York	4,885	5,368	5,455	5,615	5,922	5,893	5,747	5,578	5,921	5,878
North Carolina	2,333	2,467	2,560	2,734	2,873	3,000	2,933	3,035	3,183	3,338
North Dakota	2,709	2,777	2,999	3,148	3,197	3,200	3,552	3,674	3,843	3,925
Ohio	2,767	2,865	2,958	3,158	3,165	3,191	3,326	3,455	3,565	3,674
Oklahoma	2,265	2,369	2,535	2,637	2,760	2,865	3,011	3,247	3,394	3,640
Oregon	3,449	3,600	3,844	4,028	4,009	4,187	4,430	4,546	4,668	4,888
Pennsylvania	3,334	3,434	3,738	4,119	4,044	4,146	4,294	4,445	4,593	4,655
Rhode Island	3,300	3,396	3,577	3,815	3,905	4,164	3,406	4,304	4,631	4,837
South Carolina	2,320	2,359	2,456	2,701	2,686	2,783	2,795	2,894	3,096	3,125
South Dakota	2,684	2,853	2,931	3,042	3,053	3,051	3,411	3,343	3,410	3,563
Tennessee	2,171	2,289	2,380	2,453	2,531	2,788	2,574	3,085	3,061	3,092
Texas	2,254	2,396	2,622	2,774	2,726	2,880	3,178	3,275	3,518	3,447
Utah	2,434	2,482	2,619	2,678	2,706	2,779	2,934	3,058	3,189	3,285
Vermont	3,229	3,367	3,664	3,636	3,688	3,774	3,591	3,759	3,877	3,939
Virginia	2,677	2,875	3,057	3,181	3,226	3,303	3,369	3,509	3,408	3,485
Washington	3,489	3,365	3,570	3,682	3,787	3,856	3,990	4,093	4,520	4,548
West Virginia	2,541	2,620	2,875	2,777	2,749	2,833	3,094	3,259	3,348	3,361
Wisconsin	3,244	3,445	3,596	3,674	3,666	3,794	4,019	4,150	4,304	4,495
Wyoming	3,292	3,405	3,727	3,899	3,853	3,965	4,360	4,355	4,490	4,556
Outlying areas										
American Samoa	—	—	2,534	2,709	—	2,106	2,113	1,842	—	—
Guam	3,135	2,698	3,520	3,399	3,976	5,026	3,164	3,784	—	—
Northern Marianas	—	—	—	—	—	—	—	—	—	1,875
Puerto Rico	—	1,515	1,772	1,795	—	—	1,690	1,697	—	—
Trust Territories	—	—	—	—	—	—	—	—	—	—
Virgin Islands	—	—	4,744	3,767	—	4,161	3,749	3,683	3,631	4,172

Table 42.—Current expenditures (in constant 1995–96 dollars[1]) per pupil in fall enrollment in public elementary and secondary schools, by state: 1969–70 to 1995–96—Continued

State or other area	1979–80	1980–81	1981–82	1982–83	1983–84	1984–85	1985–86	1986–87	1987–88	1988–89
1	12	13	14	15	16	17	18	19	20	21
United States	**$4,156**	**$4,115**	**$4,145**	**$4,307**	**$4,462**	**$4,707**	**$4,940**	**$5,114**	**$5,237**	**$5,491**
Alabama	3,026	3,275	3,144	3,232	2,937	3,261	3,423	3,362	3,426	3,849
Alaska	8,492	9,821	9,952	11,018	10,702	10,543	10,822	9,904	9,442	8,848
Arizona	3,712	3,733	3,731	3,834	3,974	3,960	4,273	4,773	4,665	4,752
Arkansas	2,929	2,826	2,838	2,916	3,174	3,394	3,557	3,553	3,696	3,854
California	4,431	4,348	4,353	4,279	4,508	4,743	5,018	5,239	5,171	5,360
Colorado	4,494	4,475	4,526	4,636	4,751	5,003	5,205	5,298	5,172	5,291
Connecticut	4,313	4,836	5,014	5,537	5,780	6,608	6,589	7,154	7,876	8,260
Delaware	5,148	4,852	4,752	4,999	5,377	5,622	5,984	6,151	6,143	6,321
District of Columbia	5,595	5,262	5,409	5,875	6,341	6,484	6,634	7,157	7,551	8,781
Florida	3,650	3,941	3,920	3,973	4,132	4,398	4,628	4,883	5,038	5,367
Georgia	2,967	2,818	3,072	3,172	3,324	3,616	3,919	4,123	4,261	4,609
Hawaii	4,152	4,268	4,289	4,711	4,683	4,651	4,977	4,866	4,882	4,897
Idaho	3,081	3,097	2,980	3,094	3,071	3,282	3,348	3,419	3,342	3,386
Illinois	4,460	4,292	4,205	4,277	4,368	4,509	4,716	4,919	5,097	5,437
Indiana	3,399	3,207	3,417	3,526	3,754	4,049	4,190	4,463	4,607	5,014
Iowa	4,307	4,468	4,454	4,596	4,677	4,759	4,810	4,931	5,157	5,134
Kansas	3,906	4,116	4,183	4,376	4,531	4,741	4,926	4,963	4,966	5,117
Kentucky	3,099	2,920	2,886	2,983	3,175	3,139	3,164	3,421	3,615	3,836
Louisiana	3,242	4,055	3,899	3,832	3,701	3,997	4,203	3,948	3,850	4,000
Maine	3,367	3,217	3,396	3,600	3,910	4,217	4,744	4,988	5,288	5,520
Maryland	4,563	4,603	4,692	4,770	5,158	5,304	5,569	5,849	6,101	6,486
Massachusetts	5,070	4,878	4,634	4,836	5,006	5,336	5,723	6,236	6,622	6,993
Michigan	4,966	5,157	4,970	5,030	4,998	5,205	5,479	5,590	5,802	6,035
Minnesota	4,570	4,493	4,555	4,568	4,850	5,124	5,311	5,505	5,511	5,756
Mississippi	3,121	2,680	2,624	2,924	3,189	3,209	3,189	3,099	3,223	3,459
Missouri	3,431	3,470	3,441	3,476	3,751	3,877	4,067	4,365	4,568	4,894
Montana	4,505	4,368	4,473	4,717	4,962	5,092	5,240	5,289	5,172	4,963
Nebraska	4,029	4,001	4,201	4,442	4,623	4,785	4,871	4,930	4,951	5,228
Nevada	3,798	3,433	3,669	3,800	3,776	3,827	4,537	4,419	4,399	4,541
New Hampshire	3,447	3,632	3,728	3,953	4,117	4,357	4,609	5,004	5,442	5,518
New Jersey	5,623	5,223	5,584	5,828	6,171	6,077	7,296	7,650	8,080	8,621
New Mexico	3,722	3,684	3,967	4,182	4,061	4,205	4,134	4,265	4,255	4,253
New York	5,872	5,751	6,052	6,361	6,742	7,001	7,413	7,843	8,264	8,484
North Carolina	3,255	3,336	3,244	3,166	3,279	3,589	3,911	4,087	4,205	4,582
North Dakota	3,864	3,879	4,291	4,286	4,377	4,496	4,544	4,387	4,320	4,633
Ohio	3,770	3,781	3,768	3,893	4,196	4,453	4,635	4,735	4,794	5,365
Oklahoma	3,601	3,684	4,119	4,136	4,059	3,903	4,173	3,998	3,863	4,028
Oregon	4,801	4,962	4,858	4,978	5,011	5,100	5,274	5,401	5,689	5,862
Pennsylvania	4,634	4,629	4,605	4,859	5,104	5,717	5,694	5,954	6,139	6,590
Rhode Island	4,658	4,734	4,516	5,107	5,412	5,706	6,041	6,273	6,568	7,137
South Carolina	3,179	2,898	2,956	2,997	3,301	3,772	3,999	4,120	4,191	4,386
South Dakota	3,544	3,362	3,577	3,711	3,881	4,013	4,122	4,077	4,096	4,299
Tennessee	3,031	2,988	2,915	2,999	3,005	3,282	3,474	3,679	3,808	4,140
Texas	3,462	3,266	3,322	3,924	3,880	4,322	4,372	4,394	4,447	4,566
Utah	3,097	3,050	2,891	2,986	2,933	3,047	3,191	3,114	3,070	3,086
Vermont	3,841	4,186	4,352	4,605	4,872	5,076	5,451	5,704	6,571	6,624
Virginia	3,630	3,611	3,636	3,895	4,060	4,306	4,669	4,907	5,166	5,387
Washington	4,750	4,217	4,036	4,698	4,894	5,057	5,118	5,123	5,168	5,174
West Virginia	3,480	3,511	3,929	4,019	4,042	4,389	4,621	4,852	4,773	4,564
Wisconsin	4,428	4,374	4,373	4,624	4,812	5,054	5,348	5,584	5,730	6,068
Wyoming	4,715	4,920	5,234	5,917	6,488	6,547	6,750	6,739	6,325	6,413
Outlying areas										
American Samoa	—	—	—	—	—	—	—	2,450	2,394	2,418
Guam	—	—	3,272	3,137	3,137	—	4,282	4,235	3,927	4,620
Northern Marianas	—	—	—	—	1,867	2,835	—	—	4,514	3,380
Puerto Rico	—	1,784	1,525	1,655	1,779	1,806	1,742	1,783	1,854	1,985
Trust Territories	—	—	—	—	—	—	—	—	—	—
Virgin Islands	—	—	3,988	4,347	4,091	—	4,282	5,547	4,954	6,064

Table 42.—Current expenditures (in constant 1995–96 dollars[1]) per pupil in fall enrollment in public elementary and secondary schools, by state: 1969–70 to 1995–96—Continued

State or other area	1989–90	1990–91	1991–92	1992–93	1993–94	1994–95	1995–96	Percentage change			
								1969–70 to 1995–96	1985–86 to 1990–91	1990–91 to 1995–96	1985–86 to 1995–96
1	22	23	24	25	26	27	28	29	30	31	32
United States	**$5,649**	**$5,655**	**$5,615**	**$5,593**	**$5,629**	**$5,679**	**$5,689**	**85.1**	**14.5**	**0.6**	**15.2**
Alabama	3,825	3,956	3,817	3,868	4,043	4,221	4,343	107.5	15.6	9.8	26.9
Alaska	9,220	8,655	8,778	8,565	8,411	8,252	8,189	89.0	–20.0	–5.4	–24.3
Arizona	4,523	4,453	4,423	4,432	4,336	4,380	4,476	62.3	4.2	0.5	4.8
Arkansas	3,929	3,993	4,222	4,183	4,240	4,300	4,401	110.6	12.2	10.2	23.7
California	5,479	5,301	5,187	4,996	4,987	4,929	4,937	44.9	5.6	–6.9	–1.6
Colorado	5,301	5,310	5,192	5,167	4,995	5,185	5,121	82.5	2.0	–3.6	–1.6
Connecticut	9,081	8,707	8,518	8,299	8,397	8,608	8,430	126.3	32.1	–3.2	27.9
Delaware	6,481	6,297	6,259	6,236	6,446	6,679	6,696	96.4	5.2	6.3	11.9
District of Columbia ...	9,578	9,263	9,393	8,983	9,344	8,516	8,510	119.7	39.6	–8.1	28.3
Florida	5,594	5,606	5,389	5,286	5,350	5,362	5,275	88.9	21.1	–5.9	14.0
Georgia	4,867	4,813	4,610	4,735	4,828	4,960	5,056	129.5	22.8	5.1	29.0
Hawaii	5,025	5,560	5,659	5,780	5,846	5,749	5,560	71.6	11.7	(2)	11.7
Idaho	3,554	3,699	3,767	3,763	3,834	4,064	4,194	78.9	10.5	13.4	25.3
Illinois	5,501	5,658	5,592	5,753	5,625	5,704	5,519	65.4	20.0	–2.5	17.0
Indiana	5,196	5,293	5,309	5,414	5,542	5,559	5,621	107.9	26.3	6.2	34.2
Iowa	5,098	5,097	5,360	5,387	5,357	5,383	5,481	67.9	5.9	7.5	13.9
Kansas	5,220	5,116	5,091	5,339	5,369	5,364	5,374	88.0	3.9	5.0	9.1
Kentucky	4,117	4,497	4,689	4,672	4,760	4,669	4,807	134.1	42.1	6.9	51.9
Louisiana	4,411	4,445	4,488	4,347	4,368	4,475	4,447	84.5	5.8	0.0	5.8
Maine	5,966	5,743	5,793	6,097	5,884	6,193	6,151	131.7	21.0	7.1	29.7
Maryland	6,781	6,841	6,624	6,569	6,541	6,602	6,593	99.2	22.8	–3.6	18.4
Massachusetts	7,016	6,785	6,653	6,657	6,786	6,968	7,033	117.5	18.6	3.7	22.9
Michigan	6,193	6,223	6,423	6,444	6,486	6,641	6,785	97.1	13.6	9.0	23.8
Minnesota	5,716	5,706	5,689	5,648	5,644	5,779	5,801	65.9	7.4	1.7	9.2
Mississippi	3,569	3,469	3,407	3,425	3,604	3,901	3,951	111.5	8.8	13.9	23.9
Missouri	4,953	4,928	4,789	4,680	4,856	4,999	5,092	108.9	21.2	3.3	25.2
Montana	5,159	5,430	5,394	5,319	5,328	5,277	5,249	76.4	3.6	–3.3	0.2
Nebraska	5,540	5,462	5,524	5,489	5,611	5,706	5,688	98.7	12.1	4.1	16.8
Nevada	4,643	4,954	5,081	5,035	4,928	4,859	4,892	69.5	9.2	–1.2	7.8
New Hampshire	5,823	5,943	5,854	5,819	5,741	5,719	5,740	110.7	28.9	–3.4	24.5
New Jersey	9,182	9,421	9,731	9,507	9,589	9,428	9,361	147.7	29.1	–0.6	28.3
New Mexico	4,193	4,334	4,390	4,259	4,339	4,523	4,604	69.3	4.9	6.2	11.4
New York	8,579	8,665	8,364	8,423	8,526	8,537	8,361	71.2	16.9	–3.5	12.8
North Carolina	4,889	4,889	4,746	4,798	4,798	4,831	4,719	102.3	25.0	–3.5	20.7
North Dakota	4,744	4,510	4,640	4,666	4,633	4,604	4,677	72.6	–0.8	3.7	2.9
Ohio	5,513	5,477	5,718	5,539	5,620	5,679	5,669	104.9	18.1	3.5	22.3
Oklahoma	4,007	4,199	4,312	4,434	4,688	4,656	4,549	100.9	0.6	8.3	9.0
Oregon	5,919	5,993	5,889	6,054	5,835	5,803	5,790	67.9	13.6	–3.4	9.8
Pennsylvania	6,981	6,978	6,849	6,907	6,808	6,744	6,922	107.6	22.5	–0.8	21.6
Rhode Island	7,189	6,846	6,810	7,047	7,182	7,320	7,304	121.4	13.3	6.7	20.9
South Carolina	4,587	4,626	4,570	4,553	4,581	4,624	4,779	106.0	15.7	3.3	19.5
South Dakota	4,272	4,299	4,402	4,455	4,327	4,387	4,220	57.3	4.3	–1.8	2.4
Tennessee	4,143	4,062	3,835	3,979	4,031	4,126	4,172	92.1	16.9	2.7	20.1
Texas	4,666	4,671	4,746	4,628	4,742	4,909	5,016	122.5	6.8	7.4	14.7
Utah	3,136	3,192	3,176	3,216	3,388	3,501	3,604	48.1	(2)	12.9	13.0
Vermont	7,021	7,217	6,979	6,778	6,621	6,540	6,488	100.9	32.4	–10.1	19.0
Virginia	5,706	5,728	5,493	5,492	5,500	5,568	5,528	106.5	22.7	–3.5	18.4
Washington	5,332	5,367	5,477	5,659	5,644	5,626	5,611	60.8	4.9	4.5	9.6
West Virginia	4,891	5,274	5,250	5,538	5,592	5,818	5,881	131.4	14.1	11.5	27.3
Wisconsin	6,108	6,209	6,308	6,476	6,473	6,472	6,517	100.9	16.1	5.0	21.9
Wyoming	6,375	6,126	5,978	5,921	5,847	5,910	5,826	77.0	–9.2	–4.9	–13.7
Outlying areas											
American Samoa	2,168	2,309	2,256	1,831	1,836	2,037	2,084	—	—	–9.7	—
Guam	4,645	5,089	5,227	5,820	5,495	5,152	4,803	53.2	18.8	–5.6	12.2
Northern Marianas	4,084	4,798	5,120	5,199	4,236	5,485	4,999	—	—	4.2	—
Puerto Rico	1,953	2,045	2,101	2,204	2,277	2,483	2,657	—	17.4	29.9	52.5
Trust Territories	—	—	—	—	—	—	—	—	—	—	—
Virgin Islands	7,353	6,363	6,086	5,708	5,599	5,423	5,378	—	48.6	–15.5	25.6

[1] Based on the Consumer Price Index, prepared by the Bureau of Labor Statistics, U.S. Department of Labor, adjusted to a school-year basis. These data do not reflect differences in inflation rates from state to state.

[2] Change of less than .05 percent.

— Data not available or not applicable.

NOTE—Beginning in 1980–81, expenditures for state administration are excluded. Beginning in 1988–89, survey was expanded and coverage of state expenditures for public school districts was improved. Because of rounding, details may not add to totals.

SOURCE: U.S. Department of Education, National Center for Education Statistics, *Revenues and Expenditures for Public Elementary and Secondary Schools*, various years; *Statistics of State School Systems*, various years; and Common Core of Data surveys. (This table was prepared July 1998.)

CHAPTER 3
Postsecondary Education

Postsecondary education in this country is diverse; American colleges and universities offer a wide range of programs. For example, a community college may offer vocational training or the first 2 years of training at the college level. A university typically offers a full undergraduate course of study leading to a bachelor's degree as well as first-professional and graduate programs leading to advanced degrees. Other 4-year colleges focus on undergraduate education. Vocational and technical institutions offer training programs that are designed to prepare students for specific careers. Community groups, churches, libraries, and businesses provide other types of educational opportunities for adults.

Students pursue higher education through both public and private institutions. Public and various types of privately controlled institutions—denominationally affiliated, nonprofit, and proprietary—offer both 4-year and 2-year programs. Public institutions are directly or indirectly controlled through state or local governments, and receive much of their funding through direct government appropriations. Private institutions are self-governed or controlled through nongovernment organizations. While they may receive significant amounts of funding through government organizations, the funding through direct appropriations is generally relatively small. Four-year institutions offer at least an undergraduate education, but many have graduate and first-professional programs as well. Two-year institutions award only associate degrees and other types of awards below the baccalaureate. Some 2-year colleges have only vocational or only academic programs, but many have both types of programs. Two-year colleges serve a wide diversity of students, including those who are taking academic courses in preparation for transferring to a 4-year college as well as those who are taking programs to prepare for specific occupations.

This chapter highlights historical data that enable the reader to observe long-range trends in American higher education. This chapter also provides an overview of some of the latest statistics on higher education. Statistics on vocational/technical institutions and adult education data are excluded because these data have not been gathered on a consistent basis during the time period covered by this publication. Also, enrollment and finance data for vocational/ technical institutions have never been available at the state level. Similar types of data limitations prohibit the presentation of state time-series data for adult education activities. Substantial amounts of vocational and technical education activities are reflected in the 2-year college data that include the academic as well as vocational education programs.

Demographics and Enrollment

College enrollment remains at nearly historic highs. The long-term expansion of higher education enrollment reflects a variety of factors including higher college enrollment rates for new high school graduates, higher college enrollment for older age groups, and higher enrollment rates for women. [1]

The college enrollment/population ratio for states is affected by the proportion of a state's population in the traditional college age, and by the migration of college students from state to state, as well as by a variety of policy measures such as the physical and financial accessibility of higher education. In 1996, the college enrollment/population ratio ranged from 4.0 percent in Arkansas, 4.1 in New Jersey and 4.3 percent in Georgia, to highs of 7.2 in Nebraska, 7.3 in Rhode Island, and 7.6 percent in Utah (table 43 and figure 12). The District of Columbia had the highest ratio of 13.7 percent, mostly because of the disproportionately large number of out-of-district students attending private universities. All of the southern states were below the national average of 5.4 percent. Many states (20) were within half of a percentage point of the national average.

There was a modest increase in the enrollment/ population ratio from 5.3 percent in 1980 to 5.6 percent in 1990, but the ratio dropped slightly to 5.4 in 1996. Overall, between 1980 and 1996, most states experienced small increases, with 11 states experiencing a decrease. Washington, California and Arizona had relatively large decreases of at least one percentage point in the ratio. In contrast, Wyoming, New Mexico, Nebraska, Iowa, Utah, and North Dakota had enrollment ratio increases of at least one percentage point.

---

[1] U.S. Department of Education, National Center for Education Statistics, *Digest of Education Statistics, 1997.*

Figure 12.– Higher education enrollment as a percentage of total population, by state: 1996

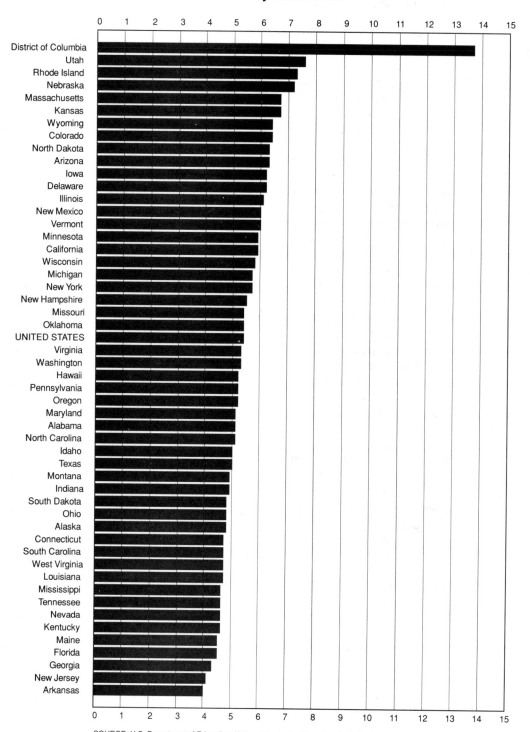

SOURCE: U.S. Department of Education, National Center for Education Statistics, Integrated Postsecondary Education Data System (IPEDS), "Fall Enrollment" survey; and U.S. Department of Commerce, Bureau of the Census, Current Population Reports, Series P-25, unpublished data. (This figure was prepared January 1998.)

Between fall 1990 and fall 1996, there were small shifts in the proportion of students attending public and private 2-year and 4-year institutions. The percentage of students at private 4-year institutions rose from 20 to 21 percent, while the proportion at private 2-year colleges fell slightly by less than 1 point (table 48). There was a small decrease in the proportion of students at public 4-year colleges, from 42 to 41 percent, and the proportion of students at public 2-year colleges rose from 36 to 37 percent.

The distribution of different types of institutions varies from state to state as a result of government policies, student preferences, and historical precedents. In the early days of the nation, most colleges were privately controlled and located in the relatively densely settled eastern part of the country. Even in 1996, out of the top 10 states in terms of percent of private enrollment, only Missouri was not part of the original 13 colonies. Of the 10 states with the lowest percentage of total enrollment in private colleges, only 2, Mississippi and Alabama, are east of the Mississippi River (figure 13 and table 48).

The actual percentages of enrollment in different types of institutions vary widely among the states. The jurisdictions with the highest percentage of students in private schools in 1996 were the District of Columbia (90 percent), Massachusetts (58 percent), and Rhode Island (48 percent). The states with the lowest percentages were New Mexico (6 percent), Alaska (4 percent), Wyoming (3 percent), and Nevada (2 percent). The structure of the public college sector also ranged widely among the states. Some states, such as South Dakota, Alaska, and West Virginia, had relatively small public 2-year college systems with fewer than 10 percent of students enrolled (figure 14). The District of Columbia had no public or private 2-year colleges. In Wyoming, California, Washington, Nevada, and Arizona, more than half of all college students attended public 2-year colleges.

The proportion of college students in each state who attend full-time also is associated with the prevalence of public 2-year colleges (table 44). The national proportion of college students attending full-time was 57 percent in 1996. The percentage was higher (71 percent) for public and private 4-year colleges and somewhat lower (60 percent) at private 2-year colleges. At public 2-year colleges, however, the percentage of students attending full-time was 35 percent. Students at public 2-year colleges were less likely to attend college full-time than students in public 4-year colleges in every state.

The percentage of college students who attended full-time showed significant variation from state to state in 1996, partly due to larger or smaller proportions of students at 2-year institutions. But some states had very low or very high full-time enrollment rates for both public 4-year and public 2-year institu-

tions. North Dakota and Montana each had an average full-time overall enrollment percentage that exceeded 75 percent. The states were characterized by high full-time enrollment rates for both public 4-year and public 2-year institutions. At the other end of the spectrum, New Mexico, Maryland, Florida, Arizona, California, Alaska, and Nevada had full-time enrollment rates below 50 percent. Except for Alaska, all of these states had relatively large public 2-year college systems. The lower percentage of full-time students at the 2-year colleges was an important factor in the attendance patterns in each of the 7 states.

Unlike many other higher education enrollment comparisons, the percentage of students who were women showed little variation from state to state in 1996 (table 45). At the national level, there was only a little variation among types of institutions, ranging from 50 percent women at private 2-year colleges to 58 percent at public 2-year colleges. Only 5 states and the U.S. Service schools had averages that were 3 percentage points or more different from the national average for all institutions.

Despite the sizable numbers of small colleges, most students attend the larger colleges. In fall 1996, 36 percent of higher education campuses had fewer than 1,000 students; yet altogether, these campuses enrolled 4 percent of college students. On the other hand, though 11 percent of the campuses enrolled over 10,000 students each, they accounted for 50 percent of total college enrollment (table 46).

Fewer than 11 percent of all public college students attended postbaccalaureate programs in 1996, compared to about 27 percent of students at private colleges and universities (table 47). Some of this difference is due to the relatively large 2-year college sector within the public college group. State college systems differed significantly in terms of the proportion of students in postbaccalaureate programs. In Connecticut, West Virginia, Virginia, South Carolina, and Michigan the proportion of public college students enrolled in postbaccalaureate programs exceeded 14 percent. The proportion was under 8 percent in California, Washington, Alaska, and the District of Columbia. The proportion of postbaccalaureate students in private colleges was higher than in public colleges in more than three-quarters of the states. The proportions of postbaccalaureate students at private colleges was particularly high in the District of Columbia, California, and Maryland, where it exceeded 40 percent.

There has been a general increase in the proportion of college students who are members of minority groups. The proportion of minority students rose from 16.5 percent in 1980 to 26.1 percent in 1996 (table 49). There were some increases in the proportion of black students (9.4 to 10.8 percent) and American Indian/Alaskan Native students (.7 to 1.0 percent). The

Figure 13. – Enrollment in private institutions of higher education as a percentage of total higher education enrollment, by state: 1996

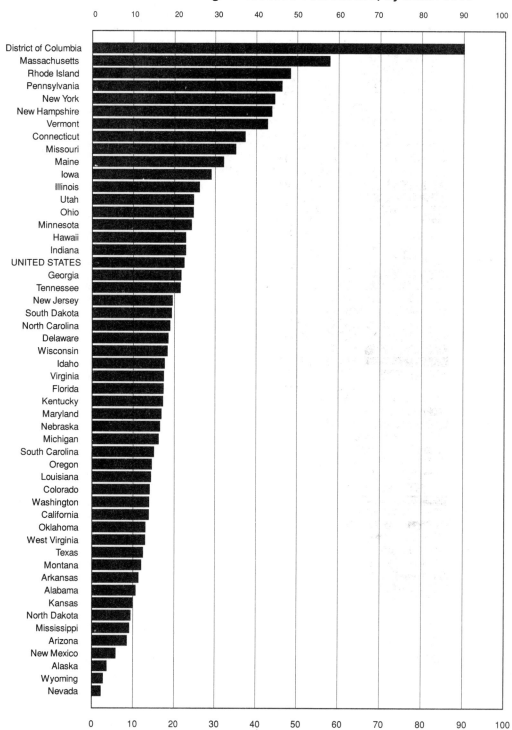

SOURCE: U.S. Department of Education, National Center for Education Statistics, Integrated Postsecondary Education Data System (IPEDS), "Fall Enrollment" survey; and U.S. Department of Commerce, Bureau of the Census, Current Population Reports, Series P-25, unpublished data. (This figure was prepared May 1998.)

Figure 14.– Percentage of all college students in public 2-year institutions of higher education, by state: Fall 1996

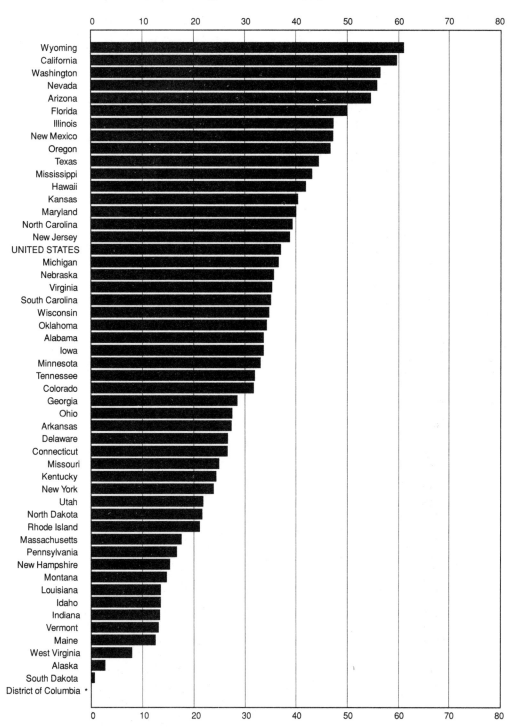

*There are no public 2-year colleges in the District of Columbia.

SOURCE: U.S. Department of Education, National Center for Education Statistics, Integrated Postsecondary Education Data System (IPEDS), "Fall Enrollment" survey. (This figure was prepared January 1998.)

proportion of Hispanic students rose much more rapidly (4.0 to 8.3 percent) as did the proportion of Asian/Pacific Islander students (2.4 to 6.0 percent). Increases in minority enrollments were reflected in all of the states. Eleven states had relatively large minority increases of 10 or more percentage points between 1980 and 1996. California had the largest increase of 22 percentage points in minority representation.

The proportion of minority students in colleges varied widely from state to state. As might be expected, the proportion was greatly affected by the predominant racial/ethnic distribution of the population (figure 15). For example, 3 states—New Hampshire, Vermont, and Maine—had 5 percent or less minority enrollment in 1996, reflecting the relatively small minority population residing in these states. In contrast, areas with substantial minority populations had high minority representation in colleges. Hawaii (71 percent), California (49 percent), the District of Columbia (46 percent), and New Mexico (44 percent) had the highest proportions of minority students in 1996.

Although state demographics are an important determinant of the enrollment profile of a state's colleges, the number of students leaving from and coming to a state to attend college can also have a significant impact. State policies on public college tuition, accessibility, and availability can affect the proportion of students who attend college in their own state. Private colleges typically attract proportionately more out-of-state students than public colleges. Four of the 5 states importing the most students relative to the enrollment of their own residents had high proportions of students enrolled in private colleges (tables 48 and 51). Variations in residence and migration of students varied widely from state to state (figure 16). In 1996, seven states—Michigan, Alabama, Texas, North Carolina, Mississippi, California, Utah—had 90 percent or more of their college bound high school graduates going to in-state colleges. Four states—Alaska, Vermont, Connecticut, and New Hampshire—and the District of Columbia had 50 percent or less of their new freshman students attend college in-state.

These percentages translated into large numbers of students migrating from state to state, with some states gaining and some states, losing. In 1996, Massachusetts, North Carolina, Pennsylvania, the District of Columbia, and Indiana had a net gain of more than 5,000 out-of-state recently graduated freshman students. In contrast, Illinois experienced a net loss of more than 8,500 freshman students and New Jersey had a net loss of 18,700 freshman students.

Enrollment Trends

Over the past several decades, college enrollments have expanded rapidly as "baby boomers" attended college in record numbers. Surging college enrollments were driven, in part, by the increasing numbers of new high school graduates and increasing enrollment rates of older adults during the 1960s through the mid-1970s. Thus, even when the pool of new high school graduates dropped during the late 1970s and the 1980s, college enrollment remained stable or increased. College enrollment finally leveled off and even decreased slightly between 1990 and 1995, in response to the low numbers of new high school graduates and the declining college-age population (table 52).

The fall 1986 to fall 1996 period was generally characterized by rising enrollment during the first half of the period, followed by small decreases or stable enrollments during the second half of the period. Enrollments decreased in fall 1993, fall 1994, and fall 1995. Overall, enrollment increased by 14 percent, between 1986 and 1996, with all of the increase occurring during the first half of the 10-year period. Most states had enrollment increases during the 10-year period. Only Massachusetts, Connecticut and the District of Columbia had decreases, of about 2 or 4 percent. Twelve states had increases of 25 percent or more, and Nevada and Georgia had enrollment increases of over 50 percent.

The increases in enrollments were not consistent for public and private 2-year and 4-year colleges from fall 1986 to fall 1996 (tables 53 to 56). In general, the increases were most rapid at the public 2-year colleges and private 4-year institutions, with moderate increases in public 4-year colleges. Enrollments dropped at private 2-year colleges. Enrollment patterns also reflected sharp differences among states for the various types of institutions.

Enrollments at public 4-year colleges increased by 10 percent during this period, slower than private 4-year colleges (19 percent) and public 2-year colleges (20 percent) (tables 53 to 56). While most states had some increase in public 4-year college enrollment, ten states, the District of Columbia, and the U.S. Service Schools had decreases. Large increases of 40 percent or more in public 4-year college enrollment were registered in Alaska, Utah, Idaho, and Florida. However, some of Alaska's apparent large increase was due to the conversion of public 2-year colleges to public 4-year colleges.

Enrollment at public 2-year colleges rose by 20 percent between 1986 and 1996, with most of the increase occurring during the first half of the 10-year period (table 54). Four states, Michigan, Pennsylvania, West Virginia, and Alaska (with both West Vir-

Figure 15. – Minority students as a percentage of resident fall enrollment in institutions of higher education, by state: 1996

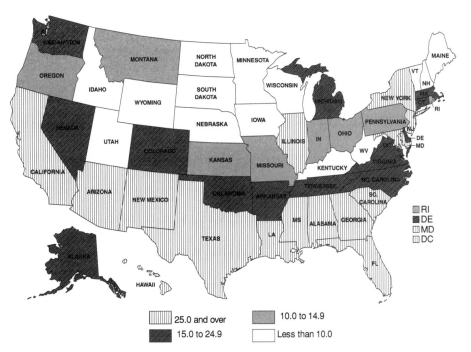

▨ RI	
▨ DE	
▥ MD	
▥ DC	

▥	25.0 and over	▨	10.0 to 14.9
▮	15.0 to 24.9	☐	Less than 10.0

SOURCE: U.S. Department of Education, National Center for Education Statistics, Integrated Postsecondary Education Data System (IPEDS), "Fall Enrollment" surveys. (This figure was prepared February 1998.)

Figure 16. – Percentage of freshmen graduating in the previous 12 months who attended higher education institutions in their home state, by state: Fall 1996

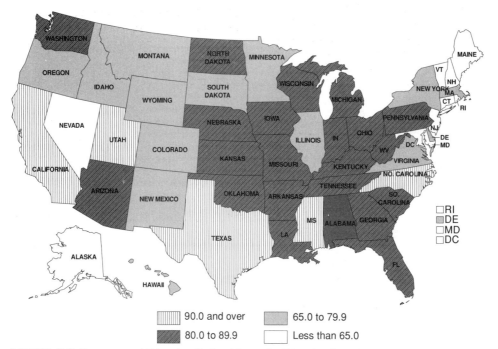

SOURCE: U.S. Department of Education, National Center for Education Statistics, Integrated Postsecondary Education Data System (IPEDS), "Residence of First-Time Students" survey, 1996. (This figure was prepared February 1998.)

ginia and Alaska reflecting conversions of 2-year colleges to 4-year colleges), had decreases in public 2-year college enrollments. In contrast, 16 states had large increases of 40 percent or more.

The enrollment pattern at private 4-year colleges was similar to the public 4-year college pattern. Enrollment rose by 19 percent at private 4-year colleges between fall 1986 and fall 1996, with most of the increase occurring during the earlier part of the decade (table 55). Enrollments increased in all states except for Alaska and Connecticut. Fourteen states had increases of 40 percent or more. Nevada, New Mexico, Colorado, and Arizona had increases of 100 percent or more.

Enrollments declined by 19 percent at private 2-year colleges during the fall 1986 to fall 1996 period, with most of the decrease occurring during the latter part of the period. There was large variation among the states with some posting very large percentage increases and others showing very large declines. However, many of the percentages for states with larger changes were based on relatively small numbers of students and institutions.

The changes in fall full-time equivalent (FTE) enrollment follow the same pattern as the total enrollment changes. The national average FTE enrollment increases were at least as high as fall enrollment changes for 4-year institutions and public 2-year institutions. (tables 57 to 61). The private 2-year colleges showed an even larger decrease in FTE enrollment than for total enrollment. The difference between the enrollment changes for the two types of enrollment statistics is due to the faster growth of full-time enrollment compared to part-time enrollment at most types of institutions.

Degrees Conferred

One measure of the output of colleges and universities is the number of degrees conferred. Comparing the number and types of degrees helps to characterize higher education systems and their focus areas. The degree data may be used to measure the access for women and minority students, the focus on undergraduate and postbaccalaureate education, and the emphasis on different types of study. In some respects, degree data provide more definitive information than enrollment statistics, because they measure final output as opposed to process. For example, racial/ethnic enrollment data may be used to measure access to higher education, but they do not describe differences in graduation rates or transfers from 2- to 4-year colleges. The degree data provide a final evaluation of the higher education process and reflect the number of students who are ready to attend higher level programs or enter the work force with a given level of credentials. The degree data suffer in

terms of timeliness since they are collected at the end of the academic year rather than the beginning and reflect a process that may take from 2 to more than 10 years to complete.

In 1994–95, higher education institutions awarded 540,000 associate degrees, 1,160,000 bachelor's degrees, 76,000 first professional degrees, 398,000 master's degrees, and 44,000 doctor's degrees (table 63). In rough terms, this amounts to slightly less than one quarter of awards at the 2-year level, slightly more than half at the bachelor's degree level, and slightly less than one quarter at the postbaccalaureate degree level (table 62). These distributions range somewhat from state to state, reflecting differences in size of the 2-year college sector, state college emphasis on graduate education, and percentages of private colleges which tend to have proportionately more students in postbaccalaureate education.

The distribution of college degrees suggests that private colleges have higher proportions of programs at the postgraduate level than public colleges (tables 48 and 62). Although 34 percent of the 4-year college enrollment was in private colleges, the private colleges awarded 61 percent of the first-professional degrees, 44 percent of the master's degrees and 35 percent of the doctor's degrees in 1994–95 (table 63).

Eight states and the District of Columbia had more than one quarter of their higher education awards at the postbaccalaureate level. Five of these states and the District had higher proportions of students in private colleges than the national average. Of the 5 states with 15 percent or fewer degrees at the postbaccalaureate level, only 1 (Maine) had a proportion of students in private colleges that exceeded the national average. All of the 5 states with the smallest proportions of graduate degrees—Montana, Idaho, Wyoming, North Dakota, and Maine—have relatively small resident populations. Without importing large numbers of students, the institutions in these low population states would find it more difficult to support diverse specialized graduate programs because of the relatively small higher education enrollment base.

Between 1980–81 and 1994–95, women increased their representation in each level of higher education (table 64). These increases were particularly notable at the postbaccalaureate level. The proportion of degrees awarded to women increased from 55 percent to 60 percent at the associate degree level between 1980–81 and 1994–95 and from 50 to 55 percent at the bachelor's degree level. The proportion of master's degrees awarded to women also rose by about 5 percentage points, reaching 55 percent in 1994–95. Significant increases occurred at the two highest degree levels: the proportion of women earning first-professional degrees rose from 27 percent to 41 percent and women's proportion of doctor's degrees rose from 31 percent to 39 percent. There was some consistency from state to state. Only in Utah (and the U.S. Service Schools) was the women's percentage of bachelor's degrees below 50 percent in 1995. The women's percentage of master's degrees was less than 50 percent in 4 states (and the U.S. Service Schools.)

In 1994–95, the proportion of associate degree recipients who were racial/ethnic minorities was 21 percent (table 65). The proportion of minority degree awards to U.S. resident graduates at the bachelor's degree was lower at 19 percent (table 66). At the master's and doctor's degree level, the percentage was lower still at 16 percent. Of the advanced degrees, only the first-professional degree minority percentage (20 percent) was higher than at the bachelor's degree level.

Degrees, by Field of Study

College degrees are awarded in a large number of different fields ranging from scientific or medical specialties offered at only a handful of institutions to programs like elementary education or business offered by hundreds of institutions. For purposes of simple analyses, the hundreds of different fields can be collapsed into several major fields to help generalize state to state differences. While there is some danger of oversimplification and differences with definitions used by other researchers, some useful points may be made.

The differences in fields of degrees from state to state are greater than might be expected. Differences in narrow specialties are to be expected because some are offered at only a small number of institutions in the United States and could not be evenly distributed across states. Differences in major categories like humanities, education, and computer science and engineering are more interesting and suggest more extensive studies of supply and demand for different fields of study from state to state (table 70 and figure 17). For example, 17 percent of all bachelor's degrees in 1994–95 were conferred in the humanities. The states ranged from 6 percent in Wyoming and North Dakota to 24 percent in Maryland and 25 percent in Vermont (and 36 percent in the U.S. Service Schools.) The range in bachelor's degrees in education around the national average of 9 percent was even wider. Colorado (less than 1 percent) and the District of Columbia, Virginia, and California (2 to 3 percent) had the smallest proportions, while Arkansas (21 percent) and Wyoming (23 percent) had the largest.

The proportions of degrees granted in major groupings at the master's degree level also varied widely. About one quarter of all master's degrees (25 percent) were awarded in the field of education. The percentage was highest in Kentucky, Washington, and Vermont where more than 40 percent of all master's degrees were in education. At the national level the proportion of master's degrees in business and management at 23 percent was the second largest major category. The state proportions in business and management ranged from a low of 6 percent in Wyoming and Vermont to 36 percent in Missouri and 40 percent in New Hampshire. The implications of these large variations in program emphasis from state to state have not been well analyzed in the context of cost variations among different types of degree programs. A better understanding of the cost differences between degree levels and variations in program emphasis across states would contribute substantially to financial studies of state higher education finances.

Trends in Degrees Conferred

Over the ten year period from 1984–85 to 1994–95, the number of degrees conferred increased at every degree level from associate degrees to doctor's degrees. Like the enrollment data, the degree numbers did not show an increase every year and there were some downturns, but the overall trend for each level has been upward (tables 71 to 75).

The number of associate degrees rose by 19 percent between 1984–85 and 1994–95, which reflects a combination of no change in the first half of the period and increases in the latter part of the period. Over the 10-year period, Utah and New Mexico had the largest increases of 101 and 88 percent, respectively. Most states had increases in the number of associate degrees during this period; 7 states and the District of Columbia had decreases.

Bachelor's degrees rose at about the same rate as the number of associate degrees, increasing by just over 18 percent between 1984–85 and 1994–95. Again, the latter part of the period showed larger increases than the beginning of the period, with degrees up 7 percent between 1984–85 and 1989–90 compared to a 10 percent rise between 1989–90 and 1994–95. The bachelor's degree increases were widely distributed among the states with Alaska (86 percent) and Nevada (72 percent) having the largest increases. Massachusetts, the District of Columbia and the U.S. Service Schools had decreases in bachelor's degrees.

The number of master's degrees rose even more rapidly than the bachelor's or associate degrees, reflecting a large (39 percent) increase over the 10-year period. About two thirds of the increase occurred in the last half of the decade when the number of master's degrees jumped by 23 percent, in contrast to the increase of 13 percent between 1984–85 and 1989–90. As might be expected by the

Figure 17. – Bachelor's degrees in business as a percent of all bachelor's degrees conferred, by state: 1994–95

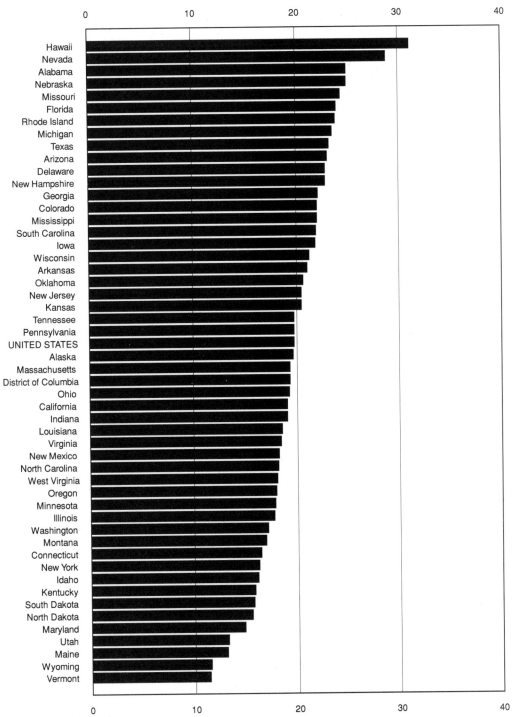

SOURCE: U.S. Department of Education, National Center for Education Statistics, Integrated Postsecondary Education Data System, "Completions" survey. (This figure was prepared February 1998.)

large national increase between 1984–85 and 1994–95, all of the states had some increase. The two states with the lowest percent increases—Indiana and Connecticut—still had rises of 10 percent. Nevada, Virginia, Delaware, and Maine had particularly large increases of nearly 100 percent or more.

Although the number of first-professional degrees (including such disciplines as medicine, dentistry, other medical specialties, theology, and law) rose between 1984–85 and 1994–95, the increase of about 1 percent was very modest compared to the increases in other types of degrees. The 10-year change includes a decrease of 5 percent between 1984–85 and 1989–90 and an increase of 7 percent between 1989–90 and 1994–95. Slightly over half of the states had a decrease over the decade, but changes varied widely. The increases ranged as high as 59 percent in Idaho and 58 percent in Delaware. Vermont had the largest decline of 57 percent, but all of the extremes in the percentage changes reflect relatively small base numbers.

The number of doctor's degrees rose nearly as fast as the number of master's degrees, increasing by 35 percent between 1984–85 and 1994–95. Unlike other types of degrees, the number of doctor's degrees rose about the same in both the first half of the 10-year period and the second half. Because of the small bases in the numbers of doctor's degrees conferred each year for many of the states, the precise percent change for many states does not mean a great deal since the percent change could vary significantly as a result of a few degrees more or less. In general terms, about 19 states had large increases of 50 percent or more and only Kansas, the District of Columbia, and Wyoming had decreases.

The degree data show systematic increases in the numbers of degrees conferred, particularly between 1989–90 and 1994–95. The master's and doctor's degrees increased at a faster rate than the associate or bachelor's degrees.

Staff and Financial Resources

Approximately 2.1 million FTE staff were employed in colleges and universities in the fall of 1995, including .7 million faculty (table 76). Staff to student ratios in both public and private 4-year colleges were considerably lower than in their 2-year counterparts. Four-year colleges are much more likely to have students residing on campus than 2-year colleges. Maintaining and operating additional facilities such as dormitories, sports and activity arenas, and food service halls require many additional staff. Many universities operate various types of research institutes that also serve to decrease student/staff ratios. In contrast, 2-year colleges have a more direct focus on instruction, instead of also providing diverse services

to students and pursuing research activities. In fall 1995, the FTE student/FTE staff ratio for public 4-year colleges was 4.2 compared to 9.2 at public 2-year colleges. The ratio at the private 4-year colleges was slightly lower than the public colleges at 3.8, and the private 2-year ratio was slightly lower, though similar, to the public 2-year college ratio.

The relationships between the various types of institutions for the FTE student to FTE faculty ratio was similar to the staff ratios. The public 4-year faculty to student ratio was 14.8, which was higher than the private 4-year ratio of 12.4. The public 2-year colleges (19.5) and the private 2-year colleges (20.1) had ratios that were considerably higher than the ratios at the 4-year colleges. Part of the reason for this difference is the emphasis of many 4-year colleges on research and postbaccalaureate education. In contrast, 2-year college faculty spend more of their time on instructional activities.[2] These staff ratios do not reflect average class sizes. For example, previous research shows that average class sizes in public 2-year colleges are smaller than the average of public and private research institutions, and higher than private liberal arts colleges.[3] Instead of spending time on research, the 2-year faculty typically spend more time teaching classes.

Because of the range in the types of 4-year college programs from liberal arts institutions to major research institutions and the diversity of program emphases from state to state, one might expect the range in student/faculty ratios to be greater for 4-year colleges than the range for public 2-year institutions. The data show that the range for the 2-year colleges is in fact greater. The highest public 2-year college ratios were in Alaska (52), Virginia (33), and Utah (32). The states with the lowest public 2-year college ratios were Wisconsin (10), New Hampshire (7), and South Dakota (5). For these 6 states, the ratio of high to low averages is more than 5:1. The states with the highest ratios for the public 4-year colleges were New Hampshire (19), Delaware (19), Utah (18), Alaska (18), and Arizona (18). The areas with the lowest ratios were the District of Columbia (11), Hawaii (10), and Oregon (10). This gives a high to low comparison of the top and bottom 3 state averages of less than 2:1. These results suggest that the variety of staffing patterns and programs among 2-year colleges is very wide, even in comparison to the well-documented contrasts among 4-year colleges (e.g., research, doctoral, comprehensive, and liberal arts).

---

[2] U.S. Department of Education, National Center for Education Statistics, *Digest of Education Statistics, 1997.*

[3] U.S. Department of Education, National Center for Education Statistics, *Condition of Education, 1997.*

Figure 18. – Average salary of faculty on 9-month contracts at public 4-year institutions of higher education, by state: 1996–97

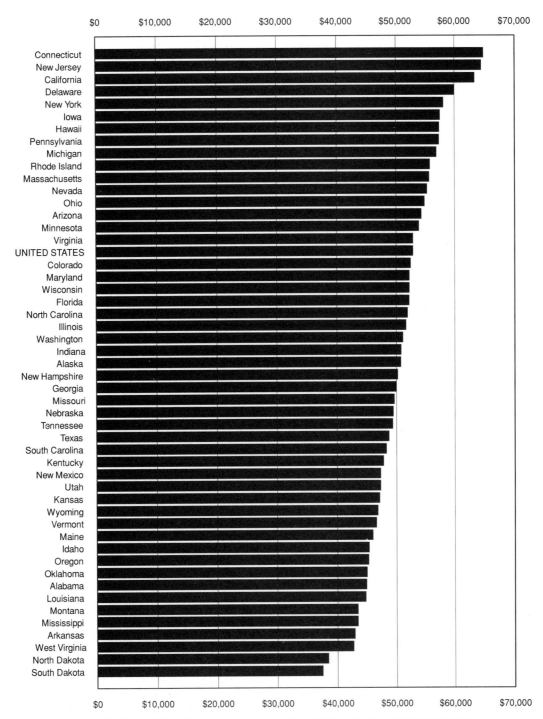

NOTE: The District of Columbia is not shown because the public 4-year faculty are not on 9-month contracts.

SOURCE: U.S. Department of Education, National Center for Education Statistics, Integrated Postsecondary Education Data System (IPEDS), "Salaries, Tenure, and Fringe Benefits of Full-Time Instructional Faculty, 1993-94" survey. (This figure was prepared February 1998.)

Faculty Salaries

The average salary for full-time instructional faculty on 9-month contracts in degree-granting institutions was $50,829 in 1996–97 (table 77). The average salary for faculty at private 4-year institutions was slightly lower than the average for faculty at public 4-year institutions. The salary average for public 2-year college faculty was $44,584. Salary averages for public 2-year faculty were consistently lower than the averages for public 4-year faculty for every state, except for Alaska where the 2-year sector is very small. The salary average for the private 2-year institutions ($32,628) was significantly lower than the averages of faculty at any other type of institution.

The range of the state averages for public 4-year college faculty reflect the differences in the cost of living among the states, in addition to other structural and policy factors. The highest average salaries were in high cost of living states with relatively large urban areas, including Connecticut, New Jersey, California, Delaware and New York (figure 18). The states with the lowest averages were Arkansas, West Virginia, North Dakota, and South Dakota, all states with relatively low cost of living indexes. [4] A comparison of the public 2-year colleges shows much the same results, with the high salary states being Alaska, Michigan, New Jersey, California, and Connecticut. The states with the relatively low average salaries for public 2-year college faculty were North Dakota, North Carolina, Arkansas, Montana, and South Dakota. Of these states, only Michigan was an exception to the generalization of high salaries in relatively high cost of living states and low salaries in relatively low cost of living states.

College faculty generally suffered losses in the purchasing power of their salaries from 1972–73 to 1980–81, when average salaries fell 17 percent after adjustment for inflation (table 79). During the 1980s, average salaries rose and recouped most of the losses. Between 1985–86 and 1996–97, average salaries for faculty on 9-month contracts rose by 7 percent, after adjustment for inflation. Virtually all of this change occurred between 1985–86 and 1989–90. The national salary average between 1989–90 and 1996–97 rose only 1 percent after adjustment for inflation. About two-thirds of the states were clustered within 5 percentage points of the national average increase between 1985–86 and 1996–97, but there were a number of states with more extreme changes. Delaware (21 percent) and New Jersey (19 percent) had the largest increases. The states with the largest declines in inflation adjusted faculty salaries were

Alaska (–20 percent), Wyoming (–15 percent), and North Dakota (–10 percent).

Institutions and Finances

During the 1995–96 academic year, higher education was provided by 3,706 institutions. The 4-year colleges were predominantly private (1,636 vs. 608) and the 2-year colleges were predominantly public (1,047 vs. 415) (table 80). Because of the typically larger size of public colleges and the narrower focus of private colleges on various baccalaureate and postbaccalaureate programs, the numbers of institutions do not provide a good description of the scope of the higher education sectors.

Revenue

Colleges and universities use a wide variety of resources to finance their institutions. Private colleges and universities are dependent to a large extent on tuition received from students, which yielded about 42 percent of their current-fund revenue in 1994–95. [5] Donations, grants, contracts, direct or indirect funding from government agencies, receipts from hospitals and other operations, endowment income, and other sources provide the balance of private institution funding. Public colleges rely on a similar set of funding resources, but differ in the relative amounts of funding from particular sources (table 82). Public colleges typically obtain the largest single share (36 percent in 1994–95) of their revenue from state governments. Other important sources of public college revenues are tuition (18 percent), federal funds (11 percent), university hospitals (11 percent), and auxiliary enterprises (10 percent).

The sources of funding for public colleges differ substantially from state to state because of policy differences and varying college missions. Large differences in the balance of revenue from appropriations and tuition may reflect basic state policies relating to the responsibility of the state and the individual in providing higher education. Relatively high proportions of revenue from auxiliary enterprises may reflect high proportions of students residing on-campus since college dormitories and food services are included in auxiliary enterprise receipts.

The states with high proportions of revenues from tuition included Vermont (43 percent), New Hampshire (40 percent), Delaware (34 percent), and Rhode Island (33 percent). The states with the lowest percentage of revenues from tuition were Hawaii (8 percent), New Mexico (8 percent), and the District of Columbia (10 percent). Some of these states came out on the opposite extreme of the list when the states were ranked by percent of revenue from

---

[4] *Wages, Amenities, & Cost of Living, Theory and Measurement of Geographical Differentials,* Research Associates of Washington, Kent Halstead, Washington, D.C., 1992.

[5] U.S. Department of Education, National Center for Education Statistics, *Digest of Education Statistics, 1997.*

state and local appropriations, grants, and contracts. The states with the highest proportion of revenue from state and local sources were the District of Columbia (74 percent), Hawaii (62 percent), and Florida (55 percent). The states with the lowest proportions of revenues from state and local sources were Virginia (27 percent), Pennsylvania (27 percent), New Hampshire (22 percent), and Vermont (14 percent).

Tuition and Fees

States vary widely in their policies regarding tuition, room, and board for students attending public institutions. Some states attempt to make tuition relatively inexpensive by providing large appropriations, while others have higher tuition. As a result, the average cost for an academic year of undergraduate education ranges widely. In 1996–97, the average cost of tuition, room, and board at a public 4-year institution, excluding books, travel, and miscellaneous expenses was $7,334 (table 81). The comparable cost at private 4-year colleges was $18,442. The average charge for tuition only was $2,987 at public 4-year colleges, $1,276 at public 2-year colleges, and $12,881 at private 4-year colleges.

The average costs for tuition, room, and board for public 4-year colleges exceeded $9,000 in Massachusetts, New Hampshire, Maryland, Connecticut, New York, Pennsylvania, Rhode Island, New Jersey, and Vermont. Average costs were less than $5,500 in Tennessee, Kentucky, North Carolina, New Mexico, Arkansas, and Oklahoma. The District of Columbia had the lowest tuition, but did not provide room and board information. The financial burden of paying for a college education reflects an interaction between the amount of the college costs and the ability to pay them.

The divergence in public 2-year tuition state averages was very large. The average tuition in public 2-year colleges was over $2,500 in South Dakota, New Hampshire, Maine, New York and Vermont. At the other extreme, North Carolina and California charged under $600 for a year's tuition. The ratio of the 3 highest to the 3 lowest states was 3.2 for public 4-year average tuition and 5.5 for public 2-year average tuition, indicating a relatively wider range for tuition for public 2-year institutions than for public 4-year institutions.

Expenditures

State expenditures for colleges and universities are heavily influenced by the size of the state population and the scope of higher education institutions. Expenditures of colleges and universities may be computed on a per student basis to compensate for the large differences in sizes of state education systems. For comparisons in this publication, the expenditure

data were restricted to educational and general expenditures, which exclude expenditures for university hospitals, dormitories, food service operations, bookstores, and other independent operations. Educational and general expenditure data are more appropriate for per student comparisons across types of institutions because they limit the expenditure categories to items that are more directly focused on education of students, rather than including all categories under financial control of the institutions.

During the 1994–95 academic year, the average educational and general expenditure per full-time equivalent student was $13,931 (table 83). The average for private 4-year colleges was the highest at $21,202 compared to $15,352 at public 4-year colleges. The averages for the 2-year colleges were substantially lower, with the public 2-year average at $6,346. Some of the institutional characteristics explored in this report directly affect these expenditures, including the low faculty and staff ratios at 4-year colleges and the relatively higher emphasis on postbaccalaureate education at private 4-year colleges. The 2-year college data are influenced by the high staff ratios and the lower faculty salaries.

The educational and general expenditures per student at public 4-year colleges varied significantly from state to state during the 1994–95 academic year (figure 20). There was some degree of grouping around the average, with about two-thirds of the states having averages that were within about 15 percent of the national average. The 3 states with the highest expenditure per FTE student, Hawaii, Washington, and Vermont, spent about 2.2 times the lowest 3 spending states, Oklahoma, West Virginia, and South Dakota. The spending range for the public 2-year colleges was at least as wide (figure 21). About half of the states spent within 15 percent of the national average. The extremes represented a wider range. The highest spending states, Alaska, Montana, and Delaware, spent 2.5 times more than the lowest spending states of Oklahoma, Louisiana, and Kentucky. The U.S. Service Schools had relatively high expenditures because of their unique programs and were excluded from the analysis.

Over the 5-year period from 1989–90 to 1994–95, educational and general expenditures per full-time equivalent student for public institutions rose about 6 percent after adjusting for the rate of inflation for colleges. Expenditures per student at private colleges rose by 12 percent, after adjusting for inflation (table 83). There were wide differences among the states in the rates of change in expenditures per student over the time period. Most states had increases, and a few states, Montana, Connecticut, Oregon, and Mississippi, had increases over 15 percent in expenditure per student in public institutions. Nine states and the District of Columbia had declines.

Figure 19. – Average tuition at public 4-year institutions of higher education (in-state): 1996-97

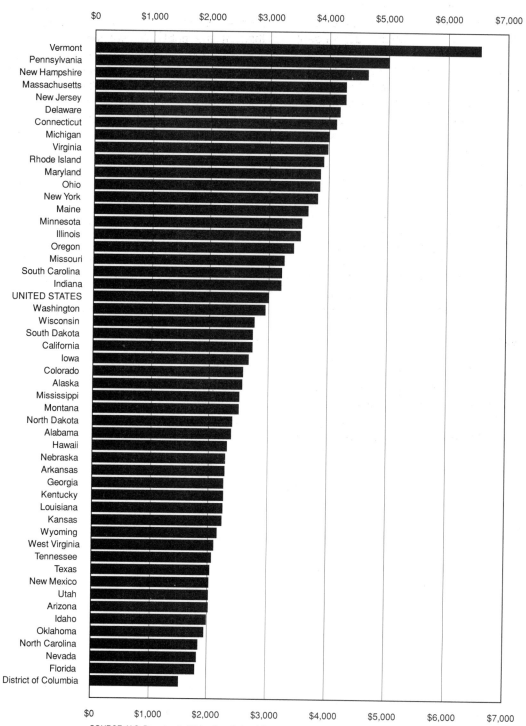

SOURCE: U.S. Department of Education, National Center for Education Statistics, Integrated Postsecondary Education Data System (IPEDS), "Fall Enrollment" and "Institutional Characteristics" survey. (This figure was prepared February 1998.)

The inflation-adjusted decline in educational and general expenditure per student at public institutions was affected by the increases in student enrollment (tables 55, 56, and 86). Even though the educational and general expenditures themselves rose by nearly 12 percent between 1989–90 and 1994–95 after adjusting for inflation, the number of FTE students rose by 6 percent. The net effect of these changes was an increase of 6 percent in the spending per student after adjusting for inflation.

Educational and general expenditures per student at private institutions rose 12 percent between 1989–90 and 1994–95, after adjustment for inflation. Thirty-nine states and the District of Columbia had an increase, but 11 states had decreases. States with particularly large percent changes may have had an administrative change, such as the opening of a new institution (table 83).

The expenditure data may be examined separately to gauge the general financial environment, without taking into account enrollment changes. Only the educational and general expenditure changes are discussed here because the current-fund expenditures show approximately the same patterns and are affected by the relatively rapid rises in hospital and other expenditures, which are not directly related to student outlays.

Educational and general expenditures at public institutions showed a pattern of increases through the 1980s and early 1990s (table 89). Between 1984–85 and 1994–95, expenditures rose by 30 percent after adjusting for inflation. The increases were significant in both halves of the 10 year period with about 16 percent in the first five years and 12 percent in the second five years. Many states had sizeable increases in expenditures, with 13 states having increases of 40 percent or more, after adjusting for inflation. The largest increases were in Nevada (88 percent), New Mexico (63 percent), and Georgia (58 percent). Only Alaska and the District of Columbia had declines.

The educational and general expenditures at the private institutions increased at a more rapid rate than at the public institutions (table 91). Between 1984–85 and 1994–95, educational and general expenditures at private institutions rose by 48 percent, after adjusting for inflation. The increase was more rapid during the early part of the 10-year period (24 percent), than in the latter half of the period (19 percent). However, both rates of increase exceeded the comparable rates for public institutions. Thirty-four of the states had increases of more than 40.0 percent, and only one state, Delaware, had a decrease. Some of the percentage changes for states show unusual patterns resulting from openings and closures of institutions, particularly in those states with very few private institutions. Despite these limitations, the data show widespread and sizeable increases in private college expenditures, particularly during the mid-1980s.

These higher education data show a steadily expanding enterprise. Recent trends in enrollments show more rapid rises at private 4-year colleges than at public 2-year or 4-year colleges. Numbers of degrees have increased, particularly at the postbaccalaureate level. The expenditures have shown increases and have maintained pace with the increases in public college enrollments and the relatively high inflation rates for colleges (Higher Education Price Index).

Figure 20. – Educational and general expenditures per full-time-equivalent student in public 4-year institutions of higher education, by state: 1994–95

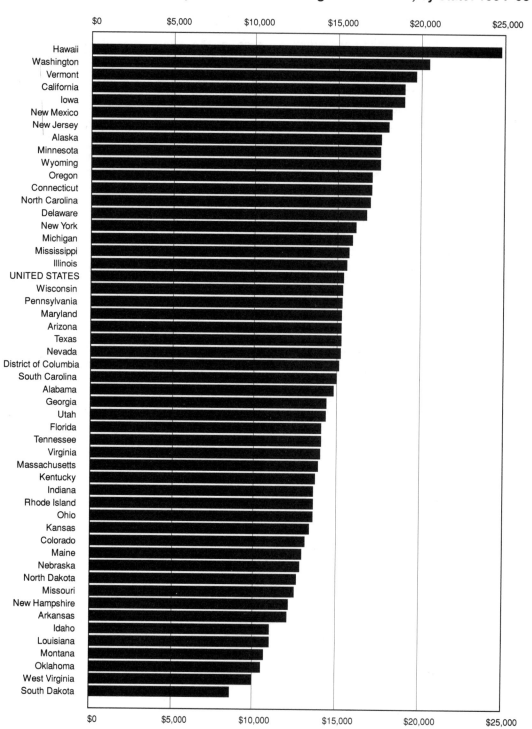

SOURCE: U.S. Department of Education, National Center for Education Statistics, Integrated Postsecondary Education Data System (IPEDS), "Finance" survey. (This figure was prepared February 1998.)

Figure 21. – Educational and general expenditures per full-time-equivalent student in public 2-year institutions of higher education, by state: 1994–95

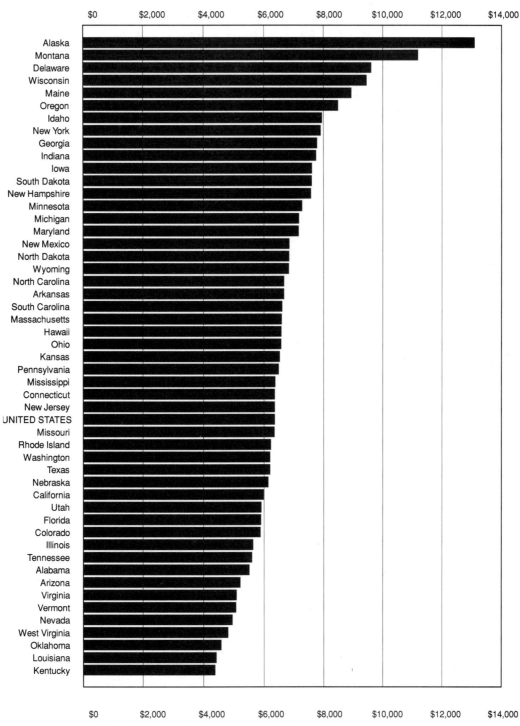

NOTE: The District of Columbia does not have any public 2-year institutions.

SOURCE: U.S. Department of Education, National Center for Education Statistics, Integrated Postsecondary Education Data System (IPEDS), "Finance" survey. (This figure was prepared February 1998.)

Table 43.—Estimated total population and total fall enrollment in higher education, by state: 1980 to 1996

[Numbers in thousands]

State or other area	Total resident population [1]						Total fall enrollment in higher education		
	1980 [2]	1985 [3]	1990 [2]	1994 [3]	1995 [3]	1996 [3]	1980	1985	1990
1	2	3	4	5	6	7	8	9	10
United States	226,546	237,924	248,710	260,372	262,890	265,284	12,096.9	12,247.0	13,818.6
Alabama	3,894	3,973	4,041	4,215	4,246	4,273	164.3	179.3	218.6
Alaska	402	532	550	601	603	607	21.3	27.5	29.8
Arizona	2,718	3,184	3,665	4,092	4,305	4,428	202.7	216.9	264.1
Arkansas	2,286	2,327	2,351	2,455	2,485	2,510	77.6	78.0	90.4
California	23,668	26,441	29,760	31,362	31,565	31,878	1,791.0	1,650.4	1,808.7
Colorado	2,890	3,209	3,294	3,663	3,748	3,823	162.9	161.3	227.1
Connecticut	3,108	3,201	3,287	3,273	3,271	3,274	159.6	159.3	168.6
Delaware	594	618	666	708	717	725	32.9	31.9	42.0
District of Columbia	638	635	607	568	555	543	86.7	78.2	79.6
Florida	9,746	11,351	12,938	13,965	14,184	14,400	411.9	451.4	588.1
Georgia	5,463	5,963	6,478	7,063	7,209	7,353	184.2	196.8	251.8
Hawaii	965	1,040	1,108	1,173	1,179	1,184	47.2	49.9	56.4
Idaho	944	994	1,007	1,136	1,166	1,189	43.0	42.7	51.9
Illinois	11,427	11,400	11,431	11,734	11,790	11,847	644.2	678.7	729.2
Indiana	5,490	5,459	5,544	5,750	5,797	5,841	247.3	250.6	284.8
Iowa	2,914	2,830	2,777	2,832	2,843	2,852	140.4	152.9	170.5
Kansas	2,364	2,427	2,478	2,550	2,564	2,572	136.6	141.4	163.7
Kentucky	3,661	3,695	3,685	3,826	3,857	3,884	143.1	141.7	177.9
Louisiana	4,206	4,408	4,220	4,315	4,338	4,351	160.1	177.2	186.8
Maine	1,125	1,163	1,228	1,238	1,239	1,243	43.3	52.2	57.2
Maryland	4,217	4,413	4,781	5,000	5,039	5,072	225.5	231.6	259.7
Massachusetts	5,737	5,881	6,016	6,042	6,071	6,092	418.4	421.2	417.8
Michigan	9,262	9,076	9,295	9,486	9,538	9,594	520.1	507.3	569.8
Minnesota	4,076	4,184	4,375	4,572	4,615	4,658	206.7	221.2	253.8
Mississippi	2,521	2,588	2,573	2,668	2,696	2,716	102.4	101.2	122.9
Missouri	4,917	5,000	5,117	5,275	5,319	5,359	234.4	241.1	289.9
Montana	787	822	799	857	870	879	35.2	36.0	35.9
Nebraska	1,570	1,585	1,578	1,626	1,639	1,652	89.5	97.8	112.8
Nevada	800	951	1,202	1,464	1,533	1,603	40.5	43.7	61.7
New Hampshire	921	997	1,109	1,135	1,148	1,162	46.8	52.3	59.5
New Jersey	7,365	7,566	7,730	7,906	7,950	7,988	321.6	297.7	324.3
New Mexico	1,303	1,438	1,515	1,659	1,690	1,713	58.3	68.3	85.5
New York	17,558	17,792	17,990	18,197	18,191	18,185	992.2	1,000.1	1,048.3
North Carolina	5,882	6,254	6,629	7,079	7,202	7,323	287.5	327.3	352.1
North Dakota	653	677	639	640	642	644	34.1	37.9	37.9
Ohio	10,798	10,735	10,847	11,097	11,134	11,173	489.1	514.7	557.7
Oklahoma	3,025	3,271	3,146	3,254	3,275	3,301	160.3	169.2	173.2
Oregon	2,633	2,673	2,842	3,094	3,149	3,204	157.5	138.0	165.7
Pennsylvania	11,864	11,771	11,882	12,058	12,060	12,056	507.7	533.2	604.1
Rhode Island	947	969	1,003	996	992	990	66.9	69.9	78.3
South Carolina	3,122	3,303	3,487	3,643	3,667	3,699	132.5	131.9	159.3
South Dakota	691	698	696	724	730	732	32.8	32.8	34.2
Tennessee	4,591	4,715	4,877	5,175	5,247	5,320	204.6	194.8	226.2
Texas	14,229	16,273	16,987	18,434	18,801	19,128	701.4	769.7	901.4
Utah	1,461	1,643	1,723	1,910	1,958	2,000	94.0	104.0	121.3
Vermont	511	530	563	581	585	589	30.6	31.4	36.4
Virginia	5,347	5,715	6,187	6,550	6,615	6,675	280.5	292.4	353.4
Washington	4,132	4,400	4,867	5,351	5,448	5,533	303.6	231.6	263.4
West Virginia	1,950	1,907	1,793	1,822	1,825	1,826	82.0	76.7	84.8
Wisconsin	4,706	4,748	4,892	5,084	5,122	5,160	269.1	275.1	299.8
Wyoming	470	500	454	476	479	481	21.1	24.2	31.3
U.S. Service Schools	—	—	—	—	—	—	49.8	54.7	48.7
Outlying areas	—	—	—	—	—	—	137.7	164.9	164.6
American Samoa	—	—	—	—	—	—	1.0	0.8	1.2
Federated States of Micronesia	—	—	—	—	—	—	—	—	1.0
Guam	—	—	—	—	—	—	3.2	4.6	4.7
Marshall Islands	—	—	—	—	—	—	—	—	—
Northern Marianas	—	—	—	—	—	—	—	0.3	0.7
Palau	—	—	—	—	—	—	—	—	0.5
Puerto Rico	—	—	—	—	—	—	131.2	155.9	154.1
Trust Territory of the Pacific	—	—	—	—	—	—	0.2	0.7	—
Virgin Islands	—	—	—	—	—	—	2.1	2.6	2.5

Table 43.—Estimated total population and total fall enrollment in higher education, by state: 1980 to 1996—Continued

[Numbers in thousands]

State or other area	Total fall enrollment in higher education			Enrollment as a percent of resident population					
	1994	1995	1996	1980	1985	1990	1994	1995	1996
1	11	12	13	14	15	16	17	18	19
United States	14,278.8	14,261.8	14,300.3	5.3	5.1	5.6	5.5	5.4	5.4
Alabama	229.5	225.6	219.5	4.2	4.5	5.4	5.4	5.3	5.1
Alaska	28.8	29.3	28.8	5.3	5.2	5.4	4.8	4.9	4.8
Arizona	274.9	274.0	276.8	7.5	6.8	7.2	6.7	6.4	6.3
Arkansas	96.3	98.2	100.7	3.4	3.4	3.8	3.9	4.0	4.0
California	1,835.8	1,817.0	1,882.6	7.6	6.2	6.1	5.9	5.8	5.9
Colorado	241.3	242.7	242.9	5.6	5.0	6.9	6.6	6.5	6.4
Connecticut	160.0	157.7	155.4	5.1	5.0	5.1	4.9	4.8	4.7
Delaware	44.2	44.3	44.8	5.5	5.2	6.3	6.2	6.2	6.2
District of Columbia	77.3	77.3	74.2	13.6	12.3	13.1	13.6	13.9	13.7
Florida	634.2	637.3	641.2	4.2	4.0	4.5	4.5	4.5	4.5
Georgia	308.6	314.7	318.0	3.4	3.3	3.9	4.4	4.4	4.3
Hawaii	64.3	63.2	61.4	4.9	4.8	5.1	5.5	5.4	5.2
Idaho	60.4	59.6	59.9	4.6	4.3	5.2	5.3	5.1	5.0
Illinois	731.4	717.9	721.0	5.6	6.0	6.4	6.2	6.1	6.1
Indiana	292.3	289.6	286.3	4.5	4.6	5.1	5.1	5.0	4.9
Iowa	172.5	173.8	177.0	4.8	5.4	6.1	6.1	6.1	6.2
Kansas	170.6	177.6	172.4	5.8	5.8	6.6	6.7	6.9	6.7
Kentucky	182.6	178.9	177.7	3.9	3.8	4.8	4.8	4.6	4.6
Louisiana	203.6	203.9	203.5	3.8	4.0	4.4	4.7	4.7	4.7
Maine	56.7	56.5	55.6	3.8	4.5	4.7	4.6	4.6	4.5
Maryland	266.2	266.3	260.8	5.3	5.2	5.4	5.3	5.3	5.1
Massachusetts	416.5	413.8	410.3	7.3	7.2	6.9	6.9	6.8	6.7
Michigan	551.3	548.3	547.0	5.6	5.6	6.1	5.8	5.7	5.7
Minnesota	289.3	280.8	275.3	5.1	5.3	5.8	6.3	6.1	5.9
Mississippi	120.9	122.7	126.2	4.1	3.9	4.8	4.5	4.6	4.6
Missouri	293.8	291.5	290.5	4.8	4.8	5.7	5.6	5.5	5.4
Montana	40.1	42.7	43.1	4.5	4.4	4.5	4.7	4.9	4.9
Nebraska	116.0	115.7	119.3	5.7	6.2	7.2	7.1	7.1	7.2
Nevada	64.1	67.8	73.5	5.1	4.6	5.1	4.4	4.4	4.6
New Hampshire	62.8	64.3	64.5	5.1	5.2	5.4	5.5	5.6	5.5
New Jersey	335.5	333.8	328.2	4.4	3.9	4.2	4.2	4.2	4.1
New Mexico	101.9	102.4	103.5	4.5	4.7	5.6	6.1	6.1	6.0
New York	1,057.8	1,041.6	1,027.9	5.7	5.6	5.8	5.8	5.7	5.7
North Carolina	369.4	372.0	373.2	4.9	5.2	5.3	5.2	5.2	5.1
North Dakota	40.2	40.4	40.6	5.2	5.6	5.9	6.3	6.3	6.3
Ohio	549.3	540.3	537.5	4.5	4.8	5.1	5.0	4.9	4.8
Oklahoma	185.2	180.7	177.3	5.3	5.2	5.5	5.7	5.5	5.4
Oregon	164.4	167.1	165.2	6.0	5.2	5.8	5.3	5.3	5.2
Pennsylvania	611.2	617.8	622.0	4.3	4.5	5.1	5.1	5.1	5.2
Rhode Island	74.7	74.1	72.4	7.1	7.2	7.8	7.5	7.5	7.3
South Carolina	173.1	174.1	174.3	4.2	4.0	4.6	4.8	4.7	4.7
South Dakota	37.8	36.7	35.4	4.7	4.7	4.9	5.2	5.0	4.8
Tennessee	243.0	246.0	247.0	4.5	4.1	4.6	4.7	4.7	4.6
Texas	954.5	952.5	955.4	4.9	4.7	5.3	5.2	5.1	5.0
Utah	146.2	147.3	151.6	6.4	6.3	7.0	7.7	7.5	7.6
Vermont	35.4	35.1	35.1	6.0	5.9	6.5	6.1	6.0	6.0
Virginia	354.1	355.9	353.8	5.2	5.1	5.7	5.4	5.4	5.3
Washington	284.7	285.8	292.2	7.3	5.3	5.4	5.3	5.2	5.3
West Virginia	87.7	86.0	85.7	4.2	4.0	4.7	4.8	4.7	4.7
Wisconsin	303.9	300.2	299.1	5.7	5.8	6.1	6.0	5.9	5.8
Wyoming	30.7	30.2	30.8	4.5	4.8	6.9	6.4	6.3	6.4
U.S. Service Schools	51.9	88.5	81.7	—	—	—	—	—	—
Outlying areas	170.7	183.7	181.7	—	—	—	—	—	—
American Samoa	1.2	1.2	1.2	—	—	—	—	—	—
Federated States of Micronesia	1.4	1.3	1.4	—	—	—	—	—	—
Guam	6.4	6.0	5.3	—	—	—	—	—	—
Marshall Islands	0.4	0.4	0.4	—	—	—	—	—	—
Northern Marianas	1.3	1.0	1.1	—	—	—	—	—	—
Palau	0.4	0.4	0.3	—	—	—	—	—	—
Puerto Rico	156.4	170.3	168.9	—	\	—	—	—	—
Trust Territory of the Pacific	—	—	—	—	—	—	—	—	—
Virgin Islands	3.1	3.1	2.9	—	—	—	—	—	—

[1] Includes Armed Forces residing in each state.
[2] As of April 1.
[3] Estimates as of July 1.
—Data not available or not applicable.

NOTE.—Some data have been revised from previously published figures. Because of rounding, details may not add to totals.

SOURCE: U.S. Department of Education, National Center for Education Statistics, Higher Education General Information Survey (HEGIS), "Fall Enrollment in Colleges and Universities"; and Integrated Postsecondary Education Data System (IPEDS), "Fall Enrollment" surveys; and U.S. Department of Commerce, Bureau of the Census, Current Population Reports, Series P-25, No. 1095, CPH-L-74 (1990 data) and forthcoming state level P-25 reports. (This table was prepared January 1998.)

Table 44.—Fall full-time enrollment as a percentage of total enrollment of institutions of higher education, by type and control of institution and by state: 1996

State or other area	Full-time enrollment, by type and control					Full-time as a percent of total enrollment, by type and control				
	Total	Public 4-year	Public 2-year	Private 4-year	Private 2-year	Total	Public 4-year	Public 2-year	Private 4-year	Private 2-year
1	2	3	4	5	6	7	8	9	10	11
United States	8,213,490	4,106,094	1,858,080	2,120,774	128,542	57.4	70.7	35.2	70.8	60.0
Alabama	150,321	88,533	42,833	18,214	741	68.5	72.1	58.1	83.3	67.4
Alaska	11,884	11,078	105	468	233	41.2	40.9	14.0	67.6	71.5
Arizona	131,139	72,507	38,926	18,767	939	47.4	70.7	25.8	83.8	97.7
Arkansas	67,715	46,283	11,333	9,742	357	67.3	74.5	41.4	90.0	87.9
California	887,392	389,789	307,350	177,667	12,586	47.1	77.2	27.4	73.0	88.3
Colorado	131,065	87,847	21,349	20,319	1,550	53.9	66.4	27.8	63.1	99.3
Connecticut	82,904	34,406	9,931	37,669	898	53.4	60.8	24.2	67.0	57.7
Delaware	26,194	18,316	4,500	3,378	—	58.4	74.1	37.9	40.9	—
District of Columbia	49,352	2,613	—	46,739	—	66.5	35.0	—	70.0	—
Florida	309,059	133,028	101,626	69,086	5,319	48.2	63.0	31.8	66.2	91.2
Georgia	213,966	113,990	42,569	53,536	3,871	67.3	71.7	47.2	83.3	86.8
Hawaii	35,325	15,195	10,896	9,234	—	57.5	70.1	42.4	65.9	—
Idaho	40,834	26,608	4,503	1,827	7,896	68.2	64.4	56.0	76.4	97.2
Illinois	370,915	139,720	106,319	121,482	3,394	51.4	72.7	31.3	65.9	82.3
Indiana	191,480	123,948	14,151	50,919	2,462	66.9	67.8	37.2	82.3	70.1
Iowa	121,858	53,426	32,176	35,474	782	68.8	80.3	54.2	70.9	74.2
Kansas	95,679	60,869	22,256	11,933	621	55.5	70.8	32.0	74.4	71.1
Kentucky	117,931	74,344	20,887	20,433	2,267	66.3	71.3	48.5	73.7	86.9
Louisiana	144,796	111,859	12,250	20,059	628	71.1	76.0	44.8	72.9	44.2
Maine	31,751	17,171	3,072	10,057	1,451	57.1	55.4	44.5	63.1	80.1
Maryland	128,218	72,741	31,431	23,157	889	49.2	64.3	30.2	54.7	75.3
Massachusetts	261,341	63,839	28,100	165,514	3,888	63.7	62.7	39.3	72.0	56.1
Michigan	278,331	175,049	53,206	49,620	456	50.9	67.5	26.7	57.5	27.0
Minnesota	164,246	70,441	48,497	42,302	3,006	59.7	59.8	53.5	68.3	63.0
Mississippi	93,466	48,096	37,159	7,616	595	74.0	79.4	68.4	71.8	83.2
Missouri	169,674	80,101	25,483	60,583	3,507	58.4	68.3	35.4	62.5	81.7
Montana	32,943	25,516	3,904	3,148	375	76.4	80.5	61.9	73.0	45.1
Nebraska	68,317	40,597	12,653	15,067	—	57.3	70.9	29.8	76.9	—
Nevada	23,834	16,920	5,719	1,171	24	32.4	54.6	14.0	77.1	100.0
New Hampshire	39,464	18,723	2,886	15,588	2,267	61.2	70.5	29.4	64.3	58.6
New Jersey	176,977	83,637	54,053	35,816	3,471	53.9	60.8	42.5	61.3	66.9
New Mexico	51,420	31,446	15,095	3,828	1,051	49.7	64.4	30.9	78.7	100.0
New York	665,143	218,279	134,227	292,342	20,295	64.7	66.4	55.1	67.8	83.3
North Carolina	240,848	117,760	64,694	57,645	749	64.5	75.2	44.2	83.3	74.2
North Dakota	32,305	22,757	6,212	3,092	244	79.7	81.1	71.3	88.0	88.7
Ohio	337,427	190,255	56,546	84,729	5,897	62.8	73.6	38.5	71.3	43.9
Oklahoma	107,364	65,360	24,294	15,900	1,810	60.6	69.7	40.1	76.3	88.9
Oregon	91,673	47,811	25,477	18,385	—	55.5	74.2	33.1	77.4	—
Pennsylvania	391,009	181,068	37,135	156,554	16,252	62.9	78.0	36.1	71.2	24.3
Rhode Island	46,371	13,939	4,866	27,566	—	64.0	62.6	31.9	78.9	—
South Carolina	111,272	63,436	25,843	20,827	1,166	63.8	72.6	42.4	84.6	88.7
South Dakota	25,761	20,864	129	4,709	59	72.8	73.6	65.5	71.3	28.9
Tennessee	161,898	84,055	32,425	43,929	1,489	65.5	72.8	41.2	86.0	79.2
Texas	521,478	287,455	148,560	79,890	5,573	54.6	69.4	35.0	71.9	90.1
Utah	96,132	49,263	14,007	31,805	1,057	63.4	60.6	42.6	87.9	84.2
Vermont	24,171	12,304	611	11,099	157	68.9	79.0	13.4	75.4	67.1
Virginia	202,230	123,645	34,465	40,984	3,136	57.2	73.7	27.7	72.2	68.0
Washington	179,599	73,346	76,080	27,981	2,192	61.5	84.0	46.2	74.1	86.8
West Virginia	59,658	47,223	3,533	8,181	721	69.6	69.4	52.6	80.3	96.5
Wisconsin	182,266	111,738	34,375	34,743	1,410	60.9	79.3	33.2	65.9	80.0
Wyoming	17,563	8,636	8,116	—	811	57.0	76.8	43.3	—	100.0
U.S. Service Schools	19,531	18,264	1,267	—	—	23.9	98.5	2.0	—	—
Outlying areas	138,062	54,679	7,767	68,177	7,439	76.0	80.9	63.2	73.4	83.1
American Samoa	877	—	877	—	—	70.8	—	70.8	—	—
Federated States of Micronesia	947	—	947	—	—	67.8	—	67.8	—	—
Guam	2,493	2,106	387	—	—	46.7	62.3	19.8	—	—
Marshall Islands	234	—	234	—	—	54.3	—	54.3	—	—
Northern Marianas	490	—	490	—	—	44.7	—	44.7	—	—
Palau	255	—	255	—	—	76.8	—	76.8	—	—
Puerto Rico	131,437	51,244	4,577	68,177	7,439	77.8	83.6	78.3	73.4	83.1
Virgin Islands	1,329	1,329	—	—	—	45.9	45.9	—	—	—

—Data not available or not applicable.

SOURCE: U.S. Department of Education, National Center for Education Statistics, Integrated Postsecondary Education Data System (IPEDS), "Fall Enrollment, 1996" survey. (This table was prepared January 1998.)

Table 45.—Fall female enrollment as a percentage of total enrollment of institutions of higher education, by type and control of institution and by state: 1996

State or other area	Female enrollment, by type and control					Female as a percent of total enrollment, by type and control				
	Total	Public 4-year	Public 2-year	Private 4-year	Private 2-year	Total	Public 4-year	Public 2-year	Private 4-year	Private 2-year
1	2	3	4	5	6	7	8	9	10	11
United States	7,956,263	3,160,127	3,042,507	1,646,807	106,822	55.6	54.4	57.6	55.0	49.9
Alabama	123,813	67,603	42,757	12,710	743	56.4	55.1	58.0	58.1	67.6
Alaska	17,270	16,158	496	417	199	59.9	59.7	66.0	60.3	61.0
Arizona	152,097	54,164	86,913	10,822	198	54.9	52.8	57.6	48.3	20.6
Arkansas	58,147	35,016	16,950	5,970	211	57.7	56.4	61.9	55.2	52.0
California	1,041,332	273,982	631,239	127,633	8,478	55.3	54.3	56.4	52.4	59.5
Colorado	132,415	70,512	44,584	16,169	1,150	54.5	53.3	58.0	50.2	73.7
Connecticut	87,769	31,389	25,002	30,313	1,065	56.5	55.5	60.9	53.9	68.4
Delaware	26,150	13,874	7,161	5,115	—	58.3	56.2	60.3	61.9	—
District of Columbia	41,208	4,324	—	36,884	—	55.5	58.0	—	55.2	—
Florida	364,210	116,937	191,077	52,804	3,392	56.8	55.4	59.7	50.6	58.1
Georgia	182,668	89,490	55,036	35,575	2,567	57.4	56.3	61.0	55.4	57.6
Hawaii	33,949	12,031	14,536	7,382	—	55.3	55.5	56.6	52.7	—
Idaho	33,147	22,236	4,878	1,421	4,612	55.3	53.8	60.6	59.5	56.8
Illinois	404,918	103,622	198,518	99,910	2,868	56.2	53.9	58.4	54.2	69.5
Indiana	155,171	98,515	21,087	33,143	2,426	54.2	53.8	55.5	53.6	69.1
Iowa	96,354	33,190	34,129	28,174	861	54.4	49.9	57.5	56.3	81.7
Kansas	94,894	45,321	39,942	9,079	552	55.1	52.7	57.5	56.6	63.2
Kentucky	103,905	58,578	27,911	15,867	1,549	58.5	56.2	64.7	57.2	59.4
Louisiana	117,920	84,574	17,602	14,613	1,131	57.9	57.4	64.4	53.1	79.6
Maine	33,334	18,391	3,192	10,322	1,429	59.9	59.4	46.2	64.7	78.9
Maryland	152,305	62,698	64,511	24,340	756	58.4	55.4	62.0	57.5	64.0
Massachusetts	231,098	54,858	44,334	126,492	5,414	56.3	53.9	61.9	55.0	78.1
Michigan	307,677	140,785	114,635	50,884	1,373	56.3	54.3	57.4	59.0	81.4
Minnesota	153,723	64,356	49,258	37,251	2,858	55.8	54.6	54.3	60.1	59.9
Mississippi	72,339	33,443	32,198	6,288	410	57.3	55.2	59.2	59.2	57.3
Missouri	163,868	65,417	43,917	52,387	2,147	56.4	55.8	60.9	54.0	50.0
Montana	23,135	15,985	3,990	2,698	462	53.6	50.4	63.3	62.5	55.6
Nebraska	65,592	30,168	23,869	11,555	—	55.0	52.7	56.2	59.0	—
Nevada	40,808	16,663	23,268	877	—	55.5	53.8	56.8	57.8	—
New Hampshire	37,125	15,499	5,389	13,491	2,746	57.6	58.4	54.9	55.7	71.0
New Jersey	185,674	76,317	74,778	32,106	2,473	56.6	55.5	58.8	55.0	47.6
New Mexico	60,174	26,794	29,856	2,861	663	58.1	54.9	61.2	58.8	63.1
New York	591,350	190,053	142,618	242,156	16,523	57.5	57.8	58.5	56.2	67.8
North Carolina	213,204	86,230	88,280	37,998	696	57.1	55.1	60.3	54.9	69.0
North Dakota	20,498	13,867	4,374	2,098	159	50.5	49.4	50.2	59.7	57.8
Ohio	297,454	138,220	89,715	65,028	4,491	55.3	53.5	61.1	54.8	33.4
Oklahoma	96,415	49,774	35,513	10,464	664	54.4	53.1	58.6	50.2	32.6
Oregon	89,278	33,691	42,571	13,016	—	54.1	52.3	55.3	54.8	—
Pennsylvania	329,142	122,862	62,144	122,140	21,996	52.9	52.9	60.4	55.6	32.8
Rhode Island	40,099	13,394	9,511	17,194	—	55.4	60.2	62.4	49.2	—
South Carolina	102,211	50,403	36,887	14,144	777	58.6	57.7	60.5	57.4	59.1
South Dakota	19,777	15,360	150	4,119	148	55.9	54.1	76.1	62.4	72.5
Tennessee	139,001	63,456	47,098	27,363	1,084	56.3	55.0	59.9	53.6	57.6
Texas	518,677	220,730	238,962	57,069	1,916	54.3	53.3	56.3	51.3	31.0
Utah	76,038	41,094	15,958	18,069	917	50.1	50.5	48.5	49.9	73.0
Vermont	20,308	8,237	3,366	8,622	83	57.9	52.9	73.8	58.6	35.5
Virginia	200,019	91,666	73,108	32,904	2,341	56.5	54.6	58.7	58.0	50.7
Washington	163,645	45,862	94,843	21,941	999	56.0	52.5	57.6	58.1	39.5
West Virginia	47,752	36,866	4,289	6,052	545	55.7	54.2	63.8	59.4	73.0
Wisconsin	166,730	76,874	58,242	30,877	737	55.7	54.5	56.2	58.6	41.8
Wyoming	17,675	5,842	11,820	—	13	57.4	51.9	63.1	—	1.6
U.S. Service Schools	12,801	2,756	10,045	—	—	15.7	14.9	15.9	—	—
Outlying areas	110,925	43,058	6,840	55,121	5,906	61.1	63.7	55.6	59.4	66.0
American Samoa	589	—	589	—	—	47.5	—	47.5	—	—
Federated States of Micronesia	741	—	741	—	—	53.1	—	53.1	—	—
Guam	3,121	2,041	1,080	—	—	58.5	60.3	55.3	—	—
Marshall Islands	191	—	191	—	—	44.3	—	44.3	—	—
Northern Marianas	652	—	652	—	—	59.5	—	59.5	—	—
Palau	161	—	161	—	—	48.5	—	48.5	—	—
Puerto Rico	103,271	38,818	3,426	55,121	5,906	61.1	63.3	58.6	59.4	66.0
Virgin Islands	2,199	2,199	—	—	—	75.9	75.9	—	—	—

—Data not available or not applicable.

SOURCE: U.S. Department of Education, National Center for Education Statistics, Integrated Postsecondary Education Data System (IPEDS), "Fall Enrollment, 1996" survey. (This table was prepared January 1998.)

Table 46.—Percentage distribution of total fall enrollment and number of institutions of higher education, by enrollment size of institution and state: 1996

State or other area	Number of institutions							Percentage distribution of students						
	Total	Under 1,000	1,000 to 2,499	2,500 to 4,999	5,000 to 9,999	10,000 to 19,999	20,000 or more	Total	Under 1,000	1,000 to 2,499	2,500 to 4,999	5,000 to 9,999	10,000 to 19,999	20,000 or more
1	2	3	4	5	6	7	8	9	10	11	12	13	14	15
United States	3,534	1,258	864	558	459	272	123	100.0	3.8	10.1	13.5	22.6	26.2	23.8
Alabama	70	22	21	12	11	3	1	100.0	4.3	16.0	19.6	29.6	20.5	9.9
Alaska	8	5	0	1	1	1	0	100.0	6.1	(¹)	12.0	26.2	55.6	(¹)
Arizona	44	14	7	7	9	3	4	100.0	1.9	4.0	9.2	21.7	17.5	45.6
Arkansas	38	15	11	7	3	2	0	100.0	8.7	19.1	23.1	24.1	25.0	(¹)
California	322	133	42	22	52	51	22	100.0	3.1	3.7	4.6	20.2	39.1	29.3
Colorado	56	21	10	8	11	4	2	100.0	3.2	7.3	13.2	32.4	21.9	22.0
Connecticut	42	10	11	8	9	3	1	100.0	1.8	12.4	17.8	32.0	22.0	14.0
Delaware	9	0	4	3	1	0	1	100.0	(¹)	14.1	23.2	15.0	(¹)	47.7
District of Columbia	19	10	3	0	2	4	0	100.0	4.9	6.5	(¹)	18.0	70.6	(¹)
Florida	104	43	19	7	12	13	10	100.0	2.9	5.3	3.4	13.4	27.7	47.4
Georgia	116	46	37	18	8	5	2	100.0	8.5	19.0	18.1	16.8	21.0	16.6
Hawaii	17	5	4	4	3	1	0	100.0	2.3	12.6	20.1	35.3	29.7	(¹)
Idaho	12	4	1	3	1	3	0	100.0	2.0	2.6	18.4	12.9	64.0	(¹)
Illinois	158	59	26	26	23	19	5	100.0	3.3	6.1	12.4	23.1	36.0	19.0
Indiana	78	30	24	10	7	4	3	100.0	5.2	13.5	11.8	17.1	18.0	34.4
Iowa	57	17	21	12	2	3	2	100.0	4.5	17.6	21.8	6.5	19.5	30.1
Kansas	54	22	14	8	6	3	1	100.0	6.9	13.8	15.5	21.5	27.9	14.4
Kentucky	57	23	19	6	4	3	2	100.0	6.3	18.5	9.5	17.8	23.2	24.6
Louisiana	34	7	7	7	5	7	1	100.0	1.9	5.8	13.3	19.8	45.8	13.5
Maine	33	19	10	1	3	0	0	100.0	15.5	31.6	8.2	44.7	(¹)	(¹)
Maryland	56	13	12	13	11	6	1	100.0	2.2	7.7	18.2	28.6	30.7	12.7
Massachusetts	116	39	28	22	20	3	4	100.0	3.6	11.4	19.0	31.0	9.8	25.1
Michigan	108	36	26	18	13	7	8	100.0	2.9	8.1	11.5	18.5	16.7	42.2
Minnesota	88	30	26	18	10	3	1	100.0	4.9	16.0	22.4	24.6	13.5	18.7
Mississippi	39	13	9	11	2	4	0	100.0	4.8	13.2	29.2	12.6	40.1	(¹)
Missouri	95	41	22	12	12	7	1	100.0	5.5	12.2	15.4	28.4	30.8	7.8
Montana	24	14	7	1	0	2	0	100.0	14.0	23.4	8.3	(¹)	54.3	(¹)
Nebraska	31	10	9	5	3	3	1	100.0	3.9	11.3	13.7	17.5	33.6	20.0
Nevada	10	4	0	2	1	2	1	100.0	2.1	(¹)	9.7	12.4	42.2	33.6
New Hampshire	26	10	6	7	2	1	0	100.0	6.9	15.8	36.7	16.6	23.9	(¹)
New Jersey	59	11	11	9	20	7	1	100.0	1.1	6.4	11.0	46.1	25.1	10.3
New Mexico	35	15	8	9	0	2	1	100.0	6.1	12.8	28.8	(¹)	29.3	22.9
New York	295	124	57	43	40	28	3	100.0	4.1	9.3	14.2	26.3	38.4	7.8
North Carolina	120	32	46	24	10	6	2	100.0	4.7	19.5	20.8	18.1	23.0	14.0
North Dakota	20	10	6	2	1	1	0	100.0	9.8	23.5	15.2	23.7	27.8	(¹)
Ohio	151	54	54	19	8	10	6	100.0	3.7	16.6	11.4	10.0	27.9	30.4
Oklahoma	44	8	18	10	4	3	1	100.0	1.7	17.8	21.6	17.3	29.0	12.6
Oregon	43	13	13	7	6	3	1	100.0	3.4	13.9	13.2	25.8	29.4	14.3
Pennsylvania	208	87	63	24	24	5	5	100.0	5.8	17.3	13.2	27.6	11.1	25.0
Rhode Island	12	1	3	2	4	2	0	100.0	0.7	9.0	9.2	41.7	39.3	(¹)
South Carolina	59	19	19	14	4	2	1	100.0	6.7	16.4	27.7	18.8	15.7	14.6
South Dakota	21	13	4	2	2	0	0	100.0	16.8	17.8	18.0	47.3	(¹)	(¹)
Tennessee	76	36	14	8	12	5	1	100.0	6.3	9.5	10.4	35.5	28.0	10.3
Texas	175	35	41	43	33	12	11	100.0	1.4	7.0	15.5	24.7	17.7	33.7
Utah	17	4	3	2	2	2	4	100.0	1.2	3.1	3.8	7.1	18.9	65.9
Vermont	22	12	6	3	0	1	0	100.0	14.2	29.0	27.9	(¹)	28.9	(¹)
Virginia	84	25	24	18	9	3	5	100.0	3.0	10.3	18.2	18.5	13.3	36.6
Washington	61	14	7	16	19	3	2	100.0	2.2	4.1	19.9	44.2	10.9	18.6
West Virginia	28	9	9	7	1	1	1	100.0	5.5	20.0	26.2	7.6	15.4	25.4
Wisconsin	64	16	17	10	13	5	3	100.0	1.9	10.2	11.7	30.3	18.1	27.7
Wyoming	9	1	3	4	0	1	0	100.0	2.6	17.0	43.9	(¹)	36.5	(¹)
U.S. Service Schools	10	4	2	3	0	0	1	100.0	3.8	3.5	14.9	(¹)	(¹)	77.7
Outlying areas	74	33	17	16	5	2	1	100.0	8.3	14.6	34.2	17.9	13.8	11.1
American Samoa	1	0	1	0	0	0	0	100.0	(¹)	100.0	(¹)	(¹)	(¹)	(¹)
Federated States of Micronesia	5	5	0	0	0	0	0	100.0	100.0	(¹)	(¹)	(¹)	(¹)	(¹)
Guam	2	0	1	1	0	0	0	100.0	(¹)	36.6	63.4	(¹)	(¹)	(¹)
Marshall Islands	1	1	0	0	0	0	0	100.0	100.0	(¹)	(¹)	(¹)	(¹)	(¹)
Northern Marianas	1	0	1	0	0	0	0	100.0	(¹)	100.0	(¹)	(¹)	(¹)	(¹)
Palau	1	1	0	0	0	0	0	100.0	100.0	(¹)	(¹)	(¹)	(¹)	(¹)
Puerto Rico	61	26	12	15	5	2	1	100.0	7.7	11.5	34.8	19.2	14.9	11.9
Virgin Islands	2	0	2	0	0	0	0	100.0	(¹)	100.0	(¹)	(¹)	(¹)	(¹)

¹ Less than .05 percent.

NOTE.—Because of rounding, details may not add to totals.

SOURCE: U.S. Department of Education, National Center for Education Statistics, Integrated Postsecondary Education Data System (IPEDS), "Fall Enrollment, 1996" survey. (This table was prepared January 1998.)

Table 47.—Total fall enrollment in institutions of higher education, by control, level of enrollment, and state: 1996

State or other area	Public enrollment			Public percentage distribution				Private enrollment			Private percentage distribution			
	Under-graduate	First-profes-sional	Graduate	Total	Under-graduate	First-profes-sional	Graduate	Under-graduate	First-profes-sional	Graduate	Total	Under-graduate	First-profes-sional	Graduate
1	2	3	4	5	6	7	8	9	10	11	12	13	14	15
United States	**9,905,339**	**116,385**	**1,068,447**	**100.0**	**89.3**	**1.0**	**9.6**	**2,354,078**	**181,354**	**674,652**	**100.0**	**73.3**	**5.6**	**21.0**
Alabama	173,387	2,236	20,908	100.0	88.2	1.1	10.6	19,592	1,905	1,471	100.0	85.3	8.3	6.4
Alaska	26,462	—	1,366	100.0	95.1	—	4.9	829	—	189	100.0	81.4	—	18.6
Arizona	227,432	1,553	24,484	100.0	89.7	0.6	9.7	15,815	—	7,548	100.0	67.7	—	32.3
Arkansas	79,878	1,667	7,912	100.0	89.3	1.9	8.8	10,962	—	269	100.0	97.6	—	2.4
California	1,518,803	7,910	98,194	100.0	93.5	0.5	6.0	147,789	25,494	84,444	100.0	57.3	9.9	32.8
Colorado	180,235	1,811	27,137	100.0	86.2	0.9	13.0	22,324	1,362	10,080	100.0	66.1	4.0	29.9
Connecticut	82,015	1,143	14,430	100.0	84.0	1.2	14.8	39,816	2,264	15,693	100.0	68.9	3.9	27.2
Delaware	32,995	—	3,584	100.0	90.2	—	9.8	5,629	1,272	1,358	100.0	68.2	15.4	16.4
District of Columbia	7,105	—	351	100.0	95.3	—	4.7	33,899	8,956	23,928	100.0	50.8	13.4	35.8
Florida	486,171	3,654	41,205	100.0	91.6	0.7	7.8	80,072	6,216	23,855	100.0	72.7	5.6	21.7
Georgia	218,359	3,070	27,855	100.0	87.6	1.2	11.2	51,808	7,152	9,755	100.0	75.4	10.4	14.2
Hawaii	41,436	456	5,478	100.0	87.5	1.0	11.6	12,002	11	2,000	100.0	85.6	0.1	14.3
Idaho	42,531	546	6,315	100.0	86.1	1.1	12.8	10,063	—	449	100.0	95.7	—	4.3
Illinois	482,623	4,368	45,479	100.0	90.6	0.8	8.5	122,318	12,840	53,359	100.0	64.9	6.8	28.3
Indiana	190,190	3,706	27,071	100.0	86.1	1.7	12.3	56,662	1,726	6,971	100.0	86.7	2.6	10.7
Iowa	110,374	2,830	12,719	100.0	87.7	2.2	10.1	43,707	3,633	3,758	100.0	85.5	7.1	7.4
Kansas	134,934	2,020	18,475	100.0	86.8	1.3	11.9	15,081	81	1,759	100.0	89.1	0.5	10.4
Kentucky	126,995	3,113	17,315	100.0	86.1	2.1	11.7	25,540	1,670	3,116	100.0	84.2	5.5	10.3
Louisiana	151,275	2,629	20,685	100.0	86.6	1.5	11.8	20,742	3,429	4,757	100.0	71.7	11.9	16.4
Maine	33,888	296	3,704	100.0	89.4	0.8	9.8	15,221	417	2,119	100.0	85.7	2.3	11.9
Maryland	189,637	3,564	24,076	100.0	87.3	1.6	11.1	24,098	741	18,641	100.0	55.4	1.7	42.9
Massachusetts	153,625	433	19,358	100.0	88.6	0.2	11.2	161,696	13,061	62,154	100.0	68.3	5.5	26.2
Michigan	393,974	6,479	58,536	100.0	85.8	1.4	12.8	73,602	3,966	10,417	100.0	83.7	4.5	11.8
Minnesota	189,171	2,696	16,673	100.0	90.7	1.3	8.0	44,916	3,527	18,279	100.0	67.3	5.3	27.4
Mississippi	103,170	1,282	10,453	100.0	89.8	1.1	9.1	9,260	585	1,484	100.0	81.7	5.2	13.1
Missouri	168,890	2,503	17,876	100.0	89.2	1.3	9.4	71,540	7,162	22,562	100.0	70.6	7.1	22.3
Montana	34,627	227	3,146	100.0	91.1	0.6	8.3	5,001	—	144	100.0	97.2	—	2.8
Nebraska	87,688	1,304	10,725	100.0	87.9	1.3	10.8	16,111	1,812	1,660	100.0	82.3	9.3	8.5
Nevada	64,848	205	6,872	100.0	90.2	0.3	9.6	987	—	555	100.0	64.0	—	36.0
New Hampshire	32,514	—	3,851	100.0	89.4	—	10.6	21,914	710	5,474	100.0	78.0	2.5	19.5
New Jersey	234,198	3,615	26,783	100.0	88.5	1.4	10.1	45,233	2,971	15,388	100.0	71.1	4.7	24.2
New Mexico	84,667	717	12,246	100.0	86.7	0.7	12.5	4,693	154	1,069	100.0	79.3	2.6	18.1
New York	509,053	4,679	58,750	100.0	88.9	0.8	10.3	320,393	22,743	112,252	100.0	70.4	5.0	24.6
North Carolina	272,790	2,878	27,271	100.0	90.0	1.0	9.0	57,948	4,291	7,990	100.0	82.5	6.1	11.4
North Dakota	33,734	438	2,593	100.0	91.8	1.2	7.1	3,640	—	149	100.0	96.1	—	3.9
Ohio	352,088	7,656	45,595	100.0	86.9	1.9	11.2	106,660	4,769	20,767	100.0	80.7	3.6	15.7
Oklahoma	134,805	1,853	17,723	100.0	87.3	1.2	11.5	17,863	1,248	3,763	100.0	78.1	5.5	16.5
Oregon	127,098	1,262	13,069	100.0	89.9	0.9	9.2	17,336	2,545	3,858	100.0	73.0	10.7	16.3
Pennsylvania	293,891	4,449	36,841	100.0	87.7	1.3	11.0	231,991	11,156	43,666	100.0	80.9	3.9	15.2
Rhode Island	32,487	34	4,966	100.0	86.7	0.1	13.2	29,772	835	4,338	100.0	85.2	2.4	12.4
South Carolina	126,001	1,923	20,439	100.0	84.9	1.3	13.8	23,507	815	1,618	100.0	90.6	3.1	6.2
South Dakota	24,583	566	3,415	100.0	86.1	2.0	12.0	6,326	106	377	100.0	92.9	1.6	5.5
Tennessee	171,244	2,766	20,087	100.0	88.2	1.4	10.3	43,042	2,924	6,980	100.0	81.3	5.5	13.2
Texas	746,237	10,067	81,787	100.0	89.0	1.2	9.8	86,794	9,823	20,731	100.0	74.0	8.4	17.7
Utah	104,747	775	8,673	100.0	91.7	0.7	7.6	33,372	479	3,591	100.0	89.1	1.3	9.6
Vermont	18,255	373	1,511	100.0	90.6	1.9	7.5	12,030	523	2,398	100.0	80.5	3.5	16.0
Virginia	247,646	4,499	40,267	100.0	84.7	1.5	13.8	50,845	2,401	8,130	100.0	82.8	3.9	13.2
Washington	237,095	1,993	12,781	100.0	94.1	0.8	5.1	28,590	1,765	9,956	100.0	70.9	4.4	24.7
West Virginia	62,826	1,420	10,509	100.0	84.0	1.9	14.1	10,453	—	481	100.0	95.6	—	4.4
Wisconsin	222,052	1,839	20,737	100.0	90.8	0.8	8.5	43,783	1,814	8,902	100.0	80.3	3.3	16.3
Wyoming	27,563	209	2,222	100.0	91.9	0.7	7.4	811	—	—	100.0	100.0	—	—
U.S. Service Schools	77,047	673	3,949	100.0	94.3	0.8	4.8	—	—	—	—	—	—	—
Outlying areas	73,509	1,272	5,080	100.0	92.0	1.6	6.4	91,644	1,860	8,295	100.0	90.0	1.8	8.1
American Samoa	1,239	—	—	100.0	100.0	—	—	—	—	—	—	—	—	—
Federated States of Micronesia	1,396	—	—	100.0	100.0	—	—	—	—	—	—	—	—	—
Guam	4,986	—	349	100.0	93.5	—	6.5	—	—	—	—	—	—	—
Marshall Islands	431	—	—	100.0	100.0	—	—	—	—	—	—	—	—	—
Northern Marianas	1,096	—	—	100.0	100.0	—	—	—	—	—	—	—	—	—
Palau	332	—	—	100.0	100.0	—	—	—	—	—	—	—	—	—
Puerto Rico	61,363	1,272	4,499	100.0	91.4	1.9	6.7	91,644	1,860	8,295	100.0	90.0	1.8	8.1
Virgin Islands	2,666	—	232	100.0	92.0	—	8.0	—	—	—	—	—	—	—

[1] Less than .05 percent.
—Data not reported or not applicable.

NOTE.—Because of rounding, details may not add to totals.

SOURCE: U.S. Department of Education, National Center for Education Statistics, Integrated Postsecondary Education Data System (IPEDS), "Fall Enrollment, 1996" survey. (This table was prepared January 1998.)

Table 48.—Percentage distribution of total fall enrollment in institutions of higher education, by type and control of institution, and by state: 1980 to 1996

State or other area	Public 4-year				Public 2-year				Private 4-year				Private 2-year			
	Fall 1980	Fall 1990	Fall 1995	Fall 1996	Fall 1980	Fall 1990	Fall 1995	Fall 1996	Fall 1980	Fall 1990	Fall 1995	Fall 1996	Fall 1980	Fall 1990	Fall 1995	Fall 1996
1	2	3	4	5	6	7	8	9	10	11	12	13	14	15	16	17
United States	**42.4**	**42.3**	**40.8**	**40.6**	**35.8**	**36.2**	**37.0**	**36.9**	**20.2**	**19.8**	**20.7**	**21.0**	**1.6**	**1.8**	**1.5**	**1.5**
Alabama	63.5	56.7	56.1	55.9	24.0	33.0	34.0	33.6	10.1	8.6	9.7	10.0	2.4	1.7	0.2	0.5
Alaska	40.2	93.2	93.9	93.9	56.3	—	2.8	2.6	3.5	5.5	2.6	2.4	—	1.3	0.7	1.1
Arizona	39.9	36.2	37.1	37.0	55.8	57.8	55.8	54.5	4.2	5.3	6.8	8.1	0.1	0.7	0.3	0.3
Arkansas	70.8	67.9	64.0	61.7	14.6	19.1	24.7	27.2	11.6	10.8	10.9	10.8	3.0	2.2	0.5	0.4
California	26.2	29.7	27.0	26.8	63.1	58.5	59.1	59.5	10.4	11.2	13.1	12.9	0.3	0.6	0.8	0.8
Colorado	61.9	56.6	54.6	54.5	27.5	31.7	32.0	31.6	10.0	9.6	11.9	13.3	0.7	2.1	1.5	0.6
Connecticut	35.0	38.5	36.6	36.4	26.3	26.4	27.2	26.4	37.8	34.1	35.3	36.2	1.0	0.9	1.0	1.0
Delaware	64.8	55.8	55.4	55.1	21.2	25.8	26.3	26.5	11.4	18.5	18.3	18.4	2.6	—	—	—
District of Columbia	16.0	15.1	12.5	10.0	—	—	—	—	84.0	84.9	87.5	90.0	—	—	—	—
Florida	31.0	30.1	32.5	32.9	50.2	53.1	50.8	49.9	17.7	15.7	15.9	16.3	1.2	1.1	0.9	0.9
Georgia	56.5	56.0	51.0	50.0	19.6	22.0	28.0	28.4	18.4	18.4	19.5	20.2	5.5	3.6	1.4	1.4
Hawaii	48.8	42.3	36.9	35.3	39.5	38.7	42.5	41.8	11.7	19.0	20.6	22.8	—	—	—	—
Idaho	67.6	68.8	69.6	69.0	12.6	10.8	12.7	13.4	4.7	4.5	3.9	4.0	15.1	15.9	13.9	13.6
Illinois	29.6	27.2	26.8	26.7	46.5	48.4	47.0	47.2	22.6	23.2	25.5	25.6	1.3	1.2	0.6	0.6
Indiana	64.3	65.4	63.6	63.9	12.3	13.2	14.0	13.3	21.8	20.1	21.2	21.6	1.6	1.3	1.2	1.2
Iowa	44.5	39.9	37.9	37.6	24.9	29.3	32.5	33.5	29.1	29.5	28.9	28.3	1.5	1.4	0.6	0.6
Kansas	62.9	55.1	48.8	49.9	26.4	36.0	41.5	40.3	9.5	8.3	9.2	9.3	1.2	0.6	0.5	0.5
Kentucky	67.7	59.8	59.0	58.7	12.6	22.9	24.2	24.3	14.5	14.0	15.3	15.6	5.2	3.2	1.5	1.5
Louisiana	76.6	73.1	72.5	72.3	8.8	11.6	13.2	13.4	14.4	14.1	13.7	13.5	0.2	1.2	0.6	0.7
Maine	57.2	60.5	55.3	55.7	16.5	12.0	12.2	12.4	23.7	24.9	29.1	28.7	2.6	2.5	3.4	3.3
Maryland	45.3	42.7	42.7	43.4	41.3	42.3	41.0	39.9	13.1	14.7	15.9	16.2	0.3	0.3	0.4	0.5
Massachusetts	26.1	26.3	24.6	24.8	17.8	18.2	18.1	17.4	51.7	52.2	55.3	56.0	4.4	3.2	1.9	1.7
Michigan	46.5	45.6	47.2	47.4	40.8	39.9	37.1	36.5	11.4	14.0	15.2	15.8	1.3	0.5	0.5	0.3
Minnesota	60.6	52.7	41.7	42.8	18.0	25.8	35.6	33.0	19.7	19.8	21.2	22.5	1.8	1.7	1.5	1.7
Mississippi	52.7	47.8	48.0	48.0	35.9	40.9	42.2	43.1	9.1	8.7	9.2	8.4	2.3	2.6	0.7	0.6
Missouri	47.9	43.2	40.4	40.3	22.8	25.8	24.7	24.8	28.6	29.6	33.3	33.4	0.6	1.4	1.6	1.5
Montana	79.8	78.1	73.6	73.5	8.8	10.7	14.1	14.6	9.0	8.5	10.1	10.0	2.3	2.7	2.2	1.9
Nebraska	58.3	53.8	50.2	48.0	23.9	30.1	32.4	35.6	17.5	15.9	16.9	16.4	0.4	0.3	0.5	—
Nevada	46.8	47.7	45.5	42.2	52.7	51.5	52.9	55.7	0.4	0.5	1.6	2.1	—	0.3	(1)	(1)
New Hampshire	41.2	40.0	41.2	41.2	10.4	14.1	14.9	15.2	44.0	41.2	37.7	37.6	4.5	4.7	6.3	6.0
New Jersey	43.8	42.5	41.3	41.9	33.0	38.2	39.9	38.7	20.7	18.2	17.4	17.8	2.5	1.1	1.4	1.6
New Mexico	76.7	56.2	48.6	47.1	17.2	41.4	46.3	47.1	6.1	2.2	4.1	4.7	—	0.2	0.9	1.0
New York	31.5	34.7	32.2	32.0	25.3	24.2	24.3	23.7	40.2	38.5	40.8	41.9	3.0	2.7	2.7	2.4
North Carolina	42.3	42.2	42.3	41.9	37.0	38.8	39.2	39.2	17.5	17.5	18.1	18.5	3.1	1.5	0.4	0.3
North Dakota	71.7	72.0	70.3	69.2	21.4	19.6	20.8	21.5	6.3	7.9	8.3	8.7	0.6	0.5	0.6	0.7
Ohio	52.0	52.0	48.5	48.1	26.1	24.7	27.4	27.3	19.9	20.1	21.7	22.1	2.0	3.2	2.5	2.5
Oklahoma	54.9	53.7	52.8	52.9	30.7	33.6	34.7	34.2	12.7	10.3	11.4	11.8	1.7	2.5	1.1	1.1
Oregon	41.7	40.8	37.7	39.0	47.3	46.4	48.2	46.6	10.7	12.7	14.0	14.4	0.3	0.1	0.1	—
Pennsylvania	37.3	38.9	37.8	37.3	20.3	17.9	17.2	16.6	39.3	35.5	35.7	35.3	3.1	7.6	9.3	10.8
Rhode Island	34.7	32.9	30.7	30.7	17.7	21.2	21.4	21.0	46.3	45.9	44.6	48.2	1.3	—	3.3	—
South Carolina	51.8	51.0	50.4	50.1	29.5	31.3	35.0	35.0	14.0	14.9	13.9	14.1	4.7	2.8	0.7	0.8
South Dakota	72.8	77.3	80.3	80.2	1.4	0.4	0.6	0.6	23.5	21.5	18.4	18.7	2.2	0.7	0.6	0.6
Tennessee	52.6	48.6	46.8	46.7	23.9	28.8	31.8	31.8	20.6	20.3	20.5	20.7	2.8	2.3	1.0	0.8
Texas	49.6	46.3	43.8	43.3	37.8	42.7	44.0	44.4	12.2	10.5	11.5	11.6	0.4	0.5	0.6	0.6
Utah	48.9	47.4	54.4	53.6	15.8	23.6	20.7	21.7	33.5	27.8	24.1	23.9	1.8	1.2	0.9	0.8
Vermont	50.2	44.2	45.2	44.4	8.5	13.3	13.2	13.0	36.5	37.0	41.0	41.9	4.7	5.6	0.6	0.7
Virginia	48.2	45.3	46.3	47.4	39.6	37.1	36.1	35.2	11.8	16.4	16.3	16.0	0.4	1.2	1.4	1.3
Washington	27.5	30.9	30.1	29.9	63.5	55.5	56.2	56.3	9.1	12.7	12.9	12.9	—	0.9	0.8	0.9
West Virginia	75.7	74.7	78.9	79.4	11.2	12.7	8.1	7.8	10.5	9.3	12.1	11.9	2.6	3.3	0.9	0.9
Wisconsin	54.3	50.9	46.4	47.1	33.1	33.6	35.5	34.7	12.3	15.0	17.6	17.6	0.3	0.4	0.6	0.6
Wyoming	42.6	40.0	37.6	36.5	57.3	57.8	59.8	60.8	—	—	—	—	0.1	2.2	2.5	2.6
U.S. Service Schools	37.5	39.3	21.3	22.7	62.5	60.7	78.7	77.3	—	—	—	—	—	—	—	—
Outlying areas	34.1	34.5	34.1	37.2	9.9	5.7	7.9	6.8	44.4	54.2	53.2	51.1	11.7	5.6	4.8	4.9
American Samoa	—	—	—	—	100.0	100.0	100.0	100.0	—	—	—	—	—	—	—	—
Federated States of Micronesia	—	—	—	—	—	100.0	100.0	100.0	—	—	—	—	—	—	—	—
Guam	100.0	54.7	60.8	63.4	—	45.3	39.2	36.6	—	—	—	—	—	—	—	—
Marshall Islands	—	—	—	—	—	—	100.0	100.0	—	—	—	—	—	—	—	—
Northern Marianas	—	—	—	—	—	100.0	100.0	100.0	—	—	—	—	—	—	—	—
Palau	—	—	—	—	—	100.0	100.0	100.0	—	—	—	—	—	—	—	—
Puerto Rico	31.6	33.6	32.8	36.3	9.6	2.5	4.6	3.5	46.5	57.9	57.4	55.0	12.2	5.9	5.2	5.3
Virgin Islands	100.0	100.0	100.0	100.0	—	—	—	—	—	—	—	—	—	—	—	—

[1] Less than 0.05 percent.

—Not applicable.

NOTE.—Because of rounding, details may not add to totals.

SOURCE: U.S. Department of Education, National Center for Education Statistics, Higher Education General Information Survey (HEGIS), "Fall Enrollment in Institutions of Higher Education", and Integrated Postsecondary Education Data System (IPEDS), "Fall Enrollment" surveys. (This table was prepared January 1998.)

Table 49.—Percentage of total fall enrollment in institutions of higher education, by race/ethnicity of student and by state: 1980, 1990, 1995, and 1996

State or other area	Total minority				Black				Hispanic	
	Fall 1980	Fall 1990	Fall 1995	Fall 1996	Fall 1980	Fall 1990	Fall 1995	Fall 1996	Fall 1980	Fall 1990
1	2	3	4	5	6	7	8	9	10	11
United States	**16.5**	**20.1**	**25.3**	**26.1**	**9.4**	**9.3**	**10.7**	**10.8**	**4.0**	**5.8**
Alabama	23.1	21.7	26.1	26.9	22.0	20.1	23.7	24.3	0.4	0.5
Alaska	11.1	17.4	19.3	19.4	2.5	3.7	3.5	3.8	1.0	2.2
Arizona	15.3	20.4	25.0	25.5	2.8	3.0	3.3	3.4	7.6	11.6
Arkansas	16.7	15.5	17.9	18.5	15.0	13.7	15.1	15.6	0.3	0.5
California	26.7	34.5	47.9	48.7	8.2	6.8	8.0	8.0	9.7	13.4
Colorado	10.8	14.1	17.7	18.2	2.9	3.0	3.6	3.5	5.7	7.7
Connecticut	8.1	12.4	16.9	17.5	5.0	6.1	7.8	7.9	1.7	3.4
Delaware	12.6	14.7	18.6	19.4	11.1	11.4	13.9	14.5	0.8	1.3
District of Columbia	39.7	42.8	46.1	45.7	34.8	34.5	35.3	33.9	2.0	3.4
Florida	19.9	24.6	31.0	32.7	10.6	10.7	13.5	14.2	8.1	11.5
Georgia	20.7	23.1	29.7	30.8	19.2	20.0	25.3	26.0	0.7	1.1
Hawaii	69.6	68.1	70.8	70.6	1.3	2.9	2.2	2.3	1.5	2.0
Idaho	4.4	5.0	6.4	6.5	0.6	0.6	0.7	0.7	1.5	2.0
Illinois	16.6	24.2	27.3	28.3	11.6	12.5	13.0	13.1	2.5	6.9
Indiana	8.5	9.1	10.9	11.1	6.4	5.7	6.4	6.4	1.2	1.6
Iowa	4.1	5.2	7.4	7.7	2.4	2.5	2.9	2.9	0.6	1.0
Kansas	7.7	9.5	12.8	12.6	4.3	4.3	5.5	4.9	1.5	2.2
Kentucky	8.4	7.4	9.1	9.5	7.2	6.0	6.9	7.1	0.4	0.4
Louisiana	25.8	28.5	31.8	32.6	23.3	24.6	26.8	27.1	1.6	1.9
Maine	1.2	2.3	4.8	4.0	0.4	0.5	1.1	0.7	0.2	0.3
Maryland	21.8	24.3	30.9	32.2	18.0	17.6	22.4	23.3	1.4	1.9
Massachusetts	6.6	12.2	17.3	17.7	3.6	4.7	5.9	6.1	1.5	3.2
Michigan	13.0	14.4	17.2	17.5	10.3	10.2	11.3	11.4	1.2	1.6
Minnesota	3.1	5.2	8.9	8.9	1.2	1.7	2.9	2.8	0.5	0.8
Mississippi	30.5	29.1	31.5	32.7	29.7	27.9	29.7	30.9	0.3	0.3
Missouri	11.1	11.4	13.4	13.8	9.1	8.2	9.0	9.2	0.8	1.2
Montana	5.7	8.4	11.4	11.2	0.4	0.3	0.4	0.3	0.4	0.8
Nebraska	5.4	5.6	7.8	7.9	3.0	2.5	3.0	3.0	1.0	1.4
Nevada	13.8	16.3	21.1	23.0	6.9	4.8	5.6	6.2	3.2	5.6
New Hampshire	2.9	3.7	5.2	5.0	1.6	1.1	1.7	1.4	0.6	0.8
New Jersey	16.4	22.4	28.6	29.5	10.2	10.6	12.2	12.2	4.3	6.9
New Mexico	31.7	37.5	43.1	43.7	2.2	2.6	2.6	2.5	24.8	28.1
New York	19.3	25.4	30.7	31.7	10.9	12.1	13.6	13.9	5.5	7.9
North Carolina	21.2	21.1	24.2	24.8	19.4	17.9	20.0	20.4	0.4	0.7
North Dakota	3.4	6.4	7.6	8.2	0.5	0.7	0.9	0.9	0.2	0.5
Ohio	11.2	11.4	13.6	14.0	9.5	8.7	9.7	9.8	0.7	1.0
Oklahoma	12.2	16.1	20.4	21.0	6.2	7.0	7.6	7.6	1.1	1.6
Oregon	5.7	8.8	13.4	13.0	1.0	1.4	1.9	1.8	1.1	2.0
Pennsylvania	9.5	11.3	14.0	14.2	7.6	7.5	8.5	8.6	0.8	1.3
Rhode Island	5.9	8.2	12.3	13.0	3.4	3.4	4.5	4.6	1.4	2.1
South Carolina	23.4	21.6	25.3	26.1	22.3	19.9	22.8	23.6	0.5	0.6
South Dakota	6.2	7.3	8.9	8.8	1.0	0.7	0.8	0.8	0.8	0.3
Tennessee	16.4	15.9	17.8	18.2	15.4	14.1	15.0	15.2	0.4	0.6
Texas	23.6	29.6	36.3	37.3	9.5	9.2	10.1	10.2	12.7	16.9
Utah	4.5	5.5	6.6	6.8	0.6	0.6	0.6	0.6	1.5	1.9
Vermont	2.0	4.2	5.9	4.5	1.1	1.1	1.4	1.1	0.5	1.2
Virginia	17.0	19.2	24.0	24.8	14.7	14.3	16.4	16.8	0.7	1.4
Washington	8.6	12.7	17.5	18.1	2.2	2.9	3.8	3.8	1.5	2.4
West Virginia	4.9	5.2	5.9	6.2	4.0	3.8	4.0	4.3	0.3	0.4
Wisconsin	6.0	7.6	9.5	9.6	3.5	3.6	4.3	4.4	1.0	1.6
Wyoming	4.0	5.9	7.4	8.0	0.8	0.9	0.9	0.9	1.7	2.9
U.S. Service Schools	13.5	16.5	19.8	19.9	11.1	13.0	13.3	13.2	1.2	1.7
Outlying areas	98.8	99.4	99.6	99.6	1.2	1.2	1.4	1.4	95.2	94.3
American Samoa	97.1	82.4	100.0	100.0	(1)	(1)	(1)	(1)	0.1	(1)
Federated States of Micronesia	—	100.0	100.0	100.0	—	(1)	(1)	(1)	—	(1)
Guam	74.9	90.5	90.4	90.9	2.3	0.8	0.7	0.6	1.7	0.8
Marshall Islands	—	—	100.0	100.0	—	—	(1)	(1)	—	—
Northern Marianas	—	87.9	92.1	92.2	—	(1)	(1)	(1)	—	0.4
Palau	—	100.0	100.0	100.0	—	(1)	(1)	(1)	—	(1)
Puerto Rico	99.5	100.0	100.0	100.0	(1)	(1)	(1)	(1)	99.5	100.0
Trust Territories	99.1	—	—	—	(1)				(1)	
Virgin Islands	87.4	89.5	94.5	95.2	83.6	84.7	89.2	89.9	3.2	4.0

Table 49.—Percentage of total fall enrollment in institutions of higher education, by race/ethnicity of student and by state: 1980, 1990, 1995, and 1996—Continued

State or other area	Hispanic		Asian/Pacific Islander				American Indian/Alaskan Native			
	Fall 1995	Fall 1996	Fall 1980	Fall 1990	Fall 1995	Fall 1996	Fall 1980	Fall 1990	Fall 1995	Fall 1996
1	12	13	14	15	16	17	18	19	20	21
United States	**7.9**	**8.3**	**2.4**	**4.3**	**5.8**	**6.0**	**0.7**	**0.8**	**1.0**	**1.0**
Alabama	0.8	0.8	0.5	0.8	1.1	1.1	0.2	0.3	0.6	0.6
Alaska	2.8	2.6	1.2	2.5	3.1	2.7	6.4	9.0	9.9	10.3
Arizona	14.5	14.9	1.3	2.4	3.2	3.3	3.6	3.4	4.0	3.9
Arkansas	0.8	0.8	0.7	0.8	1.2	1.2	0.7	0.5	0.9	0.9
California	20.6	21.3	7.5	13.1	18.1	18.2	1.3	1.2	1.2	1.2
Colorado	9.5	9.8	1.4	2.4	3.4	3.5	0.7	1.0	1.3	1.3
Connecticut	5.1	5.4	1.0	2.6	3.7	3.9	0.3	0.3	0.4	0.4
Delaware	1.8	2.1	0.6	1.7	2.5	2.3	0.1	0.2	0.5	0.4
District of Columbia	4.4	4.5	2.5	4.6	6.1	6.9	0.4	0.4	0.3	0.4
Florida	13.9	14.8	1.0	2.1	3.1	3.2	0.3	0.3	0.5	0.5
Georgia	1.5	1.6	0.7	1.7	2.7	2.9	0.2	0.2	0.3	0.3
Hawaii	2.4	2.4	65.3	62.8	65.8	65.4	0.3	0.4	0.4	0.4
Idaho	2.9	2.9	1.4	1.4	1.5	1.5	0.9	1.0	1.4	1.4
Illinois	8.3	9.1	2.2	4.5	5.6	5.7	0.4	0.3	0.3	0.3
Indiana	2.2	2.4	0.7	1.4	1.9	2.0	0.3	0.3	0.4	0.4
Iowa	1.7	1.7	0.8	1.5	2.4	2.6	0.4	0.3	0.4	0.5
Kansas	3.4	3.7	0.6	1.7	2.4	2.4	1.3	1.2	1.5	1.6
Kentucky	0.7	0.7	0.6	0.8	1.2	1.2	0.3	0.3	0.4	0.4
Louisiana	2.3	2.5	0.6	1.5	2.1	2.3	0.2	0.5	0.6	0.6
Maine	0.6	0.7	0.3	0.7	1.6	1.3	0.4	0.7	1.5	1.3
Maryland	2.4	2.5	2.1	4.5	5.7	5.9	0.3	0.3	0.4	0.5
Massachusetts	4.6	4.6	1.3	4.1	6.3	6.6	0.2	0.3	0.4	0.5
Michigan	2.2	2.2	0.9	1.9	2.9	3.0	0.5	0.6	0.8	0.8
Minnesota	1.5	1.4	1.0	2.0	3.5	3.6	0.5	0.8	1.0	1.1
Mississippi	0.5	0.6	0.3	0.6	0.9	0.8	0.2	0.3	0.4	0.4
Missouri	1.6	1.8	0.9	1.6	2.3	2.3	0.3	0.4	0.5	0.6
Montana	1.2	1.2	0.3	0.3	0.8	0.8	4.5	6.9	9.0	8.8
Nebraska	2.0	2.1	0.7	1.1	2.0	2.0	0.6	0.7	0.8	1.0
Nevada	7.8	8.7	2.2	4.2	6.1	6.4	1.5	1.7	1.6	1.7
New Hampshire	1.5	1.4	0.4	1.3	1.6	1.7	0.3	0.4	0.4	0.5
New Jersey	9.5	10.1	1.6	4.6	6.5	6.9	0.3	0.2	0.3	0.3
New Mexico	31.9	32.6	0.8	1.3	1.7	1.8	3.9	5.5	7.0	6.7
New York	10.0	10.5	2.3	5.0	6.7	6.9	0.5	0.3	0.4	0.4
North Carolina	1.2	1.4	0.6	1.6	1.9	2.1	0.7	0.9	1.0	1.0
North Dakota	0.6	0.7	0.3	0.8	0.8	0.8	2.4	4.4	5.3	5.8
Ohio	1.5	1.6	0.7	1.4	2.1	2.2	0.3	0.3	0.4	0.4
Oklahoma	2.4	2.5	1.1	1.7	2.4	2.6	3.9	5.7	8.0	8.2
Oregon	3.9	3.6	2.6	4.2	6.0	6.0	1.0	1.1	1.6	1.6
Pennsylvania	1.9	1.9	0.9	2.3	3.4	3.5	0.2	0.2	0.2	0.2
Rhode Island	3.8	4.3	1.0	2.5	3.6	3.8	0.2	0.3	0.4	0.4
South Carolina	0.9	1.0	0.5	1.0	1.3	1.3	0.1	0.2	0.3	0.3
South Dakota	0.5	0.5	0.3	0.6	0.7	0.8	4.2	5.7	6.9	6.7
Tennessee	1.0	1.1	0.4	1.0	1.5	1.6	0.2	0.2	0.3	0.3
Texas	21.1	21.8	1.1	3.2	4.6	4.8	0.4	0.3	0.5	0.6
Utah	2.7	2.8	1.2	1.9	2.2	2.3	1.1	1.1	1.1	1.1
Vermont	1.4	1.4	0.3	1.6	2.0	1.4	0.1	0.4	1.2	0.5
Virginia	2.3	2.4	1.3	3.3	5.0	5.1	0.2	0.2	0.4	0.4
Washington	3.7	4.0	3.6	6.0	8.1	8.3	1.3	1.5	1.9	2.0
West Virginia	0.6	0.6	0.4	0.8	1.1	1.1	0.2	0.2	0.2	0.3
Wisconsin	2.1	2.2	0.8	1.7	2.2	2.2	0.7	0.7	0.8	0.8
Wyoming	4.3	4.6	0.5	0.6	0.8	0.8	0.9	1.4	1.5	1.7
U.S. Service Schools	3.6	3.6	1.0	1.6	2.5	2.6	0.1	0.2	0.4	0.5
Outlying areas	93.3	93.4	2.3	4.0	4.9	4.9	(1)	(1)	(1)	(1)
American Samoa	0.0	0.0	97.0	82.4	100.0	100.0	(1)	(1)	(1)	(1)
Federated States of Micronesia	(1)	(1)	—	100.0	100.0	100.0	—	(1)	(1)	(1)
Guam	0.7	0.7	70.2	88.4	88.8	89.6	0.7	0.4	0.2	0.1
Marshall Islands	(1)	(1)	—	—	100.0	100.0	—	(1)	(1)	(1)
Northern Marianas	0.3	0.8	—	87.5	91.8	91.4	—	(1)	(1)	(1)
Palau	(1)	(1)	—	100.0	100.0	100.0	—	(1)	(1)	(1)
Puerto Rico	100.0	100.0	(1)	(1)	(1)	(1)	(1)	(1)	(1)	(1)
Trust Territories	—	—	99.1	—	—	—	(1)	—	—	—
Virgin Islands	4.1	4.0	0.7	0.5	1.1	1.2	(1)	0.3	0.1	0.1

[1] Less than .05 percent.

—Data not available or not applicable.

NOTE.—Percentages based on U.S. resident enrollment (total enrollment less enrollment of nonresident aliens). Some data revised from previously published figures. Because of rounding, details may not add to totals.

SOURCE: U.S. Department of Education, National Center for Education Statistics, Higher Education General Information Survey (HEGIS), "Fall enrollment in Colleges and Universities, 1980"; and Integrated Postsecondary Education Data System (IPEDS), "Fall Enrollment" surveys. (This table was prepared February 1998.)

Table 50.—Nonresident alien students as a percentage of total fall enrollment in institutions of higher education, by level of student and by state: 1980, 1990, 1995, and 1996

State or other area	All levels				Undergraduate				First-professional				Graduate			
	Fall 1980	Fall 1990	Fall 1995	Fall 1996	Fall 1980	Fall 1990	Fall 1995	Fall 1996	Fall 1980	Fall 1990	Fall 1995	Fall 1996	Fall 1980	Fall 1990	Fall 1995	Fall 1996
1	2	3	4	5	6	7	8	9	10	11	12	13	14	15	16	17
United States	2.5	2.8	3.2	3.3	2.0	1.8	2.2	2.2	1.0	2.0	2.5	2.6	6.9	10.5	10.4	10.5
Alabama	1.7	2.1	2.0	2.0	1.5	1.3	1.4	1.4	0.4	1.5	0.4	0.4	3.9	9.8	7.5	7.5
Alaska	0.8	1.6	2.1	3.7	0.7	1.2	1.6	3.3	(¹)	—	—	—	3.3	11.0	9.0	11.1
Arizona	2.3	2.6	2.7	2.8	1.8	1.5	1.6	1.7	0.2	0.3	0.7	0.7	6.6	12.2	10.9	11.1
Arkansas	1.3	1.6	2.4	2.4	1.1	1.3	2.0	2.0	0.0	0.1	0.2	0.2	3.6	5.6	7.1	6.9
California	3.2	3.7	4.4	4.4	2.7	3.0	3.9	3.8	1.5	2.5	2.6	3.0	8.0	9.8	9.5	9.8
Colorado	2.7	2.0	2.3	2.4	2.1	1.3	1.6	1.7	0.4	0.5	0.4	0.7	8.4	6.4	6.1	6.8
Connecticut	1.5	2.8	3.5	3.7	1.0	1.6	2.2	2.4	1.0	1.7	2.1	1.6	4.2	8.2	9.4	9.5
Delaware	2.2	1.9	2.1	2.4	1.7	0.8	0.8	1.1	—	(¹)	1.0	(¹)	9.6	14.9	13.1	13.1
District of Columbia	9.8	11.1	10.4	11.0	10.0	9.4	8.5	9.5	1.6	2.9	2.9	3.1	12.5	17.8	16.4	16.4
Florida	2.8	2.7	3.1	3.2	2.6	2.2	2.5	2.6	0.5	1.7	1.3	1.4	5.1	8.6	8.5	8.2
Georgia	2.1	2.3	2.6	2.5	1.7	1.4	1.8	1.7	1.3	2.6	3.1	3.3	5.4	8.8	8.3	8.6
Hawaii	5.1	7.1	9.1	9.2	5.2	5.7	7.9	8.1	1.7	2.0	1.8	2.1	4.7	17.7	18.6	17.9
Idaho	1.5	2.6	2.2	2.1	1.4	2.2	1.9	1.6	(¹)	2.0	1.3	1.1	3.0	5.3	4.4	6.0
Illinois	1.9	2.1	2.5	2.5	1.3	0.9	1.2	1.3	0.8	2.4	3.1	3.2	6.4	10.4	10.3	10.1
Indiana	2.6	2.7	3.0	3.2	1.8	1.4	1.6	1.7	1.2	1.9	2.3	2.2	8.5	13.0	13.2	13.6
Iowa	2.8	4.0	4.1	4.1	1.8	2.4	2.7	2.6	2.1	3.0	1.8	3.8	11.3	16.1	17.7	19.0
Kansas	3.2	3.3	3.4	3.2	2.4	2.2	2.2	2.2	0.3	0.5	0.2	0.4	7.6	11.2	12.9	11.2
Kentucky	1.6	1.3	1.7	1.8	1.4	0.8	1.2	1.2	0.7	1.4	1.4	1.3	3.0	5.4	5.9	6.3
Louisiana	4.0	2.5	2.9	2.8	3.8	1.4	1.8	1.5	0.5	1.7	2.3	1.6	6.0	11.0	10.8	11.8
Maine	0.5	0.7	1.1	1.0	0.5	0.7	1.1	1.1	0.5	1.8	0.4	0.4	0.8	0.9	0.7	0.5
Maryland	5.3	2.9	3.5	3.7	5.0	1.8	2.4	2.6	0.7	1.1	1.5	1.4	7.7	9.8	9.3	9.8
Massachusetts	3.3	5.0	5.9	6.1	2.5	3.2	3.9	4.2	2.9	3.1	4.4	4.0	8.2	14.0	13.9	14.0
Michigan	2.1	2.5	3.1	3.2	1.5	1.3	1.8	1.9	2.3	4.0	6.8	6.5	7.8	12.5	11.5	11.5
Minnesota	2.3	2.2	2.3	2.7	1.9	1.3	1.6	2.0	0.6	2.2	3.2	3.5	6.8	10.1	6.9	6.8
Mississippi	1.2	1.6	1.6	1.6	0.8	0.7	0.7	0.8	(¹)	1.0	1.3	0.9	5.3	11.2	10.3	9.2
Missouri	1.9	2.3	2.5	2.7	1.4	1.4	1.7	1.8	1.1	3.5	1.5	2.8	5.8	8.3	8.2	8.2
Montana	1.3	2.0	2.4	2.4	1.1	1.5	2.0	2.0	(¹)	(¹)	0.8	1.3	3.2	7.4	6.8	7.4
Nebraska	1.5	1.8	2.2	2.3	1.3	1.2	1.5	1.6	0.4	1.9	1.9	1.4	3.9	6.6	8.3	8.8
Nevada	1.3	1.4	2.8	2.8	1.2	1.1	2.5	2.5	(¹)	0.6	—	—	3.2	4.9	5.7	5.5
New Hampshire	1.3	1.4	1.8	2.0	1.3	1.0	1.5	1.5	0.2	1.5	2.1	3.0	1.8	3.9	3.8	4.8
New Jersey	1.5	3.8	3.4	3.5	1.0	2.7	2.4	2.4	0.7	1.1	1.5	1.2	4.3	11.7	10.4	10.5
New Mexico	2.0	1.8	1.8	1.6	1.1	1.1	0.9	0.8	0.2	(¹)	0.2	0.6	8.7	6.8	8.0	7.4
New York	2.2	3.9	4.3	4.3	1.6	2.5	2.8	2.7	0.5	1.3	1.9	2.1	6.0	11.4	11.9	12.2
North Carolina	1.3	1.4	1.5	1.7	1.1	0.7	0.9	1.0	0.6	1.4	1.8	2.2	4.4	8.5	7.6	8.1
North Dakota	1.4	3.1	3.9	3.6	1.1	2.6	3.1	2.9	0.2	1.2	2.5	2.1	6.0	10.8	14.3	13.7
Ohio	1.8	2.5	3.0	3.1	1.2	1.3	1.5	1.6	0.3	1.2	1.6	1.4	6.6	12.0	13.0	13.5
Oklahoma	4.9	3.1	4.5	4.7	4.3	1.9	3.3	3.4	1.0	0.4	0.9	0.7	10.3	12.0	13.8	14.7
Oregon	3.3	4.6	3.8	3.9	2.5	3.6	2.7	2.8	0.7	3.1	7.9	7.6	10.5	14.0	12.9	12.2
Pennsylvania	1.6	2.4	2.7	2.8	0.9	1.2	1.4	1.4	0.9	2.1	3.3	3.1	6.7	10.9	11.1	11.5
Rhode Island	1.6	2.6	3.4	3.6	1.1	1.6	2.4	2.6	1.8	3.3	2.2	2.4	5.3	9.7	10.6	11.0
South Carolina	1.0	1.5	1.7	1.7	0.7	0.7	0.9	0.9	2.3	1.4	1.4	1.8	3.5	8.4	6.6	6.6
South Dakota	1.5	1.9	2.7	2.6	1.2	1.0	1.6	1.6	1.4	1.3	2.0	1.0	4.4	9.8	11.9	11.4
Tennessee	2.1	1.9	2.0	2.0	1.7	1.2	1.3	1.2	1.8	1.7	2.0	2.0	5.6	8.4	7.6	7.7
Texas	3.6	2.7	2.8	2.8	3.0	1.6	1.6	1.6	0.5	1.3	2.2	3.0	9.3	11.8	12.0	12.1
Utah	3.9	3.9	3.6	3.4	3.2	2.7	2.8	2.7	2.3	2.2	2.2	2.2	11.2	17.2	13.5	11.9
Vermont	1.9	2.0	2.3	2.3	1.6	1.6	1.9	1.9	0.1	2.0	0.8	0.6	6.3	4.9	5.9	5.9
Virginia	1.4	1.7	2.2	2.2	1.2	1.1	1.4	1.5	0.3	0.9	2.5	1.7	3.3	6.1	6.9	7.1
Washington	3.0	2.0	3.1	3.2	2.6	1.3	2.5	2.7	0.6	1.4	2.0	1.6	8.9	10.6	10.5	10.3
West Virginia	1.7	1.9	2.0	2.0	1.4	1.4	1.4	1.5	(¹)	1.2	0.7	0.5	3.7	6.7	6.3	5.8
Wisconsin	1.6	2.1	2.3	2.3	0.9	1.1	1.4	1.4	0.8	1.6	1.5	1.7	7.9	11.3	10.7	10.3
Wyoming	1.9	1.8	1.5	1.3	1.4	1.1	0.8	0.7	1.0	(¹)	0.4	(¹)	8.5	8.8	9.5	8.4
U.S. Service Schools	0.6	1.0	0.6	0.6	0.2	0.4	0.2	0.2	(¹)	(¹)	(¹)	(¹)	11.9	10.4	8.2	9.1
Outlying areas	0.6	0.9	0.5	0.4	0.6	0.8	0.6	0.4	(¹)	(¹)	(¹)	0.1	0.6	1.4	0.1	0.1
American Samoa	(¹)	22.6	(¹)	(¹)	(¹)	22.6	(¹)	(¹)	—	—	—	—	—	—	—	—
Federated States of Micronesia	—	(¹)	0.1	0.0	—	(¹)	0.1	(¹)	—	—	—	—	—	—	—	—
Guam	10.0	10.1	8.4	6.1	11.4	10.2	8.8	6.3	—	—	—	—	3.5	6.1	1.9	2.6
Marshall Islands	—	—	2.6	0.0	—	—	2.6	(¹)	—	—	—	—	—	—	—	—
Northern Marianas	—	23.6	23.8	14.9	—	23.6	23.8	14.9	—	—	—	—	—	—	—	—
Palau	—	(¹)	(¹)	0.0	—	(¹)	(¹)	(¹)	—	—	—	—	—	—	—	—
Puerto Rico	0.1	0.2	(¹)	0.0	0.1	0.1	(¹)	0.0	(¹)	(¹)	(¹)	0.1	0.4	1.3	(¹)	(¹)
Trust Territories	(¹)	—	—	—	(¹)	—	—	—	—	—	—	—	—	—	—	—
Virgin Islands	15.5	8.8	4.7	4.3	17.1	9.8	4.9	4.5	—	—	—	—	0.9	(¹)	2.5	2.2

¹ Less than .05 percent.
—Data not available or not applicable.

SOURCE: U.S. Department of Education, National Center for Education Statistics, Higher Education General Information Survey (HEGIS), "Fall Enrollment in Colleges and Universities, 1980"; and Integrated Postsecondary Education Data System (IPEDS), "Fall Enrollment" surveys. (This table was prepared February 1998.)

Table 51.—Residence and migration of all freshmen students [1] in degree-granting institutions of higher education graduating from high school in the past 12 months, by state: Fall 1996

State or other area	Students enrolled in institutions located in the state [2]	Student residents of state		Ratio of students remaining to—		Migration of students		
		Attending college in any state [3]	Attending college in home state [4]	Students enrolled (col. 4 ÷ col. 2)	Student residents (col. 4 ÷ col. 3)	Out of (col. 3– col. 4)	Into (col. 2– col. 4)	Net (column 8– column 7)
1	2	3	4	5	6	7	8	9
United States	1,513,122	1,491,441	1,209,015	0.80	0.81	282,657	304,338	[5] 21,681
Alabama	26,841	23,512	21,115	0.79	0.90	2,397	5,726	3,329
Alaska	1,241	2,494	1,050	0.85	0.42	1,444	191	–1,253
Arizona	18,414	15,559	13,280	0.72	0.85	2,279	5,134	2,855
Arkansas	14,173	13,476	11,723	0.83	0.87	1,753	2,450	697
California	186,894	188,822	173,860	0.93	0.92	14,962	13,034	–1,928
Colorado	18,840	18,188	13,656	0.72	0.75	4,532	5,184	652
Connecticut	15,754	19,577	9,202	0.58	0.47	10,375	6,552	–3,823
Delaware	6,333	4,719	3,356	0.53	0.71	1,363	2,977	1,614
District of Columbia	7,707	2,277	973	0.13	0.43	1,304	6,734	5,430
Florida	51,221	49,999	41,265	0.81	0.83	8,734	9,956	1,222
Georgia	35,508	34,508	28,305	0.80	0.82	6,203	7,203	1,000
Hawaii	6,062	7,020	4,951	0.82	0.71	2,069	1,111	–958
Idaho	7,171	6,933	5,034	0.70	0.73	1,899	2,137	238
Illinois	68,351	76,889	60,941	0.89	0.79	15,948	7,410	–8,538
Indiana	40,481	35,079	30,605	0.76	0.87	4,474	9,876	5,402
Iowa	25,222	21,852	18,828	0.75	0.86	3,024	6,394	3,370
Kansas	18,334	16,937	14,812	0.81	0.87	2,125	3,522	1,397
Kentucky	21,902	20,979	18,210	0.83	0.87	2,769	3,692	923
Louisiana	25,332	24,118	20,941	0.83	0.87	3,177	4,391	1,214
Maine	6,391	7,422	4,136	0.65	0.56	3,286	2,255	–1,031
Maryland	23,969	27,699	17,711	0.74	0.64	9,988	6,258	–3,730
Massachusetts	49,793	41,485	29,054	0.58	0.70	12,431	20,739	8,308
Michigan	55,718	55,476	49,673	0.89	0.90	5,803	6,045	242
Minnesota	27,799	29,104	21,251	0.76	0.73	7,853	6,548	–1,305
Mississippi	18,937	17,157	15,680	0.83	0.91	1,477	3,257	1,780
Missouri	29,136	27,554	22,433	0.77	0.81	5,121	6,703	1,582
Montana	5,501	5,834	4,112	0.75	0.70	1,722	1,389	–333
Nebraska	12,653	12,329	10,180	0.80	0.83	2,149	2,473	324
Nevada	3,750	4,275	2,696	0.72	0.63	1,579	1,054	–525
New Hampshire	8,347	6,814	3,420	0.41	0.50	3,394	4,927	1,533
New Jersey	32,767	51,483	29,265	0.89	0.57	22,218	3,502	–18,716
New Mexico	8,382	9,169	6,822	0.81	0.74	2,347	1,560	–787
New York	110,563	114,907	90,527	0.82	0.79	24,380	20,036	–4,344
North Carolina	39,722	32,303	29,259	0.74	0.91	3,044	10,463	7,419
North Dakota	7,284	5,939	4,757	0.65	0.80	1,182	2,527	1,345
Ohio	64,521	63,371	54,089	0.84	0.85	9,282	10,432	1,150
Oklahoma	16,475	16,481	14,107	0.86	0.86	2,374	2,368	–6
Oregon	15,394	14,898	11,527	0.75	0.77	3,371	3,867	496
Pennsylvania	77,081	70,898	57,231	0.74	0.81	13,667	19,850	6,183
Rhode Island	9,781	5,944	3,536	0.36	0.59	2,408	6,245	3,837
South Carolina	21,789	19,357	16,656	0.76	0.86	2,701	5,133	2,432
South Dakota	4,393	4,568	3,054	0.70	0.67	1,514	1,339	–175
Tennessee	28,857	26,308	21,941	0.76	0.83	4,367	6,916	2,549
Texas	95,793	97,688	88,127	0.92	0.90	9,561	7,666	–1,895
Utah	18,328	13,657	12,612	0.69	0.92	1,045	5,716	4,671
Vermont	4,983	3,313	1,532	0.31	0.46	1,781	3,451	1,670
Virginia	38,287	34,248	27,005	0.71	0.79	7,243	11,282	4,039
Washington	30,060	30,551	25,819	0.86	0.85	4,732	4,241	–491
West Virginia	12,248	10,535	8,837	0.72	0.84	1,698	3,411	1,713
Wisconsin	32,447	33,445	27,426	0.85	0.82	6,019	5,021	–998
Wyoming	3,147	3,127	2,202	0.70	0.70	925	945	20
U.S. Service Schools	3,045	—	231	0.08	—	—	3,045	3,276
State unknown [6]	—	11,164	—	—	—	11,164	—	–11,164
Outlying areas	32,634	34,534	32,533	1.00	0.94	2,001	101	–1,900
American Samoa	—	37	—	—	—	37	—	–37
Federated States of Micronesia	320	1,078	320	1.00	0.30	758	—	–758
Guam	309	426	285	0.92	0.67	141	24	–117
Marshall Islands	113	115	107	0.95	0.93	8	6	–2
Northern Marianas	100	109	95	0.95	0.87	14	5	–9
Palau	109	114	70	0.64	0.61	44	39	–5
Puerto Rico	31,489	32,141	31,467	1.00	0.98	674	22	–652
Virgin Islands	194	514	189	0.97	0.37	325	5	–320
Foreign countries	—	19,781	—	—	—	19,781	—	–19,781

[1] Students who are enrolled at the reporting institution for the first time ever enrolled anywhere.

[2] All of the new students reported by the institutions in that state; i.e., all in-migrants and "remaining" students.

[3] All students living in a particular state when admitted to an institution in any state. Students may be enrolled in any state.

[4] Students who attend institutions in their home state.

[5] Includes students coming to U.S. colleges from foreign countries and the outlying areas.

[6] Students are reported in "state unknown" when an institution is unable to determine the student's home state.

—Data not available or not applicable.

NOTE.—Data are for 4-year and 2-year degree-granting higher education institutions that were eligible to participate in Title IV federal financial aid programs in the 1996–97 academic year.

SOURCE: U.S. Department of Education, National Center for Education Statistics, Integrated Postsecondary Education Data System (IPEDS), "Residence of First-Time Students" survey, 1996. (This table was prepared January 1998.)

Table 52.—Total fall enrollment in institutions of higher education, by state: 1970 to 1996

State or other area	Fall 1970	Fall 1971	Fall 1972	Fall 1973	Fall 1974	Fall 1975	Fall 1976	Fall 1977	Fall 1978	Fall 1979
1	2	3	4	5	6	7	8	9	10	11
United States	**8,580,887**	**8,948,644**	**9,214,820**	**9,602,123**	**10,223,729**	**11,184,859**	**11,012,137**	**11,285,787**	**11,260,092**	**11,569,899**
Alabama	103,936	111,305	118,755	126,829	143,188	164,700	156,173	162,308	161,579	159,784
Alaska	9,471	12,342	13,745	13,224	14,043	13,998	18,500	21,522	26,351	20,052
Arizona	109,821	118,434	123,722	138,188	152,299	173,542	174,687	181,503	176,612	188,976
Arkansas	52,039	53,565	53,762	53,509	56,487	65,326	67,222	71,000	72,056	74,453
California	1,257,043	1,304,738	1,375,614	1,469,738	1,597,724	1,788,356	1,727,832	1,743,448	1,650,271	1,698,788
Colorado	123,395	128,160	129,153	131,993	143,093	149,814	149,455	153,967	152,359	156,100
Connecticut	125,347	129,505	131,012	135,911	144,667	148,491	145,136	149,660	152,431	156,067
Delaware	25,260	27,704	27,761	28,888	30,357	32,389	31,182	30,960	30,918	32,308
District of Columbia	77,158	80,452	80,472	80,324	81,403	84,190	80,344	84,044	81,807	87,855
Florida	235,525	251,861	260,148	281,104	306,680	344,267	345,743	364,509	377,100	395,233
Georgia	126,511	136,232	141,179	146,601	155,924	173,585	169,643	173,708	174,867	178,017
Hawaii	36,562	40,466	42,542	42,617	44,776	47,739	48,119	48,617	49,310	48,994
Idaho	34,567	35,591	35,127	35,198	35,714	39,075	38,439	40,200	39,255	40,661
Illinois	452,888	474,080	487,071	497,906	536,106	584,856	610,034	617,004	612,237	613,874
Indiana	193,035	203,803	201,655	200,334	203,996	213,972	220,413	225,143	222,922	228,397
Iowa	108,902	111,109	109,470	109,284	113,714	121,678	120,984	125,744	129,181	132,599
Kansas	102,485	106,495	107,858	108,023	113,352	120,833	122,143	127,447	127,323	133,360
Kentucky	98,591	104,798	108,178	110,759	113,755	125,253	128,866	131,515	132,706	135,179
Louisiana	120,728	129,995	134,389	135,237	140,565	153,213	154,386	153,982	152,207	153,812
Maine	34,134	32,897	34,551	36,122	36,634	40,443	39,489	40,172	41,460	42,912
Maryland	149,677	159,045	168,128	177,501	188,114	205,285	209,238	216,330	214,438	218,447
Massachusetts	303,809	315,348	321,939	332,850	356,239	384,485	360,874	375,380	384,500	396,267
Michigan	392,359	405,495	406,457	426,049	457,179	496,253	469,269	481,616	485,161	503,839
Minnesota	160,788	158,830	158,005	163,282	167,230	184,756	186,043	188,688	189,087	193,830
Mississippi	73,967	77,284	80,276	82,314	87,167	99,962	97,703	98,420	97,569	100,272
Missouri	183,188	187,665	188,164	192,433	199,999	222,348	221,135	221,469	220,456	221,088
Montana	30,062	29,421	28,195	27,317	28,092	30,843	29,713	31,646	31,103	31,906
Nebraska	66,915	66,663	66,054	66,034	67,292	74,705	77,204	81,316	81,691	86,446
Nevada	13,669	15,065	17,271	20,044	26,274	30,187	29,995	31,412	33,539	35,935
New Hampshire	29,400	30,064	30,199	33,399	34,365	41,030	39,373	41,270	41,549	42,112
New Jersey	216,121	233,214	240,891	255,357	275,864	297,114	290,603	301,091	308,304	312,460
New Mexico	44,725	48,798	48,753	49,095	50,941	52,229	54,710	55,517	56,013	56,487
New York	805,832	826,424	850,714	904,437	947,672	1,005,355	939,018	951,031	955,678	970,286
North Carolina	171,925	184,519	198,510	204,633	224,418	251,786	248,480	257,198	262,757	269,065
North Dakota	31,495	30,642	29,765	29,460	28,544	29,743	30,187	32,199	32,325	31,904
Ohio	375,933	385,961	389,020	395,305	406,444	435,336	444,624	452,375	450,386	463,310
Oklahoma	110,155	119,089	122,183	125,963	132,829	146,613	145,196	149,501	149,397	152,683
Oregon	122,177	122,189	123,209	132,341	139,055	145,281	146,068	141,186	146,349	154,597
Pennsylvania	411,044	426,391	429,651	440,666	446,994	470,536	473,571	475,659	472,577	481,347
Rhode Island	45,898	48,354	50,004	55,122	59,436	64,479	59,626	63,691	63,553	64,435
South Carolina	69,518	76,708	93,796	96,496	114,708	133,023	121,544	125,245	130,076	131,459
South Dakota	30,639	31,191	28,900	26,530	26,855	30,260	30,186	31,110	30,931	31,294
Tennessee	135,103	142,220	147,460	155,056	164,613	181,656	181,577	188,599	194,929	199,902
Texas	442,225	463,261	487,642	503,750	547,142	624,390	621,155	647,593	656,004	676,047
Utah	81,687	83,228	82,278	80,465	81,121	86,255	84,671	86,882	87,214	88,608
Vermont	22,209	24,353	25,712	27,707	28,289	29,095	29,351	29,506	29,577	29,550
Virginia	151,915	163,554	176,484	193,277	215,851	244,671	244,276	257,529	258,368	270,599
Washington	183,544	186,783	193,122	199,478	210,018	227,168	248,389	262,961	275,299	303,469
West Virginia	63,153	65,475	63,608	68,201	71,250	78,619	80,156	81,121	79,007	81,335
Wisconsin	202,058	213,654	217,835	221,277	226,575	240,701	232,729	243,876	241,384	255,907
Wyoming	15,220	17,257	17,651	17,922	19,447	18,078	19,183	19,727	19,933	19,490
U.S. Service Schools	17,079	16,967	16,780	16,573	29,235	36,897	17,500	18,190	17,986	18,102
Outlying areas	67,237	75,077	81,451	90,542	96,135	104,270	107,956	127,855	130,220	135,898
American Samoa	—	632	848	909	833	689	836	1,114	831	856
Federated States of Micronesia	—	—	—	—	—	—	—	—	—	—
Guam	2,719	3,068	3,351	3,430	3,558	3,800	3,710	4,343	3,208	3,168
Marshall Islands	—	—	—	—	—	—	—	—	—	—
Northern Marianas	—	—	—	—	—	—	—	—	—	—
Palau	—	—	—	—	—	—	—	—	—	—
Puerto Rico	63,073	69,620	75,355	84,390	89,671	97,517	100,885	119,970	123,967	129,708
Trust Territories	—	113	121	115	155	185	403	309	366	176
Virgin Islands	1,445	1,644	1,776	1,698	1,918	2,079	2,122	2,119	1,848	1,990

Table 52.—Total fall enrollment in institutions of higher education, by state: 1970 to 1996—Continued

State or other area	Fall 1980	Fall 1981	Fall 1982	Fall 1983	Fall 1984	Fall 1985	Fall 1986	Fall 1987	Fall 1988	Fall 1989
1	12	13	14	15	16	17	18	19	20	21
United States	**12,096,895**	**12,371,672**	**12,425,780**	**12,464,661**	**12,241,940**	**12,247,055**	**12,503,511**	**12,766,642**	**13,055,337**	**13,538,560**
Alabama	164,306	166,375	167,753	171,381	171,631	179,343	181,443	183,348	197,352	208,562
Alaska	21,296	24,754	24,556	26,045	26,991	27,479	27,477	26,937	28,983	28,627
Arizona	202,716	205,169	210,683	213,437	210,029	216,854	226,595	237,233	258,792	252,625
Arkansas	77,347	75,782	76,704	76,467	78,570	77,747	79,182	79,273	84,562	88,572
California	1,791,088	1,885,842	1,843,043	1,730,924	1,665,233	1,650,516	1,727,295	1,788,170	1,754,478	1,802,884
Colorado	162,916	167,977	171,821	172,650	164,394	161,314	177,333	183,583	186,912	201,114
Connecticut	159,632	162,367	162,194	164,344	161,576	159,348	158,278	162,382	165,677	169,438
Delaware	32,939	33,746	34,074	33,590	33,494	33,401	33,895	36,637	38,261	40,562
District of Columbia	86,675	88,553	82,337	79,673	79,132	78,201	76,943	76,370	78,464	79,230
Florida	411,891	426,570	436,606	443,436	444,062	451,392	483,958	489,964	516,508	578,123
Georgia	184,159	191,384	198,367	201,453	196,869	196,826	195,124	224,066	230,893	242,289
Hawaii	49,009	50,066	53,395	53,933	51,917	51,863	51,697	52,291	52,297	54,188
Idaho	43,018	42,758	42,975	42,911	43,303	42,668	45,260	45,567	46,338	48,969
Illinois	645,288	660,695	684,998	674,196	662,226	679,725	692,018	686,954	689,326	709,952
Indiana	247,253	251,826	253,529	256,470	249,957	250,567	250,176	256,264	267,905	275,821
Iowa	140,449	143,105	147,862	152,968	153,069	152,897	155,369	158,230	162,098	169,901
Kansas	136,605	138,453	141,661	141,709	141,916	141,359	143,205	146,439	152,822	158,497
Kentucky	143,066	144,154	144,159	146,503	143,555	141,724	144,560	153,351	160,208	166,014
Louisiana	160,058	174,656	176,505	179,647	179,988	177,176	171,332	173,229	176,051	180,202
Maine	43,264	44,012	47,719	53,347	52,714	52,201	46,229	46,992	48,360	58,230
Maryland	225,180	229,583	234,243	238,867	233,949	231,317	233,492	239,362	248,136	254,533
Massachusetts	418,415	417,830	407,557	423,348	418,966	421,175	417,540	423,916	426,603	426,476
Michigan	520,131	513,033	508,240	515,760	505,334	507,293	520,392	535,486	544,399	560,320
Minnesota	206,691	210,713	214,133	214,219	215,566	221,162	226,558	237,212	244,612	253,097
Mississippi	102,364	106,029	106,010	109,728	104,339	101,180	101,104	105,510	111,262	116,370
Missouri	233,378	242,545	243,131	247,217	239,808	240,110	246,185	251,778	262,391	278,505
Montana	35,177	35,959	36,811	37,877	37,061	35,958	35,238	35,882	35,777	37,660
Nebraska	89,488	93,507	94,390	95,162	97,422	97,769	100,401	100,828	104,879	108,844
Nevada	40,455	39,936	42,212	43,768	43,007	43,656	46,796	48,063	48,831	56,471
New Hampshire	46,794	48,524	52,208	53,143	53,049	52,283	53,882	56,163	57,410	59,081
New Jersey	321,610	322,797	322,284	314,468	305,330	297,658	295,271	294,433	302,881	314,091
New Mexico	58,629	60,766	63,825	66,459	66,860	68,627	80,271	83,074	79,135	81,350
New York	992,349	1,014,975	1,012,533	1,022,633	1,007,870	1,000,198	1,000,817	992,544	1,006,494	1,029,518
North Carolina	287,537	295,771	300,910	301,675	309,249	327,288	322,980	321,251	332,226	345,502
North Dakota	34,069	35,446	36,224	37,591	37,585	37,939	37,309	36,259	38,489	40,404
Ohio	488,938	521,199	532,169	535,403	518,257	514,568	520,479	518,464	543,980	550,720
Oklahoma	160,295	162,825	168,186	174,171	168,034	169,173	170,840	172,730	176,308	175,855
Oregon	157,458	149,924	141,312	141,172	141,810	137,967	144,785	152,657	156,158	161,822
Pennsylvania	507,716	516,194	527,721	543,467	527,047	531,680	545,921	554,370	573,552	610,479
Rhode Island	66,869	68,339	68,351	70,811	69,145	69,927	69,567	71,708	74,847	76,503
South Carolina	132,476	132,394	136,727	134,532	131,479	131,902	134,115	140,841	148,168	145,730
South Dakota	32,761	35,015	35,074	34,879	32,473	32,772	30,935	31,755	31,461	32,666
Tennessee	204,841	200,433	202,074	208,012	201,144	195,056	197,071	202,006	206,367	218,866
Texas	701,391	716,297	758,839	795,741	795,337	769,692	776,023	801,771	847,310	879,335
Utah	92,159	95,103	97,824	101,456	99,927	102,068	106,218	106,792	108,631	114,815
Vermont	30,628	30,573	30,648	31,306	30,786	31,416	32,460	33,242	34,403	35,946
Virginia	280,504	286,015	281,026	288,588	283,109	292,416	308,318	319,026	320,931	344,284
Washington	303,603	278,680	227,812	229,639	230,667	231,553	242,379	245,872	254,051	255,760
West Virginia	81,973	82,375	82,891	83,202	79,009	76,659	76,781	77,256	80,540	82,455
Wisconsin	269,086	275,325	276,176	277,751	270,865	275,069	283,653	281,717	286,456	291,966
Wyoming	21,147	21,235	22,713	23,844	23,424	24,204	24,357	26,062	26,540	29,159
U.S. Service Schools	49,808	54,088	60,585	53,688	53,406	54,719	54,004	61,332	45,822	56,177
Outlying areas	137,749	146,081	162,740	169,269	158,452	164,890	165,620	156,809	163,449	162,955
American Samoa	976	987	1,007	845	871	758	759	897	908	1,011
Federated States of Micronesia	—	—	—	—	—	—	—	—	—	—
Guam	3,217	5,127	5,041	3,436	4,432	4,601	4,477	4,072	3,819	838
Marshall Islands	—	—	—	—	—	—	—	—	—	4,350
Northern Marianas	—	—	—	173	431	318	514	366	352	—
Palau	—	—	—	—	—	—	—	—	—	419
Puerto Rico	131,184	137,171	153,350	161,215	149,102	155,917	156,580	147,706	154,712	1,037
Trust Territories	224	188	598	736	796	724	795	1,223	1,187	152,603
Virgin Islands	2,148	2,608	2,744	2,864	2,820	2,572	2,495	2,545	2,471	2,697

Table 52.—Total fall enrollment in institutions of higher education, by state: 1970 to 1996—Continued

State or other area	Fall 1990	Fall 1991	Fall 1992	Fall 1993	Fall 1994	Fall 1995	Fall 1996	Percentage change			
								Fall 1970 to fall 1996	Fall 1986 to fall 1991	Fall 1991 to fall 1996	Fall 1986 to fall 1996
1	22	23	24	25	26	27	28	29	30	31	32
United States	**13,818,637**	**14,358,953**	**14,487,359**	**14,304,803**	**14,278,790**	**14,261,781**	**14,300,255**	**66.7**	**14.8**	**-0.4**	**14.4**
Alabama	218,589	224,331	230,537	233,525	229,511	225,612	219,499	111.2	23.6	-2.2	21.0
Alaska	29,833	30,793	30,902	30,638	28,798	29,348	28,846	204.6	12.1	-6.3	5.0
Arizona	264,148	272,971	274,671	272,300	274,932	273,981	276,832	152.1	20.5	1.4	22.2
Arkansas	90,425	94,340	97,578	99,262	96,294	98,180	100,688	93.5	19.1	6.7	27.2
California	1,808,740	2,024,274	1,978,003	1,836,349	1,835,791	1,817,042	1,882,634	49.8	17.2	-7.0	9.0
Colorado	227,131	235,108	241,352	239,805	241,295	242,739	242,949	96.9	32.6	3.3	37.0
Connecticut	168,604	165,824	165,874	162,300	159,990	157,695	155,361	23.9	4.8	-6.3	-1.8
Delaware	42,004	42,988	42,763	43,528	44,197	44,307	44,838	77.5	26.8	4.3	32.3
District of Columbia	79,551	77,353	81,202	81,565	77,256	77,277	74,239	-3.8	0.5	-4.0	-3.5
Florida	588,086	611,781	618,285	623,403	634,237	637,303	641,173	172.2	26.4	4.8	32.5
Georgia	251,786	277,023	293,606	302,844	308,587	314,712	317,999	151.4	42.0	14.8	63.0
Hawaii	56,436	57,302	61,162	62,871	64,322	63,198	61,383	67.9	10.8	7.1	18.7
Idaho	51,881	55,397	57,798	58,768	60,393	59,566	59,904	73.3	22.4	8.1	32.4
Illinois	729,246	753,297	748,805	734,089	731,420	717,854	720,987	59.2	8.9	-4.3	4.2
Indiana	284,832	290,301	296,912	294,685	292,276	289,615	286,326	48.3	16.0	-1.4	14.4
Iowa	170,515	171,024	172,805	172,797	172,450	173,835	177,021	62.6	10.1	3.5	13.9
Kansas	163,733	167,699	169,419	170,135	170,603	177,643	172,350	68.2	17.1	2.8	20.4
Kentucky	177,852	187,958	188,322	187,332	182,577	178,858	177,749	80.3	30.0	-5.4	23.0
Louisiana	186,840	197,438	204,379	201,987	203,567	203,935	203,517	68.6	15.2	3.1	18.8
Maine	57,186	57,178	57,977	56,294	56,724	56,547	55,645	63.0	23.7	-2.7	20.4
Maryland	259,700	267,931	268,399	268,005	266,214	266,310	260,757	74.2	14.7	-2.7	11.7
Massachusetts	417,833	419,381	422,976	420,127	416,505	413,794	410,327	35.1	0.4	-2.2	-1.7
Michigan	569,803	568,491	560,773	568,210	551,307	548,339	546,974	39.4	9.2	-3.8	5.1
Minnesota	253,789	255,054	272,920	268,118	289,300	280,816	275,262	71.2	12.6	7.9	21.5
Mississippi	122,883	125,350	123,754	122,408	120,884	122,690	126,234	70.7	24.0	0.7	24.9
Missouri	289,899	297,154	296,617	297,062	293,810	291,536	290,533	58.6	20.7	-2.2	18.0
Montana	35,876	37,821	39,644	39,557	40,095	42,674	43,145	43.5	7.3	14.1	22.4
Nebraska	112,831	113,648	122,603	115,523	116,000	115,718	119,300	78.3	13.2	5.0	18.8
Nevada	61,728	62,664	63,877	63,947	64,085	67,826	73,467	437.5	33.9	17.2	57.0
New Hampshire	59,510	63,718	63,924	64,043	62,847	64,327	64,463	119.3	18.3	1.2	19.6
New Jersey	324,286	334,641	343,232	343,029	335,480	333,831	328,188	51.9	13.3	-1.9	11.1
New Mexico	85,500	93,507	99,276	101,460	101,881	102,405	103,546	131.5	16.5	10.7	29.0
New York	1,048,286	1,056,487	1,064,822	1,062,924	1,057,841	1,041,566	1,027,870	27.6	5.6	-2.7	2.7
North Carolina	352,138	371,968	383,453	371,280	369,386	372,010	373,168	117.1	15.2	0.3	15.5
North Dakota	37,878	38,739	40,470	40,316	40,184	40,399	40,554	28.8	3.8	4.7	8.7
Ohio	557,690	569,326	573,183	562,402	549,304	540,275	537,535	43.0	9.4	-5.6	3.3
Oklahoma	173,221	183,536	187,846	183,342	185,174	180,676	177,255	60.9	7.4	-3.4	3.8
Oregon	165,741	167,107	167,415	165,834	164,447	167,145	165,168	35.2	15.4	-1.2	14.1
Pennsylvania	604,060	620,036	626,904	621,228	611,174	617,759	621,994	51.3	13.6	0.3	13.9
Rhode Island	78,273	79,112	79,165	77,407	74,718	74,100	72,432	57.8	13.7	-8.4	4.1
South Carolina	159,302	164,907	171,443	174,302	173,070	174,125	174,303	150.7	23.0	5.7	30.0
South Dakota	34,208	36,332	37,596	38,166	37,764	36,695	35,373	15.5	17.4	-2.6	14.3
Tennessee	226,238	238,042	242,970	244,936	242,966	245,962	247,043	82.9	20.8	3.8	25.4
Texas	901,437	917,443	938,526	942,178	954,495	952,525	955,439	116.1	18.2	4.1	23.1
Utah	121,303	130,419	133,083	138,139	146,196	147,324	151,637	85.6	22.8	16.3	42.8
Vermont	36,398	37,436	37,377	36,415	35,409	35,065	35,090	58.0	15.3	-6.3	8.1
Virginia	353,442	356,325	354,172	348,535	354,149	355,919	353,788	132.9	15.6	-0.7	14.7
Washington	263,384	274,760	275,556	279,845	284,662	285,819	292,180	59.2	13.4	6.3	20.5
West Virginia	84,790	88,602	90,252	88,852	87,741	86,034	85,689	35.7	15.4	-3.3	11.6
Wisconsin	299,774	308,986	307,902	309,036	303,861	300,223	299,127	48.0	8.9	-3.2	5.5
Wyoming	31,326	32,118	31,548	30,702	30,682	30,176	30,805	102.4	31.9	-4.1	26.5
U.S. Service Schools	48,692	53,532	53,329	52,998	51,939	88,451	81,669	378.2	-0.9	52.6	51.2
Outlying areas	164,618	168,771	169,759	172,989	170,686	183,657	181,660	170.2	1.9	7.6	9.7
American Samoa	1,219	1,267	1,295	1,264	1,249	1,232	1,239	—	66.9	-2.2	63.2
Federated States of Micronesia	975	837	1,028	1,148	1,374	1,296	1,396	—	—	66.8	—
Guam	4,741	5,016	4,845	5,843	6,449	6,010	5,335	96.2	12.0	6.4	19.2
Marshall Islands	—	—	374	386	424	418	431	—	—	—	—
Northern Marianas	661	847	796	1,261	1,253	959	1,096	—	64.8	29.4	113.2
Palau	491	355	445	436	403	351	332	—	—	-6.5	—
Puerto Rico	154,065	157,733	158,120	159,709	156,439	170,337	168,933	167.8	0.7	7.1	7.9
Trust Territories	—	—	—	—	—	—	—	—	—	—	—
Virgin Islands	2,466	2,716	2,856	2,942	3,095	3,054	2,898	100.6	8.9	6.7	16.2

—Data not available or not applicable.

SOURCE: U.S. Department of Education, National Center for Education Statistics, Higher Education General Information Survey (HEGIS), "Fall Enrollment in Higher Education" surveys; and Integrated Postsecondary Education Data System (IPEDS), "Fall Enrollment" surveys. (This table was prepared February 1998.)

Table 53.—Total fall enrollment in public 4–year institutions of higher education, by state: 1970 to 1996

State or other area	Fall 1970	Fall 1971	Fall 1972	Fall 1973	Fall 1974	Fall 1975	Fall 1976	Fall 1977	Fall 1978	Fall 1979
1	2	3	4	5	6	7	8	9	10	11
United States	**4,232,722**	**4,346,990**	**4,429,696**	**4,529,895**	**4,703,018**	**4,998,142**	**4,901,691**	**4,945,224**	**4,912,203**	**4,980,012**
Alabama	66,635	70,326	74,076	77,969	83,306	92,814	96,041	100,072	101,540	103,026
Alaska	7,860	3,984	4,582	6,167	6,733	7,249	9,047	7,773	8,407	6,733
Arizona	63,913	66,597	67,061	68,908	70,427	77,081	73,786	76,597	76,604	80,240
Arkansas	40,775	42,198	41,947	41,191	42,444	47,657	49,362	50,254	51,403	53,200
California	429,397	418,694	456,133	461,519	469,575	516,096	491,350	466,365	450,912	445,780
Colorado	87,469	89,755	89,910	89,572	96,880	96,001	95,500	98,093	97,231	98,140
Connecticut	48,183	50,221	50,044	50,926	53,514	57,453	55,019	54,959	53,563	54,212
Delaware	17,442	18,843	19,411	19,870	20,201	20,813	20,879	21,148	20,916	21,048
District of Columbia	9,018	10,538	10,549	9,764	14,375	15,159	13,895	13,292	13,661	15,096
Florida	81,239	84,873	94,086	100,348	108,980	117,957	111,912	117,347	120,345	123,851
Georgia	80,162	87,542	90,775	91,368	95,907	102,159	99,260	101,662	99,673	103,423
Hawaii	22,110	23,680	24,364	23,874	23,195	22,661	24,526	24,169	24,391	24,032
Idaho	24,197	25,161	25,241	25,822	25,215	27,400	26,767	27,564	25,943	27,077
Illinois	179,423	175,848	176,191	178,987	183,615	193,697	188,953	188,769	185,466	187,278
Indiana	133,421	140,961	140,442	137,370	140,115	145,748	151,237	152,739	148,365	149,991
Iowa	50,879	51,005	49,816	50,368	51,821	54,692	55,482	57,380	58,569	59,255
Kansas	70,390	73,607	72,921	73,120	75,843	80,065	79,663	82,950	82,004	84,434
Kentucky	67,453	73,165	76,729	78,684	81,094	87,903	90,038	90,531	92,066	93,312
Louisiana	93,221	100,936	104,626	107,001	109,093	118,395	117,277	116,525	115,088	117,480
Maine	23,779	19,748	21,432	22,967	23,739	25,895	24,404	24,245	24,495	24,910
Maryland	76,654	80,495	84,017	86,144	94,674	100,493	100,942	102,955	100,614	101,287
Massachusetts	80,214	85,484	90,162	93,988	100,334	105,653	101,382	103,318	104,235	102,713
Michigan	217,738	220,110	218,727	221,944	229,627	241,769	237,959	237,744	236,596	240,594
Minnesota	110,200	106,357	104,190	106,499	108,793	119,706	117,567	117,014	116,063	118,094
Mississippi	43,778	46,004	47,513	47,239	49,447	55,570	54,344	54,496	53,495	54,169
Missouri	99,962	101,428	101,856	101,560	98,410	104,826	104,394	105,068	103,884	106,685
Montana	25,220	24,901	23,299	22,481	23,191	24,883	23,939	25,771	25,072	26,554
Nebraska	47,708	47,186	46,664	46,065	46,098	48,931	48,891	50,061	50,509	51,174
Nevada	13,171	13,365	13,240	12,987	14,081	15,974	16,429	17,026	16,484	17,712
New Hampshire	15,362	16,001	15,828	16,774	16,143	18,116	18,327	18,754	18,397	18,568
New Jersey	103,581	111,995	116,411	124,446	136,528	142,494	133,437	139,211	143,173	141,494
New Mexico	37,002	39,974	39,877	39,397	40,081	41,076	43,581	43,231	43,220	44,061
New York	260,519	281,269	289,004	311,998	334,543	342,430	300,208	306,010	304,915	307,317
North Carolina	83,448	88,146	91,403	94,786	102,791	111,300	109,127	111,363	112,158	115,979
North Dakota	24,267	22,968	21,975	21,737	20,312	21,280	21,246	22,699	22,958	22,933
Ohio	227,253	229,281	225,737	224,772	227,274	237,137	237,944	240,893	237,960	243,887
Oklahoma	77,959	81,018	81,056	80,678	82,993	89,026	85,811	86,933	86,152	87,529
Oregon	66,912	62,736	61,514	61,430	62,445	64,842	63,855	61,832	62,196	64,079
Pennsylvania	171,641	176,687	176,679	183,222	186,158	193,086	192,153	189,243	183,393	183,401
Rhode Island	21,946	22,984	23,651	24,478	24,406	24,255	22,089	23,263	22,949	22,579
South Carolina	34,356	39,994	44,506	49,842	54,198	61,863	62,296	63,258	64,914	65,532
South Dakota	23,936	24,627	22,553	20,495	20,659	21,925	21,716	22,535	22,630	22,832
Tennessee	89,126	93,945	95,637	98,528	101,337	108,525	106,838	108,550	108,116	108,306
Texas	251,494	257,456	261,934	270,093	287,215	315,673	321,388	329,941	335,416	337,812
Utah	42,944	43,515	42,058	41,730	43,377	44,432	41,494	41,936	41,311	42,918
Vermont	12,041	13,075	13,344	14,129	14,507	14,501	15,426	15,100	15,149	15,075
Virginia	94,028	98,804	103,837	110,557	119,346	127,266	127,880	130,273	125,250	132,154
Washington	78,004	78,599	76,595	77,916	76,316	78,734	78,480	80,475	79,403	82,790
West Virginia	47,239	49,197	47,480	50,677	51,490	54,896	56,904	58,921	58,588	60,312
Wisconsin	132,174	134,587	131,844	130,119	131,890	134,619	134,899	137,695	139,465	141,859
Wyoming	8,800	10,153	9,989	10,816	11,264	9,026	8,847	9,031	8,910	8,993
U.S. Service Schools	17,079	16,967	16,780	16,573	17,018	16,940	17,500	18,190	17,986	18,102
Outlying areas	41,326	44,522	44,789	45,896	46,031	45,292	43,703	48,021	46,537	45,601
American Samoa	—	—	—	—	—	—	—	—	—	—
Federated States of Micronesia	—	—	—	—	—	—	—	—	—	—
Guam	2,719	3,068	3,351	3,430	3,558	3,800	3,710	4,343	3,208	3,168
Marshall Islands	—	—	—	—	—	—	—	—	—	—
Northern Marianas	—	—	—	—	—	—	—	—	—	—
Palau	—	—	—	—	—	—	—	—	—	—
Puerto Rico	37,162	39,810	39,662	40,768	40,555	39,413	37,871	41,559	41,481	40,443
Trust Territories	—	—	—	—	—	—	—	—	—	—
Virgin Islands	1,445	1,644	1,776	1,698	1,918	2,079	2,122	2,119	1,848	1,990

Table 53.—Total fall enrollment in public 4-year institutions of higher education, by state: 1970 to 1996—Continued

State or other area	Fall 1980	Fall 1981	Fall 1982	Fall 1983	Fall 1984	Fall 1985	Fall 1986	Fall 1987	Fall 1988	Fall 1989
1	12	13	14	15	16	17	18	19	20	21
United States	5,128,612	5,166,324	5,176,434	5,223,404	5,198,273	5,209,540	5,300,202	5,432,200	5,545,901	5,694,303
Alabama	104,306	104,439	104,085	105,032	102,452	104,676	103,575	105,914	112,944	121,155
Alaska	8,571	9,320	9,830	10,494	11,260	10,523	10,571	11,341	22,138	26,274
Arizona	80,858	81,475	81,881	82,184	82,669	84,119	86,731	89,373	94,317	96,276
Arkansas	54,765	53,266	53,550	52,781	54,254	53,933	54,350	53,885	55,353	58,662
California	469,538	478,650	474,640	458,393	463,747	463,726	487,515	503,253	484,181	493,719
Colorado	100,780	103,544	103,810	105,591	100,931	100,538	106,067	106,571	105,302	107,324
Connecticut	55,856	56,428	56,820	58,242	58,352	57,870	58,998	62,024	64,501	65,427
Delaware	21,337	20,745	20,766	20,347	20,292	20,452	20,958	21,456	22,328	23,080
District of Columbia	13,900	14,115	14,105	13,576	12,832	12,080	11,098	9,655	11,263	11,869
Florida	127,490	129,121	134,469	138,331	143,705	146,336	150,177	150,916	157,549	168,576
Georgia	104,075	108,638	111,746	113,258	112,706	114,619	116,634	124,991	129,693	136,239
Hawaii	23,910	24,278	25,034	25,004	23,633	23,243	22,687	22,404	22,550	23,111
Idaho	29,081	28,961	29,467	29,353	29,630	28,545	28,620	29,781	30,516	33,093
Illinois	191,237	190,744	189,957	186,276	184,593	187,244	195,648	197,057	193,442	194,913
Indiana	158,905	160,993	161,057	161,149	158,028	159,304	162,314	166,736	173,499	181,286
Iowa	62,482	63,279	65,461	68,774	69,882	69,943	70,055	69,335	68,872	68,221
Kansas	85,948	85,136	85,182	84,022	83,852	83,947	85,177	85,846	87,368	89,180
Kentucky	96,804	95,135	92,847	92,264	88,960	87,069	89,487	93,857	98,112	102,332
Louisiana	122,684	136,405	137,852	140,499	140,399	138,235	132,032	134,148	133,832	133,856
Maine	24,751	24,852	28,417	29,250	28,780	28,685	29,490	29,325	30,198	34,233
Maryland	102,024	100,705	100,521	102,146	102,584	104,065	105,534	107,196	108,338	109,374
Massachusetts	109,413	109,560	105,393	107,583	108,499	110,562	108,687	113,440	112,854	112,222
Michigan	242,109	235,027	226,758	226,999	225,479	229,020	236,622	244,288	249,484	255,555
Minnesota	125,165	125,819	125,582	124,348	124,106	127,303	130,926	132,316	133,905	134,896
Mississippi	53,904	53,869	54,097	55,358	53,025	52,558	50,416	50,382	54,272	56,716
Missouri	111,855	115,674	114,572	113,991	111,739	110,979	110,683	111,911	116,420	121,045
Montana	28,081	28,517	29,377	30,348	29,276	28,503	27,681	27,234	27,405	28,461
Nebraska	52,141	53,412	54,099	55,018	54,491	55,077	55,284	55,552	57,108	59,221
Nevada	18,943	19,803	21,065	20,976	20,670	21,292	22,498	23,425	25,179	27,085
New Hampshire	19,261	19,285	19,664	19,263	20,819	20,574	21,505	22,612	24,047	25,169
New Jersey	141,015	139,985	137,883	133,654	134,089	130,925	131,344	131,859	133,289	135,101
New Mexico	44,973	46,576	48,276	50,876	50,379	51,252	46,246	47,471	47,176	47,591
New York	312,389	313,046	311,137	323,438	321,448	320,520	338,380	342,436	352,559	358,538
North Carolina	121,637	122,956	124,147	124,911	125,929	128,731	133,415	135,340	140,025	144,413
North Dakota	24,423	25,303	26,001	27,167	27,125	27,535	27,389	26,565	27,932	29,718
Ohio	254,337	258,643	257,413	263,627	259,363	260,542	262,639	270,167	279,579	284,356
Oklahoma	88,042	88,182	90,949	95,118	90,971	91,995	93,640	93,619	94,688	94,688
Oregon	65,601	63,402	59,372	59,043	58,593	59,647	61,584	66,616	68,432	66,775
Pennsylvania	189,209	186,457	184,931	186,550	186,121	189,369	192,626	222,583	229,235	234,784
Rhode Island	23,208	23,587	22,558	22,979	22,190	22,772	22,411	23,210	24,278	25,204
South Carolina	68,656	67,934	67,893	68,482	68,666	69,098	70,304	74,799	79,252	79,252
South Dakota	23,854	25,653	25,619	26,158	24,023	23,339	24,036	24,147	23,899	25,075
Tennessee	107,820	104,458	103,108	107,022	103,694	101,430	100,457	102,702	103,791	107,780
Texas	348,144	350,941	365,003	378,506	381,975	371,035	369,910	376,076	391,942	410,392
Utah	45,080	45,999	48,215	49,617	48,771	50,281	51,942	52,622	52,633	54,444
Vermont	15,375	15,386	15,420	15,253	15,093	15,210	15,079	15,390	15,762	16,127
Virginia	135,326	135,965	137,118	137,793	138,437	141,380	147,946	151,589	154,165	158,260
Washington	83,363	80,393	78,322	78,658	78,806	77,923	77,313	77,722	78,174	78,387
West Virginia	62,045	61,979	61,695	61,555	58,633	57,404	57,528	58,311	60,733	62,227
Wisconsin	146,229	149,198	148,877	151,244	151,884	154,502	154,626	151,329	151,146	151,146
Wyoming	9,014	9,635	10,209	10,270	10,087	10,123	9,980	10,401	10,773	12,335
U.S. Service Schools	18,698	19,451	20,184	20,633	20,351	19,507	19,387	21,022	19,468	19,140
Outlying areas	46,867	46,220	48,386	63,962	56,714	57,106	59,070	57,508	57,792	56,626
American Samoa	—	—	—	—	—	—	—	—	—	—
Federated States of Micronesia	—	—	—	—	—	—	—	—	—	—
Guam	3,217	2,660	2,574	2,774	2,692	2,769	2,656	2,210	2,096	2,385
Marshall Islands	—	—	—	—	—	—	—	—	—	—
Northern Marianas	—	—	—	—	—	—	—	—	—	—
Palau	—	—	—	—	—	—	—	—	—	—
Puerto Rico	41,502	40,952	43,068	58,324	51,202	51,765	53,919	52,753	53,225	51,544
Trust Territories	—	—	—	—	—	—	—	—	—	—
Virgin Islands	2,148	2,608	2,744	2,864	2,820	2,572	2,495	2,545	2,471	2,697

Table 53.—Total fall enrollment in public 4–year institutions of higher education, by state: 1970 to 1996—Continued

| State or other area | Fall 1990 | Fall 1991 | Fall 1992 | Fall 1993 | Fall 1994 | Fall 1995 | Fall 1996 | Percentage change | | | |
| | | | | | | | | Fall 1970 to fall 1996 | Fall 1986 to fall 1991 | Fall 1991 to fall 1996 | Fall 1986 to fall 1996 |
1	22	23	24	25	26	27	28	29	30	31	32
United States	5,848,242	5,904,748	5,900,012	5,851,760	5,825,213	5,814,545	5,806,904	37.2	11.4	−1.7	9.6
Alabama	123,848	127,754	127,517	128,350	126,079	126,508	122,796	84.3	23.3	−3.9	18.6
Alaska	27,792	29,019	28,451	28,108	27,037	27,556	27,077	244.5	174.5	−6.7	156.1
Arizona	95,657	95,514	97,231	95,346	101,418	101,718	102,501	60.4	10.1	7.3	18.2
Arkansas	61,408	63,464	66,623	65,966	64,540	62,809	62,094	52.3	16.8	−2.2	14.2
California	536,789	530,942	515,109	490,479	483,332	490,231	504,803	17.6	8.9	−4.9	3.5
Colorado	128,616	131,564	131,870	132,113	132,748	132,616	132,293	51.2	24.0	0.6	24.7
Connecticut	64,994	63,557	62,147	59,904	57,867	57,711	56,548	17.4	7.7	−11.0	−4.2
Delaware	23,424	23,745	24,072	25,036	24,966	24,540	24,708	41.7	13.3	4.1	17.9
District of Columbia	11,990	11,422	11,578	10,608	10,599	9,663	7,456	−17.3	2.9	−34.7	−32.8
Florida	176,989	183,117	184,736	191,457	201,242	206,961	211,159	159.9	21.9	15.3	40.6
Georgia	141,106	151,218	154,213	155,834	157,391	160,425	159,013	98.4	29.7	5.2	36.3
Hawaii	23,900	22,656	23,281	23,911	23,741	23,345	21,691	−1.9	−0.1	−4.3	−4.4
Idaho	35,709	37,936	39,738	40,434	41,629	41,449	41,344	70.9	32.6	9.0	44.5
Illinois	198,464	202,006	199,909	197,377	194,489	192,532	192,319	7.2	3.2	−4.8	−1.7
Indiana	186,318	190,444	193,911	191,356	186,586	184,184	182,946	37.1	17.3	−3.9	12.7
Iowa	67,957	68,088	67,145	66,115	65,617	65,841	66,539	30.8	−2.8	−2.3	−5.0
Kansas	90,164	89,572	89,046	89,296	86,285	86,770	85,934	22.1	5.2	−4.1	0.9
Kentucky	106,421	109,780	109,888	107,945	106,259	105,529	104,317	54.7	22.7	−5.0	16.6
Louisiana	136,635	143,219	149,550	146,158	147,110	147,920	147,238	57.9	8.5	2.8	11.5
Maine	34,616	34,038	33,521	32,395	31,899	31,275	30,979	30.3	15.4	−9.0	5.0
Maryland	110,830	113,096	112,831	112,298	112,250	113,738	113,159	47.6	7.2	0.1	7.2
Massachusetts	110,031	105,884	104,625	101,732	101,796	101,814	101,824	26.9	−2.6	−3.8	−6.3
Michigan	259,879	259,113	256,001	263,279	258,107	258,996	259,414	19.1	9.5	0.1	9.6
Minnesota	133,622	130,665	126,484	121,591	119,233	117,188	117,831	6.9	−0.2	−9.8	−10.0
Mississippi	58,781	60,187	58,437	57,665	57,507	58,847	60,560	38.3	19.4	0.6	20.1
Missouri	125,270	126,104	122,585	119,116	117,361	117,871	117,213	17.3	13.9	−7.1	5.9
Montana	28,015	29,520	29,684	30,396	30,604	31,412	31,697	25.7	6.6	7.4	14.5
Nebraska	60,692	60,695	60,400	59,515	58,007	58,081	57,266	20.0	9.8	−5.6	3.6
Nevada	29,424	30,851	30,588	30,536	31,333	30,831	30,988	135.3	37.1	0.4	37.7
New Hampshire	23,799	25,956	25,998	26,137	26,315	26,497	26,547	72.8	20.7	2.3	23.4
New Jersey	137,691	138,129	139,672	138,391	136,654	137,829	137,493	32.7	5.2	−0.5	4.7
New Mexico	48,013	49,323	51,333	52,238	50,800	49,819	48,818	31.9	6.7	−1.0	5.6
New York	363,678	346,305	343,889	341,772	345,202	335,728	328,666	26.2	2.3	−5.1	−2.9
North Carolina	148,698	152,320	156,593	155,661	156,445	157,414	156,539	87.6	14.2	2.8	17.3
North Dakota	27,277	27,559	28,671	28,521	28,301	28,396	28,052	15.6	0.6	1.8	2.4
Ohio	289,792	290,742	283,820	274,583	267,719	262,036	258,417	13.7	10.7	−11.1	−1.6
Oklahoma	92,945	95,426	97,516	96,417	97,271	95,387	93,778	20.3	1.9	−1.7	0.1
Oregon	67,600	65,169	64,854	63,113	62,651	63,056	64,413	−3.7	5.8	−1.2	4.6
Pennsylvania	235,271	236,644	239,753	234,187	231,347	233,433	232,223	35.3	22.9	−1.9	20.6
Rhode Island	25,730	25,173	25,278	24,434	23,375	22,764	22,251	1.4	12.3	−11.6	−0.7
South Carolina	81,303	85,518	87,083	88,293	87,374	87,813	87,344	154.2	21.6	2.1	24.2
South Dakota	26,451	28,737	30,191	31,216	30,783	29,484	28,367	18.5	19.6	−1.3	18.0
Tennessee	109,944	112,789	115,098	115,774	114,151	115,042	115,467	29.6	12.3	2.4	14.9
Texas	417,777	420,161	421,906	422,811	423,647	417,431	414,021	64.6	13.6	−1.5	11.9
Utah	57,529	61,782	62,361	74,011	79,554	80,088	81,313	89.3	18.9	31.6	56.5
Vermont	16,075	16,287	15,866	15,532	15,873	15,835	15,578	29.4	8.0	−4.4	3.3
Virginia	160,200	163,232	163,418	162,567	162,432	164,782	167,809	78.5	10.3	2.8	13.4
Washington	81,433	81,189	83,016	84,695	85,523	86,080	87,304	11.9	5.0	7.5	12.9
West Virginia	63,362	70,937	71,973	70,340	68,912	67,877	68,036	44.0	23.3	−4.1	18.3
Wisconsin	152,691	154,316	149,473	145,188	142,998	139,192	140,964	6.7	−0.2	−8.7	−8.8
Wyoming	12,517	12,646	12,044	12,012	12,022	11,361	11,251	27.9	26.7	−11.0	12.7
U.S. Service Schools	19,125	19,238	19,035	19,551	18,832	18,840	18,546	8.6	−0.8	−3.6	−4.3
Outlying areas	56,846	56,008	56,126	56,824	57,588	62,568	67,569	63.5	−5.2	20.6	14.4
American Samoa	—	—	—	—	—	—	—	—	—	—	—
Federated States of Micronesia	—	—	—	—	—	—	—	—	—	—	—
Guam	2,591	2,986	3,156	3,697	4,064	3,654	3,383	24.4	12.4	13.3	27.4
Marshall Islands	—	—	—	—	—	—	—	—	—	—	—
Northern Marianas	—	—	—	—	—	—	—	—	—	—	—
Palau	—	—	—	—	50,429	55,860	61,288	—	—	—	—
Puerto Rico	51,789	50,306	50,114	50,185	—	—	—	—	−6.7	—	—
Trust Territories	—	—	—	—	—	—	—	—	—	—	—
Virgin Islands	2,466	2,716	2,856	2,942	3,095	3,054	2,898	100.6	8.9	6.7	16.2

—Data not available or not applicable.

SOURCE: U.S. Department of Education, National Center for Education Statistics, Higher Education General Information Survey (HEGIS), "Fall Enrollment in Higher Education" surveys; and Integrated Postsecondary Education Data System (IPEDS), "Fall Enrollment" surveys. (This table was prepared January 1998.)

Table 54.—Total fall enrollment in public 2–year institutions of higher education, by state: 1970 to 1996

State or other area	Fall 1970	Fall 1971	Fall 1972	Fall 1973	Fall 1974	Fall 1975	Fall 1976	Fall 1977	Fall 1978	Fall 1979
1	2	3	4	5	6	7	8	9	10	11
United States	2,195,412	2,457,319	2,640,939	2,889,621	3,285,482	3,836,366	3,751,786	3,901,769	3,873,690	4,056,810
Alabama	21,249	24,269	27,839	32,546	42,937	52,884	40,600	39,725	39,123	36,334
Alaska	703	7,297	7,847	5,820	6,187	5,969	8,970	13,394	17,451	12,677
Arizona	43,402	49,581	54,134	64,596	76,716	91,585	96,053	99,902	94,954	103,134
Arkansas	2,824	3,092	3,417	3,590	5,028	8,470	8,650	11,027	10,706	11,169
California	694,132	751,039	778,668	861,494	969,982	1,101,462	1,061,786	1,095,662	1,016,657	1,069,082
Colorado	21,093	23,735	24,598	28,406	31,004	40,369	40,317	41,595	40,499	42,180
Connecticut	25,208	27,931	29,584	32,583	39,180	36,114	34,248	37,461	39,715	41,697
Delaware	3,709	4,774	4,553	4,937	6,041	6,269	5,501	5,095	5,523	6,475
District of Columbia	3,176	3,798	4,664	4,874	—	—	—	—	—	—
Florida	108,211	120,262	120,781	133,887	149,057	169,788	172,440	183,215	190,726	200,608
Georgia	21,738	23,324	24,699	27,876	31,227	40,434	39,206	38,295	38,921	35,533
Hawaii	10,853	13,010	14,154	15,699	17,172	20,617	19,217	19,077	19,120	19,067
Idaho	2,875	2,954	2,858	2,657	3,308	3,898	3,990	4,639	4,772	5,101
Illinois	136,211	160,355	175,600	185,233	215,283	250,761	277,160	279,116	279,564	277,601
Indiana	3,318	7,977	8,156	8,208	9,849	13,705	14,760	17,904	20,108	23,392
Iowa	17,511	20,474	22,262	23,267	24,542	28,880	28,684	28,985	30,114	31,778
Kansas	17,825	19,466	22,137	22,484	25,204	27,696	28,890	30,833	31,620	34,817
Kentucky	9,787	11,452	12,109	13,181	13,672	17,362	16,746	17,512	15,828	17,136
Louisiana	7,906	8,959	9,913	8,427	10,620	13,659	15,325	15,461	14,986	13,669
Maine	1,626	3,813	4,050	4,330	3,954	5,197	4,825	5,386	5,646	6,631
Maryland	42,334	47,168	52,264	58,717	64,679	76,051	79,763	84,672	85,948	88,362
Massachusetts	35,913	41,680	44,845	45,801	55,048	67,911	62,742	60,531	64,673	68,221
Michigan	121,887	132,059	136,657	152,640	172,087	194,886	171,876	182,554	186,081	199,099
Minnesota	20,367	22,662	22,689	24,395	25,092	28,924	30,090	31,030	32,950	35,073
Mississippi	21,190	22,194	23,564	25,678	28,498	34,349	32,687	32,857	33,051	35,143
Missouri	32,578	34,739	35,268	38,600	44,035	53,370	50,646	49,435	48,336	46,635
Montana	2,067	1,864	2,353	2,147	2,145	2,915	2,725	2,760	2,665	2,161
Nebraska	3,746	5,485	5,748	6,368	7,904	12,309	14,572	16,941	16,543	20,014
Nevada	405	1,601	3,927	6,940	12,029	14,036	13,381	14,188	16,806	17,953
New Hampshire	617	496	574	2,490	3,493	6,089	4,640	5,115	4,702	4,786
New Jersey	41,792	50,172	55,261	63,252	71,944	85,270	86,872	91,116	93,365	98,558
New Mexico	3,793	4,601	4,655	5,204	6,243	6,529	6,585	8,251	8,743	8,910
New York	188,918	209,924	222,051	232,822	248,145	271,412	241,573	237,560	236,818	242,628
North Carolina	40,313	46,387	57,348	60,183	71,818	89,988	86,688	91,710	93,016	95,219
North Dakota	5,925	6,361	6,413	6,457	6,492	6,674	6,969	7,478	7,237	6,855
Ohio	53,846	62,380	67,171	73,778	81,624	99,794	107,738	112,235	112,715	118,836
Oklahoma	13,479	19,079	21,928	25,255	28,702	35,346	38,018	40,864	42,193	43,763
Oregon	41,571	45,318	47,691	56,639	62,088	64,943	66,446	63,196	67,551	73,664
Pennsylvania	61,341	68,851	73,603	78,279	82,242	94,350	95,545	95,603	97,135	98,842
Rhode Island	3,581	3,743	4,198	5,511	6,594	8,056	8,974	10,317	10,340	11,158
South Carolina	12,745	13,398	25,744	23,803	37,084	45,827	33,646	36,348	37,214	37,731
South Dakota	—	—	—	—	—	—	—	—	—	529
Tennessee	9,771	11,999	14,634	18,625	22,878	31,001	33,032	37,336	40,462	43,971
Texas	114,028	126,704	144,469	152,872	180,195	226,539	221,361	237,421	241,427	253,923
Utah	6,644	7,738	8,348	8,257	8,758	12,104	12,977	13,575	13,904	13,545
Vermont	495	456	475	2,028	2,076	2,644	2,037	2,281	2,396	1,919
Virginia	29,251	36,183	43,749	54,400	67,646	87,987	86,545	95,436	100,842	104,910
Washington	84,714	87,343	94,950	98,855	109,498	123,797	145,659	159,050	169,955	194,115
West Virginia	4,124	4,389	5,340	7,272	9,577	13,221	12,499	11,543	9,788	10,292
Wisconsin	38,200	47,679	55,337	61,152	65,505	75,916	67,796	75,386	69,778	81,417
Wyoming	6,420	7,104	7,662	7,106	8,183	9,052	10,336	10,696	11,023	10,497
U.S. Service Schools	—	—	—	—	12,217	19,957	—	—	—	—
Outlying areas	5,354	4,544	5,975	11,363	13,389	14,631	14,121	11,199	9,133	12,652
American Samoa	—	632	848	909	833	689	836	1,114	831	856
Federated States of Micronesia	—	—	—	—	—	—	—	—	—	—
Guam	—	—	—	—	—	—	—	—	—	—
Marshall Islands	—	—	—	—	—	—	—	—	—	—
Northern Marianas	—	—	—	—	—	—	—	—	—	—
Palau	—	—	—	—	—	—	—	—	—	—
Puerto Rico	5,354	3,799	5,006	10,339	12,401	13,757	12,882	9,776	7,936	11,620
Trust Territories	—	113	121	115	155	185	403	309	366	176
Virgin Islands	—	—	—	—	—	—	—	—	—	—

Table 54.—Total fall enrollment in public 2–year institutions of higher education, by state: 1970 to 1996—Continued

State or other area	Fall 1980	Fall 1981	Fall 1982	Fall 1983	Fall 1984	Fall 1985	Fall 1986	Fall 1987	Fall 1988	Fall 1989
1	12	13	14	15	16	17	18	19	20	21
United States	**4,328,782**	**4,480,708**	**4,519,653**	**4,459,330**	**4,279,097**	**4,269,733**	**4,413,691**	**4,541,054**	**4,615,487**	**4,883,660**
Alabama	39,368	40,727	42,947	44,954	47,127	54,012	56,857	56,364	60,792	66,420
Alaska	11,990	14,538	13,649	14,590	14,745	15,987	15,783	14,650	5,030	—
Arizona	113,176	114,127	118,718	119,097	113,868	117,917	126,837	139,179	148,382	143,038
Arkansas	11,303	11,301	12,345	12,702	12,499	12,190	14,410	14,428	16,601	17,754
California	1,130,300	1,212,573	1,171,476	1,070,612	995,832	980,481	1,034,166	1,077,279	1,058,170	1,096,849
Colorado	44,818	46,150	47,856	46,828	43,954	41,493	51,396	55,023	57,654	68,526
Connecticut	41,932	43,150	44,448	44,478	42,402	40,746	39,830	40,537	41,918	44,270
Delaware	6,988	7,406	7,548	7,551	7,130	7,481	7,936	8,191	9,318	9,957
District of Columbia	—	—	—	—	—	—	—	—	—	—
Florida	206,859	216,382	219,170	218,955	210,451	215,905	235,256	254,376	262,829	316,704
Georgia	36,083	37,633	40,587	40,884	37,329	34,337	30,635	49,364	48,159	50,537
Hawaii	19,359	20,807	22,176	21,237	20,173	20,003	19,906	20,342	19,979	20,533
Idaho	5,410	4,897	5,052	5,065	5,288	5,121	6,912	5,010	5,340	5,354
Illinois	300,037	313,481	338,718	330,444	319,956	332,980	334,861	324,060	328,276	341,730
Indiana	30,319	32,114	33,920	35,768	34,590	34,529	31,818	34,721	35,737	35,147
Iowa	34,972	36,581	39,296	40,878	39,918	39,822	40,384	42,672	44,396	48,668
Kansas	36,039	39,082	41,391	43,144	43,359	43,273	44,664	47,537	51,334	55,954
Kentucky	18,080	20,373	22,116	24,059	23,742	23,767	25,569	28,162	31,330	34,965
Louisiana	14,019	14,368	14,747	14,971	14,447	14,938	14,265	14,344	15,519	17,877
Maine	7,127	7,523	4,237	4,579	4,656	4,503	4,969	5,272	6,127	6,278
Maryland	93,027	96,787	101,924	104,558	99,310	94,927	93,899	96,515	103,041	107,395
Massachusetts	74,352	68,823	72,576	78,396	74,585	75,040	69,916	73,651	75,990	75,550
Michigan	212,038	210,777	213,203	217,230	207,655	205,250	209,109	215,025	216,607	224,159
Minnesota	37,214	39,610	42,950	43,911	44,620	46,681	47,864	53,780	57,287	63,714
Mississippi	36,757	41,126	40,604	42,506	39,616	38,146	39,509	42,902	44,122	46,319
Missouri	53,324	57,257	59,418	63,070	58,353	57,850	58,200	59,335	62,309	71,277
Montana	3,097	3,350	3,483	3,396	3,440	3,529	3,511	4,624	3,887	4,736
Nebraska	21,368	23,343	23,427	22,591	25,730	26,125	28,978	29,349	30,935	32,116
Nevada	21,337	19,937	20,784	22,403	22,030	22,076	23,992	24,366	23,465	29,099
New Hampshire	4,858	6,246	6,354	7,193	6,504	6,095	7,226	8,287	6,677	8,201
New Jersey	106,013	108,497	118,216	117,207	109,299	106,372	104,390	103,549	110,672	118,443
New Mexico	10,104	10,704	12,217	12,479	13,882	14,807	32,320	33,827	29,903	31,768
New York	250,862	259,397	261,976	256,027	245,703	242,731	226,864	224,610	231,291	242,440
North Carolina	106,517	113,393	117,589	117,123	123,488	138,313	129,223	123,590	127,045	132,649
North Dakota	7,286	7,544	7,550	7,603	7,316	7,267	7,509	6,990	7,690	7,837
Ohio	127,428	125,990	132,019	131,582	122,247	118,622	122,150	121,664	123,244	127,717
Oklahoma	49,146	51,519	54,098	56,170	54,851	54,832	55,403	55,287	56,722	56,722
Oregon	74,501	69,105	64,680	63,560	64,638	59,965	64,280	66,842	68,174	74,536
Pennsylvania	103,290	106,953	114,907	120,837	115,051	111,154	111,564	88,627	94,254	100,317
Rhode Island	11,844	11,721	12,149	12,602	12,317	12,617	13,096	13,107	14,715	15,400
South Carolina	39,027	41,018	40,909	38,297	36,547	36,756	37,887	38,553	41,134	39,387
South Dakota	474	616	665	—	—	—	—	—	—	—
Tennessee	49,015	48,415	51,688	52,039	49,103	46,521	48,988	51,402	51,819	59,276
Texas	265,408	274,798	302,303	324,341	321,742	306,157	315,634	333,179	361,203	372,103
Utah	14,518	15,750	17,016	18,638	18,444	19,145	21,130	21,831	21,801	25,179
Vermont	2,609	2,874	2,846	3,403	3,099	3,634	3,655	3,970	4,205	4,798
Virginia	111,174	115,112	108,061	113,306	106,667	109,374	117,741	123,994	116,207	129,364
Washington	192,665	169,344	119,749	120,733	122,051	123,609	134,955	136,485	141,116	142,975
West Virginia	9,183	9,461	9,917	10,160	9,751	9,127	9,550	9,648	9,648	10,251
Wisconsin	88,950	91,817	93,073	90,544	83,200	84,233	90,322	89,204	91,941	96,116
Wyoming	12,107	11,574	12,504	13,574	13,337	14,081	13,755	15,040	15,138	16,218
U.S. Service Schools	31,110	34,637	40,401	33,055	33,055	35,212	34,617	40,310	26,354	37,037
Outlying areas	13,825	15,967	17,772	3,649	8,420	8,305	˙8,909	9,277	9,641	10,430
American Samoa	976	987	1,007	845	871	758	759	897	908	1,011
Federated States of Micronesia	—	—	—	—	—	—	—	—	—	838
Guam	—	2,467	2,467	662	1,740	1,832	1,821	1,862	1,723	1,965
Marshall Islands	—	—	—	—	—	—	—	—	—	—
Northern Marianas	—	—	—	173	431	318	514	366	352	419
Palau	—	—	—	—	—	—	—	—	—	1,037
Puerto Rico	12,625	12,325	13,700	1,233	4,582	4,673	5,020	4,929	5,471	5,160
Trust Territories	224	188	598	736	796	724	795	1,223	1,187	—
Virgin Islands	—	—	—	—	—	—	—	—	—	—

Table 54.—Total fall enrollment in public 2–year institutions of higher education, by state: 1970 to 1996—Continued

| State or other area | Fall 1990 | Fall 1991 | Fall 1992 | Fall 1993 | Fall 1994 | Fall 1995 | Fall 1996 | Percentage change | | | |
| | | | | | | | | Fall 1970 to fall 1996 | Fall 1986 to fall 1991 | Fall 1991 to fall 1996 | Fall 1986 to fall 1996 |
1	22	23	24	25	26	27	28	29	30	31	32
United States	**4,996,475**	**5,404,815**	**5,484,555**	**5,337,328**	**5,308,467**	**5,277,829**	**5,283,267**	**140.7**	**22.5**	**−2.2**	**19.7**
Alabama	72,091	74,557	78,770	81,744	80,467	76,657	73,735	247.0	31.1	−1.1	29.7
Alaska	—	—	586	600	594	812	751	6.8	—	—	−95.2
Arizona	152,556	158,117	158,676	151,408	150,766	152,812	150,968	247.8	24.7	−4.5	19.0
Arkansas	17,237	18,688	19,206	21,976	21,061	24,258	27,363	868.9	29.7	46.4	89.9
California	1,057,921	1,273,712	1,233,540	1,113,679	1,099,505	1,073,999	1,120,104	61.4	23.2	−12.1	8.3
Colorado	72,037	75,081	80,557	77,819	76,969	77,696	76,890	264.5	46.1	2.4	49.6
Connecticut	44,562	43,764	45,639	45,542	44,583	42,828	41,040	62.8	9.9	−6.2	3.0
Delaware	10,828	11,566	11,241	10,735	11,356	11,664	11,871	220.1	45.7	2.6	49.6
District of Columbia	—	—	—	—	—	—	—	—	—	—	—
Florida	312,092	323,225	326,490	327,023	326,782	323,646	319,871	195.6	37.4	−1.0	36.0
Georgia	55,307	67,706	78,865	83,921	86,464	88,257	90,271	315.3	121.0	33.3	194.7
Hawaii	21,828	23,026	26,324	26,707	27,905	26,853	25,679	136.6	15.7	11.5	29.0
Idaho	5,606	6,213	6,869	7,090	7,365	7,537	8,048	179.9	−10.1	29.5	16.4
Illinois	352,869	369,243	366,705	352,368	351,469	337,716	340,151	149.7	10.3	−7.9	1.6
Indiana	37,635	37,934	40,713	39,903	41,684	40,611	38,021	1,045.9	19.2	0.2	19.5
Iowa	49,877	52,272	55,696	56,152	56,400	56,555	59,384	239.1	29.4	13.6	47.0
Kansas	58,953	62,777	64,353	64,720	66,513	73,679	69,495	289.9	40.6	10.7	55.6
Kentucky	40,674	45,993	47,950	48,215	45,316	43,279	43,106	340.4	79.9	−6.3	68.6
Louisiana	21,655	25,603	27,823	27,792	28,002	26,953	27,351	246.0	79.5	6.8	91.7
Maine	6,884	6,890	7,325	7,424	7,289	6,920	6,909	324.9	38.7	0.3	39.0
Maryland	109,953	115,542	115,156	114,368	111,442	109,119	104,118	145.9	23.0	−9.9	10.9
Massachusetts	76,004	74,675	78,494	79,729	78,003	74,963	71,592	99.3	6.8	−4.1	2.4
Michigan	227,480	227,188	217,321	219,866	208,651	203,394	199,575	63.7	8.6	−12.2	−4.6
Minnesota	65,589	69,088	85,674	85,540	107,782	100,061	90,709	345.4	44.3	31.3	89.5
Mississippi	50,257	51,199	51,474	51,708	50,891	51,753	54,345	156.5	29.6	6.1	37.6
Missouri	74,823	77,021	76,025	78,705	74,498	72,122	72,056	121.2	32.3	−6.4	23.8
Montana	3,850	3,933	4,081	3,930	4,323	6,023	6,303	204.9	12.0	60.3	79.5
Nebraska	33,922	33,997	42,796	36,267	37,870	37,518	42,451	1,033.2	17.3	24.9	46.5
Nevada	31,818	31,134	32,604	32,693	31,938	35,852	40,937	10,007.9	29.8	31.5	70.6
New Hampshire	8,364	8,562	9,257	9,434	8,673	9,572	9,818	1,491.2	18.5	14.7	35.9
New Jersey	123,910	132,599	138,713	139,970	135,766	133,240	127,103	204.1	27.0	−4.1	21.8
New Mexico	35,390	40,530	43,568	45,855	46,273	47,401	48,812	1,186.9	25.4	20.4	51.0
New York	253,206	259,593	262,419	263,217	259,231	252,763	243,816	29.1	14.4	−6.1	7.5
North Carolina	136,707	153,153	158,925	147,895	147,204	145,685	146,400	263.2	18.5	−4.4	13.3
North Dakota	7,413	7,659	8,112	8,123	8,338	8,414	8,713	47.1	2.0	13.8	16.0
Ohio	137,821	145,550	153,207	155,173	149,847	147,782	146,922	172.9	19.2	0.9	20.3
Oklahoma	58,128	64,740	67,212	64,484	64,477	62,639	60,603	349.6	16.9	−6.4	9.4
Oregon	76,827	79,282	80,048	80,239	78,376	80,561	77,016	85.3	23.3	−2.9	19.8
Pennsylvania	108,207	117,791	120,103	117,560	111,218	106,495	102,958	67.8	5.6	−12.6	−7.7
Rhode Island	16,620	17,330	17,986	16,399	16,001	15,889	15,236	325.5	32.3	−12.1	16.3
South Carolina	49,831	51,494	58,497	60,640	61,140	60,893	61,019	378.8	35.9	18.5	61.1
South Dakota	145	151	155	211	197	209	197	—	—	30.5	—
Tennessee	65,105	73,652	77,204	78,451	77,274	78,094	78,630	704.7	50.3	6.8	60.5
Texas	384,537	396,393	410,552	411,885	419,355	419,420	424,070	271.9	25.6	7.0	34.4
Utah	28,579	33,020	34,597	26,260	29,039	30,472	32,882	394.9	56.3	−0.4	55.6
Vermont	4,835	5,198	5,531	5,469	4,632	4,635	4,561	821.4	42.2	−12.3	24.8
Virginia	131,086	134,875	134,104	131,243	130,733	128,345	124,603	326.0	14.6	−7.6	5.8
Washington	146,199	157,156	155,747	157,118	159,249	160,555	164,565	94.3	16.5	4.7	21.9
West Virginia	10,746	7,278	7,311	7,160	7,208	6,980	6,719	62.9	−23.8	−7.7	−29.6
Wisconsin	100,838	105,766	107,417	111,481	107,248	106,578	103,664	171.4	17.1	−2.0	14.8
Wyoming	18,106	18,605	18,643	17,990	17,993	18,059	18,743	191.9	35.3	0.7	36.3
U.S. Service Schools	29,567	34,294	34,294	33,447	33,107	69,611	63,123	—	−0.9	84.1	82.3
Outlying areas	9,398	10,066	10,576	12,291	13,329	14,482	12,292	129.6	13.0	22.1	38.0
American Samoa	1,219	1,267	1,295	1,264	1,249	1,232	1,239	—	66.9	−2.2	63.2
Federated States of Micronesia	975	837	1,028	1,148	1,374	1,296	1,396	—	—	66.8	—
Guam	2,150	2,030	1,689	2,146	2,385	2,356	1,952	—	11.5	−3.8	7.2
Marshall Islands	—	—	374	386	424	418	431	—	—	—	—
Northern Marianas	661	847	796	1,261	1,253	959	1,096	—	64.8	29.4	113.2
Palau	491	355	445	436	403	351	332	—	—	−6.5	—
Puerto Rico	3,902	4,730	4,949	5,650	6,241	7,870	5,846	9.2	−5.8	23.6	16.5
Trust Territories	—	—	—	—	—	—	—	—	—	—	—
Virgin Islands	—	—	—	—	—	—	—	—	—	—	—

—Data not available or not applicable.

SOURCE: U.S. Department of Education, National Center for Education Statistics, Higher Education General Information Survey (HEGIS), "Fall Enrollment in Higher Edu- cation" surveys; and Integrated Postsecondary Education Data System (IPEDS), "Fall Enrollment" surveys. (This table was prepared January 1998.)

Table 55.—Total fall enrollment in private 4–year institutions of higher education, by state: 1970 to 1996

State or other area	Fall 1970	Fall 1971	Fall 1972	Fall 1973	Fall 1974	Fall 1975	Fall 1976	Fall 1977	Fall 1978	Fall 1979
1	2	3	4	5	6	7	8	9	10	11
United States	**2,028,780**	**2,022,365**	**2,028,938**	**2,060,128**	**2,116,717**	**2,216,598**	**2,227,125**	**2,297,621**	**2,319,422**	**2,373,221**
Alabama	14,606	15,229	15,360	15,040	15,709	16,575	16,989	18,474	16,548	15,950
Alaska	749	814	1,039	907	878	504	231	355	493	642
Arizona	2,166	1,876	1,925	2,392	4,836	4,697	4,613	4,703	4,733	5,354
Arkansas	7,184	7,210	7,448	7,760	8,064	8,352	8,450	8,789	8,498	8,498
California	133,001	134,073	139,726	145,099	156,388	168,666	172,808	178,678	178,219	179,411
Colorado	14,833	14,602	14,590	14,015	13,385	13,444	13,638	13,729	13,940	14,590
Connecticut	49,286	49,121	49,319	50,493	51,973	52,898	54,741	56,092	58,024	58,968
Delaware	448	701	567	513	502	705	670	1,882	1,894	3,497
District of Columbia	64,203	65,593	64,651	65,103	66,868	68,905	66,335	70,650	68,146	72,759
Florida	43,411	45,493	44,270	44,406	46,485	55,937	60,797	63,365	64,397	68,446
Georgia	21,259	22,077	23,412	24,885	25,977	27,204	27,896	28,361	30,622	32,561
Hawaii	3,261	3,255	3,443	3,044	4,409	4,461	4,376	5,371	5,799	5,895
Idaho	2,237	2,145	1,969	1,933	1,861	1,969	1,942	2,133	2,132	2,021
Illinois	128,759	129,632	127,406	125,945	130,210	133,105	136,202	140,622	139,061	140,513
Indiana	55,437	53,876	52,053	53,135	52,492	52,283	52,229	52,838	52,168	52,809
Iowa	37,081	36,741	34,714	32,782	34,512	36,056	34,868	37,202	37,376	39,761
Kansas	12,637	11,756	11,300	11,009	10,886	11,368	11,873	12,001	12,047	12,486
Kentucky	19,533	18,535	17,699	17,251	17,454	18,341	18,979	18,996	19,364	19,518
Louisiana	19,601	20,100	19,850	19,809	20,852	21,159	21,784	21,996	21,888	22,377
Maine	8,633	8,867	8,825	8,543	8,673	8,999	9,822	10,073	10,186	10,376
Maryland	30,326	30,989	31,386	31,575	27,382	27,454	26,932	26,847	27,205	28,072
Massachusetts	170,617	172,799	173,420	178,908	185,205	188,350	177,855	195,159	200,334	208,278
Michigan	49,433	50,010	48,035	48,711	51,855	55,014	54,542	56,460	55,846	57,113
Minnesota	29,220	28,712	29,695	30,848	31,797	34,590	36,783	38,951	38,445	38,979
Mississippi	7,020	7,229	7,537	7,840	7,837	8,906	9,201	9,059	8,832	9,145
Missouri	48,196	48,831	48,710	50,801	56,029	62,301	64,780	65,737	66,981	66,458
Montana	2,775	2,656	2,543	2,689	2,756	3,045	3,049	3,115	3,366	3,191
Nebraska	15,143	13,649	13,300	13,221	12,963	13,121	13,398	14,006	14,335	14,934
Nevada	93	99	104	117	164	177	185	198	249	270
New Hampshire	12,906	13,060	13,352	13,546	13,668	16,098	16,219	17,194	18,163	18,303
New Jersey	64,883	64,074	62,207	61,116	60,813	62,641	63,236	63,852	64,693	64,994
New Mexico	3,930	4,223	4,221	4,494	4,617	4,624	4,544	4,035	4,050	3,516
New York	344,271	324,140	328,889	341,449	348,911	371,451	374,970	381,863	388,001	392,613
North Carolina	39,719	41,319	41,844	42,557	42,849	43,656	45,209	45,761	47,984	48,531
North Dakota	1,182	1,313	1,377	1,266	1,306	1,367	1,541	1,584	1,979	1,966
Ohio	93,277	92,670	93,862	94,139	94,648	94,144	95,082	95,051	95,686	96,178
Oklahoma	15,967	16,082	16,292	16,935	17,978	18,769	19,018	19,602	19,379	19,536
Oregon	13,334	13,604	13,702	13,935	14,158	15,106	15,368	15,730	16,362	16,465
Pennsylvania	172,699	175,127	174,411	174,695	173,992	177,313	179,672	184,439	186,135	192,169
Rhode Island	20,371	21,627	22,155	25,133	28,436	32,168	28,563	29,631	29,644	30,026'
South Carolina	18,655	19,235	19,256	19,716	20,477	21,851	22,371	22,503	22,762	22,652
South Dakota	6,325	6,149	5,928	5,587	5,774	7,910	8,005	8,119	7,532	7,533
Tennessee	33,536	33,560	34,267	34,663	37,075	40,160	39,965	39,995	40,801	42,067
Texas	70,610	73,062	76,126	76,607	78,130	80,576	76,756	78,618	77,374	82,589
Utah	29,957	29,719	29,555	28,418	27,448	28,270	28,844	30,028	30,528	30,562
Vermont	8,232	9,121	10,077	10,151	10,156	10,880	10,629	10,896	10,785	11,227
Virginia	25,493	25,599	25,870	25,924	26,498	28,241	28,520	30,420	30,960	32,188
Washington	20,826	20,841	21,577	22,707	24,204	24,637	24,250	23,436	25,941	26,383
West Virginia	10,062	10,128	9,443	8,776	8,737	8,869	9,128	8,900	8,630	8,813
Wisconsin	31,397	31,042	30,231	29,540	28,440	29,281	29,267	30,122	30,905	32,038
Wyoming	—	—	—	—	—	—	—	—	—	—
Outlying areas	12,934	15,952	21,034	22,985	25,456	27,127	30,961	43,792	46,992	56,936
American Samoa	—	—	—	—	—	—	—	—	—	—
Federated States of Micronesia	—	—	—	—	—	—	—	—	—	—
Guam	—	—	—	—	—	—	—	—	—	—
Marshall Islands	—	—	—	—	—	—	—	—	—	—
Northern Marianas	—	—	—	—	—	—	—	—	—	—
Palau	—	—	—	—	—	—	—	—	—	—
Puerto Rico	12,934	15,952	21,034	22,985	25,456	27,127	30,961	43,792	46,992	56,936
Trust Territories	—	—	—	—	—	—	—	—	—	—
Virgin Islands	—	—	—	—	—	—	—	—	—	—

Table 55.—Total fall enrollment in private 4–year institutions of higher education, by state: 1970 to 1996—Continued

State or other area	Fall 1980	Fall 1981	Fall 1982	Fall 1983	Fall 1984	Fall 1985	Fall 1986	Fall 1987	Fall 1988	Fall 1989
1	12	13	14	15	16	17	18	19	20	21
United States	2,441,996	2,489,137	2,477,640	2,517,791	2,512,894	2,506,438	2,523,761	2,558,220	2,634,281	2,693,368
Alabama	16,607	16,293	16,144	17,769	17,521	16,806	16,569	17,468	18,886	17,526
Alaska	735	896	1,077	961	986	969	1,123	946	1,207	2,064
Arizona	8,534	9,405	9,871	11,032	11,213	13,459	11,004	6,888	14,104	11,382
Arkansas	8,955	8,921	8,490	8,374	8,761	8,650	8,879	9,025	9,823	9,916
California	185,714	187,531	189,601	193,604	196,192	195,067	194,213	196,348	200,657	203,584
Colorado	16,232	16,498	16,785	16,659	15,827	15,253	15,556	17,708	18,348	19,756
Connecticut	60,296	61,258	59,420	60,076	59,217	59,007	57,666	58,090	57,467	58,068
Delaware	3,752	4,727	5,004	4,915	5,335	4,860	5,001	6,990	6,615	7,525
District of Columbia	72,775	74,438	68,232	66,097	66,300	66,121	65,845	66,715	67,201	67,361
Florida	72,794	75,367	75,668	78,448	82,058	82,103	84,652	80,590	91,308	87,818
Georgia	33,921	36,350	36,810	37,354	38,099	38,737	38,921	41,651	42,554	45,304
Hawaii	5,740	4,981	6,185	7,692	8,111	8,617	9,104	9,545	9,768	10,544
Idaho	2,032	2,152	1,917	2,044	2,067	2,122	2,353	2,397	2,295	2,315
Illinois	145,663	149,472	149,432	150,867	149,544	147,379	152,488	156,401	158,008	165,000
Indiana	53,969	53,857	52,572	53,039	51,602	50,781	52,005	51,397	55,431	56,433
Iowa	40,861	41,139	40,724	40,985	40,905	40,608	41,481	42,898	45,339	50,955
Kansas	12,931	12,609	13,507	12,806	13,098	12,702	12,096	11,809	12,806	12,461
Kentucky	20,803	20,725	20,132	20,880	20,862	20,778	20,750	23,236	23,289	22,261
Louisiana	22,980	23,508	23,531	23,802	23,436	22,297	23,130	23,596	24,183	26,134
Maine	10,258	10,396	13,744	18,299	18,057	17,770	10,814	11,437	10,965	16,277
Maryland	29,435	31,022	30,531	30,793	31,713	31,960	33,299	34,799	35,882	37,043
Massachusetts	216,410	219,675	209,411	216,789	216,170	216,178	220,893	220,982	223,547	225,041
Michigan	59,148	58,904	59,337	62,218	63,118	62,958	68,183	72,557	73,402	75,567
Minnesota	40,653	41,262	41,395	41,359	42,612	42,737	43,265	46,306	48,681	49,381
Mississippi	9,352	8,631	8,750	9,847	9,715	8,982	9,494	9,914	10,251	10,329
Missouri	66,690	67,937	67,148	67,572	67,300	68,431	74,270	77,303	80,940	83,468
Montana	3,178	3,071	3,023	3,146	3,391	3,007	2,987	3,312	3,305	3,231
Nebraska	15,619	16,088	16,208	16,861	16,517	15,936	15,787	15,474	16,370	16,824
Nevada	175	196	363	389	307	288	281	247	161	264
New Hampshire	20,586	20,804	23,725	24,039	22,984	22,973	22,558	23,058	24,170	24,432
New Jersey	66,434	65,887	64,285	61,638	60,148	58,432	57,126	56,471	55,983	56,648
New Mexico	3,552	3,486	3,332	3,104	2,599	2,568	1,705	1,776	2,056	1,991
New York	399,401	410,141	404,899	406,051	402,969	400,771	400,348	394,534	393,027	401,162
North Carolina	50,377	50,452	50,374	51,452	52,646	53,424	53,784	55,535	59,265	63,306
North Dakota	2,145	2,130	2,172	2,158	2,349	2,306	2,311	2,466	2,659	2,672
Ohio	97,407	100,492	100,404	101,860	100,786	98,862	102,116	103,198	106,850	108,123
Oklahoma	20,349	20,115	20,028	19,894	19,075	18,874	17,222	18,464	18,434	18,497
Oregon	16,840	16,839	17,005	17,671	18,401	18,035	18,555	18,870	19,220	20,225
Pennsylvania	199,446	205,812	205,333	208,423	207,742	207,988	208,079	209,846	212,800	214,270
Rhode Island	30,963	31,868	32,173	33,402	34,638	34,538	34,060	35,391	35,854	35,899
South Carolina	18,568	18,415	22,729	22,033	21,142	20,899	21,342	22,381	22,980	22,490
South Dakota	7,707	8,014	8,012	7,953	7,742	8,569	6,243	6,900	7,180	7,232
Tennessee	42,219	41,646	41,190	41,181	40,592	40,884	42,029	42,302	45,075	45,666
Texas	85,345	88,578	89,745	90,716	89,680	89,648	87,025	88,975	89,969	92,247
Utah	30,915	31,700	30,928	31,051	30,805	31,161	31,655	31,220	33,171	34,164
Vermont	11,193	10,826	10,700	10,793	10,723	10,701	11,967	11,809	12,319	12,921
Virginia	32,998	33,682	34,603	36,285	36,563	40,067	40,130	42,011	47,766	54,389
Washington	27,575	28,907	29,722	30,248	29,208	28,855	28,879	30,258	33,011	32,455
West Virginia	8,606	8,603	8,336	8,770	7,806	7,640	7,109	7,105	7,488	7,196
Wisconsin	33,158	33,431	32,933	34,392	34,262	34,680	37,409	39,621	42,211	43,551
Wyoming	—	—	—	—	—	—	—	—	—	—
Outlying areas	61,001	66,861	78,194	82,677	74,269	79,569	87,191	80,536	86,164	85,727
American Samoa	—	—	—	—	—	—	—	—	—	—
Federated States of Micronesia	—	—	—	—	—	—	—	—	—	—
Guam	—	—	—	—	—	—	—	—	—	—
Marshall Islands	—	—	—	—	—	—	—	—	—	—
Northern Marianas	—	—	—	—	—	—	—	—	—	—
Palau	—	—	—	—	—	—	—	—	—	—
Puerto Rico	61,001	66,861	78,194	82,677	74,269	79,569	87,191	80,536	86,164	85,727
Trust Territories	—	—	—	—	—	—	—	—	—	—
Virgin Islands	—	—	—	—	—	—	—	—	—	—

Table 55.—Total fall enrollment in private 4–year institutions of higher education, by state: 1970 to 1996—Continued

State or other area	Fall 1990	Fall 1991	Fall 1992	Fall 1993	Fall 1994	Fall 1995	Fall 1996	Percentage change			
								Fall 1970 to fall 1996	Fall 1986 to fall 1991	Fall 1991 to fall 1996	Fall 1986 to fall 1996
1	22	23	24	25	26	27	28	29	30	31	32
United States	2,730,312	2,802,305	2,864,957	2,887,176	2,923,867	2,954,707	2,995,931	47.7	11.0	6.9	18.7
Alabama	18,838	18,788	20,900	21,399	21,609	21,949	21,869	49.7	13.4	16.4	32.0
Alaska	1,647	1,432	1,506	1,682	828	776	692	−7.6	27.5	−51.7	−38.4
Arizona	13,980	17,761	17,759	24,469	21,819	18,562	22,402	934.3	61.4	26.1	103.6
Arkansas	9,799	10,070	10,203	10,288	10,347	10,667	10,825	50.7	13.4	7.5	21.9
California	202,531	207,568	215,513	217,520	239,288	238,755	243,468	83.1	6.9	17.3	25.4
Colorado	21,719	23,158	24,817	25,981	28,224	28,804	32,205	117.1	48.9	39.1	107.0
Connecticut	57,470	57,134	56,399	55,223	55,767	55,594	56,217	14.1	−0.9	−1.6	−2.5
Delaware	7,752	7,677	7,450	7,757	7,875	8,103	8,259	1,743.5	53.5	7.6	65.1
District of Columbia	67,561	65,931	69,624	70,957	66,657	67,614	66,783	4.0	0.1	1.3	1.4
Florida	92,373	98,099	100,989	100,368	101,233	101,265	104,308	140.3	15.9	6.3	23.2
Georgia	46,344	49,783	52,262	56,569	58,559	61,480	64,257	202.3	27.9	29.1	65.1
Hawaii	10,708	11,620	11,557	12,253	12,676	13,000	14,013	329.7	27.6	20.6	53.9
Idaho	2,338	2,897	2,937	2,574	2,988	2,308	2,390	6.8	23.1	−17.5	1.6
Illinois	168,953	172,498	175,254	177,790	179,359	183,336	184,393	43.2	13.1	6.9	20.9
Indiana	57,234	58,215	58,846	59,837	60,357	61,331	61,849	11.6	11.9	6.2	18.9
Iowa	50,352	48,390	47,831	48,372	49,042	50,324	50,044	35.0	16.7	3.4	20.6
Kansas	13,638	14,462	15,018	15,161	16,888	16,316	16,048	27.0	19.6	11.0	32.7
Kentucky	24,982	26,941	25,962	26,221	26,496	27,382	27,717	41.9	29.8	2.9	33.6
Louisiana	26,308	26,624	26,325	27,435	27,251	27,884	27,507	40.3	15.1	3.3	18.9
Maine	14,262	14,675	15,528	14,767	15,664	16,437	15,946	84.7	35.7	8.7	47.5
Maryland	38,174	38,438	39,426	40,287	41,381	42,267	42,299	39.5	15.4	10.0	27.0
Massachusetts	218,307	225,175	224,689	223,667	222,237	228,964	229,983	34.8	1.9	2.1	4.1
Michigan	79,599	79,129	84,364	82,364	82,086	83,304	86,298	74.6	16.1	9.1	26.6
Minnesota	50,224	51,150	55,245	56,355	57,897	59,410	61,954	112.0	18.2	21.1	43.2
Mississippi	10,640	10,996	11,448	11,816	11,431	11,278	10,614	51.2	15.8	−3.5	11.8
Missouri	85,802	90,721	93,025	93,515	96,085	96,946	96,973	101.2	22.2	6.9	30.6
Montana	3,046	3,126	3,460	4,375	4,395	4,319	4,314	55.5	4.7	38.0	44.4
Nebraska	17,885	18,477	18,880	19,149	19,698	19,575	19,583	29.3	17.0	6.0	24.0
Nevada	313	329	660	693	787	1,116	1,518	1,532.3	17.1	361.4	440.2
New Hampshire	24,546	25,611	24,809	24,496	24,011	24,227	24,229	87.7	13.5	−5.4	7.4
New Jersey	59,011	59,893	60,614	60,506	59,079	58,045	58,402	−10.0	4.8	−2.5	2.2
New Mexico	1,917	3,034	3,538	2,801	4,157	4,231	4,865	23.8	77.9	60.3	185.3
New York	403,147	417,112	427,990	427,752	424,708	425,065	431,012	25.2	4.2	3.3	7.7
North Carolina	61,522	62,053	64,728	64,906	63,203	67,448	69,220	74.3	15.4	11.5	28.7
North Dakota	2,980	3,297	3,449	3,404	3,299	3,334	3,514	197.3	42.7	6.6	52.1
Ohio	112,219	113,972	115,229	116,587	117,273	117,115	118,757	27.3	11.6	4.2	16.3
Oklahoma	17,758	19,616	19,852	20,193	20,768	20,621	20,837	30.5	13.9	6.2	21.0
Oregon	21,080	22,369	22,208	22,296	23,252	23,359	23,739	78.0	20.6	6.1	27.9
Pennsylvania	214,417	218,144	223,267	221,793	220,321	220,269	219,848	27.3	4.8	0.8	5.7
Rhode Island	35,923	36,609	35,901	34,462	33,211	33,021	34,945	71.5	7.5	−4.5	2.6
South Carolina	23,787	25,268	23,530	23,465	23,070	24,124	24,626	32.0	18.4	−2.5	15.4
South Dakota	7,363	7,191	7,065	6,528	6,573	6,769	6,605	4.4	15.2	−8.1	5.8
Tennessee	46,032	46,848	46,669	47,498	48,722	50,388	51,065	52.3	11.5	9.0	21.5
Texas	94,305	95,897	101,159	102,486	105,376	109,724	111,166	57.4	10.2	15.9	27.7
Utah	33,687	34,592	35,011	36,669	36,405	35,505	36,186	20.8	9.3	4.6	14.3
Vermont	13,462	15,808	15,803	15,240	14,717	14,394	14,717	78.8	32.1	−6.9	23.0
Virginia	57,899	54,270	52,583	50,424	56,440	57,917	56,762	122.7	35.2	4.6	41.4
Washington	33,503	34,266	34,348	35,957	37,781	36,950	37,785	81.4	18.7	10.3	30.8
West Virginia	7,880	7,815	10,096	10,395	10,768	10,391	10,187	1.2	9.9	30.4	43.3
Wisconsin	45,095	47,376	49,231	50,474	51,809	52,744	52,736	68.0	26.6	11.3	41.0
Wyoming	—	—	—	—	—	—	—	—	—	—	—
Outlying areas	89,217	92,692	91,336	90,886	87,311	97,712	79,569	515.2	6.3	−14.2	−8.7
American Samoa	—	—	—	—	—	—	—	—	—	—	—
Federated States of Micronesia	—	—	—	—	—	—	—	—	—	—	—
Guam	—	—	—	—	—	—	—	—	—	—	—
Marshall Islands	—	—	—	—	—	—	—	—	—	—	—
Northern Marianas	—	—	—	—	—	—	—	—	—	—	—
Palau	—	—	—	—	—	—	—	—	—	—	—
Puerto Rico	89,217	92,692	91,336	90,886	87,311	97,712	92,849	617.9	6.3	0.2	6.5
Trust Territories	—	—	—	—	—	—	—	—	—	—	—
Virgin Islands	—	—	—	—	—	—	—	—	—	—	—

—Data not available or not applicable.

SOURCE: U.S. Department of Education, National Center for Education Statistics, Higher Education General Information Survey (HEGIS), "Fall Enrollment in Higher Edu-cation" surveys; and Integrated Postsecondary Education Data System (IPEDS), "Fall Enrollment" surveys. (This table was prepared January 1998.)

Table 56.—Total fall enrollment in private 2–year institutions of higher education, by state: 1970 to 1996

State or other area	Fall 1970	Fall 1971	Fall 1972	Fall 1973	Fall 1974	Fall 1975	Fall 1976	Fall 1977	Fall 1978	Fall 1979
1	2	3	4	5	6	7	8	9	10	11
United States	123,973	121,970	115,247	122,479	118,512	133,753	131,535	141,173	154,777	159,856
Alabama	1,446	1,481	1,480	1,274	1,236	2,427	2,543	4,037	4,368	4,474
Alaska	159	247	277	330	245	276	252	—	—	—
Arizona	340	380	602	2,292	320	179	235	301	321	248
Arkansas	1,256	1,065	950	968	951	847	760	930	1,449	1,586
California	513	932	1,087	1,626	1,779	2,132	1,888	2,743	4,483	4,515
Colorado	—	68	55	—	—	—	—	550	689	1,190
Connecticut	2,670	2,232	2,065	1,909	1,824	2,026	1,128	1,148	1,129	1,190
Delaware	3,661	3,386	3,230	3,568	3,613	4,602	4,132	2,835	2,585	1,288
District of Columbia	761	523	608	583	160	126	114	102	—	—
Florida	2,664	1,233	1,011	2,463	2,158	585	594	582	1,632	2,328
Georgia	3,352	3,289	2,293	2,472	2,813	3,788	3,281	5,390	5,651	6,500
Hawaii	338	521	581	—	—	—	—	—	—	—
Idaho	5,258	5,331	5,059	4,786	5,330	5,808	5,740	5,864	6,408	6,462
Illinois	8,495	8,245	7,874	7,741	6,998	7,293	7,719	8,497	8,146	8,482
Indiana	859	989	1,004	1,621	1,540	2,236	2,187	1,662	2,281	2,205
Iowa	3,431	2,889	2,678	2,867	2,839	2,050	1,950	2,177	3,122	1,805
Kansas	1,633	1,666	1,500	1,410	1,419	1,704	1,717	1,663	1,652	1,623
Kentucky	1,818	1,646	1,641	1,643	1,535	1,647	3,103	4,476	5,448	5,213
Louisiana	—	—	—	—	—	—	—	—	245	286
Maine	96	469	244	282	268	352	438	468	1,133	995
Maryland	363	393	461	1,065	1,379	1,287	1,601	1,856	671	726
Massachusetts	17,065	15,385	13,512	14,153	15,652	22,571	18,895	16,372	15,258	17,055
Michigan	3,301	3,316	3,038	2,754	3,610	4,584	4,892	4,858	6,638	7,033
Minnesota	1,001	1,099	1,431	1,540	1,548	1,536	1,603	1,693	1,629	1,684
Mississippi	1,979	1,857	1,662	1,557	1,385	1,137	1,471	2,008	2,191	1,815
Missouri	2,452	2,667	2,330	1,472	1,525	1,851	1,315	1,229	1,255	1,310
Montana	—	—	—	—	—	—	—	—	—	—
Nebraska	318	343	342	380	327	344	343	308	304	324
Nevada	—	—	—	—	—	—	—	—	—	—
New Hampshire	515	507	445	589	1,061	727	187	207	287	455
New Jersey	5,865	6,973	7,012	6,543	6,579	6,709	7,058	6,912	7,073	7,414
New Mexico	—	—	—	—	—	—	—	—	—	—
New York	12,124	11,091	10,770	18,168	16,073	20,062	22,267	25,598	25,944	27,728
North Carolina	8,445	8,667	7,915	7,107	6,960	6,842	7,456	8,364	9,599	9,336
North Dakota	121	—	—	—	434	422	431	438	151	150
Ohio	1,557	1,630	2,250	2,616	2,898	4,261	3,860	4,196	4,025	4,409
Oklahoma	2,750	2,910	2,907	3,095	3,156	3,472	2,349	2,102	1,673	1,855
Oregon	360	531	302	337	364	390	399	428	240	389
Pennsylvania	5,363	5,726	4,958	4,470	4,602	5,787	6,201	6,374	5,914	6,935
Rhode Island	—	—	—	—	—	—	—	480	620	672
South Carolina	3,762	4,081	4,290	3,135	2,949	3,482	3,231	3,136	5,186	5,544
South Dakota	378	415	419	448	422	425	465	456	769	400
Tennessee	2,670	2,716	2,922	3,240	3,323	1,970	1,742	2,718	5,550	5,558
Texas	6,093	6,039	5,113	4,178	1,602	1,602	1,650	1,613	1,787	1,723
Utah	2,142	2,256	2,317	2,060	1,538	1,449	1,356	1,343	1,471	1,583
Vermont	1,441	1,701	1,816	1,399	1,550	1,070	1,259	1,229	1,247	1,329
Virginia	3,143	2,968	3,028	2,396	2,361	1,177	1,331	1,400	1,316	1,347
Washington	—	—	—	—	—	—	—	—	—	181
West Virginia	1,728	1,761	1,345	1,476	1,446	1,633	1,625	1,757	2,001	1,918
Wisconsin	287	346	423	466	740	885	767	673	1,236	593
Wyoming	—	—	—	—	—	—	—	—	—	—
Outlying areas	7,623	10,059	9,653	10,298	11,259	17,220	19,171	24,843	27,558	20,709
American Samoa	—	—	—	—	—	—	—	—	—	—
Federated States of Micronesia	—	—	—	—	—	—	—	—	—	—
Guam	—	—	—	—	—	—	—	—	—	—
Marshall Islands	—	—	—	—	—	—	—	—	—	—
Northern Marianas	—	—	—	—	—	—	—	—	—	—
Palau	—	—	—	—	—	—	—	—	—	—
Puerto Rico	7,623	10,059	9,653	10,298	11,259	17,220	19,171	24,843	27,558	20,709
Trust Territories	—	—	—	—	—	—	—	—	—	—
Virgin Islands	—	—	—	—	—	—	—	—	—	—

Table 56.—Total fall enrollment in private 2-year institutions of higher education, by state: 1970 to 1996—Continued

State or other area	Fall 1980	Fall 1981	Fall 1982	Fall 1983	Fall 1984	Fall 1985	Fall 1986	Fall 1987	Fall 1988	Fall 1989
1	12	13	14	15	16	17	18	19	20	21
United States	**197,505**	**235,503**	**252,053**	**264,136**	**251,676**	**261,344**	**265,857**	**235,168**	**259,668**	**267,229**
Alabama	4,025	4,916	4,577	3,626	4,531	3,849	4,442	3,602	4,730	3,461
Alaska	—	—	—	—	—	—	—	—	608	289
Arizona	148	162	213	1,124	2,279	1,359	2,023	1,793	1,989	1,929
Arkansas	2,324	2,294	2,319	2,610	3,056	2,974	1,543	1,935	2,785	2,240
California	5,536	7,088	7,326	8,315	9,462	11,242	11,401	11,290	11,470	8,732
Colorado	1,086	1,785	3,370	3,572	3,682	4,030	4,314	4,281	5,608	5,508
Connecticut	1,548	1,531	1,506	1,548	1,605	1,725	1,784	1,731	1,791	1,673
Delaware	862	868	756	777	737	608	—	—	—	—
District of Columbia	—	—	—	—	—	—	—	—	—	—
Florida	4,748	5,700	7,299	7,702	7,848	7,048	13,873	4,082	4,822	5,025
Georgia	10,080	8,763	9,224	9,957	8,735	9,133	8,934	8,060	10,487	10,209
Hawaii	—	—	—	—	—	—	—	—	—	—
Idaho	6,495	6,748	6,539	6,449	6,318	6,880	7,375	8,379	8,187	8,207
Illinois	8,351	6,998	6,891	6,609	8,133	12,122	9,021	9,436	9,600	8,309
Indiana	4,060	4,862	5,980	6,514	5,737	5,953	4,039	3,410	3,238	2,955
Iowa	2,134	2,106	2,381	2,331	2,364	2,524	3,449	3,325	3,491	2,057
Kansas	1,687	1,626	1,581	1,737	1,607	1,437	1,268	1,247	1,314	902
Kentucky	7,379	7,921	9,064	9,300	9,991	10,110	8,754	8,096	7,477	6,456
Louisiana	375	375	375	375	1,706	1,706	1,905	1,141	2,517	2,335
Maine	1,128	1,241	1,321	1,219	1,221	1,243	956	958	1,070	1,442
Maryland	694	1,069	1,267	1,370	342	365	760	852	875	721
Massachusetts	18,240	19,772	20,177	20,580	19,712	19,395	18,044	15,843	14,212	13,663
Michigan	6,836	8,325	8,942	9,313	9,082	10,065	6,478	3,616	4,906	5,039
Minnesota	3,659	4,022	4,206	4,601	4,228	4,441	4,503	4,810	4,739	5,106
Mississippi	2,351	2,403	2,559	2,017	1,983	1,494	1,685	2,312	2,617	3,006
Missouri	1,509	1,677	1,993	2,584	2,416	2,850	3,032	3,229	2,722	2,715
Montana	821	1,021	928	987	954	919	1,059	712	1,180	1,232
Nebraska	360	664	656	692	684	631	352	453	466	683
Nevada	—	—	—	—	—	—	25	25	26	23
New Hampshire	2,089	2,189	2,465	2,648	2,742	2,641	2,593	2,206	2,516	1,279
New Jersey	8,148	8,428	1,900	1,969	1,794	1,929	2,411	2,554	2,937	3,899
New Mexico	—	—	—	—	—	—	—	—	—	—
New York	29,697	32,391	34,521	37,117	37,750	36,176	35,225	30,964	29,617	27,378
North Carolina	9,006	8,970	8,800	8,189	7,186	6,820	6,558	6,786	5,891	5,134
North Dakota	215	469	501	663	795	831	100	238	208	177
Ohio	9,766	36,074	42,333	38,334	35,861	36,542	33,574	23,435	34,307	30,524
Oklahoma	2,758	3,009	3,111	2,989	3,137	3,472	4,575	5,360	6,464	5,948
Oregon	516	578	255	898	178	320	366	329	332	286
Pennsylvania	15,771	16,972	22,550	27,657	18,133	23,169	33,652	33,314	37,263	61,108
Rhode Island	854	1,163	1,471	1,828	—	—	—	—	—	—
South Carolina	6,225	5,027	5,196	5,720	5,124	5,149	4,582	5,108	4,802	4,601
South Dakota	726	732	778	768	708	864	656	708	382	359
Tennessee	5,787	5,914	6,088	7,770	7,755	6,221	5,597	5,600	5,682	6,144
Texas	2,494	1,980	1,788	2,178	1,940	2,852	3,454	3,541	4,196	4,593
Utah	1,646	1,654	1,665	2,150	1,907	1,481	1,491	1,119	1,026	1,028
Vermont	1,451	1,487	1,682	1,857	1,871	1,871	1,759	2,073	2,117	2,100
Virginia	1,006	1,256	1,244	1,204	1,442	1,595	2,501	1,432	2,793	2,271
Washington	—	36	19	—	602	1,166	1,232	1,407	1,750	1,943
West Virginia	2,139	2,332	2,943	2,717	2,819	2,488	2,594	2,192	2,671	2,781
Wisconsin	749	879	1,293	1,571	1,519	1,654	1,296	1,563	1,158	1,153
Wyoming	26	26	—	—	—	—	622	621	629	606
Outlying areas	16,056	17,033	18,388	18,981	19,049	19,910	10,450	9,488	9,852	10,172
American Samoa	—	—	—	—	—	—	—	—	—	—
Federated States of Micronesia	—	—	—	—	—	—	—	—	—	—
Guam	—	—	—	—	—	—	—	—	—	—
Marshall Islands	—	—	—	—	—	—	—	—	—	—
Northern Marianas	—	—	—	—	—	—	—	—	—	—
Palau	—	—	—	—	—	—	—	—	—	—
Puerto Rico	16,056	17,033	18,388	18,981	19,049	19,910	10,450	9,488	9,852	10,172
Trust Territories	—	—	—	—	—	—	—	—	—	—
Virgin Islands	—	—	—	—	—	—	—	—	—	—

Table 56.—Total fall enrollment in private 2–year institutions of higher education, by state: 1970 to 1996—Continued

State or other area	Fall 1990	Fall 1991	Fall 1992	Fall 1993	Fall 1994	Fall 1995	Fall 1996	Percentage change			
								Fall 1970 to fall 1996	Fall 1986 to fall 1991	Fall 1991 to fall 1996	Fall 1986 to fall 1996
1	22	23	24	25	26	27	28	29	30	31	32
United States	243,608	247,085	237,835	228,539	221,243	214,700	214,153	72.7	–7.1	–13.3	–19.4
Alabama	3,812	3,232	3,350	2,032	1,356	498	1,099	–24.0	–27.2	–66.0	–75.3
Alaska	394	342	359	248	339	204	326	105.0	—	–4.7	—
Arizona	1,955	1,579	1,005	1,077	929	889	961	182.6	–21.9	–39.1	–52.5
Arkansas	1,981	2,118	1,546	1,032	346	446	406	–67.7	37.3	–80.8	–73.7
California	11,499	12,052	13,841	14,671	13,666	14,057	14,259	2,679.5	5.7	18.3	25.1
Colorado	4,759	5,305	4,108	3,892	3,354	3,623	1,561	—	23.0	–70.6	–63.8
Connecticut	1,578	1,369	1,689	1,631	1,773	1,562	1,556	–41.7	–23.3	13.7	–12.8
Delaware	—	—	—	—	—	—	—	—	—	—	—
District of Columbia	—	—	—	—	—	—	—	—	—	—	—
Florida	6,632	7,340	6,070	4,555	4,980	5,431	5,835	119.0	–47.1	–20.5	–57.9
Georgia	9,029	8,316	8,266	6,520	6,173	4,550	4,458	33.0	–6.9	–46.4	–50.1
Hawaii	—	—	—	—	—	—	—	—	—	—	—
Idaho	8,228	8,351	8,254	8,670	8,411	8,272	8,122	54.5	13.2	–2.7	10.1
Illinois	8,960	9,550	6,937	6,554	6,103	4,270	4,124	–51.5	5.9	–56.8	–54.3
Indiana	3,645	3,708	3,442	3,589	3,649	3,489	3,510	308.6	1.7	–5.3	–13.1
Iowa	2,329	2,274	2,133	2,158	1,391	1,115	1,054	–69.3	–34.1	–53.6	–69.4
Kansas	978	888	1,002	958	917	878	873	–46.5	–30.0	–1.7	–31.2
Kentucky	5,775	5,244	4,522	4,951	4,506	2,668	2,609	43.5	–40.1	–50.2	–70.2
Louisiana	2,242	1,992	681	602	1,204	1,178	1,421	—	4.6	–28.7	–25.4
Maine	1,424	1,575	1,603	1,708	1,872	1,915	1,811	1,786.5	64.7	15.0	89.4
Maryland	743	855	986	1,052	1,141	1,186	1,181	225.3	12.5	38.1	55.4
Massachusetts	13,491	13,647	15,168	14,999	14,469	8,053	6,928	–59.4	–24.4	–49.2	–61.6
Michigan	2,845	3,061	3,087	2,701	2,463	2,645	1,687	–48.9	–52.7	–44.9	–74.0
Minnesota	4,354	4,151	5,517	4,632	4,388	4,157	4,768	376.3	–7.8	14.9	5.9
Mississippi	3,205	2,968	2,395	1,219	1,055	812	715	–63.9	76.1	–75.9	–57.6
Missouri	4,004	3,308	4,982	5,726	5,866	4,597	4,291	75.0	9.1	29.7	41.5
Montana	965	1,242	2,419	856	773	920	831	—	17.3	–33.1	–21.5
Nebraska	332	479	527	592	425	544	—	—	36.1	—	—
Nevada	173	350	25	25	27	27	24	—	1,300.0	–93.1	–4.0
New Hampshire	2,801	3,589	3,860	3,976	3,848	4,031	3,869	651.3	38.4	7.8	49.2
New Jersey	3,674	4,020	4,233	4,162	3,981	4,717	5,190	–11.5	66.7	29.1	115.3
New Mexico	180	620	837	566	651	954	1,051	—	—	69.5	—
New York	28,255	33,477	30,524	30,183	28,700	28,010	24,376	101.1	–5.0	–27.2	–30.8
North Carolina	5,211	4,442	3,207	2,818	2,534	1,483	1,009	–88.1	–32.3	–77.3	–84.6
North Dakota	208	224	238	268	246	255	275	127.3	124.0	22.8	175.0
Ohio	17,858	19,062	20,927	16,059	14,465	13,342	13,439	763.1	–43.2	–29.5	–60.0
Oklahoma	4,390	3,754	3,266	2,248	2,658	2,029	2,037	–25.9	–17.9	–45.7	–55.5
Oregon	234	287	305	186	168	169	—	—	–21.6	—	—
Pennsylvania	46,165	47,457	43,781	47,688	48,288	57,562	66,965	1,148.6	41.0	41.1	99.0
Rhode Island	—	—	—	2,112	2,131	2,426	—	—	—	—	—
South Carolina	4,381	2,627	2,333	1,904	1,486	1,295	1,314	–65.1	–42.7	–50.0	–71.3
South Dakota	249	253	185	211	211	233	204	–46.0	–61.4	–19.4	–68.9
Tennessee	5,157	4,753	3,999	3,213	2,819	2,438	1,881	–29.6	–15.1	–60.4	–66.4
Texas	4,818	4,992	4,909	4,996	6,117	5,950	6,182	1.5	44.5	23.8	79.0
Utah	1,508	1,025	1,114	1,199	1,198	1,259	1,256	–41.4	–31.3	22.5	–15.8
Vermont	2,026	143	177	174	187	201	234	–83.8	–91.9	63.6	–86.7
Virginia	4,257	3,948	4,067	4,301	4,544	4,875	4,614	46.8	57.9	16.9	84.5
Washington	2,249	2,149	2,445	2,075	2,109	2,234	2,526	—	74.4	17.5	105.0
West Virginia	2,802	2,572	872	957	853	786	747	–56.8	–0.8	–71.0	–71.2
Wisconsin	1,150	1,528	1,781	1,893	1,806	1,709	1,763	514.3	17.9	15.4	36.0
Wyoming	703	867	861	700	667	756	811	—	39.4	–6.5	30.4
Outlying areas	9,157	10,005	11,721	12,988	12,458	8,895	8,950	17.4	–4.3	–10.5	–14.4
American Samoa	—	—	—	—	—	—	—	—	—	—	—
Federated States of Micronesia	—	—	—	—	—	—	—	—	—	—	—
Guam	—	—	—	—	—	—	—	—	—	—	—
Marshall Islands	—	—	—	—	—	—	—	—	—	—	—
Northern Marianas	—	—	—	—	—	—	—	—	—	—	—
Palau	—	—	—	—	—	—	—	—	—	—	—
Puerto Rico	9,157	10,005	11,721	12,988	12,458	8,895	8,950	17.4	–4.3	–10.5	–14.4
Trust Territories	—	—	—	—	—	—	—	—	—	—	—
Virgin Islands	—	—	—	—	—	—	—	—	—	—	—

—Data not available or not applicable.

NOTE.—Some data have been revised from previously published figures. Large increases in 1980 and 1981 are due to the addition of schools accredited by the Accrediting Commission of Career Schools and Colleges of Technology.

SOURCE: U.S. Department of Education, National Center for Education Statistics, Higher Education General Information Survey (HEGIS), "Fall Enrollment in Higher Education" surveys; and Integrated Postsecondary Education Data System (IPEDS), "Fall Enrollment" surveys. (This table was prepared January 1998.)

Table 57.—Full-time-equivalent fall enrollment in institutions of higher education, by state: 1970 to 1996

State or other area	Fall 1970	Fall 1971	Fall 1972	Fall 1973	Fall 1974	Fall 1975	Fall 1976	Fall 1977	Fall 1978	Fall 1979
1	2	3	4	5	6	7	8	9	10	11
United States	6,737,817	7,148,575	7,253,712	7,453,467	7,805,454	8,479,688	8,312,502	8,415,339	8,348,482	8,487,317
Alabama	89,260	96,899	101,847	105,370	117,079	138,487	130,891	136,027	139,442	135,443
Alaska	5,500	6,940	7,049	8,056	7,653	6,581	9,051	10,384	12,283	8,847
Arizona	79,036	89,351	90,414	97,849	113,692	119,027	119,819	122,740	110,721	122,995
Arkansas	47,219	49,091	47,805	46,559	47,750	54,862	56,177	58,656	64,087	61,090
California	846,400	897,152	920,758	996,201	1,049,886	1,168,414	1,113,635	1,097,975	1,047,746	1,064,217
Colorado	101,261	106,169	107,972	107,449	114,622	120,210	120,427	121,925	117,984	120,468
Connecticut	96,448	101,207	100,979	104,165	109,650	110,857	107,604	109,653	119,058	111,381
Delaware	19,015	20,827	21,313	22,045	23,423	24,372	25,048	24,512	24,813	25,401
District of Columbia	54,723	60,030	59,964	61,003	62,911	63,682	60,692	61,300	67,607	62,636
Florida	187,787	201,340	207,767	215,902	227,463	257,822	259,603	270,557	272,476	280,575
Georgia	107,774	119,618	120,852	124,674	131,676	147,064	144,426	145,742	147,835	145,424
Hawaii	31,074	33,660	35,210	35,435	36,369	39,032	39,011	38,896	38,526	38,155
Idaho	29,868	30,946	29,245	28,843	29,181	31,239	32,054	32,240	31,440	32,275
Illinois	349,261	368,509	371,629	377,620	391,638	421,878	420,928	425,201	416,951	417,229
Indiana	158,433	169,612	165,383	164,990	165,516	173,136	177,010	176,869	173,550	179,700
Iowa	98,089	101,449	99,697	98,565	101,541	107,951	106,034	109,648	111,429	113,706
Kansas	89,070	94,145	94,019	89,428	91,444	96,485	94,734	96,841	96,262	98,556
Kentucky	83,180	88,858	89,789	88,998	92,193	101,136	103,762	105,451	104,887	106,197
Louisiana	103,284	114,072	115,487	115,352	118,523	129,395	129,678	130,056	126,280	127,757
Maine	27,211	29,265	30,171	31,547	31,881	34,194	32,948	32,240	32,524	33,695
Maryland	111,026	118,013	122,959	129,408	137,574	144,233	144,947	149,406	142,441	146,678
Massachusetts	243,915	253,170	257,727	272,038	286,285	303,472	285,269	292,029	298,386	307,676
Michigan	302,439	307,406	299,878	313,098	334,405	363,806	344,330	348,513	344,934	355,618
Minnesota	136,820	137,075	134,435	134,239	137,125	147,979	150,185	151,432	151,405	153,724
Mississippi	65,550	69,605	70,802	72,257	75,275	84,576	83,958	84,281	82,976	85,567
Missouri	147,999	158,104	157,366	156,731	158,749	176,855	172,112	171,255	168,645	169,032
Montana	27,445	26,822	25,219	24,019	25,036	26,843	26,315	26,911	26,604	27,449
Nebraska	57,017	57,179	56,215	55,288	55,314	60,432	62,329	65,131	62,739	66,915
Nevada	10,307	11,494	12,499	15,852	19,679	21,442	17,609	18,443	18,198	18,935
New Hampshire	26,287	27,341	27,676	29,928	31,104	34,766	34,303	35,233	35,324	35,885
New Jersey	153,586	170,575	177,012	185,534	199,216	213,506	207,288	212,152	213,706	214,839
New Mexico	36,141	38,659	37,725	38,957	39,823	41,347	42,650	42,582	43,174	42,881
New York	608,328	643,113	671,279	677,984	715,888	766,567	727,567	735,240	728,943	745,028
North Carolina	150,217	167,243	175,148	177,257	190,860	217,136	212,155	214,524	221,359	224,219
North Dakota	28,035	27,608	26,520	26,240	25,622	26,705	27,172	29,188	29,350	28,678
Ohio	308,098	325,181	325,323	323,066	326,505	344,651	348,479	351,988	343,503	352,008
Oklahoma	94,399	99,728	100,097	100,961	104,387	114,494	115,804	117,422	117,524	114,970
Oregon	93,457	98,531	93,863	102,335	105,257	110,946	106,913	106,293	104,871	108,881
Pennsylvania	330,245	350,825	346,607	351,249	355,432	376,725	379,736	382,263	377,370	383,667
Rhode Island	36,706	38,587	39,837	41,771	43,822	51,300	47,293	49,684	48,536	49,173
South Carolina	61,410	69,798	79,417	83,376	91,812	108,223	101,754	104,825	106,208	107,820
South Dakota	27,114	26,978	25,200	23,719	23,712	26,358	26,247	26,766	27,240	26,909
Tennessee	115,945	125,066	128,539	129,881	138,385	147,413	147,983	150,543	167,340	158,135
Texas	357,029	378,366	392,643	409,609	438,150	490,652	491,599	501,676	495,396	511,322
Utah	69,232	72,019	71,074	70,674	69,613	74,950	71,090	72,583	71,239	73,271
Vermont	19,560	21,339	22,962	24,078	24,422	25,028	25,330	25,042	25,962	25,016
Virginia	119,999	131,094	139,787	147,337	158,502	178,197	177,842	185,594	184,730	192,307
Washington	143,568	151,908	152,786	155,999	159,567	168,358	171,027	175,120	175,932	188,014
West Virginia	54,070	57,527	54,830	55,655	56,809	60,114	60,232	59,807	58,935	59,726
Wisconsin	168,019	177,545	179,981	175,348	178,170	189,953	187,910	190,090	187,576	195,147
Wyoming	12,882	14,569	14,186	12,955	13,773	13,265	14,042	14,253	14,110	14,048
U.S. Service Schools ...	17,079	16,967	16,770	16,573	21,090	23,572	17,500	18,157	17,925	18,032
Outlying areas	54,948	61,789	66,612	74,934	80,031	89,532	93,718	113,278	112,216	117,406
American Samoa	—	388	428	574	505	585	688	850	526	577
Federated States of Micronesia	—	—	—	—	—	—	—	—	—	—
Guam	1,885	2,207	2,701	2,573	2,612	2,812	2,608	3,224	2,144	2,208
Marshall Islands	—	—	—	—	—	—	—	—	—	—
Northern Marianas	—	—	—	—	—	—	—	—	—	—
Palau	—	—	—	—	—	—	—	—	—	—
Puerto Rico	52,305	58,168	62,386	70,613	75,632	84,626	88,926	107,709	108,203	113,313
Trust Territories	—	113	121	115	132	167	284	251	285	160
Virgin Islands	758	913	976	1,059	1,150	1,342	1,212	1,244	1,058	1,148

Table 57.—Full-time-equivalent fall enrollment in institutions of higher education, by state: 1970 to 1996—Continued

State or other area	Fall 1980	Fall 1981	Fall 1982	Fall 1983	Fall 1984	Fall 1985	Fall 1986	Fall 1987	Fall 1988	Fall 1989
1	12	13	14	15	16	17	18	19	20	21
United States	8,819,013	9,014,521	9,091,648	9,166,398	8,951,695	8,943,433	9,064,167	9,229,736	9,464,271	9,780,881
Alabama	138,910	142,241	142,271	145,138	145,293	149,895	147,502	148,267	157,911	167,682
Alaska	10,073	11,722	13,070	13,877	13,548	14,098	15,709	15,026	17,570	17,792
Arizona	127,114	129,391	132,490	136,832	131,451	134,954	141,739	144,216	161,227	158,516
Arkansas	64,120	63,012	63,488	63,512	63,862	63,083	63,800	64,949	69,191	72,615
California	1,099,636	1,144,849	1,133,894	1,104,759	1,060,013	1,062,513	1,093,096	1,126,214	1,113,073	1,143,609
Colorado	123,589	126,813	129,455	129,409	122,762	121,804	129,517	136,244	139,781	148,341
Connecticut	112,612	112,003	111,151	112,313	110,098	107,803	109,766	111,832	113,910	116,101
Delaware	26,284	27,162	27,201	26,666	26,661	27,014	25,708	27,857	29,065	30,719
District of Columbia	62,126	64,524	61,720	60,131	59,607	58,945	58,992	59,009	60,803	61,633
Florida	290,647	298,909	303,922	307,624	304,409	308,315	324,419	322,809	346,576	376,371
Georgia	152,369	158,459	164,615	166,129	161,101	161,952	156,304	175,053	182,324	191,463
Hawaii	37,637	38,546	40,147	40,679	39,289	38,847	37,813	37,778	38,167	39,204
Idaho	33,938	33,573	34,086	33,948	32,724	32,649	35,363	36,418	37,803	39,451
Illinois	433,393	445,416	452,062	451,170	437,343	451,502	465,014	466,897	467,577	480,827
Indiana	193,445	197,385	200,514	203,352	196,418	195,630	195,825	199,031	209,039	216,170
Iowa	120,083	122,085	125,949	129,357	128,646	128,492	130,033	130,931	133,515	137,794
Kansas	101,147	101,359	101,853	102,872	101,023	100,807	104,680	106,777	111,052	114,630
Kentucky	113,709	114,548	114,431	115,110	112,855	110,539	112,969	118,523	124,168	128,509
Louisiana	132,780	141,071	142,413	148,331	149,386	148,983	143,084	144,265	146,605	149,408
Maine	34,471	34,920	35,882	38,266	38,174	37,993	35,379	35,846	36,948	41,904
Maryland	148,864	150,802	152,984	156,127	151,297	147,768	153,699	157,644	162,136	165,927
Massachusetts	315,937	321,732	311,772	321,784	319,574	321,022	320,771	325,493	327,869	325,742
Michigan	366,058	368,203	362,904	367,565	359,563	354,690	355,674	365,185	372,522	383,226
Minnesota	162,559	167,637	171,139	169,242	168,550	170,958	175,851	179,371	184,446	190,748
Mississippi	85,621	90,759	90,850	93,010	88,942	86,846	84,951	88,865	94,263	98,298
Missouri	179,128	183,863	182,405	185,279	178,473	177,092	179,695	184,754	191,854	202,878
Montana	29,428	30,225	30,592	31,392	29,967	29,992	29,379	28,942	29,584	31,561
Nebraska	68,505	70,426	72,537	71,448	71,475	70,778	72,492	72,834	75,319	78,244
Nevada	22,467	21,472	23,368	23,315	22,260	23,093	25,247	26,241	27,331	31,158
New Hampshire	39,456	39,889	40,999	41,951	41,869	41,733	42,257	42,935	44,725	43,605
New Jersey	218,838	219,456	218,649	215,538	204,712	201,270	201,470	201,562	206,751	214,090
New Mexico	44,060	45,459	46,993	47,773	46,506	47,492	53,933	55,865	56,331	57,651
New York	760,398	774,481	773,941	782,487	771,352	763,693	774,158	760,464	771,777	785,624
North Carolina	235,266	240,933	245,117	244,134	241,126	249,901	242,961	243,655	252,194	263,877
North Dakota	30,188	31,444	31,361	32,547	32,496	32,456	31,962	31,821	33,698	35,453
Ohio	369,172	389,142	398,391	401,159	386,458	383,727	388,824	390,584	408,597	412,408
Oklahoma	115,701	117,812	126,405	130,785	125,823	126,691	122,718	125,553	128,181	127,715
Oregon	110,649	110,930	106,508	107,479	103,945	102,247	106,186	108,325	114,117	116,167
Pennsylvania	404,192	411,333	421,887	430,836	418,454	421,085	428,402	439,944	445,335	475,972
Rhode Island	50,628	52,140	52,089	53,271	51,941	53,016	53,362	55,278	57,072	57,704
South Carolina	109,346	108,864	113,793	111,833	107,894	109,303	107,912	112,534	117,600	115,811
South Dakota	27,873	29,283	29,036	29,135	26,797	26,988	25,528	26,112	26,278	27,112
Tennessee	161,245	160,065	160,876	164,267	158,315	153,114	154,018	156,659	162,632	171,203
Texas	527,724	536,677	562,015	587,782	587,686	566,736	546,422	568,748	598,691	619,850
Utah	76,421	75,912	79,820	81,809	81,789	82,234	85,319	82,613	84,634	89,540
Vermont	25,572	25,174	25,135	25,597	25,530	25,649	26,531	26,924	27,635	28,784
Virginia	199,549	210,521	204,560	206,545	200,324	204,928	217,841	225,955	231,605	245,199
Washington	194,440	182,717	172,490	172,337	171,478	171,668	175,225	177,580	183,472	185,046
West Virginia	60,394	61,083	62,407	62,893	60,348	58,438	59,596	60,288	63,434	65,886
Wisconsin	206,790	208,608	213,195	217,066	212,441	211,749	223,863	219,929	223,106	225,334
Wyoming	14,725	15,515	16,592	17,359	16,713	17,037	17,656	18,878	19,422	20,842
U.S. Service Schools	49,736	53,976	60,224	53,178	52,934	54,221	53,549	60,259	45,355	55,487
Outlying areas	117,637	128,637	145,780	152,114	139,888	145,530	142,910	135,588	140,426	139,630
American Samoa	824	874	890	742	720	) 497	494	556	584	644
Federated States of Micronesia	—	—	—	—	—	—	—	—	—	504
Guam	2,115	4,496	4,128	2,585	2,921	3,049	3,020	2,547	2,436	2,708
Marshall Islands	—	—	—	—	—	—	—	—	—	—
Northern Marianas	—	—	—	69	158	183	308	196	194	226
Palau	—	—	—	—	—	—	—	—	—	836
Puerto Rico	113,285	121,748	138,678	146,410	133,730	139,627	136,940	129,934	134,932	133,122
Trust Territories	195	157	528	655	694	680	697	867	843	—
Virgin Islands	1,218	1,362	1,556	1,653	1,665	1,494	1,451	1,488	1,437	1,590

Table 57.—Full-time-equivalent fall enrollment in institutions of higher education, by state: 1970 to 1996—Continued

| State or other area | Fall 1990 | Fall 1991 | Fall 1992 | Fall 1993 | Fall 1994 | Fall 1995 | Fall 1996 | Percentage change | | | |
| | | | | | | | | Fall 1970 to fall 1996 | Fall 1986 to fall 1991 | Fall 1991 to fall 1996 | Fall 1986 to fall 1996 |
1	22	23	24	25	26	27	28	29	30	31	32
United States	9,983,436	10,360,606	10,436,776	10,351,415	10,348,072	10,334,956	10,402,260	54.4	14.3	0.4	14.8
Alabama	174,610	178,519	182,528	183,013	180,171	178,736	175,609	96.7	21.0	−1.6	19.1
Alaska	18,496	19,272	19,607	19,567	18,979	18,904	18,655	239.2	22.7	−3.2	18.8
Arizona	167,617	174,011	175,720	178,348	178,878	177,379	181,725	129.9	22.8	4.4	28.2
Arkansas	74,449	77,380	79,454	80,309	77,833	78,558	79,724	68.8	21.3	3.0	25.0
California	1,156,288	1,269,457	1,248,547	1,186,529	1,200,697	1,196,379	1,231,947	45.6	16.1	−3.0	12.7
Colorado	159,032	164,189	167,832	167,652	169,176	169,997	171,484	69.3	26.8	4.4	32.4
Connecticut	115,791	114,246	113,400	111,465	110,471	109,751	109,402	13.4	4.1	−4.2	−0.3
Delaware	31,612	32,273	31,982	32,477	32,743	32,536	33,147	74.3	25.5	2.7	28.9
District of Columbia	61,549	59,888	62,484	62,734	60,297	61,018	59,213	8.2	1.5	−1.1	0.4
Florida	383,385	407,253	411,442	412,279	419,527	422,287	426,721	127.2	25.5	4.8	31.5
Georgia	198,549	218,318	231,052	237,433	241,810	248,265	252,183	134.0	39.7	15.5	61.3
Hawaii	41,097	41,177	43,505	44,623	45,614	45,296	44,640	43.7	8.9	8.4	18.1
Idaho	41,275	44,248	45,958	47,119	47,987	47,546	48,096	61.0	25.1	8.7	36.0
Illinois	493,364	507,464	506,889	500,739	499,027	491,765	494,461	41.6	9.1	−2.6	6.3
Indiana	222,835	228,882	233,272	231,193	228,793	227,543	227,438	43.6	16.9	−0.6	16.1
Iowa	138,565	139,044	140,950	140,563	139,408	140,002	141,829	44.6	6.9	2.0	9.1
Kansas	118,969	121,661	123,070	123,397	123,775	125,896	122,882	38.0	16.2	1.0	17.4
Kentucky	137,651	144,882	145,999	145,725	142,734	140,327	140,087	68.4	28.2	−3.3	24.0
Louisiana	154,132	159,038	166,680	164,605	166,658	166,816	166,973	61.7	11.2	5.0	16.7
Maine	42,021	42,298	42,250	41,679	41,557	41,200	40,968	50.6	19.6	−3.1	15.8
Maryland	169,972	175,101	175,879	175,231	175,379	176,641	175,819	58.4	13.9	0.4	14.4
Massachusetts	320,299	323,796	325,190	321,807	319,426	318,887	317,205	30.0	0.9	−2.0	−1.1
Michigan	389,814	388,850	386,643	388,039	376,696	373,059	375,198	24.1	9.3	−3.5	5.5
Minnesota	190,608	189,435	201,777	197,504	208,377	203,130	205,483	50.2	7.7	8.5	16.9
Mississippi	103,957	106,129	104,626	103,750	101,471	103,067	105,273	60.6	24.9	−0.8	23.9
Missouri	210,104	215,962	215,859	216,343	214,043	212,551	214,329	44.8	20.2	−0.8	19.3
Montana	29,905	31,966	33,525	33,797	34,332	36,528	36,812	34.1	8.8	15.2	25.3
Nebraska	80,989	82,333	88,126	83,873	84,397	84,278	86,525	51.8	13.6	5.1	19.4
Nevada	33,814	35,462	36,294	35,709	36,443	37,991	41,255	300.3	40.5	16.3	63.4
New Hampshire	45,762	48,964	49,262	49,063	48,542	49,063	48,833	85.8	15.9	−0.3	15.6
New Jersey	221,468	228,878	234,572	235,483	231,770	232,669	232,020	51.1	13.6	1.4	15.2
New Mexico	59,517	64,219	67,168	69,106	69,300	69,528	69,843	93.3	19.1	8.8	29.5
New York	798,696	809,456	818,337	822,507	817,994	805,527	800,646	31.6	4.6	−1.1	3.4
North Carolina	269,025	279,952	288,536	283,809	282,848	285,708	287,887	91.6	15.2	2.8	18.5
North Dakota	33,118	33,735	35,013	35,207	34,977	35,279	35,393	26.2	5.5	4.9	10.7
Ohio	420,499	429,566	434,240	426,308	418,048	411,810	410,696	33.3	10.5	−4.4	5.6
Oklahoma	128,203	148,292	142,449	135,727	137,161	134,176	132,558	40.4	20.8	−10.6	8.0
Oregon	120,176	119,104	120,025	118,836	117,776	116,584	117,555	25.8	12.2	−1.3	10.7
Pennsylvania	464,179	487,534	480,324	475,632	470,296	474,269	477,723	44.7	13.8	−2.0	11.5
Rhode Island	60,168	60,350	60,106	59,215	57,189	56,856	55,969	52.5	13.1	−7.3	4.9
South Carolina	127,225	132,053	132,199	131,768	130,895	132,353	133,755	117.8	22.4	1.3	23.9
South Dakota	28,256	29,680	30,615	31,850	31,507	30,555	29,521	8.9	16.3	−0.5	15.6
Tennessee	175,961	185,764	187,884	188,253	187,442	190,706	192,564	66.1	20.6	3.7	25.0
Texas	637,742	648,761	663,608	664,476	671,482	671,478	675,896	89.3	18.7	4.2	23.7
Utah	94,012	102,500	106,461	110,574	114,829	116,368	117,006	69.0	20.1	14.2	37.1
Vermont	29,072	30,028	29,634	28,784	28,152	28,079	28,217	44.3	13.2	−6.0	6.4
Virginia	251,708	255,449	254,088	250,710	254,289	255,712	256,092	113.4	17.3	0.3	17.6
Washington	189,521	196,601	199,121	204,370	211,518	214,050	218,785	52.4	12.2	11.3	24.9
West Virginia	68,235	70,932	72,133	71,272	70,966	69,831	69,622	28.8	19.0	−1.8	16.8
Wisconsin	229,975	230,353	229,686	230,744	225,024	223,938	224,066	33.4	2.9	−2.7	0.1
Wyoming	21,888	22,767	22,232	22,040	22,101	21,938	22,130	71.8	28.9	−2.8	25.3
U.S. Service Schools	48,281	53,134	38,543	38,179	37,267	42,146	40,400	136.5	−0.8	−24.0	−24.6
Outlying areas	140,954	145,214	145,833	146,491	143,160	155,364	154,998	182.1	1.6	6.7	8.5
American Samoa	952	997	1,029	1,007	998	988	999	—	101.8	0.2	102.2
Federated States of Micronesia	549	597	690	743	1,040	1,076	1,098	—	—	83.9	—
Guam	2,956	3,250	3,107	3,820	4,208	3,819	3,522	86.8	7.6	8.4	16.6
Marshall Islands	—	—	296	374	254	249	300	—	—	—	—
Northern Marianas	376	488	476	653	653	625	693	—	58.4	42.0	124.9
Palau	423	309	382	377	357	296	281	—	—	−9.1	—
Puerto Rico	134,193	137,934	138,047	137,601	133,612	146,258	146,152	179.4	0.7	6.0	6.7
Trust Territories	—	—	—	—	—	—	—	—	—	—	—
Virgin Islands	1,505	1,639	1,806	1,916	2,038	2,053	1,953	157.7	13.0	19.2	34.6

—Data not available or not applicable.

NOTE.—Some data have been revised from previously published figures.

SOURCE: U.S. Department of Education, National Center for Education Statistics, Higher Education General Information Survey (HEGIS), "Fall Enrollment in Higher Education" surveys; and Integrated Postsecondary Education Data System (IPEDS), "Fall Enrollment" surveys. (This table was prepared January 1998.)

Table 58.—Full-time-equivalent fall enrollment in public 4-year institutions of higher education, by state: 1970 to 1996

State or other area	Fall 1970	Fall 1971	Fall 1972	Fall 1973	Fall 1974	Fall 1975	Fall 1976	Fall 1977	Fall 1978	Fall 1979
1	2	3	4	5	6	7	8	9	10	11
United States	3,468,572	3,660,624	3,706,238	3,721,035	3,847,542	4,056,500	3,998,450	4,039,071	3,996,126	4,059,304
Alabama	57,539	61,003	63,185	66,134	70,566	79,505	80,643	85,138	86,294	88,706
Alaska	4,519	2,788	2,930	3,729	3,601	3,360	4,712	4,147	4,590	4,068
Arizona	50,360	57,055	57,561	55,106	63,980	60,987	60,459	62,971	61,287	65,527
Arkansas	37,115	38,923	37,349	35,685	36,014	40,069	41,449	42,207	47,717	44,184
California	321,107	329,543	342,778	349,991	354,937	379,631	372,849	368,666	363,715	367,369
Colorado	72,062	75,370	77,120	75,763	81,259	82,441	83,124	83,890	82,034	82,915
Connecticut	37,864	39,891	39,974	41,044	42,439	45,107	43,582	43,239	41,605	42,959
Delaware	13,121	14,595	15,100	15,671	16,330	16,705	17,012	17,400	17,381	17,587
District of Columbia	5,934	8,896	8,401	7,756	10,991	11,232	10,098	8,575	7,174	7,850
Florida	68,495	74,471	83,665	86,380	89,307	97,015	91,538	94,582	96,632	98,606
Georgia	67,797	77,770	78,619	77,760	80,501	87,558	84,722	85,459	85,497	84,892
Hawaii	19,609	21,063	21,465	21,153	20,459	19,897	21,086	20,705	20,602	20,388
Idaho	20,141	21,019	19,720	20,164	19,902	21,141	21,439	21,175	20,280	21,126
Illinois	151,721	155,557	154,771	154,300	158,618	166,006	160,663	160,505	157,968	158,673
Indiana	107,125	115,828	113,799	111,578	111,846	115,748	119,251	117,981	113,943	117,493
Iowa	46,475	47,142	46,127	45,507	46,361	48,811	48,806	50,463	50,907	51,221
Kansas	60,876	65,385	64,296	60,495	62,033	65,376	63,697	65,098	64,858	65,967
Kentucky	56,900	62,206	63,768	63,176	66,294	71,673	72,642	72,885	72,823	73,636
Louisiana	81,226	89,972	90,614	92,074	93,046	101,270	100,540	101,083	97,724	99,461
Maine	17,870	17,271	18,409	19,561	20,162	21,592	19,775	19,330	19,243	19,551
Maryland	60,505	62,806	65,838	67,927	74,285	77,872	78,214	79,468	75,236	77,145
Massachusetts	63,704	68,773	72,305	79,801	82,764	88,596	82,343	80,600	81,438	81,751
Michigan	182,165	184,413	180,576	184,029	189,100	200,249	197,684	195,060	192,721	196,570
Minnesota	90,444	88,736	85,384	83,486	85,407	91,178	90,857	89,946	90,235	91,627
Mississippi	38,417	41,363	42,092	41,892	43,117	47,063	47,277	47,707	47,117	47,796
Missouri	84,878	90,113	89,861	86,570	83,431	87,309	86,638	87,602	85,906	88,320
Montana	23,490	23,127	21,474	20,477	21,123	22,384	22,010	22,933	22,338	23,459
Nebraska	39,729	39,875	38,888	37,397	37,036	38,737	38,938	39,783	39,282	41,616
Nevada	10,034	10,831	10,875	10,280	10,874	11,888	11,069	12,282	10,945	12,085
New Hampshire	13,336	14,172	14,301	14,998	15,222	15,909	16,175	16,612	16,060	16,424
New Jersey	72,001	79,906	85,428	91,585	100,965	105,976	98,776	102,468	104,085	101,650
New Mexico	30,404	32,673	31,803	32,385	32,802	34,004	35,154	34,658	34,311	34,824
New York	197,737	221,184	241,205	235,395	260,447	268,206	240,366	243,123	235,619	240,513
North Carolina	73,927	79,671	82,311	84,277	89,736	97,813	95,887	98,306	98,977	101,577
North Dakota	21,248	20,482	19,408	19,072	18,085	18,831	18,894	20,502	20,905	20,725
Ohio	190,148	198,303	194,126	188,605	188,925	195,836	195,394	197,121	193,092	196,948
Oklahoma	68,952	69,348	67,789	66,587	67,268	71,482	70,857	71,755	70,692	71,477
Oregon	54,929	55,622	53,412	51,979	53,113	53,245	52,212	51,697	51,458	53,020
Pennsylvania	135,358	142,821	142,904	147,198	149,627	155,834	155,235	156,718	152,012	151,600
Rhode Island	15,793	16,322	17,135	17,096	17,084	17,558	16,332	16,763	16,891	16,816
South Carolina	30,731	36,576	40,539	42,492	43,820	51,325	51,162	52,868	53,352	53,454
South Dakota	20,938	20,810	19,360	18,149	18,013	18,554	18,487	18,961	19,729	19,514
Tennessee	74,314	81,195	81,943	81,073	83,570	85,295	86,371	87,067	86,645	87,062
Texas	211,897	220,110	223,657	232,338	243,315	261,370	270,741	278,255	276,903	281,614
Utah	35,727	36,564	36,019	36,490	36,220	39,152	35,574	36,242	34,714	36,371
Vermont	9,821	10,640	11,355	12,053	12,300	12,353	12,974	12,575	13,546	12,552
Virginia	73,032	78,799	83,299	87,649	92,403	99,524	100,627	103,824	102,173	107,098
Washington	68,095	72,909	71,562	70,283	69,371	71,287	69,741	71,172	70,032	72,724
West Virginia	40,580	43,840	42,067	42,672	42,878	43,695	44,525	45,186	44,745	45,828
Wisconsin	113,198	117,339	114,471	108,766	110,911	114,014	114,332	115,921	116,738	118,832
Wyoming	8,105	8,586	8,430	8,434	8,666	7,917	8,017	8,240	8,030	8,101
U.S. Service Schools ...	17,079	16,967	16,770	16,573	17,018	16,920	17,500	18,157	17,925	18,032
Outlying areas	32,969	36,013	35,955	36,728	36,910	37,350	36,340	41,776	38,354	38,517
American Samoa	—	—	—	—	—	—	—	—	—	—
Federated States of Micronesia										
Guam	1,885	2,207	2,701	2,573	2,612	2,812	2,608	3,224	2,144	2,208
Marshall Islands	---	—	—	—	—	—	—	—	—	—
Northern Marianas	—	—	—	—	—	—	—	—	—	—
Palau	—	—	—	—	—	—	—	—	—	—
Puerto Rico	30,326	32,893	32,278	33,096	33,148	33,196	32,520	37,308	35,152	35,161
Trust Territories	—	—	—	—	—	—	—	—	—	—
Virgin Islands	758	913	976	1,059	1,150	1,342	1,212	1,244	1,058	1,148

Table 58.—Full-time-equivalent fall enrollment in public 4–year institutions of higher education, by state: 1970 to 1996—Continued

State or other area	Fall 1980	Fall 1981	Fall 1982	Fall 1983	Fall 1984	Fall 1985	Fall 1986	Fall 1987	Fall 1988	Fall 1989
1	12	13	14	15	16	17	18	19	20	21
United States	**4,158,267**	**4,208,506**	**4,220,648**	**4,265,807**	**4,237,895**	**4,239,622**	**4,295,494**	**4,395,728**	**4,505,774**	**4,619,828**
Alabama	89,375	90,272	89,499	89,757	87,931	89,514	86,157	87,892	93,696	100,002
Alaska	5,103	5,691	6,418	6,836	7,108	7,083	7,736	8,022	13,999	16,227
Arizona	65,276	66,169	65,782	67,227	67,683	67,081	69,864	71,834	76,175	77,865
Arkansas	45,887	44,749	45,247	45,150	44,932	44,749	45,488	45,862	47,312	50,021
California	380,565	387,769	388,909	388,720	393,099	393,084	402,115	413,474	405,129	413,311
Colorado	84,635	86,068	87,847	87,239	84,167	84,188	86,508	89,982	90,032	93,144
Connecticut	43,307	43,093	42,900	43,711	43,372	42,847	44,806	46,728	48,414	48,709
Delaware	17,759	17,573	17,499	17,205	17,048	17,547	17,809	18,193	18,962	19,524
District of Columbia	7,300	7,625	7,948	7,702	7,411	6,986	6,965	5,901	6,842	7,193
Florida	100,851	98,917	102,724	104,919	109,556	111,069	113,346	114,505	120,976	129,015
Georgia	86,241	90,475	93,731	94,644	92,979	95,218	94,694	100,976	104,988	110,202
Hawaii	19,788	20,291	20,856	20,858	19,645	19,132	18,508	18,188	18,369	18,792
Idaho	22,332	22,503	22,949	22,916	22,181	21,556	22,264	23,216	24,327	25,878
Illinois	159,974	161,963	159,743	157,849	156,543	157,749	160,812	161,655	159,448	160,744
Indiana	122,644	125,110	126,512	127,047	123,382	123,873	127,274	130,757	136,277	142,736
Iowa	54,046	55,410	57,868	59,915	60,209	60,867	60,776	59,859	59,778	59,879
Kansas	67,247	67,516	67,729	66,814	66,569	66,514	68,093	68,978	70,398	72,409
Kentucky	77,015	76,152	74,227	73,382	71,068	68,826	71,984	74,863	78,679	82,371
Louisiana	104,777	111,707	112,992	117,118	117,337	118,327	112,682	114,219	113,978	114,013
Maine	19,812	19,851	21,420	21,649	21,211	20,965	21,884	21,854	22,771	25,097
Maryland	76,518	77,304	75,744	79,002	77,367	78,817	81,185	82,738	83,071	83,448
Massachusetts	85,077	85,746	80,633	82,832	83,826	84,360	83,721	87,240	86,803	85,932
Michigan	197,258	193,759	188,469	187,671	186,486	187,165	191,982	197,775	202,042	206,687
Minnesota	96,048	98,402	98,493	96,348	94,831	96,691	101,564	98,395	100,059	101,159
Mississippi	46,723	47,826	47,538	48,543	46,835	46,752	44,512	44,628	47,900	50,463
Missouri	93,394	95,490	94,871	94,089	91,040	90,392	90,048	91,051	94,800	98,736
Montana	24,653	25,407	25,819	26,400	25,344	25,149	24,279	23,384	23,821	24,659
Nebraska	42,325	42,924	44,041	44,456	44,064	44,140	43,784	43,993	45,113	46,762
Nevada	13,713	13,994	15,169	14,934	14,644	14,874	15,440	16,227	17,331	19,172
New Hampshire	16,906	16,982	16,941	16,662	17,259	17,092	17,954	18,604	19,476	18,720
New Jersey	102,048	101,527	99,720	98,091	95,872	95,010	97,286	97,755	98,804	100,430
New Mexico	35,373	36,381	37,262	38,289	37,380	37,986	36,401	37,313	37,901	38,270
New York	240,459	239,517	239,290	248,504	245,416	242,716	264,786	260,835	268,202	271,131
North Carolina	105,882	107,385	108,272	109,234	109,765	111,903	112,418	114,125	117,798	121,568
North Dakota	21,660	22,446	22,713	23,843	23,869	23,966	23,724	23,639	24,902	26,449
Ohio	205,128	210,673	208,567	211,662	209,418	210,436	215,155	222,912	231,442	234,734
Oklahoma	72,283	71,732	76,202	78,757	75,509	76,077	75,022	75,585	76,203	76,203
Oregon	54,570	53,406	50,241	49,782	49,396	50,533	52,578	53,550	57,105	55,773
Pennsylvania	157,181	156,526	156,283	157,080	157,856	160,010	163,371	188,138	194,102	198,491
Rhode Island	17,219	17,880	17,099	17,210	16,799	17,135	17,308	18,127	18,812	19,433
South Carolina	56,226	55,852	56,595	56,896	56,518	58,074	58,656	61,931	64,756	64,756
South Dakota	20,233	21,418	21,190	21,767	19,720	18,998	19,884	19,903	20,154	20,955
Tennessee	87,428	85,801	85,050	87,468	84,624	82,798	81,978	83,023	85,697	88,580
Texas	284,553	291,598	301,711	311,318	317,851	306,823	290,961	301,826	316,087	329,247
Utah	38,071	36,183	39,453	39,743	39,908	40,038	40,129	40,644	40,910	42,416
Vermont	12,736	12,636	12,537	12,623	12,592	12,632	13,014	13,241	13,414	13,734
Virginia	110,040	117,188	113,740	114,660	114,734	116,789	122,272	126,016	129,188	132,888
Washington	74,136	72,372	70,699	71,004	71,007	70,599	69,872	70,316	71,000	71,256
West Virginia	46,541	46,974	47,741	47,841	45,691	44,663	45,675	46,677	49,070	51,116
Wisconsin	123,233	126,220	126,699	129,173	129,846	131,817	133,057	130,128	130,646	130,646
Wyoming	8,092	8,714	9,243	9,144	9,118	9,003	8,780	9,104	9,614	10,432
U.S. Service Schools	18,626	19,339	19,823	20,123	19,879	19,009	18,932	19,949	19,001	18,450
Outlying areas	39,130	40,175	42,664	57,352	50,105	50,013	50,988	49,548	49,891	48,548
American Samoa	—	—	—	—	—	—	—	—	—	—
Federated States of Micronesia	—	—	—	—	—	—	—	—	—	—
Guam	2,115	2,311	1,943	2,220	2,086	2,133	2,105	1,702	1,660	1,848
Marshall Islands	—	—	—	—	—	—	—	—	—	—
Northern Marianas	—	—	—	—	—	—	—	—	—	—
Palau	—	—	—	—	—	—	—	—	—	—
Puerto Rico	35,797	36,502	39,165	53,479	46,354	46,386	47,432	46,358	46,794	45,110
Trust Territories	—	—	—	—	—	—	—	—	—	—
Virgin Islands	1,218	1,362	1,556	1,653	1,665	1,494	1,451	1,488	1,437	1,590

Table 58.—Full-time-equivalent fall enrollment in public 4–year institutions of higher education, by state: 1970 to 1996—Continued

State or other area	Fall 1990	Fall 1991	Fall 1992	Fall 1993	Fall 1994	Fall 1995	Fall 1996	Percentage change			
								Fall 1970 to fall 1996	Fall 1986 to fall 1991	Fall 1991 to fall 1996	Fall 1986 to fall 1996
1	22	23	24	25	26	27	28	29	30	31	32
United States	4,740,049	4,795,704	4,797,884	4,765,983	4,749,524	4,757,223	4,767,248	37.4	11.6	–0.6	11.0
Alabama	102,301	105,558	105,069	105,089	103,200	104,189	101,864	77.0	22.5	–3.5	18.2
Alaska	17,087	18,006	18,039	18,072	17,810	17,823	17,508	287.4	132.8	–2.8	126.3
Arizona	78,630	78,313	79,429	78,324	82,558	83,010	84,062	66.9	12.1	7.3	20.3
Arkansas	52,363	53,812	56,106	55,685	54,540	53,057	52,468	41.4	18.3	–2.5	15.3
California	447,782	442,688	433,625	417,202	413,527	421,100	434,560	35.3	10.1	–1.8	8.1
Colorado	101,869	103,912	104,438	104,399	104,474	104,521	104,977	45.7	20.1	1.0	21.3
Connecticut	48,502	47,380	46,388	45,083	43,582	43,441	42,967	13.5	5.7	–9.3	–4.1
Delaware	19,741	20,089	20,281	20,946	20,982	20,533	20,821	58.7	12.8	3.6	16.9
District of Columbia	7,294	6,897	7,028	6,583	6,495	5,950	4,559	–23.2	–1.0	–33.9	–34.5
Florida	135,696	140,863	142,906	147,729	155,232	160,046	163,504	138.7	24.3	16.1	44.3
Georgia	113,796	122,182	125,076	126,594	128,563	132,111	131,676	94.2	29.0	7.8	39.1
Hawaii	19,398	18,435	18,660	19,311	19,437	19,158	17,680	–9.8	–0.4	–4.1	–4.5
Idaho	27,440	29,544	30,993	31,449	32,237	32,161	32,375	60.7	32.7	9.6	45.4
Illinois	163,900	165,495	165,247	163,884	161,500	159,900	159,822	5.3	2.9	–3.4	–0.6
Indiana	146,568	150,534	153,190	151,282	147,844	146,709	147,182	37.4	18.3	–2.2	15.6
Iowa	59,562	59,456	58,773	58,156	57,556	57,870	58,444	25.8	–2.2	–1.7	–3.8
Kansas	73,509	73,573	73,356	73,783	71,257	71,592	70,500	15.8	8.0	–4.2	3.5
Kentucky	86,183	88,921	89,506	88,286	87,211	86,774	86,022	51.2	23.5	–3.3	19.5
Louisiana	116,107	121,435	126,708	123,798	124,883	125,563	125,650	54.7	7.8	3.5	11.5
Maine	25,582	25,381	24,626	24,035	23,461	22,812	22,656	26.8	16.0	–10.7	3.5
Maryland	84,972	86,728	86,358	85,869	86,578	87,997	88,440	46.2	6.8	2.0	8.9
Massachusetts	84,253	81,987	81,357	79,000	78,686	78,616	78,570	23.3	–2.1	–4.2	–6.2
Michigan	210,102	208,975	206,325	209,703	205,800	206,495	207,628	14.0	8.9	–0.6	8.1
Minnesota	100,357	97,675	94,668	91,811	89,990	88,696	89,123	–1.5	–3.8	–8.8	–12.2
Mississippi	52,249	53,693	52,038	51,147	50,417	51,561	52,907	37.7	20.6	–1.5	18.9
Missouri	101,461	102,422	99,726	97,160	95,401	94,930	94,552	11.4	13.7	–7.7	5.0
Montana	24,192	25,680	26,088	26,678	26,857	27,724	27,942	19.0	5.8	8.8	15.1
Nebraska	48,035	48,504	48,846	48,511	47,248	47,537	47,036	18.4	10.8	–3.0	7.4
Nevada	20,337	21,699	21,696	21,318	21,963	21,806	22,382	123.1	40.5	3.1	45.0
New Hampshire	20,011	21,279	21,630	21,763	21,962	21,960	21,763	63.2	18.5	2.3	21.2
New Jersey	102,451	103,519	104,568	103,462	102,204	103,590	104,618	45.3	6.4	1.1	7.5
New Mexico	38,298	39,219	40,008	41,227	39,973	39,186	38,147	25.5	7.7	–2.7	4.8
New York	273,168	267,929	268,332	268,270	272,066	265,171	261,193	32.1	1.2	–2.5	–1.4
North Carolina	125,198	128,412	131,736	131,718	132,091	132,949	132,690	79.5	14.2	3.3	18.0
North Dakota	24,185	24,287	25,105	25,257	25,055	25,147	24,827	16.8	2.4	2.2	4.7
Ohio	238,947	239,094	234,763	228,303	223,580	219,518	216,875	14.1	11.1	–9.3	0.8
Oklahoma	75,060	79,792	78,795	77,877	78,501	77,450	76,320	10.7	6.4	–4.4	1.7
Oregon	57,323	54,724	53,812	52,787	52,916	53,445	54,255	–1.2	4.1	–0.9	3.2
Pennsylvania	198,579	201,401	204,341	200,053	198,056	200,590	200,854	48.4	23.3	–0.3	22.9
Rhode Island	19,890	19,518	19,476	18,836	18,015	17,634	17,143	8.5	12.8	–12.2	–1.0
South Carolina	68,783	71,835	72,719	71,698	71,132	71,984	72,543	136.1	22.5	1.0	23.7
South Dakota	21,998	23,642	24,707	26,215	25,822	24,753	23,799	13.7	18.9	0.7	19.7
Tennessee	90,423	92,917	94,401	94,910	93,976	95,789	96,234	29.5	13.3	3.6	17.4
Texas	337,368	338,908	338,888	339,313	339,801	337,321	336,716	58.9	16.5	–0.6	15.7
Utah	44,993	48,233	49,252	58,244	61,636	62,683	62,014	73.6	20.2	28.6	54.5
Vermont	13,760	14,034	13,646	13,415	13,765	13,715	13,588	38.4	7.8	–3.2	4.4
Virginia	134,660	137,445	137,313	136,339	136,115	138,030	140,484	92.4	12.4	2.2	14.9
Washington	73,758	73,712	75,079	76,501	77,461	78,111	78,855	15.8	5.5	7.0	12.9
West Virginia	52,107	57,150	57,750	56,628	55,841	55,159	55,322	36.3	25.1	–3.2	21.1
Wisconsin	130,646	129,432	126,240	123,700	122,297	121,755	123,130	8.8	–2.7	–4.9	–7.5
Wyoming	10,461	10,545	10,180	9,976	10,116	9,752	9,635	18.9	20.1	–8.6	9.7
U.S. Service Schools	18,714	18,840	18,597	18,604	17,854	17,849	18,366	7.5	–0.5	–2.5	–3.0
Outlying areas	49,235	48,527	48,186	48,931	49,518	54,519	59,787	81.3	–4.8	23.2	17.3
American Samoa	—	—	—	—	—	—	—	—	—	—	—
Federated States of Micronesia	—	—	—	—	—	—	—	—	—	—	—
Guam	2,041	2,386	2,418	2,908	3,159	2,787	2,610	38.5	13.4	9.4	24.0
Marshall Islands	—	—	—	—	—	—	—	—	—	—	—
Northern Marianas	—	—	—	—	—	—	—	—	—	—	—
Palau	—	—	—	—	44,321	49,679	55,224	—	—	—	—
Puerto Rico	45,689	44,502	43,962	44,107	—	—	—	—	–6.2	—	—
Trust Territories	—	—	—	—	—	—	—	—	—	—	—
Virgin Islands	1,505	1,639	1,806	1,916	2,038	2,053	1,953	157.7	13.0	19.2	34.6

—Data not available or not applicable.

NOTE.—Some data have been revised from previously published figures.

SOURCE: U.S. Department of Education, National Center for Education Statistics, Higher Education General Information Survey (HEGIS), "Fall Enrollment in Higher Education" surveys; and Integrated Postsecondary Education Data System (IPEDS), "Fall Enrollment" surveys. (This table was prepared January 1998.)

Table 59.—Full-time-equivalent fall enrollment in public 2–year institutions of higher education, by state: 1970 to 1996

State or other area	Fall 1970	Fall 1971	Fall 1972	Fall 1973	Fall 1974	Fall 1975	Fall 1976	Fall 1977	Fall 1978	Fall 1979
1	2	3	4	5	6	7	8	9	10	11
United States	**1,484,577**	**1,683,732**	**1,746,613**	**1,908,533**	**2,097,257**	**2,465,810**	**2,351,453**	**2,357,405**	**2,283,073**	**2,333,313**
Alabama	16,915	20,249	23,212	24,392	31,040	41,215	32,206	30,665	33,791	27,785
Alaska	302	3,430	3,236	3,463	3,272	2,591	3,942	6,016	7,402	4,455
Arizona	26,509	30,195	30,646	38,583	44,924	53,455	54,890	55,153	44,887	52,329
Arkansas	2,228	2,306	2,539	2,603	3,356	6,161	6,029	7,313	7,034	7,349
California	420,207	457,296	463,835	527,182	567,769	649,381	601,265	583,267	529,608	546,169
Colorado	16,106	17,657	17,800	19,343	21,168	26,270	25,458	25,331	23,884	24,506
Connecticut	18,181	21,041	20,858	22,056	25,343	23,062	21,834	23,283	33,589	24,314
Delaware	2,221	2,893	2,942	3,037	3,691	4,270	4,268	3,607	4,202	4,538
District of Columbia	1,945	2,849	3,550	3,509	—	—	—	—	—	—
Florida	79,977	86,852	83,929	89,383	96,720	111,375	116,407	120,764	119,464	121,708
Georgia	16,864	18,212	18,293	21,409	24,405	30,857	30,411	28,884	28,696	24,392
Hawaii	8,420	9,409	10,558	11,910	13,271	15,828	14,489	14,065	13,693	13,396
Idaho	2,568	2,565	2,544	2,231	2,443	2,744	3,371	3,526	3,452	3,621
Illinois	88,176	102,121	106,854	113,736	121,150	142,035	142,819	146,890	141,407	140,004
Indiana	3,020	6,092	5,917	5,972	6,922	10,359	10,823	12,398	12,823	14,783
Iowa	15,607	18,818	20,045	20,865	21,304	24,928	24,297	24,141	24,488	25,996
Kansas	14,854	16,103	17,576	17,393	18,083	19,145	18,646	19,409	19,095	20,115
Kentucky	7,435	8,896	9,069	9,434	9,606	12,261	12,303	12,427	10,799	11,558
Louisiana	5,828	7,311	8,241	6,538	8,083	10,338	10,828	10,312	9,653	8,667
Maine	819	2,990	3,069	3,399	3,053	3,753	3,706	3,270	3,299	4,042
Maryland	28,500	32,755	34,224	37,540	40,858	44,989	45,660	48,202	46,901	48,106
Massachusetts	25,504	29,640	29,928	32,625	38,919	45,250	42,055	40,051	40,277	41,201
Michigan	76,315	78,561	75,776	84,706	97,434	111,991	96,158	102,343	101,116	105,892
Minnesota	17,355	19,318	18,887	19,620	19,676	22,363	22,707	23,033	23,101	23,873
Mississippi	19,206	20,327	20,671	22,306	24,271	28,868	27,854	27,642	26,889	28,663
Missouri	21,846	25,328	25,045	27,362	29,948	37,672	33,025	30,431	27,886	27,444
Montana	1,452	1,373	1,527	1,542	1,545	1,921	1,795	1,533	1,508	1,342
Nebraska	3,190	4,634	5,006	5,624	6,385	9,438	11,181	12,517	10,296	11,726
Nevada	205	582	1,541	5,483	8,682	9,410	6,390	5,999	7,081	6,664
New Hampshire	482	470	470	1,972	2,489	3,785	3,394	3,386	3,374	3,410
New Jersey	28,989	34,942	37,684	42,403	45,917	54,566	54,839	57,072	55,590	59,071
New Mexico	2,708	3,039	2,966	3,324	3,773	4,177	4,510	4,942	5,484	5,389
New York	133,817	157,871	164,615	164,204	174,966	194,809	177,817	174,853	170,745	176,311
North Carolina	29,955	39,299	44,724	45,197	53,339	71,005	66,217	65,088	68,173	68,142
North Dakota	5,590	5,932	5,820	5,939	5,904	6,130	6,433	6,784	6,552	6,102
Ohio	36,418	43,192	45,900	48,545	52,773	64,899	67,378	69,390	65,350	69,237
Oklahoma	10,387	14,501	16,082	17,708	20,054	24,838	27,230	27,472	25,620	25,881
Oregon	26,025	29,821	27,474	37,421	38,983	43,838	40,577	40,127	38,872	41,138
Pennsylvania	47,099	53,933	54,496	56,829	59,376	69,651	70,039	67,973	67,351	68,444
Rhode Island	3,581	3,743	3,966	4,341	4,665	5,552	6,037	7,027	6,622	7,211
South Carolina	9,628	11,178	16,941	19,586	26,362	33,434	26,745	28,493	27,293	28,432
South Dakota	—	—	—	—	—	—	—	—	—	302
Tennessee	7,162	9,056	10,925	13,061	16,633	22,395	22,441	23,422	37,613	26,582
Texas	81,162	90,910	99,774	108,246	125,672	157,465	152,300	153,657	146,353	156,331
Utah	5,816	6,740	6,859	6,967	7,270	8,784	8,905	8,866	8,847	9,260
Vermont	489	457	473	972	1,089	1,538	1,306	1,229	1,304	1,102
Virginia	20,858	26,194	30,113	34,038	39,620	51,917	49,652	52,533	52,902	54,355
Washington	57,564	60,678	62,205	65,536	69,036	75,803	80,734	83,659	83,851	92,589
West Virginia	3,015	3,059	3,313	3,911	4,973	7,339	6,533	5,503	5,376	4,957
Wisconsin	27,300	32,931	38,739	40,566	41,863	49,955	47,524	47,444	43,400	48,482
Wyoming	4,777	5,983	5,756	4,521	5,107	5,348	6,025	6,013	6,080	5,947
U.S. Service Schools	—	—	—	—	4,072	6,652	—	—	—	—
Outlying areas	4,717	3,852	4,978	10,019	12,080	13,632	13,164	10,380	8,306	11,482
American Samoa	—	388	428	574	505	585	688	850	526	577
Federated States of Micronesia	—	—	—	—	—	—	—	—	—	—
Guam	—	—	—	—	—	—	—	—	—	—
Marshall Islands	—	—	—	—	—	—	—	—	—	—
Northern Marianas	—	—	—	—	—	—	—	—	—	—
Palau	—	—	—	—	—	—	—	—	—	—
Puerto Rico	4,717	3,351	4,429	9,330	11,443	12,880	12,192	9,279	7,495	10,745
Trust Territories	—	113	121	115	132	167	284	251	285	160
Virgin Islands	—	—	—	—	—	—	—	—	—	—

Table 59.—Full-time-equivalent fall enrollment in public 2–year institutions of higher education, by state: 1970 to 1996—Continued

State or other area	Fall 1980	Fall 1981	Fall 1982	Fall 1983	Fall 1984	Fall 1985	Fall 1986	Fall 1987	Fall 1988	Fall 1989
1	12	13	14	15	16	17	18	19	20	21
United States	2,484,027	2,572,794	2,629,941	2,615,672	2,446,769	2,428,159	2,482,551	2,541,961	2,591,131	2,751,762
Alabama	30,486	32,489	33,840	35,853	37,290	41,507	42,377	41,310	43,298	48,839
Alaska	4,526	5,491	6,068	6,481	5,823	6,370	7,140	6,265	2,123	—
Arizona	54,840	54,656	57,038	57,783	50,996	53,743	59,534	64,400	70,519	69,519
Arkansas	7,609	7,819	8,169	8,208	7,982	7,686	8,728	9,099	10,243	11,225
California	560,936	597,846	583,609	550,293	497,432	497,941	522,673	544,184	532,159	556,259
Colorado	24,730	24,740	24,624	24,867	22,180	21,238	26,908	28,214	30,072	35,074
Connecticut	24,010	23,312	23,208	23,534	21,727	20,360	19,946	19,963	20,625	21,950
Delaware	5,281	5,482	5,828	5,483	5,361	5,427	4,652	4,738	5,497	5,832
District of Columbia	—	—	—	—	—	—	—	—	—	—
Florida	124,991	131,594	132,355	131,118	121,485	123,660	130,951	140,240	146,945	172,187
Georgia	25,752	26,865	28,754	28,790	25,758	23,474	19,820	30,057	30,659	32,448
Hawaii	13,420	14,138	14,719	14,115	13,173	12,917	12,151	12,200	12,052	12,403
Idaho	4,242	3,607	3,550	3,586	3,202	3,193	4,526	3,549	3,750	3,850
Illinois	152,650	160,340	169,150	169,160	155,808	167,767	176,270	174,451	175,364	183,223
Indiana	20,284	21,230	22,912	24,227	22,525	21,895	19,089	19,882	20,590	20,261
Iowa	28,790	29,523	31,092	32,190	31,072	30,658	30,469	31,878	32,712	35,712
Kansas	21,176	21,477	21,989	23,865	22,509	22,860	25,148	26,721	28,718	30,835
Kentucky	12,362	13,815	14,726	15,536	14,869	14,731	15,872	17,486	19,644	22,115
Louisiana	7,658	9,038	9,416	10,639	10,427	9,879	8,498	8,664	9,375	10,738
Maine	4,579	4,887	3,251	3,371	3,285	3,393	3,433	3,466	3,770	3,917
Maryland	50,310	50,329	54,299	53,421	50,923	45,347	47,577	48,760	52,469	55,145
Massachusetts	43,256	41,628	44,005	46,393	43,312	43,933	41,949	44,520	46,075	45,437
Michigan	114,786	118,699	118,067	121,436	114,574	108,164	105,348	108,373	109,627	115,159
Minnesota	25,653	27,177	30,606	31,341	31,428	31,984	31,682	35,667	37,795	42,148
Mississippi	29,623	33,530	33,894	34,735	32,380	31,442	31,436	34,323	35,973	36,863
Missouri	31,285	32,759	32,829	35,130	31,999	31,296	31,476	32,395	34,273	39,354
Montana	1,689	1,768	1,938	1,792	1,817	1,879	2,063	2,600	2,333	3,493
Nebraska	12,366	12,729	13,763	12,110	12,776	12,713	15,534	15,650	16,325	16,853
Nevada	8,595	7,334	7,922	8,076	7,381	7,990	9,525	9,795	9,839	11,758
New Hampshire	3,470	4,179	4,138	4,495	3,948	3,780	3,958	4,326	3,901	4,430
New Jersey	61,270	64,150	70,362	69,810	63,303	61,496	59,231	59,252	63,224	67,927
New Mexico	6,019	6,369	7,140	7,100	7,334	7,637	16,357	17,190	16,895	17,872
New York	181,607	186,591	188,924	183,769	175,446	170,136	157,222	153,672	159,110	166,314
North Carolina	73,366	77,528	81,778	79,880	76,384	82,909	75,393	72,946	75,423	80,236
North Dakota	6,440	6,673	6,350	6,321	6,071	5,881	6,166	5,741	6,282	6,502
Ohio	72,447	75,017	78,573	78,508	72,835	69,921	70,073	68,833	69,839	72,804
Oklahoma	24,440	27,573	30,602	32,400	31,056	31,118	29,749	29,927	30,928	30,928
Oregon	41,108	42,093	41,219	41,567	38,436	35,627	37,321	37,920	39,664	42,312
Pennsylvania	69,804	73,018	78,124	80,579	77,118	73,097	68,433	50,690	54,596	58,467
Rhode Island	7,452	7,175	7,303	7,334	6,691	6,892	7,098	7,174	7,761	7,987
South Carolina	30,393	31,568	31,619	29,303	27,221	27,249	25,585	25,547	27,417	26,362
South Dakota	248	369	429	—	—	—	—	—	—	—
Tennessee	29,295	30,038	32,301	31,680	29,398	27,260	28,808	30,571	31,246	35,875
Texas	166,774	166,760	181,172	196,329	190,956	180,051	176,899	188,611	202,979	208,449
Utah	10,184	11,050	12,358	13,502	13,554	14,263	17,719	14,769	15,087	17,158
Vermont	1,453	1,534	1,504	1,664	1,677	1,847	1,730	1,812	1,924	2,214
Virginia	58,356	61,738	57,992	58,201	52,677	51,645	57,991	61,874	59,537	66,168
Washington	97,302	85,786	76,228	75,455	74,910	75,760	80,251	80,880	83,973	85,651
West Virginia	4,795	4,957	5,493	5,949	5,520	5,416	5,900	5,936	6,029	6,593
Wisconsin	54,202	52,914	56,961	57,023	52,090	49,481	59,021	55,977	56,959	58,075
Wyoming	6,607	6,775	7,349	8,215	7,595	8,034	8,254	9,153	9,179	9,804
U.S. Service Schools	31,110	34,637	40,401	33,055	33,055	35,212	34,617	40,310	26,354	37,037
Outlying areas	12,769	14,733	16,346	2,961	6,739	6,696	7,107	7,046	7,428	7,750
American Samoa	824	874	890	742	720	497	494	556	584	644
Federated States of Micronesia	—	—	—	—	—	—	—	—	—	504
Guam	—	2,185	2,185	365	835	916	915	845	776	860
Marshall Islands	—	—	—	—	—	—	—	—	—	—
Northern Marianas	—	—	—	69	158	183	308	196	194	226
Palau	—	—	—	—	—	—	—	—	—	836
Puerto Rico	11,750	11,517	12,743	1,130	4,332	4,420	4,693	4,582	5,031	4,680
Trust Territories	195	157	528	655	694	680	697	867	843	—
Virgin Islands	—	—	—	—	—	—	—	—	—	—

Table 59.—Full-time-equivalent fall enrollment in public 2–year institutions of higher education, by state: 1970 to 1996—Continued

| State or other area | Fall 1990 | Fall 1991 | Fall 1992 | Fall 1993 | Fall 1994 | Fall 1995 | Fall 1996 | Percentage change | | | |
| | | | | | | | | Fall 1970 to fall 1996 | Fall 1986 to fall 1991 | Fall 1991 to fall 1996 | Fall 1986 to fall 1996 |
1	22	23	24	25	26	27	28	29	30	31	32
United States	**2,817,933**	**3,067,141**	**3,113,817**	**3,046,411**	**3,034,872**	**2,994,592**	**3,008,050**	**102.6**	**23.5**	**−1.9**	**21.2**
Alabama	52,042	53,198	55,679	56,950	56,255	54,564	53,207	214.6	25.5	0.0	25.6
Alaska	—	—	235	253	244	326	322	6.6	—	—	−95.5
Arizona	74,870	78,410	79,433	76,627	76,262	76,822	76,541	188.7	31.7	−2.4	28.6
Arkansas	11,109	12,187	12,376	14,074	13,281	15,177	16,713	650.1	39.6	37.1	91.5
California	531,881	646,591	626,990	577,405	575,613	563,047	580,225	38.1	23.7	−10.3	11.0
Colorado	36,481	38,048	41,449	40,444	40,104	40,332	39,996	148.3	41.4	5.1	48.6
Connecticut	22,368	22,224	23,073	22,805	22,303	21,322	20,374	12.1	11.4	−8.3	2.1
Delaware	6,318	6,782	6,629	6,349	6,529	6,705	6,975	214.0	45.8	2.8	49.9
District of Columbia	—	—	—	—	—	—	—	—	—	—	—
Florida	166,883	181,328	182,004	180,327	179,177	176,817	174,897	118.7	38.5	−3.5	33.6
Georgia	35,319	44,323	52,110	54,825	55,739	56,843	58,585	247.4	123.6	32.2	195.6
Hawaii	13,098	13,541	15,729	16,025	16,692	16,222	15,859	88.3	11.4	17.1	30.5
Idaho	3,968	4,382	4,630	5,007	5,218	5,265	5,693	121.7	−3.2	29.9	25.8
Illinois	189,347	198,713	197,756	191,411	190,946	183,337	184,823	109.6	12.7	−7.0	4.9
Indiana	22,416	23,434	25,216	23,954	24,279	23,310	22,165	633.9	22.8	−5.4	16.1
Iowa	36,210	37,395	39,895	39,833	39,735	39,829	41,310	164.7	22.7	10.5	35.6
Kansas	33,061	35,306	36,435	36,132	37,568	39,813	38,116	156.6	40.4	8.0	51.6
Kentucky	25,675	28,558	30,134	30,565	29,039	28,227	28,346	281.3	79.9	−0.7	78.6
Louisiana	13,250	12,759	16,916	17,155	17,595	17,057	17,320	197.2	50.1	35.7	103.8
Maine	4,294	4,403	4,594	4,593	4,549	4,369	4,361	432.5	28.3	−1.0	27.0
Maryland	56,978	59,956	60,510	59,917	58,471	57,419	55,837	95.9	26.0	−6.9	17.4
Massachusetts	46,709	46,403	48,116	48,436	47,035	44,938	42,703	67.4	10.6	−8.0	1.8
Michigan	116,850	117,260	114,237	114,289	108,182	103,720	102,348	34.1	11.3	−12.7	−2.8
Minnesota	43,067	44,375	56,709	55,659	67,471	62,765	62,673	261.1	40.1	41.2	97.8
Mississippi	40,020	40,851	40,955	41,568	40,669	41,384	42,928	123.5	29.9	5.1	36.6
Missouri	41,492	42,940	42,758	44,231	41,935	40,677	41,119	88.2	36.4	−4.2	30.6
Montana	2,643	2,808	3,039	2,992	3,294	4,607	4,708	224.2	36.1	67.7	128.2
Nebraska	17,704	18,044	23,029	18,634	20,129	19,711	22,656	610.2	16.2	25.6	45.8
Nevada	13,055	13,188	13,998	13,807	13,855	15,191	17,544	8,458.0	38.5	33.0	84.2
New Hampshire	4,937	5,150	5,368	5,316	5,025	5,136	5,214	981.7	30.1	1.2	31.7
New Jersey	71,873	77,385	81,494	83,472	81,903	81,176	78,580	171.1	30.6	1.5	32.7
New Mexico	19,572	22,190	23,693	25,099	25,126	25,717	26,415	875.4	35.7	19.0	61.5
New York	173,211	177,556	179,438	182,769	180,543	175,517	171,022	27.8	12.9	−3.7	8.8
North Carolina	83,123	91,592	95,541	91,489	91,727	91,106	92,126	207.5	21.5	0.6	22.2
North Dakota	6,091	6,281	6,567	6,592	6,642	6,792	7,053	26.2	1.9	12.3	14.4
Ohio	78,890	85,100	91,025	92,358	88,888	87,324	86,890	138.6	21.4	2.1	24.0
Oklahoma	33,873	47,257	43,586	38,250	38,063	37,142	36,486	251.3	58.9	−22.8	22.6
Oregon	44,101	44,921	46,742	46,522	44,748	42,866	42,781	64.4	20.4	−4.8	14.6
Pennsylvania	62,726	68,138	68,492	67,024	64,045	61,233	59,234	25.8	−0.4	−13.1	−13.4
Rhode Island	8,914	9,449	9,693	8,696	8,524	8,490	8,348	133.1	33.1	−11.7	17.6
South Carolina	33,135	35,302	36,394	37,219	37,571	37,475	37,651	291.1	38.0	6.7	47.2
South Dakota	130	137	141	171	158	172	152	—	—	10.9	—
Tennessee	39,761	46,088	47,696	47,353	46,958	46,996	47,938	569.3	60.0	4.0	66.4
Texas	216,068	224,211	234,411	233,900	237,787	237,117	241,061	197.0	26.7	7.5	36.3
Utah	18,502	21,382	23,857	17,260	18,453	19,369	20,344	249.8	20.7	−4.9	14.8
Vermont	2,288	2,413	2,530	2,479	1,834	1,885	1,937	296.1	39.5	−19.7	12.0
Virginia	67,625	69,749	69,624	68,650	67,688	66,674	64,728	210.3	20.3	−7.2	11.6
Washington	87,131	93,604	94,077	96,449	101,499	103,132	105,787	83.8	16.6	13.0	31.8
West Virginia	7,122	4,942	4,947	4,840	4,930	4,792	4,603	52.7	−16.2	−6.9	−22.0
Wisconsin	61,461	61,238	62,623	65,297	59,860	58,958	57,638	111.1	3.8	−5.9	−2.3
Wyoming	10,724	11,355	11,298	11,364	11,318	11,430	11,684	144.6	37.6	2.9	41.6
U.S. Service Schools	29,567	34,294	19,946	19,575	19,413	24,297	22,034	—	−0.9	−35.7	−36.3
Outlying areas	6,673	7,507	7,950	9,021	9,886	11,238	9,287	96.9	5.6	23.7	30.7
American Samoa	952	997	1,029	1,007	998	988	999	—	101.8	0.2	102.2
Federated States of Micronesia	549	597	690	743	1,040	1,076	1,098	—	—	83.9	—
Guam	915	864	689	912	1,049	1,032	912	—	−5.6	5.6	−0.3
Marshall Islands	—	—	296	374	254	249	300	—	—	—	—
Northern Marianas	376	488	476	653	653	625	693	—	58.4	42.0	125.0
Palau	423	309	382	377	357	296	281	—	—	−9.1	—
Puerto Rico	3,458	4,252	4,388	4,955	5,535	6,972	5,004	6.1	−9.4	17.7	6.6
Trust Territories	—	—	—	—	—	—	—	—	—	—	—
Virgin Islands	—	—	—	—	—	—	—	—	—	—	—

—Data not available or not applicable.

NOTE.—Some data have been revised from previously published figures.

SOURCE: U.S. Department of Education, National Center for Education Statistics, Higher Education General Information Survey (HEGIS), "Fall Enrollment in Higher Education" surveys; and Integrated Postsecondary Education Data System (IPEDS), "Fall Enrollment" surveys. (This table was prepared January 1998.)

Table 60.—Full-time-equivalent fall enrollment in private 4-year institutions of higher education, by state: 1970 to 1996

State or other area	Fall 1970	Fall 1971	Fall 1972	Fall 1973	Fall 1974	Fall 1975	Fall 1976	Fall 1977	Fall 1978	Fall 1979
1	2	3	4	5	6	7	8	9	10	11
United States	**1,676,838**	**1,697,084**	**1,700,554**	**1,718,191**	**1,758,706**	**1,843,903**	**1,849,551**	**1,896,005**	**1,936,231**	**1,956,768**
Alabama	13,461	14,270	14,098	13,711	14,366	15,468	15,679	16,362	15,273	14,750
Alaska	547	553	682	637	587	399	176	221	291	324
Arizona	1,923	1,765	1,730	2,112	4,581	4,456	4,318	4,450	4,393	5,014
Arkansas	6,830	7,002	7,154	7,491	7,657	7,946	8,081	8,283	8,012	8,060
California	104,603	109,486	113,185	117,809	125,680	137,519	137,807	143,515	150,046	146,277
Colorado	13,093	13,085	13,007	12,343	12,195	11,499	11,845	12,197	11,578	12,011
Connecticut	38,311	38,615	38,610	39,674	40,514	41,241	41,442	42,362	43,082	43,311
Delaware	408	584	433	358	332	466	355	1,234	1,285	2,371
District of Columbia	46,096	47,783	47,421	49,172	51,773	52,330	50,485	52,627	60,433	54,786
Florida	36,785	38,806	39,181	37,736	39,463	48,857	51,075	54,640	54,784	57,984
Georgia	19,931	20,654	21,839	23,286	24,313	25,273	26,225	26,495	28,471	30,080
Hawaii	2,723	2,704	2,709	2,372	2,639	3,307	3,436	4,126	4,231	4,371
Idaho	2,036	1,941	1,781	1,758	1,693	1,769	1,742	1,877	1,849	1,785
Illinois	102,970	104,473	103,822	103,427	106,419	108,247	111,792	111,257	111,421	112,071
Indiana	47,503	46,817	44,785	46,007	45,380	44,911	45,100	45,113	44,849	45,464
Iowa	33,095	32,955	31,307	29,783	31,482	32,418	31,225	33,296	33,500	34,857
Kansas	11,956	11,204	10,764	10,314	10,084	10,447	10,827	10,847	10,804	10,991
Kentucky	17,167	16,201	15,428	14,942	14,980	15,743	15,966	16,162	16,423	16,444
Louisiana	16,230	16,789	16,632	16,740	17,394	17,787	18,310	18,661	18,658	19,343
Maine	8,439	8,582	8,466	8,326	8,413	8,538	9,176	9,263	9,147	9,337
Maryland	21,669	22,092	22,509	22,984	21,166	20,222	19,672	20,096	19,798	20,892
Massachusetts	138,930	140,355	142,873	146,625	150,822	150,884	145,121	157,142	163,405	170,752
Michigan	41,157	41,519	40,900	41,898	44,705	47,353	46,027	47,058	45,511	47,275
Minnesota	28,094	27,942	28,773	29,717	30,574	33,041	35,101	36,868	36,471	36,671
Mississippi	6,228	6,354	6,546	6,685	6,801	7,576	7,422	6,993	6,842	7,364
Missouri	39,137	40,269	40,356	41,568	44,107	50,307	51,282	52,221	53,686	52,192
Montana	2,503	2,322	2,218	2,000	2,368	2,538	2,510	2,445	2,758	2,648
Nebraska	13,795	12,344	12,000	11,907	11,589	11,926	11,887	12,533	12,871	13,266
Nevada	68	81	83	89	123	144	150	162	172	186
New Hampshire	11,974	12,203	12,468	12,427	12,347	14,532	14,555	15,050	15,632	15,697
New Jersey	48,236	50,409	48,634	46,900	47,908	48,791	48,931	47,759	49,307	49,209
New Mexico	3,029	2,947	2,956	3,248	3,248	3,166	2,986	2,982	3,379	2,668
New York	266,637	254,649	256,451	262,866	266,324	285,281	289,533	294,190	299,787	303,621
North Carolina	38,056	39,792	40,349	40,819	40,943	41,650	42,790	42,978	45,206	45,535
North Dakota	1,083	1,194	1,292	1,229	1,201	1,327	1,439	1,474	1,787	1,748
Ohio	80,178	82,232	83,466	83,706	82,270	80,750	82,586	81,941	81,553	82,006
Oklahoma	12,873	13,639	14,050	14,382	14,892	15,629	15,945	16,637	19,918	16,092
Oregon	12,153	12,595	12,666	12,607	12,807	13,485	13,756	14,057	14,310	14,342
Pennsylvania	143,063	149,020	144,859	143,428	142,650	146,298	149,154	152,209	152,996	157,721
Rhode Island	17,332	18,522	18,736	20,334	22,073	28,190	24,924	25,491	24,547	24,674
South Carolina	17,694	18,347	18,156	18,395	18,894	20,224	20,814	20,598	20,895	20,749
South Dakota	5,852	5,793	5,479	5,197	5,344	7,419	7,369	7,415	6,951	6,756
Tennessee	31,966	32,230	32,966	32,818	35,108	37,977	37,629	37,621	38,010	39,280
Texas	59,726	62,472	65,303	65,613	67,757	70,389	67,137	68,338	70,537	71,841
Utah	26,108	27,055	26,521	25,758	24,955	25,852	25,484	26,356	26,621	26,500
Vermont	7,938	8,748	9,548	9,801	9,698	10,265	10,107	10,232	10,210	10,362
Virginia	23,033	23,178	23,442	23,334	24,210	25,676	26,248	27,894	28,389	29,534
Washington	17,909	18,321	19,019	20,180	21,160	21,268	20,552	20,289	22,049	22,539
West Virginia	9,074	9,239	8,489	8,007	7,918	7,919	8,012	7,861	7,588	7,672
Wisconsin	27,236	26,952	26,412	25,671	24,799	25,203	25,366	26,127	26,515	27,345
Wyoming	—	—	—	—	—	—	—	—	—	—
Outlying areas	10,639	12,844	16,936	19,206	21,291	22,927	26,718	38,072	40,336	48,575
American Samoa	—	—	—	—	—	—	—	—	—	—
Federated States of Micronesia	—	—	—	—	—	—	—	—	—	—
Guam	—	—	—	—	—	—	—	—	—	—
Marshall Islands	—	—	—	—	—	—	—	—	—	—
Northern Marianas	—	—	—	—	—	—	—	—	—	—
Palau	—	—	—	—	—	—	—	—	—	—
Puerto Rico	10,639	12,844	16,936	19,206	21,291	22,927	26,718	38,072	40,336	48,575
Trust Territories	—	—	—	—	—	—	—	—	—	—
Virgin Islands	—	—	—	—	—	—	—	—	—	—

Table 60.—Full-time-equivalent fall enrollment in private 4–year institutions of higher education, by state: 1970 to 1996—Continued

State or other area	Fall 1980	Fall 1981	Fall 1982	Fall 1983	Fall 1984	Fall 1985	Fall 1986	Fall 1987	Fall 1988	Fall 1989
1	12	13	14	15	16	17	18	19	20	21
United States	**2,003,105**	**2,041,341**	**2,028,275**	**2,059,415**	**2,054,816**	**2,054,717**	**2,064,831**	**2,090,776**	**2,158,372**	**2,193,774**
Alabama	15,230	14,793	14,616	16,150	15,824	15,343	14,914	15,733	16,760	15,757
Alaska	444	540	584	560	617	645	833	739	840	1,310
Arizona	6,899	8,460	9,543	10,776	10,586	12,883	10,405	6,189	12,544	9,500
Arkansas	8,340	8,257	7,914	7,783	7,967	7,741	8,099	8,231	8,955	9,156
California	152,863	152,646	154,761	157,984	160,738	160,973	157,822	158,191	165,031	165,880
Colorado	13,274	14,370	13,756	13,907	12,910	12,500	12,443	14,307	14,275	14,966
Connecticut	44,114	44,388	43,849	43,857	43,762	43,341	43,673	43,846	43,522	44,182
Delaware	2,429	3,265	3,148	3,225	3,536	3,458	3,247	4,926	4,606	5,363
District of Columbia	54,826	56,899	53,772	52,429	52,196	51,959	52,027	53,108	53,961	54,440
Florida	60,109	62,767	61,647	64,002	65,658	66,673	66,856	64,043	74,055	70,173
Georgia	31,148	33,203	33,692	33,846	34,294	34,774	33,505	36,977	37,721	40,115
Hawaii	4,429	4,117	4,572	5,706	6,471	6,798	7,155	7,390	7,746	8,009
Idaho	1,815	1,852	1,725	1,743	1,747	1,808	2,112	2,137	1,874	1,833
Illinois	114,608	117,641	117,609	118,617	117,846	115,252	119,804	122,325	124,253	129,577
Indiana	46,671	46,504	45,464	45,909	45,100	44,187	45,793	45,327	49,314	50,477
Iowa	35,287	35,241	34,817	35,226	35,218	34,678	35,640	36,201	37,714	40,334
Kansas	11,198	10,901	10,711	10,659	10,508	10,143	10,295	9,954	10,741	10,575
Kentucky	17,531	17,324	17,089	17,564	17,606	17,431	17,328	18,921	19,233	18,296
Louisiana	19,970	19,951	19,630	20,199	19,916	19,071	20,007	20,247	20,822	22,325
Maine	9,175	9,125	10,093	12,126	12,587	12,533	9,164	9,688	9,505	11,731
Maryland	21,464	22,384	21,927	22,624	22,685	23,272	24,260	25,382	25,826	26,709
Massachusetts	172,554	178,623	171,471	177,222	177,989	178,559	182,015	182,274	185,001	184,696
Michigan	48,401	49,039	48,817	50,781	50,895	51,003	53,084	56,089	57,068	57,567
Minnesota	37,623	38,497	38,376	37,558	38,432	38,378	38,398	40,919	42,512	43,087
Mississippi	7,090	7,107	7,034	7,886	7,890	7,290	7,495	7,777	7,933	8,207
Missouri	53,169	54,241	53,039	53,863	53,274	52,878	55,490	58,267	60,174	62,169
Montana	2,613	2,385	2,227	2,497	2,162	2,340	2,317	2,522	2,623	2,586
Nebraska	13,470	14,240	14,164	14,273	14,154	13,401	12,842	12,789	13,482	14,038
Nevada	159	144	277	305	235	229	256	194	135	205
New Hampshire	17,241	16,839	17,920	18,577	18,253	18,624	18,357	18,381	19,509	19,187
New Jersey	50,128	48,419	46,995	46,032	44,073	43,273	43,055	42,547	42,455	42,775
New Mexico	2,668	2,709	2,591	2,384	1,792	1,869	1,175	1,362	1,535	1,509
New York	311,473	319,344	314,614	316,907	316,585	318,561	321,057	318,565	318,392	324,061
North Carolina	47,377	47,417	46,676	47,295	48,069	48,555	48,919	50,087	53,353	57,113
North Dakota	1,920	1,886	1,904	1,888	1,961	1,938	1,987	2,227	2,306	2,325
Ohio	82,854	85,174	84,651	85,922	84,301	82,871	84,662	85,069	87,965	89,055
Oklahoma	16,277	16,085	16,801	16,921	16,414	16,323	14,853	15,799	15,833	15,883
Oregon	14,487	14,875	14,796	15,233	15,935	15,767	15,922	16,526	17,017	17,797
Pennsylvania	162,888	166,377	166,625	167,294	166,752	166,587	168,225	169,959	172,215	173,496
Rhode Island	25,185	26,081	26,418	27,007	28,451	28,989	28,956	29,977	30,499	30,284
South Carolina	16,934	16,815	20,795	20,343	19,373	19,109	19,375	20,304	20,864	20,384
South Dakota	6,934	6,955	6,936	6,891	6,559	7,376	5,205	5,734	5,859	5,911
Tennessee	39,142	38,793	38,011	37,924	37,373	37,189	38,048	37,846	40,515	41,019
Texas	74,245	76,511	77,409	78,067	77,038	77,107	75,268	74,905	75,657	77,734
Utah	26,896	27,329	26,668	26,824	26,816	26,700	26,285	26,235	27,764	29,079
Vermont	10,234	9,837	9,700	9,751	9,662	9,618	10,288	10,173	10,531	11,105
Virginia	30,181	30,372	31,615	32,512	31,576	35,059	35,240	36,759	40,256	43,938
Washington	23,002	24,524	25,549	25,878	24,963	24,177	23,899	25,012	26,794	26,242
West Virginia	7,473	7,402	6,930	7,103	7,010	6,570	6,125	6,115	6,324	6,016
Wisconsin	28,663	28,693	28,347	29,385	29,057	28,914	30,651	32,501	34,503	35,598
Wyoming	—	—	—	—	—	—	—	—	—	—
Outlying areas	51,301	58,036	69,729	74,102	65,459	70,382	75,199	70,271	74,102	74,183
American Samoa	—	—	—	—	—	—	—	—	—	—
Federated States of Micronesia	—	—	—	—	—	—	—	—	—	—
Guam	—	——	—	—	—	—	—	—	—	—
Marshall Islands	—	—	—	—	—	—	—	—	—	—
Northern Marianas	—	—	—	—	—	—	—	—	—	—
Palau	—	—	—	—	—	—	—	—	—	—
Puerto Rico	51,301	58,036	69,729	74,102	65,459	70,382	75,199	70,271	74,102	74,183
Trust Territories	—	—	—	—	—	—	—	—	—	—
Virgin Islands	—	—	—	—	—	—	—	—	—	—

Table 60.—Full-time-equivalent fall enrollment in private 4–year institutions of higher education, by state: 1970 to 1996—Continued

State or other area	Fall 1990	Fall 1991	Fall 1992	Fall 1993	Fall 1994	Fall 1995	Fall 1996	Percentage change			
								Fall 1970 to fall 1996	Fall 1986 to fall 1991	Fall 1991 to fall 1996	Fall 1986 to fall 1996
1	22	23	24	25	26	27	28	29	30	31	32
United States	2,227,959	2,285,750	2,331,495	2,354,938	2,387,817	2,415,621	2,464,432	47.0	10.7	7.8	19.4
Alabama	16,943	16,989	18,830	19,224	19,485	19,533	19,655	46.0	13.9	15.7	31.8
Alaska	1,015	924	974	1,004	622	588	555	1.5	10.9	−39.9	−33.4
Arizona	12,206	15,834	15,853	22,320	19,129	16,658	20,174	949.1	52.2	27.4	93.9
Arkansas	9,024	9,303	9,446	9,599	9,666	9,975	10,167	48.9	14.9	9.3	25.5
California	165,955	169,340	175,364	178,651	199,213	199,346	203,916	94.9	7.3	20.4	29.2
Colorado	16,150	17,139	17,934	18,942	21,477	21,702	24,957	90.6	37.7	45.6	100.6
Connecticut	43,742	43,604	42,727	42,414	43,398	43,831	44,901	17.2	−0.2	3.0	2.8
Delaware	5,553	5,402	5,072	5,182	5,232	5,298	5,351	1,211.5	66.4	−0.9	64.8
District of Columbia	54,255	52,991	55,456	56,151	53,802	55,068	54,654	18.6	1.9	3.1	5.0
Florida	74,623	78,365	80,717	79,769	80,234	80,301	82,796	125.1	17.2	5.7	23.8
Georgia	41,342	44,497	46,568	50,329	52,189	55,179	57,817	190.1	32.8	29.9	72.6
Hawaii	8,601	9,201	9,116	9,287	9,485	9,916	11,101	307.7	28.6	20.6	55.2
Idaho	1,878	2,168	2,279	2,141	2,252	1,998	2,042	0.3	2.7	−5.8	−3.3
Illinois	132,348	134,676	137,704	139,625	141,160	144,744	146,132	41.9	12.4	8.5	22.0
Indiana	50,870	51,745	52,037	53,004	53,673	54,658	55,213	16.2	13.0	6.7	20.6
Iowa	40,706	40,187	40,369	40,644	40,905	41,377	41,185	24.4	12.8	2.5	15.6
Kansas	11,533	12,006	12,411	12,663	14,166	13,756	13,545	13.3	16.6	12.8	31.6
Kentucky	20,553	22,545	22,079	22,256	22,331	22,965	23,316	35.8	30.1	3.4	34.6
Louisiana	22,542	22,854	22,376	23,050	23,195	23,442	23,060	42.1	14.2	0.9	15.3
Maine	10,967	11,160	11,657	11,545	11,945	12,364	12,357	46.4	21.8	10.7	34.8
Maryland	27,393	27,675	28,175	28,575	29,393	30,193	30,537	40.9	14.1	10.3	25.9
Massachusetts	180,290	186,478	185,982	184,779	184,199	189,336	190,839	37.4	2.5	2.3	4.8
Michigan	60,727	60,390	63,802	62,076	61,100	61,116	64,277	56.2	13.8	6.4	21.1
Minnesota	43,439	43,906	45,596	46,201	47,395	48,406	49,981	77.9	14.3	13.8	30.2
Mississippi	8,769	8,941	9,589	9,928	9,425	9,400	8,795	41.2	19.3	−1.6	17.3
Missouri	63,655	67,790	69,008	69,802	71,773	73,005	74,840	91.2	22.2	10.4	34.9
Montana	2,468	2,570	2,807	3,556	3,652	3,597	3,606	44.1	10.9	40.3	55.6
Nebraska	14,984	15,382	15,823	16,285	16,682	16,627	16,833	22.0	19.8	9.4	31.1
Nevada	249	273	575	559	598	967	1,305	1,819.1	6.6	378.0	409.8
New Hampshire	18,930	19,824	19,216	18,876	18,603	18,845	18,952	58.3	8.0	−4.4	3.2
New Jersey	44,150	44,703	45,071	45,114	44,368	44,052	44,668	−7.4	3.8	−0.1	3.7
New Mexico	1,467	2,271	2,705	2,214	3,550	3,671	4,230	39.7	93.3	86.3	260.0
New York	327,088	333,933	342,511	343,641	339,369	339,528	346,514	30.0	4.0	3.8	7.9
North Carolina	55,690	55,736	58,312	58,064	56,789	60,326	62,219	63.5	13.9	11.6	27.2
North Dakota	2,634	2,945	3,107	3,094	3,038	3,091	3,257	200.7	48.2	10.6	63.9
Ohio	91,816	93,186	94,134	95,266	95,994	96,059	98,040	22.3	10.1	5.2	15.8
Oklahoma	15,325	17,741	17,292	17,652	18,138	17,675	17,852	38.7	19.4	0.6	20.2
Oregon	18,518	19,179	19,172	19,345	19,949	20,115	20,519	68.8	20.5	7.0	28.9
Pennsylvania	174,003	176,509	179,575	179,371	179,269	179,812	181,249	26.7	4.9	2.7	7.7
Rhode Island	31,364	31,383	30,937	29,658	28,720	28,583	30,478	75.8	8.4	−2.9	5.3
South Carolina	21,162	22,511	20,969	21,103	20,849	21,694	22,336	26.2	16.2	−0.8	15.3
South Dakota	6,001	5,774	5,651	5,336	5,384	5,487	5,454	−6.8	10.9	−5.5	4.8
Tennessee	41,071	42,335	42,201	43,144	44,083	45,903	46,748	46.2	11.3	10.4	22.9
Texas	79,604	80,862	85,507	86,388	87,907	91,399	92,304	54.5	7.4	14.2	22.6
Utah	29,127	31,945	32,383	33,985	33,661	33,170	33,512	28.4	21.5	4.9	27.5
Vermont	11,377	13,449	13,295	12,729	12,390	12,301	12,504	57.5	30.7	−7.0	21.5
Virginia	45,772	44,847	43,721	42,023	46,742	46,992	47,157	104.7	27.3	5.2	33.8
Washington	26,399	27,176	27,593	29,432	30,620	30,744	31,818	77.7	13.7	17.1	33.1
West Virginia	6,834	6,762	8,575	8,860	9,349	9,104	8,966	−1.2	10.4	32.6	46.4
Wisconsin	36,847	38,344	39,242	40,082	41,269	41,724	41,748	53.3	25.1	8.9	36.2
Wyoming	—	—	—	—	—	—	—	—	—	—	—
Outlying areas	76,707	79,912	78,952	77,146	73,595	81,801	77,884	632.1	6.3	−2.5	3.6
American Samoa	—	—	—	—	—	—	—	—	—	—	—
Federated States of — —											
Micronesia	—	—	—	—	—	—	—	—	—	—	—
Guam	—	—	—	—	—	—	—	—	—	—	—
Marshall Islands	—	—	—	—	—	—	—	—	—	—	—
Northern Marianas	—	—	—	—	—	—	—	—	—	—	—
Palau	—	—	—	—	—	—	—	—	—	—	—
Puerto Rico	76,707	79,912	78,952	77,146	73,595	81,801	77,884	632.1	6.3	−2.5	3.6
Trust Territories	—	—	—	—	—	—	—	—	—	—	—
Virgin Islands	—	—	—	—	—	—	—	—	—	—	—

—Data not available or not applicable.

NOTE.—Some data have been revised from previously published figures.

SOURCE: U.S. Department of Education, National Center for Education Statistics, Higher Education General Information Survey (HEGIS), "Fall Enrollment in Higher Education" surveys; and Integrated Postsecondary Education Data System (IPEDS), "Fall Enrollment" surveys. (This table was prepared January 1998.)

Table 61.—Full-time-equivalent fall enrollment in private 2-year institutions of higher education, by state: 1970 to 1996

State or other area	Fall 1970	Fall 1971	Fall 1972	Fall 1973	Fall 1974	Fall 1975	Fall 1976	Fall 1977	Fall 1978	Fall 1979
1	2	3	4	5	6	7	8	9	10	11
United States	**107,827**	**107,135**	**100,308**	**105,708**	**101,949**	**113,475**	**113,048**	**122,858**	**133,052**	**137,932**
Alabama	1,345	1,377	1,351	1,133	1,107	2,299	2,363	3,862	4,084	4,202
Alaska	132	169	201	227	193	231	221	—	—	—
Arizona	244	336	477	2,048	207	129	152	166	154	125
Arkansas	1,033	860	763	780	723	686	618	853	1,324	1,497
California	483	827	961	1,219	1,500	1,883	1,714	2,527	4,377	4,402
Colorado	—	57	45	—	—	—	—	507	488	1,036
Connecticut	2,092	1,660	1,537	1,391	1,354	1,447	746	769	782	797
Delaware	3,265	2,755	2,838	2,979	3,070	2,931	3,413	2,271	1,945	905
District of Columbia	748	502	592	566	147	120	109	98	—	—
Florida	2,530	1,211	991	2,403	1,973	575	583	571	1,596	2,277
Georgia	3,182	2,982	2,101	2,219	2,457	3,376	3,068	4,904	5,171	6,060
Hawaii	322	484	478	—	—	—	—	—	—	—
Idaho	5,123	5,421	5,200	4,690	5,143	5,585	5,502	5,662	5,859	5,743
Illinois	6,394	6,358	6,182	6,157	5,451	5,590	5,654	6,549	6,155	6,481
Indiana	785	875	882	1,433	1,368	2,118	1,836	1,377	1,935	1,960
Iowa	2,912	2,534	2,218	2,410	2,394	1,794	1,706	1,748	2,534	1,632
Kansas	1,384	1,453	1,384	1,226	1,244	1,517	1,564	1,487	1,505	1,483
Kentucky	1,678	1,555	1,524	1,446	1,313	1,459	2,851	3,977	4,842	4,559
Louisiana	—	—	—	—	—	—	—	—	245	286
Maine	83	422	227	261	253	311	291	377	835	765
Maryland	352	360	388	957	1,265	1,150	1,401	1,640	506	535
Massachusetts	15,777	14,402	12,621	12,987	13,780	18,742	15,750	14,236	13,266	13,972
Michigan	2,802	2,913	2,626	2,465	3,166	4,213	4,461	4,052	5,586	5,881
Minnesota	927	1,079	1,391	1,416	1,468	1,397	1,520	1,585	1,598	1,553
Mississippi	1,699	1,561	1,493	1,374	1,086	1,069	1,405	1,939	2,128	1,744
Missouri	2,138	2,394	2,104	1,231	1,263	1,567	1,167	1,001	1,167	1,076
Montana	—	—	—	—	—	—	—	—	—	—
Nebraska	303	326	321	360	304	331	323	298	290	307
Nevada	—	—	—	—	—	—	—	—	—	—
New Hampshire	495	496	437	531	1,046	540	179	185	258	354
New Jersey	4,360	5,318	5,266	4,646	4,426	4,173	4,742	4,853	4,724	4,909
New Mexico	—	—	—	—	—	—	—	—	—	—
New York	10,137	9,409	9,008	15,519	14,151	18,271	19,851	23,074	22,792	24,583
North Carolina	8,279	8,481	7,764	6,964	6,842	6,668	7,261	8,152	9,003	8,965
North Dakota	114	—	—	—	432	417	406	428	106	103
Ohio	1,354	1,454	1,831	2,210	2,537	3,166	3,121	3,536	3,508	3,817
Oklahoma	2,187	2,240	2,176	2,284	2,173	2,545	1,772	1,558	1,294	1,520
Oregon	350	493	311	328	354	378	368	412	231	381
Pennsylvania	4,725	5,051	4,348	3,794	3,779	4,942	5,308	5,363	5,011	5,902
Rhode Island	—	—	—	—	—	—	—	403	476	472
South Carolina	3,357	3,697	3,781	2,903	2,736	3,240	3,033	2,866	4,668	5,185
South Dakota	324	375	361	373	355	385	391	390	560	337
Tennessee	2,508	2,585	2,705	2,929	3,074	1,746	1,542	2,433	5,072	5,211
Texas	4,244	4,874	3,909	3,412	1,406	1,428	1,421	1,426	1,603	1,536
Utah	1,586	1,660	1,675	1,459	1,168	1,162	1,127	1,119	1,057	1,140
Vermont	1,312	1,494	1,586	1,252	1,335	872	943	1,006	902	1,000
Virginia	3,076	2,923	2,933	2,316	2,269	1,080	1,315	1,343	1,266	1,320
Washington	—	—	—	—	—	—	—	—	—	162
West Virginia	1,401	1,389	962	1,065	1,040	1,161	1,162	1,257	1,226	1,269
Wisconsin	285	323	359	345	597	781	688	598	923	488
Wyoming	—	—	—	—	—	—	—	—	—	—
Outlying areas	6,623	9,080	8,744	8,981	9,750	15,623	17,496	23,050	25,220	18,832
American Samoa	—	—	—	—	—	—	—	—	—	—
Federated States of Micronesia	—	—	—	—	—	—	—	—	—	—
Guam	—	—	—	—	—	—	—	—	—	—
Marshall Islands	—	—	—	—	—	—	—	—	—	—
Northern Marianas	—	—	—	—	—	—	—	—	—	—
Palau	—	—	—	—	—	—	—	—	—	—
Puerto Rico	6,623	9,080	8,744	8,981	9,750	15,623	17,496	23,050	25,220	18,832
Trust Territories	—	—	—	—	—	—	—	—	—	—
Virgin Islands	—	—	—	—	—	—	—	—	—	—

Table 61.—Full-time-equivalent fall enrollment in private 2–year institutions of higher education, by state: 1970 to 1996—Continued

State or other area	Fall 1980	Fall 1981	Fall 1982	Fall 1983	Fall 1984	Fall 1985	Fall 1986	Fall 1987	Fall 1988	Fall 1989
1	12	13	14	15	16	17	18	19	20	21
United States	173,614	191,880	212,784	225,504	212,215	220,935	221,291	201,269	208,994	215,517
Alabama	3,819	4,687	4,316	3,378	4,248	3,531	4,054	3,332	4,157	3,084
Alaska	—	—	—	—	—	—	—	—	608	255
Arizona	99	106	127	1,046	2,186	1,247	1,937	1,793	1,989	1,632
Arkansas	2,284	2,187	2,158	2,371	2,981	2,907	1,485	1,757	2,681	2,213
California	5,272	6,588	6,615	7,762	8,744	10,515	10,486	10,365	10,754	8,159
Colorado	950	1,635	3,228	3,396	3,505	3,878	3,657	3,741	5,402	5,157
Connecticut	1,181	1,210	1,194	1,211	1,237	1,255	1,341	1,295	1,349	1,260
Delaware	815	842	726	753	716	582	—	—	—	—
District of Columbia	—	—	—	—	—	—	—	—	—	—
Florida	4,696	5,631	7,196	7,585	7,710	6,913	13,266	4,021	4,600	4,996
Georgia	9,228	7,916	8,438	8,849	8,070	8,486	8,284	7,043	8,956	8,698
Hawaii	—	—	—	—	—	—	—	—	—	—
Idaho	5,549	5,611	5,862	5,703	5,594	6,092	6,460	7,516	7,852	7,890
Illinois	6,161	5,472	5,560	5,544	7,146	10,734	8,129	8,466	8,512	7,283
Indiana	3,846	4,541	5,626	6,169	5,411	5,675	3,669	3,065	2,858	2,696
Iowa	1,960	1,911	2,172	2,026	2,147	2,289	3,148	2,993	3,311	1,869
Kansas	1,526	1,465	1,424	1,534	1,437	1,290	1,144	1,124	1,195	811
Kentucky	6,801	7,257	8,389	8,628	9,312	9,551	7,785	7,253	6,612	5,727
Louisiana	375	375	375	375	1,706	1,706	1,897	1,135	2,430	2,332
Maine	905	1,057	1,118	1,120	1,091	1,102	898	838	902	1,159
Maryland	572	785	1,014	1,080	322	332	678	764	770	625
Massachusetts	15,050	15,735	15,663	15,337	14,447	14,170	13,087	11,459	9,990	9,677
Michigan	5,613	6,706	7,551	7,677	7,608	8,358	5,260	2,948	3,785	3,813
Minnesota	3,235	3,561	3,664	3,995	3,859	3,905	4,207	4,390	4,080	4,354
Mississippi	2,185	2,296	2,384	1,846	1,837	1,362	1,508	2,137	2,457	2,765
Missouri	1,280	1,373	1,666	2,197	2,160	2,526	2,680	3,041	2,607	2,619
Montana	473	665	608	703	644	624	721	436	807	823
Nebraska	344	533	569	609	481	524	333	402	399	591
Nevada	—	—	—	—	—	—	25	25	26	23
New Hampshire	1,839	1,889	2,000	2,217	2,409	2,237	1,988	1,624	1,839	1,268
New Jersey	5,392	5,360	1,572	1,605	1,464	1,491	1,898	2,008	2,268	2,958
New Mexico	—	—	—	—	—	—	—	—	—	—
New York	26,859	29,029	31,113	33,307	33,905	32,280	31,093	27,392	26,073	24,118
North Carolina	8,641	8,603	8,391	7,725	6,908	6,534	6,231	6,497	5,620	4,960
North Dakota	168	439	394	495	595	671	86	214	208	177
Ohio	8,743	18,278	26,600	25,067	19,904	20,499	18,934	13,770	19,351	15,815
Oklahoma	2,701	2,422	2,800	2,707	2,844	3,173	3,094	4,242	5,217	4,701
Oregon	484	556	252	897	178	320	366	329	331	285
Pennsylvania	14,319	15,412	20,855	25,883	16,728	21,391	28,373	31,157	24,422	45,518
Rhode Island	772	1,004	1,269	1,720	—	—	—	—	—	—
South Carolina	5,793	4,629	4,784	5,291	4,782	4,871	4,296	4,752	4,563	4,309
South Dakota	458	541	481	477	518	614	438	475	265	246
Tennessee	5,380	5,433	5,514	7,195	6,920	5,867	5,184	5,219	5,174	5,729
Texas	2,152	1,808	1,723	2,068	1,841	2,755	3,295	3,406	3,968	4,420
Utah	1,270	1,350	1,341	1,740	1,511	1,233	1,185	965	873	887
Vermont	1,149	1,167	1,394	1,559	1,599	1,552	1,498	1,698	1,766	1,731
Virginia	972	1,223	1,213	1,172	1,337	1,435	2,337	1,306	2,624	2,205
Washington	—	35	35	14	—	598	1,132	1,204	1,372	1,705	1,897
West Virginia	1,585	1,750	2,243	2,000	2,127	1,789	1,896	1,560	2,011	2,161
Wisconsin	692	781	1,188	1,485	1,448	1,537	1,134	1,323	998	1,015
Wyoming	26	26	—	—	—	—	622	621	629	606
Outlying areas	14,437	15,693	17,041	17,699	17,585	18,439	9,616	8,723	9,005	9,149
American Samoa	—	—	—	—	—	—	—	—	—	—
Federated States of Micronesia	—	—	—	—	—	—	—	—	—	—
Guam	—	—	—	—	—	—	—	—	—	—
Marshall Islands	—	—	—	—	—	—	—	—	—	—
Northern Marianas	—	—	—	—	—	—	—	—	—	—
Palau	—	—	—	—	—	—	—	—	—	—
Puerto Rico	14,437	15,693	17,041	17,699	17,585	18,439	9,616	8,723	9,005	9,149
Trust Territories	—	—	—	—	—	—	—	—	—	—
Virgin Islands	—	—	—	—	—	—	—	—	—	—

Table 61.—Full-time-equivalent fall enrollment in private 2-year institutions of higher education, by state: 1970 to 1996—Continued

State or other area	Fall 1990	Fall 1991	Fall 1992	Fall 1993	Fall 1994	Fall 1995	Fall 1996	Percentage change Fall 1970 to fall 1996	Fall 1986 to fall 1991	Fall 1991 to fall 1996	Fall 1986 to fall 1996
1	22	23	24	25	26	27	28	29	30	31	32
United States	197,495	212,011	193,580	184,083	175,859	167,520	162,530	50.7	-4.2	-23.3	-26.6
Alabama	3,324	2,774	2,950	1,750	1,231	450	883	-34.3	-31.6	-68.2	-78.2
Alaska	394	342	359	238	303	167	270	104.5	—	-21.1	—
Arizona	1,911	1,454	1,005	1,077	929	889	948	288.5	-24.9	-34.8	-51.1
Arkansas	1,953	2,078	1,526	951	346	349	376	-63.6	39.9	-81.9	-74.7
California	10,670	10,838	12,568	13,271	12,344	12,886	13,246	2,642.4	3.4	22.2	26.3
Colorado	4,532	5,090	4,011	3,867	3,121	3,442	1,554	—	39.2	-69.5	-57.5
Connecticut	1,179	1,038	1,212	1,163	1,188	1,157	1,160	-44.6	-22.6	11.8	-13.5
Delaware	—	—	—	—	—	—	—				
District of Columbia	—	—	—	—	—	—	—	—	—	—	—
Florida	6,183	6,697	5,815	4,454	4,884	5,123	5,524	118.3	-49.5	-17.5	-58.4
Georgia	8,092	7,316	7,298	5,685	5,319	4,132	4,105	29.0	-11.7	-43.9	-50.4
Hawaii	—	—	—	—	—	—	—				
Idaho	7,989	8,154	8,056	8,522	8,280	8,122	7,986	55.9	26.2	-2.1	23.6
Illinois	7,769	8,580	6,182	5,819	5,421	3,784	3,684	-42.4	5.5	-57.1	-54.7
Indiana	2,981	3,169	2,829	2,953	2,997	2,866	2,878	266.6	-13.6	-9.2	-21.6
Iowa	2,087	2,006	1,913	1,930	1,212	926	890	-69.4	-36.3	-55.6	-71.7
Kansas	866	776	868	819	784	735	721	-47.9	-32.2	-7.1	-37.0
Kentucky	5,240	4,858	4,280	4,618	4,153	2,361	2,403	43.2	-37.6	-50.5	-69.1
Louisiana	2,233	1,990	680	602	985	754	943	—	4.9	-52.6	-50.3
Maine	1,178	1,354	1,373	1,506	1,602	1,655	1,594	1,820.5	50.8	17.7	77.5
Maryland	629	742	836	870	937	1,032	1,005	185.5	9.4	35.4	48.2
Massachusetts	9,047	8,928	9,735	9,592	9,506	5,997	5,093	-67.7	-31.8	-43.0	-61.1
Michigan	2,135	2,225	2,279	1,971	1,614	1,728	945	-66.3	-57.7	-57.5	-82.0
Minnesota	3,745	3,479	4,804	3,833	3,521	3,263	3,706	299.8	-17.3	6.5	-11.9
Mississippi	2,919	2,644	2,044	1,107	960	722	643	-62.2	75.3	-75.7	-57.4
Missouri	3,496	2,810	4,367	5,150	4,934	3,939	3,818	78.6	4.9	35.9	42.5
Montana	602	908	1,591	571	529	600	556	—	25.9	-38.8	-22.9
Nebraska	266	403	428	443	338	403	—	—	21.0	—	—
Nevada	173	302	25	25	27	27	24	—	1,108.0	-92.1	-4.0
New Hampshire	1,884	2,711	3,048	3,108	2,952	3,122	2,904	486.7	36.4	7.1	46.1
New Jersey	2,994	3,271	3,439	3,435	3,295	3,851	4,154	-4.7	72.3	27.0	118.9
New Mexico	180	539	762	566	651	954	1,051	—	—	95.0	—
New York	25,229	30,038	28,056	27,827	26,016	25,311	21,917	116.2	-3.4	-27.0	-29.5
North Carolina	5,014	4,212	2,947	2,538	2,241	1,327	852	-89.7	-32.4	-79.8	-86.3
North Dakota	208	222	234	264	242	249	256	124.6	158.1	15.3	197.7
Ohio	10,846	12,186	14,318	10,381	9,586	8,909	8,891	556.6	-35.6	-27.0	-53.0
Oklahoma	3,945	3,502	2,776	1,948	2,459	1,909	1,900	-13.1	13.2	-45.7	-38.6
Oregon	234	280	299	182	163	158	—	—	—	-23.5	—
Pennsylvania	28,871	41,486	27,916	29,184	28,926	32,634	36,386	670.1	46.2	-12.3	28.2
Rhode Island	—	—	—	—	2,025	1,930	2,149	—	—	—	—
South Carolina	4,145	2,405	2,117	1,748	1,343	1,200	1,225	-63.5	-44.0	-49.1	-71.5
South Dakota	127	127	116	128	143	143	116	-64.2	-71.0	-8.7	-73.5
Tennessee	4,706	4,424	3,586	2,846	2,425	2,018	1,644	-34.4	-14.7	-62.8	-68.3
Texas	4,702	4,780	4,802	4,875	5,987	5,641	5,815	37.0	45.1	21.7	76.5
Utah	1,390	940	969	1,085	1,079	1,146	1,136	-28.4	-20.7	20.9	-4.1
Vermont	1,647	132	163	161	163	178	188	-85.7	-91.2	42.4	-87.4
Virginia	3,651	3,408	3,430	3,698	3,744	4,016	3,723	21.0	45.8	9.2	59.3
Washington	2,233	2,109	2,372	1,988	1,938	2,063	2,325	—	75.2	10.2	93.1
West Virginia	2,172	2,078	861	944	846	776	731	-47.8	9.6	-64.8	-61.4
Wisconsin	1,021	1,339	1,581	1,665	1,598	1,501	1,550	443.9	18.1	15.8	36.7
Wyoming	703	867	754	700	667	756	811	—	39.4	-6.5	30.4
Outlying areas	8,339	9,268	10,745	11,393	10,161	7,806	8,040	21.4	-3.6	-13.2	-16.4
American Samoa	—	—	—	—	—	—	—	—	—	—	—
Federated States of Micronesia	—	—	—	—	—	—	—	—	—	—	—
Guam	—	—	—	—	—	—	—	—	—	—	—
Marshall Islands	—	—	—	—	—	—	—	—	—	—	—
Northern Marianas	—	—	—	—	—	—	—	—	—	—	—
Palau	—	—	—	—	—	—	—	—	—	—	—
Puerto Rico	8,339	9,268	10,745	11,393	10,161	7,806	8,040	21.4	-3.6	-13.2	-16.4
Trust Territories	—	—	—	—	—	—	—	—	—	—	—
Virgin Islands	—	—	—	—	—	—	—	—	—	—	—

—Data not available or not applicable.

NOTE.—Some data have been revised from previously published figures. Large increases in 1980 and 1981 are due to the addition of schools accredited by the Accrediting Commission of Career Schools and Colleges of Technology.

SOURCE: U.S. Department of Education, National Center for Education Statistics, Higher Education General Information Survey (HEGIS), "Fall Enrollment in Higher Education" surveys; and Integrated Postsecondary Education Data System (IPEDS), "Fall Enrollment" surveys. (This table was prepared January 1998.)

Table 62.—Percentage distribution of degrees awarded by institutions of higher education, by level of degree and state: 1980–81, 1990–91, and 1994–95

State or other area	1980–81					1990–91					1994–95				
	Associate degrees	Bachelor's degrees	First professional degrees [1]	Master's degrees	Doctor's degrees (Ph.D., Ed.D., etc.)	Associate degrees	Bachelor's degrees	First professional degrees [1]	Master's degrees	Doctor's degrees (Ph.D., Ed.D., etc.)	Associate degrees	Bachelor's degrees	First professional degrees [1]	Master's degrees	Doctor's degrees (Ph.D., Ed.D., etc.)
1	2	3	4	5	6	7	8	9	10	11	12	13	14	15	16
United States	23.8	53.4	4.1	16.9	1.9	23.8	54.1	3.6	16.7	1.9	24.3	52.3	3.4	17.9	2.0
Alabama	17.4	59.4	3.4	18.9	0.9	21.0	58.5	2.7	16.5	1.3	22.3	56.7	2.7	17.0	1.2
Alaska	43.8	39.8	—	16.3	0.2	30.5	55.0	—	14.1	0.5	32.3	51.4	—	15.6	0.6
Arizona	24.5	51.2	1.9	20.6	1.9	18.5	55.0	1.3	23.1	2.0	22.2	52.7	1.4	21.2	2.6
Arkansas	16.2	63.1	3.5	16.3	1.0	21.8	61.4	2.8	13.1	1.0	18.1	62.5	3.5	14.8	1.1
California	32.2	44.3	4.7	16.6	2.2	27.9	49.2	3.8	16.9	2.2	27.2	49.3	3.9	17.1	2.4
Colorado	17.6	57.5	3.3	18.9	2.8	20.8	56.5	2.6	17.7	2.4	19.6	55.9	2.3	19.9	2.2
Connecticut	20.6	50.9	3.1	23.7	1.8	17.5	53.7	3.6	23.0	2.2	17.9	52.1	3.4	23.9	2.6
Delaware	24.4	65.2	0.0	9.2	1.2	19.5	60.1	6.3	12.1	2.0	15.6	61.2	5.7	15.1	2.3
District of Columbia	4.0	42.1	15.2	35.4	3.3	2.1	48.1	14.6	32.4	2.9	1.2	41.9	14.7	39.4	2.8
Florida	43.0	40.9	2.5	11.9	1.7	40.0	43.4	2.6	12.6	1.4	38.9	42.9	2.4	14.1	1.6
Georgia	19.0	54.0	4.9	20.4	1.8	20.0	56.4	4.9	16.6	2.1	19.4	55.9	4.4	18.4	2.0
Hawaii	31.8	49.2	2.3	15.0	1.7	31.4	50.3	1.6	14.7	2.0	27.3	51.5	1.8	17.4	1.9
Idaho	35.9	49.2	1.6	12.2	1.1	43.1	43.4	1.7	10.8	1.1	42.9	43.5	1.7	11.1	0.8
Illinois	23.9	50.3	5.0	18.5	2.3	24.0	49.6	4.4	19.6	2.4	24.6	47.5	4.0	21.3	2.6
Indiana	16.4	58.6	3.6	19.0	2.5	18.8	61.5	2.9	14.6	2.2	19.9	59.8	2.9	15.0	2.3
Iowa	22.7	58.5	6.4	10.2	2.3	26.6	55.9	4.8	10.4	2.3	26.2	55.6	4.9	11.1	2.2
Kansas	22.4	57.3	2.8	15.7	1.8	25.0	56.1	2.7	14.6	1.6	25.8	54.2	2.2	16.1	1.7
Kentucky	21.5	51.3	5.9	20.1	1.2	23.8	53.7	4.7	16.4	1.3	24.1	54.4	4.2	15.8	1.5
Louisiana	9.2	65.8	6.3	17.4	1.2	11.3	64.4	6.5	16.2	1.6	11.7	62.2	5.8	18.6	1.7
Maine	24.1	67.1	1.2	7.3	0.3	25.2	62.2	2.1	10.2	0.4	25.7	61.9	1.9	10.0	0.4
Maryland	23.1	54.0	3.0	17.8	2.0	21.5	54.0	2.8	19.4	2.4	21.9	50.5	2.5	22.8	2.2
Massachusetts	20.1	53.2	4.8	19.3	2.7	16.1	53.8	4.4	23.0	2.6	15.9	50.2	4.6	26.5	2.8
Michigan	24.8	50.6	3.5	19.5	1.7	26.4	52.1	3.0	16.7	1.8	26.2	51.2	2.9	17.9	1.8
Minnesota	21.0	61.7	5.2	10.5	1.7	20.8	61.4	3.8	11.9	2.1	27.5	54.1	3.5	13.0	2.0
Mississippi	24.8	53.3	4.1	16.4	1.4	29.2	52.0	2.6	14.3	1.9	28.5	53.4	2.5	13.5	2.1
Missouri	16.5	56.7	6.0	19.4	1.5	17.2	56.5	5.0	19.9	1.5	17.8	55.6	4.6	20.6	1.4
Montana	10.4	74.4	1.4	13.0	0.7	15.8	68.8	1.1	13.4	1.0	19.9	65.1	1.2	12.8	1.0
Nebraska	18.8	59.7	5.8	13.8	1.9	20.4	61.5	5.1	11.6	1.5	20.0	60.1	4.9	13.4	1.5
Nevada	24.1	55.6	1.8	17.4	1.1	24.9	58.3	0.9	15.1	0.9	24.3	58.0	0.9	15.4	1.3
New Hampshire	21.4	65.3	2.0	10.6	0.7	22.0	59.0	1.5	16.8	0.7	26.2	54.8	1.4	16.8	0.8
New Jersey	22.2	55.2	3.5	17.4	1.8	24.1	53.3	3.7	17.0	1.8	26.5	50.8	3.4	17.0	2.2
New Mexico	16.7	56.9	2.4	22.0	2.0	24.7	52.2	1.7	19.1	2.3	26.1	50.8	1.4	19.4	2.3
New York	27.9	48.0	3.7	18.6	1.9	26.2	47.7	3.8	20.1	2.1	26.7	45.7	3.7	21.9	1.9
North Carolina	25.4	56.7	3.6	12.6	1.7	23.4	58.8	3.3	12.6	1.8	24.9	57.1	3.0	13.1	1.8
North Dakota	27.6	61.8	1.9	7.6	1.1	25.3	63.6	1.9	8.3	0.9	24.6	62.7	2.6	8.9	1.2
Ohio	20.6	55.1	4.7	17.6	2.0	21.6	57.0	3.7	15.7	2.0	22.3	54.8	3.4	17.0	2.4
Oklahoma	18.4	59.8	3.6	16.4	1.8	25.1	55.3	3.6	14.6	1.5	24.5	53.5	3.3	17.2	1.4
Oregon	23.2	52.7	5.5	16.5	2.2	21.5	57.4	4.2	15.0	1.9	24.2	53.7	3.8	16.3	2.1
Pennsylvania	18.2	61.0	4.2	14.8	1.9	19.3	60.3	3.3	15.1	2.1	18.8	57.5	3.6	17.9	2.2
Rhode Island	25.9	59.6	0.6	12.5	1.4	25.5	59.4	0.5	12.9	1.8	25.5	58.8	0.5	13.4	1.9
South Carolina	26.5	54.8	3.4	14.4	0.9	21.0	58.8	2.4	16.2	1.5	22.9	56.5	2.3	16.8	1.5
South Dakota	21.6	65.7	2.3	9.8	0.6	16.4	66.6	2.0	14.1	0.9	13.2	67.8	2.2	15.9	1.0
Tennessee	18.9	58.3	5.1	15.7	2.0	21.4	57.5	4.0	15.0	2.0	18.9	57.7	4.0	17.5	1.9
Texas	18.8	57.2	4.5	17.6	1.9	19.2	58.2	3.8	16.8	2.1	20.5	55.6	3.8	18.0	2.2
Utah	16.2	62.6	2.4	16.1	2.6	22.0	60.9	2.1	13.2	1.9	24.1	60.3	1.5	12.6	1.5
Vermont	19.4	59.8	3.0	17.4	0.5	17.2	63.9	3.2	15.0	0.7	18.4	64.3	1.3	15.3	0.8
Virginia	18.4	60.3	4.7	15.0	1.6	18.4	59.9	3.6	16.4	1.8	19.6	56.0	3.3	19.3	1.9
Washington	33.0	49.6	3.0	12.9	1.5	37.1	46.7	2.0	12.6	1.6	37.8	43.2	1.8	15.7	1.4
West Virginia	18.9	61.2	2.7	16.3	0.8	21.3	61.1	2.9	13.8	0.9	19.9	60.6	2.5	15.9	1.1
Wisconsin	20.0	61.0	2.7	14.4	2.0	20.9	60.9	2.3	13.8	2.0	20.8	60.5	2.2	14.5	2.0
Wyoming	31.8	50.2	2.4	12.7	3.0	44.0	44.2	1.9	8.2	1.8	41.9	44.8	1.8	10.0	1.6
U.S. Service Schools	48.5	39.4	0.8	11.2	0.1	67.2	23.0	1.0	8.6	0.2	71.1	19.5	0.9	8.3	0.3
Outlying areas	25.5	66.1	2.3	6.0	0.1	22.8	66.9	3.4	6.6	0.3	20.7	67.4	3.1	8.5	0.3
American Samoa	100.0	—	—	—	—	100.0	—	—	—	—	100.0	—	—	—	—
Federated States of Micronesia	—	—	—	—	—	100.0	—	—	—	—	100.0	—	—	—	—
Guam	7.9	71.2	—	21.0	—	11.0	81.9	—	7.0	—	12.4	76.0	—	11.6	—
Marshall Islands	—	—	—	—	—	—	—	—	—	—	100.0	—	—	—	—
Northern Marianas	—	—	—	—	—	100.0	—	—	—	—	100.0	—	—	—	—
Palau	—	—	—	—	—	—	—	—	—	—	100.0	—	—	—	—
Puerto Rico	25.0	66.8	2.4	5.7	0.1	22.1	67.5	3.5	6.5	0.3	17.6	70.1	3.3	8.6	0.3
Trust Territories	100.0	—	—	—	—	—	—	—	—	—					
Virgin Islands	32.9	51.9	—	15.2	—	23.3	58.0	—	18.7	—	17.8	61.9	—	20.3	—

[1] Includes degrees which require at least 6 years of college work for completion (including at least 2 years of preprofessional training). See Definitions for details.

—Data not available or not applicable.

NOTE.—Due to rounding, details may not sum to 100.0.

SOURCE: U.S. Department of Education, National Center for Education Statistics, Higher Education General Information Survey (HEGIS), "Degrees and Other Formal Awards Conferred" survey, and and Integrated Postsecondary Education Data System (IPEDS), "Completions" surveys. (This table was prepared February 1998.)

Table 63.—Degrees awarded by institutions of higher education, by control, level of degree, and state: 1994–95

State or other area	Public					Private				
	Associate degrees	Bachelor's degrees	First-professional degrees [1]	Master's degrees	Doctor's degrees (Ph.D., Ed.D., etc.)	Associate degrees	Bachelor's degrees	First-professional degrees [1]	Master's degrees	Doctor's degrees (Ph.D., Ed.D., etc.)
1	2	3	4	5	6	7	8	9	10	11
United States	451,539	776,670	29,871	224,152	28,917	88,152	383,464	45,929	173,477	15,529
Alabama	7,176	16,821	591	5,540	435	659	3,103	372	443	3
Alaska	834	1,428	—	386	19	126	98	—	77	—
Arizona	5,886	13,877	445	4,850	787	923	2,298	—	1,648	—
Arkansas	2,416	7,141	482	1,982	155	76	1,482	—	59	—
California	53,982	83,300	2,200	18,187	2,847	6,521	26,414	6,583	19,878	2,520
Colorado	5,126	16,054	463	4,531	666	1,858	3,875	370	2,580	122
Connecticut	4,009	7,368	310	2,384	265	791	6,604	610	4,035	442
Delaware	934	3,552	—	738	139	207	914	418	364	30
District of Columbia	73	542	—	120	—	132	6,485	2,467	6,487	474
Florida	34,286	30,885	942	8,449	961	6,447	14,039	1,552	6,344	692
Georgia	7,193	19,302	692	6,705	712	1,950	7,010	1,369	1,939	222
Hawaii	2,109	3,156	121	1,070	155	278	1,344	39	450	11
Idaho	1,140	3,870	167	934	80	3,041	365	—	143	—
Illinois	24,273	30,170	1,103	9,858	1,358	2,853	22,100	3,257	13,629	1,492
Indiana	7,918	20,941	948	5,648	1,013	2,145	9,312	537	1,949	139
Iowa	7,608	9,429	554	2,540	667	583	7,992	981	938	19
Kansas	6,482	11,522	572	3,748	450	479	3,072	19	602	—
Kentucky	4,937	11,576	739	3,676	284	1,509	2,994	388	543	113
Louisiana	2,879	14,880	711	3,933	373	490	3,040	969	1,413	126
Maine	1,710	3,491	79	730	40	735	2,402	101	223	2
Maryland	8,186	15,864	808	4,658	587	446	4,044	193	4,333	290
Massachusetts	8,333	12,510	99	3,264	379	4,475	27,769	3,557	18,012	1,904
Michigan	19,578	33,837	1,493	13,720	1,493	3,118	10,480	1,003	1,740	55
Minnesota	8,623	15,996	682	3,508	685	3,593	8,072	856	2,252	204
Mississippi	5,340	8,602	346	2,227	340	179	1,733	146	394	59
Missouri	6,075	15,656	663	3,805	341	2,853	12,275	1,633	6,550	378
Montana	1,162	3,880	78	836	66	167	474	—	21	—
Nebraska	3,014	6,961	368	1,839	249	351	3,144	457	413	6
Nevada	1,379	3,291	54	895	77	32	80	—	2	—
New Hampshire	2,000	3,839	—	684	51	1,530	3,556	193	1,578	61
New Jersey	12,012	18,138	906	4,846	584	843	6,489	764	3,415	469
New Mexico	3,199	5,582	172	2,218	285	78	781	—	220	—
New York	41,340	41,447	1,171	13,560	1,375	13,331	52,102	6,465	31,166	2,599
North Carolina	13,195	22,583	709	5,645	750	912	9,738	987	1,785	272
North Dakota	1,682	3,812	187	595	84	56	628	—	33	—
Ohio	17,030	32,988	1,901	10,421	1,644	3,153	16,600	1,168	4,966	547
Oklahoma	6,568	12,480	602	3,595	347	443	2,827	353	1,333	67
Oregon	5,488	9,219	321	2,705	430	325	3,698	583	1,209	63
Pennsylvania	12,801	31,872	1,200	8,742	1,283	7,768	31,155	2,742	10,895	1,119
Rhode Island	1,579	3,334	4	898	108	2,311	5,644	72	1,143	187
South Carolina	5,435	11,573	539	4,102	365	730	3,603	75	423	26
South Dakota	488	3,474	124	931	58	346	819	13	76	5
Tennessee	5,658	13,209	704	4,366	452	1,063	7,254	732	1,827	213
Texas	23,210	54,752	2,577	17,075	2,355	2,590	15,296	2,198	5,665	372
Utah	5,390	7,757	218	1,663	272	422	6,784	155	1,382	86
Vermont	664	2,323	90	384	53	647	2,268	—	707	1
Virginia	8,941	23,265	1,172	8,381	1,048	1,941	7,841	645	2,325	29
Washington	18,210	16,843	453	3,610	651	892	4,985	456	4,337	36
West Virginia	2,124	7,349	358	2,140	159	716	1,307	—	128	—
Wisconsin	8,396	19,868	526	5,043	833	866	7,075	451	1,403	74
Wyoming	1,491	1,777	70	396	63	172	—	—	—	—
U.S. Service Schools	11,977	3,284	157	1,391	44	—	—	—	—	—
Outlying areas	2,075	6,417	267	737	32	2,328	7,885	390	1,062	35
American Samoa	419	—	—	—	—	—	—	—	—	—
Federated States of Micronesia	163	—	—	—	—	—	—	—	—	—
Guam	48	295	—	45	—	—	—	—	—	—
Marshall Islands	40	—	—	—	—	—	—	—	—	—
Northern Marianas	180	—	—	—	—	—	—	—	—	—
Palau	21	—	—	—	—	—	—	—	—	—
Puerto Rico	1,148	5,927	267	628	32	2,328	7,885	390	1,062	35
Virgin Islands	56	195	—	64	—	—	—	—	—	—

[1] Includes degrees which require at least 6 years of college work for completion (including at least 2 years of preprofessional training). See *Definitions* for details.

—Data not available or not applicable.

SOURCE: U.S. Department of Education, National Center for Education Statistics, Integrated Postsecondary Education Data System (IPEDS), ''Completions'' survey. (This table was prepared April 1997.)

Table 64.—Percentage of degrees awarded to women by institutions of higher education, by level of degree and state: 1980–81, 1990–91, and 1994–95

State or other area	1980–81					1990–91					1994–95				
	Associate degrees	Bachelor's degrees	First professional degrees[1]	Master's degrees	Doctor's degrees (Ph.D., Ed.D., etc.)	Associate degrees	Bachelor's degrees	First professional degrees[1]	Master's degrees	Doctor's degrees (Ph.D., Ed.D., etc.)	Associate degrees	Bachelor's degrees	First professional degrees[1]	Master's degrees	Doctor's degrees (Ph.D., Ed.D., etc.)
1	2	3	4	5	6	7	8	9	10	11	12	13	14	15	16
United States	54.7	49.8	26.6	50.3	31.1	58.8	53.9	39.1	53.6	37.0	59.5	54.6	40.8	55.1	39.4
Alabama	62.5	50.4	23.7	58.2	34.3	62.9	55.5	32.5	60.6	41.8	63.7	56.4	38.6	58.0	45.7
Alaska	49.8	54.0	—	46.3	—	62.1	61.4	—	46.9	10.0	63.2	59.8	—	52.7	42.1
Arizona	52.1	48.1	30.2	46.8	30.6	50.7	47.8	45.4	46.6	31.7	57.7	52.4	46.7	53.5	38.1
Arkansas	57.8	51.1	21.5	56.6	21.0	63.4	56.6	32.8	61.1	33.3	69.3	57.2	43.2	63.6	38.7
California	55.0	49.2	30.1	43.3	29.2	60.7	53.4	42.7	50.4	36.5	59.7	54.2	43.6	53.0	40.0
Colorado	44.6	48.4	28.0	49.2	28.7	55.1	52.4	48.1	49.1	34.5	57.5	52.5	44.5	51.5	37.6
Connecticut	60.8	51.1	33.5	53.0	34.2	65.8	55.3	41.7	55.3	39.8	64.7	55.8	43.2	56.2	43.0
Delaware	64.5	53.1	—	48.0	37.9	68.0	59.0	37.3	58.8	29.3	66.5	60.3	43.1	54.0	40.2
District of Columbia	53.1	53.5	34.0	45.8	39.8	57.5	57.2	45.3	49.5	43.4	52.7	57.6	44.2	51.5	42.8
Florida	55.1	46.7	27.1	52.5	35.6	58.2	53.0	41.5	53.1	41.7	59.4	53.8	42.1	51.3	46.6
Georgia	55.6	50.7	23.7	58.0	31.8	59.9	55.2	37.3	55.0	35.9	62.9	56.2	40.3	58.3	41.5
Hawaii	47.0	49.7	34.6	53.3	28.1	56.8	55.2	41.5	54.5	38.9	55.9	56.2	45.0	53.9	39.8
Idaho	60.7	44.1	19.8	40.1	18.3	59.9	52.0	31.1	52.4	38.2	62.2	51.8	40.1	50.7	25.0
Illinois	55.2	50.6	24.9	48.7	27.9	59.5	53.1	38.2	52.7	35.4	61.1	53.9	40.5	54.2	40.4
Indiana	48.4	47.4	21.3	55.5	27.0	50.6	51.8	34.0	49.5	34.0	54.2	52.6	41.1	48.7	36.3
Iowa	52.7	49.6	18.8	47.9	26.6	56.0	52.7	28.6	50.8	31.3	60.1	54.0	36.9	54.5	34.1
Kansas	56.5	50.3	26.1	54.5	29.8	60.4	53.5	38.5	58.5	37.7	59.9	53.7	39.3	58.3	38.7
Kentucky	58.6	50.9	20.1	63.3	15.5	68.1	56.7	32.0	61.7	29.0	70.6	57.4	34.7	62.6	34.5
Louisiana	59.2	51.1	22.3	57.4	27.9	60.5	56.0	34.3	57.4	36.7	64.4	57.9	38.0	57.2	32.3
Maine	60.2	51.1	37.3	54.8	12.0	64.3	57.4	37.0	58.8	36.4	66.1	56.9	37.8	61.0	35.7
Maryland	60.1	52.1	29.0	55.7	37.5	63.2	56.3	39.0	53.8	43.2	64.9	56.6	43.0	57.3	42.4
Massachusetts	63.1	51.6	32.9	46.5	31.8	65.5	55.7	44.7	54.6	36.2	65.8	54.3	44.3	57.1	39.4
Michigan	54.8	47.9	25.1	47.9	30.6	62.5	54.2	37.8	52.1	36.0	64.3	53.9	41.1	52.5	37.5
Minnesota	60.9	51.6	25.7	47.0	31.6	60.5	55.7	40.6	57.1	36.8	54.8	55.7	44.9	59.1	38.4
Mississippi	59.7	53.8	19.3	61.4	32.8	68.3	57.9	33.2	59.5	37.6	67.6	57.5	31.3	58.3	35.1
Missouri	54.4	49.1	18.7	44.0	28.2	56.6	53.7	31.6	49.4	37.0	61.2	55.3	34.4	51.0	38.2
Montana	52.6	45.9	31.0	42.5	23.7	67.9	50.6	31.1	50.9	33.9	62.3	51.9	41.0	48.7	37.9
Nebraska	44.5	50.8	23.3	50.5	24.4	48.7	54.0	35.9	60.0	44.7	49.5	56.1	41.6	58.8	39.6
Nevada	45.2	45.4	29.2	52.3	43.3	63.8	55.2	34.2	56.6	33.3	62.2	54.1	44.4	59.1	40.3
New Hampshire	50.8	46.9	33.0	39.2	22.1	60.1	53.6	41.3	53.0	36.0	64.8	56.1	37.3	53.4	44.6
New Jersey	62.2	51.7	27.2	50.3	28.7	62.8	55.4	36.5	50.4	35.2	62.3	55.3	39.3	54.6	37.7
New Mexico	56.0	47.5	39.7	48.6	36.4	62.1	53.5	44.9	56.7	34.5	64.0	55.3	57.6	55.2	36.8
New York	55.3	51.1	31.8	54.1	36.1	60.2	53.9	42.5	58.4	40.7	60.5	55.2	41.1	59.4	42.2
North Carolina	56.0	53.3	25.7	57.6	33.1	65.8	55.9	39.8	56.4	38.8	65.4	56.5	40.0	56.6	39.0
North Dakota	50.1	50.7	20.3	44.8	20.3	52.9	51.4	40.6	49.6	34.9	54.6	51.3	39.0	54.6	47.6
Ohio	54.1	49.4	25.8	50.4	37.3	60.1	53.6	37.9	54.1	38.8	62.2	54.3	41.1	56.4	41.7
Oklahoma	53.3	48.3	21.5	48.5	25.9	58.2	52.7	34.3	52.6	40.5	61.1	55.1	37.7	53.2	42.5
Oregon	49.5	48.2	26.3	47.5	31.6	54.4	52.0	32.7	53.0	30.3	54.4	53.8	36.0	57.1	37.5
Pennsylvania	53.3	49.4	27.5	48.8	31.9	54.5	53.4	39.7	52.1	36.1	56.9	54.2	41.0	53.7	40.7
Rhode Island	49.2	49.2	28.4	49.3	23.4	46.9	53.1	48.8	50.1	37.8	51.3	53.8	51.3	56.0	39.0
South Carolina	50.3	50.7	20.8	61.7	35.2	60.7	55.8	35.2	61.0	35.9	58.9	56.5	35.5	58.8	38.1
South Dakota	64.8	46.1	23.1	40.9	24.2	80.6	54.3	29.2	51.7	34.7	72.9	53.7	43.8	55.2	50.8
Tennessee	56.0	48.7	21.1	57.6	36.4	55.1	54.4	33.0	59.4	45.2	64.7	54.6	39.2	58.8	39.2
Texas	50.4	49.8	24.0	50.1	29.9	58.8	54.7	38.7	51.1	36.3	57.1	55.1	37.1	51.2	35.1
Utah	55.9	39.3	16.4	33.4	23.8	58.0	46.0	23.8	39.6	27.0	58.1	49.4	37.0	41.3	28.8
Vermont	63.9	53.3	21.9	62.8	20.0	61.5	55.0	40.5	62.7	41.7	65.0	53.2	56.7	68.8	42.6
Virginia	55.3	54.2	25.9	54.9	29.0	63.8	56.5	41.5	54.8	38.7	61.6	55.9	40.6	56.9	38.5
Washington	52.7	48.7	28.3	45.3	27.4	53.9	53.9	43.4	55.7	34.5	56.5	54.7	45.8	59.8	36.5
West Virginia	58.8	48.6	18.9	54.2	29.0	66.9	53.9	36.8	59.2	35.5	62.0	52.2	40.8	58.3	44.0
Wisconsin	54.3	50.7	26.4	49.5	29.0	59.8	54.9	38.2	55.3	31.4	59.9	55.7	41.8	57.3	35.6
Wyoming	56.2	46.1	23.8	36.6	24.4	56.8	51.6	32.9	47.0	29.9	59.5	54.4	50.0	43.9	30.2
U.S. Service Schools ...	4.0	6.5	20.9	2.4	—	14.7	10.6	14.8	10.1	—	17.3	12.1	22.3	11.4	20.5
Outlying areas	66.6	62.1	32.7	63.4	58.3	69.2	63.5	44.8	68.9	66.1	69.3	64.9	48.2	66.6	68.7
American Samoa	55.7	—	—	—	—	62.1	—	—	—	—	61.6	—	—	—	—
Federated States of Micronesia						43.5	—	—	—	—	50.9	—	—	—	—
Guam	88.9	54.0	—	68.8	—	44.0	54.3	—	75.0	—	56.3	65.1	—	53.3	—
Marshall Islands	—	—	—	—	—	—	—	—	—	—	27.5	—	—	—	—
Northern Marianas	—	—	—	—	—	57.1	—	—	—	—	67.8	—	—	—	—
Palau	—	—	—	—	—	—	—	—	—	—	57.1	—	—	—	—
Puerto Rico	67.1	62.0	32.7	62.7	58.3	69.7	63.5	44.8	68.4	66.1	71.9	64.7	48.2	66.7	68.7
Trust Territories	38.2	—	—	—	—	—	—	—	—	—	—	—	—	—	—
Virgin Islands	76.9	80.5	—	79.2	—	91.8	77.6	—	81.6	—	71.4	80.0	—	75.0	—

[1] Includes degrees which require at least 6 years of college work for completion (including at least 2 years of preprofessional training). See Definitions for details.

—Data not available or not applicable.

SOURCE: U.S. Department of Education, National Center for Education Statistics, Higher Education General Information Survey (HEGIS), "Degrees and Other Formal Awards Conferred" survey, and Integrated Postsecondary Education Data System (IPEDS), "Completions" surveys. (This table was prepared February 1998.)

Table 65.—Percentage distribution of associate degrees conferred by institutions of higher education, by race/ethnicity and state: 1994–95

State or other area	Total	Total resident	Percentage distribution of resident degrees by race/ethnicity							Total, nonresident alien
			Total	White, non-Hispanic	Total, minority	Black, non-Hispanic	Hispanic	American Indian/ Alaskan Native	Asian/ Pacific Islander	
1	2	3	4	5	6	7	8	9	10	11
United States	100.0	98.1	100.0	79.3	20.7	8.9	6.8	1.0	3.9	1.9
Alabama	100.0	99.6	100.0	79.4	20.6	18.0	0.9	0.7	1.0	0.4
Alaska	100.0	98.8	100.0	78.9	21.1	6.9	2.5	9.4	2.4	1.2
Arizona	100.0	99.6	100.0	72.8	27.2	3.1	14.7	6.2	3.2	0.4
Arkansas	100.0	99.4	100.0	89.5	10.5	8.7	0.5	0.5	0.7	0.6
California	100.0	94.1	100.0	58.2	41.8	7.4	18.4	1.2	14.8	5.9
Colorado	100.0	97.3	100.0	81.0	19.0	5.4	10.3	1.5	1.9	2.7
Connecticut	100.0	98.7	100.0	84.3	15.7	8.6	4.8	0.4	2.0	1.3
Delaware	100.0	99.4	100.0	84.7	15.3	11.5	2.5	0.4	1.0	0.6
District of Columbia	100.0	96.2	100.0	19.4	80.6	71.4	4.0	0.6	4.6	3.8
Florida	100.0	98.0	100.0	76.8	23.2	9.2	11.2	0.5	2.4	2.0
Georgia	100.0	98.4	100.0	78.9	21.1	17.9	1.4	0.4	1.4	1.6
Hawaii	100.0	99.9	100.0	30.0	70.0	3.9	2.4	0.3	63.5	0.1
Idaho	100.0	97.1	100.0	96.2	3.8	0.4	1.6	1.0	0.7	2.9
Illinois	100.0	99.4	100.0	80.4	19.6	10.7	5.7	0.3	2.9	0.6
Indiana	100.0	99.1	100.0	91.8	8.2	5.2	1.8	0.5	0.7	0.9
Iowa	100.0	98.9	100.0	96.5	3.5	1.4	0.6	0.3	1.1	1.1
Kansas	100.0	98.7	100.0	85.4	14.6	7.4	3.4	2.4	1.5	1.3
Kentucky	100.0	99.5	100.0	93.3	6.7	5.5	0.5	0.3	0.5	0.5
Louisiana	100.0	99.9	100.0	72.0	28.0	23.2	2.6	0.7	1.5	0.1
Maine	100.0	99.0	100.0	97.5	2.5	0.4	0.3	1.5	0.4	1.0
Maryland	100.0	98.0	100.0	79.7	20.3	15.2	1.6	0.7	2.9	2.0
Massachusetts	100.0	97.6	100.0	87.5	12.5	6.0	3.2	0.4	2.9	2.4
Michigan	100.0	99.2	100.0	87.0	13.0	9.1	1.5	0.9	1.5	0.8
Minnesota	100.0	99.1	100.0	93.5	6.5	2.4	1.1	1.0	2.0	0.9
Mississippi	100.0	99.9	100.0	76.7	23.3	22.3	0.3	0.2	0.5	0.1
Missouri	100.0	99.6	100.0	87.7	12.3	9.6	1.4	0.5	0.9	0.4
Montana	100.0	99.0	100.0	83.6	16.4	0.2	1.0	15.0	0.2	1.0
Nebraska	100.0	99.6	100.0	94.6	5.4	2.0	1.2	1.2	1.0	0.4
Nevada	100.0	97.5	100.0	82.7	17.3	5.0	6.1	1.7	4.4	2.5
New Hampshire	100.0	99.0	100.0	97.7	2.3	1.0	0.5	0.4	0.5	1.0
New Jersey	100.0	96.9	100.0	79.8	20.2	10.2	6.3	0.3	3.4	3.1
New Mexico	100.0	99.4	100.0	57.7	42.3	3.4	29.1	8.5	1.2	0.6
New York	100.0	98.4	100.0	72.9	27.1	13.0	10.2	0.4	3.5	1.6
North Carolina	100.0	99.8	100.0	83.8	16.2	13.2	1.1	1.1	0.9	0.2
North Dakota	100.0	100.0	100.0	90.0	10.0	1.0	0.2	8.1	0.7	—
Ohio	100.0	99.4	100.0	89.8	10.2	7.9	1.0	0.4	0.9	0.6
Oklahoma	100.0	99.4	100.0	80.1	19.9	6.8	2.5	9.0	1.5	0.6
Oregon	100.0	97.8	100.0	90.6	9.4	1.1	2.0	1.7	4.5	2.2
Pennsylvania	100.0	99.5	100.0	89.3	10.7	7.7	1.2	0.2	1.7	0.5
Rhode Island	100.0	97.3	100.0	88.3	11.7	6.2	3.1	0.4	2.1	2.7
South Carolina	100.0	99.3	100.0	78.8	21.2	18.8	0.9	0.4	1.2	0.7
South Dakota	100.0	94.1	100.0	81.5	18.5	0.8	0.6	16.5	0.6	5.9
Tennessee	100.0	99.6	100.0	86.2	13.8	11.8	0.8	0.3	0.9	0.4
Texas	100.0	99.0	100.0	66.8	33.2	10.9	19.1	0.6	2.6	1.0
Utah	100.0	95.7	100.0	93.3	6.7	0.5	2.3	1.6	2.3	4.3
Vermont	100.0	99.6	100.0	96.8	3.2	0.6	0.9	0.6	1.2	0.4
Virginia	100.0	99.5	100.0	80.1	19.9	14.5	1.8	0.3	3.4	0.5
Washington	100.0	94.7	100.0	85.7	14.3	2.9	3.1	1.6	6.7	5.3
West Virginia	100.0	99.2	100.0	96.0	4.0	2.9	0.3	0.2	0.6	0.8
Wisconsin	100.0	99.6	100.0	93.1	6.9	3.6	1.5	0.7	1.1	0.4
Wyoming	100.0	98.9	100.0	92.5	7.5	0.9	3.5	1.6	1.6	1.1
U.S. Service Schools	100.0	98.5	100.0	76.9	23.1	9.5	8.1	1.1	4.3	1.5
Outlying areas	100.0	98.5	100.0	0.9	99.1	0.8	79.5	(1)	18.7	1.5
American Samoa	100.0	100.0	100.0	—	100.0	—	—	—	100.0	—
Federated States of Micronesia	100.0	100.0	100.0	—	100.0	—	—	—	100.0	—
Guam	100.0	89.6	100.0	18.6	81.4	2.3	2.3	2.3	74.4	10.4
Marshall Islands	100.0	100.0	100.0	—	100.0	—	—	—	100.0	—
Northern Marianas	100.0	80.0	100.0	5.6	94.4	—	—	—	94.4	20.0
Palau	100.0	100.0	100.0	—	100.0	—	—	—	100.0	—
Puerto Rico	100.0	99.7	100.0	0.5	99.5	(1)	99.4	—	(1)	0.3
Virgin Islands	100.0	75.0	100.0	9.5	90.5	81.0	9.5	—	—	25.0

1 Less than .05 percent.

—Data not available or not applicable.

NOTE.—Excludes degree recipients whose race was not reported. Because of rounding, details may not add to totals.

SOURCE: U.S. Department of Education, National Center for Education Statistics, Integrated Postsecondary Education Data System (IPEDS), "Completions" survey. (This table was prepared March 1997.)

Table 66.—Percentage distribution of bachelor's degrees conferred by institutions of higher education, by race/ethnicity and state: 1994–95

State or other area	Total	Total resident	Percentage distribution of resident degrees by race/ethnicity							Total, nonresident alien
			Total	White, non-Hispanic	Total, minority	Black, non-Hispanic	Hispanic	American Indian/ Alaskan Native	Asian/ Pacific Islander	
1	2	3	4	5	6	7	8	9	10	11
United States	**100.0**	**96.7**	**100.0**	**81.4**	**18.6**	**7.8**	**4.8**	**0.6**	**5.4**	**3.3**
Alabama	100.0	97.9	100.0	79.2	20.8	18.8	0.7	0.3	1.0	2.1
Alaska	100.0	97.1	100.0	84.2	15.8	3.7	2.0	7.7	2.3	2.9
Arizona	100.0	95.6	100.0	82.5	17.5	2.5	9.4	2.2	3.5	4.4
Arkansas	100.0	96.1	100.0	87.2	12.8	10.4	0.7	0.7	1.0	3.9
California	100.0	95.8	100.0	61.5	38.5	4.8	13.1	1.0	19.6	4.2
Colorado	100.0	98.1	100.0	86.4	13.6	2.7	6.6	1.0	3.3	1.9
Connecticut	100.0	97.2	100.0	88.1	11.9	4.3	3.2	0.3	4.1	2.8
Delaware	100.0	98.7	100.0	87.6	12.4	9.1	1.1	0.2	2.0	1.3
District of Columbia	100.0	90.2	100.0	57.5	42.5	32.1	4.3	0.2	5.9	9.8
Florida	100.0	96.5	100.0	74.2	25.8	10.8	11.6	0.2	3.1	3.5
Georgia	100.0	97.7	100.0	77.2	22.8	18.7	1.4	0.2	2.6	2.3
Hawaii	100.0	87.0	100.0	28.7	71.3	2.0	1.8	0.4	67.2	13.0
Idaho	100.0	96.8	100.0	94.6	5.4	0.8	2.2	0.6	1.8	3.2
Illinois	100.0	97.7	100.0	80.8	19.2	8.8	4.2	0.2	5.9	2.3
Indiana	100.0	97.6	100.0	91.6	8.4	4.0	1.9	0.3	2.1	2.4
Iowa	100.0	95.0	100.0	94.2	5.8	2.5	1.1	0.2	1.9	5.0
Kansas	100.0	95.0	100.0	91.6	8.4	3.3	2.1	0.7	2.3	5.0
Kentucky	100.0	97.6	100.0	93.5	6.5	5.0	0.4	0.2	0.9	2.4
Louisiana	100.0	97.5	100.0	72.9	27.1	22.8	2.1	0.3	1.9	2.5
Maine	100.0	95.6	100.0	95.9	4.1	1.1	0.6	0.5	1.8	4.4
Maryland	100.0	97.1	100.0	74.2	25.8	17.0	2.1	0.3	6.4	2.9
Massachusetts	100.0	94.2	100.0	85.0	15.0	4.2	3.4	0.3	7.1	5.8
Michigan	100.0	96.4	100.0	87.5	12.5	7.1	1.8	0.6	3.0	3.6
Minnesota	100.0	97.1	100.0	94.4	5.6	1.4	0.9	0.6	2.7	2.9
Mississippi	100.0	98.2	100.0	73.7	26.3	25.0	0.4	0.2	0.7	1.8
Missouri	100.0	97.1	100.0	89.3	10.7	6.4	1.7	0.4	2.2	2.9
Montana	100.0	95.2	100.0	94.6	5.4	0.5	1.1	3.0	0.8	4.8
Nebraska	100.0	97.3	100.0	94.1	5.9	2.3	1.6	0.3	1.7	2.7
Nevada	100.0	93.8	100.0	84.7	15.3	4.8	4.8	1.0	4.7	6.2
New Hampshire	100.0	97.7	100.0	94.7	5.3	1.6	1.4	0.6	1.7	2.3
New Jersey	100.0	96.8	100.0	77.7	22.3	8.6	6.7	0.2	6.7	3.2
New Mexico	100.0	98.5	100.0	66.2	33.8	2.5	27.1	2.7	1.5	1.5
New York	100.0	96.7	100.0	75.3	24.7	10.1	6.9	0.3	7.5	3.3
North Carolina	100.0	98.6	100.0	79.7	20.3	16.2	1.1	0.7	2.3	1.4
North Dakota	100.0	97.6	100.0	96.3	3.7	0.5	0.5	1.8	0.9	2.4
Ohio	100.0	97.2	100.0	90.7	9.3	5.9	1.1	0.2	2.1	2.8
Oklahoma	100.0	93.6	100.0	83.1	16.9	5.8	1.9	6.8	2.4	6.4
Oregon	100.0	93.8	100.0	89.5	10.5	1.2	2.5	1.1	5.7	6.2
Pennsylvania	100.0	97.7	100.0	90.5	9.5	4.6	1.3	0.1	3.5	2.3
Rhode Island	100.0	95.7	100.0	89.8	10.2	3.0	2.4	0.2	4.6	4.3
South Carolina	100.0	98.4	100.0	79.9	20.1	17.8	0.8	0.1	1.3	1.6
South Dakota	100.0	97.8	100.0	96.0	4.0	0.6	0.5	2.1	0.8	2.2
Tennessee	100.0	97.9	100.0	86.2	13.8	11.2	0.9	0.2	1.5	2.1
Texas	100.0	97.2	100.0	73.7	26.3	7.1	14.6	0.4	4.1	2.8
Utah	100.0	94.7	100.0	95.1	4.9	0.6	1.8	0.6	1.8	5.3
Vermont	100.0	97.7	100.0	96.0	4.0	1.2	1.2	0.3	1.2	2.3
Virginia	100.0	98.2	100.0	79.1	20.9	14.0	1.7	0.3	5.0	1.8
Washington	100.0	95.4	100.0	84.5	15.5	2.4	2.8	1.3	9.0	4.6
West Virginia	100.0	97.5	100.0	94.4	5.6	3.5	0.6	0.3	1.2	2.5
Wisconsin	100.0	97.2	100.0	93.8	6.2	2.1	1.4	0.5	2.2	2.8
Wyoming	100.0	97.9	100.0	95.8	4.2	0.6	2.4	0.6	0.6	2.1
U.S. Service Schools	100.0	98.7	100.0	83.7	16.3	6.0	4.7	0.9	4.7	1.3
Outlying areas	100.0	99.5	100.0	0.4	99.6	0.9	96.9	—	1.8	0.5
American Samoa	—	—	—	—	—	—	—	—	—	—
Federated States of Micronesia	—	—	—	—	—	—	—	—	—	—
Guam	100.0	98.6	100.0	10.0	90.0	—	1.4	—	88.7	1.4
Marshall Islands	—	—	—	—	—	—	—	—	—	—
Northern Marianas	—	—	—	—	—	—	—	—	—	—
Palau	—	—	—	—	—	—	—	—	—	—
Puerto Rico	100.0	99.9	100.0	0.1	99.9	—	99.9	—	—	0.1
Virgin Islands	100.0	74.4	100.0	9.0	91.0	86.9	2.1	—	2.1	25.6

—Data not available or not applicable.

NOTE.—Excludes degree recipients whose race was not reported. Because of rounding, details may not add to totals.

SOURCE: U.S. Department of Education, National Center for Education Statistics, Integrated Postsecondary Education Data System (IPEDS), "Completions" survey. (This table was prepared March 1997.)

Table 67.—Percentage distribution of master's degrees conferred by institutions of higher education, by race/ethnicity and state: 1994–95

State or other area	Total	Total resident	Percentage distribution of resident degrees by race/ethnicity							Total, nonresident alien
			Total	White, non-Hispanic	Total, minority	Black, non-Hispanic	Hispanic	American Indian/ Alaskan Native	Asian/ Pacific Islander	
1	2	3	4	5	6	7	8	9	10	11
United States	100.0	87.1	100.0	84.1	15.9	6.9	3.7	0.5	4.8	12.9
Alabama	100.0	92.4	100.0	83.4	16.6	12.9	0.9	0.4	2.4	7.6
Alaska	100.0	85.7	100.0	89.7	10.3	2.3	1.3	3.3	3.3	14.3
Arizona	100.0	84.6	100.0	86.5	13.5	2.0	6.5	1.6	3.4	15.4
Arkansas	100.0	90.6	100.0	91.7	8.3	6.6	0.7	0.5	0.5	9.4
California	100.0	85.6	100.0	72.6	27.4	5.2	7.9	0.7	13.6	14.4
Colorado	100.0	91.0	100.0	89.4	10.6	2.3	4.4	0.5	3.4	9.0
Connecticut	100.0	86.6	100.0	90.5	9.5	4.0	2.5	0.2	2.7	13.4
Delaware	100.0	87.3	100.0	85.3	14.7	10.2	2.1	0.7	1.8	12.7
District of Columbia	100.0	78.5	100.0	76.0	24.0	14.5	3.1	0.4	6.0	21.5
Florida	100.0	90.1	100.0	79.2	20.8	8.1	9.8	0.3	2.6	9.9
Georgia	100.0	91.6	100.0	80.8	19.2	14.7	1.5	0.1	3.0	8.4
Hawaii	100.0	89.9	100.0	43.1	56.9	2.5	1.4	0.8	52.2	10.1
Idaho	100.0	92.0	100.0	94.8	5.2	0.3	2.6	0.5	1.7	8.0
Illinois	100.0	88.5	100.0	84.2	15.8	7.9	2.5	0.2	5.3	11.5
Indiana	100.0	86.9	100.0	91.5	8.5	3.8	1.7	0.2	2.8	13.1
Iowa	100.0	82.5	100.0	92.8	7.2	3.4	1.5	0.3	2.0	17.5
Kansas	100.0	82.3	100.0	92.2	7.8	3.0	1.7	0.5	2.6	17.7
Kentucky	100.0	93.2	100.0	94.5	5.5	3.7	0.5	0.1	1.2	6.8
Louisiana	100.0	84.5	100.0	77.2	22.8	15.8	2.0	0.3	4.7	15.5
Maine	100.0	96.9	100.0	96.7	3.3	0.4	0.1	0.3	2.5	3.1
Maryland	100.0	90.1	100.0	81.5	18.5	11.9	1.7	0.3	4.6	9.9
Massachusetts	100.0	83.8	100.0	87.1	12.9	5.3	2.6	0.3	4.8	16.2
Michigan	100.0	85.9	100.0	83.4	16.6	10.1	2.2	0.5	3.8	14.1
Minnesota	100.0	90.7	100.0	94.7	5.3	1.8	0.9	0.5	2.0	9.3
Mississippi	100.0	88.5	100.0	79.2	20.8	18.4	0.5	0.2	1.7	11.5
Missouri	100.0	89.7	100.0	86.3	13.7	8.2	2.4	0.5	2.7	10.3
Montana	100.0	88.4	100.0	96.0	4.0	0.4	0.7	2.4	0.4	11.6
Nebraska	100.0	92.2	100.0	94.2	5.8	1.9	1.6	0.5	1.8	7.8
Nevada	100.0	87.2	100.0	89.5	10.5	1.9	3.3	0.8	4.5	12.8
New Hampshire	100.0	91.5	100.0	95.7	4.3	1.5	1.0	—	1.9	8.5
New Jersey	100.0	85.1	100.0	83.6	16.4	6.2	3.1	0.3	6.7	14.9
New Mexico	100.0	88.6	100.0	77.8	22.2	1.6	17.3	1.9	1.5	11.4
New York	100.0	85.1	100.0	79.6	20.4	9.0	5.3	0.3	5.8	14.9
North Carolina	100.0	92.3	100.0	85.7	14.3	10.4	1.3	0.5	2.1	7.7
North Dakota	100.0	90.1	100.0	93.6	6.4	0.4	1.4	1.9	2.7	9.9
Ohio	100.0	85.2	100.0	89.7	10.3	6.7	1.1	0.3	2.3	14.8
Oklahoma	100.0	76.6	100.0	85.6	14.4	6.3	1.7	3.9	2.4	23.4
Oregon	100.0	84.2	100.0	92.7	7.3	0.9	1.8	0.9	3.8	15.8
Pennsylvania	100.0	87.1	100.0	89.0	11.0	5.7	1.5	0.2	3.6	12.9
Rhode Island	100.0	84.5	100.0	91.8	8.2	2.9	2.0	0.1	3.2	15.5
South Carolina	100.0	87.7	100.0	88.5	11.5	10.0	0.4	0.1	1.1	12.3
South Dakota	100.0	86.3	100.0	96.7	3.3	0.5	0.5	1.8	0.6	13.7
Tennessee	100.0	92.4	100.0	89.0	11.0	8.2	0.9	0.2	1.7	7.6
Texas	100.0	85.7	100.0	79.9	20.1	6.0	9.3	0.5	4.4	14.3
Utah	100.0	88.0	100.0	95.0	5.0	0.6	1.6	0.6	2.1	12.0
Vermont	100.0	91.8	100.0	96.1	3.9	1.9	0.5	0.5	1.0	8.2
Virginia	100.0	93.1	100.0	85.7	14.3	8.5	1.5	0.3	3.9	6.9
Washington	100.0	88.2	100.0	88.1	11.9	2.5	2.7	1.4	5.3	11.8
West Virginia	100.0	91.4	100.0	95.4	4.6	2.8	0.6	0.3	0.9	8.6
Wisconsin	100.0	88.6	100.0	93.6	6.4	2.6	1.3	0.4	2.2	11.4
Wyoming	100.0	86.2	100.0	97.2	2.8	0.6	1.3	0.3	0.6	13.8
U.S. Service Schools	100.0	78.8	100.0	95.7	4.3	2.3	—	0.3	0.3	21.2
Outlying areas	100.0	99.1	100.0	1.4	98.6	2.6	94.7	—	1.2	0.9
American Samoa	—	—	—	—	—	—	—	—	—	—
Federated States of Micronesia	—	—	—	—	—	—	—	—	—	—
Guam	100.0	86.4	100.0	36.8	63.2	2.6	2.6	—	57.9	13.6
Marshall Islands	—	—	—	—	—	—	—	—	—	—
Northern Marianas	—	—	—	—	—	—	—	—	—	—
Palau	—	—	—	—	—	—	—	—	—	—
Puerto Rico	100.0	100.0	100.0	—	100.0	—	100.0	—	—	—
Virgin Islands	100.0	92.2	100.0	18.6	81.4	78.0	3.4	—	—	7.8

—Data not available or not applicable.

NOTE.—Excludes degree recipients whose race was not reported. Because of rounding, details may not add to totals.

SOURCE: U.S. Department of Education, National Center for Education Statistics, Integrated Postsecondary Education Data System (IPEDS), "Completions" survey. (This table was prepared March 1997.)

Table 68.—Percentage distribution of first-professional degrees [1] conferred by institutions of higher education, by race/ethnicity and state: 1994–95

State or other area	Total	Total resident	Percentage distribution of resident degrees by race/ethnicity							Total, nonresident alien
			Total	White, non-Hispanic	Total, minority	Black, non-Hispanic	Hispanic	American Indian/ Alaskan Native	Asian/ Pacific Islander	
1	2	3	4	5	6	7	8	9	10	11
United States	**100.0**	**97.8**	**100.0**	**80.1**	**19.9**	**6.4**	**4.4**	**0.6**	**8.6**	**2.2**
Alabama	100.0	99.6	100.0	87.6	12.4	7.6	0.8	0.5	3.5	0.4
Alaska	—	—	—	—	—	—	—	—	—	—
Arizona	100.0	99.3	100.0	72.7	27.3	5.5	13.1	2.6	6.2	0.7
Arkansas	100.0	100.0	100.0	89.6	10.4	7.1	0.4	0.6	2.3	—
California	100.0	97.6	100.0	68.3	31.7	4.3	7.4	0.7	19.3	2.4
Colorado	100.0	99.1	100.0	83.3	16.7	2.9	7.0	2.2	4.5	0.9
Connecticut	100.0	98.5	100.0	80.2	19.8	6.9	4.1	0.6	8.3	1.5
Delaware	100.0	100.0	100.0	92.5	7.5	3.1	1.7	0.2	2.4	—
District of Columbia	100.0	96.9	100.0	67.8	32.2	17.7	5.4	0.4	8.7	3.1
Florida	100.0	98.8	100.0	76.6	23.4	7.7	11.5	0.3	3.8	1.2
Georgia	100.0	98.3	100.0	82.7	17.3	10.8	2.3	0.1	4.1	1.7
Hawaii	100.0	100.0	100.0	23.1	76.9	0.6	—	0.6	75.6	—
Idaho	100.0	97.0	100.0	93.1	6.9	—	3.8	0.6	2.5	3.0
Illinois	100.0	96.9	100.0	77.3	22.7	5.7	4.1	0.2	12.7	3.1
Indiana	100.0	97.9	100.0	88.8	11.2	4.2	2.2	0.3	4.4	2.1
Iowa	100.0	95.7	100.0	87.9	12.1	4.0	2.7	0.8	4.7	4.3
Kansas	100.0	99.7	100.0	89.1	10.9	3.1	2.8	0.5	4.5	0.3
Kentucky	100.0	98.1	100.0	94.2	5.8	2.4	0.5	0.1	2.8	1.9
Louisiana	100.0	98.8	100.0	77.5	22.5	13.6	3.4	0.2	5.3	1.2
Maine	100.0	99.4	100.0	95.4	4.6	1.1	2.9	—	0.6	0.6
Maryland	100.0	97.9	100.0	72.8	27.2	15.9	1.7	—	9.6	2.1
Massachusetts	100.0	95.7	100.0	82.1	17.9	5.2	3.5	0.3	9.0	4.3
Michigan	100.0	95.5	100.0	81.7	18.3	8.3	3.6	0.6	5.9	4.5
Minnesota	100.0	98.2	100.0	90.1	9.9	3.2	1.8	0.6	4.3	1.8
Mississippi	100.0	99.8	100.0	93.6	6.4	3.3	0.2	0.6	2.3	0.2
Missouri	100.0	97.0	100.0	87.7	12.3	3.0	1.3	0.6	7.3	3.0
Montana	100.0	100.0	100.0	97.3	2.7	—	—	2.7	—	—
Nebraska	100.0	97.8	100.0	89.2	10.8	3.5	2.9	0.5	4.0	2.2
Nevada	100.0	100.0	100.0	84.3	15.7	—	2.0	—	13.7	—
New Hampshire	100.0	99.5	100.0	91.0	9.0	2.1	1.1	0.5	5.3	0.5
New Jersey	100.0	98.7	100.0	74.7	25.3	10.4	5.3	0.1	9.5	1.3
New Mexico	100.0	99.4	100.0	64.9	35.1	1.8	25.1	2.3	5.8	0.6
New York	100.0	98.2	100.0	76.8	23.2	6.0	5.9	0.3	11.0	1.8
North Carolina	100.0	97.2	100.0	84.5	15.5	10.3	0.8	0.5	3.8	2.8
North Dakota	100.0	96.8	100.0	92.3	7.7	—	0.6	4.4	2.8	3.2
Ohio	100.0	99.0	100.0	85.5	14.5	6.9	1.6	0.5	5.5	1.0
Oklahoma	100.0	98.9	100.0	87.8	12.2	2.0	2.0	5.5	2.7	1.1
Oregon	100.0	96.7	100.0	89.4	10.6	1.1	2.1	1.2	6.2	3.3
Pennsylvania	100.0	98.2	100.0	82.7	17.3	5.3	2.7	0.2	9.0	1.8
Rhode Island	100.0	98.7	100.0	62.7	37.3	2.7	2.7	—	32.0	1.3
South Carolina	100.0	98.9	100.0	90.9	9.1	6.4	1.2	—	1.5	1.1
South Dakota	100.0	100.0	100.0	97.1	2.9	—	—	1.5	1.5	—
Tennessee	100.0	97.7	100.0	82.9	17.1	12.1	1.4	0.2	3.4	2.3
Texas	100.0	97.5	100.0	76.5	23.5	5.8	8.7	0.4	8.6	2.5
Utah	100.0	97.0	100.0	91.8	8.2	0.6	2.2	1.3	4.1	3.0
Vermont	100.0	96.7	100.0	90.8	9.2	—	—	2.3	6.9	3.3
Virginia	100.0	99.0	100.0	83.2	16.8	9.3	1.8	0.1	5.6	1.0
Washington	100.0	99.2	100.0	82.2	17.8	3.3	3.8	1.7	9.0	0.8
West Virginia	100.0	99.4	100.0	90.2	9.8	2.0	0.8	1.7	5.3	0.6
Wisconsin	100.0	97.4	100.0	83.4	16.6	4.2	4.7	0.8	6.8	2.6
Wyoming	100.0	100.0	100.0	95.4	4.6	—	3.1	—	1.5	—
U.S. Service Schools	100.0	100.0	100.0	89.8	10.2	1.9	3.2	0.6	4.5	—
Outlying areas	100.0	100.0	100.0	0.6	99.4	—	99.1	—	0.3	—
American Samoa	—	—	—	—	—	—	—	—	—	—
Federated States of Micronesia	—	—	—	—	—	—	—	—	—	—
Guam	—	—	—	—	—	—	—	—	—	—
Marshall Islands	—	—	—	—	—	—	—	—	—	—
Northern Marianas	—	—	—	—	—	—	—	—	—	—
Palau	—	—	—	—	—	—	—	—	—	—
Puerto Rico	100.0	100.0	100.0	0.6	99.4	—	99.1	—	0.3	—
Virgin Islands	—	—	—	—	—	—	—	—	—	—

[1] Includes degrees which require at least 6 years of college work for completion (including at least 2 years of preprofessional training.) See *Definitions* for details.

—Data not available or not applicable.

NOTE.—Excludes degree recipients whose race was not reported. Because of rounding, details may not add to totals.

SOURCE: U.S. Department of Education, National Center for Education Statistics, Integrated Postsecondary Education Data System (IPEDS), "Completions" survey. (This table was prepared March 1997.)

Table 69.—Percentage distribution of doctor's degrees conferred by institutions of higher education, by race/ethnicity and state: 1994–95

State or other area	Total	Total resident	Percentage distribution of resident degrees by race/ethnicity							Total, nonresident alien
			Total	White, non-Hispanic	Total, minority	Black, non-Hispanic	Hispanic	American Indian/ Alaskan Native	Asian/ Pacific Islander	
1	2	3	4	5	6	7	8	9	10	11
United States	100.0	74.1	100.0	83.6	16.4	5.0	3.0	0.4	8.0	25.9
Alabama	100.0	74.5	100.0	89.0	11.0	5.7	0.9	0.3	4.1	25.5
Alaska	100.0	50.0	100.0	100.0	—	—	—	—	—	50.0
Arizona	100.0	78.4	100.0	81.4	18.6	3.3	6.6	1.2	7.5	21.6
Arkansas	100.0	81.3	100.0	84.9	15.1	2.4	—	2.4	10.3	18.7
California	100.0	78.2	100.0	78.8	21.2	3.2	5.0	0.8	12.1	21.8
Colorado	100.0	77.4	100.0	91.9	8.1	1.0	3.4	0.3	3.3	22.6
Connecticut	100.0	71.3	100.0	89.1	10.9	2.8	2.4	0.2	5.5	28.7
Delaware	100.0	79.8	100.0	89.6	10.4	5.2	0.7	0.7	3.7	20.2
District of Columbia	100.0	74.1	100.0	74.9	25.1	19.9	2.0	—	3.2	25.9
Florida	100.0	84.5	100.0	78.1	21.9	10.7	4.9	0.3	6.0	15.5
Georgia	100.0	77.9	100.0	80.4	19.6	10.4	1.8	0.1	7.3	22.1
Hawaii	100.0	100.0	100.0	48.7	51.3	0.6	2.5	—	48.1	—
Idaho	100.0	71.4	100.0	94.5	5.5	—	1.8	—	3.6	28.6
Illinois	100.0	70.4	100.0	84.9	15.1	5.0	2.9	0.4	6.8	29.6
Indiana	100.0	69.9	100.0	86.0	14.0	2.2	1.6	0.7	9.4	30.1
Iowa	100.0	64.6	100.0	82.2	17.8	2.7	1.6	0.2	13.3	35.4
Kansas	100.0	70.5	100.0	86.9	13.1	3.4	2.4	0.3	7.1	29.5
Kentucky	100.0	83.1	100.0	91.8	8.2	2.7	1.5	—	4.0	16.9
Louisiana	100.0	75.5	100.0	82.3	17.7	5.6	1.9	—	10.2	24.5
Maine	100.0	93.1	100.0	92.6	7.4	—	—	—	7.4	6.9
Maryland	100.0	68.4	100.0	80.4	19.6	8.5	1.3	—	9.7	31.6
Massachusetts	100.0	68.5	100.0	85.5	14.5	4.3	3.4	0.1	6.7	31.5
Michigan	100.0	68.4	100.0	80.9	19.1	8.2	3.1	0.2	7.6	31.6
Minnesota	100.0	75.8	100.0	89.6	10.4	3.6	3.3	0.7	2.8	24.2
Mississippi	100.0	72.9	100.0	84.2	15.8	6.9	0.3	—	8.6	27.1
Missouri	100.0	72.5	100.0	88.6	11.4	3.6	0.6	1.0	6.2	27.5
Montana	100.0	81.7	100.0	98.0	2.0	—	—	—	2.0	18.3
Nebraska	100.0	76.1	100.0	90.2	9.8	1.5	0.5	0.5	7.2	23.9
Nevada	100.0	87.0	100.0	88.3	11.7	1.7	1.7	1.7	6.7	13.0
New Hampshire	100.0	73.9	100.0	95.1	4.9	—	1.2	—	3.7	26.1
New Jersey	100.0	71.6	100.0	78.3	21.7	6.0	3.6	0.4	11.7	28.4
New Mexico	100.0	77.1	100.0	82.6	17.4	0.9	14.2	0.5	1.8	22.9
New York	100.0	70.9	100.0	81.4	18.6	4.4	3.0	0.2	10.9	29.1
North Carolina	100.0	80.6	100.0	85.1	14.9	6.6	1.6	0.2	6.6	19.4
North Dakota	100.0	84.5	100.0	87.3	12.7	1.4	2.8	1.4	7.0	15.5
Ohio	100.0	72.0	100.0	81.7	18.3	9.1	1.5	0.5	7.2	28.0
Oklahoma	100.0	77.4	100.0	83.3	16.7	6.9	3.1	2.5	4.1	22.6
Oregon	100.0	70.3	100.0	94.6	5.4	1.0	1.3	0.3	2.9	29.7
Pennsylvania	100.0	70.9	100.0	86.3	13.7	4.6	2.1	0.2	6.7	29.1
Rhode Island	100.0	74.1	100.0	90.9	9.1	1.4	3.3	—	4.3	25.9
South Carolina	100.0	76.3	100.0	88.5	11.5	8.8	1.0	—	1.7	23.7
South Dakota	100.0	90.2	100.0	98.2	1.8	—	—	1.8	—	9.8
Tennessee	100.0	83.9	100.0	87.4	12.6	5.9	0.9	0.2	5.6	16.1
Texas	100.0	72.2	100.0	82.0	18.0	4.4	4.3	0.3	9.1	27.8
Utah	100.0	65.7	100.0	90.9	9.1	1.0	2.0	1.0	5.1	34.3
Vermont	100.0	94.3	100.0	100.0	—	—	—	—	—	5.7
Virginia	100.0	81.2	100.0	86.2	13.8	6.2	1.4	0.1	6.2	18.8
Washington	100.0	77.8	100.0	88.2	11.8	1.0	1.8	0.4	8.6	22.2
West Virginia	100.0	69.2	100.0	97.3	2.7	1.8	—	—	0.9	30.8
Wisconsin	100.0	71.9	100.0	90.0	10.0	1.7	2.1	0.3	5.8	28.1
Wyoming	100.0	76.4	100.0	100.0	—	—	—	—	—	23.6
U.S. Service Schools	100.0	82.4	100.0	57.1	42.9	—	—	—	42.9	17.6
Outlying areas	100.0	100.0	100.0	—	100.0	—	100.0	—	—	—
American Samoa	—	—	—	—	—	—	—	—	—	—
Federated States of Micronesia	—	—	—	—	—	—	—	—	—	—
Guam	—	—	—	—	—	—	—	—	—	—
Marshall Islands	—	—	—	—	—	—	—	—	—	—
Northern Marianas	—	—	—	—	—	—	—	—	—	—
Palau	—	—	—	—	—	—	—	—	—	—
Puerto Rico	100.0	100.0	100.0	—	100.0	—	100.0	—	—	—
Virgin Islands	—	—	—	—	—	—	—	—	—	—

—Data not available or not applicable.

NOTE.—Excludes degree recipients whose race was not reported. Because of rounding, details may not add to totals.

SOURCE: U.S. Department of Education, National Center for Education Statistics, Integrated Postsecondary Education Data System (IPEDS), "Completions" survey. (This table was prepared March 1997.)

Table 70.—Percentage distribution of bachelor's and master's degrees conferred by institutions of higher education, by major field and state: 1994–95

State or other area	Humanities [1]		Social and behavioral sciences [2]		Natural sciences [3]		Computer sciences and engineering [4]		Education		Business and management		Other technical/ professional [5]	
	Bachelor's degrees	Master's degrees	Bachelor's degrees	Master's degrees	Bachelor's degrees	Master's degrees	Bachelor's degrees	Master's degrees	Bachelor's degrees	Master's degrees	Bachelor's degrees	Master's degrees	Bachelor's degrees	Master's degrees
1	2	3	4	5	6	7	8	9	10	11	12	13	14	15
United States	16.6	8.7	17.3	7.2	7.7	3.9	8.8	10.1	9.1	25.5	19.7	23.4	20.8	21.3
Alabama	8.5	3.5	10.3	6.0	6.4	3.4	10.1	9.6	15.7	38.9	24.9	17.1	24.0	21.6
Alaska	13.3	9.3	13.9	8.4	5.7	6.3	6.9	16.4	19.2	34.6	19.6	12.3	21.4	12.7
Arizona	11.5	6.0	13.7	5.0	6.3	3.8	10.9	10.4	12.6	28.9	23.0	30.9	22.0	15.0
Arkansas	9.2	4.9	11.8	6.6	7.1	2.8	7.2	5.7	20.6	37.4	21.0	15.2	23.2	27.3
California	22.8	10.8	21.5	10.7	9.4	3.5	9.1	11.8	3.1	18.7	19.0	24.7	15.0	19.8
Colorado	15.7	7.9	20.2	10.5	9.2	4.4	10.6	16.7	0.3	18.2	22.0	23.4	22.0	18.9
Connecticut	21.1	8.9	25.0	8.1	9.2	4.0	5.8	6.9	3.9	24.2	16.4	29.4	18.6	18.6
Delaware	9.3	14.0	22.1	9.9	6.5	4.1	6.0	7.4	13.8	23.9	22.8	25.9	19.5	14.9
District of Columbia	15.7	9.0	32.7	13.5	6.1	3.2	6.7	13.8	2.2	10.2	19.3	20.9	17.3	29.4
Florida	12.7	4.4	14.5	6.5	5.4	3.2	8.9	10.6	12.0	22.6	23.9	28.6	22.7	24.0
Georgia	13.1	4.7	14.5	4.8	7.5	3.5	10.2	10.2	15.1	32.9	22.1	24.3	17.6	19.6
Hawaii	16.0	9.3	17.2	8.1	5.3	4.1	6.9	5.3	7.2	12.2	31.1	31.8	16.3	29.1
Idaho	10.6	7.8	11.8	9.5	7.7	5.2	8.5	10.1	19.5	39.1	16.1	8.9	25.8	19.4
Illinois	20.3	9.4	15.5	6.1	7.2	4.2	9.1	7.5	10.5	24.4	17.7	28.8	19.6	19.7
Indiana	13.1	11.6	13.6	6.0	6.9	4.4	11.5	9.7	12.0	20.4	19.0	25.3	23.8	22.6
Iowa	15.1	13.4	14.6	5.0	7.6	6.0	7.6	9.4	13.0	25.5	21.8	19.0	20.3	21.6
Kansas	13.1	8.4	13.0	7.2	6.7	4.4	8.6	8.3	14.0	25.5	20.4	20.7	24.2	25.5
Kentucky	11.8	7.8	15.2	5.3	7.4	3.5	7.7	7.6	16.1	42.0	15.8	8.7	26.0	25.2
Louisiana	13.8	10.3	14.0	5.3	6.9	5.0	9.5	10.3	13.2	25.3	18.5	15.9	24.1	27.9
Maine	19.6	6.8	18.1	4.2	7.9	5.5	6.5	4.0	13.2	32.6	13.1	20.4	21.6	26.5
Maryland	23.9	9.8	19.9	11.4	8.4	3.2	8.3	12.9	8.1	19.7	14.8	24.1	16.7	18.9
Massachusetts	18.0	7.3	22.4	6.6	8.1	2.9	9.4	9.7	4.2	25.1	19.3	24.1	18.6	24.3
Michigan	12.2	6.0	14.0	4.7	6.5	3.9	12.3	12.4	8.0	20.0	23.5	33.1	23.5	19.9
Minnesota	18.4	8.4	17.7	7.0	8.5	3.1	6.7	6.7	11.6	31.6	17.8	22.9	19.3	20.4
Mississippi	7.6	6.2	11.9	6.4	8.5	4.8	8.2	9.5	14.7	36.5	22.0	17.9	27.2	18.6
Missouri	11.3	6.6	13.3	11.0	6.5	2.4	8.6	7.0	11.1	18.9	24.3	36.2	24.9	17.8
Montana	12.0	13.4	12.2	7.9	7.1	8.8	11.7	11.1	16.1	25.7	16.9	12.6	24.0	20.5
Nebraska	9.6	6.3	10.9	4.4	8.0	5.2	4.7	6.5	14.6	36.9	24.9	19.1	27.3	21.4
Nevada	9.1	5.4	13.3	5.5	4.8	4.0	6.7	15.4	13.2	37.6	28.8	14.6	24.2	17.6
New Hampshire	16.7	5.0	20.6	4.6	8.3	3.0	7.1	6.6	8.0	24.8	22.8	39.7	16.5	16.4
New Jersey	15.5	6.8	22.1	4.3	8.1	4.8	8.4	14.6	7.9	27.8	20.4	24.3	17.6	17.4
New Mexico	15.8	10.5	12.9	5.4	6.4	6.3	11.8	12.7	15.8	34.4	18.2	12.4	19.2	18.3
New York	20.9	10.4	20.6	6.9	6.9	3.1	8.1	9.0	7.4	29.1	16.2	17.4	19.9	24.1
North Carolina	12.2	9.8	19.2	6.5	10.2	6.2	8.0	8.0	9.6	22.6	18.1	23.3	22.6	23.6
North Dakota	6.4	5.6	8.6	6.2	6.0	9.4	11.7	9.2	15.4	29.8	15.5	7.8	36.5	32.0
Ohio	14.4	11.1	14.8	7.7	6.9	4.8	9.1	9.3	12.1	27.9	19.2	20.6	23.5	18.5
Oklahoma	10.3	6.5	10.6	12.3	6.1	3.3	9.3	10.8	19.6	27.5	20.6	22.9	23.4	16.8
Oregon	21.6	7.7	24.1	7.7	7.7	4.9	6.6	7.4	5.1	36.3	17.9	14.6	17.0	21.4
Pennsylvania	13.9	8.3	16.1	6.0	8.8	3.1	8.9	10.2	11.6	21.2	19.7	26.8	21.0	24.4
Rhode Island	16.1	8.6	16.6	7.4	6.5	6.5	5.3	7.4	7.6	22.4	23.8	27.3	24.1	20.3
South Carolina	13.9	6.8	17.7	4.2	9.3	4.8	6.9	9.6	13.6	32.5	21.9	19.6	16.7	22.4
South Dakota	7.8	5.8	15.3	11.1	8.1	6.6	10.9	12.9	14.4	31.6	15.7	11.9	27.8	20.2
Tennessee	18.0	7.0	16.1	5.8	7.9	4.0	8.5	8.3	6.6	34.3	19.7	20.0	23.2	20.7
Texas	20.3	10.9	14.2	6.3	7.1	4.4	8.3	11.6	3.7	20.9	23.2	25.9	23.2	20.0
Utah	16.8	8.2	18.6	5.6	7.3	4.9	9.7	12.5	13.5	16.2	13.2	32.1	21.0	20.5
Vermont	24.8	21.8	24.5	15.2	7.6	3.9	4.1	2.2	7.6	41.1	11.4	6.0	19.9	9.8
Virginia	19.9	9.5	24.2	7.6	9.5	4.1	8.7	11.8	2.9	30.4	18.4	20.1	16.3	16.6
Washington	23.0	7.1	18.9	7.2	7.5	3.4	7.7	6.5	7.3	41.8	17.1	15.6	18.5	18.5
West Virginia	15.3	6.7	13.0	4.5	6.0	2.4	7.6	12.1	13.6	37.5	18.0	12.5	26.5	24.3
Wisconsin	13.0	6.6	16.2	6.3	7.7	3.7	8.2	8.6	10.7	31.1	21.2	19.2	23.0	24.6
Wyoming	5.5	9.6	13.4	11.4	8.7	17.2	10.0	13.6	23.0	18.2	11.5	5.6	27.9	24.5
U.S. Service Schools	36.2	15.4	17.7	—	10.7	8.1	27.4	19.8	—	—	1.2	19.9	6.7	36.7
Outlying areas	4.3	2.5	7.6	6.1	8.4	3.1	9.9	3.9	13.9	25.5	40.8	29.5	15.1	29.4
American Samoa	—	—	—	—	—	—	—	—	—	—	—	—	—	—
Federated States of Micronesia														
Guam	2.7	—	8.5	—	1.4	22.2	5.1	—	35.9	40.0	28.5	37.8	18.0	—
Marshall Islands	—	—	—	—	—	—	—	—	—	—	—	—	—	—
Northern Marianas	—	—	—	—	—	—	—	—	—	—	—	—	—	—
Palau	—	—	—	—	—	—	—	—	—	—	—	—	—	—
Puerto Rico	4.4	2.7	7.6	6.5	8.5	2.7	10.1	4.1	13.4	24.0	40.9	29.1	15.2	30.8
Virgin Islands	5.6	—	8.2	—	10.3	—	—	—	14.4	53.1	53.8	34.4	7.7	12.5

[1] Includes degrees in area and ethnic studies; foreign languages; letters; liberal/general studies; multi/interdisciplinary studies; philosophy and religion; theology; and visual and performing arts.

[2] Includes psychology and social sciences and history.

[3] Includes life sciences; physical sciences and science technologies; and mathematics.

[4] Includes computer and information sciences; engineering; and engineering technologies.

[5] Includes agriculture and natural resources; architecture and environmental design; communications and communications technologies; health sciences; home economics and vocational home economics; law; library and archival sciences; military sciences; parks and recreation; protective services; precision production; public affairs; construction trades; mechanics and repairers; and transportation and material moving.

—Data not available or not applicable.

NOTE.—Because of rounding, details may not add to totals.

SOURCE: U.S. Department of Education, National Center for Education Statistics, Integrated Postsecondary Education Data System (IPEDS), "Completions" survey. (This table was prepared April 1997.)

Table 71.—Associate degrees conferred by institutions of higher education, by state: 1969–70 to 1994–95

State or other area	1969–70	1970–71	1971–72	1972–73	1973–74	1974–75	1975–76	1976–77	1977–78	1978–79
1	2	3	4	5	6	7	8	9	10	11
United States	206,023	252,311	292,014	316,174	343,924	360,171	391,454	406,377	412,246	402,702
Alabama	1,772	2,115	2,522	3,191	3,161	3,425	4,831	5,191	5,600	4,954
Alaska	79	93	143	239	319	325	370	401	387	388
Arizona	2,289	2,696	3,146	3,199	3,802	4,179	5,149	5,304	5,238	5,357
Arkansas	422	627	656	781	993	1,130	1,148	1,410	1,636	1,599
California	51,302	61,124	66,707	66,223	67,703	68,835	70,355	70,176	66,762	60,057
Colorado	1,895	2,631	3,025	3,144	3,519	3,514	3,908	4,338	4,820	4,652
Connecticut	2,650	3,313	3,592	4,035	4,670	4,785	4,974	5,263	5,400	5,329
Delaware	1,026	1,126	1,265	1,180	1,165	1,193	1,450	1,666	1,664	1,351
District of Columbia	694	834	772	887	892	980	928	1,040	814	695
Florida	17,096	18,840	23,559	24,242	24,395	26,398	28,812	28,089	28,236	29,925
Georgia	3,052	3,673	4,054	4,835	4,963	5,133	5,962	5,913	6,280	5,930
Hawaii	733	967	1,170	1,248	1,427	1,653	1,867	1,976	2,233	2,331
Idaho	1,243	2,118	1,598	1,224	1,355	1,518	1,534	1,616	1,483	1,818
Illinois	8,382	11,340	14,043	17,405	18,846	19,513	19,880	20,930	20,889	20,119
Indiana	1,957	2,337	2,991	3,322	3,684	4,094	4,532	5,085	5,590	5,318
Iowa	2,760	3,366	4,492	4,044	4,109	4,210	4,550	4,647	4,711	4,740
Kansas	2,448	3,473	3,691	3,901	4,016	4,135	4,047	4,271	4,270	4,480
Kentucky	1,440	1,602	1,705	2,273	2,427	3,013	3,290	3,937	5,056	4,539
Louisiana	310	364	433	665	983	1,066	1,661	1,696	1,784	1,851
Maine	336	612	807	1,013	1,221	1,291	1,475	1,690	1,792	1,758
Maryland	2,494	3,427	4,295	5,130	6,626	4,610	7,781	8,028	8,156	7,223
Massachusetts	9,133	10,028	10,777	11,261	12,425	13,448	15,554	16,362	16,351	15,160
Michigan	7,980	9,869	12,200	13,730	15,273	16,223	16,482	17,624	17,890	18,547
Minnesota	4,016	4,232	4,880	5,310	5,590	5,432	5,559	5,699	5,995	5,740
Mississippi	3,258	3,119	3,534	3,720	3,745	3,666	3,919	4,054	3,941	4,039
Missouri	3,239	4,201	4,568	5,150	5,090	5,106	7,564	7,101	6,719	6,658
Montana	125	242	236	368	404	369	513	451	488	464
Nebraska	558	723	1,038	1,190	1,212	1,598	1,805	1,952	2,123	2,148
Nevada	152	144	191	237	357	424	551	539	634	716
New Hampshire	461	664	806	947	1,344	1,350	1,938	1,730	1,949	1,642
New Jersey	3,461	5,897	7,241	7,419	8,652	9,136	9,755	10,421	10,647	9,619
New Mexico	397	448	482	740	852	881	950	1,049	1,255	1,259
New York	27,158	30,975	34,651	37,872	43,973	46,098	47,408	48,572	47,527	48,140
North Carolina	3,210	5,852	6,716	7,490	7,876	8,232	9,926	11,022	11,392	11,088
North Dakota	938	1,028	1,021	1,163	1,297	1,410	1,476	1,550	1,674	1,716
Ohio	4,633	5,684	7,263	9,506	11,489	12,385	12,493	13,548	14,319	14,311
Oklahoma	1,864	2,352	2,836	3,074	3,193	3,400	3,673	4,174	3,947	3,795
Oregon	1,819	2,320	2,966	3,161	3,269	3,253	3,807	4,008	4,330	4,180
Pennsylvania	7,782	9,098	10,720	11,127	11,550	11,642	12,170	12,908	13,816	13,073
Rhode Island	1,041	1,288	1,577	1,499	1,602	2,137	3,089	3,214	2,842	2,782
South Carolina	1,056	1,781	2,467	3,316	3,380	3,966	4,630	5,541	4,893	5,473
South Dakota	311	418	406	497	551	621	743	955	1,055	1,214
Tennessee	1,020	1,721	2,180	2,732	3,125	3,327	3,986	4,254	4,849	5,627
Texas	6,195	7,913	9,573	11,092	13,440	14,860	16,565	17,620	18,308	17,364
Utah	1,332	1,478	1,603	1,624	1,720	2,081	1,975	2,003	2,175	2,184
Vermont	818	885	846	893	1,068	1,217	1,311	1,292	1,306	1,186
Virginia	1,891	2,983	3,754	4,443	5,651	6,382	6,474	6,812	6,715	6,675
Washington	4,098	5,860	7,453	8,317	8,907	8,879	10,083	9,836	10,343	10,095
West Virginia	825	985	1,122	1,389	1,503	1,690	1,953	1,957	2,041	2,104
Wisconsin	2,287	2,797	3,604	4,042	4,451	5,232	5,859	6,374	6,770	7,097
Wyoming	585	648	637	684	659	726	739	758	901	859
U.S. Service Schools	—	—	—	—	—	—	—	330	2,250	3,333
Outlying areas	652	1,230	1,884	1,987	3,143	2,674	3,820	3,457	4,565	4,663
American Samoa	—	—	18	23	58	68	73	87	87	51
Federated States of Micronesia	—	—	—	—	—	—	—	—	—	—
Guam	3	18	34	39	47	46	73	64	78	60
Marshall Islands	—	—	—	—	—	—	—	—	—	—
Northern Marianas	—	—	—	—	—	—	—	—	—	—
Palau	—	—	—	—	—	—	—	—	—	—
Puerto Rico	622	1,186	1,754	1,846	2,951	2,479	3,562	3,155	4,256	4,413
Trust Territories	—	—	42	51	53	49	86	123	121	105
Virgin Islands	27	26	36	28	34	32	26	28	23	34

Table 71.—Associate degrees conferred by institutions of higher education, by state: 1969–70 to 1994–95—Continued

State or other area	1979–80	1980–81	1981–82	1982–83	1983–84	1984–85	1985–86	1986–87	1987–88	1988–89
1	12	13	14	15	16	17	18	19	20	21
United States	400,910	416,377	434,526	449,620	452,240	454,712	446,047	436,304	435,085	436,764
Alabama	5,146	4,839	5,036	4,820	5,067	6,012	6,107	6,212	5,974	5,877
Alaska	453	512	586	676	582	611	686	742	661	606
Arizona	4,834	5,180	5,450	6,156	5,702	5,797	6,657	5,040	5,466	6,167
Arkansas	1,766	1,785	1,935	2,360	2,064	2,119	1,990	2,263	2,412	2,432
California	58,892	59,490	59,246	57,194	54,647	55,181	47,467	46,724	47,503	47,560
Colorado	4,450	4,483	4,616	5,301	5,271	5,235	5,282	5,756	5,825	5,943
Connecticut	5,289	5,381	5,387	5,714	5,995	5,763	5,268	4,842	4,781	4,703
Delaware	1,209	1,195	1,340	1,302	1,291	1,196	1,175	1,153	1,131	1,138
District of Columbia	477	639	574	496	495	629	461	369	391	407
Florida	29,842	31,503	35,190	35,517	32,542	32,767	33,401	29,396	30,666	32,244
Georgia	5,663	5,978	6,633	6,496	6,618	6,400	6,521	6,732	6,653	7,126
Hawaii	2,159	2,140	2,319	2,444	2,504	2,314	2,423	2,350	2,309	2,120
Idaho	1,911	2,015	2,002	2,491	2,579	2,423	2,291	2,297	2,600	2,589
Illinois	19,965	21,213	21,333	22,013	22,771	23,492	24,590	23,961	24,720	23,205
Indiana	5,578	6,932	7,710	9,017	9,223	9,266	8,723	8,681	8,949	8,902
Iowa	5,127	5,603	6,200	6,852	6,831	6,780	7,076	7,236	7,013	8,145
Kansas	4,453	4,564	5,024	4,826	5,331	5,263	5,012	5,410	4,759	5,171
Kentucky	4,756	4,818	5,283	5,338	5,720	6,122	5,713	5,150	4,915	4,938
Louisiana	1,944	2,066	2,215	2,258	2,328	2,645	2,650	2,603	2,532	2,542
Maine	1,825	1,731	1,987	2,029	2,035	2,223	2,084	2,030	2,069	1,884
Maryland	6,952	6,778	7,157	7,020	7,345	7,314	7,038	7,129	7,061	6,938
Massachusetts	14,638	14,632	15,155	15,042	15,072	14,781	14,352	13,616	13,047	13,003
Michigan	18,312	18,938	20,351	21,918	22,702	22,859	21,384	21,834	19,249	20,351
Minnesota	6,257	6,590	7,043	6,774	6,921	6,942	6,443	7,527	7,591	6,947
Mississippi	4,327	4,190	4,448	4,764	4,624	4,472	4,316	4,332	4,448	4,810
Missouri	5,983	6,344	6,644	6,993	7,106	7,207	6,791	6,492	6,711	6,898
Montana	425	534	697	715	697	719	663	734	714	683
Nebraska	2,244	2,331	2,531	2,813	2,986	2,883	2,805	2,918	2,546	2,734
Nevada	582	641	778	911	1,074	927	936	884	857	885
New Hampshire	1,761	1,980	2,348	2,612	2,477	2,685	2,491	2,372	2,377	2,366
New Jersey	9,889	9,834	9,927	10,231	10,374	10,126	9,869	9,534	9,379	9,337
New Mexico	1,386	1,347	1,478	1,672	1,882	1,743	1,779	1,766	1,760	1,698
New York	47,405	48,679	48,595	49,607	50,865	50,006	49,694	47,956	46,888	46,957
North Carolina	10,909	10,608	10,934	10,960	11,308	11,053	10,854	10,655	10,333	9,894
North Dakota	1,621	1,695	1,711	1,724	1,734	1,755	1,941	1,980	1,886	1,797
Ohio	14,214	15,455	17,112	18,225	18,880	18,940	18,351	17,850	17,656	18,827
Oklahoma	3,850	3,947	4,096	4,184	4,277	4,442	5,607	5,338	5,341	6,172
Oregon	4,076	4,309	4,784	5,229	5,184	5,157	4,872	4,673	4,823	4,456
Pennsylvania	13,005	16,278	17,175	18,585	19,049	19,032	18,612	18,629	18,283	17,108
Rhode Island	2,956	3,150	3,161	3,385	3,588	3,461	3,642	3,822	3,659	3,663
South Carolina	6,194	5,501	5,385	5,880	5,831	5,245	5,114	4,766	4,776	4,949
South Dakota	1,170	1,272	1,279	1,331	1,369	1,045	1,081	793	831	789
Tennessee	5,379	5,659	6,273	6,816	6,470	6,503	5,937	5,568	5,906	5,605
Texas	18,043	17,626	17,751	19,231	20,248	21,521	20,865	20,816	21,993	22,595
Utah	2,182	2,390	2,481	3,156	2,955	2,897	2,941	3,151	3,552	3,572
Vermont	1,148	1,285	1,249	1,141	1,232	1,238	1,179	1,128	1,149	1,136
Virginia	6,460	6,755	6,856	7,604	7,451	7,381	6,801	7,037	8,192	7,438
Washington	10,586	11,097	11,600	10,469	10,853	10,421	11,841	12,278	11,664	12,284
West Virginia	2,179	2,386	2,377	2,534	2,527	2,881	2,791	2,563	2,419	2,640
Wisconsin	6,525	7,222	7,774	8,735	9,355	9,171	8,921	8,723	8,570	8,614
Wyoming	794	838	951	1,039	1,188	1,163	1,313	1,309	1,386	1,507
U.S. Service Schools ...	3,719	4,019	4,359	5,020	5,020	6,504	9,246	9,184	8,709	6,412
Outlying areas	4,800	4,533	5,474	5,674	5,611	4,375	5,211	4,508	5,556	4,894
American Samoa	82	97	71	106	125	125	84	—	—	89
Federated States of Micronesia	—	—	—	—	—	—	—	—	—	44
Guam	34	18	37	54	65	51	66	67	64	65
Marshall Islands	—	—	—	—	—	—	—	—	—	—
Northern Marianas	—	—	—	—	14	28	27	15	23	23
Palau	—	—	—	—	—	—	—	—	—	16
Puerto Rico	4,541	4,298	5,129	5,275	5,306	4,006	4,925	4,350	5,324	4,601
Trust Territories	103	68	189	189.00	54	87	47	10	71	—
Virgin Islands	40	52	48	50	47	78	62	66	74	56

Table 71.—Associate degrees conferred by institutions of higher education, by state: 1969–70 to 1994–95—Continued

State or other area	1989–90	1990–91	1991–92	1992–93	1993–94	1994–95	Percentage change			
							1969–70 to 1994–95	1984–85 to 1989–90	1989–90 to 1994–95	1984–85 to 1994–95
1	22	23	24	25	26	27	28	29	30	31
United States	455,102	481,720	504,231	514,756	530,632	539,691	162.0	0.1	18.6	18.7
Alabama	6,265	6,584	7,257	7,484	7,781	7,835	342.2	4.2	25.1	30.3
Alaska	603	636	753	940	1,002	960	1,115.2	–1.3	59.2	57.1
Arizona	6,361	6,066	6,776	6,928	6,796	6,809	197.5	9.7	7.0	17.5
Arkansas	2,605	2,741	2,592	2,618	2,808	2,492	490.5	22.9	–4.3	17.6
California	48,353	56,943	53,008	54,688	56,417	60,503	17.9	–12.4	25.1	9.6
Colorado	6,144	6,163	6,301	6,294	6,746	6,984	268.5	17.4	13.7	33.4
Connecticut	4,721	4,758	4,994	5,094	5,081	4,800	81.1	–18.1	1.7	–16.7
Delaware	1,288	1,304	1,152	1,313	1,191	1,141	11.2	7.7	–11.4	–4.6
District of Columbia	403	325	399	435	305	205	–70.5	–35.9	–49.1	–67.4
Florida	33,756	35,876	39,062	39,405	40,620	40,733	138.3	3.0	20.7	24.3
Georgia	7,389	7,938	8,480	8,316	9,419	9,143	199.6	15.5	23.7	42.9
Hawaii	2,247	2,317	2,466	2,515	2,391	2,387	225.6	–2.9	6.2	3.2
Idaho	2,979	3,117	3,243	3,544	4,068	4,181	236.4	22.9	40.3	72.6
Illinois	23,327	24,464	26,276	27,620	27,022	27,126	223.6	–0.7	16.3	15.5
Indiana	8,947	8,851	8,770	9,236	9,589	10,063	414.2	–3.4	12.5	8.6
Iowa	7,888	8,079	8,859	8,344	8,314	8,191	196.8	16.3	3.8	20.8
Kansas	5,547	5,821	6,371	6,312	6,716	6,961	184.4	5.4	25.5	32.3
Kentucky	5,387	5,759	5,930	6,546	6,416	6,446	347.6	–12.0	19.7	5.3
Louisiana	2,642	2,866	2,660	2,865	3,303	3,369	986.8	–0.1	27.5	27.4
Maine	1,859	2,118	2,471	2,433	2,463	2,445	627.7	–16.4	31.5	10.0
Maryland	7,429	7,656	8,166	8,425	8,292	8,632	246.1	1.6	16.2	18.0
Massachusetts	13,409	13,330	13,434	13,354	13,084	12,808	40.2	–9.3	–4.5	–13.3
Michigan	21,156	22,422	23,108	24,231	24,215	22,696	184.4	–7.5	7.3	–0.7
Minnesota	7,674	8,008	9,183	9,766	9,708	12,216	204.2	10.5	59.2	76.0
Mississippi	4,995	5,119	5,431	5,575	5,538	5,519	69.4	11.7	10.5	23.4
Missouri	6,903	7,563	7,818	8,023	8,424	8,928	175.6	–4.2	29.3	23.9
Montana	782	890	883	801	1,031	1,329	963.2	8.8	69.9	84.8
Nebraska	2,678	2,965	3,730	2,494	3,189	3,365	503.0	–7.1	25.7	16.7
Nevada	949	1,013	1,171	1,311	1,295	1,411	828.3	2.4	48.7	52.2
New Hampshire	2,512	2,657	2,943	3,343	3,350	3,530	665.7	–6.4	40.5	31.5
New Jersey	9,935	10,703	12,287	12,299	12,625	12,855	271.4	–1.9	29.4	27.0
New Mexico	2,455	2,479	2,874	3,007	3,065	3,277	725.4	40.8	33.5	88.0
New York	48,956	50,865	53,043	53,393	53,784	54,671	101.3	–2.1	11.7	9.3
North Carolina	10,647	11,469	11,865	12,164	13,621	14,107	339.5	–3.7	32.5	27.6
North Dakota	1,875	1,784	1,615	1,696	1,718	1,738	85.3	6.8	–7.3	–1.0
Ohio	17,552	18,446	19,589	19,881	20,117	20,183	335.6	–7.3	15.0	6.6
Oklahoma	6,204	6,375	6,175	6,304	6,689	7,011	276.1	39.7	13.0	57.8
Oregon	4,769	4,844	4,829	5,676	5,986	5,813	219.6	–7.5	21.9	12.7
Pennsylvania	17,763	19,884	20,932	20,091	21,172	20,569	164.3	–6.7	15.8	8.1
Rhode Island	3,495	3,930	4,043	4,156	3,941	3,890	273.7	1.0	11.3	12.4
South Carolina	5,202	5,097	6,191	5,953	6,218	6,165	483.8	–0.8	18.5	17.5
South Dakota	791	906	798	848	873	834	168.2	–24.3	5.4	–20.2
Tennessee	5,642	6,717	6,661	6,801	6,894	6,721	558.9	–13.2	19.1	3.4
Texas	22,834	21,521	23,056	24,804	25,787	25,800	316.5	6.1	13.0	19.9
Utah	3,750	4,099	4,556	4,839	5,318	5,812	336.3	29.4	55.0	100.6
Vermont	1,262	1,227	1,317	1,264	1,268	1,311	60.3	1.9	3.9	5.9
Virginia	8,378	8,883	9,735	10,232	11,339	10,882	475.5	13.5	29.9	47.4
Washington	14,319	15,246	16,436	16,619	18,365	19,102	366.1	37.4	33.4	83.3
West Virginia	2,841	2,632	2,803	2,919	3,012	2,840	244.2	–1.4	(1)	–1.4
Wisconsin	8,537	9,049	9,622	9,481	9,394	9,262	305.0	–6.9	8.5	1.0
Wyoming	1,629	1,633	1,891	1,850	1,862	1,663	184.3	40.1	2.1	43.0
U.S. Service Schools ...	9,068	9,582	10,226	10,226	11,010	11,977	—	39.4	32.1	84.1
Outlying areas	4,399	4,577	4,473	4,342	4,125	4,403	575.3	0.5	0.1	0.6
American Samoa	87	87	41	43	44	419	—	–30.4	381.6	235.2
Federated States of Micronesia	58	62	81	56	105	163	—	—	181.0	—
Guam	51	25	52	36	25	48	1,500.0	—	–5.9	–5.9
Marshall Islands	—	—	—	35	40	40	—	—	—	—
Northern Marianas	25	42	52	87	69	180	—	–10.7	620.0	542.9
Palau	6	—	—	4	13	21	—	—	250.0	—
Puerto Rico	4,119	4,300	4,180	4,017	3,769	3,476	458.8	2.8	–15.6	–13.2
Trust Territories	—	—	—	—	—	—	—	—	—	—
Virgin Islands	53	61	67	64	60	56	107.4	–32.1	5.7	–28.2

[1] Less than 0.05 percent.
—Data not available or not applicable.

NOTE.—Some data have been revised from previously published figures.

SOURCE: U.S. Department of Education, National Center for Education Statistics, Higher Education General Information Survey (HEGIS), "Degrees and Other Formal Awards Conferred" surveys, and Integrated Postsecondary Education Data System, "Completions" surveys. (This table was prepared February 1998.)

Table 72.—Bachelor's degrees conferred by institutions of higher education, by state: 1969–70 to 1994–95

State or other area	1969–70	1970–71	1971–72	1972–73	1973–74	1974–75	1975–76	1976–77	1977–78	1978–79
1	2	3	4	5	6	7	8	9	10	11
United States	792,316	839,730	887,273	922,362	945,776	922,933	925,746	919,549	921,204	921,390
Alabama	12,868	13,000	13,792	13,790	14,365	14,236	14,792	15,280	16,100	16,345
Alaska	315	369	520	508	638	610	475	423 357	370	
Arizona	7,918	8,291	7,907	8,351	8,672	8,994	9,230	9,354	9,486	9,905
Arkansas	7,287	7,284	7,111	7,124	7,035	6,997	6,959	6,581	6,522	6,708
California	67,814	73,814	78,669	82,741	86,185	82,879	83,562	82,811	84,275	82,608
Colorado	11,923	12,401	13,432	13,536	14,041	14,073	14,176	14,208	14,480	13,864
Connecticut	10,918	11,499	12,565	13,617	14,257	13,647	13,628	13,396	13,433	12,701
Delaware	1,533	1,602	2,103	2,417	2,551	2,776	2,808	3,016	2,997	3,053
District of Columbia	5,854	5,997	6,377	6,535	6,864	6,641	6,989	6,611	6,727	6,833
Florida	19,773	20,933	22,817	24,252	26,837	26,313	27,540	28,300	27,770	28,523
Georgia	13,911	15,117	15,913	16,032	16,921	16,759	16,791	16,377	16,351	16,135
Hawaii	2,612	3,051	3,472	3,546	3,860	3,924	3,628	3,783	3,765	3,362
Idaho	2,743	2,744	2,950	2,945	3,038	2,805	2,847	2,754	2,877	2,694
Illinois	38,600	42,016	45,245	46,949	47,602	44,577	44,795	45,204	43,610	43,619
Indiana	22,202	23,660	24,215	26,164	25,621	24,480	24,080	23,794	23,607	23,677
Iowa	14,307	14,784	15,054	14,453	14,502	13,480	13,423	13,047	13,199	13,378
Kansas	12,161	12,360	12,811	12,896	12,638	12,198	11,598	11,834	11,621	11,786
Kentucky	12,018	12,459	12,309	12,716	12,539	12,000	11,819	11,337	11,226	11,220
Louisiana	13,617	14,051	14,259	15,228	15,975	16,061	15,969	15,370	15,307	14,765
Maine	4,118	4,482	4,390	4,602	4,757	4,690	4,716	4,600	4,679	4,559
Maryland	12,176	12,598	13,815	14,792	16,181	16,486	16,098	16,337	16,401	15,550
Massachusetts	29,455	30,632	33,067	34,942	36,465	36,569	37,459	37,405	38,434	37,803
Michigan	35,281	36,774	37,791	39,276	38,413	36,813	37,026	35,941	36,279	36,875
Minnesota	18,040	18,674	19,447	20,066	19,395	18,429	18,263	18,163	18,185	18,467
Mississippi	8,784	8,816	9,054	9,215	9,843	9,643	9,061	9,055	8,784	8,687
Missouri	18,201	19,378	20,279	21,457	21,751	21,222	21,265	21,501	21,659	21,900
Montana	3,746	3,991	4,120	4,260	3,873	3,722	3,842	3,660	3,577	3,812
Nebraska	9,417	9,876	9,564	9,496	9,146	8,381	7,744	7,478	7,657	7,398
Nevada	1,006	1,253	1,346	1,382	1,393	1,428	1,490	1,370	1,543	1,391
New Hampshire	4,180	4,328	4,701	4,925	5,259	5,023	5,254	5,300	6,177	5,418
New Jersey	18,007	19,690	22,194	23,760	24,812	25,188	25,812	25,534	25,086	25,233
New Mexico	4,107	4,365	4,765	5,031	5,245	4,751	5,078	4,742	4,672	4,652
New York	67,481	72,235	78,805	82,167	83,907	82,932	85,547	86,844	85,221	85,601
North Carolina	18,587	19,847	20,776	22,094	22,943	23,406	23,410	23,244	23,792	23,640
North Dakota	3,867	4,017	3,963	4,028	4,007	3,627	3,541	3,367	3,436	3,613
Ohio	41,811	44,313	46,786	47,475	47,710	45,327	42,968	41,147	40,394	40,650
Oklahoma	12,012	12,488	13,164	13,457	13,873	13,494	13,328	12,778	12,744	12,855
Oregon	9,923	10,069	10,388	10,416	10,810	10,118	10,455	10,626	10,329	10,014
Pennsylvania	47,315	50,074	52,618	56,262	56,989	55,545	54,571	53,786	53,514	54,213
Rhode Island	4,793	5,107	5,605	6,261	6,307	6,479	6,495	6,545	6,859	7,187
South Carolina	7,835	8,039	8,715	9,525	10,378	10,796	11,136	11,168	11,343	11,406
South Dakota	4,636	4,796	4,816	4,976	4,852	4,165	3,695	3,794	3,750	3,689
Tennessee	15,916	16,575	17,211	17,723	17,985	17,623	17,807	17,806	17,801	17,599
Texas	40,178	43,329	45,856	47,889	49,399	50,231	51,439	51,699	52,306	53,656
Utah	8,837	9,386	9,595	9,279	9,496	9,154	8,629	9,301	8,503	9,254
Vermont	2,885	3,045	3,345	3,553	3,821	3,781	4,130	4,001	3,768	3,782
Virginia	13,744	14,762	15,733	16,725	18,372	19,056	20,069	20,017	20,709	21,251
Washington	14,614	16,556	17,294	16,880	17,178	16,929	16,892	16,297	16,139	16,053
West Virginia	7,996	7,901	8,077	8,555	8,959	8,413	7,834	7,708	7,638	7,382
Wisconsin	20,936	22,700	23,908	23,390	23,520	21,735	21,161	20,803	21,347	21,734
Wyoming	1,357	1,315	1,389	1,444	1,436	1,306	1,281	1,283	1,359	1,289
U.S. Service Schools ...	2,701	2,887	3,175	3,259	3,160	3,021	3,141	2,769	3,409	3,231
Outlying areas	5,754	6,373	6,829	7,905	8,593	8,724	8,686	8,671 8,994	9,944	
American Samoa	—	—	—	—	—	—	—	—	—	—
Federated States of Micronesia	—	—	—	—	—	—	—	—	—	—
Guam	79	97	157	134	190	169	249	192 180	183	
Marshall Islands	—	—	—	—	—	—	—	—	—	—
Northern Marianas	—	—	—	—	—	—	—	—	—	—
Palau	—	—	—	—	—	—	—	—	—	—
Puerto Rico	5,646	6,228	6,601	7,691	8,303	8,478	8,355	8,399	8,741	9,689
Trust Territories	—	—	—	—	—	—	—	—	—	—
Virgin Islands	29	48	71	80	100	77	82	80	73	72

Table 72.—Bachelor's degrees conferred by institutions of higher education, by state: 1969–70 to 1994–95—Continued

State or other area	1979–80	1980–81	1981–82	1982–83	1983–84	1984–85	1985–86	1986–87	1987–88	1988–89
1	12	13	14	15	16	17	18	19	20	21
United States	929,417	935,140	952,998	969,510	974,309	979,477	987,823	991,264	994,829	1,018,755
Alabama	16,306	16,534	16,623	16,217	15,909	16,334	16,068	15,975	16,270	16,508
Alaska	419	465	535	671	685	820	786	898	927	1,011
Arizona	10,187	10,826	11,279	11,797	11,370	12,236	11,987	12,287	12,348	13,767
Arkansas	6,965	6,955	7,243	7,282	7,431	7,153	7,283	7,036	7,017	7,300
California	83,095	81,848	84,376	85,358	87,683	87,397	88,615	90,003	88,553	91,498
Colorado	14,128	14,677	15,226	15,175	14,886	14,921	15,095	15,218	15,144	15,561
Connecticut	13,011	13,312	13,215	13,120	13,308	13,516	14,017	13,499	13,680	13,525
Delaware	3,276	3,194	3,224	3,281	3,324	3,137	3,198	3,246	3,527	3,414
District of Columbia	6,532	6,807	6,785	6,914	6,774	7,093	6,875	6,711	6,933	7,482
Florida	28,629	29,988	28,556	31,184	30,102	31,289	32,056	31,430	32,406	34,244
Georgia	16,579	17,014	17,325	17,920	17,741	18,401	18,734	19,103	19,481	19,883
Hawaii	3,311	3,312	3,349	3,392	3,527	3,447	3,539	3,701	3,724	3,628
Idaho	2,907	2,759	2,883	3,133	3,086	2,986	3,086	3,035	3,043	3,017
Illinois	44,336	44,653	45,361	46,421	47,606	46,553	47,418	47,636	47,958	48,865
Indiana	24,224	24,834	25,682	26,470	26,001	26,390	26,627	26,623	26,408	26,874
Iowa	13,511	14,441	14,463	14,494	14,854	15,268	15,844	16,450	16,747	16,859
Kansas	11,706	11,672	11,961	12,483	12,335	12,179	12,016	11,714	11,891	12,198
Kentucky	11,491	11,509	11,586	11,591	11,717	11,572	11,773	11,707	12,074	12,337
Louisiana	14,774	14,821	15,313	15,533	16,020	16,070	16,535	16,221	16,367	16,210
Maine	4,848	4,817	4,678	4,879	4,882	5,019	5,178	5,122	5,168	5,173
Maryland	15,698	15,859	16,111	16,056	15,840	15,690	16,582	16,760	17,334	17,928
Massachusetts	38,285	38,792	39,916	39,171	40,145	40,458	40,383	41,570	41,801	42,500
Michigan	37,589	38,647	38,919	39,083	39,244	38,132	37,468	38,181	38,939	40,860
Minnesota	18,634	19,392	19,748	20,664	20,555	20,673	20,229	20,669	21,167	21,901
Mississippi	8,805	8,982	8,577	9,020	8,987	8,644	8,911	9,173	8,486	8,227
Missouri	21,655	21,858	22,645	22,677	22,865	22,951	23,309	23,250	23,024	23,700
Montana	3,880	3,815	3,963	4,065	4,194	4,324	4,356	4,140	4,170	3,887
Nebraska	7,553	7,404	7,767	8,054	8,151	8,330	8,331	8,410	8,288	8,406
Nevada	1,423	1,477	1,532	1,799	1,949	1,962	1,943	1,929	1,943	2,023
New Hampshire	5,751	6,025	6,111	6,701	6,316	6,313	6,558	6,770	6,803	6,948
New Jersey	24,431	24,474	24,892	25,507	24,068	23,764	23,450	23,328	22,327	22,898
New Mexico	4,768	4,585	4,562	4,547	4,467	4,674	4,725	4,548	4,778	4,959
New York	85,140	83,783	86,140	86,364	87,094	87,603	87,185	86,632	87,981	88,573
North Carolina	23,689	23,712	24,113	24,448	25,225	25,008	25,125	24,919	25,688	26,981
North Dakota	3,702	3,795	3,755	3,936	4,072	4,189	4,263	4,209	4,110	4,287
Ohio	40,707	41,300	42,197	42,930	42,527	43,073	43,115	43,975	43,909	45,141
Oklahoma	12,741	12,818	12,419	12,404	12,598	13,287	13,498	13,545	13,173	13,617
Oregon	10,448	9,783	10,946	11,394	11,104	10,842	10,938	10,922	11,251	11,823
Pennsylvania	55,003	54,446	55,487	56,972	56,337	56,871	56,669	57,147	58,348	58,890
Rhode Island	7,058	7,263	7,500	7,588	7,701	7,636	7,809	7,737	7,934	8,493
South Carolina	11,924	11,358	11,590	12,289	12,387	12,422	12,814	12,547	12,136	12,524
South Dakota	3,948	3,868	3,909	4,160	4,089	4,125	3,979	3,738	3,627	3,689
Tennessee	17,894	17,409	17,685	16,977	17,218	17,029	17,512	17,329	17,175	17,398
Texas	53,604	53,589	53,562	54,895	55,277	56,505	57,963	57,438	55,575	56,987
Utah	9,207	9,236	9,653	9,861	10,259	10,159	10,516	11,085	10,820	10,682
Vermont	3,968	3,971	4,285	3,885	3,902	4,076	3,999	4,068	4,273	4,193
Virginia	21,736	22,078	22,778	23,090	23,696	23,958	24,391	24,010	25,149	26,028
Washington	16,216	16,648	18,159	18,139	17,985	17,549	17,331	17,767	17,552	18,118
West Virginia	7,423	7,720	7,465	7,490	7,676	7,897	7,862	7,518	7,260	7,033
Wisconsin	21,807	22,026	22,371	23,186	23,827	24,151	24,531	25,322	25,057	25,604
Wyoming	1,332	1,320	1,328	1,381	1,487	1,608	1,657	1,625	1,631	1,647
U.S. Service Schools ...	3,163	3,269	3,250	3,462	3,826	3,793	3,691	3,388	3,454	3,456
Outlying areas	10,834	11,737	11,045	11,169	12,036	11,400	12,381	12,268	12,671	12,535
American Samoa	—	—	—	—	—	—	—	—	—	—
Federated States of Micronesia	—	—	—	—	—	—	—	—	—	—
Guam	191	163	183	181	177	205	175	171	227	186
Marshall Islands	—	—	—	—	—	—	—	—	—	—
Northern Marianas	—	—	—	—	—	—	—	—	—	—
Palau	—	—	—	—	—	—	—	—	—	—
Puerto Rico	10,560	11,492	10,777	10,871	11,737	11,058	12,108	11,952	12,298	12,231
Trust Territories	—	—	—	—	—	—	—	—	—	—
Virgin Islands	83	82	85	117	122	137	98	145	146	118

Table 72.—Bachelor's degrees conferred by institutions of higher education, by state: 1969-70 to 1994-95—Continued

State or other area	1989–90	1990–91	1991–92	1992–93	1993–94	1994–95	Percentage change 1969–70 to 1994–95	1984–85 to 1989–90	1989–90 to 1994–95	1984–85 to 1994–95
1	22	23	24	25	26	27	28	29	30	31
United States	1,051,344	1,094,538	1,136,553	1,165,178	1,169,275	1,160,134	46.4	7.3	10.3	18.4
Alabama	17,111	18,308	19,628	20,525	21,150	19,924	54.8	4.8	16.4	22.0
Alaska	1,043	1,148	1,114	1,260	1,396	1,526	384.4	27.2	46.3	86.1
Arizona	14,265	18,068	14,680	15,807	16,093	16,175	104.3	16.6	13.4	32.2
Arkansas	7,486	7,729	8,133	8,449	8,549	8,623	18.3	4.7	15.2	20.6
California	98,157	100,484	107,462	111,010	111,848	109,714	61.8	12.3	11.8	25.5
Colorado	16,435	16,728	17,646	18,925	18,954	19,929	67.1	10.1	21.3	33.6
Connecticut	14,179	14,630	15,019	14,931	13,929	13,972	28.0	4.9	-1.5	3.4
Delaware	3,539	4,008	4,121	4,119	4,187	4,466	191.3	12.8	26.2	42.4
District of Columbia	7,483	7,614	8,206	8,095	7,184	7,027	20.0	5.5	-6.1	-0.9
Florida	35,600	38,927	41,090	43,212	44,075	44,924	127.2	13.8	26.2	43.6
Georgia	21,415	22,322	23,493	25,390	26,283	26,312	89.1	16.4	22.9	43.0
Hawaii	3,720	3,711	3,821	4,186	4,314	4,500	72.3	7.9	21.0	30.5
Idaho	3,169	3,136	3,529	3,923	4,203	4,235	54.4	6.1	33.6	41.8
Illinois	49,757	50,508	53,263	51,482	52,330	52,270	35.4	6.9	5.1	12.3
Indiana	27,668	28,886	30,770	31,453	30,769	30,253	36.3	4.8	9.3	14.6
Iowa	16,129	16,996	17,162	17,598	17,846	17,421	21.8	5.6	8.0	14.1
Kansas	12,428	13,035	13,690	14,282	14,599	14,594	20.0	2.0	17.4	19.8
Kentucky	12,225	12,973	13,861	14,396	14,629	14,570	21.2	5.6	19.2	25.9
Louisiana	15,905	16,309	16,985	17,825	17,787	17,920	31.6	-1.0	12.7	11.5
Maine	4,944	5,227	5,778	5,976	5,953	5,893	43.1	-1.5	19.2	17.4
Maryland	18,493	19,235	20,324	20,427	20,720	19,908	63.5	17.9	7.7	26.9
Massachusetts	43,491	44,487	45,051	42,747	42,351	40,279	36.7	7.5	-7.4	-0.4
Michigan	42,428	44,213	44,789	45,711	44,925	44,317	25.6	11.3	4.5	16.2
Minnesota	22,881	23,619	24,453	24,762	24,746	24,068	33.4	10.7	5.2	16.4
Mississippi	8,808	9,106	10,054	10,673	10,524	10,335	17.7	1.9	17.3	19.6
Missouri	24,651	24,917	26,552	26,954	27,494	27,931	53.5	7.4	13.3	21.7
Montana	3,862	3,872	4,161	4,194	4,357	4,354	16.2	-10.7	12.7	0.7
Nebraska	8,677	8,945	9,417	9,522	10,087	10,105	7.3	4.2	16.5	21.3
Nevada	2,235	2,373	2,694	3,029	3,276	3,371	235.1	13.9	50.8	71.8
New Hampshire	6,745	7,128	7,430	7,524	7,546	7,395	76.9	6.8	9.6	17.1
New Jersey	22,859	23,624	24,207	25,185	25,234	24,627	36.8	-3.8	7.7	3.6
New Mexico	5,022	5,242	5,501	5,667	6,118	6,363	54.9	7.4	26.7	36.1
New York	89,567	92,629	95,611	97,104	93,134	93,549	38.6	2.2	4.4	6.8
North Carolina	27,288	28,795	30,826	31,852	32,730	32,321	73.9	9.1	18.4	29.2
North Dakota	4,202	4,487	4,755	4,555	4,558	4,440	14.8	0.3	5.7	6.0
Ohio	47,044	48,799	50,557	51,487	50,982	49,588	18.6	9.2	5.4	15.1
Oklahoma	13,601	14,067	14,542	15,002	15,734	15,307	27.4	2.4	12.5	15.2
Oregon	12,586	12,963	13,375	13,139	13,272	12,917	30.2	16.1	2.6	19.1
Pennsylvania	60,495	62,184	64,304	65,073	64,326	63,027	33.2	6.4	4.2	10.8
Rhode Island	8,789	9,153	9,249	9,341	9,145	8,978	87.3	15.1	2.2	17.6
South Carolina	13,215	14,250	14,219	15,254	15,318	15,176	93.7	6.4	14.8	22.2
South Dakota	3,617	3,680	4,075	4,252	4,164	4,293	-7.4	-12.3	18.7	4.1
Tennessee	17,577	18,063	19,139	20,371	19,992	20,463	28.6	3.2	16.4	20.2
Texas	61,030	65,112	64,313	67,598	69,298	70,048	74.3	8.0	14.8	24.0
Utah	10,907	11,340	12,016	12,901	14,191	14,541	64.5	7.4	33.3	43.1
Vermont	4,517	4,553	4,521	4,707	4,671	4,591	59.1	10.8	1.6	12.6
Virginia	27,119	28,960	30,320	30,858	31,226	31,106	126.3	13.2	14.7	29.8
Washington	18,359	19,201	19,737	20,829	21,321	21,928	49.4	4.6	18.9	24.4
West Virginia	7,414	7,533	8,191	8,606	9,045	8,656	8.3	-6.1	16.8	9.6
Wisconsin	26,276	26,343	27,542	27,709	27,484	26,943	28.7	8.8	2.5	11.6
Wyoming	1,646	1,641	1,781	1,856	1,794	1,777	31.0	2.4	8.0	10.5
U.S. Service Schools ...	3,285	3,277	3,396	3,445	3,434	3,284	21.6	-13.4	(1)	-13.4
Outlying areas	12,427	13,459	13,519	14,100	13,866	14,302	148.6	9.0	15.1	25.5
American Samoa	—	—	—	—	—	—	—	—	—	—
Federated States of Micronesia	—	—	—	—	—	—	—	—	—	—
Guam	166	186	198	178	208	295	273.4	-19.0	77.7	43.9
Marshall Islands	—	—	—	—	—	—	—	—	—	—
Northern Marianas	—	—	—	—	—	—	—	—	—	—
Palau	—	—	—	—	—	—	—	—	—	—
Puerto Rico	12,105	13,121	13,182	13,746	13,486	13,812	144.6	9.5	14.1	24.9
Trust Territories	—	—	—	—	—	—	—	—	—	—
Virgin Islands	156	152	139	176	172	195	572.4	13.9	25.0	42.3

[1] Less than 0.05 percent.

—Data not available or not applicable.

NOTE.—Some data have been revised from previously published figures.

SOURCE: U.S. Department of Education, National Center for Education Statistics, Higher Education General Information Survey (HEGIS), "Degrees and Other Formal Awards Conferred" surveys, and Integrated Postsecondary Education Data System (IPEDS), "Completions" surveys. (This table was prepared February 1998.)

Table 73.—Master's degrees conferred by institutions of higher education, by state: 1969–70 to 1994–95

State or other area	1969–70	1970–71	1971–72	1972–73	1973–74	1974–75	1975–76	1976–77	1977–78	1978–79
1	2	3	4	5	6	7	8	9	10	11
United States	208,291	230,509	251,633	263,371	277,033	292,450	311,771	317,164	311,620	301,079
Alabama	2,344	2,561	3,261	3,814	4,262	5,180	6,116	5,757	6,139	6,020
Alaska	174	231	258	250	211	243	211	195	160	175
Arizona	2,825	3,155	3,550	3,530	3,678	3,866	4,278	4,327	4,097	3,940
Arkansas	1,159	1,185	1,243	1,307	1,234	1,408	1,640	1,800	1,772	1,680
California	19,467	21,097	22,265	22,881	24,567	27,611	30,828	31,160	31,711	31,255
Colorado	3,330	3,571	3,593	3,857	4,262	3,940	5,186	5,130	5,353	4,853
Connecticut	4,143	4,525	4,863	5,402	5,999	5,863	6,403	6,316	6,019	5,743
Delaware	364	472	511	491	464	485	459	362	495	453
District of Columbia	4,077	4,632	4,683	5,338	5,027	5,070	5,046	5,513	5,702	5,187
Florida	4,327	5,069	5,799	6,010	6,530	7,258	8,227	8,535	8,990	9,435
Georgia	3,278	4,541	4,911	5,751	6,819	7,360	8,168	8,233	7,539	7,133
Hawaii	1,017	1,104	1,554	1,661	1,423	1,298	1,131	1,019	1,046	1,105
Idaho	385	462	507	551	567	599	615	659	676	613
Illinois	12,715	13,767	14,906	15,042	16,040	16,611	17,735	17,923	17,423	16,550
Indiana	8,105	8,632	9,263	9,851	10,155	10,046	9,697	9,802	9,472	8,616
Iowa	2,241	2,666	2,606	2,476	2,413	2,377	2,411	2,624	2,470	2,535
Kansas	2,883	2,849	3,027	3,080	3,133	3,046	3,272	3,542	3,645	3,268
Kentucky	2,560	2,765	3,424	3,636	4,231	4,517	4,877	4,900	4,976	5,006
Louisiana	3,086	3,343	3,699	4,204	4,235	4,326	4,339	4,442	4,458	4,053
Maine	595	746	710	610	728	736	695	666	565	618
Maryland	2,984	3,226	3,660	4,119	4,294	5,059	5,379	5,456	5,366	5,135
Massachusetts	10,811	11,236	12,166	13,033	12,797	13,887	14,079	14,633	14,546	14,243
Michigan	12,043	13,261	13,649	13,503	13,817	14,887	16,005	16,098	15,558	14,896
Minnesota	2,582	2,781	2,904	2,668	2,786	2,918	2,941	3,509	3,554	3,317
Mississippi	1,433	1,656	1,873	2,166	2,465	2,850	3,299	3,665	3,518	2,982
Missouri	5,308	6,009	6,101	6,025	6,229	6,700	7,534	8,285	8,147	7,714
Montana	586	682	662	665	672	613	680	672	635	606
Nebraska	1,247	1,374	1,548	1,547	1,521	1,517	1,552	1,771	1,816	1,721
Nevada	222	260	303	326	461	443	469	476	479	426
New Hampshire	565	598	623	714	751	721	797	853	1,001	882
New Jersey	5,048	5,694	6,835	6,685	7,666	8,163	8,108	8,560	7,992	7,862
New Mexico	1,282	1,319	1,508	1,584	1,620	1,391	1,619	1,714	1,791	1,739
New York	26,628	29,798	33,314	36,011	36,686	38,688	40,012	37,752	35,086	33,734
North Carolina	3,216	3,443	3,909	4,215	4,530	4,480	4,957	5,596	5,740	5,537
North Dakota	703	665	709	575	580	466	453	516	488	465
Ohio	8,761	9,762	10,642	11,037	11,212	11,811	12,240	12,884	12,631	12,996
Oklahoma	2,892	2,898	3,228	3,278	3,758	3,850	4,082	4,030	3,885	3,667
Oregon	2,932	3,251	3,223	2,915	3,006	3,132	3,068	3,276	3,403	3,259
Pennsylvania	11,055	12,434	14,096	13,674	14,405	14,515	14,327	13,983	13,701	13,468
Rhode Island	1,072	1,304	1,494	1,823	1,758	1,787	1,737	1,885	1,588	1,572
South Carolina	769	1,092	1,398	1,791	2,402	3,116	3,737	3,810	3,559	3,461
South Dakota	899	866	897	780	738	695	720	777	659	683
Tennessee	3,054	3,236	3,868	4,280	4,621	4,719	5,310	5,300	4,958	4,599
Texas	8,489	9,603	10,583	11,535	12,712	13,803	15,549	16,738	16,774	16,236
Utah	1,827	2,016	2,165	2,162	2,371	2,293	2,260	2,471	2,255	2,487
Vermont	618	704	853	904	1,014	1,146	1,246	1,108	1,181	1,181
Virginia	2,564	3,174	3,600	3,990	4,303	4,661	5,284	5,346	5,669	5,178
Washington	2,964	3,427	3,402	3,337	3,536	3,616	3,824	3,955	3,895	4,045
West Virginia	1,179	1,265	1,493	1,696	1,775	1,969	2,219	2,159	2,254	2,176
Wisconsin	4,249	4,815	4,880	5,221	5,319	5,386	5,712	5,661	5,438	5,320
Wyoming	341	329	376	337	348	352	388	378	414	353
U.S. Service Schools ...	893	958	1,038	1,033	902	976	850	942	931	901
Outlying areas	1,096	977	1,141	1,154	1,226	1,201	1,230	1,077	1,196	996
American Samoa	—	—	—	—	—	—	—	—	—	—
Federated States of Micronesia	—	—	—	—	—	—	—	—	—	—
Guam	45	63	68	86	80	88	119	55	74	51
Marshall Islands	—	—	—	—	—	—	—	—	—	—
Northern Marianas	—	—	—	—	—	—	—	—	—	—
Palau	—	—	—	—	—	—	—	—	—	—
Puerto Rico	1,051	914	1,073	1,068	1,146	1,113	1,103	1,017	1,115	936
Trust Territories	—	—	—	—	—	—	—	—	—	—
Virgin Islands	—	—	—	—	—	—	8	5	7	9

Table 73.—Master's degrees conferred by institutions of higher education, by state: 1969–70 to 1994–95—Continued

State or other area	1979–80	1980–81	1981–82	1982–83	1983–84	1984–85	1985–86	1986–87	1987–88	1988–89
1	12	13	14	15	16	17	18	19	20	21
United States	298,081	295,739	295,546	289,921	284,263	286,251	288,567	289,349	299,317	310,621
Alabama	5,527	5,271	4,863	4,819	4,101	4,372	4,096	3,946	4,559	4,233
Alaska	184	190	199	256	252	280	300	320	318	286
Arizona	3,890	4,350	3,890	4,020	4,288	4,891	4,868	4,826	4,970	4,885
Arkansas	1,754	1,794	1,854	1,771	1,690	1,731	1,697	1,883	1,746	1,801
California	31,161	30,626	30,528	31,190	31,767	30,790	31,136	31,246	31,506	33,101
Colorado	4,953	4,811	4,429	4,216	4,084	4,098	4,117	4,088	4,397	4,574
Connecticut	5,639	6,190	5,826	5,711	5,833	5,828	6,301	5,755	5,892	6,022
Delaware	468	452	508	495	570	552	568	586	649	691
District of Columbia	5,488	5,712	5,583	5,484	5,123	5,145	5,241	4,993	5,062	5,028
Florida	8,299	8,716	8,824	8,326	7,615	8,599	9,112	9,044	9,849	10,563
Georgia	6,820	6,414	6,540	6,208	6,289	6,267	6,099	5,652	5,883	6,099
Hawaii	1,009	1,008	1,052	992	1,008	967	911	925	969	1,017
Idaho	660	684	651	633	602	596	644	722	703	706
Illinois	16,298	16,423	17,175	17,155	16,888	16,566	17,208	17,075	17,783	18,666
Indiana	8,313	8,031	7,934	7,591	6,973	6,882	6,610	6,943	7,079	7,514
Iowa	2,584	2,511	2,466	2,345	2,643	2,633	2,890	2,775	3,001	3,218
Kansas	3,126	3,202	3,182	3,078	2,959	2,984	3,048	2,986	2,983	3,132
Kentucky	5,210	4,518	4,161	3,703	3,620	3,419	3,473	3,256	3,333	3,491
Louisiana	4,190	3,925	3,855	4,006	3,917	4,100	4,109	3,972	3,941	3,859
Maine	599	527	544	535	493	483	534	503	548	633
Maryland	5,098	5,232	5,109	5,066	4,994	5,217	5,128	5,334	5,394	5,949
Massachusetts	14,653	14,049	14,491	13,666	13,517	14,446	14,686	15,066	15,692	16,967
Michigan	15,056	14,916	14,368	13,295	12,668	11,804	11,468	11,534	11,904	12,720
Minnesota	3,222	3,299	3,535	3,499	4,032	3,480	3,463	3,607	3,839	4,114
Mississippi	2,845	2,769	2,563	2,174	2,062	2,271	2,288	2,037	2,082	2,108
Missouri	7,555	7,464	7,917	8,008	7,081	7,487	7,806	7,673	7,920	8,569
Montana	638	669	574	686	643	701	740	765	724	674
Nebraska	1,689	1,710	1,549	1,676	1,563	1,668	1,634	1,609	1,722	1,776
Nevada	425	461	470	457	452	425	431	419	434	502
New Hampshire	880	974	998	1,099	1,235	1,289	1,399	1,649	1,635	1,723
New Jersey	7,965	7,737	7,520	7,222	6,801	6,656	6,303	6,454	6,397	7,101
New Mexico	1,741	1,773	1,783	1,699	1,764	1,703	1,771	1,732	1,798	1,868
New York	32,860	32,470	33,154	32,660	31,622	32,068	31,569	32,905	34,360	35,204
North Carolina	5,252	5,289	5,573	5,465	5,356	5,291	5,665	5,678	5,938	5,872
North Dakota	474	466	463	464	560	552	534	587	584	579
Ohio	12,964	13,199	13,465	12,964	12,593	12,235	12,088	12,170	12,287	12,791
Oklahoma	3,485	3,508	3,478	3,462	3,493	3,729	3,800	3,935	4,118	4,112
Oregon	3,203	3,063	3,050	2,884	2,827	2,685	2,649	2,784	2,869	3,120
Pennsylvania	13,060	13,171	13,450	13,254	13,032	13,239	13,217	13,501	13,791	14,587
Rhode Island	1,472	1,524	1,517	1,567	1,524	1,558	1,573	1,720	1,625	1,774
South Carolina	3,268	2,985	3,037	3,165	2,995	3,065	3,098	3,269	3,535	3,269
South Dakota	604	577	728	737	719	731	745	719	756	802
Tennessee	4,876	4,685	4,396	4,230	3,828	4,133	4,008	4,000	4,423	4,840
Texas	16,750	16,521	16,185	16,250	16,925	17,147	17,702	17,164	17,559	17,163
Utah	2,333	2,376	2,367	2,372	2,238	2,401	2,288	2,403	2,574	2,345
Vermont	1,164	1,152	1,145	854	849	886	865	819	830	991
Virginia	5,282	5,488	5,485	5,463	5,302	5,208	5,468	5,473	6,056	6,545
Washington	4,281	4,344	4,551	4,328	3,923	4,219	4,370	4,066	4,262	4,275
West Virginia	2,167	2,054	2,058	2,012	1,945	1,779	1,820	1,751	1,824	1,691
Wisconsin	5,323	5,200	5,317	5,130	5,275	5,351	5,355	5,394	5,479	5,398
Wyoming	295	333	311	350	339	347	380	345	343	335
U.S. Service Schools ...	1,029	926	875	1,229	1,391	1,297	1,294	1,291	1,392	1,338
Outlying areas	1,014	1,059	1,034	1,010	1,199	962	1,262	1,183	1,358	1,265
American Samoa	—	—	—	—	—	—	—	—	—	—
Federated States of Micronesia	—	—	—	—	—	—	—	—	—	—
Guam	41	48	34	41	50	34	37	30	35	40
Marshall Islands	—	—	—	—	—	—	—	—	—	—
Northern Marianas	—	—	—	—	—	—	—	—	—	—
Palau	—	—	—	—	—	—	—	—	—	—
Puerto Rico	945	987	970	953	1,110	896	1,200	1,120	1,291	1,192
Trust Territories	—	—	—	—	—	—	—	—	—	—
Virgin Islands	28	24	30	16	39	32	25	33	32	33

Table 73.—Master's degrees conferred by institutions of higher education, by state: 1969–70 to 1994–95—Continued

| State or other area | 1989–90 | 1990–91 | 1991–92 | 1992–93 | 1993–94 | 1994–95 | Percentage change | | | |
| | | | | | | | 1969–70 to 1994–95 | 1984–85 to 1989–90 | 1989–90 to 1994–95 | 1984–85 to 1994–95 |
1	22	23	24	25	26	27	28	29	30	31
United States	**324,301**	**337,168**	**352,838**	**369,585**	**387,070**	**397,629**	**90.9**	**13.3**	**22.6**	**38.9**
Alabama	4,510	5,162	5,544	5,636	5,763	5,983	155.2	3.2	32.7	36.8
Alaska	324	294	367	363	422	463	166.1	15.7	42.9	65.4
Arizona	5,178	7,597	5,093	5,694	6,399	6,498	130.0	5.9	25.5	32.9
Arkansas	1,700	1,649	1,774	1,836	1,995	2,041	76.1	–1.8	20.1	17.9
California	34,489	34,419	35,429	37,046	38,708	38,065	95.5	12.0	10.4	23.6
Colorado	5,099	5,241	5,655	6,391	6,859	7,111	113.5	24.4	39.5	73.5
Connecticut	6,285	6,281	6,563	6,590	6,649	6,419	54.9	7.8	2.1	10.1
Delaware	791	809	857	954	955	1,102	202.7	43.3	39.3	99.6
District of Columbia	5,073	5,136	5,380	5,941	6,176	6,607	62.1	–1.4	30.2	28.4
Florida	10,802	11,295	11,864	13,145	14,056	14,793	241.9	25.6	36.9	72.0
Georgia	6,427	6,566	7,022	7,958	8,326	8,644	163.7	2.6	34.5	37.9
Hawaii	1,007	1,086	1,199	1,383	1,369	1,520	49.5	4.1	50.9	57.2
Idaho	790	778	921	1,005	1,017	1,077	179.7	32.6	36.3	80.7
Illinois	19,288	19,948	21,674	22,440	23,689	23,487	84.7	16.4	21.8	41.8
Indiana	7,370	6,843	6,650	6,874	6,962	7,597	–6.3	7.1	3.1	10.4
Iowa	3,006	3,168	3,369	3,517	3,488	3,478	55.2	14.2	15.7	32.1
Kansas	3,309	3,402	3,791	3,920	4,618	4,350	50.9	10.9	31.5	45.8
Kentucky	3,681	3,968	4,059	4,195	4,028	4,219	64.8	7.7	14.6	23.4
Louisiana	3,993	4,100	4,235	4,723	5,205	5,346	73.2	–2.6	33.9	30.4
Maine	731	854	890	917	896	953	60.2	51.3	30.4	97.3
Maryland	6,448	6,924	7,496	7,982	8,182	8,991	201.3	23.6	39.4	72.3
Massachusetts	17,832	19,014	19,740	19,215	20,745	21,276	96.8	23.4	19.3	47.3
Michigan	13,297	14,139	14,374	14,944	15,474	15,460	28.4	12.6	16.3	31.0
Minnesota	4,366	4,585	4,853	5,217	5,678	5,760	123.1	25.5	31.9	65.5
Mississippi	2,370	2,511	2,547	2,672	2,630	2,621	82.9	4.4	10.6	15.4
Missouri	8,600	8,790	9,405	9,303	10,130	10,355	95.1	14.9	20.4	38.3
Montana	709	753	730	756	803	857	46.2	1.1	20.9	22.3
Nebraska	1,713	1,691	1,909	2,007	2,201	2,252	80.6	2.7	31.5	35.0
Nevada	543	613	710	845	922	897	304.1	27.8	65.2	111.1
New Hampshire	1,944	2,029	2,101	2,267	2,228	2,262	300.4	50.8	16.4	75.5
New Jersey	7,246	7,538	7,901	8,110	8,274	8,261	63.6	8.9	14.0	24.1
New Mexico	1,838	1,916	2,224	2,142	2,348	2,438	90.2	7.9	32.6	43.2
New York	37,418	39,079	41,213	42,539	42,903	44,726	68.0	16.7	19.5	39.5
North Carolina	6,015	6,185	6,644	6,864	7,276	7,430	131.0	13.7	23.5	40.4
North Dakota	620	587	572	649	675	628	–10.7	12.3	1.3	13.8
Ohio	13,021	13,436	13,760	14,613	14,992	15,387	75.6	6.4	18.2	25.8
Oklahoma	3,943	3,717	4,267	4,457	4,954	4,928	70.4	5.7	25.0	32.2
Oregon	3,276	3,397	3,918	3,650	3,617	3,914	33.5	22.0	19.5	45.8
Pennsylvania	14,821	15,611	16,899	17,649	18,906	19,637	77.6	11.9	32.5	48.3
Rhode Island	1,795	1,984	2,038	2,070	2,019	2,041	90.4	15.2	13.7	31.0
South Carolina	3,828	3,935	3,911	4,245	4,452	4,525	488.4	24.9	18.2	47.6
South Dakota	769	781	785	913	1,038	1,007	12.0	5.2	30.9	37.8
Tennessee	4,839	4,716	4,946	5,016	5,740	6,193	102.8	17.1	28.0	49.8
Texas	18,148	18,794	19,749	20,887	21,838	22,740	167.9	5.8	25.3	32.6
Utah	2,479	2,452	2,550	2,868	2,837	3,045	66.7	3.2	22.8	26.8
Vermont	1,002	1,066	1,056	1,103	1,174	1,091	76.5	13.1	8.9	23.1
Virginia	7,159	7,913	8,339	9,325	9,980	10,706	317.6	37.5	49.5	105.6
Washington	5,284	5,200	6,088	6,745	7,268	7,947	168.1	25.2	50.4	88.4
West Virginia	1,740	1,707	1,912	1,916	2,032	2,268	92.4	–2.2	30.3	27.5
Wisconsin	5,788	5,977	6,252	6,340	6,267	6,446	51.7	8.2	11.4	20.5
Wyoming	361	304	350	342	457	396	16.1	4.0	9.7	14.1
U.S. Service Schools	1,236	1,228	1,263	1,406	1,450	1,391	55.8	–4.7	12.5	7.2
Outlying areas	1,068	1,330	1,369	1,388	1,938	1,799	64.1	11.0	68.4	87.0
American Samoa	—	—	—	—	—	—	—	—	—	—
Federated States of Micronesia	—	—	—	—	—	—	—	—	—	—
Guam	18	16	16	15	26	45	—	–47.1	150.0	32.4
Marshall Islands	—	—	—	—	—	—	—	—	—	—
Northern Marianas	—	—	—	—	—	—	—	—	—	—
Palau	—	—	—	—	—	—	—	—	—	—
Puerto Rico	1,019	1,265	1,301	1,330	1,858	1,690	60.8	13.7	65.8	88.6
Trust Territories	—	—	—	—	—	—	—	—	—	—
Virgin Islands	31	49	52	43	54	64	—	–3.1	106.5	100.0

—Data not available or not applicable.

NOTE.—Some data have been revised from previously published figures.

SOURCE: U.S. Department of Education, National Center for Education Statistics, Higher Education General Information Survey (HEGIS), "Degrees and Other Formal Awards Conferred" surveys, and Integrated Postsecondary Education Data System (IPEDS), "Completions" surveys. (This table was prepared February 1998.)

Table 74.—First-professional degrees [1] conferred by institutions of higher education, by state: 1969–70 to 1994–95

State or other area	1969–70	1970–71	1971–72	1972–73	1973–74	1974–75	1975–76	1976–77	1977–78	1978–79
1	2	3	4	5	6	7	8	9	10	11
United States	34,918	37,946	43,411	50,018	53,816	55,916	62,649	64,359	66,581	68,848
Alabama	413	425	486	510	720	838	727	747	809	870
Alaska	—	—	—	—	—	—	—	—	—	—
Arizona	132	212	254	392	343	284	289	319	335	349
Arkansas	191	206	208	262	248	218	299	327	350	379
California	3,153	3,893	4,682	4,878	5,662	5,784	7,600	7,885	8,280	8,628
Colorado	427	502	609	663	657	673	700	716	712	722
Connecticut	440	449	593	609	574	551	642	644	668	725
Delaware	—	—	—	—	—	—	—	—	—	—
District of Columbia	1,453	1,544	1,933	2,109	2,289	2,267	2,257	2,315	2,331	2,359
Florida	632	666	916	1,133	1,212	1,187	1,380	1,699	1,714	1,702
Georgia	759	769	789	997	1,033	1,130	1,261	1,193	1,263	1,355
Hawaii	—	—	—	—	—	62	105	110	125	121
Idaho	26	34	46	65	77	75	99	70	83	73
Illinois	2,254	2,461	2,832	3,116	3,458	3,631	4,262	4,103	4,643	4,670
Indiana	906	866	573	1,329	1,393	1,206	1,307	1,486	1,501	1,426
Iowa	526	598	701	733	876	1,347	1,550	1,583	1,592	1,428
Kansas	379	387	452	509	592	563	675	616	660	725
Kentucky	731	844	930	1,050	1,166	1,135	1,171	1,196	1,303	1,352
Louisiana	784	820	844	952	1,056	1,134	1,213	1,277	1,308	1,377
Maine	45	58	60	84	84	69	88	95	109	100
Maryland	624	602	643	917	971	1,029	894	918	899	921
Massachusetts	1,845	2,111	2,429	2,699	2,902	3,082	3,325	3,469	3,335	3,157
Michigan	1,408	1,481	1,683	1,886	1,992	2,072	2,354	2,373	2,601	2,702
Minnesota	785	738	880	878	982	1,067	1,300	1,412	1,454	1,654
Mississippi	188	195	218	266	391	294	391	421	460	461
Missouri	1,391	1,405	1,593	1,924	1,880	1,954	2,107	2,120	2,177	2,276
Montana	34	35	39	64	51	61	65	75	65	74
Nebraska	407	402	517	583	657	716	748	716	680	809
Nevada	—	—	—	—	—	—	—	—	—	—
New Hampshire	—	—	—	45	20	57	123	59	58	169
New Jersey	672	683	860	1,194	1,244	1,208	1,217	1,321	1,364	1,454
New Mexico	58	82	105	130	152	162	165	190	166	179
New York	3,517	4,195	4,580	4,785	4,773	5,111	5,361	5,559	5,649	6,225
North Carolina	665	737	870	1,010	1,120	1,090	1,262	1,218	1,284	1,384
North Dakota	37	34	46	63	61	47	143	118	96	137
Ohio	1,769	1,730	2,051	2,574	2,618	2,693	3,150	3,162	3,366	3,378
Oklahoma	404	352	420	495	571	736	705	789	859	857
Oregon	397	489	507	664	707	749	895	886	948	972
Pennsylvania	2,215	2,386	2,896	3,139	3,232	3,269	3,463	3,495	3,577	3,757
Rhode Island	—	—	—	—	—	58	60	60	64	60
South Carolina	233	278	277	434	471	541	534	559	623	581
South Dakota	48	58	65	76	83	68	86	123	124	119
Tennessee	814	868	1,007	1,140	1,382	1,222	1,373	1,320	1,311	1,409
Texas	2,073	2,112	2,381	2,812	3,166	3,201	3,498	3,691	3,589	3,596
Utah	153	166	179	227	198	233	378	386	359	334
Vermont	58	46	66	78	63	69	151	209	182	162
Virginia	657	808	890	1,014	993	1,028	1,154	1,183	1,232	1,346
Washington	346	387	377	514	548	804	962	960	1,031	1,011
West Virginia	158	184	199	221	225	226	237	252	293	335
Wisconsin	522	614	685	740	838	854	861	864	890	900
Wyoming	31	34	40	55	85	61	62	70	59	68
U.S. Service Schools ...	158	—	—	—	—	—	—	—	—	—
Outlying Areas	334	330	363	417	462	343	412	421	383	374
American Samoa	—	—	—	—	—	—	—	—	—	—
Federated States of Micronesia	—	—	—	—	—	—	—	—	—	—
Guam	—	—	—	—	—	—	—	—	—	—
Marshall Islands	—	—	—	—	—	—	—	—	—	—
Northern Marianas	—	—	—	—	—	—	—	—	—	—
Palau	—	—	—	—	—	—	—	—	—	—
Puerto Rico	334	330	363	417	462	343	412	421	383	374
Trust Territories	—	—	—	—	—	—	—	—	—	—
Virgin Islands	—	—	—	—	—	—	—	—	—	—

Table 74.—First-professional degrees[1] conferred by institutions of higher education, by state: 1969–70 to 1994–95—Continued

State or other area	1979–80	1980–81	1981–82	1982–83	1983–84	1984–85	1985–86	1986–87	1987–88	1988–89
1	12	13	14	15	16	17	18	19	20	21
United States	**70,131**	**71,956**	**72,032**	**73,054**	**74,468**	**75,063**	**73,910**	**71,617**	**70,735**	**70,856**
Alabama	893	940	878	902	921	855	842	797	817	787
Alaska	—	—	—	—	—	—	—	—	—	—
Arizona	348	401	361	347	372	374	349	352	404	420
Arkansas	345	391	382	363	342	354	355	319	369	343
California	8,528	8,616	8,313	8,384	8,998	8,546	8,209	7,850	7,889	7,651
Colorado	800	839	831	836	837	882	904	853	872	873
Connecticut	946	799	803	889	879	967	931	947	918	920
Delaware	—	—	221	222	238	265	265	245	284	317
District of Columbia	2,375	2,460	2,550	2,503	2,678	2,558	2,643	2,681	2,437	2,467
Florida	1,799	1,804	1,762	1,762	1,731	1,823	1,878	2,105	1,984	2,051
Georgia	1,603	1,540	1,775	1,812	1,831	1,946	2,083	1,990	1,875	1,846
Hawaii	128	153	137	132	131	139	131	137	126	119
Idaho	80	91	89	93	80	105	82	68	71	67
Illinois	4,532	4,471	4,553	4,468	4,579	4,679	4,552	4,429	4,353	4,404
Indiana	1,513	1,522	1,537	1,555	1,619	1,545	1,476	1,518	1,422	1,442
Iowa	1,675	1,587	1,363	1,544	1,584	1,650	1,661	1,315	1,518	1,489
Kansas	643	571	687	674	717	712	665	655	628	590
Kentucky	1,330	1,319	1,320	1,283	1,219	1,281	1,168	1,113	1,161	1,167
Louisiana	1,396	1,427	1,546	1,559	1,449	1,522	1,521	1,392	1,400	1,505
Maine	110	83	122	135	174	189	170	163	157	139
Maryland	907	894	918	905	891	899	1,124	968	932	973
Massachusetts	3,480	3,496	3,568	3,644	3,497	3,645	3,557	3,732	3,721	3,605
Michigan	2,705	2,638	2,631	2,676	2,557	2,722	2,697	2,504	2,341	2,212
Minnesota	1,501	1,622	1,756	1,616	1,553	1,591	1,580	1,529	1,560	1,486
Mississippi	375	684	469	387	409	500	491	461	473	414
Missouri	2,333	2,321	2,355	2,539	2,436	2,409	2,470	2,275	2,264	2,300
Montana	74	71	73	78	64	75	66	74	78	59
Nebraska	776	721	808	765	772	742	755	752	706	727
Nevada	36	48	45	42	48	70	75	42	46	46
New Hampshire	175	185	179	122	178	163	167	173	172	154
New Jersey	1,497	1,547	1,642	1,570	1,703	1,743	1,690	1,753	1,723	1,618
New Mexico	165	194	179	176	186	166	191	170	164	181
New York	6,266	6,512	6,512	6,709	7,102	7,037	6,765	6,943	6,628	7,139
North Carolina	1,468	1,508	1,519	1,582	1,630	1,662	1,573	1,620	1,594	1,632
North Dakota	111	118	126	132	130	157	134	117	114	115
Ohio	3,528	3,549	3,404	3,517	3,603	3,627	3,533	3,341	3,199	3,225
Oklahoma	960	767	956	992	1,009	1,020	1,022	999	1,031	950
Oregon	1,033	1,014	980	1,062	1,075	994	938	899	845	906
Pennsylvania	3,691	3,723	3,621	3,680	3,672	3,614	3,715	3,727	3,637	3,575
Rhode Island	61	67	64	63	70	80	78	78	84	80
South Carolina	405	696	690	658	647	661	690	738	683	738
South Dakota	124	134	118	120	157	123	134	140	121	130
Tennessee	1,349	1,523	1,527	1,566	1,540	1,482	1,392	1,305	1,348	1,343
Texas	3,860	4,207	4,167	4,331	4,465	4,624	4,557	4,028	3,999	4,146
Utah	371	360	376	382	389	379	361	365	378	376
Vermont	177	196	196	209	201	208	206	77	98	85
Virginia	1,352	1,715	1,520	1,517	1,669	1,651	1,666	1,597	1,699	1,695
Washington	934	1,006	924	1,016	963	1,000	908	901	898	809
West Virginia	351	338	353	396	348	362	319	329	308	315
Wisconsin	934	958	963	950	945	991	950	838	988	1,017
Wyoming	60	63	60	68	59	122	68	59	69	57
U.S. Service Schools	28	67	103	121	121	152	153	154	149	151
Outlying Areas	395	413	522	433	493	499	671	503	729	552
American Samoa	—	—	—	—	—	—	—	—	—	—
Federated States of Micronesia	—	—	—	—	—	—	—	—	—	—
Guam	—	—	—	—	—	—	—	—	—	—
Marshall Islands	—	—	—	—	—	—	—	—	—	—
Northern Marianas	—	—	—	—	—	—	—	—	—	—
Palau	—	—	—	—	—	—	—	—	—	—
Puerto Rico	395	413	522	433	493	499	671	503	729	552
Trust Territories	—	—	—	—	—	—	—	—	—	—
Virgin Islands	—	—	—	—	—	—	—	—	—	—

Table 74.—First-professional degrees [1] conferred by institutions of higher education, by state:
1969–70 to 1994–95—Continued

State or other area	1989–90	1990–91	1991–92	1992–93	1993–94	1994–95	Percentage change			
							1969–70 to 1994–95	1984–85 to 1989–90	1989–90 to 1994–95	1984–85 to 1994–95
1	22	23	24	25	26	27	28	29	30	31
United States	70,988	71,948	74,146	75,387	75,418	75,800	117.1	−5.4	6.8	1.0
Alabama	832	850	850	866	908	963	133.2	−2.7	15.7	12.6
Alaska	—	—	—	—	—	—	—	—	—	—
Arizona	408	425	424	436	462	445	237.1	9.1	9.1	19.0
Arkansas	324	354	363	449	441	482	152.4	−8.5	48.8	36.2
California	7,814	7,685	8,918	9,195	9,228	8,783	178.6	−8.6	12.4	2.8
Colorado	794	772	788	813	809	833	95.1	−10.0	4.9	−5.6
Connecticut	956	980	896	679	769	920	109.1	−1.1	−3.8	−4.9
Delaware	329	418	578	550	461	418	—	24.2	27.1	57.7
District of Columbia	2,498	2,310	2,254	2,321	2,420	2,467	69.8	−2.3	−1.2	−3.6
Florida	2,138	2,303	2,312	2,322	2,382	2,494	294.6	17.3	16.7	36.8
Georgia	1,835	1,952	1,833	1,949	2,015	2,061	171.5	−5.7	12.3	5.9
Hawaii	113	118	116	176	172	160	—	−18.7	41.6	15.1
Idaho	124	122	135	146	148	167	542.3	18.1	34.7	59.0
Illinois	4,412	4,476	4,364	4,410	4,321	4,360	93.4	−5.7	−1.2	−6.8
Indiana	1,420	1,384	1,512	1,496	1,454	1,485	63.9	−8.1	4.6	−3.9
Iowa	1,427	1,462	1,493	1,534	1,442	1,535	191.8	−13.5	7.6	−7.0
Kansas	566	629	614	601	619	591	55.9	−20.5	4.4	−17.0
Kentucky	1,127	1,130	896	985	1,118	1,127	54.2	−12.0	0.0	−12.0
Louisiana	1,459	1,640	1,562	1,502	1,582	1,680	114.3	−4.1	15.1	10.4
Maine	162	173	179	168	173	180	300.0	−14.3	11.1	−4.8
Maryland	971	997	946	1,050	972	1,001	60.4	8.0	3.1	11.3
Massachusetts	3,653	3,674	3,651	3,677	3,771	3,656	98.2	0.2	0.1	0.3
Michigan	2,418	2,536	2,575	2,581	2,746	2,496	77.3	−11.2	3.2	−8.3
Minnesota	1,561	1,454	1,829	1,854	1,536	1,538	95.9	−1.9	−1.5	−3.3
Mississippi	477	452	513	466	478	492	161.7	−4.6	3.1	−1.6
Missouri	2,283	2,186	2,157	2,171	2,206	2,296	65.1	−5.2	0.6	−4.7
Montana	71	61	70	68	70	78	129.4	−5.3	9.9	4.0
Nebraska	658	736	732	806	811	825	102.7	−11.3	25.4	11.2
Nevada	49	38	44	54	39	54	—	−30.0	10.2	−22.9
New Hampshire	165	184	185	195	182	193	—	1.2	17.0	18.4
New Jersey	1,763	1,648	1,719	1,679	1,709	1,670	148.5	1.1	−5.3	−4.2
New Mexico	179	167	176	178	192	172	196.6	7.8	−3.9	3.6
New York	7,200	7,468	7,543	7,476	7,442	7,636	117.1	2.3	6.1	8.5
North Carolina	1,597	1,625	1,537	1,709	1,673	1,696	155.0	−3.9	6.2	2.0
North Dakota	109	133	127	142	189	187	405.4	−30.6	71.6	19.1
Ohio	3,076	3,148	3,176	3,225	3,251	3,069	73.5	−15.2	−0.2	−15.4
Oklahoma	923	909	989	928	846	955	136.4	−9.5	3.5	−6.4
Oregon	928	942	1,032	988	946	904	127.7	−6.6	−2.6	−9.1
Pennsylvania	3,462	3,382	3,561	3,774	3,745	3,942	78.0	−4.2	13.9	9.1
Rhode Island	82	80	86	81	87	76	—	2.5	−7.3	−5.0
South Carolina	587	591	621	604	627	614	163.5	−11.2	4.6	−7.1
South Dakota	102	113	135	130	141	137	185.4	−17.1	34.3	11.4
Tennessee	1,289	1,268	1,352	1,341	1,296	1,436	76.4	−13.0	11.4	−3.1
Texas	4,109	4,208	4,817	4,882	4,768	4,775	130.3	−11.1	16.2	3.3
Utah	380	383	364	388	367	373	143.8	0.3	−1.8	−1.6
Vermont	87	227	91	96	93	90	55.2	−58.2	3.4	−56.7
Virginia	1,732	1,739	1,627	1,811	1,839	1,817	176.6	4.9	4.9	10.1
Washington	852	832	886	920	918	909	162.7	−14.8	6.7	−9.1
West Virginia	302	353	329	320	367	358	126.6	−16.6	18.5	−1.1
Wisconsin	967	1,012	946	971	966	977	87.2	−2.4	1.0	−1.4
Wyoming	67	70	64	69	66	70	125.8	−45.1	4.5	−42.6
U.S. Service Schools	151	149	179	155	155	157	−0.6	−0.7	4.0	3.3
Outlying Areas	683	688	655	681	582	657	96.7	36.9	−3.8	31.7
American Samoa	—	—	—	—	—	—	—	—	—	—
Federated States of Micronesia	—	—	—	—	—	—	—	—	—	—
Guam	—	—	—	—	—	—	—	—	—	—
Marshall Islands	—	—	—	—	—	—	—	—	—	—
Northern Marianas	—	—	—	—	—	—	—	—	—	—
Palau	—	—	—	—	—	—	—	—	—	—
Puerto Rico	683	688	655	681	582	657	96.7	36.9	−3.8	31.7
Trust Territories	—	—	—	—	—	—	—	—	—	—
Virgin Islands	—	—	—	—	—	—	—	—	—	—

[1] Includes degrees which require at least 6 years of college work for completion (including at least 2 years of preprofessional training). See *Definitions* for details.
—Data not available or not applicable.

NOTE.—Some data have been revised from previously published figures.

SOURCE: U.S. Department of Education, National Center for Education Statistics, Higher Education General Information Survey (HEGIS), "Degrees and Other Formal Awards Conferred" surveys, and Integrated Postsecondary Education Data System (IPEDS), "Completions" surveys. (This table was prepared February 1998.)

Table 75.—Doctor's degrees conferred by institutions of higher education, by state: 1969–70 to 1994–95

State or other area	1969–70	1970–71	1971–72	1972–73	1973–74	1974–75	1975–76	1976–77	1977–78	1978–79
1	2	3	4	5	6	7	8	9	10	11
United States	**29,866**	**32,107**	**33,363**	**34,777**	**33,816**	**34,083**	**34,064**	**33,232**	**32,131**	**32,730**
Alabama	221	265	276	268	273	196	226	257	269	267
Alaska	7	12	3	6	9	10	8	5	3	5
Arizona	383	396	386	384	421	413	387	417	403	392
Arkansas	124	116	147	118	116	105	120	106	108	93
California	3,175	3,349	3,490	3,917	3,699	3,628	3,799	3,683	3,644	3,718
Colorado	636	656	714	697	715	701	726	703	679	655
Connecticut	511	519	578	559	577	584	579	527	530	503
Delaware	60	75	85	76	68	76	68	49	75	57
District of Columbia	498	576	554	567	559	568	524	553	511	512
Florida	668	702	761	734	762	1,141	1,411	1,418	1,321	1,517
Georgia	345	456	489	544	545	548	568	570	563	530
Hawaii	53	78	80	94	109	97	116	134	129	122
Idaho	45	57	58	44	69	65	70	49	59	64
Illinois	1,887	2,086	2,142	2,229	2,165	2,131	2,025	2,061	1,874	1,943
Indiana	1,313	1,355	1,316	1,260	1,298	1,300	1,208	1,089	1,015	1,030
Iowa	617	702	625	643	565	551	568	520	515	552
Kansas	389	387	382	412	447	448	385	370	480	384
Kentucky	173	190	198	205	259	251	259	251	242	261
Louisiana	348	391	449	365	406	386	332	303	319	322
Maine	24	25	28	42	29	26	41	38	41	22
Maryland	576	552	617	623	584	649	612	602	578	587
Massachusetts	1,676	1,791	1,818	2,190	2,022	2,018	2,018	1,980	1,952	1,865
Michigan	1,577	1,793	1,710	1,758	1,582	1,635	1,498	1,504	1,338	1,417
Minnesota	546	613	599	557	575	540	497	519	501	474
Mississippi	178	225	253	278	241	255	280	276	269	216
Missouri	630	645	751	762	706	704	686	689	593	688
Montana	63	76	72	75	103	81	70	63	49	50
Nebraska	213	223	210	230	237	229	178	218	206	200
Nevada	11	19	21	24	11	15	24	33	18	19
New Hampshire	49	54	63	63	51	62	67	55	52	63
New Jersey	565	551	621	609	597	718	691	760	713	719
New Mexico	182	182	188	213	218	143	167	166	155	158
New York	3,292	3,370	3,607	3,953	3,681	3,451	3,626	3,478	3,400	3,398
North Carolina	634	723	763	787	824	825	734	716	742	739
North Dakota	86	118	83	90	82	67	66	66	47	69
Ohio	1,262	1,419	1,475	1,519	1,490	1,565	1,665	1,542	1,600	1,549
Oklahoma	484	467	509	505	474	498	416	406	390	421
Oregon	441	494	573	524	481	465	409	411	331	375
Pennsylvania	1,492	1,636	1,817	1,825	1,663	1,771	1,809	1,628	1,645	1,658
Rhode Island	187	207	208	191	220	204	194	204	188	189
South Carolina	115	125	130	126	134	162	207	174	198	227
South Dakota	63	52	51	50	51	46	45	48	50	45
Tennessee	452	484	524	561	570	578	585	570	513	565
Texas	1,241	1,358	1,457	1,476	1,486	1,541	1,502	1,595	1,502	1,612
Utah	413	394	491	460	442	455	407	445	357	393
Vermont	33	28	35	29	38	41	39	33	32	27
Virginia	306	372	331	407	501	479	534	516	538	555
Washington	466	574	541	613	538	539	512	462	453	511
West Virginia	143	102	134	131	109	110	121	121	117	115
Wisconsin	934	960	861	902	911	917	899	765	757	807
Wyoming	67	88	78	73	85	78	57	69	58	55
U.S. Service Schools ...	12	19	11	9	18	17	29	15	9	15
Outlying Areas	6	6	6	13	10	3	12	12	25	26
American Samoa	—	—	—	—	—	—	—	—	—	—
Federated States of Micronesia	—	—	—	—	—	—	—	—	—	—
Guam	—	—	—	—	—	—	—	—	—	—
Marshall Islands	—	—	—	—	—	—	—	—	—	—
Northern Marianas	—	—	—	—	—	—	—	—	—	—
Palau	—	—	—	—	—	—	—	—	—	—
Puerto Rico	6	6	6	13	10	3	12	12	25	26
Trust Territories	—	—	—	—	—	—	—	—	—	—
Virgin Islands	—	—	—	—	—	—	—	—	—	—

**Table 75.—Doctor's degrees conferred by institutions of higher education, by state:
1969–70 to 1994–95—Continued**

State or other area	1979–80	1980–81	1981–82	1982–83	1983–84	1984–85	1985–86	1986–87	1987–88	1988–89
1	12	13	14	15	16	17	18	19	20	21
United States	32,615	32,958	32,707	32,775	33,209	32,943	33,653	34,041	34,870	35,720
Alabama	249	254	275	281	267	264	270	279	289	341
Alaska	—	2	6	5	6	8	12	7	15	14
Arizona	417	392	442	459	434	431	458	506	495	559
Arkansas	108	105	126	258	128	128	134	112	101	96
California	3,982	4,154	4,011	4,106	4,041	3,913	4,140	4,083	4,116	4,209
Colorado	618	711	611	680	655	601	588	636	667	665
Connecticut	499	483	482	470	515	472	462	533	496	553
Delaware	70	58	105	58	3	93	100	96	107	114
District of Columbia	487	535	556	571	531	517	556	475	542	503
Florida	1,536	1,226	1,060	1,038	1,044	982	1,030	1,109	1,200	1,201
Georgia	549	553	575	601	595	713	666	654	737	800
Hawaii	103	114	111	120	101	138	132	145	116	172
Idaho	55	60	55	49	49	54	42	47	63	60
Illinois	1,872	2,043	1,932	1,896	1,910	2,027	2,007	2,062	2,152	2,176
Indiana	1,036	1,045	1,000	1,035	1,006	1,022	974	967	941	962
Iowa	532	557	582	489	552	558	537	608	658	574
Kansas	388	369	389	360	380	456	351	389	376	379
Kentucky	271	264	240	271	279	255	248	281	313	332
Louisiana	314	269	262	280	244	256	290	301	346	384
Maine	21	25	32	22	25	23	29	25	25	36
Maryland	529	594	594	598	657	696	663	690	705	703
Massachusetts	1,839	2,005	1,822	1,822	1,840	1,777	1,912	1,908	1,937	1,986
Michigan	1,334	1,310	1,438	1,383	1,387	1,259	1,289	1,321	1,238	1,333
Minnesota	503	535	479	487	593	529	577	529	549	568
Mississippi	226	241	280	274	339	245	268	272	241	245
Missouri	637	578	585	567	632	566	579	545	531	621
Montana	56	38	48	51	53	52	60	49	65	57
Nebraska	221	238	214	220	226	196	210	215	248	248
Nevada	21	30	34	26	29	31	28	32	28	35
New Hampshire	58	68	65	67	58	49	57	78	69	90
New Jersey	645	781	790	812	709	690	735	670	824	743
New Mexico	166	165	151	170	174	189	209	206	222	217
New York	3,375	3,255	3,259	3,181	3,310	3,360	3,411	3,367	3,497	3,541
North Carolina	757	714	732	725	769	697	753	788	796	724
North Dakota	83	69	47	49	47	64	67	76	66	61
Ohio	1,487	1,489	1,525	1,492	1,471	1,443	1,449	1,611	1,434	1,652
Oklahoma	377	379	362	405	415	404	412	342	349	358
Oregon	346	405	392	457	460	421	433	349	409	414
Pennsylvania	1,669	1,664	1,812	1,761	1,858	1,850	1,832	1,802	1,882	2,027
Rhode Island	203	175	202	178	179	196	183	212	237	222
South Carolina	191	196	207	207	208	224	258	266	302	266
South Dakota	37	33	41	48	47	53	60	65	51	48
Tennessee	545	604	585	585	626	598	609	576	541	582
Texas	1,660	1,753	1,662	1,676	1,811	1,839	1,978	2,079	2,067	2,113
Utah	453	383	408	371	371	358	371	361	418	367
Vermont	32	35	26	28	39	29	53	41	45	49
Virginia	550	589	574	627	656	647	689	687	746	764
Washington	512	493	531	573	550	514	527	599	576	583
West Virginia	145	107	130	128	113	115	113	110	131	112
Wisconsin	760	723	779	696	742	797	747	788	812	771
Wyoming	76	78	64	49	55	122	75	68	73	73
U.S. Service Schools ...	15	12	17	13	20	22	20	24	26	17
Outlying Areas	17	24	28	24	31	29	24	185	58	35
American Samoa	—	—	—	—	—	—	—	—	—	—
Federated States of Micronesia	—	—	—	—	—	—	—	—	—	—
Guam	—	—	—	—	—	—	—	—	—	—
Marshall Islands	—	—	—	—	—	—	—	—	—	—
Northern Marianas	—	—	—	—	—	—	—	—	—	—
Palau	—	—	—	—	—	—	—	—	—	—
Puerto Rico	17	24	28	24	31	29	24	185	58	35
Trust Territories	—	—	—	—	—	—	—	—	—	—
Virgin Islands	—	—	—	—	—	—	—	—	—	—

Table 75.—Doctor's degrees conferred by institutions of higher education, by state: 1969–70 to 1994–95—Continued

State or other area	1989–90	1990–91	1991–92	1992–93	1993–94	1994–95	Percentage change			
							1969–70 to 1994–95	1984–85 to 1989–90	1989–90 to 1994–95	1984–85 to 1994–95
1	22	23	24	25	26	27	28	29	30	31
United States	**38,371**	**39,294**	**40,659**	**42,132**	**43,185**	**44,446**	**48.8**	**16.5**	**15.8**	**34.9**
Alabama	354	392	374	406	476	438	98.2	34.1	23.7	65.9
Alaska	8	10	13	10	24	19	171.4	—	137.5	137.5
Arizona	545	668	633	690	754	787	105.5	26.5	44.4	82.6
Arkansas	135	123	112	120	146	155	25.0	5.5	14.8	21.1
California	4,747	4,540	4,703	4,987	5,034	5,367	69.0	21.3	13.1	37.2
Colorado	718	715	707	768	765	788	23.9	19.5	9.7	31.1
Connecticut	572	610	604	630	646	707	38.4	21.2	23.6	49.8
Delaware	114	133	167	144	121	169	181.7	22.6	48.2	81.7
District of Columbia	540	456	473	562	489	474	−4.8	4.4	−12.2	−8.3
Florida	1,251	1,249	1,430	1,661	1,644	1,653	147.5	27.4	32.1	68.3
Georgia	800	827	880	899	813	934	170.7	12.2	16.8	31.0
Hawaii	114	144	145	168	175	166	213.2	−17.4	45.6	20.3
Idaho	90	76	76	65	88	80	77.8	66.7	−11.1	48.1
Illinois	2,409	2,449	2,581	2,601	2,592	2,850	51.0	18.8	18.3	40.6
Indiana	1,040	1,028	1,114	1,107	1,103	1,152	−12.3	1.8	10.8	12.7
Iowa	604	694	698	683	689	686	11.2	8.2	13.6	22.9
Kansas	346	369	447	387	415	450	15.7	−24.1	30.1	−1.3
Kentucky	320	324	311	328	401	397	129.5	25.5	24.1	55.7
Louisiana	405	417	423	428	447	499	43.4	58.2	23.2	94.9
Maine	34	33	51	40	53	42	75.0	47.8	23.5	82.6
Maryland	816	838	928	949	934	877	52.3	17.2	7.5	26.0
Massachusetts	2,122	2,172	2,256	2,276	2,228	2,283	36.2	19.4	7.6	28.5
Michigan	1,313	1,487	1,549	1,513	1,483	1,548	−1.8	4.3	17.9	23.0
Minnesota	750	823	684	674	917	889	62.8	41.8	18.5	68.1
Mississippi	293	340	302	303	352	399	124.2	19.6	36.2	62.9
Missouri	619	643	764	711	778	719	14.1	9.4	16.2	27.0
Montana	71	56	65	57	57	66	4.8	36.5	−7.0	26.9
Nebraska	230	219	236	238	244	255	19.7	17.3	10.9	30.1
Nevada	38	36	45	39	52	77	600.0	22.6	102.6	148.4
New Hampshire	83	89	79	118	136	112	128.6	69.4	34.9	128.6
New Jersey	855	816	994	965	1,032	1,053	86.4	23.9	23.2	52.6
New Mexico	223	232	229	243	243	285	56.6	18.0	27.8	50.8
New York	3,842	4,019	3,816	4,045	4,025	3,974	20.7	14.3	3.4	18.3
North Carolina	861	872	923	980	988	1,022	61.2	23.5	18.7	46.6
North Dakota	71	63	79	74	74	84	−2.3	10.9	18.3	31.3
Ohio	1,709	1,751	1,766	1,973	2,127	2,191	73.6	18.4	28.2	51.8
Oklahoma	408	380	398	416	387	414	−14.5	1.0	1.5	2.5
Oregon	452	436	511	535	531	493	11.8	7.4	9.1	17.1
Pennsylvania	2,036	2,120	2,201	2,267	2,247	2,402	61.0	10.1	18.0	29.8
Rhode Island	190	270	241	269	255	295	57.8	−3.1	55.3	50.5
South Carolina	342	370	374	408	459	391	240.0	52.7	14.3	74.6
South Dakota	44	49	60	52	60	63	—	−17.0	43.2	18.9
Tennessee	626	642	741	721	672	665	47.1	4.7	6.2	11.2
Texas	2,268	2,304	2,481	2,546	2,732	2,727	119.7	23.3	20.2	48.3
Utah	361	356	378	376	338	358	−13.3	0.8	−0.8	—
Vermont	59	48	47	53	62	54	63.6	103.4	−8.5	86.2
Virginia	839	874	963	998	1,006	1,077	252.0	29.7	28.4	66.5
Washington	632	656	594	618	696	687	47.4	23.0	8.7	33.7
West Virginia	128	110	116	99	127	159	11.2	11.3	24.2	38.3
Wisconsin	862	872	830	851	956	907	−2.9	8.2	5.2	13.8
Wyoming	58	67	50	50	73	63	−6.0	−52.5	8.6	−48.4
U.S. Service Schools	24	27	17	31	39	44	266.7	9.1	83.3	100.0
Outlying Areas	43	56	68	74	76	67	1,016.7	48.3	55.8	131.0
American Samoa	—	—	—	—	—	—	—	—	—	—
Federated States of Micronesia	—	—	—	—	—	—	—	—	—	—
Guam	—	—	—	—	—	—	—	—	—	—
Marshall Islands	—	—	—	—	—	—	—	—	—	—
Northern Marianas	—	—	—	—	—	—	—	—	—	—
Palau	—	—	—	—	—	—	—	—	—	—
Puerto Rico	43	56	68	74	76	67	1,016.7	48.3	55.8	131.0
Trust Territories	—	—	—	—	—	—	—	—	—	—
Virgin Islands	—	—	—	—	—	—	—	—	—	—

—Data not available or not applicable.

NOTE.—Some data have been revised from previously published figures.

SOURCE: U.S. Department of Education, National Center for Education Statistics, Higher Education General Information Survey (HEGIS), "Degrees and Other Formal Awards Conferred" surveys, and Integrated Postsecondary Education Data System (IPEDS), "Completions" surveys. (This table was prepared February 1998.)

Table 76.—Staff and student/staff ratios in institutions of higher education, by type and control of institution and by state: Fall 1995

State or other area	Full-time-equivalent staff				Full-time-equivalent faculty				Full-time-equivalent students per FTE staff	
	Public		Private		Public		Private		Public	
	4-year	2-year	4-year	2-year	4-year	2-year	4-year	2-year	4-year	2-year
1	2	3	4	5	6	7	8	9	10	11
United States	1,143,594	325,546	639,524	20,595	321,664	153,545	194,189	8,338	4.2	9.2
Alabama	32,599	5,113	3,913	103	7,004	2,670	1,393	35	3.2	10.7
Alaska	3,116	29	169	47	1,016	6	47	28	5.7	11.3
Arizona	19,732	6,654	1,802	101	4,742	2,939	791	32	4.2	11.5
Arkansas	15,010	2,037	1,888	94	3,979	950	645	38	3.5	7.4
California	92,969	42,432	45,518	1,605	29,354	20,832	14,391	605	4.5	13.3
Colorado	21,434	4,672	4,362	410	7,956	2,090	1,302	193	4.9	8.6
Connecticut	10,341	2,586	15,072	238	2,987	1,283	5,091	90	4.2	8.2
Delaware	4,486	775	761	—	1,097	293	388	—	4.6	8.6
District of Columbia	974	—	24,214	—	522	—	5,269	—	6.1	—
Florida	32,694	21,272	18,977	784	9,456	8,983	5,953	289	4.9	8.3
Georgia	32,561	7,901	12,200	530	7,835	3,789	4,848	239	4.1	7.2
Hawaii	5,146	1,436	1,241	—	1,881	868	509	—	3.7	11.3
Idaho	5,591	679	363	845	2,000	297	165	358	5.8	7.8
Illinois	43,829	19,683	40,654	523	11,336	9,074	12,861	220	3.6	9.3
Indiana	32,658	3,329	11,968	268	8,955	1,473	3,684	112	4.5	7.0
Iowa	17,502	4,805	8,121	117	4,001	1,963	2,834	51	3.3	8.3
Kansas	15,532	5,272	2,529	174	4,726	2,378	1,074	52	4.6	7.6
Kentucky	21,006	2,702	4,258	283	6,001	1,535	1,455	118	4.1	10.4
Louisiana	25,612	1,448	6,190	94	7,847	692	2,037	48	4.9	11.8
Maine	4,960	643	2,949	137	1,498	308	882	60	4.6	6.8
Maryland	20,655	8,437	13,466	158	6,936	3,790	3,723	44	4.3	6.8
Massachusetts	18,867	5,488	56,511	873	5,214	2,502	15,151	361	4.2	8.2
Michigan	45,738	10,476	10,134	328	14,104	4,936	3,633	133	4.5	9.9
Minnesota	22,480	6,050	8,752	440	5,317	3,242	3,231	204	3.9	10.4
Mississippi	15,867	4,873	1,575	130	3,168	2,530	563	44	3.2	8.5
Missouri	23,276	4,983	17,752	743	7,711	2,150	5,819	308	4.1	8.2
Montana	5,306	631	623	94	1,666	341	209	31	5.2	7.3
Nebraska	13,760	2,441	4,013	54	3,383	1,015	1,450	38	3.5	8.1
Nevada	4,544	1,654	137	14	1,628	821	68	5	4.8	9.2
New Hampshire	3,681	1,170	5,174	265	1,144	787	1,456	108	6.0	4.4
New Jersey	26,971	8,008	11,708	397	6,835	3,208	3,291	159	3.8	10.1
New Mexico	12,313	3,163	480	53	2,702	1,239	175	23	3.2	8.1
New York	52,989	22,351	104,750	2,644	16,916	10,428	30,515	1,144	5.0	7.9
North Carolina	33,513	14,575	26,912	341	8,755	7,957	5,722	129	4.0	6.3
North Dakota	5,332	926	404	170	1,831	383	173	34	4.7	7.3
Ohio	50,420	9,426	20,436	837	13,807	4,528	7,153	373	4.4	9.3
Oklahoma	15,896	4,411	3,461	393	4,802	1,803	1,231	152	4.9	8.4
Oregon	15,723	6,733	3,990	17	5,471	2,955	1,585	11	3.4	6.4
Pennsylvania	52,022	7,414	50,477	3,361	16,146	4,091	16,094	1,174	3.9	8.3
Rhode Island	3,327	673	7,174	212	1,013	287	1,796	109	5.3	12.6
South Carolina	15,904	4,821	4,100	228	5,028	2,173	1,353	85	4.5	7.8
South Dakota	4,215	56	1,070	35	1,485	34	414	5	5.9	3.1
Tennessee	27,278	5,021	17,161	304	6,929	2,240	4,427	150	3.5	9.4
Texas	83,986	28,587	21,891	644	20,276	13,226	6,944	263	4.0	8.3
Utah	15,447	1,777	4,805	157	3,545	612	1,740	84	4.1	10.9
Vermont	3,866	266	3,194	176	1,198	157	974	104	3.5	7.1
Virginia	37,812	4,688	10,216	585	9,250	1,999	3,379	261	3.7	14.2
Washington	24,840	9,934	5,735	228	6,299	4,940	2,338	100	3.1	10.4
West Virginia	10,301	586	1,837	92	3,698	259	570	39	5.4	8.2
Wisconsin	29,113	10,809	14,440	127	7,634	5,795	3,396	57	4.2	5.5
Wyoming	2,826	1,563	—	141	848	697	—	39	3.5	7.3
U.S. Service Schools ...	7,575	88	—	—	2,731	—	—	—	2.4	276.1
Outlying areas	11,629	1,976	7,802	584	3,797	766	2,722	298	4.7	5.7
American Samoa	—	182	—	—	—	98	—	—	—	5.4
Federated States of Micronesia	—	240	—	—	—	107	—	—	—	4.5
Guam	573	288	—	—	212	135	—	—	4.9	3.6
Marshall Islands	—	32	—	—	—	8	—	—	—	—
Northern Marianas	—	206	—	—	—	49	—	—	—	3.0
Palau	—	140	—	—	—	35	—	—	—	2.1
Puerto Rico	10,509	888	7,802	584	3,404	334	2,722	298	4.7	7.9
Virgin Islands	548	—	—	—	180	—	—	—	3.7	—

Table 76.—Staff and student/staff ratios in institutions of higher education, by type and control of institution and by state: Fall 1995

State or other area	Full-time-equivalent students per FTE staff		Full-time-equivalent students per FTE faculty				Full-time-equivalent faculty as a percent of FTE staff			
	Private		Public		Private		Public		Private	
	4-year	2-year	4-year	2-year	4-year	2-year	4-year	2-year	4-year	2-year
1	12	13	14	15	16	17	18	19	20	21
United States	**3.8**	**8.1**	**14.8**	**19.5**	**12.4**	**20.1**	**28.1**	**47.2**	**30.4**	**40.5**
Alabama	5.0	4.4	14.9	20.4	14.0	12.7	21.5	52.2	35.6	34.2
Alaska	3.5	3.6	17.5	51.5	12.5	6.0	32.6	22.0	27.9	59.4
Arizona	9.2	8.8	17.5	26.1	21.1	27.7	24.0	44.2	43.9	31.7
Arkansas	5.3	3.7	13.3	16.0	15.5	9.2	26.5	46.6	34.1	40.6
California	4.4	8.0	14.3	27.0	13.9	21.3	31.6	49.1	31.6	37.7
Colorado	5.0	8.4	13.1	19.3	16.7	17.9	37.1	44.7	29.8	47.0
Connecticut	2.9	4.9	14.5	16.6	8.6	12.9	28.9	49.6	33.8	37.6
Delaware	7.0	—	18.7	22.9	13.6	—	24.5	37.8	51.0	—
District of Columbia	2.3	—	11.4	—	10.5	—	53.6	—	21.8	—
Florida	4.2	6.5	16.9	19.7	13.5	17.7	28.9	42.2	31.4	36.8
Georgia	4.5	7.8	16.9	15.0	11.4	17.3	24.1	48.0	39.7	45.2
Hawaii	8.0	—	10.2	18.7	19.5	—	36.6	60.4	41.0	—
Idaho	5.5	9.6	16.1	17.7	12.1	22.7	35.8	43.8	45.3	42.3
Illinois	3.6	7.2	14.1	20.2	11.3	17.2	25.9	46.1	31.6	42.1
Indiana	4.6	10.7	16.4	15.8	14.8	25.5	27.4	44.2	30.8	41.9
Iowa	5.1	7.9	14.5	20.3	14.6	18.3	22.9	40.9	34.9	43.1
Kansas	5.4	4.2	15.1	16.7	12.8	14.2	30.4	45.1	42.5	29.8
Kentucky	5.4	8.3	14.5	18.4	15.8	20.0	28.6	56.8	34.2	41.7
Louisiana	3.8	8.0	16.0	24.6	11.5	15.7	30.6	47.8	32.9	51.2
Maine	4.2	12.1	15.2	14.2	14.0	27.6	30.2	47.8	29.9	43.8
Maryland	2.2	6.5	12.7	15.1	8.1	23.6	33.6	44.9	27.6	27.6
Massachusetts	3.4	6.9	15.1	18.0	12.5	16.6	27.6	45.6	26.8	41.4
Michigan	6.0	5.3	14.6	21.0	16.8	13.0	30.8	47.1	35.9	40.6
Minnesota	5.5	7.4	16.7	19.4	15.0	16.0	23.7	53.6	36.9	46.3
Mississippi	6.0	5.6	16.3	16.4	16.7	16.5	20.0	51.9	35.7	33.7
Missouri	4.1	5.3	12.3	18.9	12.5	12.8	33.1	43.1	32.8	41.4
Montana	5.8	6.4	16.6	13.5	17.2	19.1	31.4	54.0	33.5	33.5
Nebraska	4.1	7.5	14.0	19.4	11.5	10.6	24.6	41.6	36.1	70.4
Nevada	7.1	1.9	13.4	18.5	14.2	5.4	35.8	49.6	49.7	36.1
New Hampshire	3.6	11.8	19.2	6.5	12.9	29.0	31.1	67.2	28.1	40.7
New Jersey	3.8	9.7	15.2	25.3	13.4	24.2	25.3	40.1	28.1	40.0
New Mexico	7.6	18.0	14.5	20.8	21.0	42.0	21.9	39.2	36.5	42.9
New York	3.2	9.6	15.7	16.8	11.1	22.1	31.9	46.7	29.1	43.3
North Carolina	2.2	3.9	15.2	11.4	10.5	10.3	26.1	54.6	21.3	37.9
North Dakota	7.7	1.5	13.7	17.7	17.8	7.3	34.3	41.4	43.0	20.1
Ohio	4.7	10.7	15.9	19.3	13.4	23.9	27.4	48.0	35.0	44.6
Oklahoma	5.1	4.9	16.1	20.6	14.4	12.6	30.2	40.9	35.6	38.6
Oregon	5.0	9.0	9.8	14.5	12.7	14.3	34.8	43.9	39.7	63.4
Pennsylvania	3.6	9.7	12.4	15.0	11.2	27.8	31.0	55.2	31.9	34.9
Rhode Island	4.0	—	17.4	29.6	15.9	—	30.4	42.6	25.0	—
South Carolina	5.3	5.3	14.3	17.2	16.0	14.2	31.6	45.1	33.0	37.1
South Dakota	5.1	4.1	16.7	5.1	13.2	28.4	35.2	60.2	38.7	14.5
Tennessee	2.7	6.6	13.8	21.0	10.4	13.4	25.4	44.6	25.8	49.4
Texas	4.2	8.8	16.6	17.9	13.2	21.4	24.1	46.3	31.7	40.9
Utah	6.9	7.3	17.7	31.7	19.1	13.6	22.9	34.4	36.2	53.8
Vermont	3.9	1.0	11.4	12.0	12.6	1.7	31.0	59.0	30.5	59.1
Virginia	4.6	6.9	14.9	33.4	13.9	15.4	24.5	42.6	33.1	44.6
Washington	5.4	9.0	12.4	20.9	13.2	20.7	25.4	49.7	40.8	43.6
West Virginia	5.0	8.4	14.9	18.5	16.0	19.9	35.9	44.2	31.1	42.4
Wisconsin	2.9	11.8	15.9	10.2	12.3	26.2	26.2	53.6	23.5	45.1
Wyoming	—	5.4	11.5	16.4	—	19.5	30.0	44.6	—	27.5
U.S. Service Schools	—	—	6.5	—	—	—	36.1	—	—	—
Outlying areas	10.5	13.4	14.4	14.7	30.1	26.2	32.6	38.8	34.9	51.0
American Samoa	—	—	—	10.1	—	—	—	53.8	—	—
Federated States of Micronesia	—	—	—	10.0	—	—	—	44.8	—	—
Guam	—	—	13.1	7.6	—	—	37.1	46.9	—	—
Marshall Islands	—	—	—	—	—	—	—	25.3	—	—
Northern Marianas	—	—	—	12.8	—	—	—	23.8	—	—
Palau	—	—	—	8.5	—	—	—	25.0	—	—
Puerto Rico	10.5	13.4	14.6	20.9	30.1	26.2	32.4	37.6	34.9	51.0
Virgin Islands	—	—	11.4	—	—	—	33.0	—	—	—

—Data not reported or not applicable.

NOTE.—Data include imputations for nonrespondent institutions. Because of rounding, details may not add to totals.

SOURCE: U.S. Department of Education, National Center for Education Statistics, Integrated Postsecondary Education Data System (IPEDS), "Fall Staff, 1995" and "Fall Enrollment" surveys. (This table was prepared January 1998.)

Table 77.—Average salary of full-time instructional faculty on 9–month contracts in institutions of higher education, by type and control of institution and by state: 1996–97

State or other area	All institutions	Public institutions					Private institutions				
		Total	4-year institutions			2-year	Total	4-year institutions			2-year
			Total	University	Other 4-year			Total	University	Other 4-year	
1	2	3	4	5	6	7	8	9	10	11	12
United States	$50,829	$50,303	$52,718	$57,047	$49,836	$44,584	$52,112	$52,443	67,457	45,938	32,628
Alabama	42,006	42,843	44,785	48,913	42,219	37,708	37,530	37,701	—	37,701	25,023
Alaska	50,091	50,725	50,657	50,914	50,494	59,281	38,307	38,307	—	38,307	—
Arizona	52,605	52,681	54,206	57,275	45,889	49,601	50,636	50,636	—	50,636	—
Arkansas	39,488	39,915	42,800	48,836	40,820	31,780	37,269	38,059	—	38,059	16,681
California	59,870	59,543	63,276	75,604	60,987	54,529	61,172	61,394	75,175	54,043	36,992
Colorado	50,095	49,784	52,336	58,381	47,221	37,225	52,270	52,270	55,228	48,623	
Connecticut	61,592	61,598	64,695	70,883	58,855	52,640	61,584	62,293	79,548	55,058	35,069
Delaware	56,948	57,203	59,872	62,295	46,688	43,846	54,483	54,483	—	54,483	—
District of Columbia	59,385	—	—	—	—	—	59,385	59,385	60,978	45,531	—
Florida	47,598	47,576	52,100	57,386	49,010	41,436	47,685	47,718	59,180	43,449	26,720
Georgia	47,193	47,721	49,929	55,990	48,444	37,663	45,767	46,227	69,677	39,794	30,492
Hawaii	52,175	52,488	57,364	58,846	48,142	44,264	48,572	48,572	—	48,572	—
Idaho	44,016	44,179	45,201	49,095	43,360	37,295	43,460	40,100	—	40,100	44,970
Illinois	52,548	50,970	51,532	55,988	47,655	50,034	55,292	55,746	72,650	44,627	28,830
Indiana	48,588	48,299	50,719	53,481	45,021	34,590	49,193	49,429	71,279	43,084	30,265
Iowa	47,191	51,033	57,503	60,581	49,273	36,710	40,880	40,897	51,200	39,593	29,025
Kansas	41,655	43,272	47,067	49,907	40,890	35,437	31,478	31,768	—	31,768	25,910
Kentucky	43,410	45,097	47,773	54,298	43,871	35,627	37,369	37,369	—	37,369	—
Louisiana	44,884	43,530	44,635	52,901	42,521	34,416	51,281	51,340	58,881	38,830	48,630
Maine	45,199	43,882	45,874	49,583	43,866	35,831	48,616	49,255	—	49,255	28,944
Maryland	50,802	49,781	52,144	59,221	48,566	45,594	54,379	54,441	71,669	45,791	25,000
Massachusetts	58,697	51,427	55,611	64,374	52,029	41,536	62,790	63,061	71,789	53,799	35,212
Michigan	54,248	56,393	56,869	63,355	51,451	54,698	43,242	43,459	47,513	42,919	20,074
Minnesota	48,877	50,390	53,763	64,476	48,163	45,176	45,347	45,591	—	45,591	36,638
Mississippi	39,644	40,232	43,302	45,240	42,010	36,257	34,896	35,749	—	35,749	23,554
Missouri	47,063	47,579	49,568	58,603	47,753	40,596	46,023	46,424	62,112	37,842	29,963
Montana	40,589	41,731	43,338	45,089	39,402	31,758	33,714	34,360	—	34,360	26,100
Nebraska	44,701	46,030	49,374	56,249	44,649	34,332	40,574	40,574	47,592	36,828	—
Nevada	51,959	52,050	55,194	58,997	52,647	44,829	37,946	37,946	—	37,946	—
New Hampshire	49,425	47,339	50,127	51,630	47,545	36,029	52,143	52,991	—	52,991	27,236
New Jersey	61,538	61,419	64,359	71,997	61,765	54,694	61,850	61,989	75,071	51,694	25,845
New Mexico	43,322	43,552	47,244	49,782	40,250	32,627	38,532	38,532	—	38,532	—
New York	56,996	55,913	58,051	62,459	57,349	52,120	58,092	58,546	69,356	51,389	29,503
North Carolina	47,462	49,096	51,803	62,388	47,500	32,153	43,687	43,978	61,504	37,234	31,300
North Dakota	36,366	37,103	38,347	39,434	36,099	32,190	31,158	32,623	—	32,623	23,785
Ohio	50,240	51,914	54,747	56,462	48,586	42,722	46,526	46,769	67,470	44,502	29,678
Oklahoma	41,961	42,514	44,841	50,253	40,482	35,991	39,830	40,329	50,222	35,806	25,654
Oregon	44,506	44,212	45,121	47,702	42,250	43,161	45,546	45,546	—	45,546	—
Pennsylvania	55,132	56,029	57,330	62,407	54,469	48,938	54,040	54,457	73,122	48,846	31,440
Rhode Island	54,797	52,382	55,721	60,085	48,226	42,341	56,582	56,582	—	56,582	—
South Carolina	42,246	43,199	48,228	53,983	42,235	32,486	38,030	38,169	—	38,169	31,540
South Dakota	36,482	37,279	37,382	38,107	36,391	26,212	33,685	33,738	—	33,738	28,800
Tennessee	45,532	45,994	49,315	56,243	46,955	35,625	44,488	44,636	67,787	35,955	23,582
Texas	46,434	45,576	48,678	55,528	43,062	39,963	50,117	50,292	59,321	43,378	26,395
Utah	46,735	45,037	47,232	51,683	39,984	36,352	50,704	50,859	51,750	39,229	37,370
Vermont	44,722	46,461	46,461	49,695	38,167	—	43,140	44,403	—	44,403	20,261
Virginia	48,468	49,391	52,734	57,209	49,924	38,940	45,405	45,503	—	45,503	28,018
Washington	46,038	46,051	51,042	54,807	44,925	39,662	45,989	45,989	—	45,989	—
West Virginia	40,929	41,942	42,570	49,056	39,510	33,520	35,534	35,534	—	35,534	—
Wisconsin	49,325	50,747	52,106	63,364	48,066	48,694	43,320	43,320	54,490	40,117	—
Wyoming	39,855	39,855	46,743	46,743		33,007	—	—	—	—	—
U.S. Service Schools	61,536	61,536	61,536	—	61,536						
Outlying areas	33,163	34,652	34,840	36,820	33,761	33,380	21,412	21,412	—	21,412	—
American Samoa	29,072	29,072	—	—	—	29,072	—	—	—	—	—
Federated States of Micronesia	17,695	17,695	—	—	—	17,695	—	—	—	—	—
Guam	47,679	47,679	51,109	—	51,109	43,155	—	—	—	—	—
Marshall Islands	—	—	—	—	—	—	—	—	—	—	—
Northern Marianas	35,628	35,628	—	—	—	35,628	—	—	—	—	—
Palau	17,743	17,743	—	—	—	17,743	—	—	—	—	—
Puerto Rico	32,030	33,641	33,495	36,820	31,389	36,361	21,412	21,412	—	21,412	—
Virgin Islands	44,976	44,976	44,976	—	44,976		—	—	—	—	—

—Data not reported or not applicable.

NOTE.—Data include imputations for nonrespondent institutions. Data are for degree granting institutions.

SOURCE: U.S. Department of Education, National Center for Education Statistics, Integrated Postsecondary Education Data System (IPEDS), "Salaries, Tenure, and Fringe Benefits of Full-Time Instructional Faculty, 1996–97" survey. (This table was prepared February 1998).

Table 78.—Average salary (in current dollars) of full-time faculty on 9-month contracts in institutions of higher education, by state: 1970–71 to 1996–97

State or other area	1970–71	1971–72	1972–73	1974–75	1975–76	1976–77	1977–78	1978–79	1979–80
1	2	3	4	5	6	7	8	9	10
United States	$12,710	$13,300	$13,856	$15,622	$16,659	$17,560	$18,709	$19,820	$21,348
Alabama	10,778	10,937	11,385	13,466	13,840	15,091	16,378	17,426	17,887
Alaska	13,929	14,420	15,027	17,304	24,741	26,207	—	28,638	29,091
Arizona	12,940	13,665	14,106	16,534	17,574	18,702	19,679	21,365	23,710
Arkansas	10,241	10,960	11,446	13,008	13,783	14,727	15,420	16,466	17,756
California	13,922	14,639	15,582	18,129	19,614	20,786	22,155	22,757	25,715
Colorado	12,501	12,582	13,284	14,776	16,129	17,091	17,890	19,097	20,537
Connecticut	13,805	14,297	14,600	16,720	17,488	18,170	20,048	21,387	22,782
Delaware	12,312	12,878	13,546	15,480	16,463	18,398	19,620	20,493	21,586
District of Columbia	13,422	14,116	14,872	16,214	17,446	18,749	20,332	21,426	22,855
Florida	11,424	12,954	13,568	15,194	15,211	16,265	17,332	18,294	19,438
Georgia	11,947	12,106	12,612	13,987	14,176	14,806	16,094	17,611	19,351
Hawaii	13,777	14,323	14,663	15,577	18,723	20,179	20,857	21,185	22,455
Idaho	10,825	11,526	11,625	13,890	14,695	15,536	16,736	17,952	19,378
Illinois	14,193	13,673	14,214	15,992	17,251	18,269	19,083	20,341	21,550
Indiana	12,681	13,366	13,773	14,962	16,056	16,821	17,784	18,883	20,099
Iowa	12,100	12,449	12,824	14,100	15,290	16,293	17,185	18,129	19,326
Kansas	11,207	11,482	12,019	13,682	14,875	15,920	16,801	17,880	19,095
Kentucky	11,453	12,035	12,535	13,820	14,651	15,569	16,394	17,551	18,559
Louisiana	11,292	11,419	12,138	13,417	14,546	15,046	16,636	17,388	19,352
Maine	11,917	12,283	12,921	14,099	14,333	15,358	16,156	16,983	18,232
Maryland	12,577	13,096	13,842	15,614	16,914	17,599	19,051	19,966	21,447
Massachusetts	13,524	15,570	15,242	17,039	17,760	18,393	19,470	20,615	22,463
Michigan	13,448	14,089	14,797	16,754	17,525	18,663	19,729	20,982	22,422
Minnesota	12,866	13,215	13,887	15,198	16,046	17,303	18,367	19,430	20,802
Mississippi	9,975	10,534	10,958	12,284	13,422	13,749	15,010	16,069	17,083
Missouri	11,887	12,473	12,848	14,471	15,354	16,045	17,151	18,461	19,670
Montana	11,546	11,958	12,467	13,618	15,436	16,137	17,313	17,873	19,212
Nebraska	11,562	12,060	12,237	13,763	14,583	15,667	16,379	17,640	18,666
Nevada	10,258	13,998	14,395	15,643	17,256	18,202	19,673	21,018	22,876
New Hampshire	12,226	13,017	13,053	14,678	15,715	16,263	17,108	18,155	19,273
New Jersey	13,152	14,025	14,647	16,678	17,382	18,742	19,790	21,265	22,233
New Mexico	12,122	12,835	13,429	14,651	16,089	16,924	18,074	19,378	20,802
New York	14,144	14,495	15,546	17,401	18,242	18,750	20,315	21,522	22,972
North Carolina	11,804	12,988	13,438	14,479	14,858	15,233	16,394	17,505	18,836
North Dakota	10,579	10,876	11,414	12,668	14,707	15,575	16,406	17,410	18,742
Ohio	12,157	13,028	13,475	15,104	16,339	17,421	18,393	19,453	20,858
Oklahoma	11,268	11,485	11,777	13,158	14,263	15,063	16,489	17,557	18,980
Oregon	12,406	12,739	12,961	14,582	16,185	17,493	18,403	19,862	20,491
Pennsylvania	12,207	12,491	13,969	16,215	17,484	18,365	19,155	20,428	21,795
Rhode Island	12,658	13,211	13,910	15,868	16,544	17,921	19,255	20,735	22,241
South Carolina	11,146	11,750	12,083	13,485	13,782	14,212	15,189	16,897	18,578
South Dakota	10,257	10,473	10,757	12,563	13,501	14,342	14,741	16,030	17,184
Tennessee	11,295	12,215	12,701	14,247	14,593	15,691	16,819	18,050	19,433
Texas	11,947	12,294	12,662	14,157	15,741	16,706	17,667	18,531	19,755
Utah	12,324	12,702	13,180	14,691	16,191	17,533	18,696	20,044	21,230
Vermont	11,575	12,100	12,522	13,379	14,548	15,143	16,042	16,930	18,353
Virginia	11,634	12,267	12,844	14,134	15,045	16,058	16,796	18,050	19,312
Washington	12,883	12,886	13,390	15,008	16,346	17,178	18,754	19,775	21,561
West Virginia	10,723	11,256	11,526	13,094	13,749	14,743	15,400	16,732	17,997
Wisconsin	12,219	12,947	13,902	15,462	16,502	17,498	18,553	19,804	21,256
Wyoming	12,120	12,594	13,114	14,251	16,179	17,302	18,977	19,842	22,236
U.S. Service Schools ...	16,621	15,722	20,165	21,343	22,805	23,896	25,690	28,666	29,995
Outlying areas	10,514	10,759	11,761	12,686	13,592	14,079	15,123	15,066	16,333
American Samoa	—	15,834	7,895	8,446	7,827	9,350	10,286	—	11,384
Federated States of Micronesia	—	—	—	—	—	—	—	—	—
Guam	—	11,499	—	14,078	14,481	14,374	14,797	18,282	18,664
Marshall Islands	—	—	—	—	—	—	—	—	—
Northern Marianas	—	—	—	—	—	—	—	—	—
Palau	—	—	—	—	—	—	—	—	—
Puerto Rico	10,500	10,585	11,755	12,590	13,611	14,083	15,199	14,842	16,250
Trust Territories	—	—	—	—	—	—	—	—	—
Virgin Islands	11,116	14,376	13,559	14,315	14,414	15,308	15,189	17,055	17,702

Table 78.—Average salary (in current dollars) of full-time faculty on 9-month contracts in institutions of higher education, by state: 1970–71 to 1996–97—Continued

State or other area	1980–81	1981–82	1982–83	1984–85	1985–86	1987–88	1989–90	1990–91	1991–92
1	11	12	13	14	15	16	17	18	19
United States	**$23,302**	**$25,449**	**$27,196**	**$30,447**	**$32,392**	**$35,897**	**$40,133**	**$42,165**	**$43,851**
Alabama	20,421	21,200	22,883	26,732	29,108	31,328	33,308	36,055	36,335
Alaska	35,387	37,467	41,313	41,204	42,696	41,045	44,789	43,486	44,854
Arizona	25,654	28,293	29,854	32,048	34,118	38,080	40,903	43,425	44,503
Arkansas	18,991	20,903	22,613	25,621	27,427	28,911	31,588	33,110	35,031
California	28,628	30,847	31,887	36,413	39,002	42,611	47,681	51,394	52,728
Colorado	22,455	24,613	26,184	28,852	31,003	34,373	38,450	40,733	42,284
Connecticut	24,861	27,087	29,663	33,894	36,464	41,437	47,057	49,246	52,456
Delaware	23,367	25,750	26,813	30,147	32,134	35,706	40,682	42,899	46,274
District of Columbia	24,622	27,132	28,592	32,408	35,014	39,028	44,872	47,876	49,564
Florida	21,381	23,126	24,947	28,248	29,334	34,375	38,027	37,806	39,642
Georgia	21,466	23,236	24,733	28,129	30,378	33,171	36,261	37,759	38,595
Hawaii	24,008	25,548	28,008	28,577	30,444	35,489	39,917	41,887	46,638
Idaho	20,867	22,292	23,872	26,952	28,266	30,825	32,118	34,539	35,060
Illinois	23,571	25,608	27,025	30,551	32,789	35,509	40,546	42,480	44,359
Indiana	22,156	23,766	25,431	28,348	30,279	33,716	37,442	39,943	42,401
Iowa	20,972	22,710	24,730	26,994	27,959	31,894	38,028	39,912	40,683
Kansas	20,533	22,213	24,193	26,749	28,274	29,957	34,185	35,426	36,338
Kentucky	20,495	22,439	23,920	25,863	27,324	30,257	32,687	35,213	37,729
Louisiana	21,385	23,519	24,837	27,301	28,202	30,463	33,275	37,103	38,900
Maine	19,931	21,774	23,630	26,457	27,444	31,836	36,794	38,737	40,026
Maryland	23,427	24,802	27,410	30,595	32,797	36,874	41,877	43,871	44,737
Massachusetts	24,097	27,061	29,603	33,499	36,582	40,273	46,104	48,060	49,526
Michigan	24,423	26,193	27,894	31,183	33,039	36,947	41,270	40,667	45,877
Minnesota	22,609	24,400	26,291	30,728	32,373	34,719	39,376	41,718	42,640
Mississippi	18,889	20,795	20,792	23,680	24,273	26,763	30,595	31,688	31,687
Missouri	21,485	22,536	24,396	27,269	29,033	31,979	35,621	37,658	38,714
Montana	20,342	23,110	25,269	26,845	27,730	28,746	29,780	32,647	34,401
Nebraska	20,527	22,477	23,568	26,940	27,693	29,747	34,745	37,384	39,306
Nevada	24,117	27,054	29,121	28,877	32,394	36,250	39,414	42,057	44,160
New Hampshire	21,190	23,046	24,450	28,316	30,237	34,333	38,783	40,764	42,111
New Jersey	24,237	25,845	29,739	32,376	35,313	40,151	44,968	48,047	52,254
New Mexico	23,131	24,529	26,846	28,460	29,485	31,086	34,661	36,398	37,961
New York	24,549	27,410	29,474	33,923	35,845	39,727	44,604	47,200	49,014
North Carolina	21,176	23,072	23,391	27,082	29,585	32,908	37,207	39,159	40,205
North Dakota	20,244	23,563	24,815	24,823	27,618	28,591	30,907	32,511	33,701
Ohio	23,093	24,967	26,823	30,695	32,212	36,026	40,147	42,339	44,163
Oklahoma	21,337	23,772	26,552	27,450	29,479	30,461	34,508	36,225	36,911
Oregon	21,786	23,559	24,809	26,857	28,629	31,608	34,342	35,692	38,011
Pennsylvania	23,620	25,583	27,457	30,514	31,956	36,148	41,191	43,290	45,970
Rhode Island	24,298	25,984	28,042	31,285	33,519	36,907	43,971	47,055	47,780
South Carolina	20,371	22,402	23,017	26,555	27,895	30,382	34,017	35,543	35,959
South Dakota	18,806	20,123	21,101	23,306	25,234	27,388	29,437	32,122	33,111
Tennessee	20,956	21,814	24,056	27,699	29,389	32,935	36,126	37,813	38,641
Texas	21,381	24,726	26,952	29,712	31,311	33,990	37,608	38,809	39,736
Utah	23,702	25,278	27,222	29,565	31,475	32,208	38,319	37,664	39,277
Vermont	19,839	22,437	24,110	27,787	28,843	32,013	36,018	37,841	39,888
Virginia	21,260	23,346	24,946	27,891	30,769	35,987	40,984	42,761	43,188
Washington	23,329	25,651	26,330	28,715	30,376	33,182	36,675	38,828	41,127
West Virginia	19,253	21,408	21,728	24,139	26,225	28,287	29,758	33,930	34,348
Wisconsin	23,118	25,128	27,002	28,908	31,233	35,034	38,498	40,695	41,775
Wyoming	24,133	26,993	29,129	30,747	32,065	32,819	34,438	35,583	37,502
U.S. Service Schools ...	32,409	33,983	35,269	38,269	38,205	42,299	42,924	45,537	50,243
Outlying areas	19,534	20,850	20,396	21,356	23,580	17,346	22,303	21,387	24,370
American Samoa	13,028	14,514	13,885	16,482	—	—	20,694	21,416	21,411
Federated States of Micronesia	—	—	—	—	—	—	16,348	16,637	17,001
Guam	22,176	23,270	24,304	23,819	27,575	9,336	36,263	47,741	48,459
Marshall Islands	—	—	—	—	—	—	—	—	—
Northern Marianas	—	—	—	—	—	—	—	—	30,520
Palau	—	—	—	—	—	—	30,873	25,918	30,898
Puerto Rico	19,522	20,712	20,202	21,129	23,180	16,717	19,961	18,610	22,294
Trust Territories	—	—	—	8,628	13,406	12,468	—	—	—
Virgin Islands	18,638	22,343	23,832	24,435	25,804	33,500	40,888	40,254	43,609

Table 78.—Average salary (in current dollars) of full-time faculty on 9-month contracts in institutions of higher education, by state: 1970–71 to 1996–97—Continued

State or other area	1992–93	1993–94	1994–95	1995–96	1996–97[1]	1970–71 to 1996–97	1985–86 to 1991–92	1991–92 to 1996–97	1985–86 to 1996–97
						Percentage change			
1	20	21	22	23	24	25	26	27	28
United States	**$44,714**	**$46,364**	**$47,811**	**$49,309**	**$50,829**	**299.9**	**35.4**	**15.9**	**56.9**
Alabama	36,813	38,418	40,576	40,505	42,006	289.7	24.8	15.6	44.3
Alaska	45,765	47,917	49,023	49,036	50,091	259.6	5.1	11.7	17.3
Arizona	43,030	46,825	48,863	50,841	52,605	306.5	30.4	18.2	54.2
Arkansas	36,127	37,222	37,655	38,782	39,488	285.6	27.7	12.7	44.0
California	51,516	54,259	55,247	57,716	59,870	330.0	35.2	13.5	53.5
Colorado	43,474	44,008	46,350	47,874	50,095	300.7	36.4	18.5	61.6
Connecticut	53,238	55,458	56,559	59,253	61,592	346.2	43.9	17.4	68.9
Delaware	48,247	49,780	52,773	55,148	56,948	362.5	44.0	23.1	77.2
District of Columbia	51,556	52,586	54,560	56,994	59,385	342.4	41.6	19.8	69.6
Florida	39,989	41,543	43,078	45,677	47,598	316.6	35.1	20.1	62.3
Georgia	39,738	40,707	42,852	45,188	47,193	295.0	27.0	22.3	55.4
Hawaii	50,519	49,958	51,978	51,470	52,175	278.7	53.2	11.9	71.4
Idaho	35,626	38,813	40,248	42,271	44,016	306.6	24.0	25.5	55.7
Illinois	46,055	47,435	49,511	51,065	52,548	270.2	35.3	18.5	60.3
Indiana	43,734	44,921	45,395	47,351	48,588	283.2	40.0	14.6	60.5
Iowa	42,349	43,491	44,571	46,113	47,191	290.0	45.5	16.0	68.8
Kansas	37,433	38,481	40,538	41,497	41,655	271.7	28.5	14.6	47.3
Kentucky	38,101	39,393	40,463	41,791	43,410	279.0	38.1	15.1	58.9
Louisiana	38,989	39,304	39,725	40,689	44,884	297.5	37.9	15.4	59.2
Maine	40,621	41,232	41,499	43,075	45,199	279.3	45.8	12.9	64.7
Maryland	45,307	46,212	48,051	49,835	50,802	303.9	36.4	13.6	54.9
Massachusetts	51,232	54,233	55,110	56,498	58,697	334.0	35.4	18.5	60.5
Michigan	47,606	49,152	50,804	52,555	54,248	303.4	38.9	18.2	64.2
Minnesota	44,328	44,617	46,147	46,617	48,877	279.9	31.7	14.6	51.0
Mississippi	33,516	35,214	37,250	39,565	39,644	297.4	30.5	25.1	63.3
Missouri	40,306	41,786	43,280	44,993	47,063	295.9	33.3	21.6	62.1
Montana	36,545	36,549	36,728	38,784	40,589	251.5	24.1	18.0	46.4
Nebraska	41,051	41,663	42,293	43,443	44,701	286.6	41.9	13.7	61.4
Nevada	44,959	45,505	46,820	49,235	51,959	406.5	36.3	17.7	60.4
New Hampshire	45,448	45,173	47,424	48,438	49,425	304.3	39.3	17.4	63.5
New Jersey	53,308	55,629	59,200	60,408	61,538	367.9	48.0	17.8	74.3
New Mexico	38,749	40,008	41,898	42,565	43,322	257.4	28.7	14.1	46.9
New York	50,015	52,503	53,915	55,764	56,996	303.0	36.7	16.3	59.0
North Carolina	40,473	42,202	44,472	45,065	47,462	302.1	35.9	18.0	60.4
North Dakota	34,113	34,379	35,213	35,303	36,366	243.8	22.0	7.9	31.7
Ohio	44,558	45,830	47,164	48,468	50,240	313.3	37.1	13.8	56.0
Oklahoma	37,899	39,255	39,686	40,798	41,961	272.4	25.2	13.7	42.3
Oregon	39,950	42,161	42,639	44,272	44,506	258.7	32.8	17.1	55.5
Pennsylvania	47,856	50,390	52,303	53,987	55,132	351.6	43.9	19.9	72.5
Rhode Island	48,679	49,560	51,818	52,805	54,797	332.9	42.5	14.7	63.5
South Carolina	36,789	37,101	39,333	40,820	42,246	279.0	28.9	17.5	51.4
South Dakota	34,269	34,877	35,269	35,982	36,482	255.7	31.2	10.2	44.6
Tennessee	38,820	41,382	43,721	44,431	45,532	303.1	31.5	17.8	54.9
Texas	40,869	43,158	43,892	45,164	46,434	288.7	26.9	16.9	48.3
Utah	42,688	42,111	43,744	45,437	46,735	279.2	24.8	19.0	48.5
Vermont	40,517	40,842	42,053	43,171	44,722	286.4	38.3	12.1	55.1
Virginia	43,227	44,226	45,710	47,365	48,468	316.6	40.4	12.2	57.5
Washington	42,428	43,782	44,107	45,703	46,038	257.4	35.4	11.9	51.6
West Virginia	34,646	36,486	37,812	39,793	40,929	281.7	31.0	19.2	56.1
Wisconsin	43,961	45,306	47,633	48,332	49,325	303.7	33.8	18.1	57.9
Wyoming	37,397	37,422	39,291	39,998	39,855	228.8	17.0	6.3	24.3
U.S. Service Schools ...	53,230	56,353	56,032	61,758	61,536	270.2	31.5	22.5	61.1
Outlying areas	22,421	24,793	32,230	31,663	33,163	215.4	3.4	36.1	40.6
American Samoa	34,170	37,530	33,334	32,522	29,072	—	—	35.8	—
Federated States of Micronesia	18,520	20,001	18,681	26,884	17,695	—	—	4.1	—
Guam	47,510	46,374	46,839	47,021	47,679	—	75.7	-1.6	72.9
Marshall Islands	—	—	16,032	14,722	—	—	—	—	—
Northern Marianas	30,526	30,005	33,706	32,321	35,628	—	—	16.7	—
Palau	34,160	36,360	15,143	15,143	17,743	—	—	-42.6	—
Puerto Rico	19,233	21,222	30,626	30,321	32,030	205.0	-3.8	43.7	38.2
Trust Territories	—	—	—	—	—	—	—	—	—
Virgin Islands	43,161	43,801	42,821	45,452	44,976	304.6	69.0	3.1	74.3

[1] Data for degree-granting institutions. Survey coverage is slightly wider than data for higher education institutions reported for earlier years.

—Data not available or not applicable.

NOTE.—Data for 1973–74, 1983–84, 1986–87, and 1988–89 are not available.

SOURCE: U.S. Department of Education, National Center for Education Statistics, Higher Education General Information Survey (HEGIS), "Salaries and Tenure of Full-Time Instructional Faculty" surveys; and Integrated Postsecondary Education Data System (IPEDS), "Salaries, Tenure, and Fringe Benefits of Full-Time Instructional Faculty" surveys. (This table was prepared February 1998.)

Table 79.—Average salary (in constant 1996–97 dollars [1]) of full-time faculty on 9-month contracts in institutions of higher education, by state: 1970–71 to 1996–97

State or other area	1970–71	1971–72	1972–73	1974–75	1975–76	1976–77	1977–78	1978–79	1979–80
1	2	3	4	5	6	7	8	9	10
United States	$50,843	$51,360	$51,436	$44,103	$44,103	$47,543	$47,467	$45,980	$43,698
Alabama	43,114	42,236	42,262	41,316	39,658	40,859	41,553	40,425	36,613
Alaska	55,719	55,686	55,782	53,092	70,891	70,955	—	66,435	59,547
Arizona	51,763	52,770	52,363	50,729	50,355	50,635	49,928	49,563	48,532
Arkansas	40,966	42,325	42,489	39,912	39,494	39,873	39,123	38,198	36,345
California	55,691	56,531	57,842	55,622	56,201	56,278	56,210	52,792	52,636
Colorado	50,007	48,587	49,312	45,335	46,216	46,274	45,389	44,302	42,037
Connecticut	55,223	55,211	54,197	51,299	50,111	49,195	50,864	49,614	46,633
Delaware	49,250	49,732	50,284	47,496	47,173	49,812	49,778	47,540	44,185
District of Columbia	53,691	54,510	55,206	49,748	49,990	50,763	51,585	49,705	46,782
Florida	45,698	50,024	50,366	46,618	43,586	44,037	43,974	42,439	39,788
Georgia	47,790	46,750	46,817	42,914	40,620	40,087	40,833	40,854	39,610
Hawaii	55,111	55,311	54,431	47,793	53,647	54,634	52,917	49,145	45,963
Idaho	43,302	44,510	43,153	42,617	42,106	42,064	42,461	41,645	39,665
Illinois	56,775	52,799	52,764	49,065	49,431	49,463	48,416	47,188	44,111
Indiana	50,727	51,617	51,127	45,905	46,008	45,543	45,120	43,805	41,141
Iowa	48,402	48,072	47,604	43,260	43,812	44,113	43,601	42,056	39,559
Kansas	44,830	44,341	44,616	41,979	42,621	43,103	42,626	41,478	39,086
Kentucky	45,814	46,477	46,531	42,404	41,980	42,153	41,594	40,715	37,989
Louisiana	45,170	44,096	45,058	41,166	41,679	40,737	42,208	40,337	39,612
Maine	47,670	47,433	47,964	43,257	41,069	41,582	40,990	39,398	37,319
Maryland	50,311	50,571	51,383	47,908	48,465	47,649	48,335	46,318	43,900
Massachusetts	54,099	60,126	56,580	52,278	50,888	49,799	49,398	47,823	45,980
Michigan	53,795	54,408	54,928	51,403	50,215	50,530	50,055	48,675	45,896
Minnesota	51,467	51,030	51,550	46,631	45,978	46,848	46,599	45,074	42,580
Mississippi	39,902	40,680	40,677	37,690	38,460	37,225	38,082	37,277	34,967
Missouri	47,550	48,166	47,693	44,398	43,994	43,442	43,514	42,826	40,263
Montana	46,186	46,179	46,279	41,784	44,229	43,691	43,925	41,462	39,325
Nebraska	46,250	46,572	45,425	42,228	41,785	42,418	41,556	40,922	38,208
Nevada	41,034	54,057	53,436	47,996	49,445	49,282	49,913	48,758	46,825
New Hampshire	48,906	50,267	48,454	45,036	45,030	44,032	43,405	42,116	39,450
New Jersey	52,611	54,161	54,371	51,172	49,806	50,744	50,210	49,331	45,509
New Mexico	48,490	49,564	49,850	44,952	46,100	45,822	45,856	44,954	42,580
New York	56,579	55,976	57,708	53,390	52,269	50,765	51,542	49,927	47,022
North Carolina	47,218	50,154	49,883	44,435	42,574	41,243	41,594	40,609	38,556
North Dakota	42,318	42,000	42,370	38,867	42,142	42,169	41,624	40,388	38,363
Ohio	48,630	50,309	50,021	46,340	46,817	47,167	46,665	45,128	42,695
Oklahoma	45,074	44,351	43,718	40,372	40,870	40,783	41,835	40,729	38,850
Oregon	49,626	49,194	48,113	44,739	46,375	47,362	46,691	46,076	41,943
Pennsylvania	48,830	48,238	51,854	49,750	50,098	49,723	48,599	47,389	44,612
Rhode Island	50,635	51,016	51,635	48,685	47,405	48,521	48,852	48,102	45,525
South Carolina	44,586	45,376	44,853	41,376	39,490	38,479	38,536	39,198	38,028
South Dakota	41,030	40,445	39,931	38,546	38,686	38,831	37,400	37,187	35,174
Tennessee	45,182	47,171	47,148	43,714	41,814	42,483	42,672	41,873	39,778
Texas	47,790	47,475	47,003	43,438	45,103	45,231	44,823	42,989	40,437
Utah	49,298	49,053	48,926	45,074	46,393	47,470	47,434	46,499	43,456
Vermont	46,302	46,728	46,483	41,049	41,684	41,000	40,701	39,275	37,567
Virginia	46,538	47,371	47,678	43,365	43,108	43,477	42,614	41,873	39,530
Washington	51,535	49,761	49,705	46,047	46,838	46,509	47,581	45,875	44,133
West Virginia	42,894	43,467	42,786	40,176	39,396	39,917	39,072	38,815	36,838
Wisconsin	48,878	49,995	51,606	47,440	47,284	47,376	47,071	45,942	43,509
Wyoming	48,482	48,633	48,681	43,726	46,359	46,845	48,147	46,030	45,515
U.S. Service Schools	66,487	60,714	74,855	65,485	65,344	64,698	65,179	66,500	61,397
Outlying areas	42,058	41,548	43,658	38,923	38,946	38,119	38,369	34,950	33,432
American Samoa	—	61,145	29,307	25,914	22,427	25,315	26,097	—	—
Federated States of Micronesia	—	—	—	—	—	—	—	—	—
Guam	—	44,407	—	43,193	41,492	38,917	37,542	42,411	38,204
Marshall Islands	—	—	—	—	—	—	—	—	—
Northern Marianas	—	—	—	—	—	—	—	—	—
Palau	—	—	—	—	—	—	—	—	—
Puerto Rico	42,002	40,876	43,636	38,630	39,001	38,130	38,562	34,431	33,262
Trust Territories	—	—	—	—	—	—	—	—	—
Virgin Islands	44,466	55,515	50,332	43,922	41,302	41,446	38,536	39,565	36,234

Table 79.—Average salary (in constant 1996–97 dollars [1]) of full-time faculty on 9-month contracts in institutions of higher education, by state: 1970–71 to 1996–97—Continued

State or other area	1980–81	1981–82	1982–83	1984–85	1985–86	1987–88	1989–90	1990–91	1991–92
1	11	12	13	14	15	16	17	18	19
United States	**$42,746**	**$42,972**	**$44,031**	**$45,745**	**$47,303**	**$49,242**	**$50,226**	**$50,034**	**$50,419**
Alabama	37,461	35,798	37,048	40,163	42,507	42,975	41,685	42,783	41,777
Alaska	64,915	63,266	66,887	61,906	62,350	56,304	56,053	51,601	51,572
Arizona	47,061	47,775	48,335	48,150	49,823	52,237	51,190	51,529	51,168
Arkansas	34,838	35,296	36,611	38,494	40,052	39,659	39,532	39,289	40,278
California	52,516	52,087	51,626	54,708	56,956	58,452	59,672	60,985	60,625
Colorado	41,192	41,561	42,393	43,348	45,274	47,152	48,120	48,334	48,617
Connecticut	45,606	45,738	48,025	50,924	53,249	56,842	58,891	58,436	60,313
Delaware	42,865	43,481	43,411	45,294	46,926	48,980	50,913	50,905	53,205
District of Columbia	45,167	45,814	46,291	48,691	51,132	53,537	56,157	56,810	56,987
Florida	39,222	39,050	40,390	42,441	42,837	47,154	47,590	44,861	45,579
Georgia	39,378	39,236	40,044	42,262	44,362	45,503	45,380	44,805	44,376
Hawaii	44,041	43,140	45,346	42,935	44,458	48,683	49,956	49,704	53,623
Idaho	38,279	37,642	38,650	40,494	41,277	42,285	40,195	40,985	40,311
Illinois	43,239	43,241	43,754	45,901	47,883	48,710	50,743	50,407	51,003
Indiana	40,644	40,131	41,174	42,591	44,217	46,250	46,858	47,397	48,752
Iowa	38,472	38,347	40,039	40,557	40,829	43,751	47,592	47,360	46,776
Kansas	37,666	37,508	39,169	40,189	41,289	41,094	42,782	42,037	41,780
Kentucky	37,597	37,890	38,727	38,857	39,902	41,505	40,907	41,784	43,380
Louisiana	39,229	39,713	40,212	41,018	41,184	41,788	41,643	44,027	44,726
Maine	36,562	36,767	38,258	39,750	40,077	43,672	46,047	45,966	46,021
Maryland	42,975	41,880	44,378	45,967	47,894	50,582	52,409	52,058	51,437
Massachusetts	44,204	45,694	47,928	50,330	53,422	55,245	57,699	57,029	56,944
Michigan	44,802	44,229	45,161	46,850	48,248	50,683	51,649	48,256	52,748
Minnesota	41,475	41,201	42,566	46,167	47,275	47,626	49,279	49,503	49,026
Mississippi	34,651	35,114	33,663	35,578	35,446	36,713	38,289	37,601	36,433
Missouri	39,413	38,054	39,498	40,970	42,398	43,868	44,579	44,686	44,512
Montana	37,316	39,023	40,911	40,333	40,495	39,433	37,269	38,739	39,553
Nebraska	37,655	37,954	38,157	40,476	40,441	40,806	43,483	44,360	45,193
Nevada	44,241	45,683	47,148	43,386	47,306	49,726	49,326	49,905	50,774
New Hampshire	38,872	38,915	39,585	42,543	44,156	47,097	48,537	48,371	48,418
New Jersey	44,461	43,641	48,148	48,643	51,568	55,078	56,277	57,013	60,080
New Mexico	42,432	41,419	43,465	42,759	43,058	42,643	43,378	43,190	43,647
New York	45,034	46,284	47,719	50,967	52,345	54,496	55,821	56,008	56,355
North Carolina	38,846	38,959	37,871	40,689	43,204	45,142	46,564	46,467	46,227
North Dakota	37,136	39,788	40,176	37,295	40,331	39,220	38,680	38,578	38,749
Ohio	42,363	42,159	43,427	46,117	47,040	49,419	50,244	50,240	50,777
Oklahoma	39,141	40,141	42,989	41,242	43,049	41,785	43,186	42,985	42,439
Oregon	39,965	39,781	40,167	40,351	41,808	43,359	42,979	42,353	43,704
Pennsylvania	43,329	43,199	44,454	45,845	46,666	49,587	51,550	51,369	52,855
Rhode Island	44,573	43,876	45,401	47,004	48,949	50,628	55,029	55,836	54,936
South Carolina	37,369	37,827	37,265	39,897	40,736	41,677	42,572	42,176	41,345
South Dakota	34,498	33,979	34,163	35,016	36,850	37,570	36,840	38,116	38,070
Tennessee	38,442	36,834	38,947	41,616	42,917	45,179	45,211	44,869	44,428
Texas	39,222	41,752	43,636	44,640	45,724	46,626	47,066	46,051	45,687
Utah	43,480	42,684	44,073	44,419	45,964	44,182	47,956	44,693	45,160
Vermont	36,393	37,887	39,035	41,748	42,120	43,914	45,076	44,903	45,862
Virginia	39,000	39,421	40,388	41,904	44,933	49,366	51,291	50,741	49,656
Washington	42,796	43,314	42,629	43,142	44,359	45,518	45,898	46,074	47,287
West Virginia	35,318	36,149	35,178	36,267	38,297	38,803	37,242	40,262	39,492
Wisconsin	42,408	42,431	43,717	43,432	45,610	48,058	48,180	48,289	48,032
Wyoming	44,270	45,580	47,161	46,195	46,825	45,020	43,099	42,223	43,119
U.S. Service Schools	59,452	57,382	57,102	57,497	55,792	58,024	53,719	54,035	57,768
Outlying areas	35,834	35,206	33,022	32,086	34,434	23,795	27,912	25,378	28,020
American Samoa	23,899	24,508	22,480	24,763	—	—	25,898	25,413	24,618
Federated States of Micronesia	—	—	—	—	—	—	20,459	19,742	19,547
Guam	40,680	39,293	39,349	35,786	40,268	12,807	45,383	56,650	55,717
Marshall Islands	—	—	—	—	—	—	—	—	—
Northern Marianas	—	—	—	—	—	—	—	—	35,091
Palau	—	—	—	—	—	—	38,637	30,755	35,526
Puerto Rico	35,812	34,973	32,708	31,745	33,850	22,932	24,981	22,083	25,633
Trust Territories	—	—	—	12,963	19,577	17,103	—	—	—
Virgin Islands	34,190	37,727	38,585	36,712	37,682	45,954	51,171	47,766	50,141

Table 79.—Average salary (in constant 1996–97 dollars¹) of full-time faculty on 9-month contracts in institutions of higher education, by state: 1970–71 to 1996–97—Continued

State or other area	1992–93	1993–94	1994–95	1995–96	1996–97²	Percentage change			
						1970–71 to 1996–97	1985–86 to 1991–92	1991–92 to 1996–97	1985–86 to 1996–97
1	20	21	22	23	24	25	26	27	28
United States	$49,855	$50,389	$50,513	$50,716	$50,829	(³)	6.6	0.8	7.5
Alabama	41,045	41,753	42,869	41,661	42,006	−2.6	−1.7	0.5	−1.2
Alaska	51,026	52,076	51,793	50,435	50,091	−10.1	−17.3	−2.9	−19.7
Arizona	47,976	50,889	51,624	52,292	52,605	1.6	2.7	2.8	5.6
Arkansas	40,280	40,453	39,783	39,888	39,488	−3.6	0.6	−2.0	−1.4
California	57,438	58,968	58,369	59,363	59,870	7.5	6.4	−1.2	5.1
Colorado	48,471	47,828	48,969	49,240	50,095	0.2	7.4	3.0	10.6
Connecticut	59,358	60,272	59,755	60,944	61,592	11.5	13.3	2.1	15.7
Delaware	53,793	54,101	55,755	56,721	56,948	15.6	13.4	7.0	21.4
District of Columbia	57,482	57,150	57,643	58,620	59,385	10.6	11.5	4.2	16.1
Florida	44,586	45,149	45,512	46,980	47,598	4.2	6.4	4.4	11.1
Georgia	44,306	44,240	45,274	46,477	47,193	−1.3	(³)	6.3	6.4
Hawaii	56,326	54,294	54,915	52,938	52,175	−5.3	20.6	−2.7	17.4
Idaho	39,721	42,182	42,523	43,477	44,016	1.6	−2.3	9.2	6.6
Illinois	51,349	51,552	52,309	52,522	52,548	−7.4	6.5	3.0	9.7
Indiana	48,761	48,820	47,960	48,702	48,588	−4.2	10.3	−0.3	9.9
Iowa	47,217	47,266	47,090	47,429	47,191	−2.5	14.6	0.9	15.6
Kansas	41,736	41,821	42,829	42,681	41,655	−7.1	1.2	−0.3	0.9
Kentucky	42,481	42,812	42,750	42,983	43,410	−5.2	8.7	0.1	8.8
Louisiana	43,471	42,715	41,970	41,850	44,884	−0.6	8.6	0.4	9.0
Maine	45,290	44,811	43,844	44,304	45,199	−5.2	14.8	−1.8	12.8
Maryland	50,515	50,223	50,767	51,257	50,802	1.0	7.4	−1.2	6.1
Massachusetts	57,121	58,940	58,224	58,110	58,697	8.5	6.6	3.1	9.9
Michigan	53,078	53,418	53,675	54,054	54,248	0.8	9.3	2.8	12.4
Minnesota	49,423	48,490	48,755	47,947	48,877	−5.0	3.7	−0.3	3.4
Mississippi	37,369	38,270	39,355	40,694	39,644	−0.6	2.8	8.8	11.8
Missouri	44,939	45,413	45,726	46,277	47,063	−1.0	5.0	5.7	11.0
Montana	40,746	39,721	38,804	39,891	40,589	−12.1	−2.3	2.6	0.2
Nebraska	45,770	45,279	44,683	44,682	44,701	−3.3	11.8	−1.1	10.5
Nevada	50,127	49,455	49,466	50,640	51,959	26.6	7.3	2.3	9.8
New Hampshire	50,672	49,094	50,104	49,820	49,425	1.1	9.7	2.1	11.9
New Jersey	59,436	60,457	62,546	62,131	61,538	17.0	16.5	2.4	19.3
New Mexico	43,203	43,481	44,266	43,779	43,322	−10.7	1.4	−0.7	0.6
New York	55,764	57,060	57,060	57,355	56,996	0.7	7.7	1.1	8.9
North Carolina	45,125	45,865	46,985	46,351	47,462	0.5	7.0	2.7	9.9
North Dakota	38,034	37,363	37,203	36,310	36,366	−14.1	−3.9	−6.1	−9.8
Ohio	49,680	49,808	49,829	49,851	50,240	3.3	7.9	−1.1	6.8
Oklahoma	42,255	42,662	41,929	41,962	41,961	−6.9	−1.4	−1.1	−2.5
Oregon	44,542	45,820	45,049	45,535	44,506	−10.3	4.5	1.8	6.5
Pennsylvania	53,357	54,764	55,259	55,527	55,132	12.9	13.3	4.3	18.1
Rhode Island	54,275	53,862	54,746	54,312	54,797	8.2	12.2	−0.3	11.9
South Carolina	41,018	40,321	41,556	41,985	42,246	−5.2	1.5	2.2	3.7
South Dakota	38,208	37,904	37,262	37,009	36,482	−11.1	3.3	−4.2	−1.0
Tennessee	43,282	44,974	46,192	45,699	45,532	0.8	3.5	2.5	6.1
Texas	45,567	46,904	46,372	46,453	46,434	−2.8	−0.1	1.6	1.6
Utah	47,595	45,766	46,216	46,733	46,735	−5.2	−1.7	3.5	1.7
Vermont	45,174	44,387	44,430	44,403	44,722	−3.4	8.9	−2.5	6.2
Virginia	48,196	48,065	48,293	48,716	48,468	4.1	10.5	−2.4	7.9
Washington	47,305	47,582	46,600	47,007	46,038	−10.7	6.6	−2.6	3.8
West Virginia	38,628	39,653	39,949	40,928	40,929	−4.6	3.1	3.6	6.9
Wisconsin	49,014	49,238	50,325	49,711	49,325	0.9	5.3	2.7	8.1
Wyoming	41,696	40,670	41,511	41,139	39,855	−17.8	−7.9	−7.6	−14.9
U.S. Service Schools ...	59,349	61,244	59,199	63,520	61,536	−7.4	3.5	6.5	10.3
Outlying areas	24,998	26,945	34,051	32,566	33,163	−21.1	−18.6	18.4	−3.7
American Samoa	38,098	40,787	35,218	33,450	29,072	—	—	18.1	—
Federated States of Micronesia	20,649	21,737	19,737	27,651	17,695	—	—	−9.5	—
Guam	52,971	50,399	49,486	48,363	47,679	—	38.4	−14.4	18.4
Marshall Islands	—	—	16,938	15,142	—	—	—	—	—
Northern Marianas	34,035	32,609	35,611	33,243	35,628	—	—	1.5	—
Palau	38,087	39,516	15,999	15,575	17,743	—	—	−50.1	—
Puerto Rico	21,444	23,064	32,357	31,186	32,030	−23.7	−24.3	25.0	−5.4
Trust Territories	—	—	—	—	—	—	—	—	—
Virgin Islands	48,122	47,603	45,241	46,749	44,976	1.1	33.1	−10.3	19.4

¹Based on the Consumer Price Index, prepared by the Bureau of Labor Statistics, U.S. Department of Labor, adjusted to a school-year basis. These data do not reflect differences in inflation rates from state to state.

²Data are for degree-granting institutions. Survey coverage is slightly wider than data for higher education institutions reported for earlier years.

³Change of less than 0.05 percent.

—Data not available or not applicable.

NOTE.—Data for 1973–74, 1983–84, 1986–87, and 1988–89 are not available.

SOURCE: U.S. Department of Education, National Center for Education Statistics, Higher Education General Information Survey (HEGIS), "Salaries and Tenure of Full-Time Instructional Faculty" surveys; and Integrated Postsecondary Education Data System (IPEDS), "Salaries, Tenure, and Fringe Benefits of Full-Time Instructional Faculty" surveys. (This table was prepared February 1998.)

Table 80.—Institutions of higher education and branches, by type, control of institution, and state: 1995–96

State or other area	Total	Public 4-year institutions						Public 2-year	Private 4-year institutions						Private 2-year
		Total	Research[1]	Doctoral[2]	Master's[3]	Baccalaureate[4]	Other 4-year[5]		Total	Research[1]	Doctoral[2]	Master's[3]	Baccalaureate[4]	Other 4-year[5]	
1	2	3	4	5	6	7	8	9	10	11	12	13	14	15	16
United States	3,706	608	85	66	278	114	65	1,047	1,636	40	49	293	633	621	415
Alabama	82	18	2	2	13	1	0	35	18	0	0	4	10	4	11
Alaska	9	3	0	1	2	0	0	1	3	0	0	1	1	1	2
Arizona	45	5	2	1	1	0	1	18	18	0	0	1	1	16	4
Arkansas	38	10	1	0	6	2	1	16	10	0	0	2	6	2	2
California	349	31	9	1	19	0	2	107	169	3	9	35	26	96	42
Colorado	59	14	2	3	2	5	2	16	20	0	1	3	4	12	9
Connecticut	42	7	1	0	4	1	1	12	19	1	0	7	6	5	4
Delaware	9	2	1	0	1	0	0	3	4	0	0	2	1	1	0
District of Columbia	18	1	0	0	1	0	0	0	17	3	2	3	1	8	0
Florida	114	9	3	3	3	0	0	29	59	1	2	11	22	23	17
Georgia	120	19	2	1	12	1	3	54	37	1	2	2	21	11	10
Hawaii	17	3	1	0	0	2	0	7	7	0	0	2	1	4	0
Idaho	12	4	1	1	1	1	0	2	4	0	0	0	3	1	2
Illinois	169	12	3	2	7	0	0	49	95	2	3	15	28	47	13
Indiana	78	14	2	3	7	2	0	14	40	1	0	6	22	11	10
Iowa	59	3	2	0	1	0	0	17	36	0	0	5	25	6	3
Kansas	54	10	2	1	4	1	2	21	21	0	0	5	13	3	2
Kentucky	61	8	1	1	6	0	0	14	29	0	0	4	17	8	10
Louisiana	36	14	1	3	9	0	1	6	13	1	0	3	4	5	3
Maine	33	8	0	1	1	5	1	6	13	0	1	1	7	4	6
Maryland	57	13	1	1	9	1	1	20	21	1	0	4	6	10	3
Massachusetts	116	15	1	1	8	2	3	17	73	6	3	12	25	27	11
Michigan	109	15	3	2	10	0	0	30	56	0	2	6	22	26	8
Minnesota	106	11	1	0	6	4	0	51	36	0	1	4	16	15	8
Mississippi	46	9	2	0	3	2	2	22	12	0	0	2	5	5	3
Missouri	101	13	1	3	6	2	1	17	57	2	0	9	18	28	14
Montana	28	6	0	2	3	1	0	13	7	0	0	0	4	3	2
Nebraska	35	7	1	0	4	1	1	11	15	0	0	2	9	4	2
Nevada	10	2	0	1	1	0	0	4	3	0	0	0	1	2	1
New Hampshire	30	5	0	1	2	2	0	7	14	0	2	2	6	4	4
New Jersey	61	14	1	2	7	3	1	19	21	1	2	5	7	6	7
New Mexico	35	6	2	0	3	0	1	18	9	0	0	1	5	3	2
New York	310	42	3	3	19	8	9	47	169	8	9	29	44	79	52
North Carolina	121	16	2	1	9	3	1	58	42	1	1	7	26	7	5
North Dakota	21	6	0	2	1	3	0	9	5	0	0	1	1	3	1
Ohio	156	24	4	6	1	11	2	37	68	1	1	11	32	23	27
Oklahoma	45	14	2	0	6	4	2	15	11	0	1	4	3	3	5
Oregon	45	8	2	1	2	1	2	14	22	0	0	4	9	9	1
Pennsylvania	217	45	3	2	16	21	3	20	101	3	3	19	45	31	51
Rhode Island	12	2	1	0	1	0	0	1	8	1	0	1	2	4	1
South Carolina	59	12	2	0	6	3	1	21	22	0	0	2	17	3	4
South Dakota	21	8	0	1	2	2	3	1	10	0	0	0	8	2	2
Tennessee	76	10	0	1	3	5	1	14	42	1	0	5	24	12	10
Texas	179	40	4	6	22	2	6	67	58	1	3	14	21	19	14
Utah	17	5	2	0	1	2	0	5	4	1	0	2	1	0	3
Vermont	22	5	1	0	2	2	0	1	14	0	0	3	9	2	2
Virginia	89	15	3	3	6	3	0	24	39	0	0	13	19	7	11
Washington	64	8	2	0	5	1	0	29	24	0	0	11	2	11	3
West Virginia	28	13	1	0	3	9	0	3	10	0	0	3	6	1	2
Wisconsin	66	13	2	0	11	0	0	17	31	0	1	5	14	11	2
Wyoming	9	1	1	0	0	0	0	7	0	0	0	0	0	0	1
U.S. Service Schools	11	10	0	0	0	0	10	1	0	0	0	0	0	0	0
Outlying areas	74	13	0	1	4	4	4	14	37	0	0	6	19	12	10
American Samoa	1	0	0	0	0	0	0	1	0	0	0	0	0	0	0
Guam	2	1	0	0	1	0	0	1	0	0	0	0	0	0	0
Marshall Islands	1	0	0	0	0	0	0	1	0	0	0	0	0	0	0
Micronesia	5	0	0	0	0	0	0	5	0	0	0	0	0	0	0
Northern Marianas	1	0	0	0	0	0	0	1	0	0	0	0	0	0	0
Palau	1	0	0	0	0	0	0	1	0	0	0	0	0	0	0
Puerto Rico	61	10	0	1	1	4	4	4	37	0	0	6	19	12	10
Virgin Islands	2	2	0	0	2	0	0	0	0	0	0	0	0	0	0

[1] Research institutions are committed to graduate education through the doctorate, give high priority to research, and receive more than $15.5 million in federal research funds annually.

[2] Offer a full range of baccalaureate programs and are committed to eduation through the doctorate. They award at least 40 doctoral degrees annually in 5 or more disciplines.

[3] Offer a full range of baccalaureate programs and are committed to education through the master's degree. They award at least 20 master's degrees per year.

[4] Primarily undergraduate colleges with major emphasis on baccalaureate degrees.

[5] Other specialized 4-year institutions awarding degrees primarily in single fields of study, such as medicine, business, fine arts, theology and engineering. Also, includes some institutions which have 4-year programs, but have not reported sufficient data to identify program category.

NOTE.—New institutions which do not have sufficient data to report by detailed level are included under "Other 4-year" or "2-year" depending on level reported by institution.

SOURCE: U.S. Department of Education, National Center for Education Statistics, Integrated Postsecondary Education Data System (IPEDS), "Institutional Characteristics, 1995–96" survey. (This table was prepared October 1997.)

Table 81.—Average undergraduate tuition and fees and room and board (in current dollars) paid by students in institutions of higher education, by type and control of institution and by state: 1986–87 to 1996–97

State	Public 4-year, 1986–87		Public 4-year, 1987–88		Public 4-year, 1988–89		Public 4-year, 1989–90		Public 4-year, 1990–91		Public 4-year, 1991–92	
	Total	Tuition (in-state)	Total	Tuition (in-state)	Total	Tuition (in-state)	Total	Tuition (in-state)	Total	Tuition (in-state)	Total	Tuition (in-state)
1	2	3	4	5	6	7	8	9	10	11	12	13
United States	$4,138	$1,414	$4,403	$1,537	$4,678	$1,646	$4,975	$1,780	$5,243	$1,888	$5,693	$2,117
Alabama	3,406	1,275	4,174	1,447	3,831	1,411	4,113	1,521	4,357	1,593	4,686	1,700
Alaska	3,983	975	3,956	1,063	4,164	1,087	4,341	1,256	4,572	1,382	5,022	1,510
Arizona	3,832	1,136	3,964	1,196	4,318	1,278	5,556	1,362	4,731	1,478	5,228	1,528
Arkansas	2,793	931	3,066	1,100	3,026	1,186	4,165	1,372	3,844	1,418	4,198	1,541
California	5,189	1,031	4,942	984	5,375	1,068	5,530	1,118	5,894	1,220	6,450	1,442
Colorado	4,438	1,482	4,474	1,547	4,678	1,629	4,955	1,830	5,212	1,919	5,718	2,221
Connecticut	4,317	1,527	4,368	1,672	4,897	1,832	5,430	2,005	5,976	2,313	6,790	2,772
Delaware	—	2,157	4,886	2,341	5,305	2,556	6,182	2,760	6,208	2,910	6,826	3,265
District of Columbia	—	634	—	634	—	664	—	664	—	664	—	800
Florida	3,870	1,055	4,107	1,097	4,283	1,158	—	—	4,802	1,337	5,457	1,484
Georgia	3,623	1,369	3,934	1,536	4,256	1,736	4,257	1,621	4,373	1,680	4,931	1,761
Hawaii	4,249	972	3,726	947	4,266	1,194	4,524	1,290	4,966	1,290	4,754	1,351
Idaho	3,744	1,036	3,841	1,050	4,377	1,055	3,810	1,122	4,287	1,189	4,535	1,256
Illinois	4,450	1,708	4,653	1,853	5,131	2,152	5,550	2,362	5,776	2,465	6,025	2,564
Indiana	4,822	1,627	4,242	1,580	4,611	1,858	4,961	1,969	5,331	2,067	5,695	2,239
Iowa	3,457	1,385	4,186	1,561	4,123	1,703	4,344	1,823	4,251	1,880	4,847	2,044
Kansas	3,529	1,271	3,622	1,176	3,920	1,391	3,524	1,468	4,164	1,569	4,524	1,687
Kentucky	3,273	1,152	3,474	1,226	3,607	1,288	4,050	1,314	4,459	1,444	4,397	1,574
Louisiana	3,575	1,341	3,928	1,422	3,994	1,607	4,307	1,764	4,567	1,791	4,467	1,795
Maine	4,535	1,561	4,878	1,803	5,035	1,796	5,418	1,978	6,004	2,263	6,616	2,537
Maryland	5,325	1,682	5,577	1,787	5,953	1,946	6,423	2,123	6,791	2,287	7,156	2,479
Massachusetts	4,220	1,388	4,371	1,523	5,045	1,750	5,471	2,045	6,465	2,580	7,604	3,705
Michigan	4,738	1,877	5,062	2,075	5,432	2,271	5,844	2,473	6,284	2,635	6,769	2,879
Minnesota	4,005	1,814	4,202	1,861	4,328	1,893	4,651	2,055	4,881	2,216	5,207	2,410
Mississippi	3,865	1,603	3,931	1,661	3,967	1,677	4,245	1,858	5,005	1,927	4,591	2,125
Missouri	3,406	1,277	3,555	1,372	3,729	1,424	4,082	1,526	4,345	1,733	4,857	1,953
Montana	4,118	1,205	4,469	1,263	4,618	1,275	5,039	1,531	5,180	1,553	5,427	1,547
Nebraska	3,342	1,292	3,506	1,315	3,742	1,430	3,939	1,512	3,304	1,592	4,522	1,695
Nevada	3,527	988	3,268	988	4,362	1,100	4,010	1,103	5,473	1,275	6,096	1,338
New Hampshire	4,534	2,190	5,147	2,385	5,847	2,838	5,484	2,196	6,578	3,110	6,940	3,257
New Jersey	4,920	1,861	5,475	2,103	5,818	2,251	6,379	2,499	6,922	2,860	7,484	3,130
New Mexico	3,618	915	3,408	1,102	4,099	1,242	4,015	1,324	4,257	1,409	4,548	1,523
New York	4,704	1,431	5,206	1,701	5,077	1,540	5,241	1,563	5,495	1,587	6,543	2,332
North Carolina	3,057	818	3,045	862	3,364	905	3,784	1,015	4,066	1,112	4,256	1,224
North Dakota	3,130	1,198	3,288	1,327	3,591	1,399	4,349	1,602	4,338	1,930	4,938	2,052
Ohio	4,835	1,982	5,088	2,054	5,876	2,264	5,798	2,426	6,623	2,622	6,768	2,839
Oklahoma	2,925	757	3,007	893	3,519	1,141	3,751	1,307	3,827	1,340	4,289	1,505
Oregon	3,938	1,296	4,218	1,534	4,504	1,615	4,779	1,738	5,189	1,906	5,882	2,529
Pennsylvania	5,147	2,496	5,589	2,749	6,397	3,093	6,350	3,204	6,776	3,401	7,437	3,801
Rhode Island	5,398	1,845	5,626	1,971	5,815	1,976	6,325	2,266	6,631	2,311	7,559	2,842
South Carolina	4,224	1,733	4,470	1,846	4,733	1,997	5,088	2,160	5,441	2,317	5,821	2,470
South Dakota	3,408	1,409	3,627	1,565	3,580	1,453	4,236	1,715	3,827	1,854	4,168	1,940
Tennessee	3,375	1,133	3,694	1,202	3,968	1,308	4,160	1,403	4,356	1,518	4,497	1,586
Texas	3,853	885	4,145	915	3,975	910	4,180	958	4,123	986	4,397	1,143
Utah	3,949	1,159	3,664	1,233	4,216	1,318	4,335	1,427	4,265	1,524	4,737	1,723
Vermont	6,357	2,942	6,711	3,122	7,193	3,350	7,568	3,628	8,159	4,092	8,866	4,654
Virginia	4,983	2,070	5,232	2,213	5,816	2,381	5,987	2,529	6,295	2,691	6,778	3,024
Washington	3,940	1,339	4,927	1,560	4,720	1,614	4,631	1,710	5,060	1,823	6,010	1,992
West Virginia	4,106	1,003	4,354	1,081	4,538	1,138	5,137	1,594	4,822	1,543	5,240	1,622
Wisconsin	3,597	1,271	3,963	1,627	4,167	1,730	4,480	1,861	4,771	1,951	5,045	2,019
Wyoming	—	778	—	778	3,613	833	3,880	1,003	4,227	1,148	4,464	1,293

Table 81.—Average undergraduate tuition and fees and room and board (in current dollars) paid by students in institutions of higher education, by type and control of institution and by state: 1986–87 to 1996–97—Continued

State	Public 4-year, 1992–93		Public 4-year, 1993–94		Public 4-year, 1994–95		Public 4-year, 1995–96		Public 4-year, 1996–97 [1]			
	Total	Tuition (in-state)	Total	Tuition (in-state)	Total	Tuition (in-state)	Total	Tuition (in-state)	Total	Tuition (in-state)	Room	Board
1	14	15	16	17	18	19	20	21	22	23	24	25
United States	$6,020	$2,349	$6,365	$2,537	$6,670	$2,681	$7,014	$2,848	$7,334	$2,987	$2,214	$2,133
Alabama	4,990	1,876	5,295	1,986	5,429	2,107	5,735	2,239	6,002	2,362	1,813	1,827
Alaska	5,416	1,695	5,978	1,909	6,153	2,039	6,663	2,488	6,892	2,550	2,406	1,937
Arizona	5,705	1,555	5,463	1,819	5,825	1,894	5,996	1,926	6,312	2,009	2,363	1,941
Arkansas	4,954	1,661	5,296	1,805	4,912	1,954	5,055	2,028	5,402	2,258	1,675	1,470
California	8,755	1,990	7,524	2,388	7,924	2,696	8,209	2,664	8,304	2,720	3,031	2,552
Colorado	5,943	2,220	6,190	2,267	6,524	2,380	7,030	2,472	7,321	2,561	2,127	2,633
Connecticut	7,580	3,247	7,915	3,476	8,491	3,737	8,755	3,850	9,256	4,111	2,740	2,405
Delaware	7,269	3,465	7,790	3,663	8,118	3,805	8,512	4,003	8,886	4,170	2,533	2,183
District of Columbia	—	830	—	974	—	1,046	—	1,118	—	1,502		
Florida	5,942	1,703	5,861	1,784	6,201	1,783	6,251	1,766	6,559	1,789	2,452	2,318
Georgia	5,034	1,836	5,063	1,886	5,382	1,964	5,690	2,104	6,508	2,241	2,149	2,118
Hawaii	5,905	1,399	1,452	1,452	—	1,504	—	1,578	—	2,294	—	—
Idaho	4,721	1,415	4,977	1,497	5,203	1,581	5,306	1,678	5,681	1,979	1,583	2,120
Illinois	6,504	2,824	6,999	3,031	7,498	3,195	7,841	3,355	8,193	3,522	2,132	2,539
Indiana	6,281	2,448	6,640	2,621	6,920	2,862	7,388	3,038	8,110	3,198	1,991	2,921
Iowa	5,213	2,228	5,439	2,352	5,701	2,462	5,945	2,564	6,174	2,655	1,771	1,748
Kansas	4,933	1,801	5,137	1,890	5,441	2,019	5,688	2,116	5,895	2,219	1,781	1,895
Kentucky	4,755	1,704	5,027	1,914	5,327	2,057	5,454	2,162	5,460	2,241	1,439	1,780
Louisiana	4,802	1,831	5,214	2,177	5,268	2,212	5,503	2,221	5,637	2,233	1,502	1,903
Maine	7,026	2,889	7,503	3,131	7,763	3,303	7,899	3,424	8,262	3,648	2,287	2,326
Maryland	7,556	2,766	8,147	3,111	8,300	3,321	8,731	3,575	9,179	3,849	2,826	2,504
Massachusetts	7,874	3,834	8,503	4,163	8,562	4,148	8,770	4,262	9,045	4,272	2,525	2,247
Michigan	7,205	3,172	7,668	3,492	7,948	3,733	8,189	3,895	8,645	3,988	2,112	2,544
Minnesota	5,691	2,662	5,929	2,783	6,203	2,931	6,734	3,229	7,148	3,546	2,064	1,539
Mississippi	5,120	2,366	5,088	2,368	5,250	2,446	5,416	2,459	5,532	2,499	1,480	1,553
Missouri	5,622	2,234	5,833	2,476	6,347	2,797	6,768	3,024	7,204	3,245	2,150	1,809
Montana	6,013	1,833	5,668	1,889	6,004	2,109	7,803	2,369	6,511	2,490	1,857	2,163
Nebraska	4,739	1,853	4,925	1,936	5,187	2,058	5,503	2,189	5,722	2,269	1,477	1,976
Nevada	6,388	1,529	6,379	1,532	6,905	1,601	7,400	1,686	7,707	1,815	3,200	2,691
New Hampshire	7,273	3,452	7,801	3,835	8,181	4,039	8,730	4,445	9,123	4,641	2,710	1,772
New Jersey	7,988	3,351	8,251	3,517	8,727	3,776	9,118	3,972	9,661	4,269	3,228	2,165
New Mexico	4,776	1,613	5,062	1,726	5,365	1,836	5,299	1,940	5,428	2,014	1,528	1,885
New York	7,329	2,893	7,721	2,920	7,926	2,944	8,971	3,715	9,294	3,802	3,044	2,448
North Carolina	4,529	1,265	4,706	1,408	4,857	1,502	5,119	1,641	5,440	1,841	1,804	1,795
North Dakota	5,053	2,008	5,253	2,124	5,514	2,248	5,641	2,247	5,924	2,381	1,059	2,484
Ohio	7,286	3,106	6,992	3,265	7,732	3,403	8,157	3,606	8,490	3,841	2,537	2,113
Oklahoma	3,832	1,551	4,027	1,643	4,196	1,672	4,296	1,848	5,076	1,937	1,282	1,857
Oregon	6,618	2,653	6,630	2,831	6,930	3,064	7,395	3,246	7,988	3,408	1,893	2,688
Pennsylvania	7,816	4,041	8,277	4,316	8,672	4,517	9,138	4,731	9,501	4,994	2,305	2,201
Rhode Island	8,090	3,150	8,604	3,404	9,067	3,706	9,453	3,861	9,648	3,903	3,045	2,700
South Carolina	6,153	2,641	6,206	2,895	6,756	3,020	6,964	3,096	7,238	3,205	2,117	1,916
South Dakota	4,613	2,071	4,917	2,338	5,271	2,509	5,613	2,644	5,814	2,722	1,292	1,800
Tennessee	4,813	1,713	5,019	1,796	5,131	1,897	5,373	1,989	5,498	2,052	1,729	1,717
Texas	4,717	1,356	4,934	1,504	5,177	1,606	5,471	1,824	5,911	2,028	1,981	1,903
Utah	4,872	1,834	5,125	1,868	5,334	1,943	5,389	2,006	5,559	2,011	1,527	2,021
Vermont	9,666	5,314	10,054	5,532	10,327	5,682	10,657	5,922	11,360	6,533	3,160	1,668
Virginia	7,228	3,338	7,725	3,645	7,958	3,776	8,207	3,917	8,450	3,968	2,295	2,187
Washington	5,973	2,070	6,476	2,334	7,068	2,685	7,129	2,792	7,320	2,933	2,236	2,151
West Virginia	5,412	1,755	5,687	1,875	5,912	1,961	6,119	2,020	6,348	2,091	2,084	2,173
Wisconsin	5,260	2,170	5,249	2,316	5,613	2,468	5,839	2,614	6,075	2,748	1,775	1,552
Wyoming	4,652	1,430	4,900	1,648	5,237	1,908	5,429	2,005	6,016	2,144	1,596	2,276

Table 81.—Average undergraduate tuition and fees and room and board (in current dollars) paid by students in institutions of higher education, by type and control of institution and by state: 1986–87 to 1996–97—Continued

State	Private 4-year, 1986–87		Private 4-year, 1987–88		Private 4-year, 1988–89		Private 4-year, 1989–90		Private 4-year, 1990–91		Private 4-year, 1991–92	
	Total	Tuition	Total	Tuition	Total	Tuition	Total	Tuition	Total	Tuition	Total	Tuition
1	26	27	28	29	30	31	32	33	34	35	36	37
United States	$10,039	$6,658	$10,659	$7,116	$11,474	$7,722	$12,284	$8,396	$13,237	$9,083	$14,258	$9,759
Alabama	6,777	4,316	7,259	4,506	7,641	4,897	8,213	5,480	9,077	5,942	9,709	6,355
Alaska	7,245	3,719	8,031	4,493	9,127	4,893	9,023	5,076	8,436	5,842	10,036	5,868
Arizona	4,530	2,462	7,331	5,004	6,074	3,867	6,421	4,095	7,470	4,660	8,228	5,393
Arkansas	5,287	3,310	5,458	3,446	5,906	3,745	6,136	3,733	7,226	4,464	7,904	5,042
California	11,782	8,073	12,062	8,032	13,096	8,790	14,315	9,551	16,000	10,863	17,162	11,767
Colorado	10,689	7,913	10,684	6,688	12,121	8,630	12,849	9,127	13,662	9,516	15,236	10,215
Connecticut	12,567	8,534	14,044	9,673	15,022	10,282	16,037	11,216	17,200	12,315	18,424	13,266
Delaware	5,811	2,794	8,282	4,758	8,967	5,040	8,670	5,410	9,463	5,831	9,903	6,154
District of Columbia	11,466	7,128	12,398	7,762	13,379	8,520	14,575	9,438	17,990	11,939	17,620	11,579
Florida	—	1,367	8,755	5,777	10,239	6,825	10,934	7,309	11,820	7,992	12,650	8,550
Georgia	8,819	5,688	8,895	5,846	10,205	6,668	10,213	7,016	11,482	7,542	12,436	8,149
Hawaii	5,153	3,020	5,704	3,428	6,965	3,603	7,263	4,192	8,111	4,448	8,733	4,703
Idaho	8,539	5,774	8,472	5,364	9,273	6,004	9,406	6,296	10,745	7,203	11,607	7,951
Illinois	9,955	6,560	10,716	7,020	11,198	7,673	12,115	8,201	12,745	8,853	13,577	9,377
Indiana	9,530	6,762	10,442	7,518	10,049	7,130	11,429	8,230	11,677	8,451	11,926	8,566
Iowa	8,260	5,847	9,483	6,786	9,997	7,265	10,753	7,924	11,798	8,703	12,894	9,421
Kansas	6,349	4,121	6,831	4,225	7,746	5,062	8,316	5,510	8,985	5,997	9,666	6,537
Kentucky	6,380	3,868	6,552	4,091	6,886	4,427	7,415	4,727	7,915	5,200	8,847	5,669
Louisiana	10,359	6,812	11,309	7,494	12,460	8,268	13,161	9,009	14,124	9,783	14,798	10,374
Maine	12,674	9,032	13,784	9,987	14,633	10,617	13,878	9,599	15,713	10,928	15,917	11,149
Maryland	11,140	7,274	12,068	8,008	13,440	8,922	14,625	9,913	15,798	10,698	16,878	11,435
Massachusetts	13,474	8,953	14,289	9,621	15,469	10,375	16,690	11,258	18,089	12,446	19,207	13,174
Michigan	7,727	5,093	8,313	5,287	9,067	5,904	9,764	6,520	10,023	6,885	11,118	7,534
Minnesota	9,436	6,843	9,769	7,053	10,869	7,945	11,893	8,769	12,812	9,507	13,813	10,346
Mississippi	5,535	3,890	6,612	4,341	6,948	4,666	7,170	4,803	7,552	5,238	7,993	5,593
Missouri	8,162	5,474	9,047	6,117	9,848	6,647	10,586	7,087	11,093	7,487	12,070	8,180
Montana	6,364	3,867	7,000	4,177	7,211	4,521	7,983	5,014	8,605	5,565	9,573	6,055
Nebraska	7,536	5,090	8,011	5,469	8,510	5,929	9,055	6,392	9,995	6,893	10,466	7,314
Nevada	4,900	3,100	—	3,100	—	4,200	7,400	5,400	—	6,200	9,050	6,950
New Hampshire	12,337	8,401	13,016	8,611	13,679	9,447	14,823	10,362	15,757	11,154	16,870	11,863
New Jersey	11,955	8,221	11,787	7,958	13,307	8,515	14,374	9,347	15,604	10,281	16,781	11,031
New Mexico	6,504	3,649	7,938	5,043	9,583	6,788	10,360	7,157	11,545	8,187	12,551	8,936
New York	11,344	7,364	12,264	8,026	13,119	8,707	14,029	9,524	15,443	10,340	16,656	11,088
North Carolina	8,004	5,597	8,810	6,057	9,704	6,511	10,330	7,304	11,061	7,826	12,090	8,491
North Dakota	5,897	4,162	7,207	4,953	7,318	4,734	7,862	5,089	7,860	5,389	8,400	5,710
Ohio	8,950	6,176	10,201	7,063	10,895	7,588	11,333	8,015	12,296	8,729	13,749	9,742
Oklahoma	6,151	3,662	7,189	4,584	7,487	4,717	8,110	5,127	8,900	5,852	9,472	6,101
Oregon	10,270	7,122	10,530	7,403	11,666	8,466	12,152	8,725	13,231	9,606	14,368	10,382
Pennsylvania	10,607	7,140	11,507	7,939	13,088	8,725	13,344	9,369	14,046	9,848	15,619	11,040
Rhode Island	11,941	8,187	12,531	8,519	13,577	9,320	14,128	10,148	15,613	10,685	17,182	11,765
South Carolina	7,023	4,534	7,876	5,195	8,180	5,425	8,877	6,007	9,295	6,434	10,724	7,353
South Dakota	7,800	5,202	7,667	4,973	8,312	5,855	8,543	6,164	9,080	6,346	10,139	6,907
Tennessee	7,696	5,075	8,166	5,423	8,865	5,918	9,592	6,486	10,413	6,889	11,065	7,477
Texas	8,569	5,510	8,219	5,138	8,569	5,448	9,406	6,051	10,000	6,497	10,638	6,980
Utah	—	1,498	4,521	1,904	4,596	1,870	4,970	1,975	5,168	2,182	5,476	2,281
Vermont	9,369	6,393	11,472	8,288	12,743	9,126	14,589	10,815	15,147	10,649	17,300	12,507
Virginia	8,875	5,724	9,332	6,110	10,095	6,672	10,148	7,033	11,084	7,621	12,154	8,273
Washington	10,109	8,837	10,647	7,127	10,532	7,284	11,550	8,418	13,159	9,463	14,206	10,119
West Virginia	8,989	6,164	9,501	6,087	9,900	6,748	10,074	7,159	11,816	8,751	12,528	9,014
Wisconsin	8,968	6,055	9,440	6,479	10,097	6,967	10,954	7,568	11,026	8,237	12,699	8,865
Wyoming	—	—	—	—	—	—	—	—	—	—	—	—

Table 81.—Average undergraduate tuition and fees and room and board (in current dollars) paid by students in institutions of higher education, by type and control of institution and by state: 1986–87 to 1996–97—Continued

State	Private 4-year, 1992–93		Private 4-year, 1993–94		Private 4-year, 1994–95		Private 4-year, 1995–96		Private 4-year, 1996–97			
	Total	Tuition	Total	Tuition	Total	Tuition	Total	Tuition	Total	Tuition	Room	Board
1	38	39	40	41	42	43	44	45	46	47	48	49
United States	**$15,009**	**$10,294**	**$15,904**	**$10,952**	**$16,602**	**$11,481**	**$17,612**	**$12,243**	**$18,442**	**$12,881**	**$2,889**	**$2,672**
Alabama	10,092	6,562	10,551	6,905	11,208	7,318	11,636	7,580	12,164	8,002	1,832	2,330
Alaska	11,057	6,738	12,134	7,637	12,849	8,302	12,568	7,996	12,707	8,131	1,845	2,730
Arizona	9,201	5,688	9,406	5,716	10,358	6,225	11,290	7,008	12,330	7,886	2,123	2,321
Arkansas	8,398	5,411	8,866	5,721	9,615	6,197	10,157	6,553	10,784	7,037	1,558	2,188
California	17,432	11,863	19,277	13,249	17,696	11,847	20,040	13,905	20,760	14,429	3,288	3,043
Colorado	15,235	10,499	15,960	11,007	16,262	11,060	17,188	11,899	18,137	12,003	2,651	3,483
Connecticut	19,708	14,058	20,740	14,785	21,739	15,521	22,954	16,601	23,916	17,458	3,740	2,717
Delaware	10,132	6,477	10,595	6,817	11,349	7,159	11,450	7,285	12,602	7,444	2,816	2,341
District of Columbia	18,004	11,851	18,581	12,573	20,311	14,021	21,406	14,734	22,599	15,586	4,164	2,849
Florida	13,722	9,143	13,778	9,422	14,329	9,785	15,130	10,447	16,029	11,112	2,509	2,408
Georgia	13,066	8,518	13,696	9,040	14,329	9,562	15,215	10,221	16,409	10,942	3,042	2,425
Hawaii	9,514	4,932	10,185	5,578	11,020	5,971	11,610	6,230	14,151	6,541	2,950	4,660
Idaho	12,751	8,942	14,176	10,103	14,451	11,130	15,258	11,806	15,722	12,210	1,377	2,135
Illinois	14,299	9,843	15,242	10,471	16,009	11,078	16,671	11,649	17,606	12,376	2,820	2,410
Indiana	14,196	10,458	14,974	11,094	15,920	11,842	16,853	12,621	17,670	13,234	2,045	2,391
Iowa	13,566	10,098	14,499	10,820	15,184	11,349	15,878	11,894	16,562	12,403	1,912	2,247
Kansas	10,398	7,041	11,138	7,602	11,698	8,063	12,345	8,605	12,995	9,129	1,617	2,249
Kentucky	9,559	6,248	10,019	6,519	10,679	7,046	11,267	7,564	12,085	8,138	1,831	2,116
Louisiana	15,785	11,033	16,150	11,179	16,748	11,768	17,313	12,081	18,407	12,885	2,786	2,736
Maine	18,754	13,486	19,827	14,421	20,520	15,058	22,003	16,338	22,619	16,956	2,776	2,887
Maryland	18,275	12,282	18,962	12,847	20,120	13,805	21,076	14,561	21,967	15,332	3,613	3,022
Massachusetts	20,223	14,000	21,384	14,826	22,330	15,689	23,353	16,430	24,339	17,188	3,926	3,225
Michigan	11,411	7,722	12,253	8,362	12,849	8,771	13,425	9,259	13,930	9,580	2,152	2,198
Minnesota	14,569	10,831	15,594	11,637	16,339	12,233	17,177	12,864	17,980	13,623	2,128	2,229
Mississippi	8,125	5,546	8,763	5,960	9,312	6,384	9,965	6,835	10,482	7,210	1,662	1,610
Missouri	12,417	8,469	13,005	8,722	14,057	9,577	14,160	9,611	14,763	9,990	2,305	2,468
Montana	9,944	6,546	9,446	6,084	10,438	6,999	11,049	7,540	11,701	7,858	1,662	2,181
Nebraska	11,221	7,881	11,811	8,338	12,541	8,861	13,201	9,409	13,748	9,797	1,861	2,090
Nevada	8,797	6,397	9,773	7,173	—	7,532	—	7,388	13,331	7,731	3,300	2,300
New Hampshire	17,698	12,644	18,738	13,359	17,180	12,148	20,984	14,965	21,436	15,839	3,174	2,422
New Jersey	17,855	11,653	18,208	12,375	18,949	12,928	19,753	13,579	20,984	14,371	3,431	3,181
New Mexico	13,126	9,429	14,637	10,261	13,489	9,104	14,251	9,717	14,823	9,944	2,301	2,578
New York	17,673	11,674	18,364	12,161	19,663	13,069	20,910	13,909	21,528	14,544	3,896	3,088
North Carolina	12,743	8,979	13,543	9,635	14,658	10,493	15,334	10,916	16,311	11,651	2,219	2,441
North Dakota	8,768	6,050	9,194	6,437	9,520	6,663	9,924	7,020	10,437	7,434	1,292	1,711
Ohio	14,361	10,167	15,396	11,055	16,282	11,735	17,186	12,425	17,905	12,980	2,430	2,495
Oklahoma	10,096	6,737	10,706	7,126	11,562	7,781	11,615	7,700	11,563	7,622	1,706	2,235
Oregon	15,458	11,411	16,617	12,311	17,592	12,971	18,841	13,856	19,869	14,769	2,380	2,721
Pennsylvania	16,642	11,791	18,137	12,710	18,979	13,418	19,894	14,131	20,887	14,927	3,074	2,886
Rhode Island	18,340	12,595	19,695	13,617	20,957	14,604	22,015	15,340	22,490	15,675	3,751	3,064
South Carolina	11,617	8,001	12,138	8,570	12,651	9,073	13,464	9,669	14,125	10,207	1,899	2,020
South Dakota	10,927	7,355	11,652	8,019	12,352	8,536	13,111	9,184	13,756	9,617	1,631	2,507
Tennessee	11,267	8,059	11,967	8,579	13,235	9,257	13,953	9,745	14,970	10,450	2,324	2,195
Texas	11,322	7,437	11,847	7,936	12,390	8,386	13,022	8,848	13,684	9,373	2,048	2,263
Utah	5,645	2,439	6,796	2,679	7,060	2,761	7,366	2,940	7,697	3,094	1,436	3,167
Vermont	18,339	13,458	19,555	14,263	20,596	14,960	21,589	15,646	22,855	16,474	3,566	2,815
Virginia	13,217	9,152	13,852	9,679	14,166	9,943	15,032	10,614	15,775	11,165	2,149	2,461
Washington	15,357	10,976	16,108	11,713	16,988	12,408	17,956	13,147	18,461	13,656	2,559	2,245
West Virginia	12,281	8,546	13,179	9,284	13,354	9,460	14,412	10,185	15,184	10,774	1,966	2,444
Wisconsin	13,012	9,490	13,872	10,160	14,693	10,761	15,732	11,629	16,864	12,478	1,935	2,451
Wyoming	—	—	—	—	—	—	—	—	—	—	—	—

Table 81.—Average undergraduate tuition and fees and room and board (in current dollars) paid by students in institutions of higher education, by type and control of institution and by state: 1986–87 to 1996–97—Continued

| State | Public 2-year, tuition only (in-state) | | | | | | | | | | | Percent change, 1986–87 to 1996–97 | | |
	1986–87	1987–88	1988–89	1989–90	1990–91	1991–92	1992–93	1993–94	1994–95	1995–96	1996–97	Public 4-year tuition	Public 2-year tuition	Private 4-year tuition
1	50	51	52	53	54	55	56	57	58	59	60	61	62	63
United States	$660	$706	$730	$756	$824	$936	$1,025	$1,125	$1,192	$1,239	$1,276	111.2	93.3	93.5
Alabama	666	585	656	661	689	1,046	1,129	1,107	1,132	1,316	1,359	85.3	104.0	85.4
Alaska	824	847	741	—	—	601	1,162	1,268	1,320	2,120	1,850	161.5	124.5	118.6
Arizona	358	413	450	521	579	601	681	727	735	764	783	76.8	118.8	220.3
Arkansas	472	575	606	641	648	714	766	842	884	912	937	142.5	98.5	112.6
California	96	235	113	112	114	137	208	345	365	361	371	163.8	286.1	78.7
Colorado	623	707	816	800	943	1,017	1,126	1,201	1,282	1,340	1,395	72.8	124.0	51.7
Connecticut	573	715	831	910	972	1,169	1,314	1,398	1,520	1,646	1,722	169.2	200.5	104.6
Delaware	932	771	810	882	936	1,044	1,044	—	1,266	1,266	1,330	360.3	42.7	166.4
District of Columbia	-	-	-	—	—	—	—	—	—	—	—	136.9	—	118.7
Florida	608	669	685	730	788	905	999	1,074	1,113	1,103	1,151	69.6	89.4	712.9
Georgia	799	731	741	862	946	934	937	974	1,023	1,060	1,093	63.7	36.7	92.4
Hawaii	281	311	363	410	413	434	458	480	500	524	789	136.0	180.6	116.6
Idaho	690	566	774	779	802	850	902	914	991	991	1,043	91.0	51.2	111.5
Illinois	866	780	836	868	906	984	1,075	1,134	1,193	1,232	1,290	106.2	49.0	88.7
Indiana	1,211	1,242	1,308	1,369	1,423	1,598	1,628	1,743	1,848	1,928	2,331	96.6	92.5	95.7
Iowa	1,057	1,046	1,169	1,200	1,298	1,410	1,531	1,615	1,700	1,785	1,845	91.7	74.5	112.1
Kansas	537	659	671	714	748	783	875	982	1,051	1,133	1,248	74.6	132.4	121.5
Kentucky	540	658	695	696	771	817	837	966	1,088	1,124	1,215	94.5	125.0	110.4
Louisiana	619	658	839	841	852	853	934	955	1,023	1,026	1,047	66.5	69.1	89.2
Maine	880	875	1,007	1,140	1,497	1,570	1,626	1,907	2,151	2,376	2,545	133.7	189.2	87.7
Maryland	906	932	1,050	1,169	1,244	1,355	1,599	1,676	1,843	1,969	2,102	128.8	132.0	110.8
Massachusetts	750	923	1,085	1,280	1,528	2,162	2,212	2,344	2,437	2,361	2,341	207.8	212.2	92.0
Michigan	917	901	976	1,045	1,124	1,201	1,268	1,357	1,436	1,527	1,576	112.5	71.9	88.1
Minnesota	1,229	1,329	1,358	1,492	1,578	1,658	1,740	1,845	1,965	2,050	2,187	95.5	78.0	99.1
Mississippi	489	618	636	676	722	817	932	937	938	941	954	55.9	95.1	85.3
Missouri	524	693	771	813	891	978	1,066	1,138	1,204	1,252	1,281	154.1	144.5	82.5
Montana	423	436	717	855	964	991	1,083	1,162	1,376	1,516	1,610	106.6	280.6	103.2
Nebraska	740	665	846	920	990	975	1,029	1,088	1,102	1,132	1,227	75.6	65.8	92.5
Nevada	573	564	522	520	651	723	753	817	843	974	1,010	83.7	76.3	149.4
New Hampshire	1,514	1,496	1,519	1,609	1,899	2,053	2,150	2,259	2,316	2,419	2,858	111.9	88.8	88.5
New Jersey	763	983	998	1,131	1,235	1,385	1,482	1,540	1,754	1,880	1,949	129.4	155.4	74.8
New Mexico	407	432	451	498	536	556	598	620	675	674	659	120.1	62.0	172.5
New York	1,340	1,378	1,398	1,413	1,419	1,773	2,041	2,112	2,151	2,426	2,519	165.7	88.0	97.5
North Carolina	216	244	276	288	334	504	577	578	582	581	581	125.1	169.1	108.2
North Dakota	1,074	992	1,232	1,287	1,584	1,576	1,595	1,637	1,689	1,697	1,783	98.7	66.0	78.6
Ohio	1,181	1,342	1,502	1,634	1,768	1,827	2,002	2,088	2,166	2,266	2,335	93.8	97.7	110.2
Oklahoma	456	547	714	840	864	981	1,011	1,107	1,149	1,253	1,268	155.9	178.2	108.1
Oregon	484	652	711	751	794	930	1,051	1,185	1,322	1,342	1,526	163.0	215.3	107.4
Pennsylvania	1,626	1,170	1,528	1,426	1,505	1,710	1,611	1,672	1,755	1,906	2,013	100.1	23.8	109.1
Rhode Island	844	900	950	1,004	1,100	1,368	1,496	1,546	1,686	1,726	1,736	111.5	105.7	91.5
South Carolina	645	629	749	821	813	915	1,053	1,058	1,048	1,066	1,114	84.9	72.7	125.1
South Dakota	—	—	—	—	1,920	1,920	—	2,640	3,430	3,430	3,430	93.2	—	84.9
Tennessee	660	674	722	803	848	849	911	950	976	1,022	1,047	81.1	58.6	105.9
Texas	300	373	438	457	495	552	586	625	689	768	791	129.2	163.8	70.1
Utah	884	1,346	1,069	1,138	1,173	1,215	1,290	1,289	1,340	1,390	1,390	73.5	57.3	106.5
Vermont	1,966	1,865	2,011	2,227	2,424	2,501	2,555	2,726	2,196	2,370	2,516	122.1	28.0	157.7
Virginia	775	764	874	814	867	1,059	1,231	1,332	1,384	1,433	1,466	91.7	89.2	95.1
Washington	654	726	757	800	844	952	1,014	1,143	1,313	1,370	1,447	119.0	121.3	54.5
West Virginia	517	552	702	809	930	1,031	1,142	1,237	1,303	1,319	1,373	108.5	165.6	74.8
Wisconsin	887	981	1,068	1,157	1,234	1,321	1,467	1,527	1,682	1,835	1,947	116.2	119.5	106.1
Wyoming	516	554	586	613	662	720	793	874	892	948	1,048	175.6	103.0	—

—Data not reported or not applicable.

NOTE.—Data are for the entire academic year and are average charges. Tuition and fees were weighted by the number of full-time-equivalent undergraduates, but are not adjusted to reflect student residency. Room and board are based on full-time students. Because of rounding, details may not add to totals.

SOURCE: U.S. Department of Education, National Center for Education Statistics, Higher Education General Information Survey (HEGIS), "Institutional Characteristics" surveys; and Integrated Postsecondary Education Data System (IPEDS), "Fall Enrollment" and "Institutional Characteristics" surveys. (This table was prepared February 1998.)

Table 82.—Current-fund revenue of public institutions of higher education, by source of funds and state: 1994–95 [1]

State or other area	Total, in thousands	Percentage distribution								
		Tuition and fees	Federal appropriations, grants, and contracts [2]	State appropriations, grants, and contracts	Local appropriations, grants, and contracts	Private gifts, grants, and contracts	Endowment income	Auxiliary enterprises	Hospitals	Educational activities and other
1	2	3	4	5	6	7	8	9	10	11
United States	$119,312,493	18.4	11.1	35.9	4.0	4.0	0.6	9.5	10.5	6.1
Alabama	2,805,154	14.1	10.3	33.2	0.5	3.9	0.7	7.0	24.5	5.8
Alaska	344,877	12.8	15.4	53.1	0.4	2.5	1.3	6.1	—	8.3
Arizona	1,931,523	21.6	15.0	35.1	10.7	4.9	0.3	8.9	—	3.5
Arkansas	1,113,954	14.2	8.0	38.5	0.4	2.6	0.1	8.2	23.6	4.4
California	14,558,144	13.2	10.2	35.3	9.9	3.2	0.6	6.7	12.3	8.6
Colorado	1,914,233	27.7	18.9	26.8	1.6	4.9	0.4	12.7	1.1	6.0
Connecticut	1,148,389	21.0	6.4	42.1	(3)	2.5	(3)	7.4	16.4	4.2
Delaware	496,696	33.9	9.2	29.0	1.3	3.7	3.9	12.8	—	6.2
District of Columbia	103,770	10.4	6.9	—	74.0	0.5	0.7	0.7	—	6.7
Florida	3,584,085	17.6	9.3	54.3	0.3	4.8	(3)	9.5	—	4.3
Georgia	2,760,323	15.3	9.4	49.0	0.9	5.2	0.1	8.5	8.8	2.8
Hawaii	651,282	7.6	18.2	61.5	0.1	2.4	0.3	8.5	—	1.3
Idaho	492,918	16.6	8.3	47.4	2.1	4.9	1.7	12.5	—	6.6
Illinois	4,360,136	18.0	9.4	35.0	9.5	2.9	0.1	10.1	6.7	8.2
Indiana	3,080,345	21.7	8.0	32.4	0.1	4.3	0.3	16.4	10.9	6.0
Iowa	2,106,504	14.5	13.8	30.6	1.3	3.2	0.1	10.0	19.4	7.0
Kansas	1,553,593	17.4	8.8	34.4	8.0	2.3	2.1	8.1	13.2	5.6
Kentucky	1,778,568	17.3	7.1	40.7	0.4	2.4	0.6	7.9	14.3	9.2
Louisiana	1,968,669	18.3	6.7	36.7	0.2	2.7	0.2	11.0	11.8	12.3
Maine	400,426	23.8	9.4	42.5	(3)	3.7	0.6	13.1	—	6.9
Maryland	2,074,521	25.7	11.2	36.0	6.5	4.1	0.3	11.8	—	4.5
Massachusetts	1,586,319	30.8	9.2	41.5	0.5	3.0	0.2	10.7	0.4	3.8
Michigan	5,798,882	22.8	9.9	26.7	4.7	4.8	0.5	13.6	12.0	4.9
Minnesota	2,671,566	16.9	10.5	35.3	0.5	7.7	0.4	8.5	13.1	7.0
Mississippi	1,443,162	14.7	11.6	40.0	2.4	2.9	0.1	10.7	13.4	4.3
Missouri	1,978,783	22.5	5.9	34.0	3.6	3.9	0.6	9.7	11.4	8.5
Montana	385,984	21.8	17.1	33.0	1.4	3.8	0.1	14.4	—	8.5
Nebraska	1,124,836	12.7	11.0	33.5	5.0	4.8	0.3	10.4	18.4	3.9
Nevada	484,276	15.4	10.8	50.8	1.4	5.8	0.3	9.5	—	6.0
New Hampshire	391,619	40.5	9.4	21.9	0.6	4.6	0.6	18.6	—	3.9
New Jersey	3,106,652	20.6	6.4	37.9	5.3	3.0	0.4	7.6	13.3	5.5
New Mexico	1,316,934	8.5	18.8	33.1	3.5	4.6	0.9	6.9	17.7	5.9
New York	6,887,321	19.6	7.4	42.6	5.8	3.9	0.2	6.0	11.9	2.4
North Carolina	3,521,601	11.2	11.7	48.8	2.3	4.6	0.7	16.2	—	4.6
North Dakota	467,926	19.3	14.8	32.6	2.3	2.0	0.6	18.0	2.8	7.7
Ohio	4,976,134	26.5	6.8	30.1	2.1	4.2	0.9	9.4	15.5	4.4
Oklahoma	1,300,779	16.3	14.0	45.2	1.3	3.6	0.2	15.8	—	3.5
Oregon	1,816,031	17.1	14.5	26.5	5.9	4.6	0.3	9.2	17.2	4.8
Pennsylvania	4,684,460	28.6	10.8	25.3	1.9	4.0	0.8	10.2	14.5	4.0
Rhode Island	344,171	33.1	11.8	36.0	—	1.4	—	13.7	—	4.1
South Carolina	1,997,203	17.5	8.9	31.7	1.3	3.7	0.1	9.1	24.7	3.0
South Dakota	260,853	23.6	13.6	40.2	(3)	3.3	0.4	12.0	—	6.9
Tennessee	2,053,495	15.4	8.6	42.3	0.7	4.5	0.7	8.4	14.8	4.6
Texas	8,123,435	14.4	10.3	42.4	4.2	4.2	1.7	6.8	3.3	12.7
Utah	1,402,962	13.2	12.7	29.5	1.9	2.8	0.7	7.9	18.3	12.8
Vermont	329,679	42.8	11.9	14.4	(3)	8.0	1.5	11.4	—	10.0
Virginia	3,483,691	21.8	8.7	26.4	0.8	4.9	0.9	12.8	21.7	2.0
Washington	2,877,386	17.8	16.4	34.4	0.7	4.9	0.4	12.3	8.6	4.6
West Virginia	693,159	25.3	9.6	47.1	0.3	2.6	—	12.2	—	3.0
Wisconsin	3,033,547	17.4	11.9	31.2	8.6	4.8	0.5	7.6	10.1	7.9
Wyoming	293,209	14.0	13.0	43.8	5.1	7.0	0.9	13.3	—	3.0
U.S. Service Schools	1,248,328	—	88.8	—	—	0.6	—	5.9	4.6	—
Outlying areas	750,676	10.0	8.8	73.1	2.6	1.1	0.1	1.7	—	2.6
American Samoa	4,817	1.7	43.9	54.4	—	—	—	—	—	—
Federated States of Micronesia	6,517	47.0	4.6	0.8	37.9	1.1	0.1	7.8	—	0.8
Guam	71,873	9.7	9.9	55.3	16.4	1.2	0.7	3.8	—	3.0
Marshall Islands	1,633	31.9	42.7	19.2	—	0.7	0.8	4.1	—	0.7
Northern Marianas	12,174	19.4	24.8	52.5	1.2	—	—	0.3	—	1.8
Palau	4,083	19.1	12.8	48.8	—	—	—	14.6	—	4.6
Puerto Rico	615,912	9.2	7.7	78.0	0.4	0.9	—	1.0	—	2.7
Virgin Islands	33,668	13.5	14.1	50.8	6.9	4.8	0.7	8.2	—	1.0

[1] Preliminary data.

[2] Includes independent operations (federally funded research and development centers).

[3] Less than 0.05 percent.

NOTE.—Because of rounding, details may not add to 100 percent.

SOURCE: U.S. Department of Education, National Center for Education Statistics, Integrated Postsecondary Education Data System (IPEDS), "Finance FY 95" survey. (This table was prepared January 1998.)

Table 83.—Educational and general expenditures (in current dollars) per full-time-equivalent student in institutions of higher education, by type and control of institution and state: 1989–90, 1993–94, and 1994–95

State or other area	All public and private institutions, 1994–95	Public institutions						Private institutions					Percent change, 1989–90 to 1994–95, in constant dollars	
		All public, 1989–90	All public, 1993–94	1994–95				All private, 1989–90	All private, 1993–94	1994–95			Public	Private
				All public	All public U.S.=100	4-year	2-year			All private	All private U.S.=100	4-year		
1	2	3	4	5	6	7	8	9	10	11	12	13	14	15
United States	$13,931	$9,383	$11,154	$11,841	100.0	$15,352	$6,346	$15,117	$19,254	$20,277	100.0	$21,202	5.6	12.3
Alabama	11,699	8,771	10,559	11,505	97.2	14,782	5,493	10,630	12,637	13,191	65.1	13,631	9.8	3.9
Alaska	17,494	15,615	17,287	17,525	148.0	17,586	13,070	11,148	14,606	16,898	83.3	18,876	-6.1	26.9
Arizona	9,931	8,391	9,833	10,413	87.9	15,230	5,199	7,229	4,762	6,111	30.1	6,086	3.9	-29.2
Arkansas	11,106	9,371	10,137	11,001	92.9	12,059	6,657	7,951	10,329	11,818	58.3	12,047	-1.7	24.4
California	13,252	9,529	10,793	11,405	96.3	18,968	5,971	18,335	22,750	21,887	107.9	22,636	0.2	-0.1
Colorado	11,332	9,108	10,558	11,099	93.7	13,107	5,867	11,083	13,025	12,702	62.6	13,076	2.0	-4.1
Connecticut	21,047	8,807	11,371	13,414	113.3	17,028	6,351	23,287	31,280	32,326	159.4	32,814	27.5	16.2
Delaware	13,565	11,959	14,208	15,037	127.0	16,730	9,597	7,368	5,604	5,824	28.7	5,824	5.3	-33.8
District of Columbia	25,892	13,548	14,556	15,095	127.5	15,095	—	20,211	24,502	27,195	134.1	27,195	-6.7	12.6
Florida	10,879	8,453	9,453	9,674	81.7	14,050	5,882	12,122	14,654	15,614	77.0	16,050	-4.2	7.8
Georgia	14,334	10,393	11,231	12,359	104.4	14,352	7,762	14,493	20,040	20,664	101.9	22,097	-0.5	19.4
Hawaii	14,720	12,327	15,751	16,341	138.0	24,737	6,565	3,821	8,281	8,546	42.1	8,546	11.0	87.2
Idaho	10,044	9,038	10,294	10,566	89.2	10,991	7,936	5,635	7,777	8,191	40.4	12,632	-2.1	21.7
Illinois	13,566	8,176	9,562	10,166	85.9	15,544	5,617	15,458	20,188	21,739	107.2	22,342	4.1	17.7
Indiana	13,514	10,252	12,016	12,758	107.7	13,584	7,730	11,909	14,855	15,808	78.0	16,491	4.2	11.1
Iowa	14,264	11,275	13,826	14,315	120.9	18,958	7,590	9,670	13,462	14,147	69.8	14,385	6.3	22.5
Kansas	10,939	8,570	10,321	10,992	92.8	13,355	6,511	10,245	11,061	10,549	52.0	10,503	7.4	-13.8
Kentucky	11,299	9,498	10,558	11,368	96.0	13,700	4,365	8,660	10,270	10,995	54.2	12,149	0.2	6.3
Louisiana	11,839	8,058	9,503	10,172	85.9	10,984	4,408	13,837	19,439	21,658	106.8	22,209	5.7	31.0
Maine	13,331	10,263	11,834	12,269	103.6	12,919	8,920	12,068	15,316	15,527	76.6	16,935	0.1	7.7
Maryland	17,318	9,374	11,477	11,977	101.1	15,243	7,140	32,776	41,354	42,860	211.4	43,809	7.0	9.5
Massachusetts	21,386	8,193	10,509	11,142	94.1	13,872	6,577	20,103	26,354	28,035	138.3	29,206	13.9	16.7
Michigan	12,746	9,567	11,994	12,875	108.7	15,887	7,146	9,167	11,405	12,104	59.7	12,118	12.6	10.5
Minnesota	13,442	9,910	13,139	13,135	110.9	17,544	7,256	13,785	13,571	14,391	71.0	14,836	11.0	-12.6
Mississippi	11,481	8,243	9,916	11,520	97.3	15,677	6,368	7,454	9,837	11,130	54.9	11,212	17.0	25.0
Missouri	14,182	7,846	9,474	10,605	89.6	12,482	6,337	16,437	19,389	20,585	101.5	21,453	13.1	4.8
Montana	10,689	6,376	10,229	10,709	90.4	10,653	11,165	6,957	9,331	10,544	52.0	11,051	40.6	26.9
Nebraska	12,070	8,541	10,521	10,805	91.2	12,796	6,130	13,690	16,257	17,080	84.2	17,229	5.9	4.4
Nevada	11,234	8,326	10,794	11,226	94.8	15,195	4,935	15,639	10,271	11,670	57.6	10,670	12.9	-37.5
New Hampshire	15,392	8,907	10,919	11,282	95.3	12,135	7,553	15,307	19,411	20,537	101.3	23,062	6.0	12.3
New Jersey	14,608	10,484	11,969	12,837	108.4	18,037	6,349	16,215	20,190	21,448	105.8	22,244	2.5	10.7
New Mexico	13,522	11,157	12,162	13,818	116.7	18,206	6,837	16,545	12,618	8,929	44.0	9,726	3.7	-54.8
New York	17,752	9,720	11,968	12,814	108.2	16,085	7,886	17,928	22,384	23,868	117.7	24,996	10.4	11.4
North Carolina	15,431	10,411	11,967	12,730	107.5	16,946	6,660	16,875	23,391	25,670	126.6	26,377	2.4	27.3
North Dakota	11,270	8,566	10,807	11,398	96.3	12,610	6,826	8,762	9,463	10,034	49.5	9,281	11.4	-4.1
Ohio	12,655	9,104	10,487	11,575	97.8	13,571	6,556	11,519	15,013	15,850	78.2	16,902	6.4	15.2
Oklahoma	9,191	7,113	8,207	8,553	72.2	10,483	4,572	10,826	12,668	12,804	63.1	13,362	0.7	-1.0
Oregon	13,661	9,296	12,031	13,120	110.8	17,043	8,482	12,570	15,339	16,287	80.3	16,355	18.1	8.5
Pennsylvania	16,640	10,107	12,284	13,122	110.8	15,269	6,483	13,288	19,733	21,069	103.9	23,304	8.7	32.7
Rhode Island	15,263	9,139	10,379	11,214	94.7	13,580	6,213	13,531	17,203	18,769	92.6	19,321	2.7	16.1
South Carolina	12,171	11,117	11,428	12,057	101.8	14,942	6,595	9,600	11,741	12,727	62.8	12,856	-9.2	11.0
South Dakota	9,067	7,731	8,682	8,576	72.4	8,582	7,579	11,229	10,864	11,374	56.1	11,501	-7.1	-15.2
Tennessee	13,538	9,597	10,390	11,225	94.8	14,043	5,585	13,941	19,450	20,550	101.3	21,368	-2.1	23.4
Texas	12,522	8,958	11,082	11,503	97.1	15,218	6,192	15,107	18,115	18,794	92.7	19,582	7.5	4.1
Utah	11,536	11,024	12,199	12,374	104.5	14,315	5,889	6,846	9,058	9,605	47.4	9,735	-6.0	17.5
Vermont	18,833	13,950	17,067	17,942	151.5	19,659	5,055	16,315	18,042	19,940	98.3	19,587	7.7	2.3
Virginia	11,856	9,082	10,365	11,032	93.2	13,996	5,123	11,206	15,363	15,179	74.9	15,766	1.7	13.4
Washington	12,578	9,971	11,995	12,358	104.4	20,436	6,193	10,105	13,174	13,785	68.0	14,149	3.7	14.2
West Virginia	10,330	7,138	9,117	9,533	80.5	9,952	4,795	10,155	12,875	15,082	74.4	15,872	11.8	24.3
Wisconsin	14,149	10,235	12,668	13,383	113.0	15,313	9,440	12,900	16,793	17,404	85.8	17,873	9.5	12.9
Wyoming	11,931	9,612	10,834	11,872	100.3	17,535	6,811	6,772	14,894	13,821	68.2	—	3.4	70.9
U.S. Service Schools ...	31,697	13,568	30,638	31,697	267.7	66,161	—	—	—	—	—	—	95.6	—
Outlying areas	7,295	8,914	10,995	11,793	99.6	12,785	6,821	2,149	3,618	4,105	20.2	4,330	10.7	59.9
American Samoa	3,490	4,471	3,392	3,490	29.5	—	3,490	—	—	—	—	—	-34.7	—
Federated States of Micronesia	4,412	2,680	4,167	4,412	37.3	—	4,412	—	—	—	—	—	37.8	—
Guam	18,485	17,496	16,627	18,485	156.1	19,415	15,684	—	—	—	—	—	-11.6	—
Marshall Islands	—	—	3,888	—	—	—	—	—	—	—	—	—	—	—
Northern Marianas	18,843	3,390	4,347	18,843	159.1	—	18,843	—	—	—	—	—	365.3	—
Palau	8,841	3,944	7,551	8,841	74.7	—	8,841	—	—	—	—	—	87.6	—
Puerto Rico	6,818	8,571	10,787	11,376	96.1	12,204	4,745	2,149	3,618	4,105	20.2	4,330	11.1	59.9
Virgin Islands	15,156	12,218	16,045	15,156	128.0	15,156	—	—	—	—	—	—	3.8	—

[1] Includes 2-year institutions not shown separately.

—Data not available or not applicable.

NOTE.—Because of rounding, details may not add to totals. Percent change reflects mergers, openings and closings of institutions. Educational and general expenditures in- clude all current-fund expenditures, except hospitals, auxiliary enterprises, and independ- ent operations.

SOURCE: U.S. Department of Education, National Center for Education Statistics, In- tegrated Postsecondary Education Data System (IPEDS), "Finance" surveys. (This table was prepared January 1998.)

Table 84.—Current-fund expenditures (in current dollars) of public institutions of higher education, by state: 1969–70 to 1994–95

[Amounts in thousands]

State or other area	1969–70	1970–71	1971–72	1972–73	1973–74	1974–75	1975–76	1976–77	1977–78	1978–79
1	2	3	4	5	6	7	8	9	10	11
United States	$13,249,546	$14,996,042	$16,484,325	$18,203,746	$20,336,284	$23,489,981	$26,183,956	$28,634,846	$30,725,119	$33,732,873
Alabama	208,085	226,786	264,493	307,583	354,497	423,231	501,072	561,642	618,994	690,175
Alaska	27,990	36,738	41,664	46,819	49,900	65,986	87,761	98,560	115,958	126,693
Arizona	164,117	195,070	232,083	259,082	293,099	341,338	367,135	425,787	480,612	529,602
Arkansas	102,615	108,694	119,208	127,809	144,520	175,584	202,718	218,251	248,536	276,021
California	1,907,868	2,032,668	2,149,912	2,390,155	2,714,692	3,259,945	3,710,956	4,265,046	4,113,539	4,304,077
Colorado	244,338	276,736	307,847	337,342	366,552	419,550	472,147	517,209	550,845	609,764
Connecticut	119,132	134,960	154,690	166,080	170,656	205,649	215,132	233,723	274,497	298,487
Delaware	42,770	49,569	53,667	62,966	72,738	87,129	95,543	103,675	109,200	125,884
District of Columbia	24,858	28,007	38,875	42,103	43,362	44,125	46,202	46,227	55,157	57,839
Florida	360,898	414,844	453,420	516,890	591,554	679,780	725,845	788,183	870,718	929,948
Georgia	232,931	268,277	288,851	322,692	368,838	410,458	441,397	480,831	539,993	603,112
Hawaii	85,590	105,072	110,867	115,146	118,418	135,403	145,344	146,356	166,005	178,919
Idaho	50,324	54,383	61,743	64,798	74,587	87,781	100,507	111,440	122,302	137,360
Illinois	667,631	789,890	827,301	903,461	961,153	1,062,946	1,166,066	1,224,767	1,299,148	1,433,311
Indiana	387,099	433,578	473,101	503,126	521,667	628,121	672,724	721,671	781,285	856,631
Iowa	238,739	258,694	279,072	299,243	346,141	400,536	440,125	523,992	562,025	630,314
Kansas	193,493	219,644	229,698	249,721	267,378	309,174	335,962	386,187	422,195	485,315
Kentucky	196,573	219,154	243,109	272,493	304,748	348,908	403,261	435,827	473,890	527,931
Louisiana	192,633	221,570	217,323	263,438	289,592	333,508	340,970	390,759	447,523	488,140
Maine	48,275	55,460	62,231	68,264	81,477	90,392	102,447	104,858	113,307	121,234
Maryland	222,270	270,242	306,494	347,152	378,938	447,411	501,371	561,475	607,423	667,001
Massachusetts	150,552	186,813	225,977	242,315	275,788	327,719	325,946	358,873	387,477	455,469
Michigan	797,887	859,806	927,663	999,681	1,087,727	1,235,651	1,343,680	1,423,988	1,592,811	1,723,983
Minnesota	314,217	350,721	368,409	434,515	465,373	524,107	592,514	594,539	645,891	706,972
Mississippi	144,205	167,189	186,060	211,621	236,751	273,799	318,258	350,524	390,841	435,680
Missouri	255,520	272,634	300,876	323,793	355,966	409,430	440,229	480,111	508,668	556,366
Montana	56,427	65,024	66,332	71,415	74,352	83,835	92,736	103,217	108,489	112,079
Nebraska	115,813	130,148	142,022	152,000	170,539	195,041	224,472	257,102	285,775	314,037
Nevada	29,823	32,459	35,923	38,255	45,368	49,810	62,256	66,944	72,950	85,392
New Hampshire	42,932	48,096	51,993	56,802	66,487	76,052	82,961	91,336	102,760	111,540
New Jersey	237,637	280,643	330,507	340,016	441,023	492,944	547,224	612,949	693,621	729,939
New Mexico	100,971	111,219	119,694	133,833	147,939	137,909	163,777	180,643	210,548	243,745
New York	826,458	1,003,046	1,128,416	1,236,479	1,480,510	1,739,842	1,937,122	1,876,945	1,988,514	2,135,793
North Carolina	326,146	370,529	427,826	452,891	520,881	642,140	649,452	715,794	794,172	899,072
North Dakota	61,334	66,454	69,005	73,554	80,439	94,401	112,270	122,060	133,691	147,448
Ohio	594,980	704,269	764,622	833,217	883,270	996,691	1,091,375	1,193,941	1,289,431	1,438,363
Oklahoma	188,409	209,337	231,465	241,714	248,800	274,536	308,625	368,932	404,816	445,006
Oregon	212,263	227,893	246,849	263,117	292,759	335,116	391,777	432,487	465,533	515,105
Pennsylvania	546,472	616,979	731,559	809,385	873,998	963,368	1,071,276	1,142,046	1,204,896	1,277,485
Rhode Island	51,333	59,964	62,541	72,714	81,267	91,446	98,796	110,439	118,983	129,647
South Carolina	133,117	150,619	173,420	204,287	250,753	313,200	341,210	361,572	419,029	480,370
South Dakota	58,073	65,239	70,928	71,877	76,506	82,967	83,526	88,182	93,518	103,957
Tennessee	191,920	219,318	250,185	281,534	312,398	364,942	401,732	450,149	502,188	567,619
Texas	594,124	712,708	794,652	892,113	1,054,530	1,246,924	1,512,928	1,703,248	1,886,515	2,112,397
Utah	129,553	144,901	158,919	174,466	185,532	207,032	237,794	269,379	296,182	330,210
Vermont	40,832	46,201	50,408	55,264	61,558	69,621	77,484	83,784	89,700	97,097
Virginia	273,611	318,661	358,466	413,522	473,022	538,067	626,401	689,461	765,082	903,503
Washington	319,797	356,608	358,623	415,914	465,713	544,422	590,298	635,627	719,261	806,783
West Virginia	105,213	116,023	105,940	113,466	116,876	132,736	151,325	164,863	174,701	259,482
Wisconsin	429,447	477,661	537,998	605,037	644,935	707,518	799,305	873,994	909,918	1,002,505
Wyoming	38,150	42,368	46,326	49,862	53,706	59,624	71,353	75,800	80,203	90,335
U.S. Service Schools	164,097	182,477	245,073	272,726	297,011	322,135	361,171	409,451	415,805	437,805
Outlying areas	100,121	116,435	116,834	137,346	150,971	185,367	182,128	194,851	213,212	226,768
American Samoa	972	1,088	744	818	982	1,159	1,060	718	1,195	1,001
Federated States of Micronesia	—	—	—	—	—	—	—	—	—	—
Guam	4,993	5,021	6,727	7,633	8,825	10,360	8,424	8,575	9,760	9,489
Marshall Islands	—	—	—	—	—	—	—	—	—	—
Northern Marianas	—	—	—	—	—	—	—	—	—	—
Palau	—	—	—	—	—	—	—	—	—	—
Puerto Rico	90,026	105,058	109,363	128,895	141,164	173,848	164,874	178,127	194,114	206,694
Trust Territories	—	—	—	—	—	—	547	546	1,095	622
Virgin Islands	4,130	5,268	—	—	—	—	7,223	6,886	7,048	8,962

Table 84.—Current-fund expenditures (in current dollars) of public institutions of higher education, by state: 1969–70 to 1994–95—Continued

[Amounts in thousands]

State or other area	1979–80	1980–81	1981–82	1982–83	1983–84	1984–85	1985–86	1986–87	1987–88	1988–89
1	12	13	14	15	16	17	18	19	20	21
United States	$37,767,970	$42,279,806	$46,219,134	$49,572,918	$53,086,644	$58,314,550	$63,193,853	$67,653,838	$72,641,301	$78,945,618
Alabama	751,398	839,366	904,216	955,520	1,040,356	1,191,478	1,324,774	1,351,761	1,511,246	1,669,401
Alaska	148,397	158,700	185,400	213,083	224,589	235,168	224,042	213,286	221,296	240,913
Arizona	595,852	691,481	780,780	819,504	889,573	934,587	1,017,203	1,098,146	1,193,764	1,317,954
Arkansas	306,206	340,621	374,283	393,679	425,497	485,363	528,831	543,200	622,442	692,970
California	5,019,441	5,775,482	6,126,818	6,390,339	6,630,635	7,705,638	8,515,440	9,079,890	9,493,900	10,182,106
Colorado	681,868	738,363	821,963	881,518	935,447	993,440	1,057,558	1,123,508	1,225,193	1,331,091
Connecticut	333,418	367,850	394,270	426,462	489,917	522,006	562,696	621,183	680,087	774,179
Delaware	140,990	158,332	170,323	181,356	190,636	207,584	229,377	255,335	279,084	314,003
District of Columbia	60,328	71,791	67,800	73,650	78,839	82,660	80,764	83,787	86,465	93,710
Florida	1,054,042	1,170,305	1,329,291	1,366,801	1,497,560	1,650,338	1,782,180	1,973,533	2,182,947	2,443,879
Georgia	669,134	754,060	846,337	921,021	1,054,899	1,142,836	1,255,964	1,404,747	1,507,960	1,622,707
Hawaii	195,758	222,718	242,489	267,258	273,105	288,217	312,248	317,294	349,791	379,799
Idaho	149,634	166,844	180,352	192,701	204,783	226,142	238,438	246,847	269,697	289,148
Illinois	1,591,213	1,780,403	1,892,135	1,951,623	2,079,772	2,320,251	2,571,409	2,707,123	2,789,932	3,015,395
Indiana	933,703	1,064,395	1,138,511	1,252,380	1,367,711	1,472,807	1,602,203	1,758,524	1,841,317	2,005,740
Iowa	713,898	767,590	836,464	909,647	944,211	1,027,080	1,092,542	1,162,266	1,229,142	1,491,442
Kansas	513,087	579,857	639,475	664,708	733,372	794,588	848,602	886,190	928,956	1,028,578
Kentucky	605,151	673,775	677,795	741,846	806,091	845,505	898,718	992,842	1,068,927	1,143,612
Louisiana	612,723	716,702	808,068	862,911	914,211	1,000,470	1,039,177	1,065,692	1,112,935	1,172,325
Maine	138,278	153,658	166,905	184,042	197,915	210,749	216,737	244,432	271,928	315,700
Maryland	704,407	795,100	902,008	886,798	901,569	1,021,140	1,064,430	1,144,897	1,249,730	1,389,900
Massachusetts	492,512	553,019	631,786	687,245	740,329	878,644	980,585	1,100,445	1,235,566	1,306,814
Michigan	1,904,616	2,053,795	2,188,662	2,356,196	2,512,255	2,706,362	2,946,336	3,094,481	3,507,141	3,745,488
Minnesota	786,017	876,632	990,681	1,043,667	1,110,870	1,220,404	1,324,691	1,427,227	1,565,491	1,809,757
Mississippi	488,894	539,222	581,252	582,401	628,647	660,816	706,380	701,795	775,821	864,611
Missouri	608,690	687,643	713,641	782,706	831,884	899,740	999,869	1,071,224	1,132,628	1,237,603
Montana	112,353	121,894	142,334	156,492	170,366	185,588	182,102	182,795	192,382	198,475
Nebraska	341,734	378,928	418,332	444,133	469,817	506,752	537,858	582,939	610,064	676,527
Nevada	99,675	111,347	125,867	132,724	140,646	156,584	180,107	198,714	217,330	240,711
New Hampshire	121,882	134,391	143,648	151,983	153,461	168,453	183,959	200,211	222,842	247,686
New Jersey	805,448	903,169	964,378	1,070,511	1,166,525	1,285,926	1,406,490	1,579,018	1,770,521	1,968,859
New Mexico	282,439	325,960	349,373	379,595	382,998	422,740	456,600	500,674	524,181	751,405
New York	2,337,898	2,519,104	2,822,661	3,132,439	3,359,316	3,636,384	3,802,602	4,227,556	4,494,943	4,732,811
North Carolina	988,975	1,128,383	1,231,966	1,284,630	1,439,145	1,633,304	1,799,173	1,955,910	2,076,493	2,238,155
North Dakota	167,202	192,046	215,787	232,038	254,455	263,909	288,214	309,961	303,762	319,583
Ohio	1,612,495	1,784,754	1,936,750	2,149,696	2,328,494	2,536,913	2,718,408	2,933,615	3,172,348	3,494,228
Oklahoma	501,400	583,174	658,176	747,590	728,923	765,599	844,829	826,461	844,428	887,293
Oregon	586,355	642,411	699,525	734,767	788,183	832,296	880,696	959,238	1,023,206	1,116,966
Pennsylvania	1,398,891	1,544,586	1,701,884	1,872,341	2,004,320	2,159,745	2,392,145	2,608,557	2,874,641	3,147,180
Rhode Island	144,002	158,365	167,888	175,371	187,412	197,849	213,253	225,033	246,258	270,411
South Carolina	553,866	617,963	646,241	683,829	743,385	853,452	951,848	980,264	1,079,002	1,179,216
South Dakota	123,662	124,103	131,745	135,637	141,986	140,885	149,092	152,274	157,736	169,308
Tennessee	582,038	665,885	723,472	781,885	839,477	958,612	1,081,052	1,275,950	1,311,921	1,411,226
Texas	2,391,570	2,736,276	3,189,782	3,538,762	3,847,643	4,087,570	4,375,082	4,451,215	4,771,023	5,166,389
Utah	359,536	405,314	457,248	515,087	533,836	595,755	669,714	700,774	757,976	835,250
Vermont	109,954	122,708	134,910	146,712	159,763	174,051	188,112	201,435	216,972	241,314
Virginia	1,018,187	1,143,755	1,267,236	1,367,587	1,465,098	1,681,173	1,825,156	2,003,090	2,201,018	2,431,539
Washington	905,936	993,171	1,044,135	1,088,315	1,205,410	1,331,849	1,399,780	1,512,376	1,575,333	1,779,855
West Virginia	298,859	317,482	345,152	364,875	404,735	357,335	376,293	392,671	406,170	451,503
Wisconsin	1,104,035	1,208,396	1,306,457	1,410,280	1,493,528	1,605,692	1,754,395	1,872,979	2,022,712	2,159,069
Wyoming	105,604	126,082	145,698	166,762	181,300	186,652	203,307	198,934	208,663	212,813
U.S. Service Schools	514,316	592,454	656,787	719,812	791,770	865,472	912,393	951,539	1,025,992	739,019
Outlying areas	239,769	268,310	304,565	361,327	419,255	418,141	451,370	429,481	491,892	494,087
American Samoa	1,424	1,609	1,235	1,399	1,369	1,092	1,092	1,162	1,257	2,642
Federated States of Micronesia	—	—	—	—	—	—	—	—	—	1,789
Guam	14,163	16,100	24,058	25,574	25,912	25,576	31,310	30,780	33,481	38,488
Marshall Islands	—	—	—	—	—	—	—	—	—	—
Northern Marianas	—	—	—	—	1,212	1,293	1,350	2,787	2,292	950
Palau	—	—	—	—	—	—	—	—	—	3,513
Puerto Rico	212,461	237,319	263,571	315,465	371,696	368,536	394,046	370,455	427,572	424,125
Trust Territories	1,227	1,447	1,695	3,960	4,038	5,525	5,992	5,444	6,455	—
Virgin Islands	10,494	11,835	14,006	14,929	15,028	16,120	17,580	18,853	20,834	22,580

Table 84.—Current-fund expenditures (in current dollars) of public institutions of higher education, by state: 1969–70 to 1994–95—Continued

[Amounts in thousands]

State or other area	1989–90	1990–91	1991–92	1992–93	1993–94	1994–95	Percentage change			
							1969–70 to 1994–95	1984–85 to 1989–90	1989–90 to 1994–95	1984–85 to 1994–95
1	22	23	24	25	26	27	28	29	30	31
United States	**$85,770,530**	**$92,961,093**	**$98,847,180**	**$104,570,101**	**$109,309,541**	**$115,464,975**	**771.5**	**47.1**	**34.6**	**98.0**
Alabama	1,831,657	2,054,798	2,189,029	2,428,620	2,510,081	2,648,077	1,172.6	53.7	44.6	122.3
Alaska	268,057	289,606	306,218	322,620	336,405	336,584	1,102.5	14.0	25.6	43.1
Arizona	1,446,388	1,586,891	1,620,019	1,621,716	1,754,682	1,854,180	1,029.8	54.8	28.2	98.4
Arkansas	751,336	797,291	878,783	976,735	1,002,908	1,070,668	943.4	54.8	42.5	120.6
California	11,230,941	12,023,304	12,910,152	13,537,367	13,244,130	13,899,338	628.5	45.7	23.8	80.4
Colorado	1,374,188	1,452,137	1,546,642	1,670,921	1,760,679	1,862,438	662.2	38.3	35.5	87.5
Connecticut	811,282	886,846	957,627	981,286	1,026,593	1,134,014	851.9	55.4	39.8	117.2
Delaware	342,119	367,012	396,947	416,699	442,488	469,085	996.8	64.8	37.1	126.0
District of Columbia	99,120	97,556	99,535	98,826	97,072	99,351	299.7	19.9	0.2	20.2
Florida	2,766,267	2,896,046	2,988,794	3,179,353	3,408,957	3,549,470	883.5	67.6	28.3	115.1
Georgia	1,769,744	1,929,993	2,015,816	2,227,608	2,453,100	2,728,682	1,071.5	54.9	54.2	138.8
Hawaii	424,473	498,307	575,337	602,346	613,356	653,303	663.3	47.3	53.9	126.7
Idaho	314,398	353,561	391,441	409,167	445,463	473,733	841.4	39.0	50.7	109.5
Illinois	3,310,763	3,528,967	3,644,740	3,877,243	4,053,858	4,293,437	543.1	42.7	29.7	85.0
Indiana	2,186,604	2,391,173	2,643,997	2,671,055	2,858,990	2,967,184	666.5	48.5	35.7	101.5
Iowa	1,617,626	1,734,476	1,776,217	1,899,159	1,981,068	2,051,631	759.4	57.5	26.8	99.8
Kansas	1,131,558	1,190,573	1,262,215	1,329,587	1,429,200	1,495,926	673.1	42.4	32.2	88.3
Kentucky	1,236,680	1,400,529	1,514,985	1,516,017	1,577,584	1,663,738	746.4	46.3	34.5	96.8
Louisiana	1,286,648	1,439,415	1,541,126	1,800,188	1,835,151	1,909,675	891.4	28.6	48.4	90.9
Maine	344,435	355,074	362,905	375,090	387,991	391,269	710.5	63.4	13.6	85.7
Maryland	1,522,145	1,684,341	1,674,918	1,829,812	1,940,403	1,997,636	798.7	49.1	31.2	95.6
Massachusetts	1,357,588	1,435,063	1,474,589	1,605,121	1,496,856	1,557,225	934.3	54.5	14.7	77.2
Michigan	4,076,519	4,416,914	4,741,682	4,925,759	5,095,422	5,395,759	576.3	50.6	32.4	99.4
Minnesota	1,802,133	2,012,225	2,219,016	2,286,336	2,459,437	2,624,464	735.2	47.7	45.6	115.0
Mississippi	922,574	978,366	1,012,544	1,102,806	1,200,196	1,358,795	842.3	39.6	47.3	105.6
Missouri	1,349,451	1,453,608	1,501,166	1,582,746	1,694,484	1,836,878	618.9	50.0	36.1	104.2
Montana	218,231	254,175	320,876	337,189	350,943	376,618	567.4	17.6	72.6	102.9
Nebraska	762,480	848,778	916,814	968,407	1,004,263	1,076,670	829.7	50.5	41.2	112.5
Nevada	281,018	330,592	363,306	377,786	415,785	447,901	1,401.9	79.5	59.4	186.0
New Hampshire	259,157	281,542	307,217	335,575	360,833	371,554	765.5	53.8	43.4	120.6
New Jersey	2,165,562	2,309,968	2,489,088	2,630,533	2,809,931	2,982,535	1,155.1	68.4	37.7	131.9
New Mexico	828,157	896,299	1,010,859	1,069,497	1,142,903	1,278,741	1,166.4	95.9	54.4	202.5
New York	5,058,750	5,605,621	5,681,964	6,096,863	6,481,594	6,922,118	737.6	39.1	36.8	90.4
North Carolina	2,420,825	2,581,156	2,770,977	3,002,915	3,192,215	3,406,215	944.4	48.2	40.7	108.5
North Dakota	357,832	367,959	408,219	419,268	432,190	456,730	644.7	35.6	27.6	73.1
Ohio	3,726,135	4,084,840	4,359,943	4,389,408	4,640,316	4,907,686	724.8	46.9	31.7	93.5
Oklahoma	973,213	1,057,248	1,158,696	1,177,061	1,214,084	1,263,002	570.4	27.1	29.8	65.0
Oregon	1,219,341	1,329,794	1,484,621	1,560,699	1,623,771	1,756,424	727.5	46.5	44.0	111.0
Pennsylvania	3,390,869	3,602,685	3,904,332	4,004,062	4,240,094	4,506,833	724.7	57.0	32.9	108.7
Rhode Island	287,194	292,199	303,606	330,038	331,359	344,457	571.0	45.2	19.9	74.1
South Carolina	1,324,647	1,475,074	1,595,552	1,702,419	1,766,671	1,817,631	1,265.4	55.2	37.2	113.0
South Dakota	184,153	197,853	217,756	240,061	259,120	252,443	334.7	30.7	37.1	79.2
Tennessee	1,519,680	1,585,614	1,621,202	1,776,066	1,911,953	2,042,171	964.1	58.5	34.4	113.0
Texas	5,604,164	5,959,584	6,370,847	6,982,016	7,414,174	7,817,433	1,215.8	37.1	39.5	91.2
Utah	914,771	993,625	1,116,845	1,174,239	1,260,797	1,354,017	945.1	53.5	48.0	127.3
Vermont	260,371	274,746	294,045	298,626	306,100	316,455	675.0	49.6	21.5	81.8
Virginia	2,682,902	2,812,109	2,939,683	3,072,851	3,301,020	3,414,167	1,147.8	59.6	27.3	103.1
Washington	1,922,673	2,157,074	2,278,549	2,486,455	2,639,504	2,807,168	777.8	44.4	46.0	110.8
West Virginia	493,825	548,802	582,453	609,447	650,642	674,664	541.2	38.2	36.6	88.8
Wisconsin	2,307,325	2,469,260	2,596,853	2,726,350	2,872,001	2,941,034	584.8	43.7	27.5	83.2
Wyoming	227,131	240,216	265,048	260,592	271,396	294,334	671.5	21.7	29.6	57.7
U.S. Service Schools	805,430	1,150,209	1,241,392	1,267,497	1,309,330	1,313,438	700.4	–6.9	63.1	51.8
Outlying areas	543,925	516,958	574,988	654,292	662,130	727,524	626.6	30.1	33.8	74.0
American Samoa	2,879	3,187	3,228	3,356	3,416	3,483	258.2	163.8	21.0	219.1
Federated States of Micronesia	1,842	3,777	3,765	3,294	3,520	5,056	—	—	174.5	—
Guam	48,954	57,645	67,220	71,917	66,913	81,148	1,525.4	91.4	65.8	217.3
Marshall Islands	—	—	3,588	1,298	1,527	1,237	—	—	—	—
Northern Marianas	1,003	2,798	3,194	2,505	3,214	12,366	—	–22.5	1,133.5	856.5
Palau	3,870	3,837	3,687	4,485	3,476	3,667	—	—	–5.2	—
Puerto Rico	460,897	385,511	434,032	536,917	546,575	586,910	551.9	25.1	27.3	59.3
Trust Territories	—	—	—	—	—	—	—	—	—	—
Virgin Islands	24,480	60,202	56,274	30,520	33,489	33,656	715.0	51.9	37.5	108.8

—Data not available or not applicable.

NOTE.—Because of rounding, details may not add to totals.

SOURCE: U.S. Department of Education, National Center for Education Statistics, Higher Education General Information Survey (HEGIS), "Financial Statistics of Institutions of Higher Education" surveys; and Integrated Postsecondary Education Data System (IPEDS), "Financial Statistics" surveys. (This table was prepared January 1998.)

Table 85.—Current-fund expenditures (in constant 1994–95 dollars[1]) of public institutions of higher education, by state: 1969–70 to 1994–95

[Amounts in thousands]

State or other area	1969–70	1970–71	1971–72	1972–73	1973–74	1974–75	1975–76	1976–77	1977–78	1978–79
1	2	3	4	5	6	7	8	9	10	11
United States	$51,455,200	$54,641,160	$57,081,163	$59,795,603	$62,516,754	$66,360,279	$69,491,676	$71,424,153	$71,738,711	$73,398,903
Alabama	886,075	906,066	1,004,236	1,107,825	1,194,919	1,311,002	1,458,136	1,536,067	1,584,699	1,646,631
Alaska	119,189	146,779	158,192	168,630	168,199	204,399	255,389	269,558	296,867	302,267
Arizona	698,848	779,353	881,181	933,139	987,960	1,057,331	1,068,375	1,164,509	1,230,424	1,263,532
Arkansas	436,960	434,260	452,613	460,330	487,138	543,890	589,917	596,909	636,281	658,535
California	8,124,138	8,121,017	8,162,870	8,608,652	9,150,526	10,098,026	10,799,009	11,664,728	10,531,160	10,268,734
Colorado	1,040,445	1,105,629	1,168,847	1,215,011	1,235,552	1,299,601	1,373,964	1,414,544	1,410,230	1,454,783
Connecticut	507,291	539,198	587,333	598,173	575,239	637,019	626,043	639,222	702,747	712,135
Delaware	182,126	198,041	203,765	226,787	245,180	269,891	278,034	283,547	279,564	300,335
District of Columbia	105,852	111,894	147,602	151,645	146,162	136,681	134,450	126,430	141,210	137,993
Florida	1,536,786	1,657,405	1,721,563	1,861,688	1,993,975	2,105,690	2,112,235	2,155,650	2,229,145	2,218,685
Georgia	991,875	1,071,833	1,096,720	1,162,242	1,243,257	1,271,438	1,284,480	1,315,053	1,382,447	1,438,914
Hawaii	364,464	419,790	420,943	414,723	399,157	419,426	422,956	400,279	424,993	426,867
Idaho	214,293	217,272	234,429	233,385	251,412	271,910	292,480	304,784	313,108	327,716
Illinois	2,842,924	3,155,806	3,141,131	3,254,008	3,239,799	3,292,587	3,393,293	3,349,688	3,325,978	3,419,617
Indiana	1,648,357	1,732,252	1,796,287	1,812,115	1,758,405	1,945,672	1,957,650	1,973,742	2,000,185	2,043,764
Iowa	1,016,605	1,033,546	1,059,593	1,077,786	1,166,751	1,240,703	1,280,778	1,433,096	1,438,854	1,503,813
Kansas	823,938	877,531	872,127	899,423	901,262	957,698	977,662	1,056,205	1,080,871	1,157,873
Kentucky	837,052	875,574	923,045	981,443	1,027,228	1,080,781	1,173,502	1,191,970	1,213,215	1,259,546
Louisiana	820,275	885,226	825,142	948,827	976,140	1,033,076	992,234	1,068,709	1,145,713	1,164,612
Maine	205,567	221,578	236,280	245,868	274,639	280,000	298,123	286,782	290,080	289,242
Maryland	946,476	1,079,686	1,163,710	1,250,341	1,277,300	1,385,903	1,459,007	1,535,612	1,555,076	1,591,343
Massachusetts	641,087	746,365	858,000	872,751	929,611	1,015,143	948,514	981,503	991,987	1,086,665
Michigan	3,397,586	3,435,138	3,522,189	3,600,564	3,666,445	3,827,560	3,910,156	3,894,549	4,077,791	4,113,107
Minnesota	1,338,006	1,401,216	1,398,789	1,564,997	1,568,653	1,623,476	1,724,238	1,626,040	1,653,560	1,686,704
Mississippi	614,059	667,963	706,439	762,197	798,027	848,120	926,141	958,669	1,000,601	1,039,452
Missouri	1,088,063	1,089,242	1,142,378	1,166,211	1,199,870	1,268,253	1,281,082	1,313,085	1,302,251	1,327,387
Montana	240,278	259,788	251,853	257,216	250,621	259,686	269,864	282,295	277,745	267,399
Nebraska	493,156	519,975	539,236	547,459	574,844	604,159	653,221	703,162	731,620	749,235
Nevada	126,994	129,681	136,394	137,785	152,922	154,293	181,166	183,089	186,760	203,730
New Hampshire	182,813	192,157	197,411	204,584	224,110	235,579	241,418	249,799	263,078	266,113
New Jersey	1,011,914	1,121,238	1,254,881	1,224,639	1,486,575	1,526,948	1,592,440	1,676,392	1,775,755	1,741,499
New Mexico	429,957	444,347	454,459	482,027	498,664	427,187	476,596	494,052	539,027	581,531
New York	3,519,247	4,007,417	4,284,415	4,453,441	4,990,416	5,389,344	5,637,091	5,133,369	5,090,837	5,095,609
North Carolina	1,388,802	1,480,357	1,624,387	1,631,185	1,755,755	1,989,098	1,889,928	1,957,668	2,033,177	2,145,019
North Dakota	261,173	265,501	262,000	264,922	271,139	292,419	326,708	333,830	342,266	351,783
Ohio	2,533,561	2,813,730	2,903,146	3,001,009	2,977,275	3,087,357	3,175,940	3,265,379	3,301,100	3,431,668
Oklahoma	802,289	836,355	878,835	870,583	838,641	850,405	898,111	1,009,015	1,036,379	1,061,702
Oregon	903,863	910,489	937,248	947,673	986,815	1,038,059	1,140,086	1,182,836	1,191,821	1,228,946
Pennsylvania	2,327,003	2,464,986	2,777,614	2,915,172	2,946,021	2,984,135	3,117,450	3,123,449	3,084,681	3,047,844
Rhode Island	218,587	239,570	237,457	261,894	273,929	283,264	287,501	302,045	304,611	309,315
South Carolina	566,842	601,759	658,450	735,783	845,222	970,172	992,931	988,885	1,072,765	1,146,075
South Dakota	247,289	260,647	269,303	258,880	257,883	256,999	243,063	241,174	239,417	248,023
Tennessee	817,239	876,229	949,914	1,014,003	1,053,011	1,130,446	1,169,055	1,231,138	1,285,662	1,354,235
Texas	2,529,913	2,847,445	3,017,165	3,213,136	3,554,548	3,862,479	4,402,671	4,658,314	4,829,707	5,039,789
Utah	551,668	578,914	603,388	628,376	625,381	641,304	691,988	736,741	758,262	787,651
Vermont	173,872	184,584	191,392	199,046	207,498	215,657	225,481	229,146	229,643	231,656
Virginia	1,165,099	1,273,130	1,361,037	1,489,387	1,594,436	1,666,720	1,822,848	1,885,648	1,958,703	2,155,591
Washington	1,361,770	1,424,736	1,361,632	1,498,002	1,569,798	1,686,404	1,717,787	1,738,413	1,841,397	1,924,835
West Virginia	448,021	463,543	402,238	408,673	393,960	411,165	440,362	450,894	447,256	619,076
Wisconsin	1,828,684	1,908,374	2,042,692	2,179,169	2,173,909	2,191,613	2,326,004	2,390,339	2,329,501	2,391,793
Wyoming	162,450	169,271	175,891	179,588	181,028	184,691	207,640	207,310	205,330	215,524
U.S. Service Schools	698,763	729,043	930,502	982,279	1,001,146	997,848	1,051,021	1,119,831	1,064,511	1,044,522
Outlying areas	426,337	465,186	443,600	494,680	508,885	574,194	530,000	532,909	545,849	541,026
American Samoa	4,141	4,347	2,823	2,946	3,310	3,590	3,085	1,964	3,059	2,388
Federated States of Micronesia	—	—	—	—	—	—	—	—	—	—
Guam	21,259	20,061	25,542	27,493	29,748	32,090	24,515	23,451	24,986	22,640
Marshall Islands	—	—	—	—	—	—	—	—	—	—
Northern Marianas	—	—	—	—	—	—	—	—	—	—
Palau	—	—	—	—	—	—	—	—	—	—
Puerto Rico	383,352	419,731	415,234	464,241	475,827	538,514	479,789	487,169	496,956	493,133
Trust Territories	—	—	—	—	—	—	1,591	1,492	2,804	1,485
Virgin Islands	17,586	21,047	—	—	—	—	21,020	18,833	18,045	21,381

Table 85.—Current-fund expenditures (in constant 1994–95 dollars [1]) of public institutions of higher education, by state: 1969–70 to 1994–95—Continued

[Amounts in thousands]

State or other area	1979–80	1980–81	1981–82	1982–83	1983–84	1984–85	1985–86	1986–87	1987–88	1988–89
1	12	13	14	15	16	17	18	19	20	21
United States	$74,756,214	$75,591,168	$75,506,019	$76,044,856	$77,705,068	$80,735,126	$83,352,855	$85,840,353	$88,367,769	$91,191,700
Alabama	1,630,776	1,645,471	1,619,692	1,607,185	1,669,732	1,808,724	1,915,967	1,880,614	2,015,794	2,114,407
Alaska	322,070	311,111	332,100	358,405	360,457	356,997	324,022	296,730	295,179	305,133
Arizona	1,293,192	1,355,560	1,398,586	1,378,406	1,427,730	1,418,751	1,471,139	1,527,777	1,592,317	1,669,276
Arkansas	664,566	667,743	670,441	662,168	682,907	736,806	764,826	755,718	830,251	877,693
California	10,893,806	11,322,099	10,974,768	10,748,550	10,641,917	11,697,547	12,315,537	12,632,237	12,663,552	12,896,312
Colorado	1,479,873	1,447,467	1,472,356	1,482,714	1,501,356	1,508,092	1,529,504	1,563,060	1,634,239	1,685,915
Connecticut	723,624	721,124	706,244	717,309	786,299	792,432	813,805	864,210	907,143	980,549
Delaware	305,994	310,390	305,094	305,041	305,963	315,123	331,739	355,230	372,260	397,705
District of Columbia	130,931	140,736	121,447	123,880	126,533	125,481	116,806	116,567	115,332	118,690
Florida	2,287,611	2,294,233	2,381,115	2,298,959	2,403,527	2,505,296	2,577,495	2,745,643	2,911,749	3,095,334
Georgia	1,452,236	1,478,239	1,516,015	1,549,157	1,693,073	1,734,883	1,816,450	1,954,330	2,011,411	2,055,266
Hawaii	424,857	436,611	434,363	449,528	438,323	437,529	451,591	441,430	466,572	481,041
Idaho	324,754	327,076	323,058	324,124	328,669	343,295	344,843	343,421	359,739	366,226
Illinois	3,453,446	3,490,254	3,389,319	3,282,630	3,337,954	3,522,258	3,718,925	3,766,238	3,721,384	3,819,197
Indiana	2,026,437	2,086,611	2,039,378	2,106,504	2,195,124	2,235,796	2,317,202	2,446,516	2,456,063	2,540,403
Iowa	1,549,390	1,504,763	1,498,331	1,530,027	1,515,423	1,559,160	1,580,100	1,616,982	1,639,506	1,889,011
Kansas	1,113,565	1,136,737	1,145,470	1,118,039	1,177,034	1,206,225	1,227,299	1,232,897	1,239,100	1,302,762
Kentucky	1,313,372	1,320,849	1,214,113	1,247,785	1,293,745	1,283,519	1,299,780	1,381,274	1,425,801	1,448,461
Louisiana	1,329,807	1,405,004	1,447,466	1,451,417	1,467,273	1,518,764	1,502,920	1,482,625	1,484,501	1,484,827
Maine	300,109	301,228	298,972	309,559	317,646	319,928	313,457	340,061	362,715	399,855
Maryland	1,528,791	1,558,692	1,615,737	1,491,595	1,446,984	1,550,142	1,539,442	1,592,818	1,666,968	1,760,401
Massachusetts	1,068,911	1,084,123	1,131,698	1,155,946	1,188,200	1,333,826	1,418,181	1,530,975	1,648,074	1,655,166
Michigan	4,133,632	4,026,204	3,920,479	3,963,121	4,032,073	4,108,395	4,261,167	4,305,143	4,678,042	4,743,909
Minnesota	1,705,910	1,718,526	1,774,574	1,755,447	1,782,904	1,852,635	1,915,848	1,985,604	2,088,148	2,292,177
Mississippi	1,061,058	1,057,076	1,041,178	979,599	1,008,954	1,003,152	1,021,609	976,360	1,034,839	1,095,087
Missouri	1,321,053	1,348,037	1,278,322	1,316,512	1,335,142	1,365,851	1,446,070	1,490,321	1,510,769	1,567,506
Montana	243,842	238,959	254,958	263,219	273,430	281,731	263,367	254,310	256,610	251,381
Nebraska	741,673	742,839	749,344	747,032	754,038	769,275	777,882	811,004	813,741	856,866
Nevada	216,327	218,282	225,461	223,242	225,732	237,703	260,481	276,457	289,888	304,876
New Hampshire	264,524	263,456	257,312	255,636	246,299	255,721	266,052	278,540	297,240	313,711
New Jersey	1,748,083	1,770,548	1,727,459	1,800,599	1,872,228	1,952,100	2,034,150	2,196,782	2,361,631	2,493,691
New Mexico	612,984	639,003	625,821	638,479	614,696	641,740	660,362	696,554	699,186	951,704
New York	5,073,994	4,938,384	5,056,140	5,268,762	5,391,575	5,520,214	5,499,551	5,881,513	5,995,633	5,994,418
North Carolina	2,146,395	2,212,051	2,206,780	2,160,747	2,309,772	2,479,438	2,602,071	2,721,125	2,769,755	2,834,772
North Dakota	362,883	376,481	386,531	390,287	408,391	400,627	416,832	431,228	405,177	404,773
Ohio	3,499,635	3,498,784	3,469,236	3,615,789	3,737,144	3,851,162	3,931,524	4,081,340	4,231,475	4,425,671
Oklahoma	1,088,200	1,143,239	1,178,970	1,257,446	1,169,893	1,162,219	1,221,841	1,149,800	1,126,350	1,123,816
Oregon	1,272,579	1,259,365	1,253,036	1,235,878	1,265,004	1,263,467	1,273,714	1,334,523	1,364,816	1,414,711
Pennsylvania	3,036,046	3,027,965	3,048,529	3,149,278	3,216,858	3,278,602	3,459,663	3,629,108	3,834,374	3,986,112
Rhode Island	312,531	310,454	300,733	294,975	300,788	300,344	308,419	313,073	328,474	342,493
South Carolina	1,202,068	1,211,438	1,157,590	1,150,200	1,193,104	1,295,583	1,376,620	1,363,776	1,439,240	1,493,556
South Dakota	268,386	243,289	235,990	228,141	227,883	213,870	215,625	211,849	210,398	214,440
Tennessee	1,263,210	1,305,383	1,295,931	1,315,131	1,347,329	1,455,221	1,563,481	1,775,143	1,749,921	1,787,412
Texas	5,190,478	5,364,121	5,713,751	5,952,198	6,175,287	6,205,138	6,327,504	6,192,674	6,363,886	6,543,574
Utah	780,310	794,566	819,054	866,376	856,787	904,386	968,580	974,939	1,011,036	1,057,900
Vermont	238,636	240,553	241,659	246,770	256,414	264,219	272,059	280,243	289,411	305,640
Virginia	2,209,793	2,242,187	2,269,959	2,300,281	2,351,426	2,552,105	2,639,649	2,786,764	2,935,854	3,079,706
Washington	1,966,174	1,946,985	1,870,324	1,830,545	1,934,636	2,021,813	2,024,445	2,104,067	2,101,276	2,254,305
West Virginia	648,621	622,384	618,260	613,719	649,584	542,452	544,217	546,296	541,775	571,858
Wisconsin	2,396,111	2,368,906	2,340,214	2,372,091	2,397,055	2,437,521	2,537,311	2,605,750	2,698,018	2,734,603
Wyoming	229,195	247,169	260,984	280,494	290,980	283,347	294,035	276,764	278,327	269,541
U.S. Service Schools	1,116,232	1,161,431	1,176,481	1,210,724	1,270,760	1,313,830	1,319,558	1,323,812	1,368,532	936,016
Outlying areas	520,375	525,988	545,558	607,753	672,888	634,759	652,798	597,507	656,116	625,794
American Samoa	3,090	3,154	2,213	2,354	2,198	1,657	1,579	1,617	1,677	3,346
Federated States of Micronesia	—	—	—	—	—	—	—	—	—	2,266
Guam	30,738	31,563	43,095	43,015	41,588	38,825	45,282	42,822	44,659	48,748
Marshall Islands	—	—	—	—	—	—	—	—	—	—
Northern Marianas	—	—	—	—	—	1,963	1,952	3,878	3,058	1,204
Palau	—	—	—	—	—	—	—	—	—	4,449
Puerto Rico	461,109	465,234	472,126	530,612	596,557	559,457	569,894	515,389	570,322	537,182
Trust Territories	2,663	2,836	3,036	6,661	6,481	8,388	8,667	7,573	8,610	—
Virgin Islands	22,775	23,201	25,089	25,111	24,119	24,470	25,425	26,229	27,790	28,599

Table 85.—Current-fund expenditures (in constant 1994–95 dollars[1]) of public institutions of higher education, by state: 1969–70 to 1994–95—Continued

[Amounts in thousands]

State or other area	1989–90	1990–91	1991–92	1992–93	1993–94	1994–95	Percentage change 1969–70 to 1994–95	Percentage change 1984–85 to 1989–90	Percentage change 1989–90 to 1994–95	Percentage change 1984–85 to 1994–95
1	22	23	24	25	26	27	28	29	30	31
United States	$93,446,018	$96,222,886	$98,847,180	$111,391,330	$112,589,496	$115,464,975	124.4	15.7	23.6	43.0
Alabama	2,188,101	2,332,099	2,400,226	2,587,041	2,585,398	2,648,077	198.9	21.0	21.0	46.4
Alaska	320,221	328,689	335,762	343,665	346,499	336,584	182.4	–10.3	5.1	–5.7
Arizona	1,727,858	1,801,046	1,776,318	1,727,502	1,807,333	1,854,180	165.3	21.8	7.3	30.7
Arkansas	897,548	904,888	963,568	1,040,449	1,033,001	1,070,668	145.0	21.8	19.3	45.3
California	13,416,508	13,645,882	14,155,721	14,420,425	13,641,535	13,899,338	71.1	14.7	3.6	18.8
Colorado	1,641,608	1,648,107	1,695,862	1,779,917	1,813,510	1,862,438	79.0	8.9	13.5	23.5
Connecticut	969,160	1,006,529	1,050,019	1,045,297	1,057,397	1,134,014	123.5	22.3	17.0	43.1
Delaware	408,696	416,542	435,245	443,880	455,765	469,085	157.6	29.7	14.8	48.9
District of Columbia	118,409	110,722	109,138	105,273	99,985	99,351	–6.1	–5.6	–16.1	–20.8
Florida	3,304,588	3,286,876	3,277,153	3,386,746	3,511,247	3,549,470	131.0	31.9	7.4	41.7
Georgia	2,114,140	2,190,451	2,210,302	2,372,917	2,526,708	2,728,682	175.1	21.9	29.1	57.3
Hawaii	507,076	565,554	630,845	641,638	631,761	653,303	79.3	15.9	28.8	49.3
Idaho	375,581	401,275	429,207	435,857	458,829	473,733	121.1	9.4	26.1	38.0
Illinois	3,955,045	4,005,211	3,996,383	4,130,160	4,175,499	4,293,437	51.0	12.3	8.6	21.9
Indiana	2,612,122	2,713,869	2,899,089	2,845,291	2,944,777	2,967,184	80.0	16.8	13.6	32.7
Iowa	1,932,419	1,968,548	1,947,586	2,023,044	2,040,512	2,051,631	101.8	23.9	6.2	31.6
Kansas	1,351,762	1,351,244	1,383,993	1,416,318	1,472,084	1,495,926	81.6	12.1	10.7	24.0
Kentucky	1,477,340	1,589,534	1,661,150	1,614,909	1,624,922	1,663,738	98.8	15.1	12.6	29.6
Louisiana	1,537,032	1,633,668	1,689,813	1,917,617	1,890,217	1,909,675	132.8	1.2	24.2	25.7
Maine	411,463	402,993	397,918	399,558	399,634	391,269	90.3	28.6	–4.9	22.3
Maryland	1,818,358	1,911,647	1,836,514	1,949,172	1,998,627	1,997,636	111.1	17.3	9.9	28.9
Massachusetts	1,621,778	1,628,729	1,616,857	1,709,825	1,541,771	1,557,225	142.9	21.6	–4.0	16.7
Michigan	4,869,819	5,012,989	5,199,158	5,247,072	5,248,316	5,395,757	58.8	18.5	10.8	31.3
Minnesota	2,152,833	2,283,781	2,433,106	2,435,477	2,533,235	2,624,464	96.1	16.2	21.9	41.7
Mississippi	1,102,109	1,110,399	1,110,234	1,174,743	1,236,209	1,358,795	121.3	9.9	23.3	35.5
Missouri	1,612,057	1,649,776	1,645,998	1,685,990	1,745,329	1,836,878	68.8	18.0	13.9	34.5
Montana	260,700	288,476	351,834	359,184	361,473	376,618	56.7	–7.5	44.5	33.7
Nebraska	910,860	963,323	1,005,268	1,031,577	1,034,397	1,076,670	118.3	18.4	18.2	40.0
Nevada	335,704	375,207	398,358	402,429	428,261	447,901	252.7	41.2	33.4	88.4
New Hampshire	309,590	319,537	336,857	357,465	371,660	371,554	103.2	21.1	20.0	45.3
New Jersey	2,586,985	2,621,704	2,729,234	2,802,125	2,894,246	2,982,535	194.7	32.5	15.3	52.8
New Mexico	989,318	1,017,257	1,108,386	1,139,262	1,177,197	1,278,741	197.4	54.2	29.3	99.3
New York	6,043,194	6,362,116	6,230,158	6,494,569	6,676,082	6,922,118	96.7	9.5	14.5	25.4
North Carolina	2,891,923	2,929,490	3,038,320	3,198,799	3,288,001	3,406,215	145.3	16.6	17.8	37.4
North Dakota	427,468	417,616	447,604	446,618	445,158	456,730	74.9	6.7	6.8	14.0
Ohio	4,451,250	4,636,100	4,780,590	4,675,734	4,779,554	4,907,686	93.7	15.6	10.3	27.4
Oklahoma	1,162,602	1,199,927	1,270,486	1,253,842	1,250,514	1,263,002	57.4	0.0	8.6	8.7
Oregon	1,456,628	1,509,253	1,627,857	1,662,505	1,672,494	1,756,424	94.3	15.3	20.6	39.0
Pennsylvania	4,050,740	4,088,877	4,281,021	4,265,251	4,367,323	4,506,833	93.7	23.6	11.3	37.5
Rhode Island	343,083	331,632	332,898	351,567	341,302	344,457	57.6	14.2	0.4	14.7
South Carolina	1,582,426	1,674,139	1,749,490	1,813,470	1,819,682	1,817,631	220.7	22.1	14.9	40.3
South Dakota	219,989	224,554	238,765	255,721	266,895	252,443	2.1	2.9	14.8	18.0
Tennessee	1,815,413	1,799,597	1,777,615	1,891,921	1,969,324	2,042,171	149.9	24.8	12.5	40.3
Texas	6,694,747	6,763,846	6,985,505	7,437,461	7,636,645	7,817,433	209.0	7.9	16.8	26.0
Utah	1,092,788	1,127,718	1,224,598	1,250,835	1,298,629	1,354,017	145.4	20.8	23.9	49.7
Vermont	311,040	311,824	322,414	318,106	315,285	316,455	82.0	17.7	1.7	19.8
Virginia	3,205,001	3,191,611	3,223,303	3,273,297	3,400,071	3,414,167	193.0	25.6	6.5	33.8
Washington	2,296,830	2,448,177	2,498,383	2,648,650	2,718,706	2,807,168	106.1	13.6	22.2	38.8
West Virginia	589,924	622,864	638,648	649,202	670,165	674,664	50.6	8.8	14.4	24.4
Wisconsin	2,756,335	2,802,493	2,847,397	2,904,193	2,958,179	2,941,034	60.8	13.1	6.7	20.7
Wyoming	271,332	272,634	290,620	277,591	279,539	294,334	81.2	–4.2	8.5	3.9
U.S. Service Schools	962,169	1,305,433	1,361,161	1,350,177	1,348,618	1,313,438	88.0	–26.8	36.5	(2)
Outlying areas	649,774	586,723	630,463	696,972	681,998	727,524	70.6	2.4	12.0	14.6
American Samoa	3,440	3,617	3,540	3,575	3,518	3,483	–15.9	107.6	1.3	110.2
Federated States of Micronesia	2,200	4,287	4,128	3,509	3,626	5,056	—	—	129.8	—
Guam	58,481	65,425	73,705	76,608	68,920	81,148	281.7	50.6	38.8	109.0
Marshall Islands	—	—	3,934	1,382	1,573	1,237	—	—	—	—
Northern Marianas	1,198	3,175	3,502	2,668	3,310	12,366	—	–39.0	932.6	530.1
Palau	4,623	4,355	4,042	4,778	3,580	3,667	—	—	–20.7	—
Puerto Rico	550,589	437,537	475,907	571,941	562,976	586,910	53.1	–1.6	6.6	4.9
Trust Territories	—	—	—	—	—	—	—	—	—	—
Virgin Islands	29,244	68,327	61,703	32,511	34,494	33,656	91.4	19.5	15.1	37.5

[1] Based on the Higher Education Price Index, prepared by Research Associates of Washington. These data do not reflect differences in inflation rates from state to state.

[2] Less than 0.05 percent.

—Data not available or not applicable.

NOTE.—Percentages reflect mergers, openings, and closures of institutions over time. Some data have been revised from previously published figures. Because of rounding, details may not add to totals.

SOURCE: U.S. Department of Education, National Center for Education Statistics, Higher Education General Information Survey (HEGIS), "Financial Statistics of Institutions of Higher Education" surveys; and Integrated Postsecondary Education Data System (IPEDS), "Financial Statistics" surveys. (This table was prepared January 1998.)

Table 86.—Current-fund expenditures (in current dollars) of private institutions of higher education, by state: 1969–70 to 1994–95

[Amounts in thousands]

State or other area	1969–70	1970–71	1971–72	1972–73	1973–74	1974–75	1975–76	1976–77	1977–78	1978–79
1	2	3	4	5	6	7	8	9	10	11
United States	$7,793,567	$8,379,155	$9,075,235	$9,751,877	$10,377,297	$11,567,582	$12,719,221	$13,964,750	$15,245,671	$16,988,111
Alabama	46,089	49,114	51,350	57,562	63,201	68,318	75,673	79,897	90,989	97,774
Alaska	3,021	3,200	5,788	4,021	4,309	4,591	4,564	4,243	4,842	6,690
Arizona	7,010	8,349	8,532	10,949	10,004	12,302	11,142	12,542	13,715	14,888
Arkansas	18,212	19,749	20,851	23,001	25,450	30,169	31,833	34,743	37,868	38,608
California	728,213	774,755	865,658	930,578	999,075	1,134,223	1,260,884	1,465,548	1,547,038	1,725,588
Colorado	45,497	49,260	50,929	54,773	59,318	63,228	68,098	72,275	80,357	90,458
Connecticut	214,832	232,290	244,682	259,729	278,451	300,090	326,326	356,645	380,301	418,449
Delaware	5,052	6,482	6,672	6,948	7,405	8,682	9,037	9,912	10,426	11,163
District of Columbia	238,885	272,137	305,279	335,600	369,547	416,282	473,140	533,710	573,189	641,994
Florida	136,131	150,936	162,619	177,082	199,111	231,706	250,670	285,761	317,421	348,396
Georgia	117,204	127,369	135,943	150,490	167,751	196,240	216,531	233,615	258,346	296,450
Hawaii	6,365	7,178	7,820	8,484	9,012	9,270	9,575	9,850	11,962	14,285
Idaho	10,588	11,984	13,105	13,888	14,352	16,140	20,100	22,181	24,676	28,352
Illinois	576,237	612,834	731,567	763,527	803,920	929,680	1,050,199	1,184,921	1,317,489	1,487,535
Indiana	150,807	163,855	168,977	176,250	185,821	195,378	214,856	234,028	248,063	273,761
Iowa	102,727	104,735	108,119	111,518	112,342	135,033	146,640	157,103	173,030	188,575
Kansas	34,263	35,644	36,489	36,827	39,825	43,023	48,258	53,055	57,334	63,748
Kentucky	49,285	52,639	53,310	55,240	57,757	63,707	65,050	72,504	87,078	99,438
Louisiana	72,468	77,797	79,018	83,073	86,071	92,596	103,245	121,797	141,676	158,389
Maine	31,353	33,391	35,254	36,306	39,787	43,316	47,325	52,580	58,032	64,416
Maryland	180,106	199,428	220,604	240,560	259,159	282,014	303,660	323,559	360,016	403,842
Massachusetts	848,749	893,832	948,374	1,022,734	1,049,949	1,139,526	1,232,292	1,314,857	1,453,353	1,621,408
Michigan	116,569	125,923	131,739	143,140	158,235	180,744	203,008	216,076	239,720	261,797
Minnesota	90,029	95,503	100,362	109,750	120,344	224,896	154,272	207,460	236,436	253,366
Mississippi	19,266	20,343	21,241	23,336	24,977	29,984	33,148	35,022	38,232	40,807
Missouri	187,755	197,030	208,628	225,018	242,990	293,296	333,990	371,266	405,956	453,749
Montana	5,399	5,852	6,201	6,339	6,821	7,702	8,482	9,181	9,766	11,216
Nebraska	41,800	43,967	42,397	46,819	49,809	55,225	61,529	66,636	73,430	79,655
Nevada	46	59	70	81	91	167	161	0	306	333
New Hampshire	56,971	62,790	69,351	75,347	79,819	85,729	94,896	102,945	111,465	123,445
New Jersey	185,684	203,785	212,791	227,401	244,714	272,470	306,955	336,853	352,214	384,173
New Mexico	6,413	8,186	10,423	8,721	10,143	9,830	12,090	13,168	13,245	14,295
New York	1,434,458	1,553,023	1,640,517	1,736,080	1,881,026	1,994,976	2,178,178	2,311,061	2,493,546	2,812,591
North Carolina	201,581	216,413	252,871	273,554	294,374	324,705	348,097	381,469	416,713	468,333
North Dakota	3,246	3,736	3,798	4,402	4,764	6,567	7,263	8,218	8,886	9,391
Ohio	287,479	306,539	327,881	347,485	367,825	377,897	408,385	442,156	478,108	522,794
Oklahoma	32,688	34,958	38,172	41,407	46,835	54,196	60,536	71,342	81,600	96,798
Oregon	37,329	39,245	42,037	43,964	48,534	53,404	62,319	69,874	77,750	89,419
Pennsylvania	632,640	666,338	721,321	798,302	813,199	908,442	1,068,238	1,171,385	1,301,747	1,443,592
Rhode Island	66,614	71,668	75,868	82,540	90,150	100,520	110,924	118,307	130,922	146,438
South Carolina	51,495	55,767	59,485	64,284	69,510	76,535	81,936	89,551	97,020	111,200
South Dakota	15,090	16,369	17,395	18,099	18,693	22,175	26,962	27,955	28,478	32,243
Tennessee	153,048	175,054	199,223	223,385	223,101	255,798	285,187	299,691	325,039	352,200
Texas	208,749	223,830	241,039	271,552	291,041	327,652	357,087	398,802	430,779	468,179
Utah	58,659	67,184	67,207	73,910	77,762	84,187	89,937	95,559	106,032	115,347
Vermont	33,306	37,290	43,038	44,301	45,226	48,925	54,122	56,778	62,979	68,007
Virginia	79,595	84,321	92,032	98,479	106,796	116,992	133,619	144,298	163,632	180,048
Washington	46,457	51,756	55,126	59,774	66,086	75,760	85,239	94,321	103,940	119,151
West Virginia	24,933	25,787	27,007	26,904	29,163	31,436	35,960	37,390	40,500	44,280
Wisconsin	93,172	99,481	107,075	118,365	123,654	131,857	147,602	152,664	170,023	191,057
Wyoming	—	—	—	—	—	—	—	—	—	—
U.S. Service Schools	—	—	—	—	—	—	—	—	—	—
Outlying areas	18,444	23,594	35,227	42,113	44,947	49,803	64,171	78,304	96,308	102,861
American Samoa	—	—	—	—	—	—	—	—	—	—
Federated States of Micronesia	—	—	—	—	—	—	—	—	—	—
Guam	—	—	—	—	—	—	—	—	—	—
Marshall Islands	—	—	—	—	—	—	—	—	—	—
Northern Marianas	—	—	—	—	—	—	—	—	—	—
Palau	—	—	—	—	—	—	—	—	—	—
Puerto Rico	18,444	23,594	35,227	42,113	44,947	49,803	64,171	78,304	96,308	102,861
Trust Territories	—	—	—	—	—	—	—	—	—	—
Virgin Islands	—	—	—	—	—	—	—	—	—	—

Table 86.—Current-fund expenditures (in current dollars) of private institutions of higher education, by state: 1969–70 to 1994–95—Continued

[Amounts in thousands]

State or other area	1979–80	1980–81	1981–82	1982–83	1983–84	1984–85	1985–86	1986–87	1987–88	1988–89
1	12	13	14	15	16	17	18	19	20	21
United States	$19,145,618	$21,773,132	$24,120,314	$26,362,831	$28,906,716	$31,636,713	$34,341,889	$38,109,719	$41,145,174	$44,921,566
Alabama	107,761	115,275	128,272	138,156	146,316	181,172	186,596	179,589	195,821	211,418
Alaska	6,055	6,459	7,551	8,672	8,534	10,106	10,171	14,110	15,901	23,230
Arizona	16,938	25,919	30,011	32,230	41,506	49,437	52,887	108,992	82,342	89,558
Arkansas	42,281	50,501	55,466	59,145	62,394	67,069	70,755	79,769	90,052	98,600
California	1,976,260	2,143,974	2,339,270	2,591,997	2,886,125	3,253,339	3,644,031	4,271,745	4,466,429	4,824,768
Colorado	101,894	117,004	131,220	143,842	153,465	161,350	160,193	213,656	195,062	215,641
Connecticut	473,590	531,921	597,281	649,916	709,565	772,262	836,949	905,945	998,845	1,093,482
Delaware	12,993	15,116	21,214	22,716	24,451	27,760	29,569	32,508	36,219	37,388
District of Columbia	735,348	847,964	947,978	1,032,749	1,115,209	1,214,024	1,307,317	1,420,576	1,550,952	1,709,835
Florida	393,931	462,879	507,086	557,949	615,004	666,774	723,270	858,316	928,429	1,035,335
Georgia	337,793	391,409	455,535	509,725	562,510	624,773	696,734	851,540	865,200	1,010,840
Hawaii	16,103	18,939	20,773	22,219	25,099	27,923	32,553	59,695	64,711	69,778
Idaho	32,200	35,851	38,913	42,326	45,196	49,784	49,768	53,552	60,913	65,346
Illinois	1,652,278	1,899,973	2,036,045	2,192,661	2,397,957	2,575,493	2,729,672	2,776,192	2,993,577	3,267,036
Indiana	305,091	356,713	391,780	419,410	460,321	492,798	530,163	599,905	654,986	706,247
Iowa	204,948	234,415	259,493	279,576	308,880	330,922	353,753	379,510	419,662	441,408
Kansas	71,338	82,188	87,955	91,619	100,285	99,841	105,193	124,003	120,672	127,456
Kentucky	107,674	120,638	134,060	146,783	156,024	175,260	194,873	207,593	227,793	233,359
Louisiana	175,701	209,710	245,076	276,414	303,778	324,687	353,433	381,628	427,935	471,954
Maine	72,277	82,416	92,524	101,794	108,405	122,332	133,778	148,665	158,746	173,505
Maryland	472,817	525,414	579,731	643,372	714,540	790,381	896,251	1,012,230	1,124,171	1,255,564
Massachusetts	1,863,610	2,130,640	2,373,007	2,633,829	2,939,165	3,222,875	3,544,867	3,924,351	4,234,020	4,532,630
Michigan	295,350	328,904	352,036	356,481	395,196	428,118	447,436	487,570	538,939	582,011
Minnesota	279,257	324,936	370,932	404,120	440,592	482,548	521,441	576,897	631,183	684,852
Mississippi	45,801	50,297	52,728	54,529	59,057	63,102	64,054	69,724	72,950	84,424
Missouri	498,407	573,097	643,871	713,716	759,788	827,259	904,573	1,060,164	1,082,391	1,184,366
Montana	12,337	15,377	18,498	20,077	20,327	21,369	22,349	21,596	23,494	28,433
Nebraska	90,336	105,503	116,739	132,976	142,701	151,298	161,066	167,941	184,796	202,777
Nevada	318	365	447	734	1,121	1,246	2,448	4,363	2,091	2,261
New Hampshire	138,816	164,923	184,480	205,275	226,934	241,452	264,440	288,346	308,173	335,947
New Jersey	417,528	486,422	544,693	597,949	660,582	700,757	714,733	749,981	804,172	879,042
New Mexico	15,226	18,105	17,525	18,980	19,896	21,359	22,196	16,375	19,941	22,644
New York	3,123,347	3,527,430	3,916,780	4,240,555	4,612,806	5,129,897	5,596,257	5,929,789	6,509,272	7,084,517
North Carolina	530,465	587,101	623,982	673,347	721,364	778,205	837,291	1,111,217	1,306,506	1,445,473
North Dakota	11,115	11,768	14,524	15,449	16,888	18,509	18,853	15,607	15,950	24,777
Ohio	577,484	654,637	722,046	780,865	851,962	920,689	976,303	1,106,174	1,160,274	1,253,124
Oklahoma	107,175	127,066	147,207	159,442	167,556	171,261	178,905	197,807	221,224	241,510
Oregon	99,733	113,122	125,406	131,787	147,198	160,702	171,604	186,107	206,573	227,910
Pennsylvania	1,640,302	1,916,417	2,169,006	2,412,451	2,643,848	2,874,245	3,155,505	3,455,512	3,728,079	4,073,729
Rhode Island	165,796	193,080	215,284	237,599	264,113	287,400	315,651	354,910	390,167	424,240
South Carolina	121,889	122,523	132,894	138,058	174,171	186,770	196,271	229,559	250,297	272,883
South Dakota	35,461	41,344	39,875	43,247	47,202	48,044	51,675	58,207	59,589	65,222
Tennessee	396,524	460,523	494,926	533,552	578,041	632,194	686,514	753,952	828,714	914,899
Texas	539,675	618,063	701,467	776,517	858,211	935,868	993,824	1,115,858	1,174,184	1,272,592
Utah	125,723	138,390	146,317	154,949	164,932	176,486	183,000	210,210	205,492	234,232
Vermont	79,675	91,908	105,093	112,467	123,705	138,726	150,689	178,365	192,278	223,378
Virginia	211,214	234,720	265,944	290,495	320,047	347,864	387,455	429,728	474,750	538,619
Washington	136,093	151,978	174,457	189,082	203,810	220,666	227,211	244,546	271,361	301,813
West Virginia	53,878	53,695	60,394	62,655	66,666	72,700	73,716	79,191	75,958	87,335
Wisconsin	217,813	255,757	282,140	308,377	333,272	357,616	373,533	404,976	491,413	531,380
Wyoming	—	360	380	—	—	—	—	977	2,527	2,797
U.S. Service Schools	—	—	—	—	—	—	—	—	—	—
Outlying areas	111,532	120,413	139,664	151,369	174,551	188,667	198,653	209,285	231,581	224,988
American Samoa	—	—	—	—	—	—	—	—	—	—
Federated States of Micronesia	—	—	—	—	—	—	—	—	—	—
Guam	—	—	—	—	—	—	—	—	—	—
Marshall Islands	—	—	—	—	—	—	—	—	—	—
Northern Marianas	—	—	—	—	—	—	—	—	—	—
Palau	—	—	—	—	—	—	—	—	—	—
Puerto Rico	111,532	120,413	139,664	151,369	174,551	188,667	198,653	209,285	231,581	224,988
Trust Territories	—	—	—	—	—	—	—	—	—	—
Virgin Islands	—	—	—	—	—	—	—	—	—	—

Table 86.—Current-fund expenditures (in current dollars) of private institutions of higher education, by state: 1969–70 to 1994–95—Continued

[Amounts in thousands]

State or other area	1989–90	1990–91	1991–92	1992–93	1993–94	1994–95	Percentage change			
							1969–70 to 1994–95	1984–85 to 1989–90	1989–90 to 1994–95	1984–85 to 1994–95
1	22	23	24	25	26	27	28	29	30	31
United States	$48,885,041	$53,126,743	$57,341,982	$60,670,938	$64,041,076	$67,503,635	766.1	54.5	38.1	113.4
Alabama	229,369	244,425	263,052	286,584	299,982	310,329	573.3	26.6	35.3	71.3
Alaska	20,050	22,127	18,454	22,693	23,199	19,825	556.2	98.4	-1.1	96.2
Arizona	90,409	121,482	94,564	106,478	118,954	130,973	1,768.3	82.9	44.9	164.9
Arkansas	108,888	114,655	118,373	124,091	130,253	140,758	672.9	62.4	29.3	109.9
California	5,077,597	5,525,201	5,957,016	6,171,590	6,419,322	6,841,207	839.5	56.1	34.7	110.3
Colorado	250,811	288,865	305,244	306,824	327,275	342,407	652.6	55.4	36.5	112.2
Connecticut	1,193,877	1,293,468	1,376,756	1,437,827	1,527,283	1,608,612	648.8	54.6	34.7	108.3
Delaware	43,184	23,875	27,215	29,293	31,836	32,995	553.1	55.6	-23.6	18.9
District of Columbia	1,873,297	1,955,110	2,100,279	2,307,943	2,386,469	2,533,020	960.7	54.3	35.3	108.7
Florida	1,162,843	1,274,196	1,386,602	1,510,855	1,561,498	1,672,960	1,128.9	74.4	43.9	150.9
Georgia	1,099,658	1,227,745	1,371,887	1,514,055	1,683,308	1,798,384	1,434.4	76.0	63.5	187.8
Hawaii	35,223	42,881	41,760	91,016	95,803	100,596	1,480.3	26.1	185.6	260.3
Idaho	69,032	74,519	82,255	87,532	95,011	98,011	825.7	38.7	42.0	96.9
Illinois	3,544,542	3,955,777	4,366,966	4,694,688	4,778,173	5,103,123	785.6	37.6	44.0	98.1
Indiana	773,866	847,885	889,004	941,404	1,000,966	1,073,603	611.9	57.0	38.7	117.9
Iowa	490,214	533,300	595,007	634,046	676,124	701,059	582.4	48.1	43.0	111.9
Kansas	135,958	144,471	147,336	157,139	171,402	180,052	425.5	36.2	32.4	80.3
Kentucky	251,329	282,937	304,780	315,147	330,341	348,262	606.6	43.4	38.6	98.7
Louisiana	531,135	572,049	629,158	673,080	739,368	624,279	761.5	63.6	17.5	92.3
Maine	186,175	200,149	210,328	223,573	238,196	250,032	697.5	52.2	34.3	104.4
Maryland	1,356,011	1,461,897	1,550,526	1,622,871	1,729,558	1,797,362	897.9	71.6	32.5	127.4
Massachusetts	4,922,923	5,339,793	5,580,304	5,850,688	6,116,367	6,416,410	656.0	52.7	30.3	99.1
Michigan	637,849	699,193	738,699	789,175	826,746	855,969	634.3	49.0	34.2	99.9
Minnesota	753,255	730,974	776,325	812,893	800,291	859,388	854.6	56.1	14.1	78.1
Mississippi	93,959	101,330	110,325	115,789	123,506	129,945	574.5	48.9	38.3	105.9
Missouri	1,340,923	1,493,892	1,645,969	1,666,001	1,769,749	1,897,323	910.5	62.1	41.5	129.4
Montana	27,990	33,471	33,238	39,500	44,193	50,343	832.5	31.0	79.9	135.6
Nebraska	226,173	245,142	269,968	287,540	303,472	319,962	665.5	49.5	41.5	111.5
Nevada	3,893	4,507	5,971	5,490	6,768	8,194	17,712.4	212.4	110.5	557.5
New Hampshire	363,330	407,903	432,080	455,312	487,785	507,227	790.3	50.5	39.6	110.1
New Jersey	944,968	982,070	1,082,717	1,167,222	1,208,726	1,252,185	574.4	34.8	32.5	78.7
New Mexico	28,022	33,272	46,252	33,162	40,520	42,331	560.1	31.2	51.1	98.2
New York	7,640,442	8,246,193	9,003,453	9,536,982	10,157,945	10,653,695	642.7	48.9	39.4	107.7
North Carolina	1,599,803	1,704,643	1,911,631	2,008,628	2,166,337	2,329,951	1,055.8	105.6	45.6	199.4
North Dakota	25,646	27,978	34,323	33,758	36,380	37,350	1,050.7	38.6	45.6	101.8
Ohio	1,402,876	1,510,387	1,613,085	1,696,377	1,807,756	1,905,659	562.9	52.4	35.8	107.0
Oklahoma	262,526	280,889	256,332	266,152	286,118	298,275	812.5	53.3	13.6	74.2
Oregon	256,067	277,152	287,800	307,280	334,424	365,448	879.0	59.3	42.7	127.4
Pennsylvania	4,437,071	4,914,117	5,452,687	5,667,740	6,008,469	6,246,550	887.4	54.4	40.8	117.3
Rhode Island	486,764	518,425	559,922	590,911	636,510	667,901	902.6	69.4	37.2	132.4
South Carolina	297,112	319,782	274,300	293,819	318,200	333,278	547.2	59.1	12.2	78.4
South Dakota	79,252	84,903	71,462	63,406	66,315	69,866	363.0	65.0	-11.8	45.4
Tennessee	1,005,210	1,097,066	1,199,755	1,226,183	1,352,769	1,410,990	821.9	59.0	40.4	123.2
Texas	1,397,222	1,528,755	1,633,787	1,716,860	1,833,288	1,955,975	837.0	49.3	40.0	109.0
Utah	252,753	272,883	317,586	454,442	458,878	492,298	739.2	43.2	94.8	178.9
Vermont	245,813	266,539	287,261	300,593	269,666	288,223	765.4	77.2	17.3	107.8
Virginia	609,665	671,912	706,344	748,902	807,849	874,960	999.3	75.3	43.5	151.5
Washington	330,200	368,077	401,261	435,993	475,565	513,782	1,005.9	49.6	55.6	132.8
West Virginia	96,910	108,334	114,586	129,367	143,742	172,925	593.6	33.3	78.4	137.9
Wisconsin	588,850	645,774	651,420	702,292	775,629	827,317	787.9	64.7	40.5	131.3
Wyoming	4,104	4,370	6,578	9,752	12,788	11,142	—	—	171.5	—
U.S. Service Schools	—	—	—	—	—	—	—	—	—	—
Outlying areas	192,950	271,237	284,662	306,098	337,721	360,203	1,853.0	2.3	86.7	90.9
American Samoa	—	—	—	—	—	—	—	—	—	—
Federated States of Micronesia	—	—	—	—	—	—	—	—	—	—
Guam	—	—	—	—	—	—	—	—	—	—
Marshall Islands	—	—	—	—	—	—	—	—	—	—
Northern Marianas	—	—	—	—	—	—	—	—	—	—
Palau	—	—	—	—	—	—	—	—	—	—
Puerto Rico	192,950	271,237	284,662	306,098	337,721	360,203	1,853.0	2.3	86.7	90.9
Trust Territories	—	—	—	—	—	—	—	—	—	—
Virgin Islands	—	—	—	—	—	—	—	—	—	—

—Data not available or not applicable.

NOTE.—Percentages reflect mergers, openings, and closures of institutions over time. Some data have been revised from previously published figures. Because of rounding, details may not add to totals.

SOURCE: U.S. Department of Education, National Center for Education Statistics, Higher Education General Information Survey (HEGIS), "Financial Statistics of Institutions of Higher Education" surveys; and Integrated Postsecondary Education Data System (IPEDS), "Financial Statistics" surveys. (This table was prepared January 1998.)

Table 87.—Current-fund expenditures (in constant 1994–95 dollars [1]) of private institutions of higher education, by state: 1969–70 to 1994–95
[Amounts in thousands]

State or other area	1969–70	1970–71	1971–72	1972–73	1973–74	1974–75	1975–76	1976–77	1977–78	1978–79
1	2	3	4	5	6	7	8	9	10	11
United States	$33,186,783	$33,476,813	$34,457,212	$35,123,464	$34,979,185	$35,831,809	$37,013,372	$38,193,024	$39,030,773	$40,530,501
Alabama	196,257	196,223	194,969	207,322	213,033	211,621	220,212	218,514	232,943	233,270
Alaska	12,865	12,786	21,975	14,483	14,526	14,221	13,281	11,606	12,397	15,961
Arizona	29,852	33,355	32,393	39,435	33,721	38,106	32,424	34,301	35,113	35,519
Arkansas	77,551	78,900	79,166	82,841	85,786	93,453	92,635	95,021	96,947	92,112
California	3,100,896	3,095,339	3,286,765	3,351,674	3,367,625	3,513,377	3,669,215	4,008,213	3,960,605	4,116,935
Colorado	193,736	196,805	193,368	197,276	199,944	195,855	198,167	197,668	205,725	215,817
Connecticut	914,803	928,057	929,020	935,471	938,585	929,560	949,620	975,410	973,618	998,342
Delaware	21,513	25,898	25,334	25,024	24,961	26,895	26,297	27,109	26,692	26,632
District of Columbia	1,017,226	1,087,254	1,159,097	1,208,734	1,245,647	1,289,479	1,376,854	1,459,676	1,467,433	1,531,680
Florida	579,678	603,027	617,440	637,799	671,152	717,734	729,458	781,544	812,637	831,209
Georgia	499,081	508,869	516,155	542,021	565,446	607,873	630,112	638,927	661,398	707,274
Hawaii	27,106	28,677	29,692	30,555	30,376	28,715	27,865	26,940	30,624	34,081
Idaho	45,085	47,878	49,759	50,019	48,378	49,996	58,491	60,665	63,173	67,642
Illinois	2,453,749	2,448,423	2,777,641	2,750,004	2,709,806	2,879,781	3,056,117	3,240,710	3,372,931	3,548,984
Indiana	642,172	654,640	641,577	634,802	626,354	605,205	625,239	640,056	635,071	653,144
Iowa	437,434	418,444	410,510	401,655	378,674	418,279	426,729	429,669	442,977	449,906
Kansas	145,898	142,407	138,543	132,639	134,238	133,268	140,432	145,104	146,782	152,091
Kentucky	209,868	210,306	202,411	198,958	194,683	197,340	189,298	198,295	222,930	237,240
Louisiana	308,587	310,818	300,017	299,206	290,124	286,824	300,447	333,108	362,709	377,886
Maine	133,507	133,407	133,854	130,763	134,111	134,176	137,718	143,804	148,570	153,685
Maryland	766,934	796,766	837,598	866,430	873,558	873,568	883,661	884,921	921,685	963,492
Massachusetts	3,614,167	3,571,084	3,600,823	3,683,593	3,539,107	3,529,801	3,586,012	3,596,080	3,720,761	3,868,380
Michigan	496,375	503,092	500,190	515,551	533,370	559,875	590,760	590,958	613,713	624,600
Minnesota	383,365	381,560	381,058	395,288	405,648	696,640	448,937	567,394	605,305	604,484
Mississippi	82,039	81,277	80,649	84,048	84,192	92,878	96,461	95,784	97,878	97,359
Missouri	799,503	787,184	792,127	810,450	819,058	908,517	971,922	1,015,397	1,039,298	1,082,561
Montana	22,989	23,379	23,543	22,831	22,992	23,859	24,682	25,110	25,000	26,758
Nebraska	177,995	175,658	160,974	168,629	167,895	171,064	179,052	182,246	187,990	190,043
Nevada	196	237	265	291	308	518	469	0	785	794
New Hampshire	242,596	250,862	263,316	271,378	269,048	265,555	276,152	281,551	285,365	294,517
New Jersey	790,683	814,174	807,934	819,034	824,869	844,006	893,251	921,278	901,711	916,566
New Mexico	27,307	32,704	39,573	31,410	34,189	30,449	35,182	36,015	33,909	34,105
New York	6,108,251	6,204,714	6,228,779	6,252,862	6,340,452	6,179,649	6,338,573	6,320,658	6,383,782	6,710,323
North Carolina	858,379	864,625	960,112	985,264	992,257	1,005,807	1,012,975	1,043,301	1,066,835	1,117,356
North Dakota	13,821	14,927	14,420	15,854	16,057	20,343	21,137	22,476	22,748	22,406
Ohio	1,224,151	1,224,701	1,244,912	1,251,541	1,239,842	1,170,577	1,188,414	1,209,278	1,224,013	1,247,290
Oklahoma	139,194	139,666	144,933	149,137	157,869	167,877	176,163	195,117	208,907	230,943
Oregon	158,956	156,794	159,609	158,346	163,595	165,425	181,351	191,103	199,050	213,338
Pennsylvania	2,693,923	2,662,188	2,738,739	2,875,254	2,741,083	2,813,994	3,108,608	3,203,691	3,332,632	3,444,144
Rhode Island	283,658	286,331	288,059	297,285	303,872	311,370	322,794	323,564	335,177	349,374
South Carolina	219,278	222,801	225,855	231,531	234,301	237,074	238,436	244,918	248,384	265,302
South Dakota	64,257	65,399	66,047	65,189	63,008	68,690	78,460	76,455	72,908	76,926
Tennessee	651,713	699,385	756,416	804,570	752,016	792,362	829,903	819,643	832,140	840,283
Texas	888,902	894,257	915,186	978,053	981,024	1,014,936	1,039,135	1,090,708	1,102,847	1,116,989
Utah	249,785	268,415	255,174	266,201	262,117	260,777	261,719	261,350	271,455	275,197
Vermont	141,826	148,981	163,410	159,561	152,444	151,550	157,497	155,286	161,233	162,252
Virginia	338,932	336,884	349,430	354,695	359,981	362,394	388,835	394,649	418,918	429,562
Washington	197,825	206,779	209,304	215,290	222,759	234,674	248,049	257,963	266,100	284,273
West Virginia	106,172	103,024	102,543	96,900	98,299	97,376	104,646	102,259	103,686	105,645
Wisconsin	396,747	397,453	406,548	426,316	416,804	408,443	429,526	417,531	435,281	455,826
Wyoming	—	—	—	—	—	—	—	—	—	—
U.S. Service Schools	—	—	—	—	—	—	—	—	—	—
Outlying areas	78,537	94,262	133,750	151,678	151,506	154,269	186,740	214,158	246,560	245,409
American Samoa	—	—	—	—	—	—	—	—	—	—
Federated States of Micronesia	—	—	—	—	—	—	—	—	—	—
Guam	—	—	—	—	—	—	—	—	—	—
Marshall Islands	—	—	—	—	—	—	—	—	—	—
Northern Marianas	—	—	—	—	—	—	—	—	—	—
Palau	—	—	—	—	—	—	—	—	—	—
Puerto Rico	78,537	94,262	133,750	151,678	151,506	154,269	186,740	214,158	246,560	245,409
Trust Territories	—	—	—	—	—	—	—	—	—	—
Virgin Islands	—	—	—	—	—	—	—	—	—	—

Table 87.—Current-fund expenditures (in constant 1994–95 dollars [1]) of private institutions of higher education, by state: 1969–70 to 1994–95—Continued

[Amounts in thousands]

State or other area	1979–80	1980–81	1981–82	1982–83	1983–84	1984–85	1985–86	1986–87	1987–88	1988–89
1	12	13	14	15	16	17	18	19	20	21
United States	$41,552,167	$42,683,459	$43,205,931	$44,342,282	$46,394,176	$48,026,129	$49,667,289	$53,019,477	$54,881,985	$56,896,140
Alabama	233,876	225,982	229,769	232,379	234,831	275,028	269,866	249,850	261,198	267,775
Alaska	13,141	12,662	13,526	14,586	13,697	15,341	14,710	19,631	21,210	29,423
Arizona	36,762	50,812	53,757	54,211	66,616	75,047	76,488	151,634	109,833	113,432
Arkansas	91,762	99,002	99,355	99,481	100,139	101,815	102,330	110,977	120,117	124,883
California	4,289,123	4,202,988	4,190,258	4,359,739	4,632,120	4,938,733	5,270,215	5,942,990	5,957,600	6,110,888
Colorado	221,142	229,371	235,051	241,942	246,306	244,937	231,680	297,245	260,186	273,124
Connecticut	1,027,843	1,042,763	1,069,889	1,093,158	1,138,825	1,172,333	1,210,446	1,260,380	1,332,322	1,384,968
Delaware	28,198	29,633	38,000	38,208	39,242	42,141	42,765	45,226	48,311	47,354
District of Columbia	1,595,942	1,662,326	1,698,082	1,737,084	1,789,868	1,842,950	1,890,806	1,976,351	2,068,756	2,165,620
Florida	854,958	907,416	908,327	938,470	987,058	1,012,197	1,046,036	1,194,117	1,238,396	1,311,321
Georgia	733,120	767,308	815,985	857,358	902,807	948,437	1,007,658	1,184,690	1,154,058	1,280,296
Hawaii	34,949	37,128	37,209	37,372	40,283	42,388	47,080	83,049	86,316	88,378
Idaho	69,884	70,282	69,704	71,192	72,537	75,575	71,977	74,504	81,250	82,765
Illinois	3,585,977	3,724,656	3,647,101	3,688,055	3,848,630	3,909,729	3,947,815	3,862,328	3,993,018	4,137,917
Indiana	662,145	699,291	701,783	705,447	738,798	748,092	766,753	834,607	873,661	894,509
Iowa	444,803	459,541	464,821	470,247	495,740	502,357	511,618	527,987	559,771	559,072
Kansas	154,826	161,120	157,552	154,104	160,953	151,564	152,137	172,517	160,959	161,432
Kentucky	233,687	236,495	240,137	246,889	250,413	266,054	281,837	288,810	303,844	295,564
Louisiana	381,328	411,110	438,997	464,928	487,553	492,891	511,157	530,933	570,806	597,760
Maine	156,865	161,566	165,734	171,218	173,986	185,706	193,478	206,827	211,745	219,756
Maryland	1,026,166	1,030,008	1,038,454	1,082,151	1,146,809	1,199,838	1,296,212	1,408,247	1,499,488	1,590,255
Massachusetts	4,044,634	4,176,850	4,250,690	4,430,100	4,717,248	4,892,487	5,126,799	5,459,684	5,647,599	5,740,877
Michigan	641,006	644,775	630,590	599,601	634,274	649,904	647,109	678,323	718,870	737,156
Minnesota	606,078	636,996	664,438	679,729	707,133	732,532	754,139	802,598	841,911	867,411
Mississippi	99,403	98,601	94,450	91,718	94,785	95,792	92,639	97,002	97,306	106,928
Missouri	1,081,703	1,123,483	1,153,346	1,200,470	1,219,430	1,255,822	1,308,247	1,474,934	1,443,760	1,500,077
Montana	26,776	30,145	33,134	33,769	32,623	32,439	32,323	30,046	31,338	36,013
Nebraska	196,058	206,826	209,110	223,666	229,030	229,677	232,943	233,645	246,492	256,830
Nevada	690	715	802	1,234	1,799	1,892	3,540	6,069	2,789	2,864
New Hampshire	301,275	323,311	330,454	345,272	364,221	366,536	382,448	401,157	411,060	425,499
New Jersey	906,170	953,569	975,690	1,005,750	1,060,210	1,063,785	1,033,689	1,043,397	1,072,655	1,113,365
New Mexico	33,046	35,492	31,392	31,925	31,932	32,425	32,101	22,782	26,599	28,680
New York	6,778,670	6,915,078	7,015,999	7,132,613	7,403,377	7,787,442	8,093,641	8,249,715	8,682,471	8,973,011
North Carolina	1,151,280	1,150,936	1,117,719	1,132,570	1,157,762	1,181,355	1,210,941	1,545,961	1,742,698	1,830,788
North Dakota	24,124	23,070	26,017	25,986	27,105	28,097	27,267	21,712	21,275	31,382
Ohio	1,253,327	1,283,332	1,293,378	1,313,415	1,367,367	1,397,652	1,411,987	1,538,946	1,547,645	1,587,165
Oklahoma	232,604	249,098	263,688	268,182	268,921	259,983	258,742	275,195	295,082	305,888
Oregon	216,454	221,761	224,636	221,666	236,247	243,953	248,184	258,917	275,540	288,663
Pennsylvania	3,559,984	3,756,892	3,885,269	4,057,742	4,243,275	4,363,250	4,563,679	4,807,421	4,972,743	5,159,648
Rhode Island	359,830	378,510	385,632	399,641	423,892	436,287	456,513	493,762	520,429	537,328
South Carolina	264,538	240,191	238,049	232,214	279,538	283,527	283,858	319,370	333,862	345,625
South Dakota	76,961	81,050	71,427	72,742	75,758	72,933	74,736	80,980	79,483	82,608
Tennessee	860,585	902,796	886,544	897,434	927,734	959,703	992,877	1,048,923	1,105,390	1,158,780
Texas	1,171,269	1,211,634	1,256,515	1,306,102	1,377,397	1,420,695	1,437,328	1,552,418	1,566,200	1,611,822
Utah	272,860	271,297	262,094	260,624	264,710	267,915	264,752	292,451	274,098	296,670
Vermont	172,920	180,174	188,250	189,169	198,541	210,592	217,935	248,147	256,472	282,923
Virginia	458,402	460,138	476,376	488,612	513,664	528,075	560,361	597,852	633,251	682,196
Washington	295,365	297,934	312,499	318,036	327,108	334,982	328,606	340,221	361,958	382,267
West Virginia	116,933	105,262	108,181	105,386	106,997	110,362	106,613	110,173	101,318	110,616
Wisconsin	472,724	501,380	505,388	518,691	534,889	542,880	540,225	563,416	655,477	673,029
Wyoming	—	706	682	—	—	—	—	1,360	3,371	3,542
U.S. Service Schools	—	—	—	—	—	—	—	—	—	—
Outlying areas	242,060	236,054	250,175	254,602	280,148	286,406	287,304	291,165	308,898	284,962
American Samoa	—	—	—	—	—	—	—	—	—	—
Federated States of Micronesia	—	—	—	—	—	—	—	—	—	—
Guam	—	—	—	—	—	—	—	—	—	—
Marshall Islands	—	—	—	—	—	—	—	—	—	—
Northern Marianas	—	—	—	—	—	—	—	—	—	—
Palau	—	—	—	—	—	—	—	—	—	—
Puerto Rico	242,060	236,054	250,175	254,602	280,148	286,406	287,304	291,165	308,898	284,962
Trust Territories	—	—	—	—	—	—	—	—	—	—
Virgin Islands	—	—	—	—	—	—	—	—	—	—

Table 87.—Current-fund expenditures (in constant 1994–95 dollars [1]) of private institutions of higher education, by state: 1969–70 to 1994–95—Continued

[Amounts in thousands]

State or other area	1989–90	1990–91	1991–92	1992–93	1993–94	1994–95	Percentage change			
							1969–70 to 1994–95	1984–85 to 1989–90	1989–90 to 1994–95	1984–85 to 1994–95
1	22	23	24	25	26	27	28	29	30	31
United States	$58,398,181	$60,296,344	$62,874,324	$64,628,574	$65,962,700	$67,503,635	103.4	21.6	15.6	40.6
Alabama	274,005	277,411	288,431	305,278	308,984	310,329	58.1	−0.4	13.3	12.8
Alaska	23,951	25,113	20,234	24,174	23,896	19,825	54.1	56.1	−17.2	29.2
Arizona	108,002	137,876	103,687	113,424	122,524	130,973	338.7	43.9	21.3	74.5
Arkansas	130,078	130,128	129,794	132,185	134,161	140,758	81.5	27.8	8.2	38.2
California	6,065,709	6,270,842	6,531,748	6,574,169	6,611,941	6,841,207	120.6	22.8	12.8	38.5
Colorado	299,620	327,848	334,694	326,839	337,095	342,407	76.7	22.3	14.3	39.8
Connecticut	1,426,209	1,468,025	1,509,586	1,531,618	1,573,111	1,608,612	75.8	21.7	12.8	37.2
Delaware	51,587	27,097	29,841	31,204	32,792	32,995	53.4	22.4	−36.0	−21.7
District of Columbia	2,237,845	2,218,957	2,302,914	2,458,493	2,458,078	2,533,943	149.1	21.4	13.2	37.5
Florida	1,389,135	1,446,152	1,520,381	1,609,410	1,608,353	1,672,960	188.6	37.2	20.4	65.3
Georgia	1,313,654	1,393,433	1,504,246	1,612,819	1,733,817	1,798,384	260.3	38.5	36.9	89.6
Hawaii	42,078	48,668	45,789	96,953	98,678	100,596	271.1	−0.7	139.1	137.3
Idaho	82,466	84,575	90,191	93,242	97,862	98,011	117.4	9.1	18.9	29.7
Illinois	4,234,318	4,489,620	4,788,290	5,000,928	4,921,548	5,103,123	108.0	8.3	20.5	30.5
Indiana	924,462	962,309	974,775	1,002,812	1,031,001	1,073,603	67.2	23.6	16.1	43.5
Iowa	585,611	605,271	652,413	675,405	696,411	701,059	60.3	16.6	19.7	39.6
Kansas	162,416	163,968	161,551	167,389	176,546	180,052	23.4	7.2	10.9	18.8
Kentucky	300,238	321,120	334,185	335,705	340,254	348,262	65.9	12.8	16.0	30.9
Louisiana	634,495	649,249	689,859	716,986	761,554	624,279	102.3	28.7	−1.6	26.7
Maine	222,405	227,160	230,621	238,157	245,344	250,032	87.3	19.8	12.4	34.6
Maryland	1,619,894	1,659,184	1,700,120	1,728,733	1,781,455	1,797,362	134.4	35.0	11.0	49.8
Massachusetts	5,880,935	6,060,413	6,118,691	6,232,336	6,299,895	6,416,410	77.5	20.2	9.1	31.1
Michigan	761,976	793,551	809,969	840,654	851,553	855,969	72.4	17.2	12.3	31.7
Minnesota	899,840	829,621	851,224	865,919	824,305	859,388	124.2	22.8	−4.5	17.3
Mississippi	112,243	115,005	120,969	123,342	127,212	129,945	58.4	17.2	15.8	35.7
Missouri	1,601,869	1,695,497	1,804,771	1,774,676	1,822,852	1,897,323	137.3	27.6	18.4	51.1
Montana	33,437	37,988	36,445	42,077	45,519	50,343	119.0	3.1	50.6	55.2
Nebraska	270,187	278,225	296,015	306,297	312,578	319,962	79.8	17.6	18.4	39.3
Nevada	4,651	5,116	6,547	5,848	6,971	8,194	4,083.1	145.9	76.2	333.2
New Hampshire	434,035	462,951	473,767	485,013	502,422	507,227	109.1	18.4	16.9	38.4
New Jersey	1,128,861	1,114,603	1,187,177	1,243,362	1,244,995	1,252,185	58.4	6.1	10.9	17.7
New Mexico	33,475	37,762	50,714	35,325	41,736	42,331	55.0	3.2	26.5	30.6
New York	9,127,289	9,359,040	9,872,104	10,159,090	10,462,746	10,653,695	74.4	17.2	16.7	36.8
North Carolina	1,911,129	1,934,690	2,096,064	2,139,653	2,231,341	2,329,951	171.4	61.8	21.9	97.2
North Dakota	30,637	31,754	37,634	35,960	37,471	37,350	170.2	9.0	21.9	32.9
Ohio	1,675,879	1,714,217	1,768,715	1,807,034	1,862,000	1,905,659	55.7	19.9	13.7	36.3
Oklahoma	313,614	318,796	281,063	283,513	294,704	298,275	114.3	20.6	−4.9	14.7
Oregon	305,899	314,555	315,567	327,325	344,458	365,448	129.9	25.4	19.5	49.8
Pennsylvania	5,300,536	5,577,291	5,978,761	6,037,453	6,188,760	6,246,550	131.9	21.5	17.8	43.2
Rhode Island	581,489	588,388	613,943	629,457	655,609	667,901	135.5	33.3	14.9	53.1
South Carolina	354,931	362,938	300,764	312,985	327,748	333,278	52.0	25.2	−6.1	17.5
South Dakota	94,675	96,361	78,357	67,542	68,305	69,866	8.7	29.8	−26.2	−4.2
Tennessee	1,200,826	1,245,118	1,315,507	1,306,169	1,393,360	1,410,990	116.5	25.1	17.5	47.0
Texas	1,669,125	1,735,065	1,791,415	1,828,853	1,888,298	1,955,975	120.0	17.5	17.2	37.7
Utah	301,939	309,710	348,226	484,085	472,647	492,298	97.1	12.7	63.0	83.8
Vermont	293,649	302,510	314,976	320,201	277,758	288,221	103.2	39.4	−1.8	36.9
Virginia	728,307	762,588	774,492	797,754	832,089	874,960	158.2	37.9	20.1	65.7
Washington	394,458	417,750	439,975	464,434	489,835	513,782	159.7	17.8	30.3	53.4
West Virginia	115,769	122,954	125,641	137,806	148,055	172,925	62.9	4.9	49.4	56.7
Wisconsin	703,441	732,923	714,269	748,103	798,903	827,317	108.5	29.6	17.6	52.4
Wyoming	4,902	4,959	7,213	10,388	13,172	11,142	—	—	127.3	—
U.S. Service Schools	—	—	—	—	—	—	—	—	—	—
Outlying areas	230,499	307,841	312,126	326,065	347,854	360,203	358.6	−19.5	56.3	25.8
American Samoa	—	—	—	—	—	—	—	—	—	—
Federated States of Micronesia	—	—	—	—	—	—	—	—	—	—
Guam	—	—	—	—	—	—	—	—	—	—
Marshall Islands	—	—	—	—	—	—	—	—	—	—
Northern Marianas	—	—	—	—	—	—	—	—	—	—
Palau	—	—	—	—	—	—	—	—	—	—
Puerto Rico	230,499	307,841	312,126	326,065	347,854	360,203	358.6	−19.5	56.3	25.8
Trust Territories	—	—	—	—	—	—	—	—	—	—
Virgin Islands	—	—	—	—	—	—	—	—	—	—

[1] Based on the Higher Education Price Index, prepared by Research Associates of Washington. These data do not reflect differences in inflation rates from state to state.
—Data not available or not applicable.

NOTE.—Percentages reflect mergers, openings, and closures of institutions over time. Some data have been revised from previously published figures. Because of rounding, details may not add to totals.

SOURCE: U.S. Department of Education, National Center for Education Statistics, Higher Education General Information Survey (HEGIS), "Financial Statistics of Institutions of Higher Education" surveys; and Integrated Postsecondary Education Data System (IPEDS), "Financial Statistics" surveys. (This table was prepared January 1998.)

Table 88.—Educational and general expenditures (in current dollars) of public institutions of higher education, by state: 1969–70 to 1994–95

[Amounts in thousands]

State or other area	1969–70	1970–71	1971–72	1972–73	1973–74	1974–75	1975–76	1976–77	1977–78	1978–79
1	2	3	4	5	6	7	8	9	10	11
United States	$10,374,191	$11,745,502	$12,906,763	$14,391,633	$16,076,536	$19,092,373	$21,283,002	$22,997,097	$25,148,911	$27,490,406
Alabama	172,760	162,614	184,949	216,812	253,947	314,022	371,203	416,197	464,296	515,123
Alaska	25,332	33,532	37,891	42,313	45,152	61,054	81,201	90,403	110,660	120,547
Arizona	131,200	154,560	181,616	204,016	229,315	279,109	302,313	347,936	392,556	425,942
Arkansas	71,806	77,474	86,263	92,710	106,890	134,754	156,227	167,043	193,330	214,462
California	1,462,541	1,595,345	1,693,762	1,912,468	2,190,646	2,513,657	2,882,278	3,182,920	3,530,952	3,674,935
Colorado	182,760	208,381	230,184	255,617	271,196	330,615	366,206	400,262	424,208	470,941
Connecticut	93,157	105,355	121,989	132,378	138,545	170,540	176,411	189,363	219,667	238,961
Delaware	34,097	39,923	44,006	51,028	60,542	73,422	80,954	88,629	93,548	108,451
District of Columbia	23,687	27,238	36,180	39,537	39,936	43,390	45,375	45,426	54,535	57,042
Florida	314,857	354,863	389,356	450,848	514,962	583,999	625,424	683,685	753,851	819,054
Georgia	186,844	217,717	237,156	267,034	308,643	347,561	372,534	405,967	451,798	503,804
Hawaii	77,212	93,949	98,945	102,715	103,604	109,213	129,360	133,615	150,969	161,543
Idaho	37,125	39,926	46,694	49,129	56,549	75,377	85,778	96,436	106,105	117,182
Illinois	527,811	624,805	644,059	713,529	762,387	890,376	977,735	1,032,865	1,094,477	1,208,786
Indiana	281,701	316,657	351,482	378,978	385,709	482,064	495,367	525,306	564,837	619,321
Iowa	185,437	205,180	224,809	241,440	285,127	304,861	322,265	367,422	384,675	426,898
Kansas	148,467	170,158	175,945	191,716	204,842	247,289	273,044	312,914	340,479	375,170
Kentucky	157,462	178,400	198,355	224,684	254,186	295,706	341,256	364,325	397,234	439,111
Louisiana	146,768	174,702	164,249	207,355	228,700	270,335	272,829	299,889	347,028	372,163
Maine	38,201	44,119	49,174	54,302	63,884	74,371	84,350	86,176	93,578	100,854
Maryland	196,619	200,051	233,907	265,540	283,476	358,046	401,888	443,551	480,634	522,007
Massachusetts	124,553	153,072	184,792	200,263	228,264	282,903	279,894	300,590	317,073	365,348
Michigan	597,950	652,034	702,984	761,231	833,708	1,006,643	1,086,991	1,146,236	1,291,805	1,384,312
Minnesota	257,330	289,645	305,460	321,496	347,206	414,379	472,583	458,744	496,319	543,532
Mississippi	99,877	119,369	131,552	150,152	166,530	203,698	241,136	259,923	294,400	328,765
Missouri	209,952	223,949	246,406	267,394	295,404	338,484	360,806	392,498	410,301	448,330
Montana	43,000	50,571	51,030	54,602	56,568	65,548	76,155	84,552	88,188	91,548
Nebraska	91,384	101,714	110,608	116,528	130,119	154,599	176,772	198,178	221,135	241,858
Nevada	27,358	30,014	32,963	35,534	42,160	47,441	59,689	63,319	68,573	80,359
New Hampshire	33,803	37,753	40,330	44,044	52,629	57,415	64,052	72,015	81,731	87,957
New Jersey	192,028	230,226	273,040	295,097	368,421	429,044	463,455	507,587	578,936	599,192
New Mexico	81,810	91,004	98,027	111,235	122,630	115,515	137,500	151,574	178,891	206,596
New York	702,844	856,570	1,009,371	1,115,042	1,270,729	1,563,039	1,745,363	1,674,645	1,772,390	1,919,930
North Carolina	247,420	284,315	319,749	363,283	423,845	546,213	550,376	613,530	680,286	771,294
North Dakota	45,845	49,225	51,237	54,771	59,482	73,031	87,833	95,650	104,964	116,365
Ohio	422,998	477,386	517,725	564,941	603,968	733,653	815,656	901,917	967,975	1,079,706
Oklahoma	117,300	132,157	141,148	156,561	167,821	197,824	226,019	261,556	287,609	317,562
Oregon	149,288	165,490	176,938	186,223	202,779	270,224	315,393	346,422	372,621	409,041
Pennsylvania	454,620	506,804	568,196	634,835	679,410	781,843	868,746	922,345	969,169	1,028,490
Rhode Island	42,260	48,865	49,788	58,604	66,800	79,407	86,156	96,915	103,836	113,537
South Carolina	90,573	103,778	120,933	145,585	184,265	247,536	267,257	281,572	323,383	375,420
South Dakota	40,512	44,040	45,054	46,900	52,650	57,636	68,011	71,056	81,152	90,810
Tennessee	151,749	169,538	194,556	220,934	246,541	300,205	326,276	366,537	405,213	457,189
Texas	470,086	582,838	651,781	735,511	884,937	1,034,054	1,261,024	1,424,999	1,587,926	1,771,457
Utah	101,870	108,058	119,578	134,844	145,869	168,996	193,367	217,414	235,749	262,660
Vermont	32,255	35,482	39,078	42,530	47,547	58,801	64,899	70,283	75,868	82,077
Virginia	182,604	214,594	241,240	284,387	323,111	379,640	444,031	477,525	527,326	631,367
Washington	275,729	310,313	308,654	360,385	387,874	463,900	498,153	537,769	612,835	686,421
West Virginia	78,102	83,909	81,469	86,698	91,716	107,409	123,852	134,238	141,292	192,425
Wisconsin	325,995	360,726	416,006	479,771	515,341	604,081	680,988	742,981	763,268	833,263
Wyoming	28,833	32,112	36,655	40,135	44,201	51,917	61,778	65,951	69,560	78,559
U.S. Service Schools	158,418	175,001	209,445	227,970	245,770	297,532	334,795	378,249	389,718	402,738
Outlying areas	88,660	104,327	104,362	122,448	135,475	181,097	176,354	189,259	207,880	219,308
American Samoa	963	1,088	704	774	982	1,159	1,056	718	1,195	1,001
Federated States of Micronesia	—	—	—	—	—	—	—	—	—	—
Guam	4,717	4,588	5,630	6,272	6,681	9,933	7,906	7,896	9,701	9,489
Marshall Islands	—	—	—	—	—	—	—	—	—	—
Northern Marianas	—	—	—	—	—	—	—	—	—	—
Palau	—	—	—	—	—	—	—	—	—	—
Puerto Rico	79,426	94,281	98,029	115,402	127,812	170,005	160,277	173,885	189,748	200,547
Trust Territories	—	—	—	—	—	—	546	545	1,006	548
Virgin Islands	3,555	4,371	—	—	—	—	6,570	6,215	6,230	7,723

Table 88.—Educational and general expenditures (in current dollars) of public institutions of higher education, by state: 1969–70 to 1994–95—Continued

[Amounts in thousands]

State or other area	1979–80	1980–81	1981–82	1982–83	1983–84	1984–85	1985–86	1986–87	1987–88	1988–89
1	12	13	14	15	16	17	18	19	20	21
United States	**$30,627,436**	**$34,173,013**	**$37,170,551**	**$39,707,421**	**$42,593,562**	**$46,873,546**	**$50,872,962**	**$54,359,434**	**$58,639,468**	**$63,444,908**
Alabama	551,897	611,409	649,849	681,447	747,005	879,006	979,770	996,174	1,102,484	1,223,329
Alaska	140,633	150,421	175,520	202,228	213,148	221,950	210,894	199,147	208,641	227,331
Arizona	477,673	554,120	621,942	651,633	699,081	783,349	862,816	932,162	1,019,287	1,122,890
Arkansas	236,359	266,522	294,708	307,913	332,283	380,554	415,800	423,721	477,369	530,691
California	4,244,523	4,847,879	5,101,040	5,287,192	5,467,785	6,371,467	7,049,635	7,419,792	7,842,747	8,352,924
Colorado	523,206	561,552	615,508	663,090	714,175	752,834	809,621	872,016	956,381	1,052,644
Connecticut	260,818	281,581	301,501	325,545	375,279	406,182	439,397	475,714	527,537	605,228
Delaware	120,261	135,164	146,322	156,842	165,002	180,947	202,331	225,753	247,116	277,543
District of Columbia	59,844	71,245	67,229	72,805	78,060	81,845	79,922	82,903	85,392	92,548
Florida	925,521	1,071,754	1,221,366	1,256,043	1,375,215	1,518,017	1,638,227	1,795,084	2,005,883	2,250,014
Georgia	559,767	628,939	705,961	762,259	876,925	952,406	1,046,341	1,178,559	1,265,156	1,364,338
Hawaii	177,610	202,154	219,560	241,176	247,944	258,802	282,058	287,357	314,832	341,609
Idaho	125,573	141,296	152,699	159,628	171,457	190,970	202,736	210,186	229,094	244,969
Illinois	1,331,451	1,487,123	1,567,716	1,600,221	1,708,394	1,922,319	2,152,955	2,291,593	2,354,360	2,556,337
Indiana	674,499	771,564	838,723	891,745	990,974	1,062,982	1,183,098	1,283,767	1,403,895	1,534,653
Iowa	483,514	512,205	546,704	616,225	634,353	697,595	736,894	778,973	883,335	987,522
Kansas	411,290	461,979	493,084	520,191	572,013	619,279	660,995	680,799	720,287	801,774
Kentucky	478,634	527,235	561,001	602,385	650,707	687,676	737,101	803,423	860,198	916,498
Louisiana	479,135	557,825	629,061	675,184	717,640	783,598	810,479	825,811	865,860	908,303
Maine	115,234	127,983	138,625	153,624	165,766	177,844	183,349	210,284	235,916	271,016
Maryland	546,005	604,419	674,500	775,937	793,291	881,583	911,562	982,303	1,063,956	1,186,989
Massachusetts	391,201	441,068	496,750	532,502	573,911	696,953	779,341	876,226	1,007,570	1,051,636
Michigan	1,519,398	1,610,016	1,702,915	1,777,059	1,949,343	2,084,114	2,278,217	2,368,290	2,729,356	2,850,114
Minnesota	603,155	667,119	756,130	786,566	855,876	943,467	1,023,324	1,113,161	1,202,304	1,330,114
Mississippi	372,803	409,942	445,276	444,958	478,961	501,386	542,022	538,471	602,499	674,608
Missouri	490,792	553,793	565,119	615,632	654,032	711,673	802,936	859,671	899,646	995,472
Montana	91,932	99,990	116,784	129,855	139,301	147,261	148,099	150,804	160,413	161,543
Nebraska	258,644	286,122	315,985	329,494	348,895	379,715	397,523	434,585	437,700	489,501
Nevada	94,324	105,177	119,012	124,720	131,310	141,080	163,714	180,492	198,938	220,033
New Hampshire	94,764	104,285	114,129	118,181	117,362	130,146	143,191	158,144	177,908	195,404
New Jersey	660,841	735,097	790,230	875,367	944,710	1,036,128	1,140,310	1,286,796	1,446,642	1,607,786
New Mexico	241,746	278,960	300,233	325,415	327,564	363,776	393,151	436,528	454,493	561,308
New York	2,100,985	2,249,821	2,484,372	2,750,318	2,957,335	3,121,328	3,238,773	3,624,574	3,820,677	3,961,073
North Carolina	850,149	971,928	1,054,886	1,102,045	1,235,261	1,396,726	1,527,535	1,656,911	1,799,484	1,941,331
North Dakota	132,308	151,372	171,649	184,750	203,604	209,899	228,609	245,905	238,453	248,612
Ohio	1,205,674	1,327,483	1,409,106	1,560,143	1,706,723	1,884,222	2,019,351	2,205,567	2,385,244	2,630,782
Oklahoma	349,038	404,178	461,734	527,172	503,812	529,560	594,561	586,653	608,121	688,953
Oregon	453,452	497,593	536,266	558,436	596,130	635,298	672,175	734,860	781,964	839,670
Pennsylvania	1,116,620	1,231,502	1,340,668	1,452,881	1,542,172	1,664,367	1,814,384	1,946,738	2,165,078	2,385,349
Rhode Island	126,857	138,965	146,605	152,746	163,119	171,733	185,215	195,498	214,627	236,790
South Carolina	434,785	481,737	496,933	524,976	577,850	669,972	741,740	749,845	832,075	903,484
South Dakota	107,794	108,632	114,854	118,096	122,632	122,969	130,825	133,995	138,428	149,457
Tennessee	458,395	515,578	559,848	602,998	649,880	754,196	865,946	1,023,986	1,037,718	1,107,583
Texas	1,993,991	2,278,337	2,667,588	2,954,902	3,215,492	3,414,903	3,674,109	3,733,581	4,038,745	4,394,333
Utah	286,467	320,278	360,261	398,877	412,515	453,185	503,557	519,875	552,193	602,628
Vermont	90,763	101,539	111,492	121,145	132,629	144,817	157,266	168,529	182,916	204,586
Virginia	705,495	796,616	872,372	922,414	986,316	1,136,322	1,241,534	1,372,892	1,500,030	1,647,075
Washington	764,495	837,281	876,286	904,402	1,004,452	1,088,208	1,143,285	1,235,106	1,270,682	1,450,608
West Virginia	224,926	228,755	248,577	256,931	287,038	294,974	310,142	321,492	331,806	371,151
Wisconsin	914,054	998,862	1,074,316	1,143,247	1,219,269	1,307,439	1,438,918	1,530,657	1,663,132	1,824,067
Wyoming	91,349	111,170	128,725	146,129	154,852	159,646	171,335	170,678	179,700	181,985
U.S. Service Schools	476,792	555,447	608,829	661,751	704,716	766,877	805,892	843,402	911,200	688,724
Outlying areas	226,600	253,820	289,129	341,259	397,494	388,570	421,500	396,895	457,094	457,344
American Samoa	1,424	1,609	1,235	1,399	1,369	1,092	1,092	1,162	1,257	2,642
Federated States of Micronesia	—	—	—	—	—	—	—	—	—	1,474
Guam	13,796	15,582	22,112	23,505	24,602	24,026	29,916	28,909	31,762	36,276
Marshall Islands	—	—	—	—	—	—	—	—	—	—
Northern Marianas	—	—	—	—	1,192	1,272	1,328	2,625	2,009	794
Palau	—	—	—	—	—	—	—	—	—	2,993
Puerto Rico	201,099	224,988	251,752	299,278	353,757	342,937	367,523	342,049	397,605	392,814
Trust Territories	1,087	1,320	1,524	3,763	3,454	4,969	5,992	5,302	5,684	—
Virgin Islands	9,195	10,322	12,506	13,314	13,119	14,275	15,649	16,849	18,777	20,351

Table 88.—Educational and general expenditures (in current dollars) of public institutions of higher education, by state: 1969–70 to 1994–95—Continued

[Amounts in thousands]

State or other area	1989–90	1990–91	1991–92	1992–93	1993–94	1994–95	Percentage change			
							1969–70 to 1994–95	1984–85 to 1989–90	1989–90 to 1994–95	1984–85 to 1994–95
1	22	23	24	25	26	27	28	29	30	31
United States	$69,163,958	$74,395,428	$78,554,534	$83,210,979	$87,139,226	$92,173,768	788.5	47.6	33.3	96.6
Alabama	1,305,463	1,415,440	1,456,605	1,580,484	1,710,955	1,834,533	961.9	48.5	40.5	108.7
Alaska	253,392	273,577	288,999	304,137	316,779	316,397	1,149.0	14.2	24.9	42.6
Arizona	1,236,696	1,364,060	1,407,819	1,409,122	1,523,655	1,653,840	1,160.6	57.9	33.7	111.1
Arkansas	573,923	633,194	604,885	676,378	707,166	746,129	939.1	50.8	30.0	96.1
California	9,238,960	9,615,356	10,341,888	11,000,665	10,734,842	11,280,758	671.3	45.0	22.1	77.1
Colorado	1,167,864	1,258,356	1,363,615	1,452,957	1,529,290	1,604,656	778.0	55.1	37.4	113.1
Connecticut	622,298	673,182	736,202	731,570	771,954	883,759	848.7	53.2	42.0	117.6
Delaware	303,220	325,838	349,369	366,801	387,810	413,692	1,113.3	67.6	36.4	128.6
District of Columbia	97,447	96,411	98,973	97,586	95,824	98,041	313.9	19.1	0.6	19.8
Florida	2,546,201	2,657,553	2,710,041	2,904,932	3,101,072	3,234,938	927.4	67.7	27.0	113.1
Georgia	1,482,499	1,617,020	1,665,009	1,834,141	2,037,534	2,277,756	1,119.1	55.7	53.6	139.2
Hawaii	384,535	454,880	526,269	546,473	556,567	590,389	664.6	48.6	53.5	128.1
Idaho	268,690	303,224	334,762	346,932	375,289	395,733	966.0	40.7	47.3	107.2
Illinois	2,812,244	2,979,768	3,068,891	3,245,802	3,397,183	3,583,012	578.8	46.3	27.4	86.4
Indiana	1,671,111	1,842,610	1,935,566	2,014,834	2,105,645	2,196,013	679.6	57.2	31.4	106.6
Iowa	1,077,810	1,172,328	1,184,382	1,267,646	1,354,777	1,392,753	651.1	54.5	29.2	99.7
Kansas	884,775	928,772	994,560	1,059,683	1,134,392	1,196,211	705.7	42.9	35.2	93.2
Kentucky	992,403	1,112,190	1,208,448	1,212,211	1,254,859	1,321,523	739.3	44.3	33.2	92.2
Louisiana	1,005,278	1,135,955	1,215,771	1,275,446	1,339,408	1,449,305	887.5	28.3	44.2	85.0
Maine	297,782	308,699	316,116	324,515	338,776	343,665	799.6	67.4	15.4	93.2
Maryland	1,299,110	1,443,669	1,428,072	1,564,259	1,673,163	1,737,204	783.5	47.4	33.7	97.1
Massachusetts	1,076,241	1,122,629	1,165,598	1,295,720	1,339,199	1,400,824	1,024.7	54.4	30.2	101.0
Michigan	3,079,227	3,325,625	3,556,178	3,727,115	3,885,984	4,042,460	576.1	47.7	31.3	94.0
Minnesota	1,420,124	1,563,054	1,728,356	1,775,640	1,937,650	2,068,280	703.7	50.5	45.6	119.2
Mississippi	719,821	756,492	772,618	842,603	919,354	1,049,356	950.6	43.6	45.8	109.3
Missouri	1,083,473	1,155,531	1,184,338	1,260,304	1,339,527	1,456,516	593.7	52.2	34.4	104.7
Montana	179,510	210,813	262,480	279,323	303,495	322,880	650.9	21.9	79.9	119.3
Nebraska	543,341	600,224	639,475	672,427	706,454	727,977	696.6	43.1	34.0	91.7
Nevada	257,526	301,487	332,246	353,875	379,154	402,097	1,369.8	82.5	56.1	185.0
New Hampshire	206,207	229,360	252,021	275,138	295,687	304,474	800.7	58.4	47.7	133.9
New Jersey	1,765,002	1,875,481	2,002,975	2,103,355	2,237,339	2,363,439	1,130.8	70.3	33.9	128.1
New Mexico	626,386	671,206	724,157	769,646	806,673	899,545	999.5	72.2	43.6	147.3
New York	4,252,153	4,680,376	4,768,772	5,113,506	5,398,182	5,799,931	725.2	36.2	36.4	85.8
North Carolina	2,101,016	2,227,060	2,406,405	2,600,325	2,671,176	2,849,310	1,051.6	50.4	35.6	104.0
North Dakota	282,247	292,978	328,738	336,361	344,187	361,276	688.0	34.5	28.0	72.1
Ohio	2,799,829	3,046,603	3,214,612	3,185,955	3,362,837	3,616,901	755.1	48.6	29.2	92.0
Oklahoma	762,034	830,929	906,908	930,102	953,027	996,963	749.9	43.9	30.8	88.3
Oregon	911,812	996,887	1,086,673	1,142,781	1,194,805	1,281,381	758.3	43.5	40.5	101.7
Pennsylvania	2,596,987	2,737,817	2,963,168	3,087,186	3,280,879	3,439,340	656.5	56.0	32.4	106.6
Rhode Island	250,604	251,992	260,123	284,957	285,742	297,597	604.2	45.9	18.8	73.3
South Carolina	1,012,928	1,065,867	1,100,035	1,172,246	1,244,696	1,310,645	1,347.1	51.2	29.4	95.6
South Dakota	162,001	173,396	192,001	211,716	229,080	222,811	450.0	31.7	37.5	81.2
Tennessee	1,194,378	1,231,619	1,228,340	1,352,125	1,478,085	1,581,929	942.5	58.4	32.4	109.8
Texas	4,816,945	5,105,246	5,439,843	5,961,535	6,352,088	6,643,734	1,313.3	41.1	37.9	94.6
Utah	656,772	730,496	826,170	856,933	921,052	991,014	872.8	44.9	50.9	118.7
Vermont	222,470	238,512	258,150	263,475	271,261	279,882	767.7	53.6	25.8	93.3
Virginia	1,807,829	1,852,416	1,892,627	1,991,591	2,124,635	2,248,402	1,131.3	59.1	24.4	97.9
Washington	1,564,535	1,757,053	1,837,095	2,007,044	2,074,451	2,211,588	702.1	43.8	41.4	103.2
West Virginia	411,950	459,984	494,733	522,173	560,380	579,349	641.8	39.7	40.6	96.4
Wisconsin	1,931,561	2,057,786	2,158,188	2,266,312	2,394,285	2,437,859	647.8	47.7	26.2	86.5
Wyoming	194,506	204,028	225,238	222,188	231,190	254,469	782.6	21.8	30.8	59.4
U.S. Service Schools	752,844	1,030,399	1,110,028	1,130,748	1,169,731	1,181,234	645.6	1.8	56.9	54.0
Outlying areas	501,855	498,958	555,054	607,730	637,164	700,528	690.1	29.2	39.6	80.3
American Samoa	2,879	3,187	3,228	3,356	3,416	3,483	261.7	163.8	21.0	219.1
Federated States of Micronesia	1,351	3,302	3,286	2,898	3,096	4,589	—	—	239.8	—
Guam	47,380	55,641	64,772	68,550	63,515	77,783	1,549.1	97.2	64.2	223.8
Marshall Islands	—	—	3,093	1,220	1,454	1,183	—	—	—	—
Northern Marianas	766	2,472	2,803	2,230	2,838	12,305	—	39.8	1,506.0	867.4
Palau	3,297	3,277	3,172	3,808	2,847	3,156	—	—	4.3	—
Puerto Rico	426,754	378,352	427,021	497,590	529,255	567,140	614.0	24.4	32.9	65.4
Trust Territories	—	—	—	—	—	—				
Virgin Islands	19,427	52,726	47,679	28,078	30,743	30,889	769.0	36.1	59.0	116.4

—Data not available or not applicable.

NOTE.—Percentages reflect mergers, openings, and closures of institutions over time. Some data have been revised from previously published figures. Because of rounding, details may not add to totals.

SOURCE: U.S. Department of Education, National Center for Education Statistics, Higher Education General Information Survey (HEGIS), "Financial Statistics of Institutions of Higher Education" surveys; and Integrated Postsecondary Education Data System (IPEDS), "Financial Statistics" surveys. (This table was prepared January 1998.)

Table 89.—Educational and general expenditures (in constant 1994–95 dollars [1]) of public institutions of higher education, by state: 1969–70 to 1994–95

[Amounts in thousands]

State or other area	1969–70	1970–71	1971–72	1972–73	1973–74	1974–75	1975–76	1976–77	1977–78	1978–79
1	2	3	4	5	6	7	8	9	10	11
United States	**$44,175,670**	**$46,926,210**	**$49,004,912**	**$51,834,531**	**$54,189,845**	**$59,140,648**	**$61,934,272**	**$62,896,126**	**$64,384,275**	**$65,587,040**
Alabama	735,651	649,685	702,223	780,895	855,988	972,715	1,080,215	1,138,281	1,188,655	1,228,990
Alaska	107,868	133,970	143,865	152,400	152,195	189,120	236,298	247,249	283,303	287,604
Arizona	558,678	617,505	689,569	734,807	772,961	864,570	879,743	951,590	1,004,991	1,016,219
Arkansas	305,767	309,527	327,526	333,915	360,300	417,415	454,625	456,857	494,948	511,667
California	6,227,832	6,373,803	6,430,941	6,888,161	7,384,102	7,786,318	8,387,528	8,705,156	9,039,667	8,767,717
Colorado	778,235	832,534	873,970	920,661	914,131	1,024,114	1,065,671	1,094,699	1,086,024	1,123,577
Connecticut	396,686	420,919	463,174	476,788	466,999	528,266	513,363	517,899	562,375	570,117
Delaware	145,193	159,502	167,084	183,787	204,072	227,434	235,578	242,397	239,495	258,745
District of Columbia	100,864	108,824	137,370	142,403	134,615	134,404	132,044	124,239	139,616	136,092
Florida	1,340,732	1,417,764	1,478,321	1,623,824	1,735,805	1,809,000	1,820,006	1,869,850	1,929,949	1,954,112
Georgia	795,623	869,832	900,443	961,782	1,040,356	1,076,606	1,084,087	1,110,303	1,156,659	1,201,984
Hawaii	328,786	375,350	375,677	369,949	349,223	338,298	376,442	365,433	386,498	385,412
Idaho	158,085	159,513	177,289	176,950	190,612	233,488	249,616	263,748	271,641	279,575
Illinois	2,247,541	2,496,254	2,445,390	2,569,927	2,569,811	2,758,033	2,845,243	2,824,844	2,801,995	2,883,940
Indiana	1,199,546	1,265,125	1,334,519	1,364,969	1,300,125	1,493,246	1,441,534	1,436,691	1,446,051	1,477,585
Iowa	789,634	819,745	853,564	869,596	961,089	944,339	937,801	1,004,883	984,816	1,018,500
Kansas	632,206	679,822	668,036	690,505	690,470	766,005	794,567	855,807	871,668	895,087
Kentucky	670,508	712,754	753,122	809,247	856,797	915,979	993,067	996,415	1,016,968	1,047,638
Louisiana	624,973	697,977	623,625	746,834	770,889	837,393	793,942	820,184	888,434	887,912
Maine	162,667	176,265	186,707	195,579	215,338	230,373	245,462	235,689	239,570	240,619
Maryland	837,247	799,252	888,108	956,399	955,526	1,109,086	1,169,507	1,213,094	1,230,483	1,245,412
Massachusetts	530,376	611,560	701,627	721,291	769,419	876,322	814,501	822,102	811,746	871,653
Michigan	2,546,208	2,605,037	2,669,119	2,741,737	2,810,215	3,118,183	3,163,183	3,134,908	3,307,178	3,302,714
Minnesota	1,095,768	1,157,202	1,159,782	1,157,935	1,170,343	1,283,583	1,375,232	1,254,646	1,270,636	1,296,767
Mississippi	425,300	476,909	499,484	540,803	561,330	630,975	701,714	710,878	753,700	784,373
Missouri	894,023	894,732	935,565	963,075	995,731	1,048,491	1,049,959	1,073,467	1,050,422	1,069,633
Montana	183,104	202,043	193,753	196,660	190,677	203,041	221,615	231,245	225,773	218,418
Nebraska	389,132	406,372	419,962	419,702	438,599	478,888	514,412	542,009	566,133	577,028
Nevada	116,497	119,912	125,155	127,984	142,111	146,953	173,696	173,175	175,554	191,722
New Hampshire	143,940	150,832	153,126	158,633	177,397	177,850	186,393	196,959	209,241	209,849
New Jersey	817,697	919,810	1,036,688	1,062,853	1,241,853	1,329,010	1,348,670	1,388,229	1,482,147	1,429,562
New Mexico	348,367	363,584	372,192	400,637	413,355	357,819	400,129	414,548	457,983	492,899
New York	2,992,872	3,422,212	3,832,418	4,016,060	4,283,300	4,841,678	5,079,065	4,580,085	4,537,535	4,580,600
North Carolina	1,053,573	1,135,910	1,214,035	1,308,440	1,428,671	1,691,952	1,601,613	1,677,978	1,741,614	1,840,164
North Dakota	195,219	196,666	194,538	197,268	200,497	226,221	255,596	261,598	268,722	277,626
Ohio	1,801,224	1,907,276	1,965,718	2,034,754	2,035,820	2,272,569	2,373,587	2,466,706	2,478,134	2,575,979
Oklahoma	499,491	528,000	535,915	563,888	565,681	612,782	657,724	715,344	736,314	757,645
Oregon	635,704	661,175	671,806	670,723	683,515	837,048	917,804	947,449	953,956	975,896
Pennsylvania	1,935,878	2,024,810	2,157,351	2,286,492	2,290,114	2,421,840	2,528,081	2,522,576	2,481,191	2,453,787
Rhode Island	179,955	195,230	189,037	211,073	225,165	245,973	250,716	265,060	265,833	270,878
South Carolina	385,680	414,618	459,163	524,357	621,109	766,769	777,727	770,088	827,900	895,682
South Dakota	172,510	175,953	171,064	168,921	177,469	178,534	197,915	194,335	207,760	216,656
Tennessee	646,183	677,348	738,699	795,740	831,026	929,918	949,473	1,002,465	1,037,394	1,090,769
Texas	2,001,734	2,328,582	2,474,708	2,649,100	2,982,895	3,203,092	3,669,624	3,897,314	4,065,285	4,226,369
Utah	433,784	431,721	454,018	485,671	491,687	523,485	562,705	594,617	603,545	626,659
Vermont	137,348	141,759	148,372	153,182	160,268	182,141	188,857	192,222	194,231	195,820
Virginia	777,570	857,357	915,950	1,024,280	1,089,123	1,175,977	1,292,144	1,306,011	1,350,018	1,506,325
Washington	1,174,117	1,239,776	1,171,909	1,298,004	1,307,422	1,436,980	1,449,644	1,470,776	1,568,933	1,637,674
West Virginia	332,557	335,238	309,326	312,260	309,151	332,712	360,414	367,137	361,724	459,090
Wisconsin	1,388,159	1,441,189	1,579,508	1,727,997	1,737,081	1,871,205	1,981,700	2,032,023	1,954,060	1,988,011
Wyoming	122,777	128,297	139,172	144,555	148,991	160,820	179,775	180,374	178,082	187,428
U.S. Service Schools	674,582	699,174	795,230	821,082	828,427	921,637	974,266	1,034,496	997,725	960,859
Outlying areas	377,535	416,814	396,245	441,023	456,653	560,968	513,195	517,615	532,197	523,228
American Samoa	4,101	4,347	2,671	2,787	3,310	3,590	3,073	1,964	3,059	2,388
Federated States of Micronesia	—	—	—	—	—	—	—	—	—	—
Guam	20,085	18,329	21,374	22,591	22,521	30,769	23,006	21,595	24,835	22,640
Marshall Islands	—	—	—	—	—	—	—	—	—	—
Northern Marianas	—	—	—	—	—	—	—	—	—	—
Palau	—	—	—	—	—	—	—	—	—	—
Puerto Rico	338,214	376,676	372,199	415,645	430,822	526,609	466,410	475,568	485,778	478,467
Trust Territories	—	—	—	—	—	—	1,588	1,490	2,576	1,307
Virgin Islands	15,136	17,461	—	—	—	—	19,118	16,999	15,950	18,426

Table 89.—Educational and general expenditures (in constant 1994–95 dollars [1]) of public institutions of higher education, by state: 1969–70 to 1994–95—Continued

[Amounts in thousands]

State or other area	1979–80	1980–81	1981–82	1982–83	1983–84	1984–85	1985–86	1986–87	1987–88	1988–89
1	12	13	14	15	16	17	18	19	20	21
United States	$66,471,416	$66,991,850	$66,582,393	$66,787,883	$68,361,041	$71,156,412	$73,575,514	$75,626,607	$78,216,958	$80,357,180
Alabama	1,197,794	1,198,589	1,164,054	1,146,194	1,198,914	1,334,376	1,417,002	1,385,910	1,470,562	1,549,427
Alaska	305,219	294,881	314,403	340,147	342,094	336,932	305,008	277,060	278,298	287,930
Arizona	1,036,705	1,086,281	1,114,065	1,096,047	1,121,999	1,189,164	1,247,856	1,296,854	1,359,589	1,422,214
Arkansas	512,974	522,483	527,900	517,909	533,301	577,700	601,355	589,494	636,744	672,156
California	9,211,984	9,503,651	9,137,326	8,893,057	8,775,586	9,672,210	10,195,603	10,322,656	10,461,142	10,579,532
Colorado	1,135,525	1,100,852	1,102,540	1,115,317	1,146,224	1,142,840	1,170,922	1,213,177	1,275,680	1,333,243
Connecticut	566,059	552,003	540,069	547,566	602,308	616,605	635,482	661,829	703,662	766,562
Delaware	261,005	264,972	262,103	263,809	264,822	274,686	292,623	314,075	329,619	351,526
District of Columbia	129,880	139,666	120,426	122,459	125,284	124,245	115,588	115,338	113,901	117,218
Florida	2,008,678	2,101,037	2,187,794	2,112,664	2,207,168	2,304,426	2,369,302	2,497,379	2,675,571	2,849,792
Georgia	1,214,876	1,232,954	1,264,564	1,282,120	1,407,431	1,445,800	1,513,281	1,639,649	1,687,543	1,728,024
Hawaii	385,471	396,298	393,290	405,659	397,941	392,874	407,929	399,780	419,942	432,670
Idaho	272,535	276,992	273,525	268,494	275,182	289,902	293,209	292,417	305,580	310,269
Illinois	2,889,678	2,915,315	2,808,198	2,691,571	2,741,907	2,918,177	3,113,732	3,188,139	3,140,391	3,237,770
Indiana	1,463,881	1,512,553	1,502,377	1,499,916	1,590,475	1,613,660	1,711,067	1,786,018	1,872,602	1,943,740
Iowa	1,049,381	1,004,113	979,293	1,036,491	1,018,112	1,058,985	1,065,740	1,083,733	1,178,247	1,250,762
Kansas	892,632	905,651	883,246	874,962	918,058	940,097	955,971	947,150	960,764	1,015,500
Kentucky	1,038,789	1,033,576	1,004,903	1,013,212	1,044,360	1,043,927	1,066,040	1,117,748	1,147,386	1,160,806
Louisiana	1,039,877	1,093,545	1,126,817	1,135,660	1,151,785	1,189,542	1,172,163	1,148,895	1,154,937	1,150,426
Maine	250,095	250,895	248,314	258,396	266,048	269,976	265,170	292,554	314,679	343,260
Maryland	1,185,006	1,184,886	1,208,209	1,305,125	1,273,202	1,338,287	1,318,356	1,366,612	1,419,170	1,503,401
Massachusetts	849,033	864,658	889,812	895,669	921,105	1,058,009	1,127,129	1,219,034	1,343,959	1,331,966
Michigan	3,297,584	3,156,232	3,050,377	2,989,014	3,128,622	3,163,790	3,294,893	3,294,842	3,640,584	3,609,858
Minnesota	1,309,042	1,307,802	1,354,431	1,323,004	1,373,649	1,432,230	1,479,993	1,548,666	1,603,708	1,684,677
Mississippi	809,102	803,639	797,608	748,420	768,715	761,130	783,905	749,139	803,650	854,436
Missouri	1,065,177	1,085,641	1,012,279	1,035,493	1,049,697	1,080,356	1,161,254	1,196,002	1,200,004	1,260,831
Montana	199,523	196,018	209,191	218,417	223,573	223,550	214,190	209,804	213,968	204,605
Nebraska	561,341	560,905	566,013	554,208	559,963	576,427	574,922	604,608	583,832	619,985
Nevada	204,714	206,186	213,182	209,779	210,747	214,166	236,773	251,106	265,355	278,686
New Hampshire	205,668	204,437	204,435	198,781	188,362	197,568	207,092	220,015	237,305	247,492
New Jersey	1,434,238	1,441,064	1,415,513	1,472,367	1,516,224	1,572,894	1,649,184	1,790,232	1,929,621	2,036,367
New Mexico	524,667	546,866	537,798	547,348	525,727	552,231	568,599	607,311	606,231	710,933
New York	4,559,816	4,410,489	4,450,175	4,626,035	4,746,411	4,738,333	4,684,107	5,042,624	5,096,256	5,016,962
North Carolina	1,845,098	1,905,341	1,889,583	1,853,639	1,982,547	2,120,301	2,209,212	2,305,148	2,400,264	2,458,824
North Dakota	287,152	296,745	307,469	310,749	326,777	318,637	330,628	342,111	318,064	314,884
Ohio	2,616,701	2,602,362	2,524,085	2,624,160	2,739,225	2,860,344	2,920,506	3,068,456	3,181,587	3,332,059
Oklahoma	757,526	792,341	827,089	886,703	808,599	803,899	859,890	816,171	811,150	872,605
Oregon	984,136	975,469	960,597	939,290	956,766	964,415	972,139	1,022,361	1,043,032	1,063,498
Pennsylvania	2,423,426	2,414,203	2,401,495	2,443,747	2,475,127	2,526,594	2,624,071	2,708,365	2,887,915	3,021,202
Rhode Island	275,321	272,424	262,608	256,920	261,800	260,700	267,868	271,983	286,283	299,910
South Carolina	943,623	944,385	890,139	883,009	927,427	1,017,051	1,072,749	1,043,209	1,109,873	1,144,322
South Dakota	233,948	212,959	205,733	198,637	196,819	186,673	189,207	186,419	184,644	189,297
Tennessee	994,865	1,010,725	1,002,838	1,014,243	1,043,033	1,144,907	1,252,383	1,424,602	1,384,173	1,402,827
Texas	4,327,603	4,466,391	4,778,364	4,970,145	5,160,742	5,183,995	5,313,716	5,194,279	5,387,129	5,565,714
Utah	621,725	627,865	645,323	670,912	662,071	687,957	728,274	723,267	736,549	763,269
Vermont	196,986	199,055	199,713	203,765	212,865	219,839	227,447	234,463	243,985	259,122
Virginia	1,531,152	1,561,665	1,562,652	1,551,500	1,583,000	1,724,995	1,795,581	1,910,011	2,000,833	2,086,130
Washington	1,659,200	1,641,383	1,569,662	1,521,204	1,612,108	1,651,955	1,653,487	1,718,320	1,694,915	1,837,291
West Virginia	488,162	448,445	445,268	432,158	460,686	447,786	448,546	447,270	442,583	470,087
Wisconsin	1,983,792	1,958,142	1,924,387	1,922,941	1,956,880	1,984,759	2,081,049	2,129,500	2,218,388	2,310,301
Wyoming	198,256	217,934	230,580	245,789	248,532	242,350	247,796	237,453	239,694	230,496
U.S. Service Schools	1,034,793	1,088,883	1,090,575	1,113,065	1,131,042	1,164,158	1,165,529	1,173,368	1,215,414	872,314
Outlying areas	491,795	497,582	517,907	573,998	637,962	589,869	609,598	552,173	609,700	579,257
American Samoa	3,090	3,154	2,213	2,354	2,198	1,657	1,579	1,617	1,677	3,346
Federated States of Micronesia	—	—	—	—	—	—	—	—	—	1,867
Guam	29,942	30,546	39,608	39,535	39,486	36,472	43,266	40,219	42,366	45,946
Marshall Islands	—	—	—	—	—	—	—	—	—	—
Northern Marianas	—	—	—	—	—	1,931	1,921	3,652	2,679	1,006
Palau	—	—	—	—	—	—	—	—	—	3,791
Puerto Rico	436,449	441,060	450,955	503,385	567,766	520,596	531,534	475,869	530,350	497,525
Trust Territories	2,359	2,588	2,729	6,329	5,544	7,543	8,667	7,377	7,582	—
Virgin Islands	19,956	20,234	22,402	22,394	21,056	21,671	22,632	23,440	25,046	25,775

Table 89.—Educational and general expenditures (in constant 1994–95 dollars [1]) of public institutions
of higher education, by state: 1969–70 to 1994–95—Continued

[Amounts in thousands]

State or other area	1989–90	1990–91	1991–92	1992–93	1993–94	1994–95	Percentage change			
							1969–70 to 1994–95	1984–85 to 1989–90	1989–90 to 1994–95	1984–85 to 1994–95
1	22	23	24	25	26	27	28	29	30	31
United States	$82,623,421	$84,435,297	$86,133,459	$88,638,927	$89,753,936	$92,173,768	108.7	16.1	11.6	29.5
Alabama	1,559,509	1,606,458	1,597,138	1,683,581	1,762,294	1,834,533	149.4	16.9	17.6	37.5
Alaska	302,703	310,497	316,882	323,977	326,284	316,397	193.3	–10.2	4.5	–6.1
Arizona	1,477,360	1,548,144	1,543,645	1,501,040	1,569,374	1,653,840	196.0	24.2	11.9	39.1
Arkansas	685,610	718,645	663,244	720,499	728,385	746,129	144.0	18.7	8.8	29.2
California	11,036,883	10,912,975	11,339,671	11,718,251	11,056,953	11,280,758	81.1	14.1	2.2	16.6
Colorado	1,395,133	1,428,175	1,495,177	1,547,735	1,575,178	1,604,656	106.2	22.1	15.0	40.4
Connecticut	743,399	764,029	807,231	779,291	795,118	883,759	122.8	20.6	18.9	43.3
Delaware	362,228	369,811	383,076	390,728	399,446	413,692	184.9	31.9	14.2	50.6
District of Columbia	116,411	109,422	108,522	103,951	98,699	98,041	–2.8	–6.3	–15.8	–21.1
Florida	3,041,697	3,016,198	2,971,506	3,094,424	3,194,123	3,234,938	141.3	32.0	6.4	40.4
Georgia	1,770,996	1,835,241	1,825,648	1,953,784	2,098,672	2,277,756	186.3	22.5	28.6	57.5
Hawaii	459,366	516,268	577,044	582,120	573,267	590,389	79.6	16.9	28.5	50.3
Idaho	320,977	344,145	367,060	369,563	386,550	395,733	150.3	10.7	23.3	36.5
Illinois	3,359,513	3,381,896	3,364,977	3,457,529	3,499,120	3,583,012	59.4	15.1	6.7	22.8
Indiana	1,996,313	2,091,275	2,122,309	2,146,264	2,168,827	2,196,013	83.1	23.7	10.0	36.1
Iowa	1,287,554	1,330,537	1,298,651	1,350,336	1,395,429	1,392,753	76.4	21.6	8.2	31.5
Kansas	1,056,954	1,054,112	1,090,515	1,128,807	1,168,430	1,196,211	89.2	12.4	13.2	27.2
Kentucky	1,185,527	1,262,284	1,325,039	1,291,284	1,292,512	1,321,523	97.1	13.6	11.5	26.6
Louisiana	1,200,908	1,289,255	1,333,068	1,358,645	1,379,598	1,449,305	131.9	1.0	20.7	21.8
Maine	355,732	350,359	346,615	345,683	348,941	343,665	111.3	31.8	–3.4	27.3
Maryland	1,551,920	1,638,496	1,565,852	1,666,297	1,723,368	1,737,204	107.5	16.0	11.9	29.8
Massachusetts	1,285,680	1,274,131	1,278,054	1,380,242	1,379,383	1,400,824	164.1	21.5	9.0	32.4
Michigan	3,678,452	3,774,427	3,899,277	3,970,239	4,002,587	4,042,460	58.8	16.3	9.9	27.8
Minnesota	1,696,483	1,773,992	1,895,107	1,891,468	1,995,791	2,068,280	88.8	18.5	21.9	44.4
Mississippi	859,900	858,582	847,160	897,567	946,940	1,049,356	146.7	13.0	22.0	37.9
Missouri	1,294,319	1,311,473	1,298,603	1,342,515	1,379,721	1,456,516	62.9	19.8	12.5	34.8
Montana	214,443	239,262	287,804	297,544	312,602	322,880	76.3	–4.1	50.6	44.4
Nebraska	649,076	681,226	701,171	716,290	727,652	727,977	87.1	12.6	12.2	26.3
Nevada	307,641	342,173	364,301	376,958	390,531	402,097	245.2	43.6	30.7	87.8
New Hampshire	246,335	260,313	276,336	293,086	304,560	304,474	111.5	24.7	23.6	54.1
New Jersey	2,108,475	2,128,583	2,196,221	2,240,559	2,304,473	2,363,439	189.0	34.1	12.1	50.3
New Mexico	748,283	761,787	794,023	819,851	830,878	899,545	158.2	35.5	20.2	62.9
New York	5,079,631	5,312,006	5,228,862	5,447,066	5,560,160	5,799,931	93.8	7.2	14.2	22.4
North Carolina	2,509,879	2,527,608	2,638,574	2,769,947	2,751,328	2,849,310	170.4	18.4	13.5	34.4
North Dakota	337,173	332,516	360,455	358,302	354,514	361,276	85.1	5.8	7.1	13.4
Ohio	3,344,682	3,457,750	3,524,757	3,393,779	3,463,743	3,616,901	100.8	16.9	8.1	26.4
Oklahoma	910,328	943,065	994,407	990,773	981,624	996,963	99.6	13.2	9.5	24.0
Oregon	1,089,252	1,131,420	1,191,515	1,217,326	1,230,656	1,281,381	101.6	12.9	17.6	32.9
Pennsylvania	3,102,366	3,107,293	3,249,054	3,288,567	3,379,325	3,439,340	77.7	22.8	10.9	36.1
Rhode Island	299,372	285,999	285,219	303,545	294,316	297,597	65.4	14.8	–0.6	14.2
South Carolina	1,210,046	1,209,708	1,206,166	1,248,713	1,282,044	1,310,645	239.8	19.0	8.3	28.9
South Dakota	193,526	196,796	210,525	225,526	235,954	222,811	29.2	3.7	15.1	19.4
Tennessee	1,426,807	1,397,830	1,346,850	1,440,326	1,522,436	1,581,929	144.8	24.6	10.9	38.2
Texas	5,754,334	5,794,213	5,964,678	6,350,413	6,542,690	6,643,734	231.9	11.0	15.5	28.2
Utah	784,581	829,079	905,879	912,832	948,689	991,014	128.5	14.0	26.3	44.1
Vermont	265,764	270,700	283,057	280,662	279,401	279,882	103.8	20.9	5.3	27.3
Virginia	2,159,637	2,102,405	2,075,227	2,121,505	2,188,387	2,248,402	189.2	25.2	4.1	30.3
Washington	1,868,998	1,994,172	2,014,338	2,137,966	2,136,697	2,211,588	88.4	13.1	18.3	33.9
West Virginia	492,116	522,060	542,465	556,234	577,195	579,349	74.2	9.9	17.7	29.4
Wisconsin	2,307,447	2,335,490	2,366,409	2,414,147	2,466,128	2,437,859	75.6	16.3	5.7	22.8
Wyoming	232,358	231,562	246,969	236,682	238,127	254,469	107.3	–4.1	9.5	5.0
U.S. Service Schools	899,349	1,169,454	1,217,124	1,204,508	1,204,830	1,181,234	75.1	–22.7	31.3	1.5
Outlying areas	599,517	566,293	608,606	647,373	656,283	700,528	85.6	1.6	16.8	18.8
American Samoa	3,440	3,617	3,540	3,575	3,518	3,483	–15.1	107.6	1.3	110.2
Federated States of Micronesia	1,613	3,747	3,603	3,087	3,189	4,589	—	—	184.4	—
Guam	56,600	63,150	71,021	73,022	65,421	77,783	287.3	55.2	37.4	113.3
Marshall Islands	—	—	3,392	1,300	1,498	1,183	—	—	—	—
Northern Marianas	915	2,806	3,074	2,376	2,924	12,305	—	–52.6	1,244.4	537.2
Palau	3,939	3,720	3,478	4,056	2,932	3,156	—	—	–19.9	—
Puerto Rico	509,802	429,412	468,220	530,048	545,136	567,140	67.7	–2.1	11.2	8.9
Trust Territories	—	—	—	—	—	—	—	—	—	—
Virgin Islands	23,208	59,842	52,279	29,909	31,666	30,889	104.1	7.1	33.1	42.5

[1] Based on the Higher Education Price Index, prepared by Research Associates of Washington. These data do not reflect differences in inflation rates from state to state.
—Data not available or not applicable.

NOTE.—Percentages reflect mergers, openings, and closures of institutions over time. Some data have been revised from previously published figures. Because of rounding, details may not add to totals.

SOURCE: U.S. Department of Education, National Center for Education Statistics, Higher Education General Information Survey (HEGIS), "Financial Statistics of Institutions of Higher Education" surveys; and Integrated Postsecondary Education Data System (IPEDS), "Financial Statistics" surveys. (This table was prepared January 1998.)

Table 90.—Educational and general expenditures (in current dollars) of private institutions of higher education, by state: 1969–70 to 1994–95

[Amounts in thousands]

State or other area	1969–70	1970–71	1971–72	1972–73	1973–74	1974–75	1975–76	1976–77	1977–78	1978–79
1	2	3	4	5	6	7	8	9	10	11
United States	**$5,414,507**	**$5,870,942**	**$6,293,742**	**$6,686,336**	**$7,180,825**	**$8,455,247**	**$9,315,684**	**$10,154,344**	**$11,107,693**	**$12,342,710**
Alabama	31,157	32,860	34,398	39,214	43,869	54,533	61,613	64,328	72,418	78,230
Alaska	2,159	2,299	4,162	3,105	3,364	3,697	3,762	3,468	4,172	5,818
Arizona	5,536	6,489	6,735	8,848	7,796	10,045	9,485	10,930	11,905	12,931
Arkansas	11,537	12,899	13,209	15,250	17,115	19,907	21,054	23,416	25,733	29,046
California	385,445	437,129	487,536	534,161	545,658	699,513	773,767	870,251	981,635	1,076,407
Colorado	35,531	38,883	40,226	43,722	46,065	53,628	57,775	61,783	69,076	78,800
Connecticut	165,374	181,641	191,881	203,933	218,608	262,781	285,173	313,304	336,639	364,778
Delaware	3,209	4,306	4,542	4,795	5,021	6,653	7,012	7,980	8,596	9,243
District of Columbia	150,081	175,335	205,023	228,526	253,589	292,811	325,715	364,332	381,676	419,582
Florida	98,497	111,316	119,649	129,993	145,372	180,746	196,442	220,944	242,087	265,427
Georgia	73,019	79,652	84,192	94,498	102,568	128,461	138,516	148,040	161,374	184,837
Hawaii	5,021	5,757	6,120	6,659	6,971	6,852	7,792	8,151	9,442	10,709
Idaho	6,897	7,979	8,818	9,293	9,575	11,711	14,548	15,947	17,787	20,526
Illinois	369,124	398,782	441,997	426,363	437,080	529,901	584,116	635,446	694,181	765,500
Indiana	103,906	112,181	114,813	119,450	127,362	151,091	166,012	181,388	190,940	209,094
Iowa	70,846	73,143	75,867	77,191	79,313	106,250	115,533	124,238	138,429	151,331
Kansas	23,585	24,174	24,668	25,179	27,636	34,323	38,289	41,709	45,424	50,296
Kentucky	33,276	35,918	36,465	37,899	39,470	48,322	53,117	59,683	66,972	77,122
Louisiana	56,389	60,416	61,093	64,102	66,576	79,049	88,563	98,935	107,937	119,696
Maine	21,329	23,165	23,856	25,027	27,528	33,984	37,717	42,278	46,423	52,210
Maryland	101,758	112,243	122,549	134,756	142,440	168,690	181,964	199,479	217,432	242,122
Massachusetts	606,629	649,329	688,039	671,954	745,214	899,993	977,385	1,050,860	1,159,172	1,311,780
Michigan	86,896	93,764	99,018	106,453	118,913	147,327	164,784	173,121	191,583	210,978
Minnesota	62,143	64,409	67,385	74,206	81,209	107,415	117,705	168,052	193,454	206,124
Mississippi	13,266	13,850	14,554	16,497	17,509	24,909	27,806	29,346	32,173	34,639
Missouri	143,860	152,421	161,466	175,145	187,608	228,357	255,602	284,166	309,986	344,278
Montana	3,675	4,107	4,282	4,420	4,621	6,007	6,672	7,206	7,630	8,653
Nebraska	29,259	31,348	31,638	33,564	36,827	40,638	46,150	48,730	54,612	59,832
Nevada	36	55	70	77	86	167	161	—	301	321
New Hampshire	40,692	45,071	50,431	54,917	58,745	69,873	76,005	84,759	89,376	102,193
New Jersey	130,224	147,154	155,601	165,929	177,041	216,073	239,585	245,935	263,962	284,805
New Mexico	4,257	5,757	7,505	6,783	7,729	8,762	10,667	11,555	11,756	12,499
New York	1,127,786	1,223,860	1,275,454	1,371,002	1,496,755	1,578,465	1,755,357	1,855,880	1,997,747	2,258,415
North Carolina	155,835	169,054	195,802	214,751	226,734	220,926	241,022	259,439	285,590	320,674
North Dakota	2,221	2,443	2,456	2,934	3,326	5,526	6,056	6,872	7,447	7,744
Ohio	209,484	221,693	236,335	251,400	268,950	310,586	337,396	366,790	397,991	435,466
Oklahoma	23,274	24,316	26,970	29,033	33,446	43,162	48,273	56,998	65,010	79,225
Oregon	26,446	28,212	30,189	31,985	35,078	43,833	50,641	57,826	64,337	74,388
Pennsylvania	424,389	440,561	469,725	497,032	537,904	663,593	716,832	790,475	873,079	959,777
Rhode Island	49,660	53,035	56,363	61,098	66,667	81,476	89,479	95,648	104,763	117,555
South Carolina	33,836	35,285	37,693	40,265	44,367	56,882	61,696	67,693	73,672	85,710
South Dakota	10,572	11,786	12,838	12,890	13,427	18,313	22,122	22,738	22,922	26,289
Tennessee	95,975	104,258	113,106	134,520	132,863	157,412	177,748	192,946	207,623	225,714
Texas	151,149	162,366	177,218	201,850	220,339	272,944	298,380	334,527	362,936	396,288
Utah	34,431	39,078	39,045	42,944	45,244	51,219	54,640	57,867	64,297	69,744
Vermont	22,009	24,858	29,613	29,932	31,011	37,229	41,131	43,440	48,770	52,334
Virginia	57,011	60,382	65,772	71,146	77,937	92,192	105,492	114,897	129,690	141,159
Washington	30,523	34,844	37,517	41,041	45,457	57,427	65,247	71,895	80,463	93,308
West Virginia	15,577	16,505	17,549	17,811	19,655	24,469	27,378	28,610	31,507	35,125
Wisconsin	69,718	74,574	82,310	92,792	93,189	107,123	126,309	130,041	145,567	163,985
Wyoming	—	—	—	—	—	—	—	—	—	—
U.S. Service Schools	—	—	—	—	—	—	—	—	—	—
Outlying areas	14,754	18,088	26,820	32,641	36,388	46,563	62,400	74,170	91,599	98,155
American Samoa	—	—	—	—	—	—	—	—	—	—
Federated States of Micronesia	—	—	—	—	—	—	—	—	—	—
Guam	—	—	—	—	—	—	—	—	—	—
Marshall Islands	—	—	—	—	—	—	—	—	—	—
Northern Marianas	—	—	—	—	—	—	—	—	—	—
Palau	—	—	—	—	—	—	—	—	—	—
Puerto Rico	14,754	18,088	26,820	32,641	36,388	46,563	62,400	74,170	91,599	98,155
Trust Territories	—	—	—	—	—	—	—	—	—	—
Virgin Islands	—	—	—	—	—	—	—	—	—	—

Table 90.—Educational and general expenditures (in current dollars) of private institutions of higher education, by state: 1969–70 to 1994–95—Continued

[Amounts in thousands]

State or other area	1979–80	1980–81	1981–82	1982–83	1983–84	1984–85	1985–86	1986–87	1987–88	1988–89
1	12	13	14	15	16	17	18	19	20	21
United States	$13,915,407	$15,900,792	$17,678,201	$19,221,796	$21,147,714	$23,187,778	$25,255,003	$28,596,121	$30,517,962	$33,358,469
Alabama	86,416	92,781	105,015	111,543	121,125	155,780	164,093	156,209	171,878	183,893
Alaska	5,204	5,772	6,408	7,359	7,255	8,959	9,106	12,427	14,046	17,606
Arizona	14,727	23,597	27,194	29,242	37,350	45,182	48,600	91,898	68,094	74,358
Arkansas	32,023	38,970	42,969	45,816	48,446	52,880	56,492	64,506	75,131	82,469
California	1,220,354	1,410,156	1,555,751	1,731,521	1,909,608	2,084,205	2,275,958	2,790,295	2,834,251	3,097,610
Colorado	88,321	101,740	115,066	124,844	135,354	143,523	142,218	193,792	171,366	186,540
Connecticut	411,877	463,791	515,591	565,950	620,216	676,790	733,144	803,781	885,475	971,844
Delaware	10,568	12,766	18,228	20,306	21,749	24,954	26,501	29,206	32,720	34,161
District of Columbia	471,554	521,714	597,344	636,930	683,777	737,607	803,566	871,087	944,373	999,347
Florida	300,226	353,522	382,450	421,276	464,580	507,374	553,391	661,732	721,415	809,958
Georgia	209,286	237,304	274,561	304,221	341,766	388,730	429,639	539,780	516,576	627,721
Hawaii	12,199	14,473	16,049	17,243	20,262	22,463	25,323	53,637	58,444	63,079
Idaho	23,488	27,049	29,228	31,867	33,836	36,985	37,736	41,804	48,823	52,283
Illinois	850,002	964,549	1,061,199	1,135,303	1,275,169	1,397,264	1,495,654	1,638,577	1,752,442	1,921,215
Indiana	233,006	277,514	307,285	330,336	362,379	393,153	426,813	487,960	536,059	575,208
Iowa	163,134	189,597	210,563	227,198	253,678	271,864	292,291	313,042	350,660	366,334
Kansas	56,707	66,384	71,580	75,143	82,534	82,185	87,719	104,658	102,082	109,069
Kentucky	84,032	94,118	104,696	115,791	123,707	141,130	159,293	170,217	188,790	191,932
Louisiana	128,817	150,584	169,618	187,465	209,890	202,727	221,928	245,088	272,899	301,663
Maine	58,105	65,564	74,173	82,385	86,824	98,201	106,912	120,581	130,265	144,309
Maryland	276,854	313,830	353,530	393,064	439,477	495,993	562,773	628,188	701,395	797,699
Massachusetts	1,508,291	1,744,928	1,921,195	2,115,308	2,331,372	2,556,877	2,817,687	3,113,886	3,353,461	3,615,146
Michigan	238,482	268,300	288,809	293,042	328,181	357,482	384,533	424,221	472,638	511,166
Minnesota	228,584	272,070	312,748	338,877	374,495	411,998	443,972	487,527	533,708	591,640
Mississippi	39,215	42,996	44,680	46,379	50,054	53,192	55,252	59,543	63,202	72,868
Missouri	381,582	435,941	490,887	539,833	582,856	650,586	713,411	767,672	856,538	931,499
Montana	9,441	12,244	14,987	16,082	16,232	17,402	18,565	17,936	19,811	24,179
Nebraska	74,729	87,005	96,925	112,968	119,234	128,665	138,929	148,340	163,951	180,547
Nevada	294	353	429	716	1,092	1,225	2,448	4,290	1,972	2,133
New Hampshire	115,645	138,845	155,783	174,767	192,086	208,447	230,657	250,879	266,989	288,569
New Jersey	318,366	360,639	400,537	423,414	462,748	503,680	540,245	576,347	618,980	677,999
New Mexico	13,327	15,878	15,561	16,922	17,638	18,991	19,678	14,018	17,857	20,369
New York	2,531,038	2,870,851	3,187,985	3,442,139	3,762,719	4,180,886	4,572,405	4,891,156	5,376,171	5,837,308
North Carolina	364,979	405,428	431,540	468,648	504,039	546,526	592,910	995,796	825,450	928,322
North Dakota	9,299	9,582	12,153	12,915	14,189	15,335	15,860	13,415	13,585	19,871
Ohio	479,878	548,989	603,849	650,484	711,429	775,274	833,879	951,304	1,003,382	1,081,053
Oklahoma	89,302	105,952	123,904	134,525	140,373	145,594	149,565	165,722	185,693	203,857
Oregon	82,992	94,768	106,424	111,172	125,548	137,961	149,289	164,362	182,383	201,591
Pennsylvania	1,086,562	1,234,971	1,390,334	1,507,827	1,670,860	1,830,108	2,033,015	2,230,583	2,426,577	2,627,790
Rhode Island	133,502	156,343	177,684	195,418	217,943	236,570	261,616	295,865	328,930	355,655
South Carolina	93,369	95,020	103,006	107,328	135,813	144,233	154,496	183,141	201,143	216,618
South Dakota	28,756	33,811	33,185	36,522	40,106	41,178	44,726	51,165	51,653	57,009
Tennessee	254,502	292,271	317,277	335,702	371,893	401,837	440,308	485,351	530,784	585,631
Texas	455,194	524,346	597,740	663,978	733,580	802,492	855,445	975,795	1,033,885	1,128,402
Utah	75,612	83,359	88,207	93,362	99,954	107,173	110,880	171,548	166,646	189,240
Vermont	61,421	71,119	83,190	90,255	101,002	114,653	126,299	150,889	162,501	189,351
Virginia	167,093	186,058	211,658	230,999	256,585	280,057	313,055	353,475	392,152	454,865
Washington	106,292	119,288	137,847	152,325	166,301	181,212	189,575	207,844	230,898	257,843
West Virginia	43,157	44,204	48,774	50,487	53,465	59,271	60,900	67,173	63,849	74,375
Wisconsin	187,605	219,100	242,023	264,602	286,944	310,923	326,254	357,437	393,616	422,644
Wyoming	—	360	380	—	—	—	—	—	977	2,374	2,628
U.S. Service Schools	—	—	—	—	—	—	—	—	—	—
Outlying areas	106,674	115,102	134,786	145,471	167,793	183,258	189,080	199,075	220,228	232,743
American Samoa	—	—	—	—	—	—	—	—	—	—
Federated States of Micronesia	—	—	—	—	—	—	—	—	—	—
Guam	—	—	—	—	—	—	—	—	—	—
Marshall Islands	—	—	—	—	—	—	—	—	—	—
Northern Marianas	—	—	—	—	—	—	—	—	—	—
Palau	—	—	—	—	—	—	—	—	—	—
Puerto Rico	106,674	115,102	134,786	145,471	167,793	183,258	189,080	199,075	220,228	232,743
Trust Territories	—	—	—	—	—	—	—	—	—	—
Virgin Islands	—	—	—	—	—	—	—	—	—	—

Table 90.—Educational and general expenditures (in current dollars) of private institutions of higher education, by state: 1969–70 to 1994–95—Continued

[Amounts in thousands]

State or other area	1989–90	1990–91	1991–92	1992–93	1993–94	1994–95	Percentage change 1969–70 to 1994–95	1984–85 to 1989–90	1989–90 to 1994–95	1984–85 to 1994–95
1	22	23	24	25	26	27	28	29	30	31
United States	$36,421,118	$39,744,472	$43,012,623	$45,766,989	$48,885,124	$51,984,234	860.1	57.1	42.7	124.2
Alabama	200,278	212,538	229,670	252,259	265,046	273,268	777.1	28.6	36.4	75.4
Alaska	17,447	19,375	15,851	18,687	18,140	15,631	623.9	94.7	−10.4	74.5
Arizona	80,478	110,015	86,087	100,150	111,414	122,573	2,114.1	78.1	52.3	171.3
Arkansas	90,390	95,560	98,442	103,347	108,969	118,323	925.6	70.9	30.9	123.8
California	3,191,054	3,484,709	3,836,270	4,051,762	4,366,131	4,630,342	1,101.3	53.1	45.1	122.2
Colorado	223,016	257,003	269,386	279,956	297,087	312,444	779.4	55.4	40.1	117.7
Connecticut	1,058,226	1,143,220	1,224,643	1,280,969	1,363,083	1,441,297	771.5	56.4	36.2	113.0
Delaware	39,515	21,598	24,741	26,575	29,040	30,471	849.7	58.4	−22.9	22.1
District of Columbia	1,100,263	1,178,178	1,246,366	1,311,616	1,375,811	1,463,154	874.9	49.2	33.0	98.4
Florida	911,193	1,001,000	1,089,712	1,193,708	1,234,246	1,329,012	1,249.3	79.6	45.9	161.9
Georgia	707,446	788,200	886,314	981,355	1,122,545	1,188,358	1,527.5	82.0	68.0	205.7
Hawaii	30,605	36,528	36,124	72,609	76,909	81,060	1,514.5	36.2	164.9	260.9
Idaho	54,790	59,252	65,018	72,006	82,923	86,269	1,150.9	48.1	57.5	133.3
Illinois	2,115,533	2,349,405	2,544,490	2,698,324	2,936,263	3,186,567	763.3	51.4	50.6	128.1
Indiana	633,221	700,346	736,784	782,734	831,223	895,861	762.2	61.1	41.5	127.9
Iowa	408,098	445,631	501,547	534,230	573,136	595,823	741.0	50.1	46.0	119.2
Kansas	116,651	124,578	126,939	136,036	149,127	157,710	568.7	41.9	35.2	91.9
Kentucky	208,042	236,191	255,870	263,722	275,986	291,198	775.1	47.4	40.0	106.3
Louisiana	341,168	372,431	397,191	439,834	459,780	523,694	828.7	68.3	53.5	158.3
Maine	155,562	167,618	176,530	187,523	199,895	210,350	886.2	58.4	35.2	114.2
Maryland	895,903	987,405	1,048,953	1,133,491	1,217,678	1,299,953	1,177.5	80.6	45.1	162.1
Massachusetts	3,907,555	4,278,151	4,600,897	4,874,439	5,122,411	5,430,455	795.2	52.8	39.0	112.4
Michigan	562,650	618,422	651,408	696,518	730,458	759,066	773.5	57.4	34.9	112.3
Minnesota	653,993	625,497	654,953	678,472	679,001	732,714	1,079.1	58.7	12.0	77.8
Mississippi	81,782	88,305	96,217	101,895	108,547	115,582	771.2	53.7	41.3	117.3
Missouri	1,064,937	1,186,195	1,306,990	1,347,644	1,453,221	1,579,030	997.6	63.7	48.3	142.7
Montana	23,716	29,165	28,567	33,873	38,509	44,086	1,099.6	36.3	85.9	153.3
Nebraska	200,268	219,054	242,660	258,485	271,942	290,697	893.5	55.7	45.2	125.9
Nevada	3,566	4,066	5,127	4,666	5,998	7,294	20,161.3	191.2	104.6	495.6
New Hampshire	313,098	355,056	374,323	395,395	426,736	442,671	987.9	50.2	41.4	112.4
New Jersey	741,565	789,649	863,322	926,131	980,224	1,022,274	685.0	47.2	37.9	103.0
New Mexico	24,967	28,754	39,813	28,659	35,079	37,509	781.2	31.5	50.2	97.5
New York	6,242,098	6,735,931	7,401,300	7,837,705	8,315,046	8,721,147	673.3	49.3	39.7	108.6
North Carolina	1,047,477	1,123,378	1,255,073	1,313,943	1,417,518	1,515,305	872.4	91.7	44.7	177.3
North Dakota	21,922	24,033	29,719	28,821	31,776	32,912	1,382.0	43.0	50.1	114.6
Ohio	1,207,973	1,308,048	1,403,786	1,486,111	1,586,086	1,673,414	698.8	55.8	38.5	115.8
Oklahoma	222,843	239,088	220,403	230,661	248,299	263,719	1,033.1	53.1	18.3	81.1
Oregon	227,291	247,671	256,162	275,352	299,529	327,566	1,138.6	64.8	44.1	137.4
Pennsylvania	2,910,308	3,242,842	3,521,644	3,802,781	4,115,506	4,386,385	933.6	59.0	50.7	139.7
Rhode Island	409,784	437,800	476,062	504,274	545,057	575,255	1,058.4	73.2	40.4	143.2
South Carolina	237,042	258,540	225,437	245,689	268,292	282,443	734.8	64.3	19.2	95.8
South Dakota	69,138	74,859	63,351	56,780	59,358	62,863	494.6	67.9	−9.1	52.7
Tennessee	651,714	706,976	785,347	827,801	894,506	955,718	895.8	62.2	46.6	137.8
Texas	1,241,102	1,365,275	1,460,510	1,540,238	1,653,269	1,764,618	1,067.5	54.7	42.2	119.9
Utah	205,138	223,238	257,271	313,342	317,681	333,683	869.1	91.4	62.7	211.4
Vermont	209,420	229,548	250,999	261,364	232,565	250,310	1,037.3	82.7	19.5	118.3
Virginia	517,098	581,094	607,724	645,752	702,430	766,327	1,244.2	84.6	48.2	173.6
Washington	284,341	316,014	345,756	375,031	413,941	448,823	1,370.5	56.9	57.8	147.7
West Virginia	83,036	93,399	98,830	112,959	126,231	153,757	887.1	40.1	85.2	159.4
Wisconsin	472,313	519,270	585,465	633,564	701,051	746,036	970.1	51.9	58.0	139.9
Wyoming	4,104	4,370	6,578	7,752	10,426	9,219	—	—	124.7	—
U.S. Service Schools	—	—	—	—	—	—	—	—	—	—
Outlying areas	179,105	256,576	267,789	290,189	320,304	343,782	2,230.0	−2.3	91.9	87.6
American Samoa	—	—	—	—	—	—	—	—	—	—
Federated States of Micronesia	—	—	—	—	—	—	—	—	—	—
Guam	—	—	—	—	—	—	—	—	—	—
Marshall Islands	—	—	—	—	—	—	—	—	—	—
Northern Marianas	—	—	—	—	—	—	—	—	—	—
Palau	—	—	—	—	—	—	—	—	—	—
Puerto Rico	179,105	256,576	267,789	290,189	320,304	343,782	2,230.0	−2.3	91.9	87.6
Trust Territories	—	—	—	—	—	—	—	—	—	—
Virgin Islands	—	—	—	—	—	—	—	—	—	—

—Data not available or not applicable.

NOTE.—Percentages reflect mergers, openings, and closures of institutions over time. Some data have been revised from previously published figures. Because of rounding, details may not add to totals.

SOURCE: U.S. Department of Education, National Center for Education Statistics, Higher Education General Information Survey (HEGIS), "Financial Statistics of Institutions of Higher Education" surveys; and Integrated Postsecondary Education Data System (IPEDS), "Financial Statistics" surveys. (This table was prepared January 1998.)

Table 91.—Educational and general expenditures (in constant 1994–95 dollars [1]) of private institutions of higher education, by state: 1969–70 to 1994–95

[Amounts in thousands]

State or other area	1969–70	1970–71	1971–72	1972–73	1973–74	1974–75	1975–76	1976–77	1977–78	1978–79
1	2	3	4	5	6	7	8	9	10	11
United States	$23,056,206	$23,455,877	$23,896,329	$24,082,263	$24,204,706	$26,191,023	$27,108,962	$27,771,719	$28,437,047	$29,447,430
Alabama	132,674	131,284	130,605	141,239	147,872	168,922	179,295	175,936	185,398	186,642
Alaska	9,194	9,186	15,803	11,184	11,338	11,452	10,948	9,485	10,680	13,881
Arizona	23,573	25,925	25,571	31,868	26,278	31,115	27,601	29,893	30,479	30,851
Arkansas	49,125	51,533	50,153	54,925	57,691	61,663	61,268	64,042	65,881	69,297
California	1,641,314	1,746,441	1,851,095	1,923,895	1,839,271	2,166,816	2,251,688	2,380,102	2,513,104	2,568,108
Colorado	151,297	155,348	152,731	157,475	155,275	166,120	168,128	168,975	176,842	188,002
Connecticut	704,201	725,703	728,541	734,509	736,871	813,992	829,862	856,873	861,837	870,293
Delaware	13,663	17,202	17,245	17,270	16,924	20,608	20,405	21,825	22,006	22,051
District of Columbia	639,079	700,507	778,440	823,085	854,784	907,012	947,841	996,432	977,136	1,001,046
Florida	419,421	444,735	454,289	468,196	490,012	559,880	571,654	604,273	619,773	633,261
Georgia	310,932	318,228	319,664	340,353	345,731	397,923	403,087	404,883	413,138	440,987
Hawaii	21,380	22,999	23,238	23,983	23,499	21,224	22,675	22,292	24,174	25,549
Idaho	29,367	31,878	33,479	33,471	32,274	36,277	42,335	43,615	45,537	48,971
Illinois	1,571,816	1,593,235	1,678,190	1,535,637	1,473,283	1,641,426	1,699,797	1,737,919	1,777,187	1,826,342
Indiana	442,455	448,190	435,928	430,224	429,305	468,020	483,100	496,090	488,828	498,861
Iowa	301,677	292,224	288,053	278,018	267,343	329,120	336,205	339,786	354,394	361,049
Kansas	100,431	96,581	93,660	90,688	93,153	106,320	111,423	114,072	116,292	119,998
Kentucky	141,698	143,502	138,450	136,502	133,042	149,681	154,572	163,231	171,457	183,999
Louisiana	240,117	241,378	231,961	230,878	224,410	244,861	257,722	270,583	276,333	285,572
Maine	90,825	92,549	90,577	90,142	92,790	105,268	109,759	115,628	118,848	124,564
Maryland	433,308	448,440	465,298	485,352	480,127	522,534	529,520	545,567	556,653	577,658
Massachusetts	2,583,165	2,594,231	2,612,374	2,420,187	2,511,925	2,787,825	2,844,225	2,874,059	2,967,622	3,129,664
Michigan	370,022	374,612	375,956	383,412	400,824	456,360	479,528	473,479	490,475	503,355
Minnesota	264,620	257,329	255,851	267,270	273,733	332,729	342,525	459,616	495,266	491,774
Mississippi	56,491	55,336	55,260	59,417	59,019	77,159	80,917	80,260	82,366	82,642
Missouri	612,591	608,962	613,062	630,823	632,378	707,359	743,811	777,182	793,602	821,385
Montana	15,649	16,408	16,257	15,918	15,576	18,607	19,416	19,708	19,533	20,645
Nebraska	124,592	125,242	120,125	120,888	124,135	125,880	134,297	133,275	139,814	142,747
Nevada	153	221	265	277	288	518	469	—	772	765
New Hampshire	173,275	180,069	191,479	197,795	198,013	216,440	221,177	231,813	228,814	243,812
New Jersey	554,523	587,917	590,792	597,628	596,761	669,310	697,200	672,623	675,774	679,493
New Mexico	18,125	23,002	28,496	24,430	26,051	27,141	31,042	31,603	30,098	29,821
New York	4,802,371	4,889,624	4,842,694	4,937,954	5,045,173	4,889,462	5,108,149	5,075,756	5,114,476	5,388,163
North Carolina	663,580	675,413	743,427	773,472	764,262	684,342	701,383	709,555	731,146	765,070
North Dakota	9,456	9,760	9,326	10,568	11,210	17,118	17,623	18,794	19,065	18,476
Ohio	892,029	885,721	897,327	905,471	906,562	962,072	981,833	1,003,156	1,018,905	1,038,943
Oklahoma	99,106	97,148	102,400	104,568	112,738	133,699	140,475	155,888	166,434	189,015
Oregon	112,614	112,713	114,623	115,202	118,238	135,776	147,366	158,151	164,711	177,476
Pennsylvania	1,807,144	1,760,152	1,783,471	1,790,167	1,813,135	2,055,550	2,086,005	2,161,918	2,235,190	2,289,851
Rhode Island	211,464	211,887	214,000	220,058	224,718	252,382	260,386	261,592	268,205	280,465
South Carolina	144,080	140,971	143,115	145,021	149,549	176,199	179,537	185,138	188,609	204,489
South Dakota	45,018	47,089	48,744	46,426	45,260	56,725	64,377	62,189	58,684	62,722
Tennessee	408,685	416,537	429,444	484,503	447,848	487,601	517,253	527,700	531,539	538,513
Texas	643,626	648,693	672,867	727,007	742,706	845,473	868,295	914,919	929,161	945,470
Utah	146,615	156,126	148,248	154,673	152,506	158,657	159,004	158,264	164,609	166,396
Vermont	93,720	99,314	112,435	107,807	104,529	115,321	119,694	118,807	124,856	124,859
Virginia	242,765	241,243	249,726	256,249	262,707	285,575	306,984	314,237	332,022	336,778
Washington	129,973	139,210	142,445	147,818	153,224	177,886	189,870	196,631	205,994	222,617
West Virginia	66,330	65,941	66,632	64,149	66,251	75,797	79,671	78,247	80,661	83,803
Wisconsin	296,877	297,941	312,518	334,210	314,117	331,826	367,565	355,658	372,668	391,238
Wyoming	—	—	—	—	—	—	—	—	—	—
U.S. Service Schools	—	—	—	—	—	—	—	—	—	—
Outlying areas	62,828	72,264	101,831	117,563	122,655	144,235	181,587	202,851	234,504	234,179
American Samoa	—	—	—	—	—	—	—	—	—	—
Federated States of Micronesia	—	—	—	—	—	—	—	—	—	—
Guam	—	—	—	—	—	—	—	—	—	—
Marshall Islands	—	—	—	—	—	—	—	—	—	—
Northern Marianas	—	—	—	—	—	—	—	—	—	—
Palau	—	—	—	—	—	—	—	—	—	—
Puerto Rico	62,828	72,264	101,831	117,563	122,655	144,235	181,587	202,851	234,504	234,179
Trust Territories	—	—	—	—	—	—	—	—	—	—
Virgin Islands	—	—	—	—	—	—	—	—	—	—

Table 91.—Educational and general expenditures (in constant 1994–95 dollars [1]) of private institutions of higher education, by state: 1969–70 to 1994–95—Continued

[Amounts in thousands]

State or other area	1979–80	1980–81	1981–82	1982–83	1983–84	1984–85	1985–86	1986–87	1987–88	1988–89
1	12	13	14	15	16	17	18	19	20	21
United States	**$30,200,923**	**$31,171,482**	**$31,666,383**	**$32,331,062**	**$33,941,274**	**$35,200,218**	**$36,525,292**	**$39,783,851**	**$40,706,751**	**$42,250,712**
Alabama	187,551	181,885	188,110	187,615	194,401	236,482	237,321	217,323	229,262	232,912
Alaska	11,293	11,315	11,478	12,377	11,645	13,601	13,169	17,289	18,736	22,299
Arizona	31,961	46,258	48,711	49,186	59,945	68,588	70,288	127,852	90,827	94,180
Arkansas	69,500	76,395	76,968	77,062	77,753	80,275	81,703	89,743	100,214	104,453
California	2,648,561	2,764,432	2,786,766	2,912,418	3,064,848	3,163,928	3,291,626	3,881,948	3,780,500	3,923,329
Colorado	191,685	199,449	206,114	209,987	217,238	217,876	205,684	269,610	228,578	236,266
Connecticut	893,907	909,204	923,562	951,928	995,423	1,027,402	1,060,317	1,118,247	1,181,101	1,230,905
Delaware	22,937	25,027	32,652	34,155	34,906	37,881	38,328	40,633	43,644	43,268
District of Columbia	1,023,423	1,022,753	1,070,002	1,071,317	1,097,436	1,119,725	1,162,164	1,211,884	1,259,663	1,265,739
Florida	651,588	693,035	685,071	708,586	745,634	770,219	800,347	920,622	962,268	1,025,865
Georgia	454,219	465,203	491,812	511,700	548,522	590,111	621,370	750,959	689,041	795,050
Hawaii	26,476	28,373	28,748	29,003	32,520	34,100	36,624	74,622	77,956	79,894
Idaho	50,976	53,027	52,355	53,601	54,305	56,145	54,576	58,159	65,123	66,220
Illinois	1,844,778	1,890,876	1,900,891	1,909,580	2,046,598	2,121,118	2,163,104	2,279,641	2,337,516	2,433,347
Indiana	505,697	544,031	550,430	555,625	581,605	596,826	617,283	678,866	715,029	728,540
Iowa	354,054	371,681	377,175	382,147	407,144	412,703	422,729	435,514	467,732	463,986
Kansas	123,073	130,137	128,220	126,391	132,464	124,761	126,865	145,604	136,164	138,143
Kentucky	182,376	184,507	187,539	194,760	198,546	214,242	230,380	236,812	251,819	243,095
Louisiana	279,574	295,200	303,831	315,316	336,865	307,750	320,966	340,974	364,009	382,077
Maine	126,107	128,530	132,864	138,572	139,348	149,074	154,622	167,756	173,756	182,777
Maryland	600,863	615,223	633,267	661,134	705,343	752,943	813,916	873,955	935,565	1,010,339
Massachusetts	3,273,478	3,420,710	3,441,374	3,557,947	3,741,763	3,881,468	4,075,108	4,332,139	4,473,054	4,578,822
Michigan	517,583	525,968	517,334	492,896	526,719	542,676	556,134	590,190	630,434	647,425
Minnesota	496,101	533,359	560,216	569,991	601,050	625,434	642,099	678,263	711,893	749,352
Mississippi	85,109	84,289	80,034	78,009	80,335	80,749	79,908	82,838	84,302	92,293
Missouri	828,156	854,607	879,310	907,999	935,462	987,623	1,031,777	1,068,011	1,142,503	1,179,805
Montana	20,491	24,003	26,845	27,049	26,052	26,417	26,850	24,953	26,425	30,625
Nebraska	162,186	170,562	173,618	190,012	191,365	195,321	200,927	206,375	218,688	228,674
Nevada	638	691	769	1,204	1,753	1,859	3,540	5,968	2,631	2,702
New Hampshire	250,986	272,189	279,049	293,957	308,290	316,433	333,590	349,031	356,126	365,492
New Jersey	690,957	706,988	717,469	712,183	742,693	764,612	781,334	801,833	825,634	858,730
New Mexico	28,924	31,127	27,874	28,462	28,308	28,829	28,460	19,502	23,819	25,799
New York	5,493,168	5,627,938	5,710,533	5,789,678	6,039,021	6,346,796	6,612,885	6,804,735	7,171,071	7,393,338
North Carolina	792,121	794,790	773,003	788,266	808,963	829,655	857,501	1,385,384	1,101,036	1,175,781
North Dakota	20,181	18,784	21,770	21,723	22,773	23,279	22,938	18,664	18,121	25,168
Ohio	1,041,490	1,076,224	1,081,654	1,094,114	1,141,816	1,176,906	1,206,005	1,323,485	1,338,373	1,369,225
Oklahoma	193,813	207,705	221,946	226,271	225,293	221,018	216,309	230,558	247,689	258,199
Oregon	180,119	185,780	190,634	186,991	201,500	209,431	215,911	228,666	243,274	255,328
Pennsylvania	2,358,189	2,421,004	2,490,460	2,536,166	2,681,666	2,778,197	2,940,268	3,103,260	3,236,719	3,328,270
Rhode Island	289,741	306,491	318,279	328,693	349,790	359,125	378,365	411,618	438,747	450,460
South Carolina	202,641	186,274	184,512	180,526	217,975	218,953	223,441	254,792	268,297	274,361
South Dakota	62,410	66,281	59,443	61,429	64,369	62,510	64,686	71,182	68,898	72,206
Tennessee	552,352	572,960	568,328	564,650	596,874	610,009	636,799	675,236	707,993	741,740
Texas	987,918	1,027,914	1,070,712	1,116,810	1,177,368	1,218,223	1,237,195	1,357,557	1,379,059	1,429,197
Utah	164,102	163,415	158,002	157,035	160,423	162,693	160,361	238,663	222,283	239,685
Vermont	133,304	139,420	149,015	151,809	162,105	174,049	182,661	209,922	216,754	239,826
Virginia	362,646	364,743	379,137	388,540	411,809	425,141	452,759	491,766	523,076	576,116
Washington	230,688	233,849	246,920	256,211	266,906	275,089	274,175	289,159	307,987	326,575
West Virginia	93,665	86,656	87,367	84,919	85,809	89,977	88,077	93,454	85,166	94,201
Wisconsin	407,163	429,517	433,528	445,061	460,535	471,997	471,849	497,278	525,030	535,307
Wyoming	—	706	682	—	—	—	—	—	1,360	3,167	3,328
U.S. Service Schools	—	—	—	—	—	—	—	—	—	—
Outlying areas	231,516	225,642	241,437	244,682	269,302	278,195	273,459	276,959	293,754	294,784
American Samoa	—	—	—	—	—	—	—	—	—	—
Federated States of Micronesia	—	—	—	—	—	—	—	—	—	—
Guam	—	—	—	—	—	—	—	—	—	—
Marshall Islands	—	—	—	—	—	—	—	—	—	—
Northern Marianas	—	—	—	—	—	—	—	—	—	—
Palau	—	—	—	—	—	—	—	—	—	—
Puerto Rico	231,516	225,642	241,437	244,682	269,302	278,195	273,459	276,959	293,754	294,784
Trust Territories	—	—	—	—	—	—	—	—	—	—
Virgin Islands	—	—	—	—	—	—	—	—	—	—

Table 91.—Educational and general expenditures (in constant 1994–95 dollars [1]) of private institutions of higher education, by state: 1969–70 to 1994–95—Continued

[Amounts in thousands]

State or other area	1989–90	1990–91	1991–92	1992–93	1993–94	1994–95	Percentage change			
							1969–70 to 1994–95	1984–85 to 1989–90	1989–90 to 1994–95	1984–85 to 1994–95
1	22	23	24	25	26	27	28	29	30	31
United States	$43,508,751	$45,108,099	$47,162,472	$48,752,423	$50,351,977	$51,984,234	125.5	23.6	19.5	47.7
Alabama	239,252	241,221	251,829	268,714	272,999	273,268	106.0	1.2	14.2	15.6
Alaska	20,842	21,990	17,380	19,905	18,685	15,631	70.0	53.2	−25.0	14.9
Arizona	96,140	124,861	94,393	106,683	114,757	122,573	420.0	40.2	27.5	78.7
Arkansas	107,980	108,456	107,940	110,089	112,238	118,323	140.9	34.5	9.6	47.4
California	3,812,040	3,954,980	4,206,392	4,316,063	4,497,142	4,630,342	182.1	20.5	21.5	46.3
Colorado	266,415	291,686	295,376	298,217	306,001	312,444	106.5	22.3	17.3	43.4
Connecticut	1,264,160	1,297,500	1,342,796	1,364,528	1,403,984	1,441,297	104.7	23.0	14.0	40.3
Delaware	47,205	24,512	27,128	28,309	29,912	30,471	123.0	24.6	−35.4	−19.6
District of Columbia	1,314,376	1,337,177	1,366,615	1,397,174	1,417,094	1,463,154	128.9	17.4	11.3	30.7
Florida	1,088,513	1,136,088	1,194,848	1,271,575	1,271,281	1,329,012	216.9	41.3	22.1	72.5
Georgia	845,117	894,570	971,826	1,045,370	1,156,228	1,188,358	282.2	43.2	40.6	101.4
Hawaii	36,561	41,457	39,609	77,346	79,217	81,060	279.1	7.2	121.7	137.7
Idaho	65,452	67,248	71,291	76,703	85,411	86,269	193.8	16.6	31.8	53.7
Illinois	2,527,221	2,666,464	2,789,982	2,874,339	3,024,369	3,186,567	102.7	19.1	26.1	50.2
Indiana	756,447	794,860	807,868	833,793	856,164	895,861	102.5	26.7	18.4	50.1
Iowa	487,515	505,770	549,936	569,078	590,333	595,823	97.5	18.1	22.2	44.4
Kansas	139,351	141,390	139,186	144,910	153,602	157,710	57.0	11.7	13.2	26.4
Kentucky	248,528	268,066	280,556	280,925	284,267	291,198	105.5	16.0	17.2	35.9
Louisiana	407,560	422,692	435,512	468,525	473,576	523,694	118.1	32.4	28.5	70.2
Maine	185,835	190,239	193,561	199,756	205,893	210,350	131.6	24.7	13.2	41.1
Maryland	1,070,247	1,120,658	1,150,156	1,207,430	1,254,216	1,299,953	200.0	42.1	21.5	72.6
Massachusetts	4,667,974	4,855,500	5,044,790	5,192,405	5,276,115	5,430,455	110.2	20.3	16.3	39.9
Michigan	672,143	701,880	714,256	741,953	752,376	759,066	105.1	23.9	12.9	39.9
Minnesota	781,262	709,909	718,143	722,730	699,375	732,714	176.9	24.9	−6.2	17.2
Mississippi	97,697	100,222	105,500	108,542	111,804	115,582	104.6	21.0	18.3	43.1
Missouri	1,272,177	1,346,276	1,433,088	1,435,552	1,496,827	1,579,030	157.8	28.8	24.1	59.9
Montana	28,332	33,101	31,323	36,083	39,664	44,086	181.7	7.2	55.6	66.9
Nebraska	239,240	248,616	266,071	275,346	280,102	290,697	133.3	22.5	21.5	48.8
Nevada	4,260	4,614	5,622	4,970	6,178	7,294	4,658.1	129.1	71.2	292.4
New Hampshire	374,028	402,972	410,438	421,187	439,540	442,671	155.5	18.2	18.4	39.9
New Jersey	885,875	896,214	946,615	986,543	1,009,636	1,022,274	84.4	15.9	15.4	33.7
New Mexico	29,825	32,635	43,654	30,528	36,132	37,509	106.9	3.5	25.8	30.1
New York	7,456,824	7,644,964	8,115,376	8,348,967	8,564,548	8,721,147	81.6	17.5	17.0	37.4
North Carolina	1,251,319	1,274,981	1,376,162	1,399,653	1,460,052	1,515,305	128.4	50.8	21.1	82.6
North Dakota	26,189	27,277	32,586	30,701	32,729	32,912	248.0	12.5	25.7	41.4
Ohio	1,443,047	1,484,573	1,539,223	1,583,051	1,633,678	1,673,414	87.6	22.6	16.0	42.2
Oklahoma	266,209	271,353	241,667	245,707	255,749	263,719	166.1	20.4	−0.9	19.3
Oregon	271,523	281,095	280,876	293,314	308,517	327,566	190.9	29.6	20.6	56.4
Pennsylvania	3,476,660	3,680,473	3,861,411	4,050,841	4,238,996	4,386,385	142.7	25.1	26.2	57.9
Rhode Island	489,528	496,882	521,993	537,169	561,413	575,255	172.0	36.3	17.5	60.2
South Carolina	283,171	293,430	247,188	261,716	276,342	282,443	96.0	29.3	−0.3	29.0
South Dakota	82,593	84,962	69,463	60,484	61,140	62,863	39.6	32.1	−23.9	0.6
Tennessee	778,539	802,384	861,118	881,799	921,347	955,718	133.9	27.6	22.8	56.7
Texas	1,482,624	1,549,523	1,601,420	1,640,710	1,702,877	1,764,618	174.2	21.7	19.0	44.9
Utah	245,058	253,365	282,093	333,781	327,213	333,683	127.6	50.6	36.2	105.1
Vermont	250,173	260,526	275,216	278,413	239,543	250,310	167.1	43.7	0.1	43.8
Virginia	617,726	659,515	666,357	687,875	723,507	766,327	215.7	45.3	24.1	80.3
Washington	339,675	358,661	379,115	399,495	426,362	448,823	245.3	23.5	32.1	63.2
West Virginia	99,195	106,004	108,366	120,327	130,018	153,757	131.8	10.2	55.0	70.9
Wisconsin	564,226	589,347	641,950	674,893	722,087	746,036	151.3	19.5	32.2	58.1
Wyoming	4,902	4,959	7,213	8,258	10,739	9,219	—	—	88.1	—
U.S. Service Schools	—	—	—	—	—	—	—	—	—	—
Outlying areas	213,959	291,201	293,625	309,118	329,915	343,782	447.2	−23.1	60.7	23.6
American Samoa	—	—	—	—	—	—	—	—	—	—
Federated States of Micronesia	—	—	—	—	—	—	—	—	—	—
Guam	—	—	—	—	—	—	—	—	—	—
Marshall Islands	—	—	—	—	—	—	—	—	—	—
Northern Marianas	—	—	—	—	—	—	—	—	—	—
Palau	—	—	—	—	—	—	—	—	—	—
Puerto Rico	213,959	291,201	293,625	309,118	329,915	343,782	447.2	−23.1	60.7	23.6
Trust Territories	—	—	—	—	—	—	—	—	—	—
Virgin Islands	—	—	—	—	—	—	—	—	—	—

[1] Based on the Higher Education Price Index, prepared by Research Associates of Washington. These data do not reflect differences in inflation rates from state to state.
—Data not available or not applicable.

NOTE.—Percentages reflect mergers, openings, and closures of institutions over time. Some data have been revised from previously published figures. Because of rounding, details may not add to totals.

SOURCE: U.S. Department of Education, National Center for Education Statistics, Higher Education General Information Survey (HEGIS), "Financial Statistics of Institutions of Higher Education" surveys; and Integrated Postsecondary Education Data System (IPEDS), "Financial Statistics" surveys. (This table was prepared January 1998.)

Table 92.—Public libraries, books and serial volumes, annual attendance, and reference transactions, by state: 1992 and 1994

State	Number of public libraries		Number of books and serial volumes (in thousands)		Number of books and serial volumes per capita		Library visits per capita[1]		Public library reference transactions per capita[2]		Circulation per capita, 1994
	1992	1994	1992	1994	1992	1994	1992	1994	1992	1994	
1	2	3	4	5	6	7	8	9	10	11	12
United States	8,946	8,921	642,617	671,815	2.7	2.7	4.0	4.1	1.0	1.1	6.4
Alabama	204	207	6,835	7,372	1.8	2.0	—	3.3	0.5	0.7	3.9
Alaska	85	87	1,855	1,867	3.2	3.1	4.7	3.8	0.7	0.7	6.3
Arizona	39	39	7,225	7,311	1.9	2.0	4.5	4.7	1.1	1.3	6.8
Arkansas	36	35	4,607	4,714	2.0	2.1	2.4	2.3	0.4	0.4	4.0
California	168	170	58,136	59,072	1.9	1.9	4.3	4.0	1.3	1.3	4.6
Colorado	120	120	8,977	9,522	2.7	2.6	3.9	4.3	1.0	1.2	7.8
Connecticut	194	194	12,523	12,854	4.1	4.3	6.5	6.3	1.1	1.1	8.1
Delaware	29	29	1,209	1,255	1.8	1.9	3.1	3.3	0.5	0.6	4.3
District of Columbia	1	1	1,881	2,165	3.1	3.6	4.0	3.5	1.8	1.6	3.1
Florida	110	97	20,954	21,961	1.7	1.7	—	—	1.4	—	5.1
Georgia	54	54	13,557	12,724	2.0	1.8	2.7	2.8	0.7	0.6	4.4
Hawaii	1	1	3,011	2,875	2.7	2.3	3.1	2.9	1.1	1.3	5.7
Idaho	107	107	2,778	2,997	3.5	3.3	4.8	4.9	0.8	0.9	7.9
Illinois	607	606	33,464	35,416	3.3	3.4	5.4	5.3	1.2	1.3	7.5
Indiana	238	238	18,732	19,653	3.6	3.7	5.6	5.7	1.0	1.1	9.6
Iowa	517	518	10,562	10,904	3.8	3.9	5.0	5.2	0.7	0.6	8.9
Kansas	320	324	8,333	9,016	4.1	4.4	5.5	5.1	1.1	1.3	9.2
Kentucky	116	116	7,123	7,160	2.0	2.0	2.6	2.6	0.3	0.3	5.1
Louisiana	64	65	9,133	9,659	2.1	2.2	2.2	2.3	0.7	0.6	4.4
Maine	226	232	4,790	4,874	4.9	4.9	4.9	—	—	—	7.6
Maryland	24	24	14,013	13,086	3.0	2.7	4.4	4.5	1.3	1.1	9.1
Massachusetts	374	373	27,203	28,015	4.6	4.7	—	—	—	0.7	6.9
Michigan	377	380	23,359	26,297	2.5	2.9	3.2	3.8	0.8	0.9	5.4
Minnesota	133	132	11,820	12,513	2.7	2.8	4.6	4.6	1.3	1.4	9.4
Mississippi	47	47	5,000	5,079	1.9	2.0	2.4	2.5	0.4	0.4	3.1
Missouri	143	147	18,107	19,475	3.8	4.0	4.1	4.3	0.6	0.9	7.8
Montana	83	82	2,480	2,541	3.1	3.1	3.5	3.5	0.6	0.7	6.0
Nebraska	269	269	4,859	4,705	3.8	3.8	—	—	—	—	7.8
Nevada	26	23	2,325	2,993	1.7	2.0	3.1	3.1	0.8	0.7	4.8
New Hampshire	232	229	4,695	4,825	5.5	4.4	6.1	4.8	0.9	0.7	7.5
New Jersey	310	309	28,263	29,234	3.7	3.8	4.9	4.7	0.8	0.9	5.8
New Mexico	74	73	4,053	3,765	3.7	3.3	—	—	—	0.8	6.5
New York	761	741	64,446	69,875	3.6	4.2	4.6	4.9	1.2	1.6	7.1
North Carolina	74	74	12,491	13,468	1.9	2.0	3.1	3.3	0.8	0.8	5.9
North Dakota	90	78	1,919	1,890	3.6	3.5	4.1	5.4	0.6	—	7.3
Ohio	250	250	38,595	40,400	3.5	3.6	5.1	5.0	1.4	1.6	11.8
Oklahoma	110	112	5,518	5,635	2.2	2.2	—	3.9	0.8	0.7	6.4
Oregon	125	124	6,382	6,479	2.3	2.4	—	—	—	0.8	9.6
Pennsylvania	446	445	23,848	24,661	2.1	2.1	2.9	3.0	0.7	0.7	4.7
Rhode Island	51	51	3,633	3,873	3.9	4.1	5.4	5.4	0.0	1.0	6.2
South Carolina	40	40	5,833	6,337	1.7	1.7	2.5	2.9	0.7	1.1	4.3
South Dakota	116	113	2,244	2,277	3.9	3.4	4.6	3.7	0.4	—	7.0
Tennessee	136	140	7,936	8,358	1.6	1.7	2.5	2.5	0.7	1.0	3.9
Texas	484	496	31,141	32,360	2.0	2.0	2.8	3.0	1.0	1.1	4.3
Utah	69	69	4,578	4,899	2.7	2.7	—	—	—	—	8.9
Vermont	205	200	2,359	2,335	4.7	4.8	—	—	—	—	7.1
Virginia	90	90	14,626	15,576	2.4	2.5	4.4	4.4	1.1	1.0	7.0
Washington	70	69	12,876	14,297	2.6	2.8	—	—	—	1.0	10.1
West Virginia	98	97	4,362	4,608	2.4	2.5	3.3	3.4	0.8	1.0	4.6
Wisconsin	380	381	15,962	16,363	3.2	3.2	5.7	5.2	1.1	1.2	8.7
Wyoming	23	23	2,006	2,225	4.3	4.7	4.6	4.7	0.8	0.7	8.1

[1] Attendance is the total number of persons entering the library including persons attending activities, meetings, and those persons requiring no staff services.

[2] A reference transaction is an information contact which involves the knowledge, use, recommendations, interpretation or instructions in the use of one or more information sources by a member of the library staff.

—Response rate less than 70 percent.

NOTE.—Totals may be underestimated due to nonresponse.

SOURCE: U.S. Department of Education, National Center for Education Statistics, *Public Libraries in the United States: 1992* and *Public Libraries in the United States: 1994*. (This table was prepared January 1998.)

Guide to Sources
Sources and Comparability of Data

The information presented in this report was obtained from many sources, including federal and state agencies, private research organizations, and professional associations. The data were collected using many research methods, including surveys of a universe (such as all colleges) or of a sample, compilations of administrative records, and statistical projections. *State Comparisons of Education Statistics* users should take particular care when comparing data from different sources. Differences in procedures, timing, phrasing of questions, interviewer training, and so forth mean that the results from the different sources may not be strictly comparable. Following the general discussion of data accuracy below, descriptions of the information sources and data collection methods are presented, grouped by sponsoring organization. More extensive documentation of a particular survey's procedures does not imply more problems with the data, only that more information is available.

Accuracy of Data

The accuracy of any statistic is determined by the joint effects of "sampling" and "nonsampling" errors. Estimates based on a sample will differ somewhat from the figures that would have been obtained if a complete census had been taken using the same survey instruments, instructions, and procedures. In addition to such sampling errors, all surveys, both universe and sample, are subject to design, reporting, and processing errors and errors due to nonresponse. To the extent possible, these nonsampling errors are kept to a minimum by methods built into the survey procedures. In general, however, the effects of nonsampling errors are more difficult to gauge than those produced by sampling variability.

Sampling Errors

The samples used in surveys are selected from a large number of possible samples of the same size that could have been selected using the same sample design. Estimates derived from the different samples would differ from each other. The difference between a sample estimate and the average of all possible samples is called the sampling deviation. The standard or sampling error of a survey estimate is a measure of the variation among the estimates from all possible samples and, thus, is a measure of the precision with which an estimate from a particular sample approximates the average result of all possible samples.

The sample estimate and an estimate of its standard error permit us to construct interval estimates with prescribed confidence that the interval includes the average result of all possible samples. If all possible samples were selected under essentially the same conditions and an estimate and its estimated standard error were calculated from each sample, then: (1) approximately 2/3 of the intervals from one standard error below the estimate to one standard error above the estimate would include the average value of all possible samples; and (2) approximately 19/20 of the intervals from two standard errors below the estimate to two standard errors above the estimate would include the average value of all possible samples. We call an interval from two standard errors below the estimate to two standard errors above the estimate a 95 percent confidence interval.

Analysis of standard errors can help assess how valid a comparison between two estimates might be. The **standard error of a difference** between two independent sample estimates is equal to the square root of the sum of the squared standard errors of the estimates. The standard error (se) of the difference between independent sample estimates "a" and "b" is:

$$se_{a,b} = (se_a^2 + se_b^2)^{1/2}$$

It should be noted that most of the standard error estimates presented in subsequent sections and in the original documents are approximations. That is, to derive estimates of standard errors that would be applicable to a wide variety of items and could be prepared at a moderate cost, a number of approximations were required. As a result, the standard error estimates provide a general order of magnitude rather than the exact standard error for any specific item. The preceding discussion on sampling variability was directed toward a situation concerning one or two estimates.

Nonsampling Errors

Universe and sample surveys are subject to nonsampling errors. Nonsampling errors may arise when respondents or interviewers interpret questions differently, when respondents must estimate values, or when coders, keyers, and other processors handle answers differently, when persons who should be included in the universe are not, or when persons fail to respond (completely or partially). Nonsampling errors usually, but not always, result in an understatement of total survey error and thus an overstatement of the precision of survey estimates. Since estimating the magnitude of nonsampling errors often would require special experiments or access to independent data, these nonsampling errors are seldom available.

To compensate for nonresponse, adjustments of the sample estimates are often made. An adjustment made for either type of nonresponse, total or partial, is often referred to as an imputation, which is often a substitution of the "average" questionnaire response for the nonresponse. Imputations are usually made separately within various groups of sample members which have similar survey characteristics. Imputation for item nonresponse is usually made by substituting for a missing item the response to that item of a respondent having characteristics that are similar to those of the nonrespondent.

Although the magnitude of nonsampling error in the data compiled in this *State Comparisons of Education Statistics* is frequently unknown, idiosyncrasies that have been identified are noted on the appropriate tables.

Department of Education

National Center for Education Statistics (NCES)

Common Core of Data

NCES uses the Common Core of Data (CCD) survey beginning in 1978 to acquire and maintain statistical data from each of the 50 states, the District of Columbia, and the outlying areas. Information about staff and students is collected annually at the school, LEA (local education agency or school district), and state levels. Information about revenues and expenditures is also collected at the state level.

Data are collected for a particular school year (July 1 through June 30) via survey instruments sent to the state education agencies during the subsequent school year. States have one year in which to modify the data originally submitted.

Since the CCD is a universe survey, the CCD information presented in this publication is not subject to sampling errors. However, nonsampling errors could come from two sources—nonreturn and inaccurate reporting. Almost all of the states submit the six CCD survey instruments each year, but submissions are sometimes incomplete or too late for publication.

Understandably, when 57 education agencies compile and submit data for approximately 85,000 public schools and 15,000 local school districts, misreporting can occur. Typically, this results from varying interpretation of NCES definitions and differing recordkeeping systems. NCES attempts to minimize these errors by working closely with the Council of Chief State School Officers (CCSSO) and its Committee on Evaluation and Information Systems (CEIS).

The state education agencies report data to NCES from data collected and edited in their regular reporting cycles. NCES encourages the agencies to incorporate into their own survey systems the NCES items they do not already collect so that those items will also be available for the subsequent CCD survey. Over time, this has meant fewer missing data cells in each state's response, reducing the need to impute data.

NCES subjects data from the education agencies to a comprehensive edit. Where data are determined to be inconsistent, missing, or out of range, NCES contacts the education agencies for verification. NCES-prepared state summary forms are returned to the state education agencies for verification. States are also given an opportunity to revise their state-level aggregates from the previous survey cycle.

Questions concerning the Common Core of Data can be directed to:

John Sietsema
Surveys and Cooperative Systems Group
National Center for Education Statistics
555 New Jersey Avenue NW
Washington, DC 20208–5651
John__Sietsema@ed.gov

Private School Universe Survey

The NCES Private School Universe Survey (PSS) was designed to build a universe of private schools to serve as a sampling frame for NCES sample surveys, and generate biennial data on the total number of private schools, teachers, and students. In order to achieve these purposes, the survey includes both a list frame and an area frame component. The basis for the 1995–96 list frame was the 1993–94 PSS.

To provide coverage for the schools founded after 1993, NCES requested and collected membership lists from 26 private school associations and religious denominations. The states and the District of Columbia were also asked to provide lists of private schools. Schools on both the private school association lists and the state lists were compared to the

NCES base lists and any school which did not match a school on the base list was added to the NCES private school universe list. As a result of these efforts, approximately 5,525 were added in 1995, for a total of 31,698 schools on the private school universe list. Additionally, questionnaires were sent out to approximately 7,000 programs identified in the 1993–94 PSS as ending with kindergarten to determine if any of the schools included at least a kindergarten in 1995–96, becoming eligible for the 1995–96 PSS.

In addition to the list frame, an area frame of 124 distinct primary sampling units (PSUs) was constructed. Within each of the 124 PSUs, the Census Bureau attempted to find all eligible private schools using local lists from associations, government agencies, and telephone books. The survey data from the area frame component were weighted to reflect the sampling rates in the PSUs. Survey data from both the list and area frame components were adjusted for school nonresponse.

After two attempts by mail and additional follow-ups by telephone and visits, a final return rate of 99 percent was achieved. Further information on the PSS may be obtained from:

Stephen Broughman
Surveys and Cooperative Systems Group
National Center for Education Statistics
555 New Jersey Avenue, NW
Washington, DC 20208-5651
Stephen_Broughman@ed.gov

Integrated Postsecondary Education Data System

The Integrated Postsecondary Education Data System (IPEDS) surveys approximately 11,000 postsecondary institutions, including universities and colleges, as well as institutions offering technical and vocational education beyond the high school level. This survey, which began in 1986, replaced the Higher Education General Information Survey (HEGIS).

IPEDS consists of eight integrated components that obtain information on who provides postsecondary education (institutions), who participates in it and completes it (students), what programs are offered and what programs are completed, and both the human and financial resources involved in the provision of institutionally based postsecondary education. Specifically, these components include: Institutional Characteristics, including instructional activity; Fall Enrollment, including age and residence; Enrollment in Occupationally Specific Programs; Completions; Finance; Staff; Salaries of Full-Time Instructional Faculty; and Academic Libraries.

The higher education portion of this survey is a census of accredited 2- and 4-year colleges. Prior to 1993, data from the technical and vocational institu-

tions were collected through a sample survey. Beginning in 1993, all data are gathered in a census of all postsecondary institutions. The tabulations on "Institutional Characteristics" developed for this edition of the State Comparisons are based on lists of all institutions and are not subject to sampling errors.

Prior to the establishment of IPEDS in 1986, HEGIS acquired and maintained statistical data on the characteristics and operations of institutions of higher education. Implemented in 1966, HEGIS was an annual universe survey of institutions accredited at the college level by an agency recognized by the Secretary of the U.S. Department of Education. These institutions were listed in NCES's Education Directory, Colleges and Universities.

The trend tables presented in this report draw on HEGIS surveys which solicited information concerning institutional characteristics, faculty salaries, finances, enrollment, and degrees. Since these surveys were distributed to all higher education institutions, the data presented are not subject to sampling error. However, they are subject to nonsampling error, the sources of which varied with the survey instrument. Information concerning the nonsampling error of the enrollment and degrees surveys draws extensively on the "HEGIS Post-Survey Validation Study" conducted in 1979.

Further information on IPEDS may be obtained from:

Roslyn A. Korb
Surveys and Cooperative Systems Group
National Center for Education Statistics
555 New Jersey Avenue NW
Washington, DC 20208–5652
Roslyn_Korb@ed.gov

Institutional Characteristics

This survey provides the basis for the universe of institutions presented in the Directory of Postsecondary Institutions. The universe comprises institutions that met certain accreditation criteria and offered at least a 1-year program of college-level studies leading toward a degree. All of these institutions were certified as eligible by the U.S. Department of Education's Division of Eligibility and Agency Evaluation. The survey collects basic information necessary to classify the institutions including control, level, and kinds of programs; information on tuition, fees, and room and board charges; and unduplicated full-year enrollment counts and instructional activity.

Fall Enrollment

This survey has been part of the HEGIS and IPEDS series since 1966. The enrollment survey response rate is relatively high; the 1996 response rate was 96.2 percent for higher education institutions, or

95 percent overall. Major sources of nonsampling error for this survey as identified in the 1979 report were classification problems, the unavailability of needed data, interpretation of definitions, the survey due date, and operational errors. Of these, the classification of students appears to have been the main source of error. Institutions had problems in correctly classifying first-time freshmen and other first-time students for both full-time and part-time categories. These problems occurred most often at 2-year institutions (private and public) and private 4-year institutions. In the 1977–78 HEGIS validation studies, the classification problem led to an estimated overcount of 11,000 full-time students and an undercount of 19,000 part-time students. Although the ratio of error to the grand total was quite small (less than 1 percent), the percentage of errors was as high as 5 percent for detailed student levels and even higher at certain aggregation levels.

Beginning with fall 1986, the survey system was redesigned with the introduction of the IPEDS (see above). The IPEDS system comprises all postsecondary institutions, but also maintains comparability with earlier surveys by allowing HEGIS institutions to be tabulated separately. The survey allows (in alternating years) for the collection of age and residence data.

Salaries, Tenure, and Fringe Benefits of Full-Time Instructional Faculty

This institutional survey has been conducted for most years from 1966–67 to 1987–88, and annually since 1989–90. Although the survey form changed a number of times during those years, only comparable data are presented in this report.

Between 1966–67 and 1985–86 this survey differed from other HEGIS surveys in that imputations were not made for nonrespondents. Thus, there is some possibility that the salary averages presented in this report may differ from the results of a complete enumeration of all colleges and universities. Beginning with the surveys for 1987–88, the IPEDS data tabulation procedures included imputations for survey nonrespondents. The response rate for the 1996–97 survey was 93.4 percent for higher education institutions, or 92.9 percent overall. Because of the higher response rate for public colleges, it is probable that the public colleges' salary data are more accurate than the data for private colleges. Although data from these surveys are not subject to sampling error, sources of nonsampling error may include computational errors and misclassification in reporting and processing. NCES reviews individual colleges' data for internal and longitudinal consistency and contacts the colleges to check inconsistent data.

Completions

This survey was part of the HEGIS series throughout its existence. Collection of degree data has been maintained through the IPEDS system.

The nonresponse rate did not appear to be a significant source of nonsampling error for this survey. The return rate over the years has been high, with the higher education response rate for the 1994–95 survey at 97 percent. The overall response rate including the noncollegiate institutions is 88 percent. Because of the high return rate for the institutions of higher education, nonsampling error caused by imputation is also minimal.

The major sources of nonsampling error for this survey were differences between the NCES program taxonomy and taxonomies used by the colleges, classification of double majors, operational problems, and survey timing. In the 1979 HEGIS validation study, these sources of nonsampling contributed to an error rate of 0.3 percent overreporting of bachelor's degrees and 1.3 percent overreporting of master's degrees. The differences, however, varied greatly among fields. Over 50 percent of the fields selected for the validation study had no errors identified. Categories of fields that had large differences were business and management, education, engineering, letters, and psychology. It was also shown that differences in proportion to the published figures were less than 1 percent for most of the selected fields that had some errors. Exceptions to these were: master's and Ph.D. programs in labor and industrial relations (20 percent and 8 percent); bachelor's and master's programs in art education (3 percent and 4 percent); bachelor's and Ph.D. programs in business and commerce, and in distributive education (5 percent and 9 percent); master's programs in philosophy (8 percent); and Ph.D. programs in psychology (11 percent).

Financial Statistics

This survey was part of the HEGIS series and has been continued under the IPEDS system. Changes were made in the financial survey instruments in fiscal years (FY) 1976, 1982, and 1987. The FY 76 survey instrument contained numerous revisions to earlier survey forms and made direct comparisons of line items very difficult. Beginning in FY 82, Pell Grant data were collected in the categories of federal restricted grants and contracts revenues and restricted scholarships and fellowships expenditures. The introduction of IPEDS in the FY 87 survey included several important changes to the survey instrument and data processing procedures. While these changes were significant, considerable effort has been made to present only comparable information on trends in this report and to note inconsistencies. Finance tables for this publication have been adjusted by subtracting the largely duplicative Pell Grant amounts from the later data to maintain comparability with pre-FY 82 data.

Possible sources of nonsampling error in the financial statistics include nonresponse, imputation, and misclassification. The response rate has been about 85 to 90 percent for most of the years reported. The response rate for the FY 1995 survey was 94 percent for higher education institutions, or 83 percent overall.

Two general methods of imputation were used in HEGIS. If the prior year's data were available for a nonresponding institution, these data were inflated using the Higher Education Price Index and adjusted according to changes in enrollments. If no previous year's data were available, current data were used from peer institutions selected for location (state or region), control, level, and enrollment size of institution. In most cases estimates for nonreporting institutions in IPEDS were made using data from peer institutions.

Beginning with FY 87, the IPEDS survey system included all postsecondary institutions, but maintained comparability with earlier surveys by allowing 2- and 4-year HEGIS institutions to be tabulated separately. The finance data tabulated for this publication reflect totals for the HEGIS or higher education institutions only. For FY 87 through FY 91, in order to maintain comparability with the historical time series of HEGIS institutions, data were combined from two of the three different survey forms that make up the IPEDS survey system. The vast majority of the data were tabulated from Form 1, which was used to collect information from public and private nonprofit 2- and 4-year colleges. Form 2, a condensed form, was used to gather data for the 2-year proprietary institutions. Because of the differences in the data requested on the two forms, several assumptions were made about the Form 2 reports so that their figures could be included in the institutions of higher education totals.

In IPEDS, the Form 2 institutions were not asked to separate appropriations from grants and contracts, nor state from local sources of funding. For the Form 2 institutions, all the federal revenues were assumed to be federal grants and contracts and all of the state and local revenues were assumed to be restricted state grants and contracts. All other Form 2 sources of revenue, except for tuition and fees and sales and services of educational activities, were included under "other." Similar adjustments were made to the expenditure accounts. The Form 2 institutions reported instruction and scholarship and fellowship expenditures only. All other educational and general expenditures were allocated to academic support.

To reduce reporting error, NCES uses national standards for reporting finance statistics. These standards are contained in *College and University Business Administration: Administrative Services (1974 Edition)*, and the *Financial Accounting and Reporting Manual for Higher Education (1990 Education)*, published by the National Association of College and University Business Officers; *Audits of Colleges and Universities* (as amended August 31, 1974), by the American Institute of Certified Public Accountants; and *HEGIS Financial Reporting Guide (1980)*, by NCES. Wherever possible, definitions and formats in the survey form are consistent with those in these four accounting texts.

Staff

The fall staff data presented in this publication were collected by NCES, through the IPEDS system, which collected data from postsecondary institutions, including all 2- and 4-year higher education institutions. The NCES collects staff data biennially in odd numbered years in institutions of postsecondary education.

The "Fall Staff" questionnaires were mailed out by NCES July 1995; the respondents reported the employment statistics in their institution that cover the payroll period closest to October 1 of the survey year.

The "Fall Staff" survey had an overall response rate of 86.9 percent. The response rate for higher education institutions was 93.6 percent.

National Assessment of Educational Progress

The National Assessment of Educational Progress (NAEP) is a series of cross-sectional studies designed and initially implemented in 1969. NAEP has gathered information about selected levels of educational achievement across the country. NAEP has surveyed the educational attainments by age and grade (9-, 13-, and 17-year-olds, and 4th-, 8th-, and 12th-graders), and young adults (ages 25–35) in 10 learning areas. Long-term trends are assessed by age and measure changes in educational achievement, while specific subject areas are assessed periodically by grade level. Different learning areas have been assessed periodically, and all areas have been reassessed in order to measure possible changes in educational achievement.

The assessment data presented in this publication were derived from tests designed and conducted by the Education Commission of the States (1969–1983) and by the Educational Testing Service (1983 to present). Three-stage probability samples have been used. The primary sampling units have been stratified by region and, within region, by state, size of community, and, for the two smaller sizes of community strata, by socioeconomic level. The first stage of sampling entails defining and selecting primary sampling units (PSUs). For each age/grade level (4, 8, and 12) the second stage entails enumerating, stratifying, and randomly selecting schools, both public and private, within each PSU selected at the first stage. The third stage involves randomly selecting students within a school for participation in NAEP. Assessment exercises have been administered either to individuals or to small groups of students by specially trained personnel.

In 1990, representative state-level data were produced for mathematics at the 8th-grade level. This was the first time NAEP had produced data on a state-by-state level. In 1996, state-level assessments were conducted in 4th- and 8th-grade mathematics and 8th-grade science.

Information from NAEP is subject to both nonsampling and sampling error. Two possible sources of nonsampling error are nonparticipation and instrumentation. Certain populations have been oversampled to assure samples of sufficient size for analysis. Instrumentation nonsampling error could result from failure of the test instruments to measure what is being taught and, in turn, what is being learned by the students.

For further information on NAEP, contact:

Gary W. Phillips
Assessment Group
National Center for Education Statistics
555 New Jersey Avenue NW
Washington, DC 20208–5653
Gary__Phillips@ed.gov

Library Statistics Program

Nationwide, public library statistics are collected using the Public Libraries Survey and disseminated annually through the Federal-State Cooperative System for public library data (FSCS). Descriptive statistics are produced for nearly 9,000 public libraries. The Public Libraries Survey includes information about staffing; operating income and expenditures; type of governance; type of administrative structure; size of collection; and service measures such as reference transactions, public service hours, interlibrary loans, circulation, and library visits. In FSCS, respondents supply the information electronically, and data are edited and tabulated in machine-readable form.

The respondents are 8,921 public libraries identified in the 50 states and the District of Columbia by state library agencies. At the state level, FSCS is administered by State Data Coordinators, appointed by the Chief Officer of each State Library Agency. The State Data Coordinator collects the requested data

from local public libraries and submits these data to NCES. An annual training conference sponsored by NCES is provided for the State Data Coordinators. A steering committee representing State Data Coordinators and other public library constituents is active in the development of FSCS data elements and software. Technical assistance to states is provided by phone and in person by the FSCS steering committee and by NCES staff and contractors. All 50 states and the District of Columbia have submitted data which are available for individual public libraries and are also aggregated to state and national levels.

Since 1990, data collections have been collected electronically. The most recent software is called DECPLUS. It includes identifying information on all known public libraries and their outlets, some state libraries, and some library systems and cooperatives. Beginning in 1994, this resource was available for drawing samples for special surveys on such topics as literacy, access for the disabled, and library construction.

Under the Academic Libraries Survey (ALS), NCES surveyed academic libraries on a 3-year cycle between 1966 and 1988. Since 1988, ALS has been a component of the Integrated Postsecondary Education Data System and is on a 2-year cycle. ALS provides data on about 3,500 academic libraries. In aggregate, these data provide an overview of the status of academic libraries nationally and statewide. The survey collects data on the libraries in the entire universe of accredited higher education institutions and on the libraries in nonaccredited institutions with a program of 4 years or more. ALS produces descriptive statistics on academic libraries in postsecondary institutions in the 50 states, the District of Columbia and the outlying areas.

The School Library Statistics Survey collected data on school libraries/media centers in 1990–91. This survey asked questions on libraries in public and private schools as part of the Schools and Staffing Survey (SASS). These questionnaires were revised and a sample survey of about 7,600 schools was conducted during school year 1993–94. The library components of the 1990–91 SASS include: number of students served and number of professional staff and aides; at the district level, number of full-time equivalent librarians/media specialists, vacant positions, positions abolished, and approved positions; and amount of librarian input in establishing curriculum. The 1993–94 survey was much more extensive and added questions concerning media centers and collections of libraries.

Additional information on these academic and school library studies is available from:

Jeff Williams
Surveys and Cooperative Systems Group
National Center for Education Statistics
555 New Jersey Avenue NW
Washington, DC 20208–5652
Jeff__Williams@ed.gov

Schools and Staffing Survey

The Schools and Staffing Survey (SASS) is a set of linked questionnaires that covers public school districts, public and private schools, principals, and teachers, as its core components. SASS was first conducted for the National Center for Education Statistics by the Bureau of the Census during the 1987–88 school year. SASS subsequently was conducted in 1990–91 and in 1993–94. The next SASS is scheduled for school year 1999–2000. SASS is a mailed questionnaire with telephone follow-up that collects data on the nation's public and private elementary and secondary teaching force, characteristics of schools and school principals, demand for teachers, and school/school district policies. The 1990–91 and 1993–94 SASS also collected data on Bureau of Indian Affairs (BIA) schools. The SASS data are collected through a sample survey of schools, the school districts associated with sampled schools, school principals, and teachers. The 1993–94 SASS expanded as well to cover school libraries and librarians, and field tested an administrative student records questionnaire.

The 1993–94 SASS estimates are based upon a sample consisting of approximately 9,900 public schools, 3,300 private schools, and 5,500 public school districts associated with the public schools in the sample. From these schools, about 57,000 public school teachers and 11,500 private school teachers were selected for the 1993–94 SASS teacher survey.

The public school sample for the 1993–94 SASS was based upon the 1991–92 school year Common Core of Data (CCD), the compilation of all the nation's public school districts and public schools. CCD is collected annually from state education agencies. The frame includes regular public schools, Department of Defense-operated military base schools in the United States, and nonregular schools such as special education, vocational, and alternative schools. SASS is designed to provide national estimates for public and private school characteristics and state estimates for school districts, public schools, principals, and teachers. The teacher survey is designed as well to allow comparisons between new and experienced teachers, and between bilingual/ESL teachers and other teachers.

The private school sample for the 1993–94 SASS was selected from the 1991–92 Private School Universe Survey (PSS), supplemented with list updates from states and some associations available in time for sample selection. PSS collects basic data on all of the nation's private schools from two sources: the list frame and the area search frame. The list frame was compiled from a set of private school associations that provide NCES with their membership lists and states that gather lists of private schools. The area search frame consisted of schools not included on the list frame that were compiled from local sources in a sample of counties around the United States. Private school estimates are available at the national level and by type of private school.

The Teacher Demand and Shortage (school district) and School Principal Questionnaires were mailed out first in October 1993, along with School Library/Media Center and Library Media Specialist/Librarian Questionnaires. The weighted response rate for the Teacher Demand and Shortage Questionnaire was 93.9 percent. Weighted response rates for the Public School Principal Questionnaire and the Private School Questionnaire were 96.6 percent and 87.6 percent, respectively.

In December 1993, public, private, and BIA school questionnaires were mailed out. The public, private, and BIA teacher questionnaires were sent out in several batches, between mid-December 1993 and early February 1994. Weighted response rates for the Public School Questionnaire and the Private School Questionnaire were 92.3 percent and 83.2 percent, respectively. Five percent of public schools and 9 percent of private schools did not provide a list of teachers in their schools and were thus ineligible for sampling. Weighted response rates were 88.2 percent for public school teachers and 80.2 percent for private school teachers.

Item response rates were varied, but generally high, ranging from 67 to 100 percent for the TDS, 65 to 100 percent for public school principal questions, 55 to 100 percent for private school principal items, 83 to 100 percent for public school items, 61 to 100 percent for private school survey items, 71 to 100 percent for public school teacher items, and 69 to 100 percent for private school teacher items.

Public-use and restricted-use microdata files are available on CD-ROM or 9-track tape. Summary data from the 1993–94 SASS can be found in *Schools and Staffing in the United States: Selected Data for Public and Private Schools, 1993–94* (NCES 95–191). More detailed results from the 1993–94 SASS are published in *Schools and Staffing in the United States: A Statistical Profile, 1993–94* (NCES 96–124). Data by state are available in *SASS by State—1993–94 Schools and Staffing Survey Selected State Results* (NCES 96–312). Further information about the sample may be obtained from *1993–94 Schools and Staffing Survey: Sample Design and Estimation* (NCES 96–086). Data from previous SASS collections are published in the 1987–88 and 1990–91 *Profile* (NCES 92–127 and 93–146, respectively), as well as the 1987–88 and 1990–91 versions of the sample design report (NCES 91–127 and 93–449, respectively).

For more information about this survey or to order reports, contact:

Kerry Gruber
Surveys and Cooperative Systems Group
National Center for Education Statistics
555 New Jersey Avenue NW
Washington, DC 20208–5651
Kerry__Gruber@ed.gov

Office for Civil Rights

Civil Rights Survey of Elementary and Secondary Schools

The Office for Civil Rights (OCR), U.S. Department of Education, conducts biennial surveys of public school districts and of schools within those districts. Data are obtained on the characteristics of pupils enrolled in public schools throughout the Nation. Such information is required under Title VI of the Civil Rights Act of 1964, Title IX of the Education Amendments of 1972, and Section 504 of the Rehabilitation Act of 1973 to enable OCR to carry out its compliance responsibilities. The 1990 survey included the 100 largest public school districts, those of special interest (i.e., court order, compliance review), and a stratified random sample of approximately 3,500 districts representing approximately 40,000 schools. School, district, and national data are currently available.

Further information is available from:

Peter McCabe
Office for Civil Rights
U.S. Department of Education
330 C Street SW
Washington, DC 20202

Office of Special Education and Rehabilitative Services

Annual Report to Congress on the Implementation of the Education of the Handicapped Act

The Individuals with Disabilities Education Act (IDEA), formerly the Education of the Handicapped Act (EHA), requires the Secretary of Education to transmit to Congress annually a report describing the progress in serving the nation's handicapped children. The annual report contains information on children served by the public schools under the provisions of Part B of the IDEA and for children served in state-operated programs (SOP) for the handicapped under Chapter I of the Elementary and Secondary Education Act (ESEA). Statistics on children receiving special education and related services in various settings and school personnel providing such services are reported in an annual submission of data to the Office of Special Education and Rehabilitative Services (OSERS), by the 50 states, the District of Columbia, and the outlying areas. The child count information is based on the number of handicapped children receiving special education and related services on December 1st of each year.

Since each participant in programs for the handicapped is reported to OSERS, the data are not subject to sampling error. However, nonsampling error can occur from a variety of sources. Some states follow a noncategorical approach to the delivery of special education services, but produce counts by handicapping condition because EHA–B requires it. In those states that do categorize their handicapped students, definitions and labeling practices vary.

Further information on the Annual Report to Congress may be obtained from:

Office of Special Education Programs
Office of Special Education and Rehabilitative Services
330 C Street SW
Washington, DC 20202

Other Governmental Agencies

Bureau of the Census

Current Population Survey

Current estimates of school enrollment, as well as social and economic characteristics of students, are based on data collected in the Census Bureau's monthly household survey of about 60,000 households. The monthly Current Population Survey (CPS) sample consists of 729 areas comprising 1,973 counties, independent cities, and minor civil divisions throughout the 50 states and the District of Columbia. The sample was initially selected from the 1980 census files and is periodically updated to reflect new housing construction.

The monthly CPS deals primarily with labor force data for the civilian noninstitutional population (i.e., excluding military personnel and their families living on post and inmates of institutions). In addition, in October of each year, supplemental questions are asked about highest grade completed, level and grade of current enrollment, attendance status, number and type of courses, degree or certificate objective, and type of organization offering instruction for each member of the household. In March of each year, supplemental questions on income are asked. The responses to these questions are combined with answers to two questions on educational attainment: highest grade of school ever attended, and whether that grade was completed.

The estimation procedure employed for the monthly CPS data involves inflating weighted sample results to independent estimates of characteristics of the civilian noninstitutional population in the United States by age, sex, and race. These independent estimates are based on statistics from decennial censuses; statistics on births, deaths, immigration, and emigration; and statistics on the population in the armed services. Generalized standard error tables are provided in the *Current Population Reports*. The data are subject to both nonsampling and sampling errors.

Further information is available in the *Current Population Reports,* Series P–20, or by contacting:

Education Branch
Population Division
Bureau of the Census
U.S. Department of Commerce
Washington, DC 20233

Educational Attainment

Data on years of school completed are derived from questions on the Current Population Survey (CPS) instrument. Formal reports documenting educational attainment are produced by the Bureau of the Census using March CPS results. The latest report is *Educational Attainment in the United States, March 1994 and 1993*, Series P–20, No. 476, which is available from the Government Printing Office.

In addition to the general constraints of the CPS, some data indicate that the respondents have a tendency to overestimate the educational level of members of their household. Some inaccuracy is due to a lack of the respondent's knowledge of the exact educational attainment of each household member and the hesitancy to acknowledge anything less than a high school education. Another cause of nonsampling variability is the change in the numbers in the armed services over the years. In 1970, 25 percent of all males 20 and 21 years old were in the armed services. By 1974, this had decreased to less than 10 percent. The exclusion of members of the armed services appears to increase the proportion of the CPS population with some college and decrease the proportion of those who finished high school but went no further. After 1974, there was more stability in the proportion of young men in the military.

Questions concerning "Educational Attainment in the United States" may be directed to:

Education Branch
Population Division
Bureau of the Census
U.S. Department of Commerce
Washington, DC 20233

1990 Census of Population—Education in the United States

This report is based on a part of the decennial census which consists of questions asked of a 1-in-6 sample of persons and housing units in the United States. This sample was asked more detailed questions about income, occupation and housing costs in addition to general demographic information.

School Enrollment

Persons classified as enrolled in school reported attending a "regular" public or private school or college at any time between February 1, 1990 and the time listed. Questions asked were whether the institution attended was public or private, and level of school in which the student was enrolled.

Educational Attainment

Data for educational attainment were tabulated for persons 15 years and over, and classified according to the highest grade completed or the highest degree received. Instructions were also given to include the level of the previous grade attended or the highest degree received for persons currently enrolled in school.

Poverty status

To determine poverty status, answers to income questions were used and compared to the appropriate poverty threshold. All persons except institutionalized persons, persons in military group quarters and in college dormitories, and unrelated persons under 15 years old were considered. If total income of each family or unrelated individual in the sample was less than the corresponding cutoff, that family or individual was classified as "below the poverty level."

Further information can be obtained from:

Population Division
Bureau of the Census
U.S. Department of Commerce
Washington, DC 20233

Other Organization Sources

Council of Chief State School Officers

The Council of Chief State School Officers (CCSSO) is a nonprofit organization of the 57 public officials who head departments of public education in every state, the outlying areas, the District of Columbia, and the Department of Defense Dependents Schools. In 1985, the CCSSO founded the State Education Assessment Center to provide a locus of leadership by the states to improve the monitoring and assessment of education. *State Education Indicators, 1993* is the principal report of the Assessment Center's program of indicators on education. Most of the data are obtained from a member questionnaire; the remainder of the data are obtained from federal government agencies. Information on mathematics education was taken from *CCSSO, State Policies on Science and Mathematics Evaluation, 1992.*

For additional information, contact:

Edward Roeber
State Education Assessment Center
Council of Chief State School Officers
One Massachusetts Avenue NW
7th Floor
Washington, DC 20001

National Education Association

The National Education Association (NEA) reports enrollment, expenditure, revenue, graduate, teacher, and instructional staff salary data in its annual publication, *Estimates of School Statistics*. Each year NEA prepares regression-based estimates of financial and other education statistics and submits them to the states for verification. Generally about 30 states adjust these estimates based on their own data. These preliminary data are published by NEA along with revised data from previous years. States are asked to revise previously submitted data as final figures become available. The most recent publication contains all changes reported to the NEA.

Research Associates of Washington

Research Associates annually compiles the Higher Education Price Index (HEPI) which measures aver-age changes in prices of goods and services purchased by colleges and universities through current-fund educational and general expenditures. Sponsored research and auxiliary enterprises are not priced by the HEPI.

The HEPI is based on the prices (or salaries) of faculty and of administrators and other professional service personnel; clerical, technical, service, and other nonprofessional personnel; and contracted services, such as data processing, communication, transportation, supplies and materials, equipment, books and periodicals, and utilities. These represent the items purchased for current operations by colleges and universities. Prices for these items are obtained from salary surveys conducted by various national higher education associations, the American Association of University Professors, the Bureau of Labor Statistics, and the National Center for Education Statistics; and from components of the Consumer Price Index (CPI) and the Producer Price Index (PPI) published by the U.S. Department of Labor, Bureau of Labor Statistics.

The quantities of these goods and services have been kept constant based on the 1971–72 buying pattern of colleges and universities. The weights assigned the various items priced, which represent their relative importance in the current-fund educational and general budget, are estimated national averages. Variance in spending patterns of individual institutions from these national averages reduces only slightly the applicability of the HEPI to any given institutional situation. Modest differences in the weights attached to expenditure categories have little effect on overall index values. This is because the HEPI is dominated by the trend in faculty salaries and similar salary trends for other personnel hired by institutions, which absorbs or diminishes the effects of price changes in other items purchased in small quantities.

For more information, contact:

Kent Halstead
Research Associates of Washington
1200 North Nash St.
#225
Arlington, VA 22209

Definitions

Academic support This category of college expenditures includes expenditures for support services that are an integral part of the institution's primary missions of instruction, research, or public service. Includes expenditures for libraries, galleries, audio/visual services, academic computing support, ancillary support, academic administration, personnel development, and course and curriculum development.

Achievement test An examination that measures the extent to which a person has acquired certain information or mastered certain skills, usually as a result of specific instruction.

Agriculture Courses designed to improve competencies in agricultural occupations. Included is the study of agricultural production, supplies, mechanization and products, agricultural science, forestry, and related services.

Appropriation (institutional revenues) An amount (other than a grant or contract) received from or made available to an institution through an act of a legislative body.

Associate degree A degree granted for the successful completion of a sub-baccalaureate program of studies, usually requiring at least 2 years (or equivalent) of full-time college-level study. This includes degrees granted in a cooperative or work-study program.

Auxiliary enterprises This category includes those essentially self-supporting operations which exist to furnish a service to students, faculty, or staff, and which charge a fee that is directly related to, although not necessarily equal to, the cost of the service. Examples are residence halls, food services, college stores, and intercollegiate athletics.

Average daily attendance (ADA) The aggregate attendance of a school during a reporting period (normally a school year) divided by the number of days school is in session during this period. Only days on which the pupils are under the guidance and direction of teachers should be considered days in session.

Average daily membership (ADM) The aggregate membership of a school during a reporting period

(normally a school year) divided by the number of days school is in session during this period. Only days on which the pupils are under the guidance and direction of teachers should be considered as days in session. The average daily membership for groups of schools having varying lengths of terms is the average of the average daily memberships obtained for the individual schools.

Bachelor's degree A degree granted for the successful completion of a baccalaureate program of studies, usually requiring at least 4 years (or equivalent) of full-time college-level study. This includes degrees granted in a cooperative or work-study program.

Business Program of instruction that prepares individuals for a variety of activities in planning, organizing, directing, and controlling business office systems and procedures.

Class size The membership of a class at a given date.

Classroom teacher A staff member assigned the professional activities of instructing pupils in self-contained classes or courses, or in classroom situations. Usually expressed in full-time equivalents.

Cohort A group of individuals that have a statistical factor in common, for example, year of birth.

College A postsecondary school which offers general or liberal arts education, usually leading to an associate, bachelor's, master's, doctor's, or first-professional degree. Junior colleges and community colleges are included under this terminology.

Combined elementary and secondary school A school which encompasses instruction at both the elementary and the secondary levels. Includes schools starting with grade 6 or below and ending with grade 9 or above.

Computer science A group of instructional programs that describes computer and information sciences, including computer programming, data processing, and information systems.

Constant dollars Dollar amounts that have been adjusted by means of price and cost indexes to eliminate inflationary factors and allow direct comparison across years.

Consumer Price Index (CPI) This price index measures the average change in the cost of a fixed market basket of goods and services purchased by consumers.

Current dollars Dollar amounts that have not been adjusted to compensate for inflation.

Current expenditures (elementary/secondary) The expenditures for operating local public schools, excluding capital outlay and interest on school debt. These expenditures include such items as salaries for school personnel, fixed charges, student transportation, school books and materials, and energy costs. Beginning in 1980–81, expenditures for state administration are excluded.

Current expenditures per pupil in average daily attendance Current expenditures for the regular school term divided by the average daily attendance of full-time pupils (or full-time equivalency of pupils) during the term. See also Current expenditures and Average daily attendance.

Current-fund expenditures (higher education) Money spent to meet current operating costs, including salaries, wages, utilities, student services, public services, research libraries, scholarships and fellowships, auxiliary enterprises, hospitals, and independent operations. Excludes loans, capital expenditures, and investments.

Current-fund revenues (higher education) Money received during the current fiscal year from revenue which can be used to pay obligations currently due, and surpluses reappropriated for the current fiscal year.

Doctor's degree An earned degree carrying the title of Doctor. The Doctor of Philosophy degree (Ph.D.) is the highest academic degree and requires mastery within a field of knowledge and demonstrated ability to perform scholarly research. Other doctorates are awarded for fulfilling specialized requirements in professional fields, such as education (Ed.D.), musical arts (D.M.A.), business administration (D.B.A.), and engineering (D.Eng. or D.E.S.). Many doctor's degrees in academic and professional fields require an earned master's degree as a prerequisite. First-professional degrees, such as M.D. and D.D.S., are not included under this heading.

Educational and general expenditures The sum of current funds expenditures on instruction, research, public service, academic support, student services, institutional support, operation and maintenance of plant, and awards from restricted and unrestricted funds.

Educational attainment The highest grade of regular school attended and completed.

Elementary education/programs Learning experiences concerned with the knowledge, skills, appreciations, attitudes, and behavioral characteristics which are considered to be needed by all pupils in terms of their awareness of life within our culture and the world of work, and which normally may be achieved during the elementary school years (usually kindergarten through grade 8 or kindergarten through grade 6), as defined by applicable state laws and regulations.

Elementary school A school classified as elementary by state and local practice and composed of any span of grades not above grade 8. A preschool or kindergarten school is included under this heading only if it is an integral part of an elementary school or a regularly established school system.

Elementary/secondary school As reported in this publication, includes only regular schools (i.e., schools that are part of state and local school systems, and also most not-for-profit private elementary/secondary schools, both religiously affiliated and nonsectarian). Schools not reported include subcollegiate departments of institutions of higher education, residential schools for exceptional children, federal schools for American Indians, and federal schools on military posts and other federal installations.

Endowment A trust fund set aside to provide a perpetual source of revenue from the proceeds of the endowment investments. Endowment funds are often created by donations from benefactors of an institution, who may designate the use of the endowment revenue. Normally, institutions or their representatives manage the investments, but they are not permitted to spend the endowment fund itself, only the proceeds from the investments. Typical uses of endowments would be an endowed chair for a particular department or for a scholarship fund. Endowment totals tabulated in this book also include funds functioning as endowments, such as funds left over from the previous year and placed with the endowment investments by the institution. These funds may be withdrawn by the institution and spent as current funds at any time. Endowments are evaluated by two different measures, book value and market value. Book value is the purchase price of the endowment investment. Market value is the current worth of the endowment investment. Thus, the book value of a stock held in an endowment fund would be the purchase price of the stock. The market value of the stock would be its selling price as of a given day.

English A group of instructional programs that describes the English language arts, including composition, creative writing, and the study of literature.

Enrollment The total number of students registered in a given school unit at a given time, generally in the fall of a year.

Expenditures Charges incurred, whether paid or unpaid, which are presumed to benefit the current fiscal year. For elementary/secondary schools, these include all charges for current outlays plus capital outlays and interest on school debt. For institutions of higher education, these include current outlays plus capital outlays. For government, these include charges net of recoveries and other correcting transactions other than for retirement of debt, investment in securities, extension of credit, or as agency transaction. Government expenditures include only external transactions, such as the provision of perquisites or other payments in kind. Aggregates for groups of governments exclude intergovernmental transactions among the governments.

Expenditures per pupil Charges incurred for a particular period of time divided by a student unit of measure, such as average daily attendance or average daily membership.

Family A group of two persons or more (one of whom is the householder) related by birth, marriage, or adoption and residing together. All such persons (including related subfamily members) are considered as members of one family.

Federal sources Includes federal appropriations, grants, and contracts, and federally-funded research and development centers (FFRDCs). Federally subsidized student loans and Pell Grants are not included.

First-professional degree A degree that signifies both completion of the academic requirements for beginning practice in a given profession and a level of professional skill beyond that normally required for a bachelor's degree. This degree usually is based on a program requiring at least 2 academic years of work prior to entrance and a total of at least 6 academic years of work to complete the degree program, including both prior required college work and the professional program itself. By NCES definition, first-professional degrees are awarded in the fields of dentistry (D.D.S. or D.M.D.), medicine (M.D.), optometry (O.D.), osteopathic medicine (D.O.), pharmacy (D.Phar.), podiatric medicine (D.P.M.), veterinary medicine (D.V.M.), chiropractic (D.C. or D.C.M.), law (J.D.), and theological professions (M.Div. or M.H.L.).

First-professional enrollment The number of students enrolled in a professional school or program which requires at least 2 years of academic college work for entrance and a total of at least 6 years for a degree. By NCES definition, first-professional enrollment includes only students in certain programs. (See First-professional degree for a list of programs.)

Foreign languages A group of instructional programs that describes the structure and use of language that is common or indigenous to people of the same community or nation, the same geographical area, or the same cultural traditions. Programs cover such features as sound, literature, syntax, phonology, semantics, sentences, prose, and verse, as well as the development of skills and attitudes used in communicating and evaluating thoughts and feelings through oral and written language.

Full-time enrollment The number of students enrolled in higher education courses with total credit load equal to at least 75 percent of the normal full-time course load.

Full-time-equivalent (FTE) enrollment For institutions of higher education, enrollment of full-time students, plus the full-time equivalent of part-time students as reported by institutions. In the absence of an equivalent reported by an institution, the FTE enrollment is estimated by adding one-third of part-time enrollment to full-time enrollment.

Full-time instructional faculty Those members of the instruction/research staff who are employed full time as defined by the institution, including faculty with released time for research and faculty on sabbatical leave. Full-time counts exclude faculty who are employed to teach less than two semesters, three quarters, two trimesters, or two 4-month sessions; replacements for faculty on sabbatical leave or those on leave without pay; faculty for preclinical and clinical medicine; faculty who are donating their services; faculty who are members of military organizations and paid on a different pay scale from civilian employees; academic officers, whose primary duties are administrative; and graduate students who assist in the instruction of courses.

Full-time worker In educational institutions, an employee whose position requires being on the job on school days throughout the school year at least the number of hours the schools are in session. For higher education, a member of an educational institution's staff who is employed full time.

General administration support services Includes salary, benefits, supplies, and contractual fees for boards of education staff and executive administration. Excludes state administration.

Government appropriation An amount (other than a grant or contract) received from or made available to an institution through an act of a legislative body.

Government grant or contract Revenues from a government agency for a specific research project or other program.

Graduate An individual who has received formal recognition for the successful completion of a prescribed program of studies.

Graduate enrollment The number of students who hold the bachelor's or first-professional degree, or the equivalent, and who are working towards a master's or doctor's degree. First-professional students are counted separately. These enrollment data measure those students who are registered at a particular time during the fall. At some institutions, graduate enrollment also includes students who are in postbaccalaureate classes but not in degree programs. In specified tables, graduate enrollment includes all students in regular graduate programs and all students in postbaccalaureate classes but not in degree programs (unclassified postbaccalaureate students).

Graduation Formal recognition given an individual for the successful completion of a prescribed program of studies.

Gross national product (GNP) The total national output of goods and services valued at market prices. GNP can be viewed in terms of expenditure categories which include purchases of goods and services by consumers and government, gross private domestic investment, and net exports of goods and services. The goods and services included are largely those bought for final use (excluding illegal transactions) in the market economy. A number of inclusions, however, represent imputed values, the most important of which is rental value of owner-occupied housing. GNP, in this broad context, measures the output attributable to the factors of production—labor and property—supplied by U.S. residents.

Handicapped Those children evaluated as having any of the following impairments, who because of these impairments need special education and related services. (These definitions apply specifically to data from the U.S. Office of Special Education and Rehabilitative Services presented in this publication.)

Deaf Having a hearing impairment which is so severe that the student is impaired in processing linguistic information through hearing (with or without amplification) and which adversely affects educational performance.

Deaf-blind Having concomitant hearing and visual impairments which cause such severe communication and other developmental and educational problems that the student cannot be accommo-

dated in special education programs solely for deaf or blind students.

Hard of hearing Having a hearing impairment, whether permanent or fluctuating, which adversely affects the student's educational performance, but which is not included under the definition of "deaf" in this section.

Mentally retarded Having significantly subaverage general intellectual functioning, existing concurrently with defects in adaptive behavior and manifested during the developmental period, which adversely affects the child's educational performance.

Multihandicapped Having concomitant impairments (such as mentally retarded-blind, mentally retarded-orthopedically impaired, etc.), the combination of which causes such severe educational problems that the student cannot be accommodated in special education programs solely for one of the impairments. Term does not include deaf-blind students but does include those students who are severely or profoundly mentally retarded.

Orthopedically impaired Having a severe orthopedic impairment which adversely affects a student's educational performance. The term includes impairment resulting from congenital anomaly, disease, or other causes.

Other health impaired Having limited strength, vitality, or alertness due to chronic or acute health problems such as a heart condition, tuberculosis, rheumatic fever, nephritis, asthma, sickle cell anemia, hemophilia, epilepsy, lead poisoning, leukemia, or diabetes which adversely affects the student's educational performance.

Seriously emotionally disturbed Exhibiting one or more of the following characteristics over a long period of time, to a marked degree, and adversely affecting educational performance: an inability to learn which cannot be explained by intellectual, sensory, or health factors; an inability to build or maintain satisfactory interpersonal relationships with peers and teachers; inappropriate types of behavior or feelings under normal circumstances; a general pervasive mood of unhappiness or depression; or a tendency to develop physical symptoms or fears associated with personal or school problems. This term does not include children who are socially maladjusted, unless they also display one or more of the listed characteristics.

Specific learning disabled Having a disorder in one or more of the basic psychological processes involved in understanding or in using spoken or written language, which may manifest itself in an imperfect ability to listen, think, speak, read, write, spell, or do mathematical calculations. The term includes such conditions as perceptual handicaps, brain injury, minimal brain dysfunction, dyslexia, and developmental aphasia. The term does not include children who have learning problems which are primarily the result of visual, hearing, or environmental, cultural, or economic disadvantage.

Speech impaired Having a communication disorder, such as stuttering, impaired articulation, language impairment, or voice impairment, which adversely affects the student's educational performance.

Visually handicapped Having a visual impairment which, even with correction, adversely affects the student's educational performance. The term includes partially seeing and blind children.

Higher education Study beyond secondary school at an institution that offers programs terminating in an associate, baccalaureate, or higher degree.

Higher education institutions (traditional classification)

4-year institution An institution legally authorized to offer and offering at least a 4-year program of college-level studies wholly or principally creditable toward a baccalaureate degree. In some tables, a further division between universities and other 4-year institutions is made. A "university" is a postsecondary institution which typically comprises one or more graduate or professional schools (also see University). For purposes of trend comparisons in this volume, the selection of universities has been held constant for all tabulations after 1982. "Other 4-year institutions" would include the rest of the nonuniversity 4-year institutions.

2-year institution An institution legally authorized to offer and offering at least a 2-year program of college-level studies which terminates in an associate degree or is principally creditable toward a baccalaureate degree. Also includes about 20 institutions that have a less than 2-year program, but were designated as institutions of higher education in the Higher Education General Information Survey.

Higher Education Price Index A price index which measures average changes in the prices of goods and services purchased by colleges and universities through current-fund education and general expenditures (excluding expenditures for sponsored research and auxiliary enterprises).

High school A secondary school offering the final years of high school work necessary for graduation, usually including grades 10, 11, 12 (in a 6–3–3 plan) or grades 9, 10, 11, and 12 (in a 6–2–4 plan).

High school program A program of studies designed to prepare students for their postsecondary education and occupation. Three types of programs are usually distinguished—academic, vocational, and general. An academic program is designed to prepare students for continued study at a college or university. A vocational program is designed to prepare students for employment in one or more semiskilled, skilled, or technical occupations. A general program is designed to provide students with the understanding and competence to function effectively in a free society and usually represents a mixture of academic and vocational components.

Household All the persons who occupy a housing unit. A house, apartment, or other group of rooms, or a single room, is regarded as a housing unit when it is occupied or intended for occupancy as separate living quarters, that is, when the occupants do not live and eat with any other persons in the structure, and there is direct access from the outside or through a common hall.

Independent operations A group of self-supporting activities under control of a college or university. For purposes of financial surveys conducted by the National Center for Education Statistics, this category is composed principally of federally funded research and development centers (FFRDCs).

Institutional support The category of higher education expenditures that includes day-to-day operational support for colleges, excluding expenditures for physical plant operations. Examples of institutional support include general administrative services, executive direction and planning, legal and fiscal operations, and community relations.

Instruction That category including expenditures of the colleges, schools, departments, and other instructional divisions of higher education institutions and expenditures for departmental research and public service which are not separately budgeted. Includes expenditures for both credit and noncredit activities. Excludes expenditures for academic administration where the primary function is administration (e.g., academic deans).

Instruction (elementary and secondary) Instruction encompasses all activities dealing directly with the interaction between teachers and students. Teaching may be provided for students in a school classroom, in another location such as a home or hospital, and in other learning situations such as those involving co-curricular activities. Instruction may be provided through some other approved medium such as television, radio, telephone, and correspondence. Instruction expenditures include: salaries, employee benefits, purchased services, supplies, and tuition to private schools.

Instructional staff Full-time-equivalent number of positions, not the number of different individuals occupying the positions during the school year. In local schools, includes all public elementary and secondary (junior and senior high) day-school positions that are in the nature of teaching or in the improvement of the teaching-learning situation. Includes consultants or supervisors of instruction, principals, teachers, guidance personnel, librarians, psychological personnel, and other instructional staff. Excludes administrative staff, attendance personnel, clerical personnel, and junior college staff.

Instructional support services Includes salary, benefits, supplies, and contractual fees for staff providing instructional improvement, educational media (library and audiovisual), and other instructional support services.

Junior high school A separately organized and administered secondary school intermediate between the elementary and senior high schools, usually including grades 7, 8, and 9 (in a 6–3–3 plan) or grades 7 and 8 (in a 6–2–4 plan).

Labor force Persons employed as civilians, unemployed (but looking for work), or in the armed services during the survey week. The "civilian labor force" comprises all civilians classified as employed or unemployed.

Local education agency See School district.

Mandatory transfer A transfer of current funds that must be made in order to fulfill a binding legal obligation of the institution. Included under mandatory transfers are debt service provisions relating to academic and administrative buildings, including (1) amounts set aside for debt retirement and interest and (2) required provisions for renewal and replacement of buildings to the extent these are not financed from other funds.

Master's degree A degree awarded for successful completion of a program generally requiring 1 or 2 years of full-time college-level study beyond the bachelor's degree. One type of master's degree, including the Master of Arts degree, or M.A., and the Master of Science degree, or M.S., is awarded in liberal arts and sciences for advanced scholarship in

a subject field or discipline and demonstrated ability to perform scholarly research. A second type of master's degree is awarded for the completion of a professionally oriented program, for example, an M.Ed. in education, an M.B.A. in business administration, an M.F.A. in fine arts, an M.M. in music, an M.S.W. in social work, and an M.P.A. in public administration. A third type of master's degree is awarded in professional fields for study beyond the first-professional degree, for example, the Master of Laws (L.L.M.) and Master of Science in various medical specializations.

Mathematics A group of instructional programs that describes the science of numbers and their operations, interrelations, combinations, generalizations, and abstractions and of space configurations and their structure, measurement, transformations, and generalizations.

National Assessment of Educational Progress (NAEP) See Guide to Sources.

Nonresident alien A person who is not a citizen of the United States and who is in this country on a temporary basis and does not have the right to remain indefinitely.

Nonsupervisory instructional staff Persons such as curriculum specialists, counselors, librarians, remedial specialists, and others possessing education certification but not responsible for day-to-day teaching of the same group of pupils.

Operation and maintenance services Includes salary, benefits, supplies, and contractual fees for supervision of operations and maintenance, operating buildings (heating, lighting, ventilating, repair, and replacement), care and upkeep of grounds and equipment, vehicle operations and maintenance (other than student transportation), security, and other operations and maintenance services.

Other support services Includes salary, benefits, supplies, and contractual fees for business support services, central support services, and other support services not otherwise classified.

Outlays The value of checks issued, interest accrued on the public debt, or other payments made, net of refunds and reimbursements.

Outlying areas Jurisdictions which are not states or the District of Columbia, but are controlled by the U.S. Government. Federal installations in foreign countries are not considered outlying areas. Data for outlying areas are tabulated to the extent reported by the respective jurisdictions. In many cases when no data for a particular outlying area are available for any year in the table, the outlying area is not included in the stub listing. Totals for outlying areas are included where data are complete for the applicable areas.

Part-time enrollment The number of students enrolled in higher education courses with a total credit load less than 75 percent of the normal full-time credit load.

Personal income Current income received by persons from all sources minus their personal contributions for social insurance. Classified as "persons" are individuals (including owners of unincorporated firms), nonprofit institutions serving individuals, private trust funds, and private noninsured welfare funds. Personal income includes transfers (payments not resulting from current production) from government and business such as social security benefits and military pensions but excludes transfers among persons.

Postbaccalaureate enrollment The number of graduate and first-professional students working towards advanced degrees and of students enrolled in graduate-level classes but not enrolled in degree programs. See also Graduate enrollment and First-professional enrollment.

Postsecondary education The provision of formal instructional programs with a curriculum designed primarily for students who have completed the requirements for a high school diploma or equivalent. This includes programs of an academic, vocational, and continuing professional education purpose, and excludes avocational and adult basic education programs.

Private school or institution A school or institution which is controlled by an individual or agency other than a state, a subdivision of a state, or the Federal Government, which is usually supported primarily by other than public funds, and the operation of whose program rests with other than publicly elected or appointed officials.

Property tax The sum of money collected from a tax levied against the value of property.

Proprietary institution An educational institution that is under private control but whose profits derive from revenues subject to taxation.

Public school or institution A school or institution controlled and operated by publicly elected or appointed officials and deriving its primary support from public funds.

Pupil-teacher ratio The enrollment of pupils at a given period of time, divided by the full-time-equivalent number of classroom teachers serving these pupils during the same period.

Racial/ethnic group Classification indicating general racial or ethnic heritage based on self-identification, as in data collected by the Bureau of the Census, or on observer identification, as in data collected by the Office for Civil Rights. These categories are in accordance with the Office of Management and Budget standard classification scheme presented below:

White A person having origins in any of the original peoples of Europe, North Africa, or the Middle East. Normally excludes persons of Hispanic origin except for tabulations produced by the Bureau of the Census, which are noted accordingly in this volume.

Black A person having origins in any of the black racial groups in Africa. Normally excludes persons of Hispanic origin except for tabulations produced by the Bureau of the Census, which are noted accordingly in this volume.

Hispanic A person of Mexican, Puerto Rican, Cuban, Central or South American, or other Spanish culture or origin, regardless of race.

Asian or Pacific Islander A person having origins in any of the original peoples of the Far East, Southeast Asia, the Indian subcontinent, or the Pacific Islands. This area includes, for example, China, India, Japan, Korea, the Philippine Islands, and Samoa.

American Indian or Alaskan Native A person having origins in any of the original peoples of North America and maintaining cultural identification through tribal affiliation or community recognition.

Resident population Includes civilian population and armed forces personnel residing within the United States. Excludes armed forces personnel residing overseas.

Revenue All funds received from external sources, net of refunds, and correcting transactions. Noncash transactions such as receipt of services, commodities, or other receipts "in kind" are excluded as are funds received from the issuance of debt, liquidation of investments, and nonroutine sale of property.

Salary The total amount regularly paid or stipulated to be paid to an individual, before deductions, for personal services rendered while on the payroll of a business or organization.

Sales and services Revenues derived from the sales of goods or services that are incidental to the conduct of instruction, research, or public service. Examples include film rentals, scientific and literary publications, testing services, university presses, and dairy products.

Sales tax Tax imposed upon the sale and consumption of goods and services. It can be imposed either as a general tax on the retail price of all goods and services sold or as a tax on the sale of selected goods and services.

Scholarships and fellowships This category of college expenditures applies only to money given in the form of outright grants and trainee stipends to individuals enrolled in formal coursework, either for credit or not. Aid to students in the form of tuition or fee remissions is included. College Work-Study funds are excluded and are reported under the program in which the student is working. In the tabulations in this volume, Pell Grants are not included in this expenditure category.

School A division of the school system consisting of students in one or more grades or other identifiable groups and organized to give instruction of a defined type. One school may share a building with another school or one school may be housed in several buildings.

School administration support services Includes salary, benefits, supplies, and contractual fees for the office of the principal, full-time department chairpersons, and graduation expenses.

School district An education agency at the local level that exists primarily to operate public schools or to contract for public school services. Synonyms are "local basic administrative unit" and "local education agency."

Science The body of related courses concerned with knowledge of the physical and biological world and with the processes of discovering and validating this knowledge.

Secondary instructional level The general level of instruction provided for pupils in secondary schools (generally covering grades 7 through 12 or 9 through 12) and any instruction of a comparable nature and difficulty provided for adults and youth beyond the age of compulsory school attendance.

Secondary school A school comprising any span of grades beginning with the next grade following an elementary or middle-school (usually 7, 8, or 9) and ending with or below grade 12. Both junior high schools and senior high schools are included.

Senior high school A secondary school offering the final years of high school work necessary for graduation.

Social studies A group of instructional programs that describes the substantive portions of behavior, past and present activities, interactions, and organizations of people associated together for religious, benevolent, cultural, scientific, political, patriotic, or other purposes.

Special education Direct instructional activities or special learning experiences designed primarily for students identified as having exceptionalities in one or more aspects of the cognitive process or as being underachievers in relation to general level or model of their overall abilities. Such services usually are directed at students with the following conditions: 1) physically handicapped; 2) emotionally handicapped; 3) culturally different, including compensatory education; 4) mentally retarded; and 5) students with learning disabilities. Programs for the mentally gifted and talented are also included in some special education programs. See also Handicapped.

Student An individual for whom instruction is provided in an educational program under the jurisdiction of a school, school system, or other education institution. No distinction is made between the terms "student" and "pupil," though "student" may refer to one receiving instruction at any level while "pupil" refers only to one attending school at the elementary or secondary level. A student may receive instruction in a school facility or in another location, such as at home or in a hospital. Instruction may be provided by direct student-teacher interaction or by some other approved medium such as television, radio, telephone, and correspondence.

Student support services Includes salary, benefits, supplies, and contractual fees for staff providing attendance and social work, guidance, health, psychological services, speech pathology, audiology, and other support to students.

Subject-matter club Organizations that are formed around a shared interest in a particular area of study and whose primary activities promote that interest. Examples of such organizations are math, science, business, and history clubs.

Supervisory staff Principals, assistant principals, and supervisors of instruction. Does not include superintendents or assistant superintendents.

Tax base The collective value of objects, assets, and income components against which a tax is levied.

Technical education A program of vocational instruction that ordinarily includes the study of the sciences and mathematics underlying a technology, as well as the methods, skills, and materials commonly used and the services performed in the technology. Technical education prepares individuals for positions—such as draftsman or lab technician—in the occupational area between the skilled craftsman and the professional person.

Tuition and fees A payment or charge for instruction or compensation for services, privileges, or the use of equipment, books, or other goods.

Unadjusted dollars See ***current dollars.***

Undergraduate students Students registered at an institution of higher education who are working in a program leading to a baccalaureate degree or other formal award below the baccalaureate, such as an associate degree.

U.S. Service Schools These institutions of higher education are controlled by the U.S. Department of Defense and the U.S. Department of Transportation. The ten institutions counted in the NCES surveys of higher education institutions include: the Air Force Institute of Technology, Community College of the Air Force, Naval Postgraduate School, Uniformed Services University of the Health Sciences, U.S. Air Force Academy, U.S Army Command and General Staff College, U.S. Coast Guard Academy, U.S. Merchant Marine Academy, U.S. Military Academy, and the U.S. Naval Academy.

University An institution of higher education consisting of a liberal arts college, a diverse graduate program, and usually two or more professional schools or faculties and empowered to confer degrees in various fields of study. For purposes of maintaining trend data in this publication, the selection of university institutions has not been revised since 1982.

Visual and performing arts A group of instructional programs that generally describes the historic development, aesthetic qualities, and creative processes of the visual and performing arts.

Vocational education Organized educational programs, services, and activities which are directly related to the preparation of individuals for paid or unpaid employment, or for additional preparation for a career, requiring other than a baccalaureate or advanced degree.

ISBN 0-16-049807-4